COLLECTORS ART PRIZE

ART LEGENDS OF OUR TIME

BY CONTEMPORARY ART CURATOR

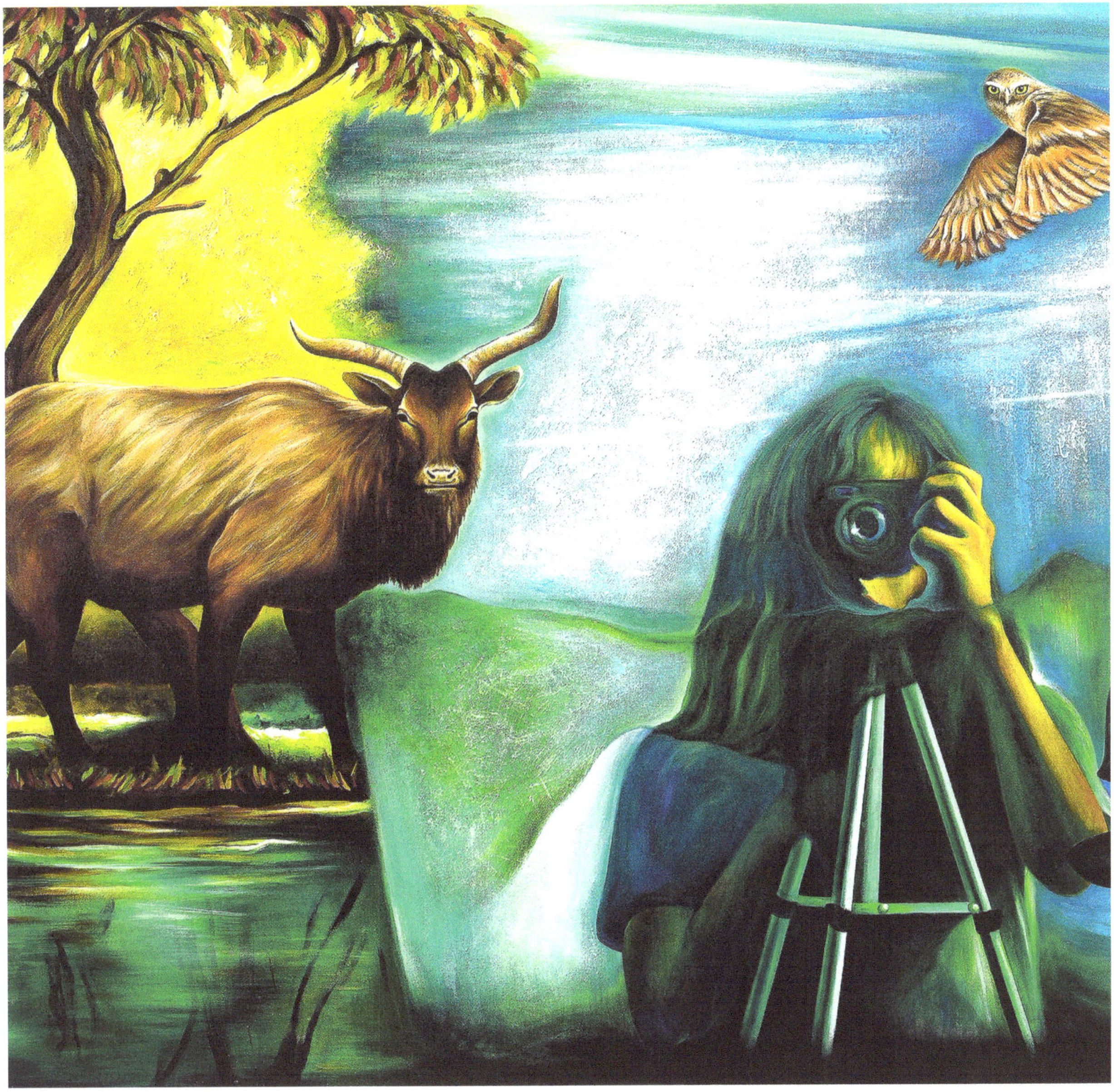

JEONG-AH ZHANG

A Breath. 2010. Acrylic on Canvas. 91 X 117 cm

COLLECTORS ART PRIZE

ART LEGENDS OF OUR TIME

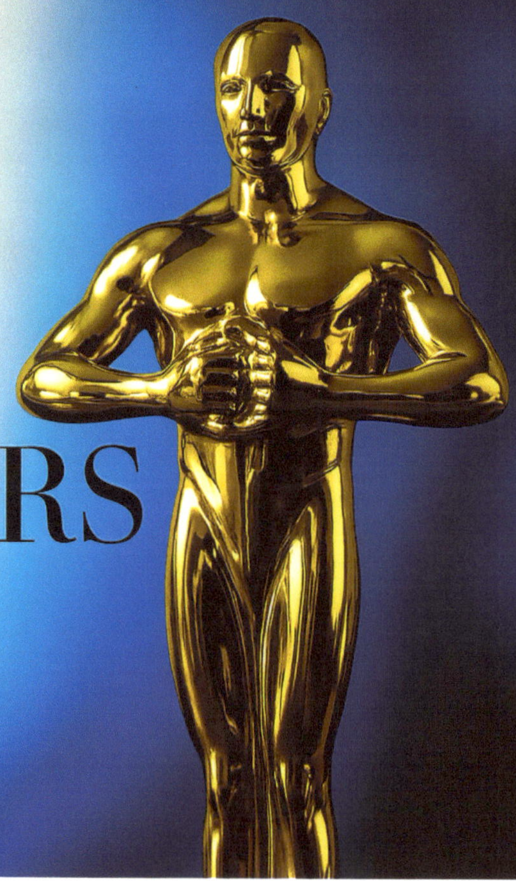

COLLECTORS ART PRIZE
ART LEGENDS OF OUR TIME

COLLECTORS ART PRIZE – SECOND EDITION
ART LEGENDS OF OUR TIME
CELEBRATING TIMELESS MASTERY

The COLLECTORS ART PRIZE | ART LEGENDS OF OUR TIME recognises a distinguished group of artists whose practices have demonstrated sustained excellence and cultural relevance. This honour is conferred by invitation only and is reserved for artists whose work extends beyond aesthetic accomplishment to engage meaningfully with the social, emotional, and intellectual conditions of our time.

The selected artists exemplify a form of mastery that endures across generations. Their work contributes to the evolving discourse of contemporary art, shaping how the field is interpreted, understood, and remembered. These artists do not merely participate in the history of art; they actively advance it.

Presented biennially, the prize is determined through a rigorous evaluation process led by respected curators, museum directors, and art historians. The selection prioritises depth, innovation, and long-term cultural impact over momentary trends or stylistic fashion.

This volume presents the artists recognised as the ART LEGENDS OF OUR TIME, highlighting their continued influence on the direction and development of contemporary artistic practice.

THE COLLECTORS ART PRIZE
A Biennial Distinction of International Standing
The COLLECTORS ART PRIZE honours artists whose contributions have significantly shaped the visual and conceptual landscape of contemporary art. The prize acknowledges practices that expand the boundaries of artistic expression and encourage critical engagement with the world we inhabit.

This is not an open competition. It is a selective recognition, extended only to artists whose work demonstrates exceptional conceptual clarity, technical proficiency, and cultural resonance.

Awarded every two years, the prize celebrates artists who challenge established frameworks, introduce new possibilities for artistic inquiry, and create work that remains compelling long after its initial reception. Their practices encourage reflection, dialogue, and an expanded understanding of contemporary visual culture.
As the prize cannot be applied for, it represents one of the highest forms of professional acknowledgement within the field. It is earned through sustained commitment, vision, and the lasting significance of the artist's oeuvre.

Founded by Contemporary Art Curator Magazine, an internationally respected publication since 2014, the prize reflects the magazine's ongoing mission to document, interpret, and elevate contemporary art. Through its publications, interviews, curated exhibitions, and collector-focused initiatives, the magazine has become a trusted resource for institutions, scholars, collectors, and artists worldwide.

To receive this prize is to be recognised as a defining figure in the art of our time — an artist whose work contributes meaningfully to the cultural record and to the future of artistic practice.

The COLLECTORS ART PRIZE is not merely an award. It is an institutional acknowledgement of artistic legacy and an affirmation of those who continue to shape the language of contemporary art.

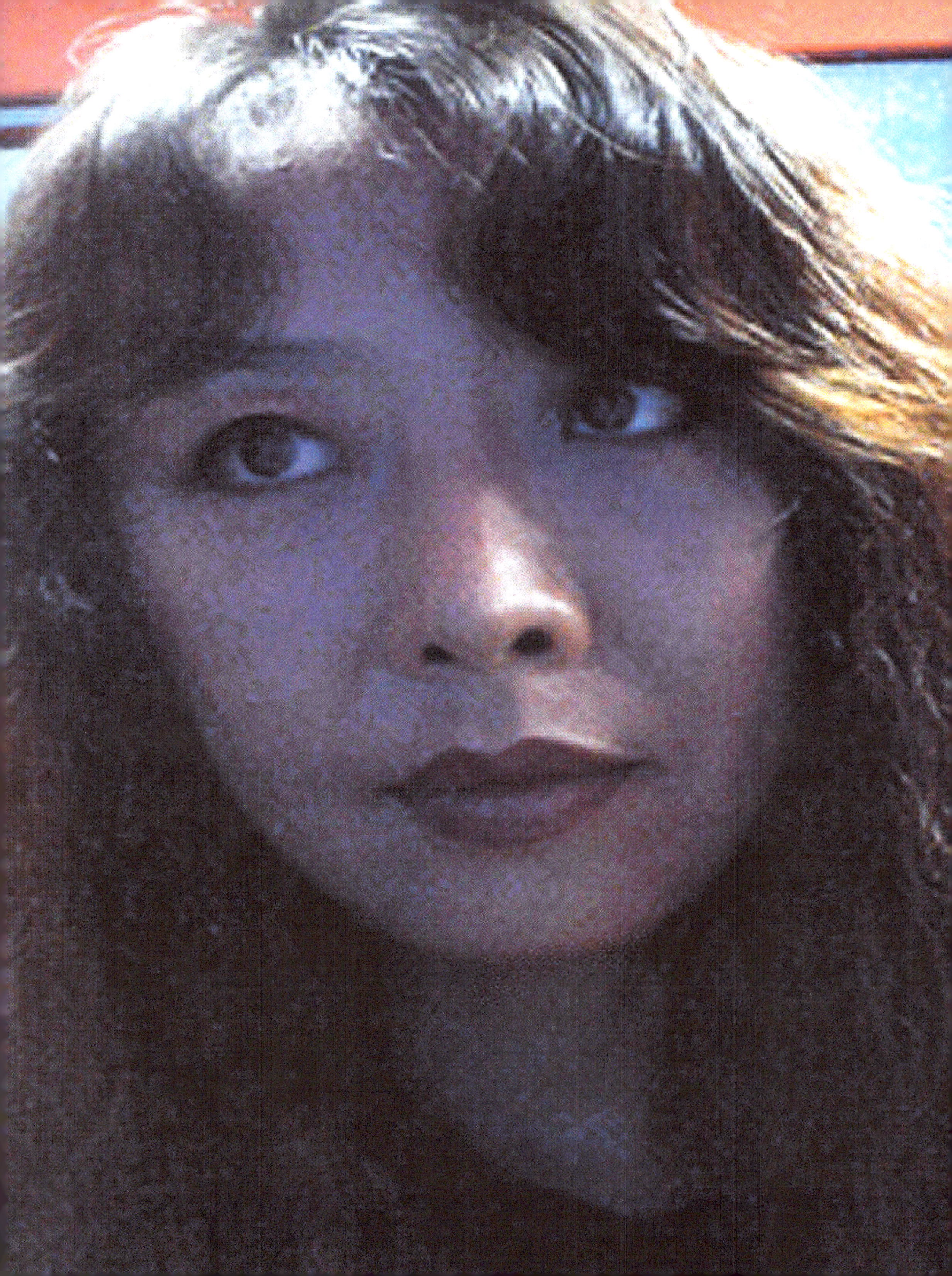

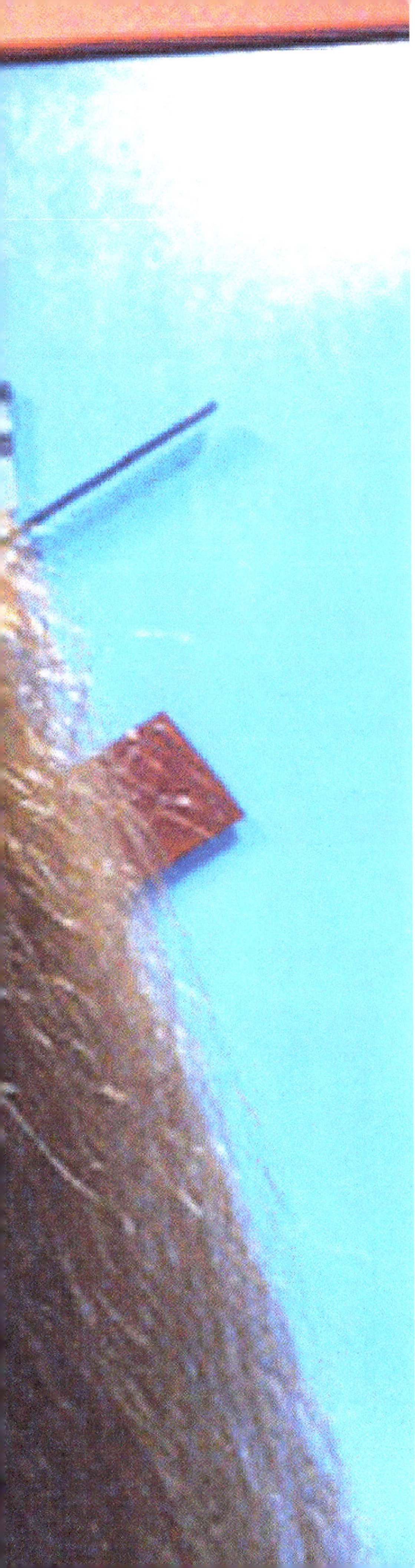

My life and art are based on my own philosophical thoughts and experiences. I am interested in the philosophy of immanence and transcendence on all beings, and this means that I try to focus on the essence of life by establishing core values, and at the same time, sublimate it into my works. I look at the relationship between human and nature and the universe from a very broader perspective. I think all thoughts and consciousness are breath, The breath is the switch between the conscious and the subconscious mind, It is a connected cycle of creation and extinction. And It is a soul resonance beyond the time frame. I try to listen to all the conceptions of all things, have an open mind and remember what resonates. Therefore, my surrealism is simply is not just an exploration of the unconscious. It is a question of will and philosophy, constant introspection. Philosophical considerations on a visible world and an invisible world. I value awakening and balance, and try to embody the meaning of existence and non-existence, and the nature of things in an implicit and artistic way. My art is intended to make the viewers think, but my delivery is intended to make the viewers listen to their own inner voice. It makes people, including myself, think beyond reality and into the essence of reality. As I look back on that afternoon so long ago that presented my life, When remembering the experience of seeing the interconnected nature of all things... The flash point of all creation in the present moment is immortality.

JEONG-AH ZHANG

zenairzhang@gmail.com

Born and based in Seoul, South Korea on July 3, 1966, Jeong-Ah Zhang is an internationally active contemporary artist who specializes in painting and has achieved significant international recognition.

In the dynamic world of contemporary art, Jeong-Ah Zhang emerges as a profound statement on existential reflection and metaphysical dialogue, capturing the spirit of a generation that seeks to transcend traditional artistic boundaries. Jeong-Ah Zhang's ability to convey complex, abstract ideas through tangible imagery sets her apart as a visionary in contemporary art. Jeong-Ah Zhang's contribution to contemporary art is not a trend. It is a legacy. She is not imitating, she is inventing. Not conforming, but transcending. In every line, every layer of pigment, there is a quiet but unshakable declaration: that art still has the power to transform consciousness, to illuminate the mysteries of existence, and to connect us all in the shared experience of being. Her art is not just singular. It is timeless.

Jeong-Ah Zhang majored in fine arts at Ewha Womans University in Seoul, and she also won the University Literature Award[-Play Literature Category] for three consecutive years separately from her major. After graduating from university, she worked as an Assistant Director for a prominent theater company in Seoul for several years, during which time she even quite seriously considered becoming a monk with profound questions about life and death (or Creation and Extinction). Afterwards she traveled to 30 countries on adventurous solo backpacking trips in her late 20s and early 30s, while her mindfulness routine fostered a harmonious balance of mental focus, creativity and originality she later needed to create the masterpieces of art.

Echoes of her own spiritual journey and meditation, an extension of the transcendental experiences of the magical realism at the age of eight that foreshadowed her identity, became a crucial trigger for her fundamental insight into a multidimensional world where the boundaries between reality and the virtual disappeared, making the meaning of time and space disappear. Building on this foundation, she began her artistic career in earnest in 1999 at the age of 33, debuting in the art world that same year by winning an award at Korea's biggest art competition, and has since dedicated herself to artistic activities for the past 25 years.

Jeong-Ah Zhang has held five solo exhibitions in Korea, Canada, and the United States, and her works has been selected for exhibitions in over 90-juried competitions, and invited to over 90 group exhibitions and art fairs in the United States, Korea, France, Italy, Spain, the Netherlands, Japan, Germany, Canada, the United Kingdom, and the United Arab Emirates. And she has also won 50 prestigious international awards in many countries around the world, including 15 art competitions in Korea, and has been featured in more than 80 international art books and art magazines.

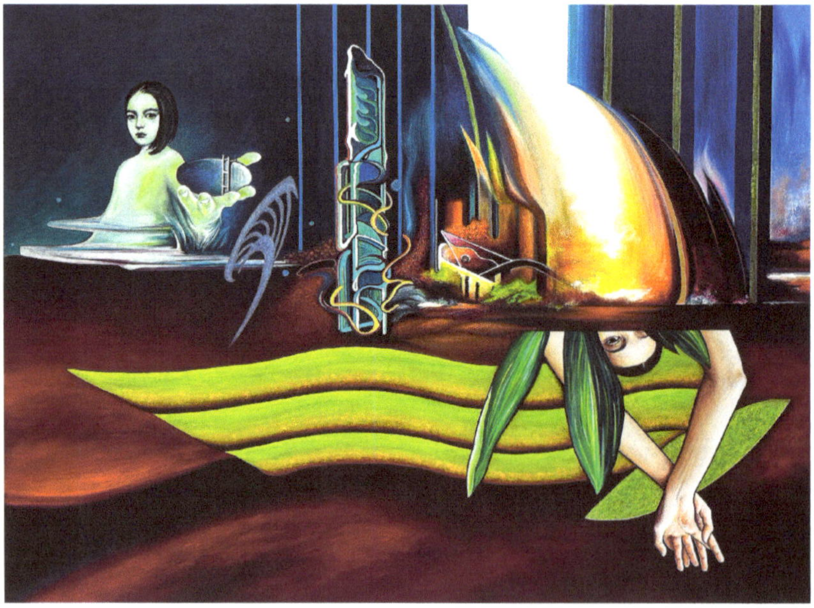

Epitaph of Time and Space. 2025. Acrylic on Canvas. 61 X 81 cm

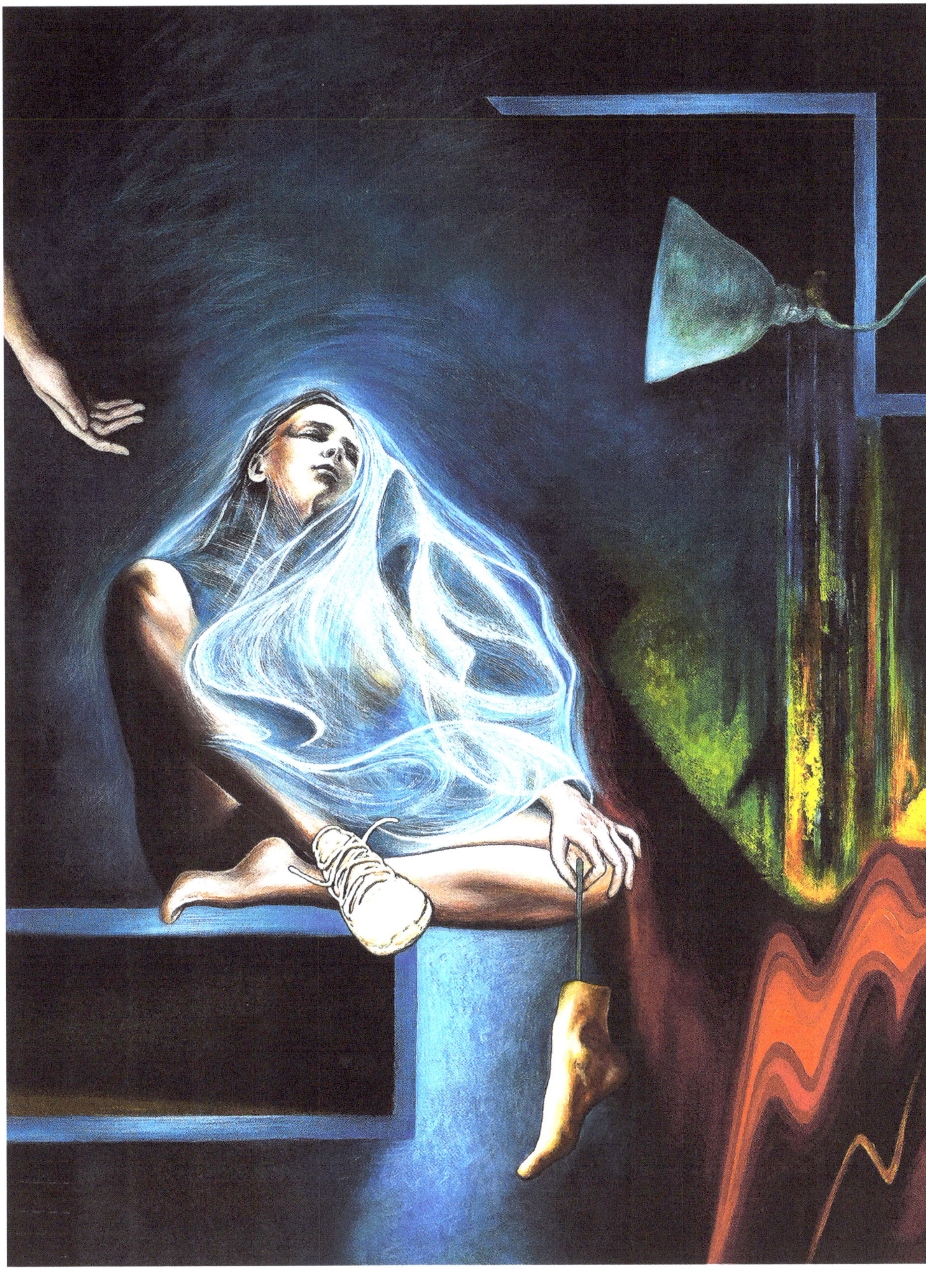

The Whispering of Zero-Gravity. 2022. Oil and Acrylic on Canvas. 73 X 53 cm

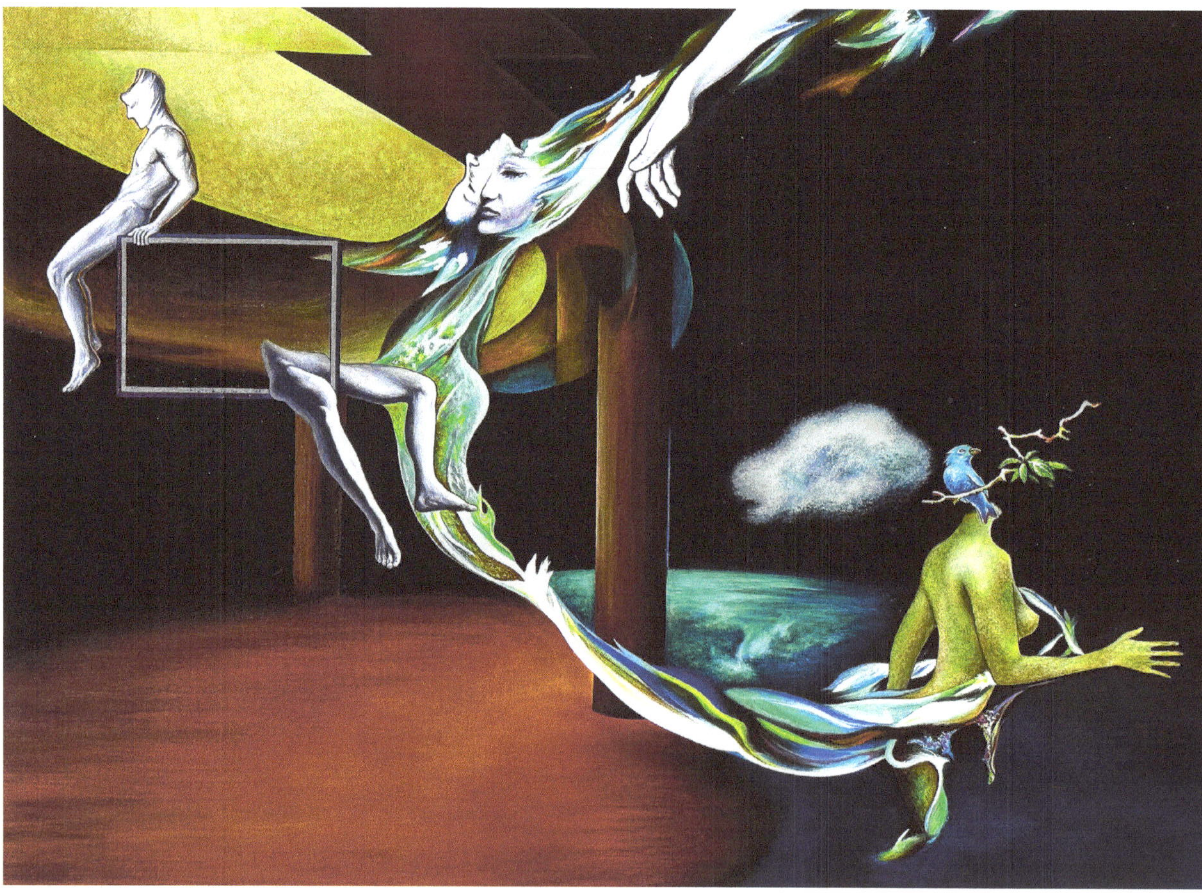

Everywhere But Nowhere. 2023. Acrylic on Canvas. 53 x 73 cm

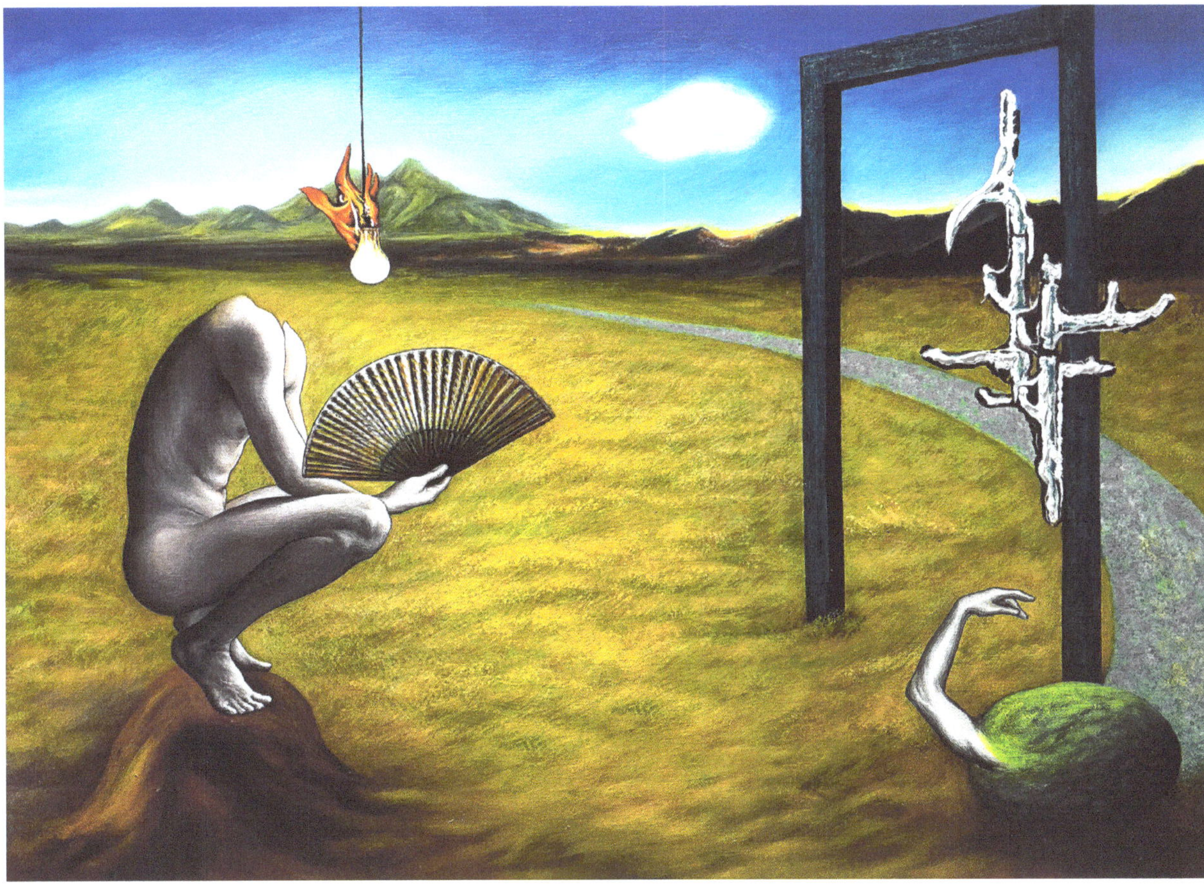

The No-Boundary Moment. 2021. Acrylic on Canvas. 53 X 73 cm

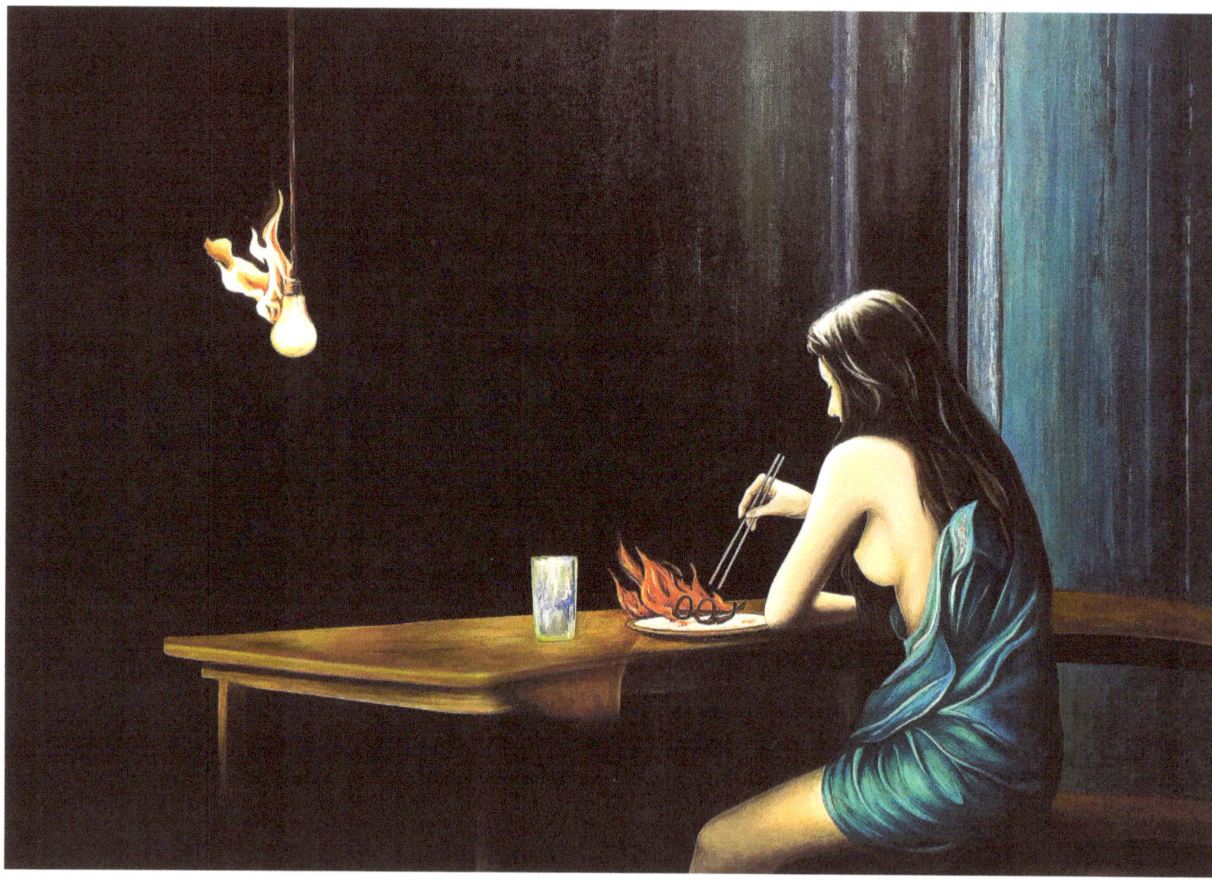

A Quiet Meal. 2016. Acrylic on Canvas. 65 X 91 cm

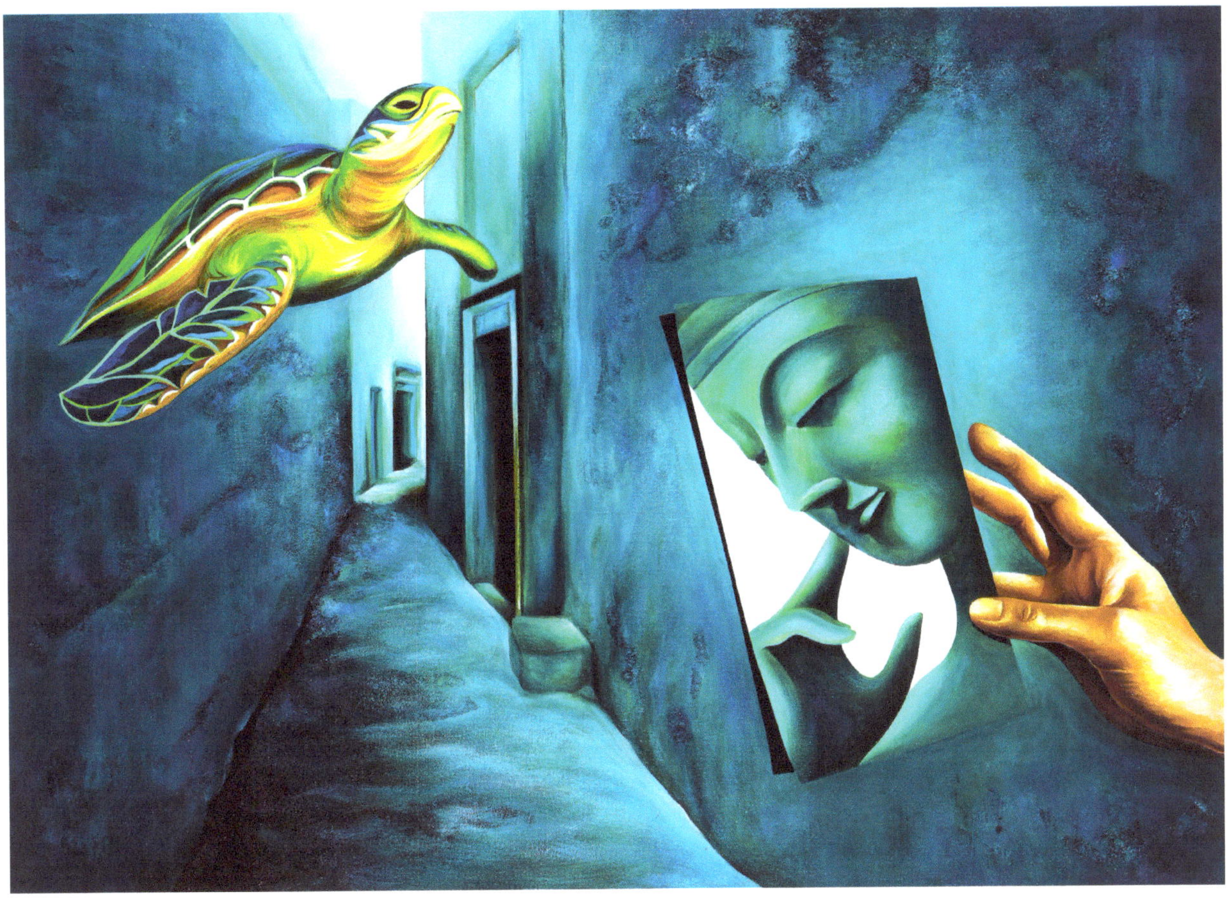

A Voyager. 2009. Acrylic on Canvas. 73 X 102 cm

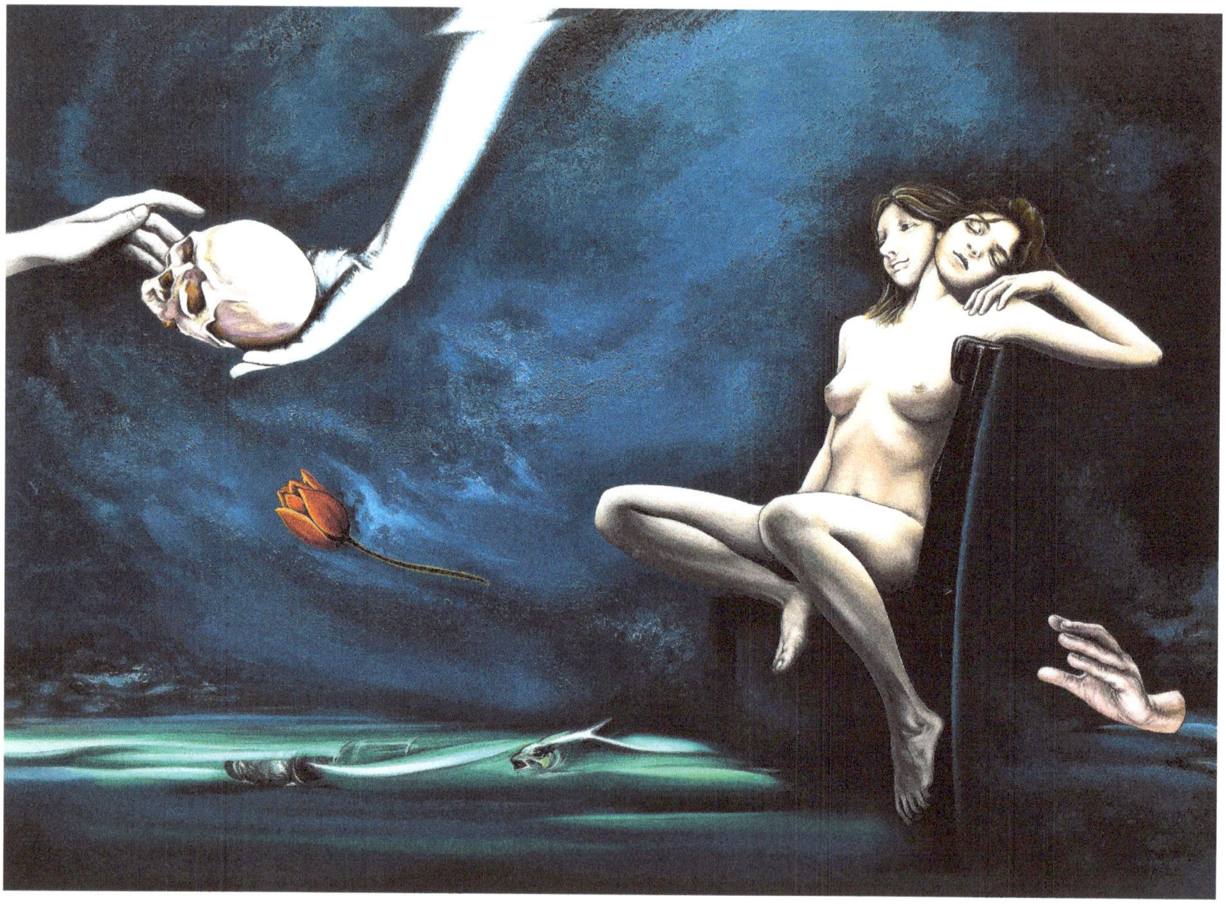

A Low Voice. 2018. Acrylic on Canvas. 53 X 73 cm

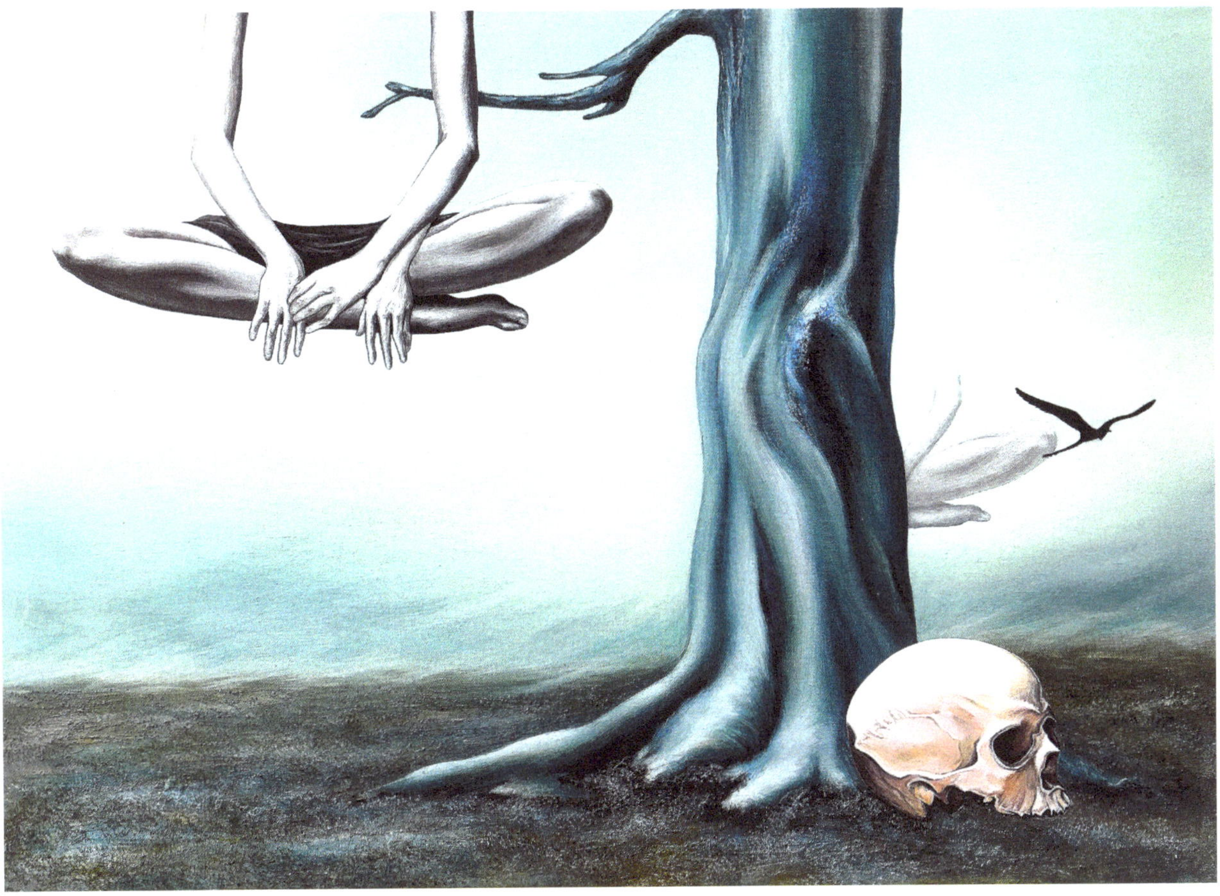

The Spirit of the Fragrance. 2021. Acrylic on Canvas. 53 X 73 cm

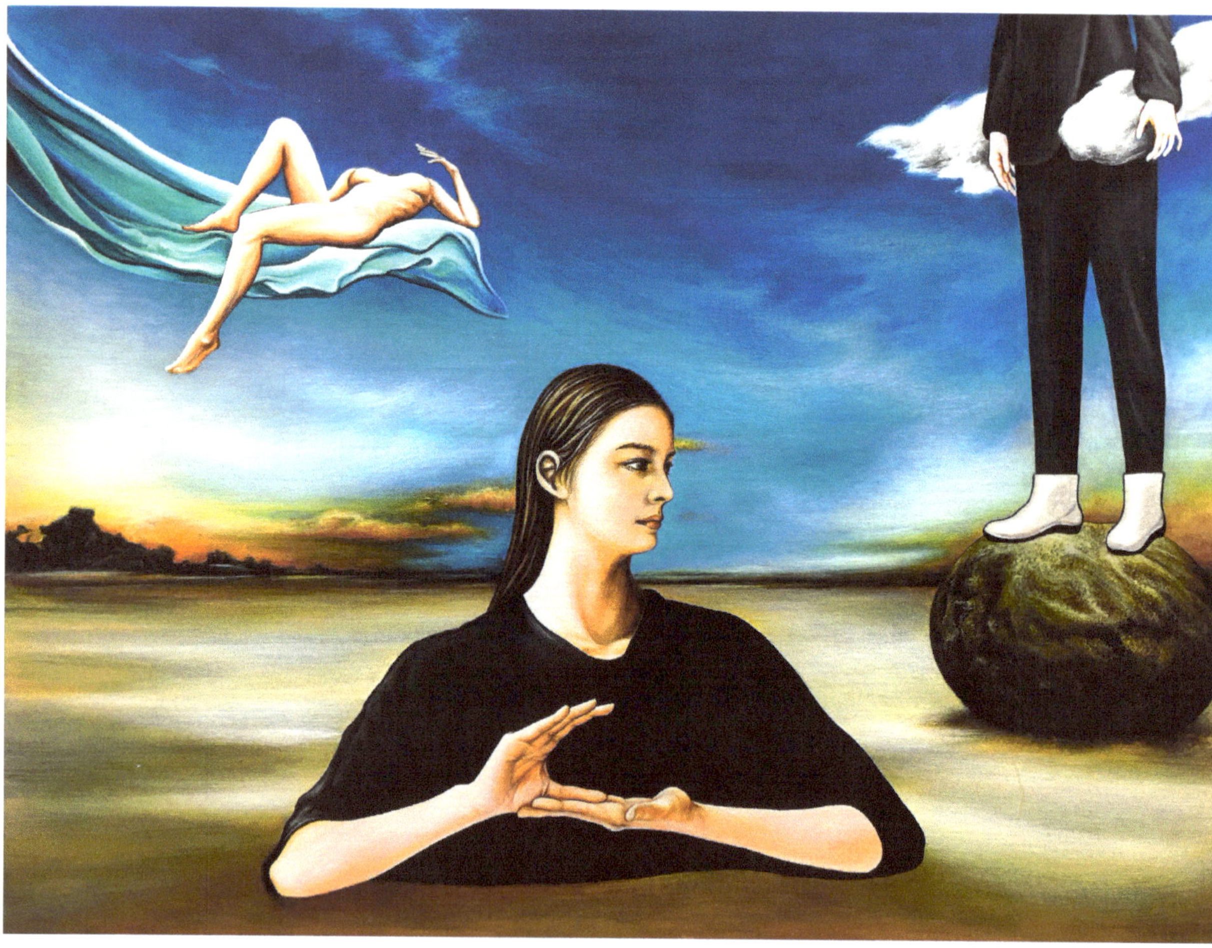

Frequency and Wavelength. 2020. Acrylic on Canvas. 50 X 65 cm

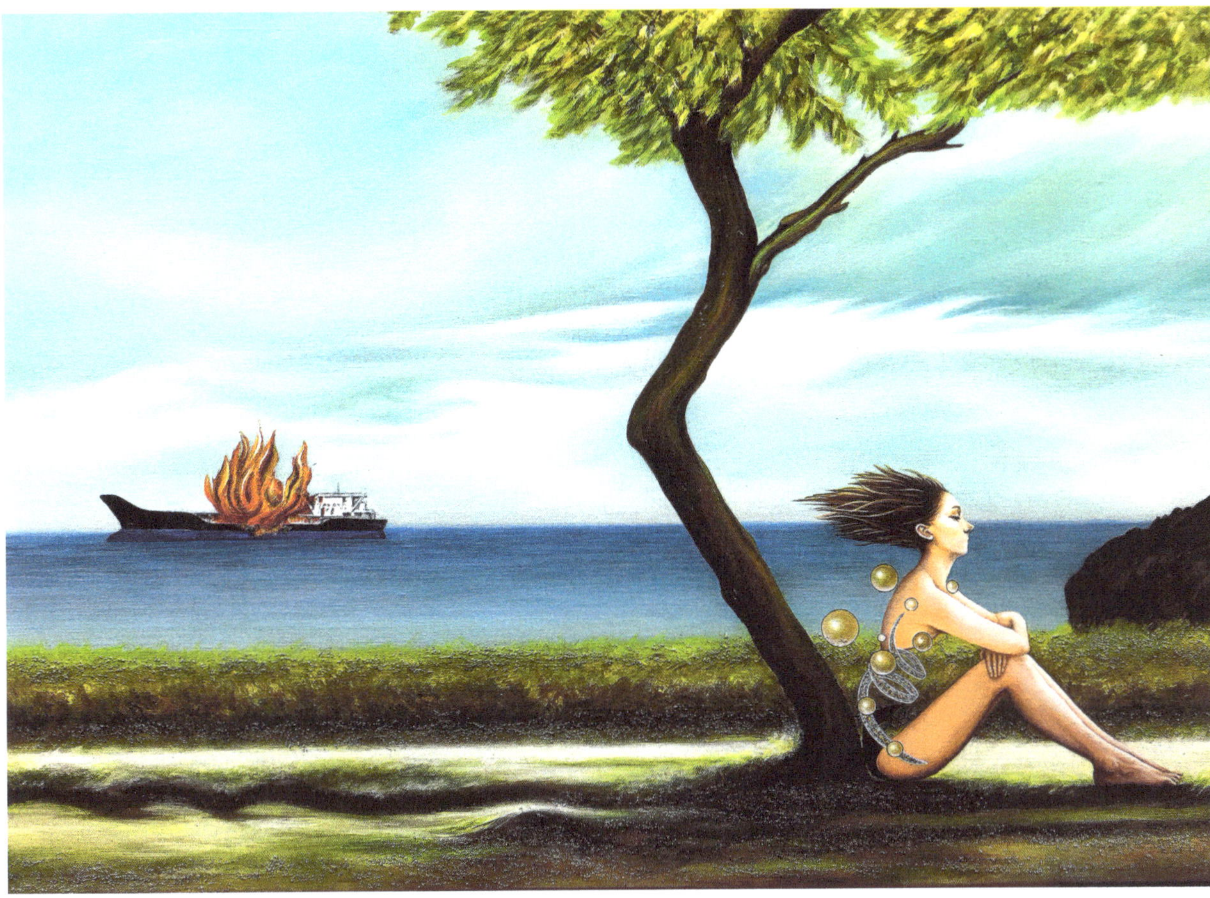

The Condition of Life. 2021. Acrylic on Canvas. 53 X 73 cm

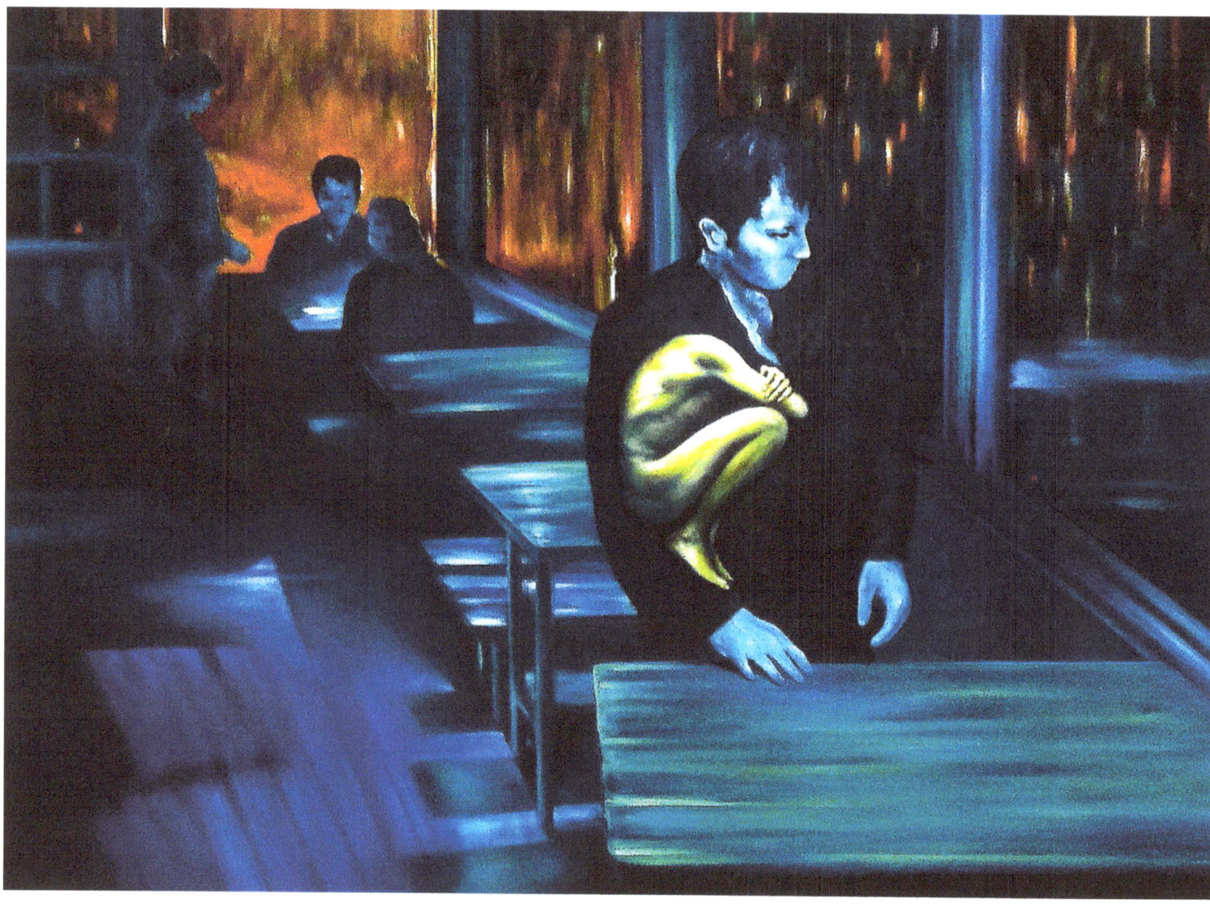

Deep Silence. 2012. Acrylic on Canvas. 53 X 73 cm

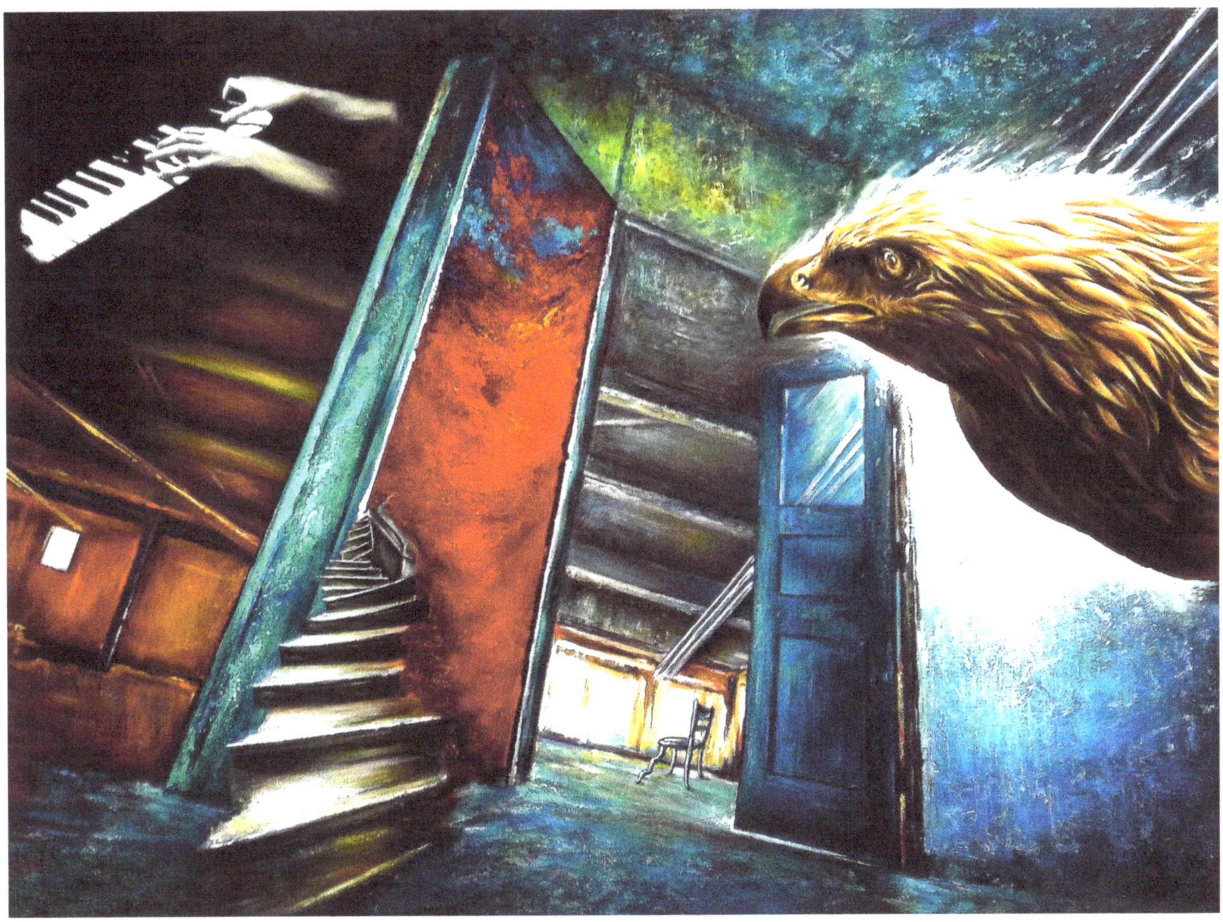

A Layer – Phenomenal World. 2013. Oil and Acrylic on Canvas. 53 X 73 cm

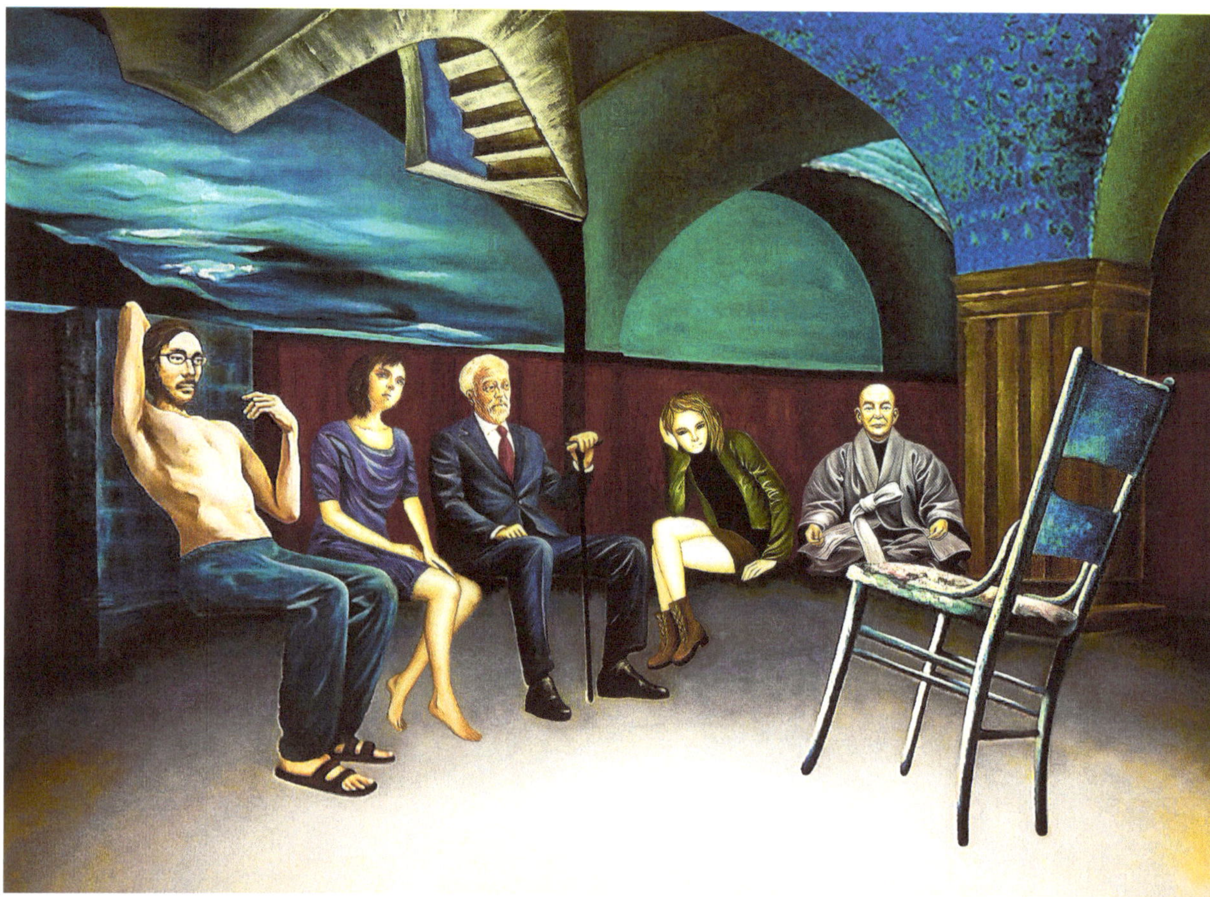

Interview – The illimitable space. 2014. Oil and Acrylic on Canvas. 53 X 73 cm

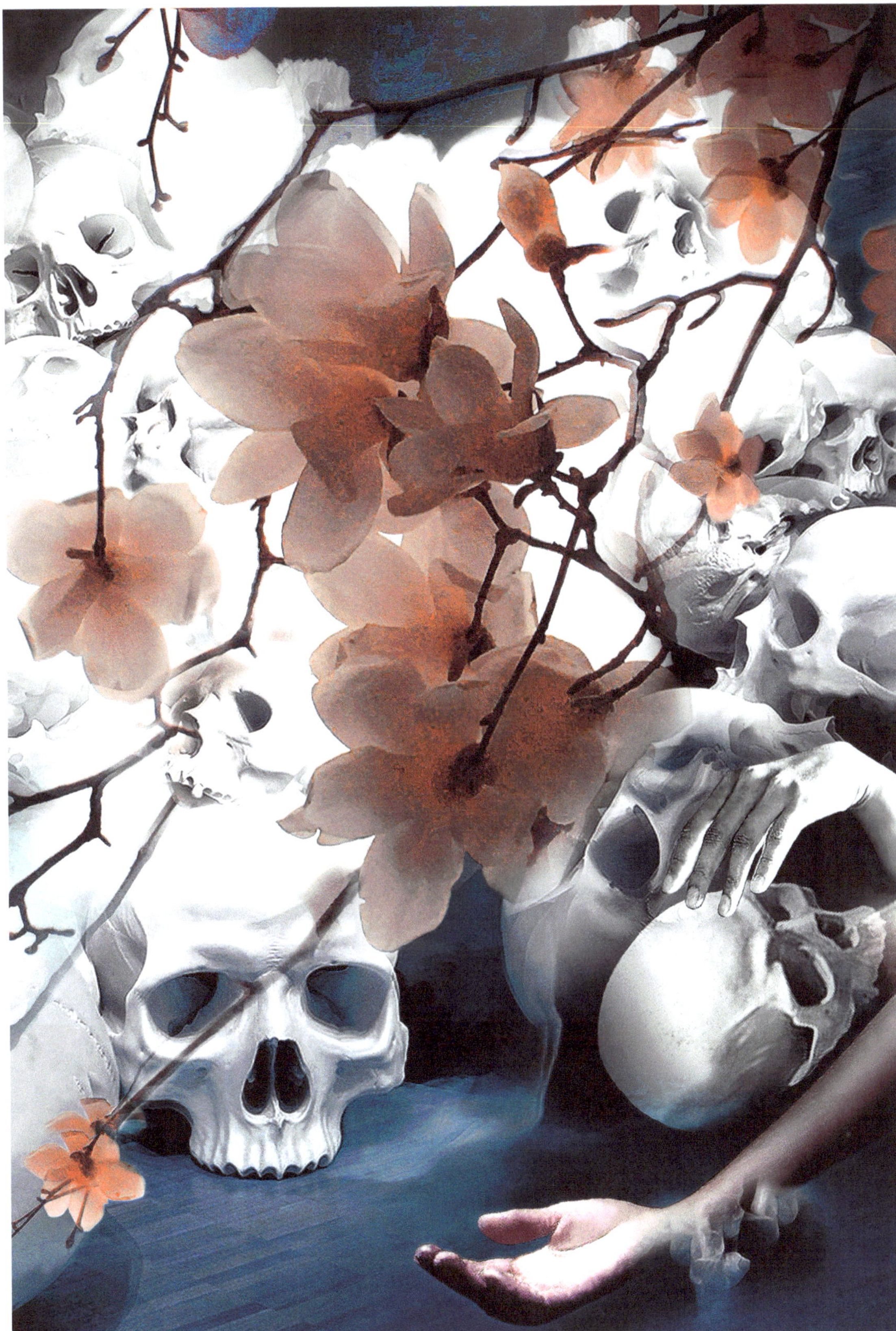

Transparent Time Scale. 2021. Mixed Media on Canvas. 91 X 61 cm

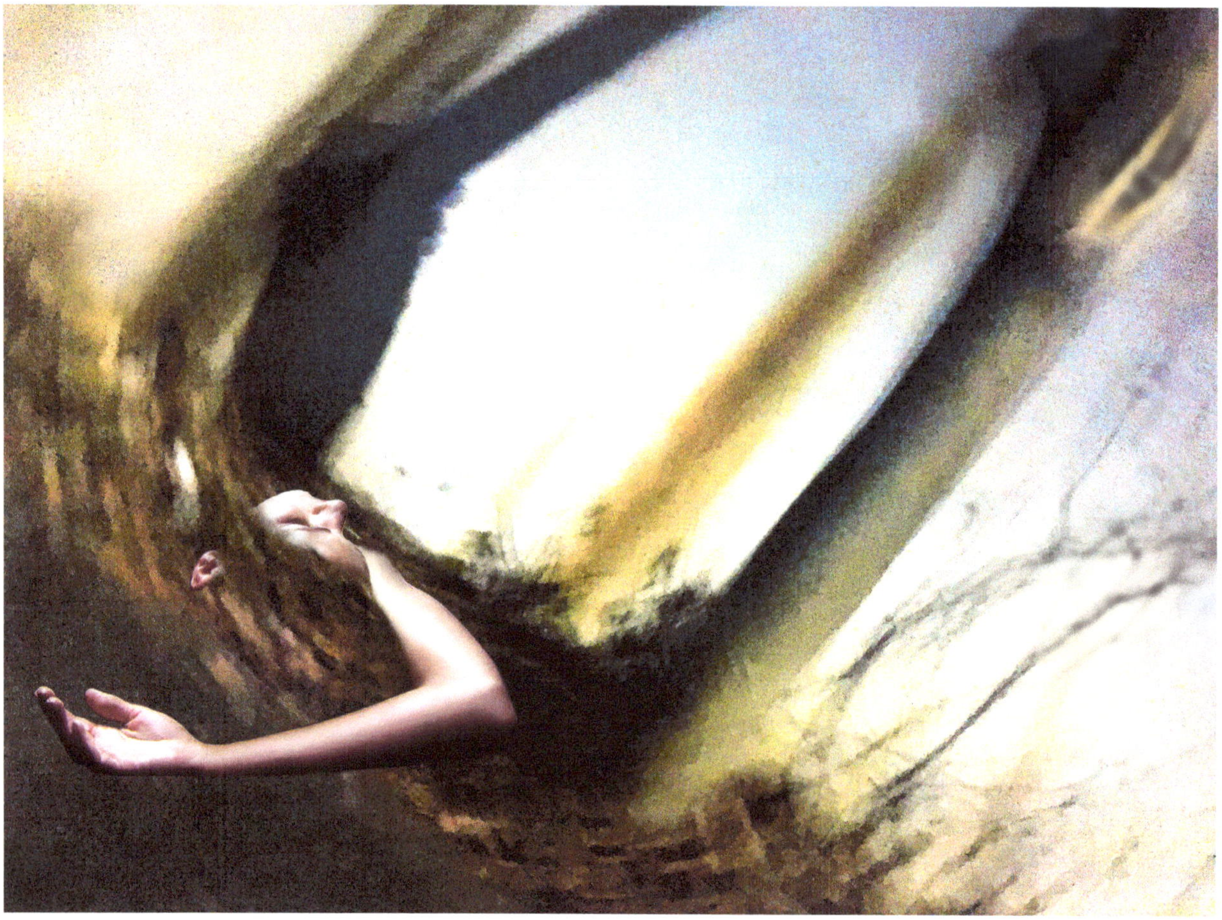

A Nap of One Spring Day. 2023. Mixed Media on Canvas. 65 X 91 cm

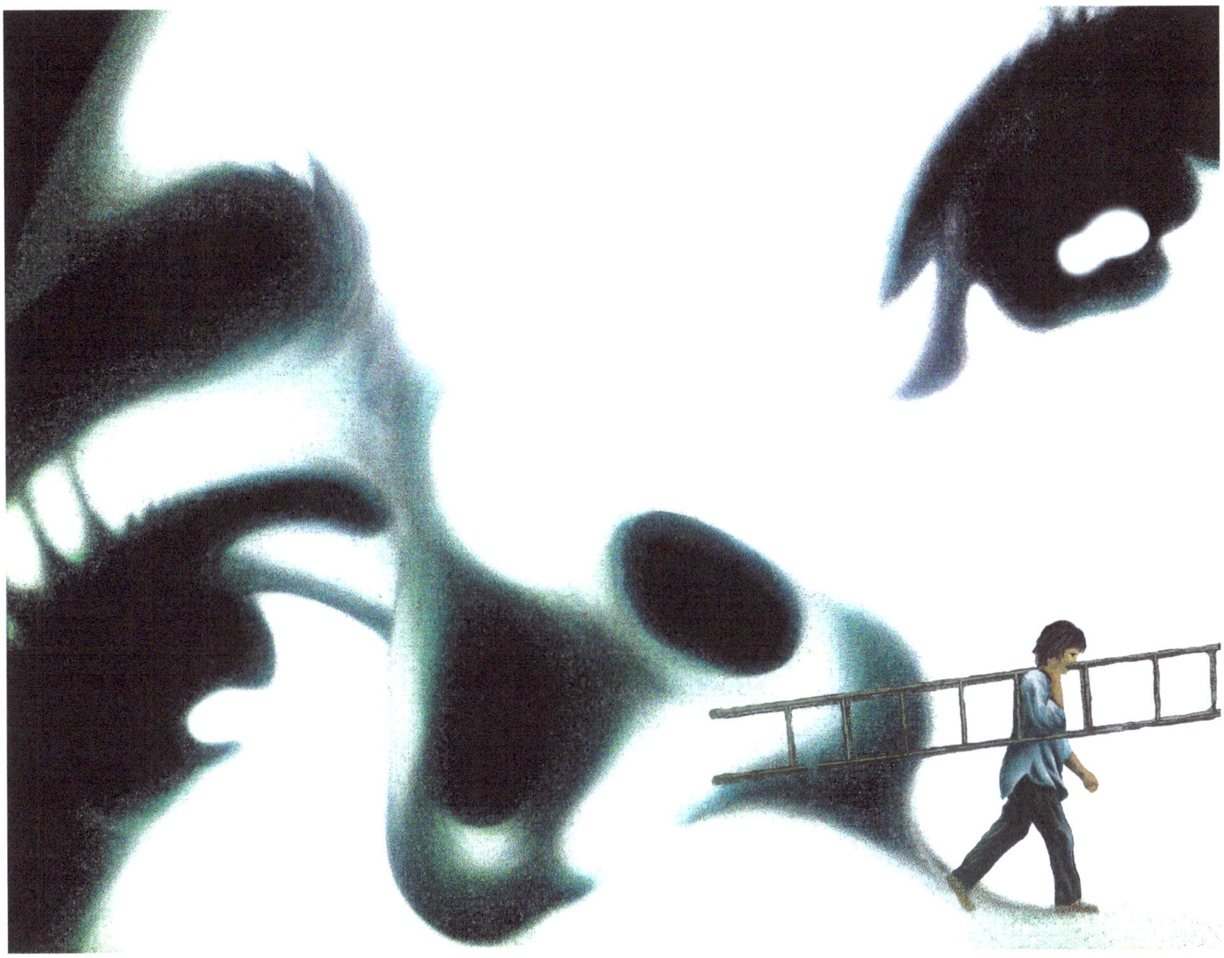

The Universe is Not Two. 2011. Acrylic on Canvas. 73 x 91 cm

GAYLE PRINTZ, A WORLD MASTER ARTIST

Https://www.GaylePrintz.com

Widely regarded as an artistic prodigy, American contemporary artist, Gayle Printz, began painting in 2020, during the height of the pandemic. Within five months, her artwork was part of the permanent physical exhibit of Le Musée de Peinture de Saint-Frajou in France. Printz soared to international fame and cemented her place in the art history books by composing an unrivaled, historically significant, visual language. Printz paintings speak a visual language never before spoken. It is a universal language layered with meaning and a dynamic figuration that changes before your eyes. It is a language of incomparable technical skill and unsurpassed emotional depth. It is a language that exposes the artistic genius of Gayle Printz and her uniquely recognizable artistic style—a style so unprecedented that it screamed for a genre of its own. It is a language heard by the world's leading art experts, who responded by naming the revolutionary style of Gayle Printz: Modern Abstractionism. Gayle Printz earned her Bachelor of Arts at the University of Pennsylvania and her Juris Doctor at Boston University School of Law. She grew up surrounded by music, paintings, and books. Yet, to this day, the world-renowned Founder of Modern Abstractionism has never taken a painting class. And, for fear of unintentionally adopting a style that already exists, Gayle may not be taking one in the future. Printz feels that, to make a meaningful contribution in any pursuit, one must precipitate change. And, in her visionary manner, Gayle Printz has transformed the absence of training into a distinct advantage. Reshaping the future of contemporary art over the course of a few short years, World Master Artist Gayle Printz, is one of the most important and influential artists of this era. Exploring freedom of expression through a captivating blend of cutting edge technique, creative innovation, and emotional depth, Gayle Printz has become a venerated leader in the contemporary art world. And, though we know her paintings are soaring in value, Gayle will only admit to that which is already public: Printz paintings are part of the illustrious international art collections of museums, galleries, art historians, curators, collectors, investors, business venues, and even rock stars. Printz paintings are showcased in leading global art publications (where her artwork can usually be found on the cover), permanent solo exhibitions, and important worldwide physical exhibitions. Gayle has won hundreds of coveted invitational prizes. And, having earned top honors in a staggering number of juried international art competitions, Printz artworks have been in thousands of highly respected group exhibitions. The extraordinary accomplishments of Gayle Printz are endless.

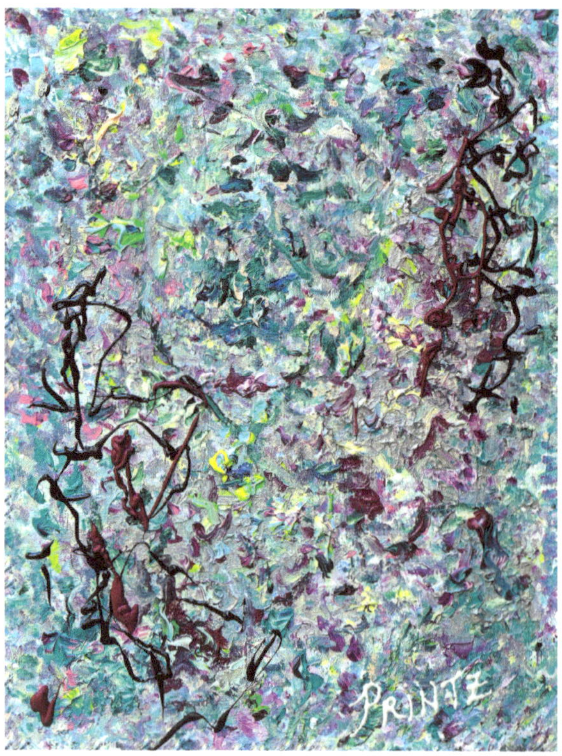

FEMME, 2024 by Gayle Printz, Acrylic on Canvas Modern Abstractionist Painting, 60.96 cm High x 45.72 Wide

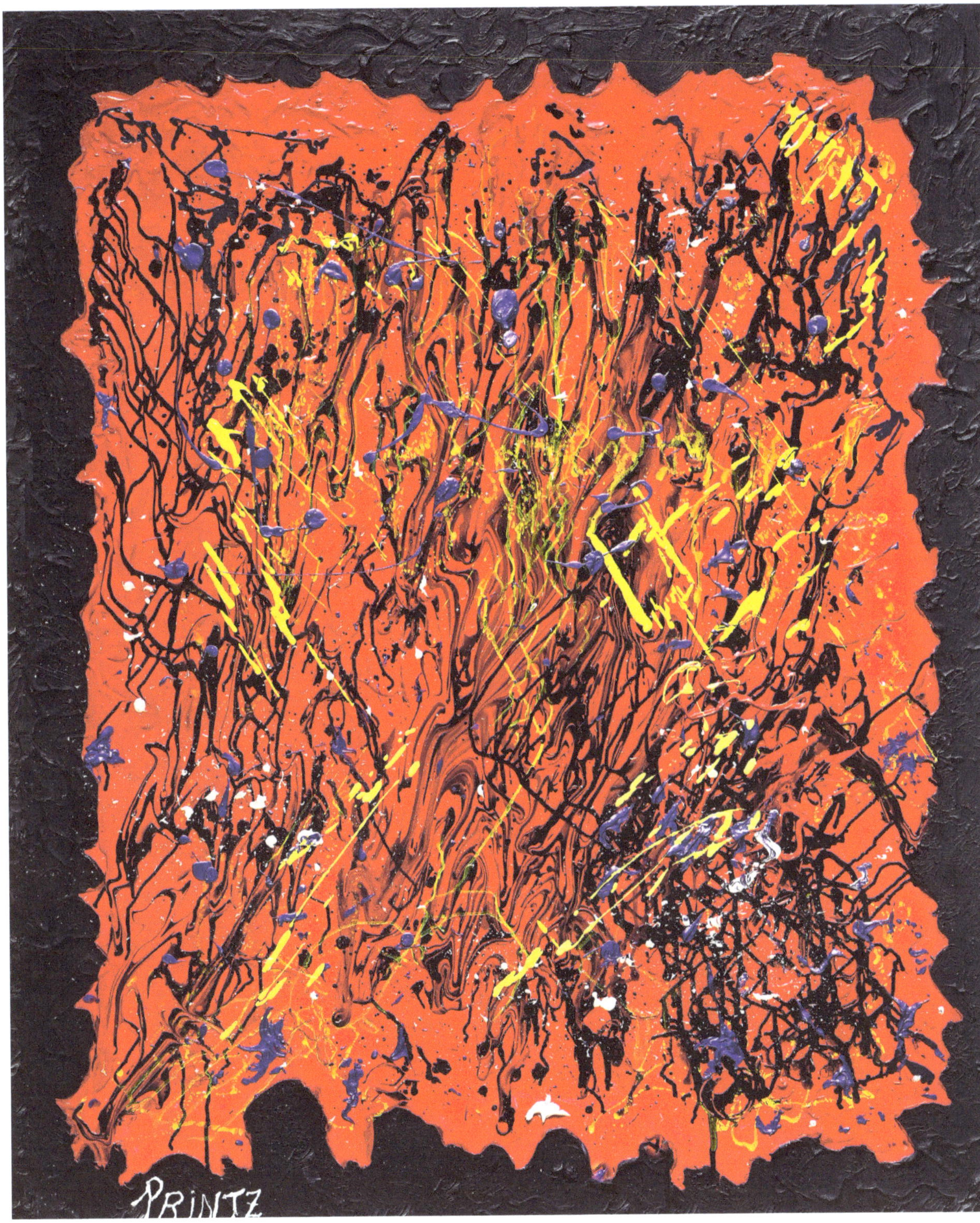

STRENGTH, 2024 by Gayle Printz, Acrylic on Canvas Modern Abstractionist Painting, 121.92 cm High x 152.4 cm Wide x 3.81 cm Deep

ALINE POUGET

https://en.alinepouget-artiste.net/

Aline Pouget is a French contemporary painter who works between Paris and Blois-Chambord. Having always been drawn to the beauty and colors of nature, her transition to creating art came naturally. She began with watercolor and quickly moved on to oil painting, which gives her greater satisfaction. She paints on canvas or wooden supports. The search for color, light, life, and the beauty of the world around us is the foundation of her art. Her approach allows her to express emotions and feelings that she transposes into her paintings with strength and depth. The intimate meaning of her thoughts, life experiences, and deepest sensations, her sense of the duality between good and evil, shapes her work. She is inspired by nature, and her masterful paintings form a visual syntax ranging from abstract compositions reflecting an organic universe to expressive portrayals of natural beauty. Revealing and profound, the whirlwind of her compositions highlights her love of nature. Interpretations can vary from palliative and pristine to intensely immersive and profound. Illuminating the very essence of nature and life by juxtaposing them in highly tangible scenes, she bridges the worlds of realism and abstraction. Her paintings capture her visceral response to the universe. Through a rainbow of colors, the artist employs a palette of varied and monochromatic tones that give each work a vibrant sense of life. This is enhanced by the dynamic style of her compositions and her energetic brushstrokes. A powerful sense of movement and emotion resonates in her work, along with a unique sense of perspective and depth. Aline Pouget, internationally awarded contemporary painter, has exhibited in remarkable places such as the Vatican Chancellery, the Vicar's Palace in the Vatican during the jubilee year, the Whitney Gallery in New York, the museums of Turin and Barcelona among others.

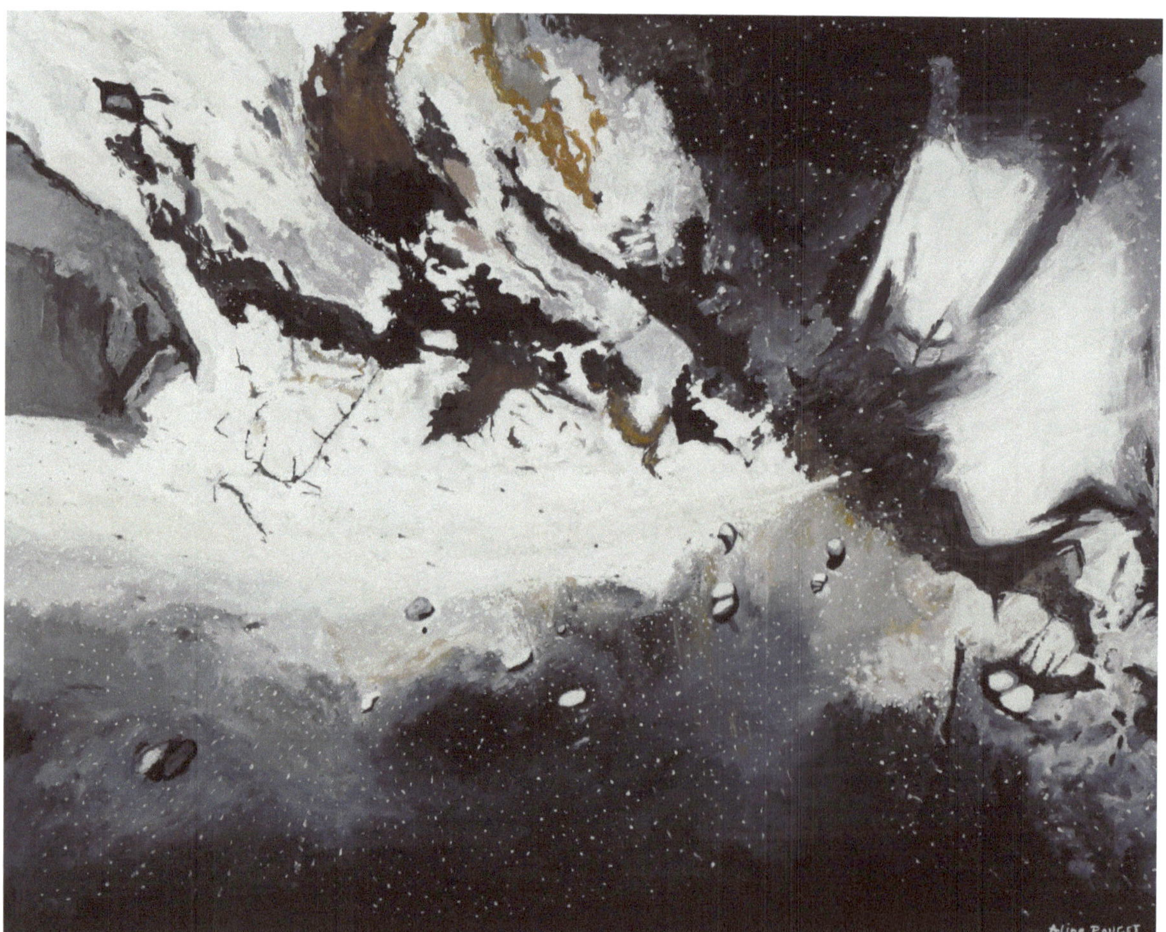

Infini, 2017, Oil on canvas, 100 x 81 cm

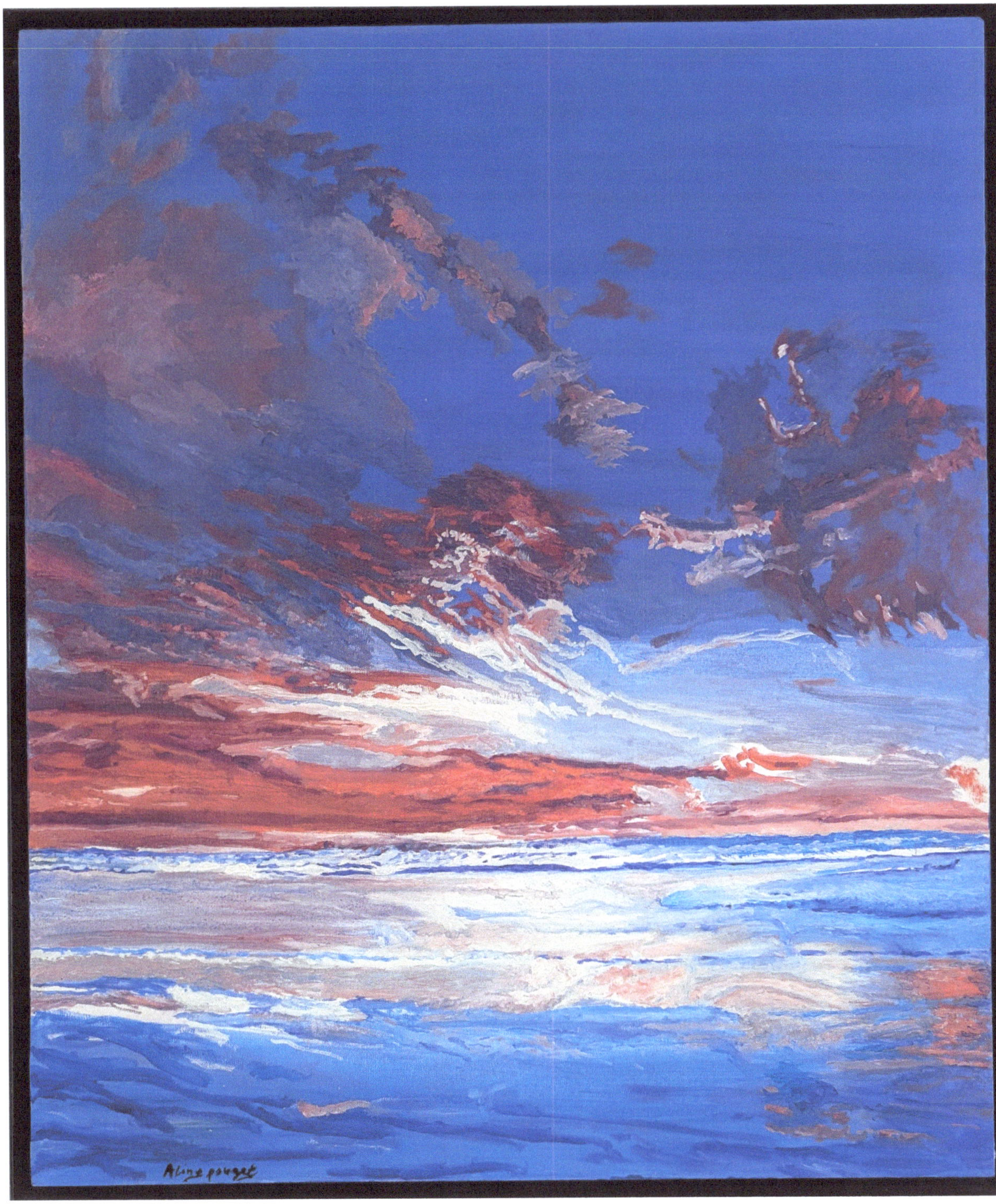

Crépuscule, 2020, Oil on wood, 54 x 65 cm

ANA CAROLINA CERAMICS

www.anacarolinaceramics.com

Ana Carolina creates through an intuitive understanding among forms, organics volumes and space, freely abstract ceramics vessels and sculptures. Fantasy and imagination are brought into the narrative, whereby the ceramics forms are to seem to be alive and to move in a world that only fantasy and imagination can reach. The main pottery techniques, wheel-throw, slab-built, pinching and coiling are used. I explore different clays highlighting natural textures and colors on the ceramics pieces. Process: pottery techniques, intuition, controlling proportions and organic volumes with sensibility. Intention: fantasy, imagination, movement. 2001 - 2006 Bachelor degree in Architecture and Urbanism, FAAP (Fundação Armando Álvares Penteado) - University of Fine Arts. 2016 - 2017 Master degree in Design: Ceramics, MMU (Manchester Metropolitan University) - Manchester School of Art.

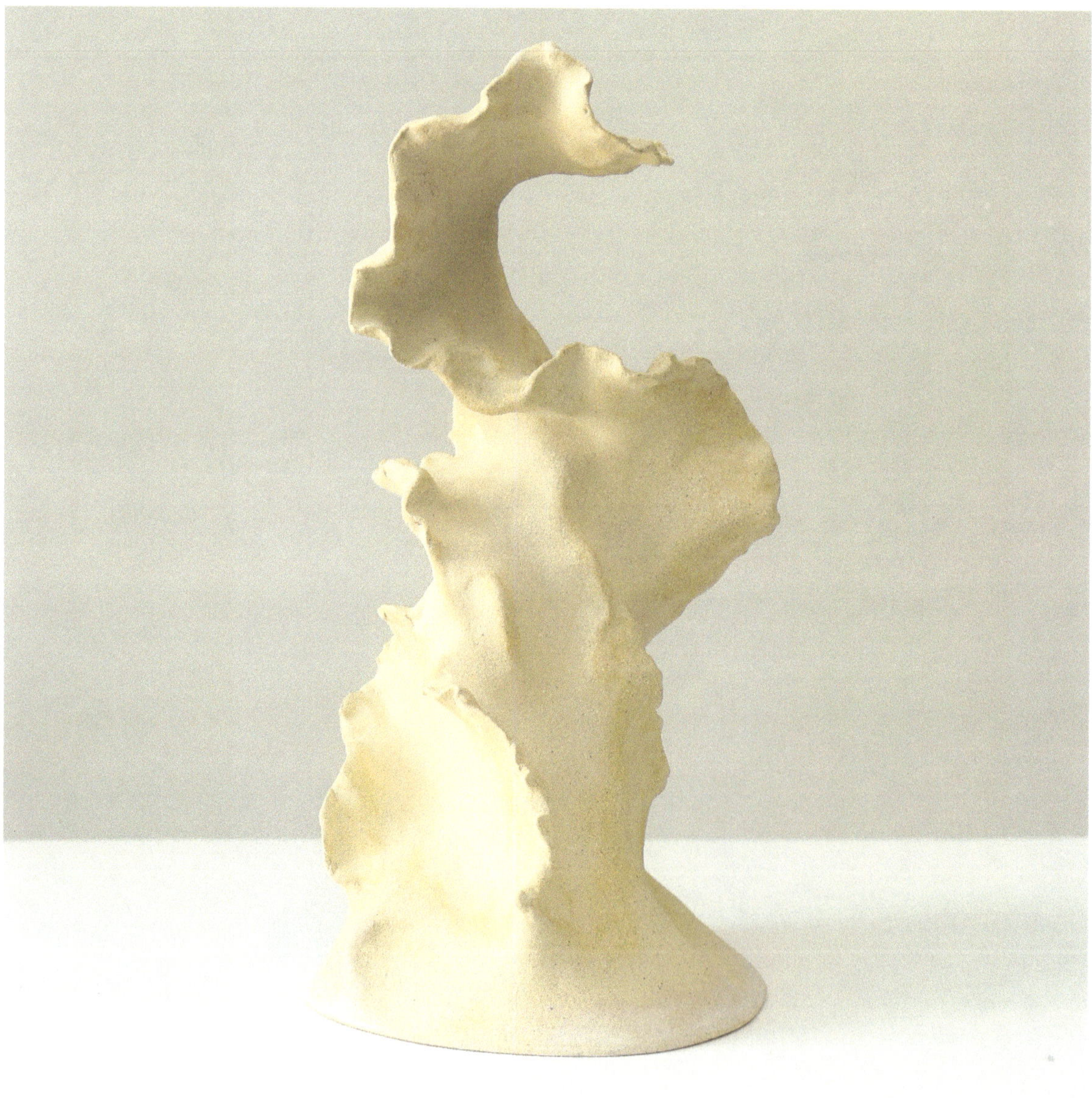

Untitled, 2024. Stoneware, pinching. H. 28 cm x W. 14 cm x D. 14 cm

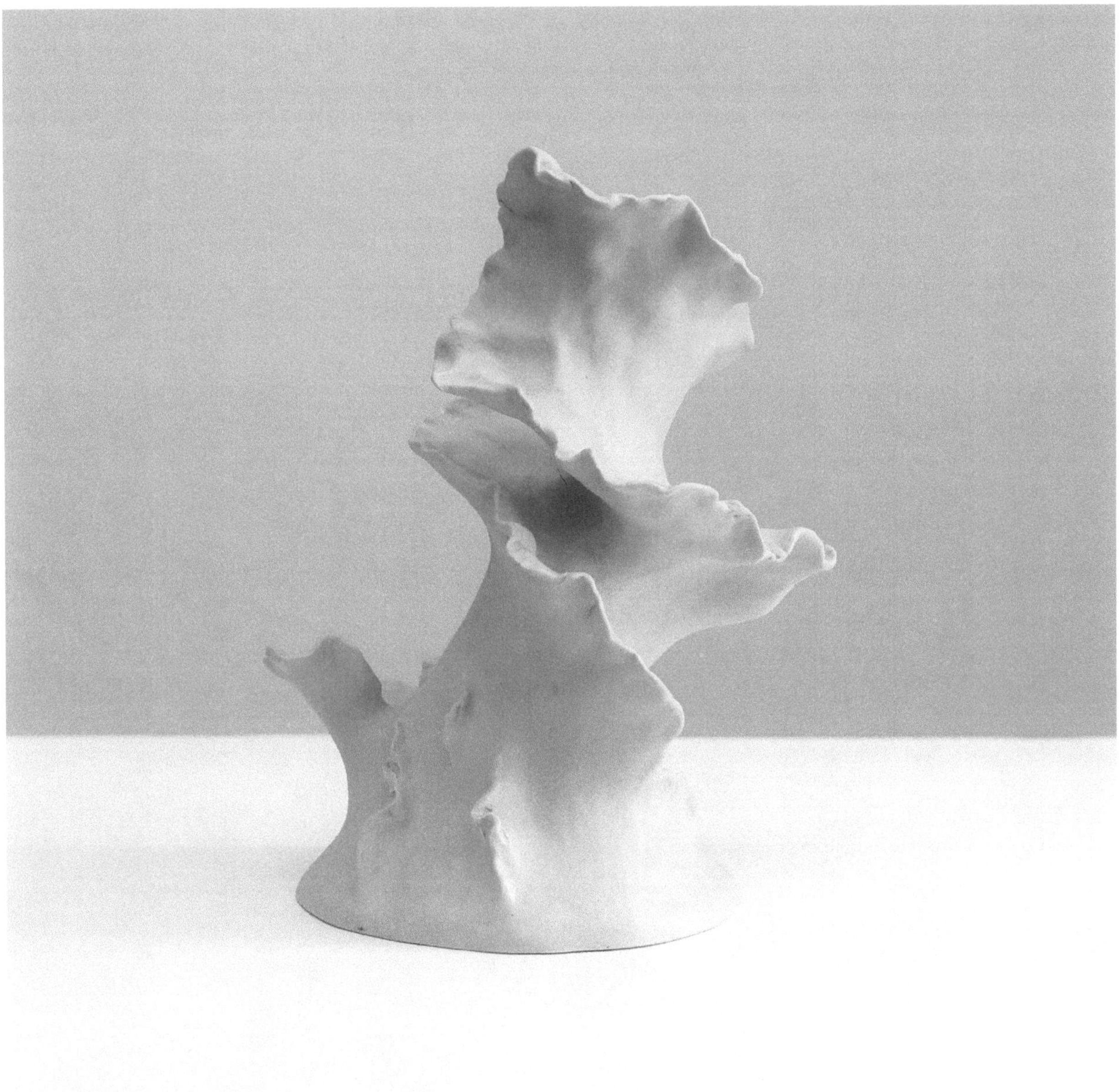

Untitled, 2024. Stoneware, pinching. H. 22 cm x W. 12 cm x D. 11 cm

ANGELE ŠIMOLIUNIENE

https://www.facebook.com/angele.simoliuniene

Paintings are an open dialogue with the world. When physical and abstract art coexist harmoniorisly. The motifs are symbolic in nature and open to various interpretations. They mostly touch on human life ,its feelings, its essence on this earth. Draws without looking, simply guiding the brush across a sheet of paper, following a feeling, without thought. This is how paintings are born - intuitively, without knowing where the information encoded in them comes from. It seems that the subconscious controls hand.

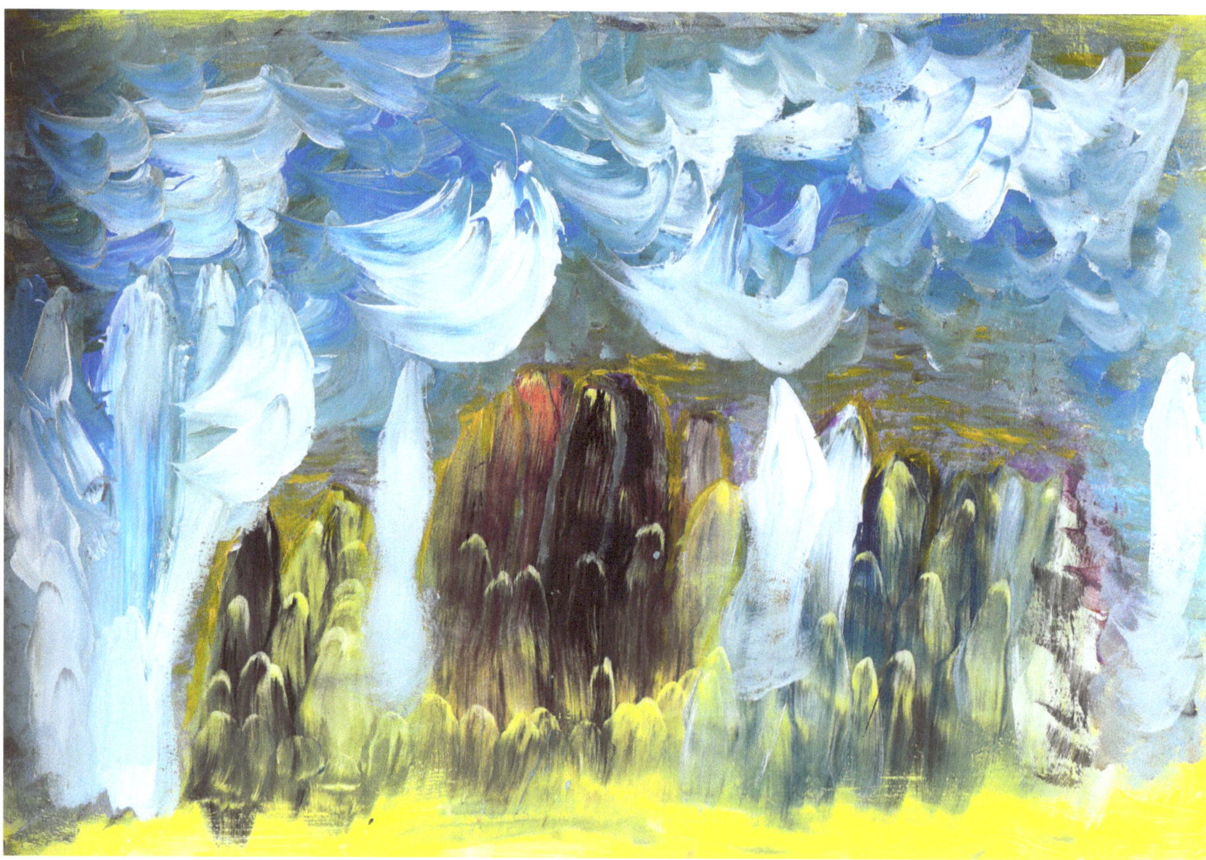

"Accompanied by spirits", 2024. Acrylic and paper, 64x44 cm.

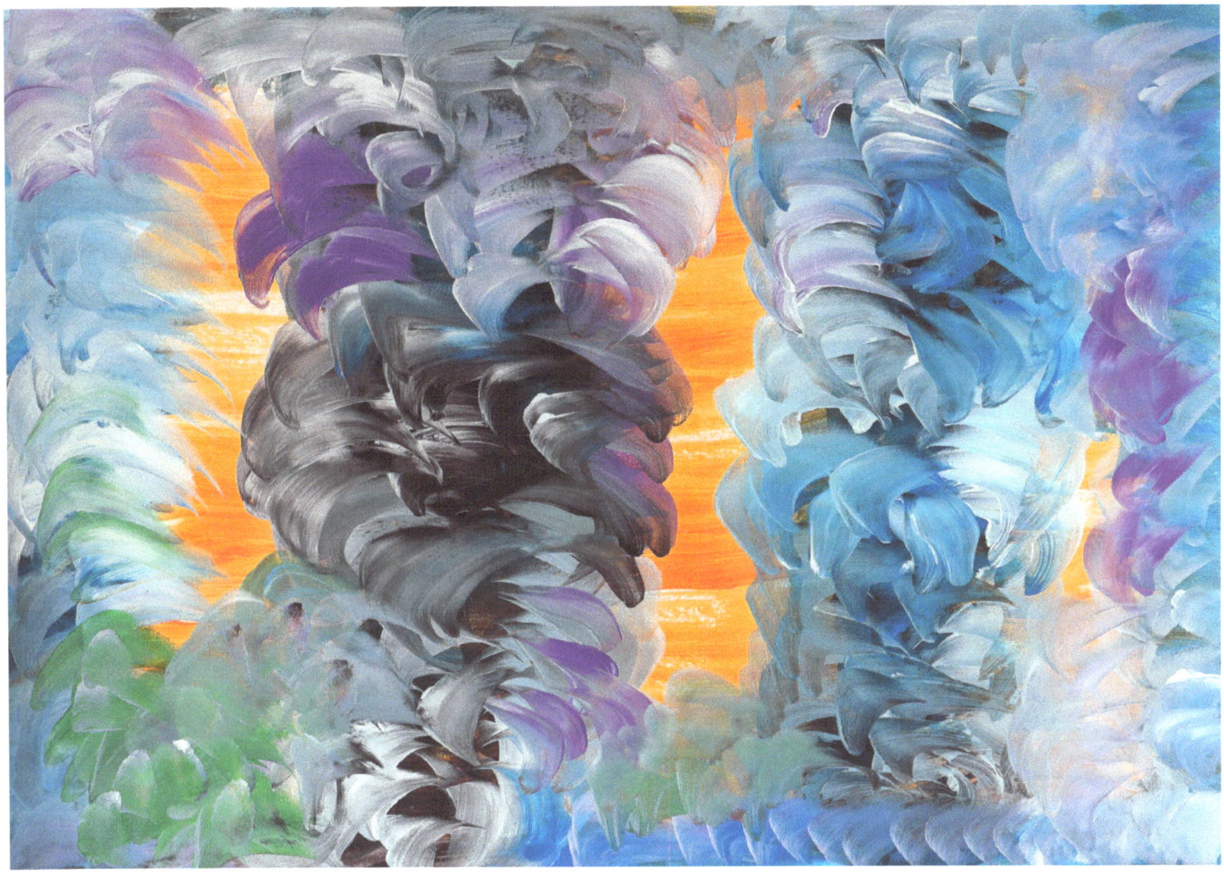

"Fairy tale characters", 2024. Acrylic and paper, 64x44 cm.

ANNABELL MOZER

https://instagram.com/annabell.m.art

Annabell Mozer is a 36-year-old self-taught artist based in Stuttgart, Germany. Her artistic journey began on her 30th birthday, when she made the decision to dedicate her life to art. A path shaped profoundly by her experience overcoming a serious illness. Painting became both a source of strength and a way to process her past. Now she's working almost every day in her own studio — her favourite place. Annabell considers art to be an interplay of music and colour. She loves and needs music while working — it inspires her and fuels her creativity. Sometimes she even dances during the process of painting. For her, painting is all about letting go and being in the moment. In 2023, she began participating in group exhibitions and international art fairs. Her works have been exhibited in cities such as Miami, Paris, Madrid, Milan, Monaco and in her hometown of Stuttgart. Many of her paintings have already found their way into private collections and the hands of art appreciators. She doesn't limit herself to one style or specific theme. Every kind of colour and variety holds its own charm and her artworks reflect this diversity. Acrylic paint is her preferred medium, as it allows her to express feelings directly and vividly. She often works with a wide range of colours and techniques, choosing them spontaneously based on her mood. One of her favourite motifs is flowers, which she finds impressive in both colour and form. She enjoys taking photographs of arranged bouquets and interpreting them on canvas with her own emotional touch. At the moment she focuses on huge and colourful acrylic paintings which she creates on canvases that are attached directly to the wall instead of yet being mounted on the frame. This approach not only provides significantly more space, but also opens up a wider range of possibilities to let her creative energy flow freely and intuitively. The direct interaction with the wall creates a unique dynamic-allowing the boundaries between artwork and space to begin to dissolve.

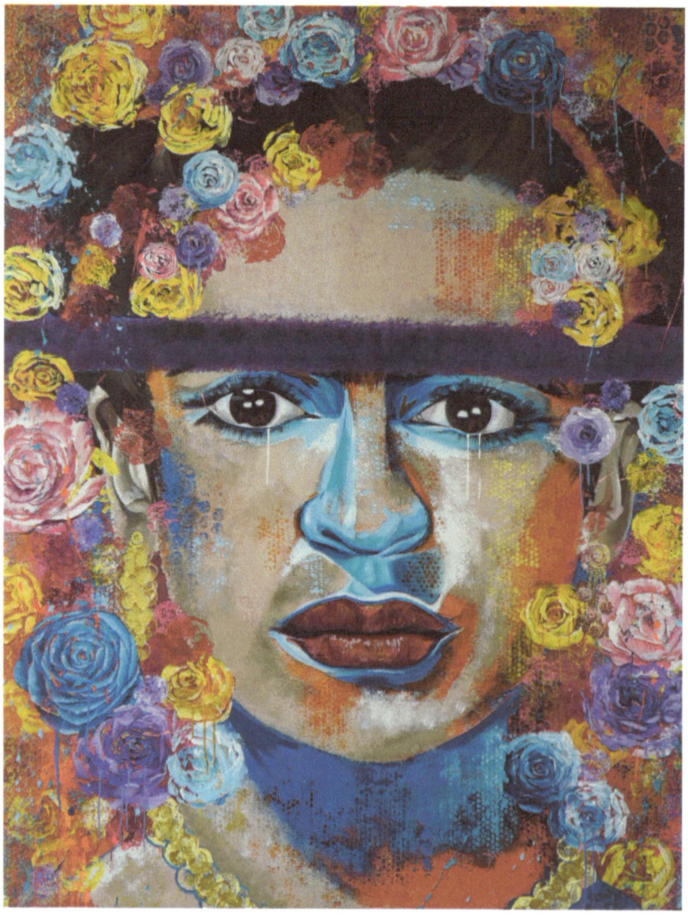

FRIDA II streetart style, 2024. Acrylic color, gouache and nail polish on canvas, 200 x 150 cm

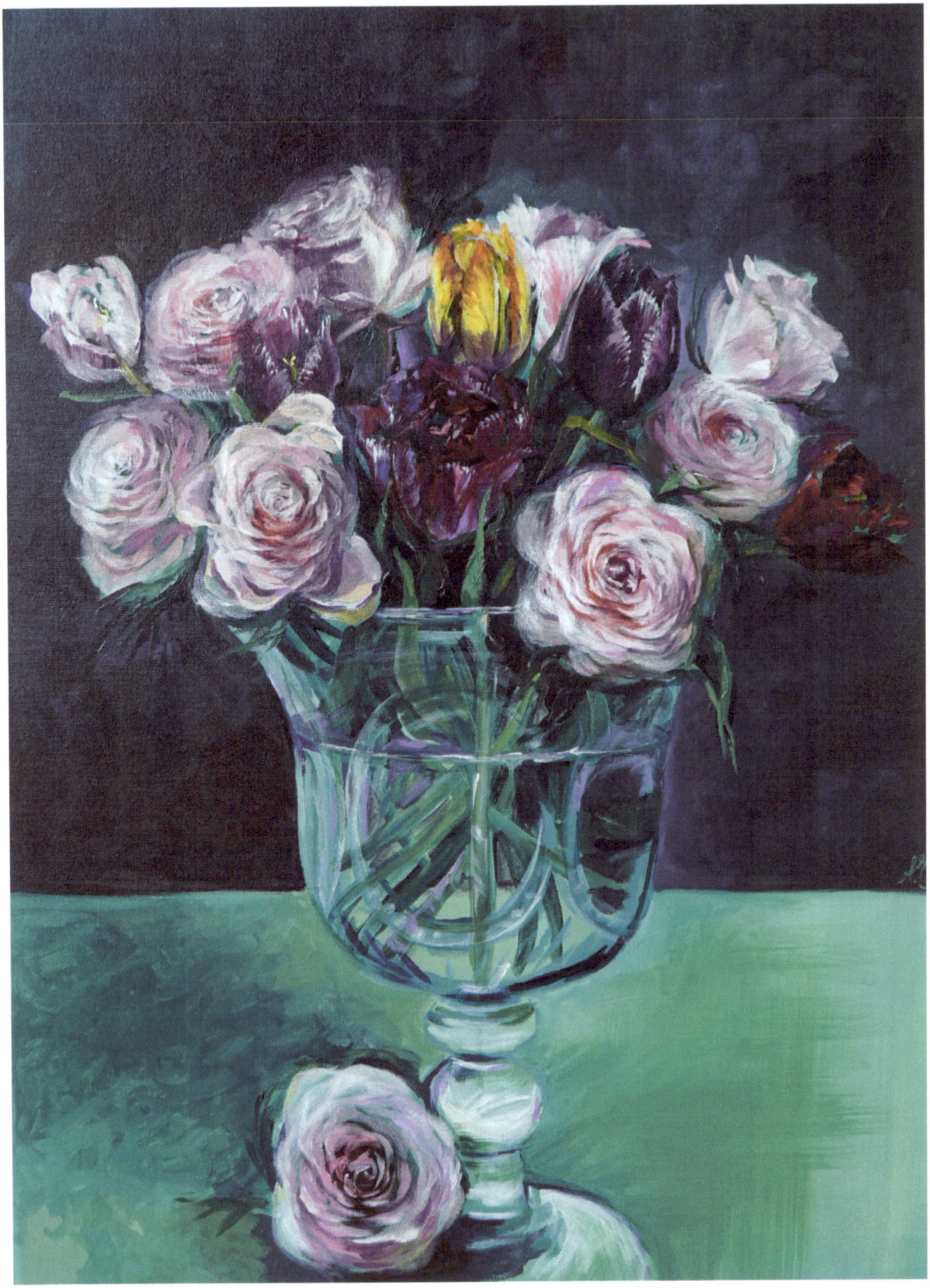

delicate roses with tulips in a vase, 2025. Acrylic color on canvas, 70 x 50 cm

ANNE WALBRING

Annewalbring.com

Anne Walbring is a contemporary visual artist whose work captivates audiences with its unique blend of vibrant colors, intricate patterns, and evocative themes. Drawing inspiration from both the natural world and urban landscapes, her pieces often explore the intersection of humanity and environment, inviting viewers to reflect on their own connection to the world around them. Walbring employs a variety of mediums, including painting, digital art, and mixed media, showcasing her versatility and innovative approach to art-making. Her exhibitions have been featured in galleries across the globe, and she continues to gain recognition for her ability to convey complex narratives through visual storytelling. Whether through abstract compositions or more representational works, Anne Walbring's art invites contemplation and sparks dialogue, making her a significant figure in the contemporary art scene.

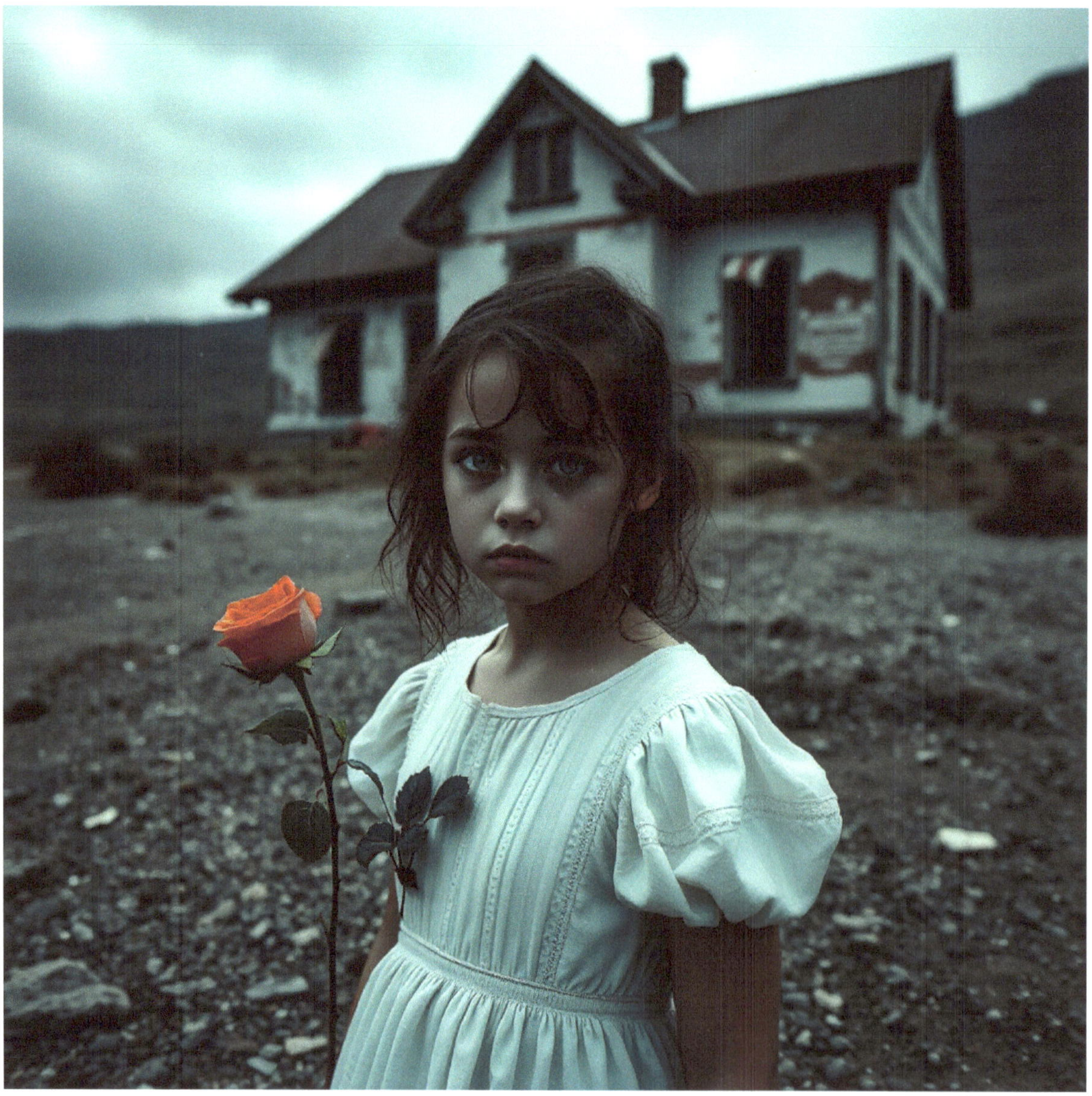

Rosas Cálidas - 2025

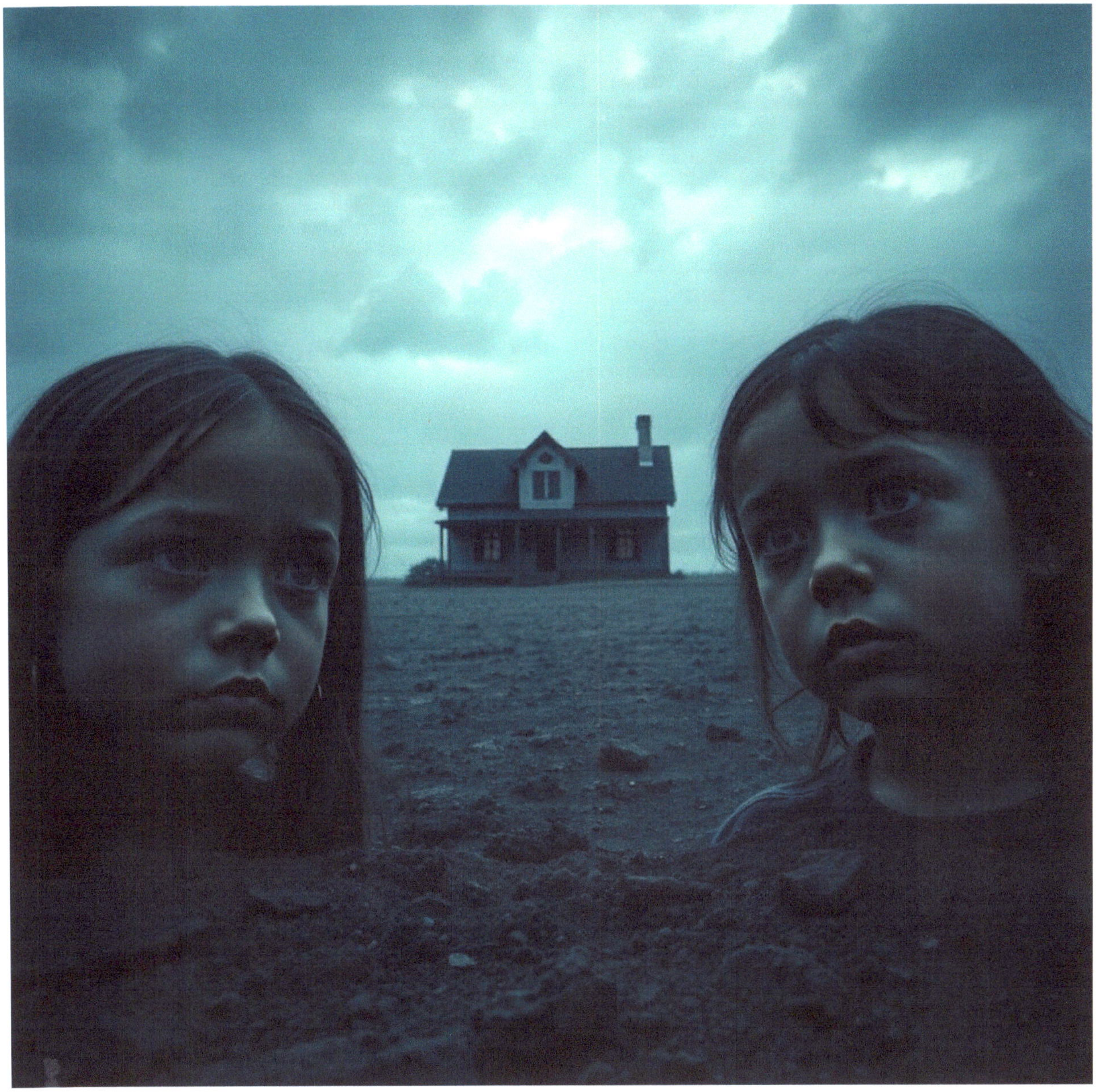

Statos quo - 2025

ANTÓNIO ADAUTA

antonio@adauta.eu

XXXV Years crafting full-time and uninterruptedly. António Adauta started working as an artisan in 1990 when student in Coimbra "rediscovered" the mosaics of Conimbriga. He adapted its patterns to create an Arraiolos stitch framed handmade embroidery. For about three years he worked on the elaboration of "master patterns" and the handcrafting of 16 prototypes. In 1992, the Secretary of State for Culture approved a "manifesto of cultural interest" for this project being sponsorable. That year he started an economic activity as artisan. Framed handmade embroidery is a new application of the Arraiolos stitch. Using cotton instead of wool, aida cloth instead of burlap, but always using the Arraiolos stitch, he manufactured an embroidery. Placed between two glasses and a frame – is displayed on a wall because of it small dimensions. The adaptation processes from the mosaic design to Arraiolos stitch master pattern were made in the following steps: Firstly - trough "on site" observation he selected the mosaics and made a chromatic study with the propose to reproduce as faithfully as possible the real colors. Secondly – based on photos and posters of the chosen mosaics- he made the master patterns of which one, making it possible to be worked in Arraiolos stitch. Finally - he handwork the embroideries with the delicate task of reproducing stitch working faithfully resembling the tesserae of the original mosaics. This work of re-invention and execution of the master patterns for Arraiolos point applied to mosaics is personal and exclusive and cannot be executed without express permission. All the master pattern has been duly registered with the D. G. E. D. A. Each work has a label (in which is identified is name and the author's) a wax seal and will be accompanied with a certified attesting origin.

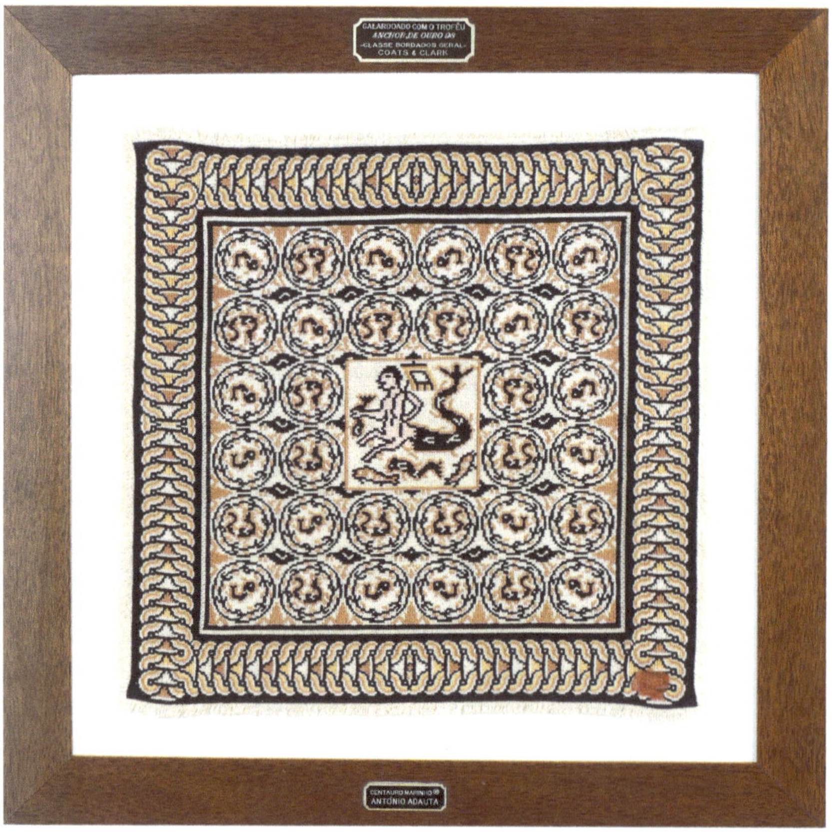

Centauro Marinho®, 1998, Cotton threads on aida cloth with Arraiolos stitch, 54 X 54 cm.

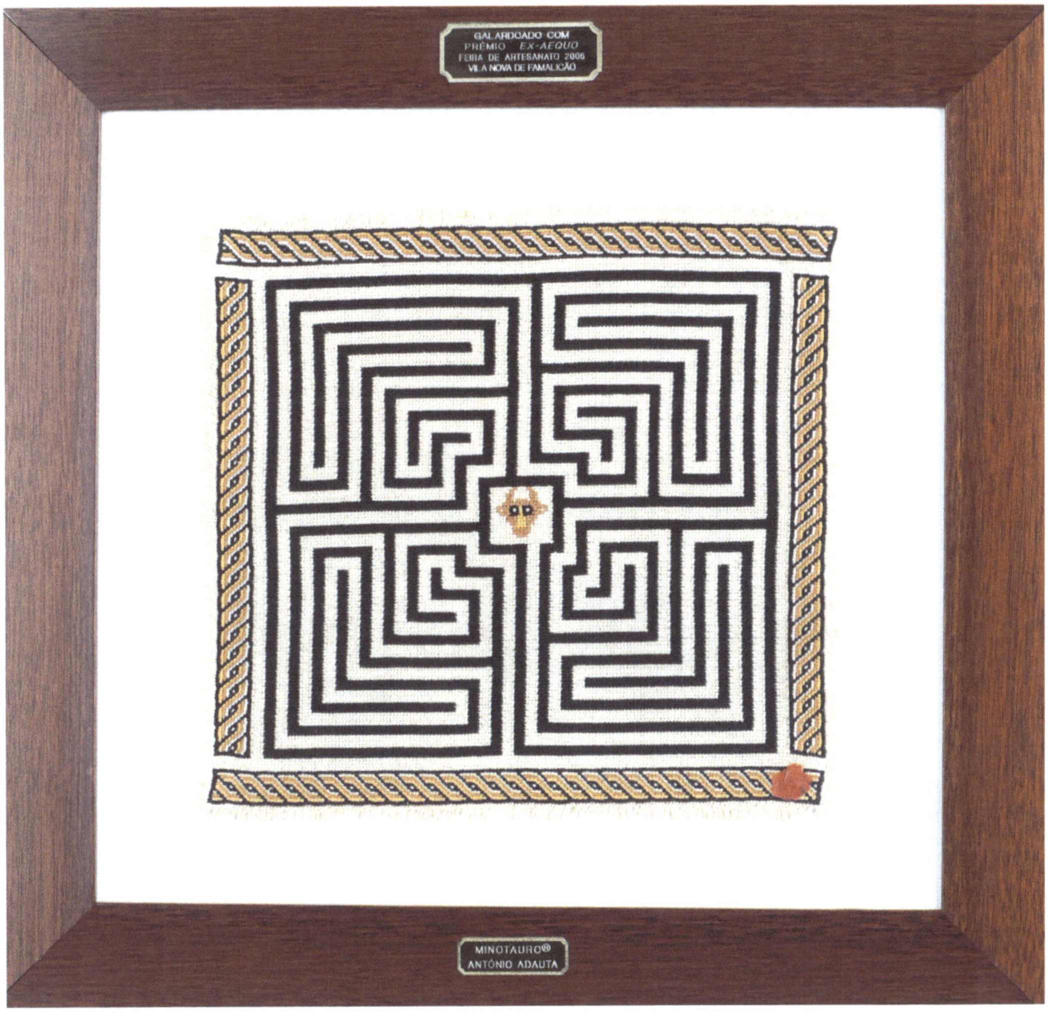

Minotauro®, 2006, Cotton threads on aida cloth with Arraiolos stitch, 40 X 40 cm.

ASHLEY GRAY

https://www.instagram.com/human3d/

Ashley Gray, known in the digital art world as Human, is a London-based artist whose work bridges technical mastery with raw emotional depth. A graduate with a master's degree in computer games art, Gray has carved a unique space in contemporary digital artistry by blending 3D modelling with philosophical introspection. His practice is rooted in both the precision of digital tools and the unpredictable nature of human emotion, resulting in a body of work that is as technically impressive as it is emotionally resonant. Gray's art explores profound themes such as duality, ego, grief, and love, often using skeletal figures and surreal compositions to evoke universal human experiences. These motifs are not merely aesthetic choices—they are symbolic representations of the internal landscapes we all navigate. His signature style combines structured digital precision with expressive chaos that invite deep contemplation and emotional engagement. Ashley's influences span both modern and classical worlds. On one hand, contemporary 3D artists such as Viky Yeo, Mike Thompson, and Raf Grassetti each offering their own level of mastery he continuously aspires to endlessly. On the other, historical figures like Edgar Allan Poe, Francisco Goya, and Edvard Munch provide thematic inspiration—their explorations of human fragility and existential depth resonate deeply with his creative philosophy. Gray's creative process begins in 3D space, using ZBrush to build complex scenes that serve as the foundation for his final compositions. The space is then rendered and transformed into 2D artworks through digital painting using Photoshop, where he blends multiple renders and painted layers to achieve a sense of emotional and visual harmony. This hybrid workflow allows Gray to maintain the mathematical integrity of 3D sculpting while introducing the expressive fluidity of traditional painting, his use of intense colours, dramatic lighting, and stark contrast draws the viewer into a focal point—often a figure or symbolic object—surrounded by deep black voids that amplify the emotional weight of the piece.

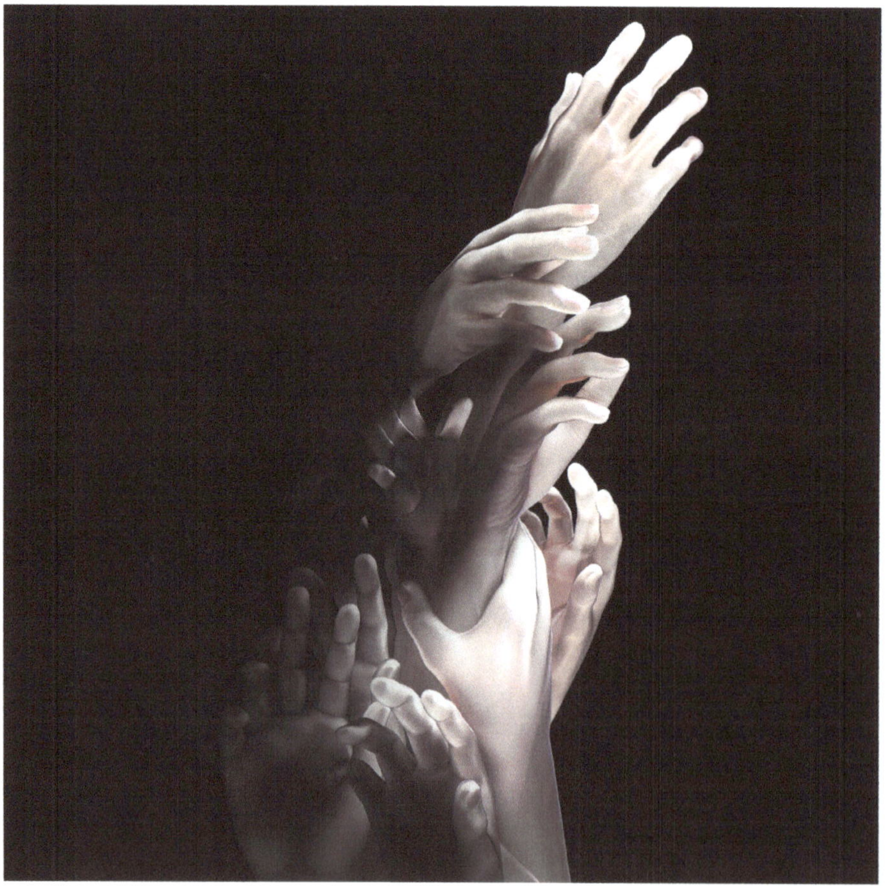

Distress Signals, 2020. Digital, 49 x 49 cm.

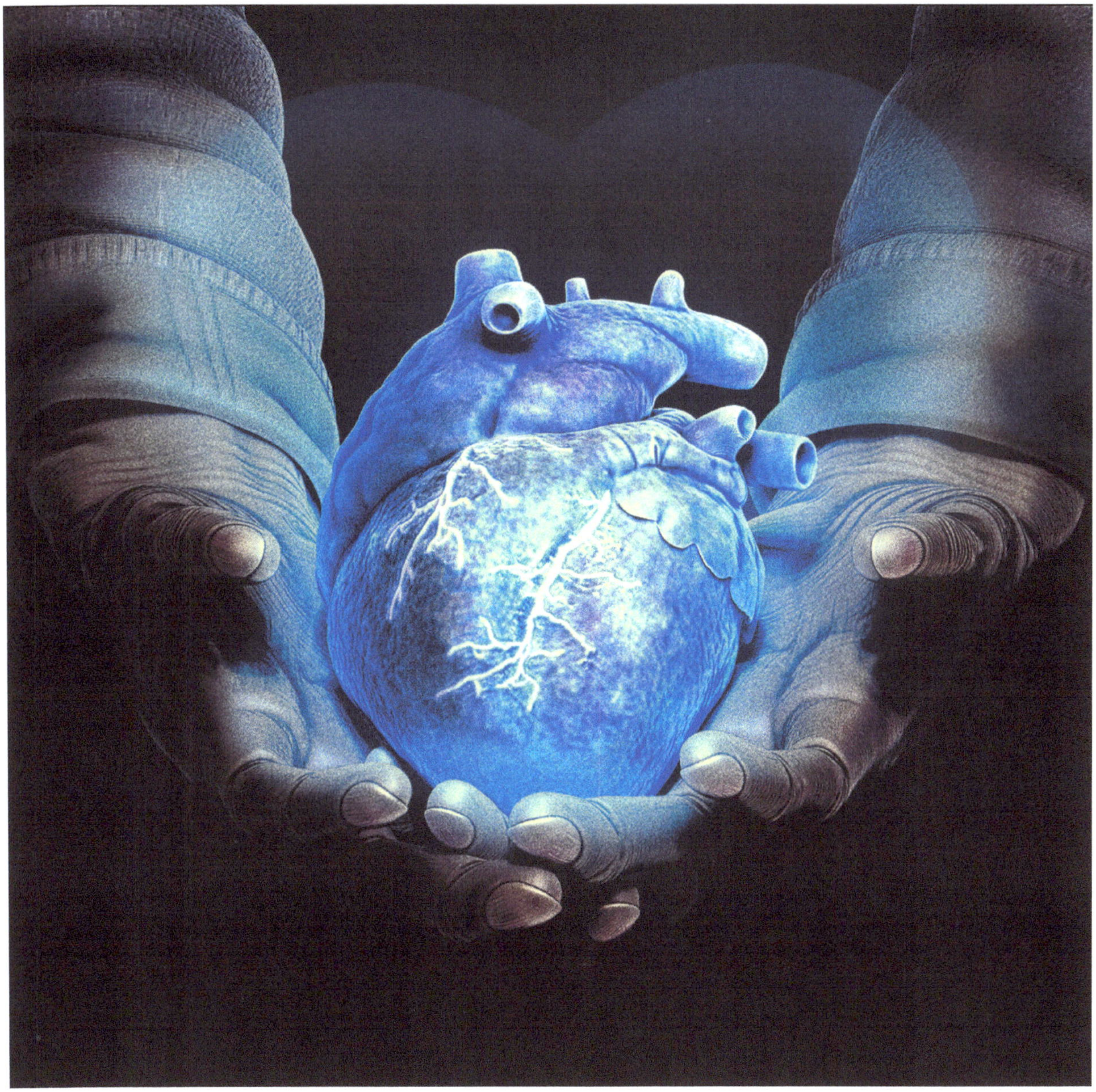

Blue Heart Forever, 2017. Digital, 49 x 49 cm.

ATOM HOVHANESYAN

arahov62@yahoo.com

Atom Hovhanesyan was a self-taught artist that worked and lived in New York. He was born in Armenia on August 19, 1981. In 1997, just as Atom graduated from high school at age 16, his family immigrated to the United States. In 1998, Atom was accepted at St. John's University where he studied Economics while continuing to work in the restaurant industry where he excelled and quickly moved into key management positions in both the New York and Los Angeles restaurant market. Atom relocated from Los Angeles to New York in 2009 and began painting- the passion of his childhood and youth. From that point his entire life was dedicated to Art. He busied himself with the study of anatomy, perspective, effects of light, color theory, art history, and the works of the Old Masters and the Modern Masters. As a faithful and respectful learner, then successor of legendary master's vision, style and performance, loved very much traditional choice of medium and ground his own colors. And after colossal dedication to art, some times, 72 hours nonstop painting or drawing, unintentionally or maybe subconsciously created unique, unrepeatable style and technique in post divisionism and ink drawings, never observed before.

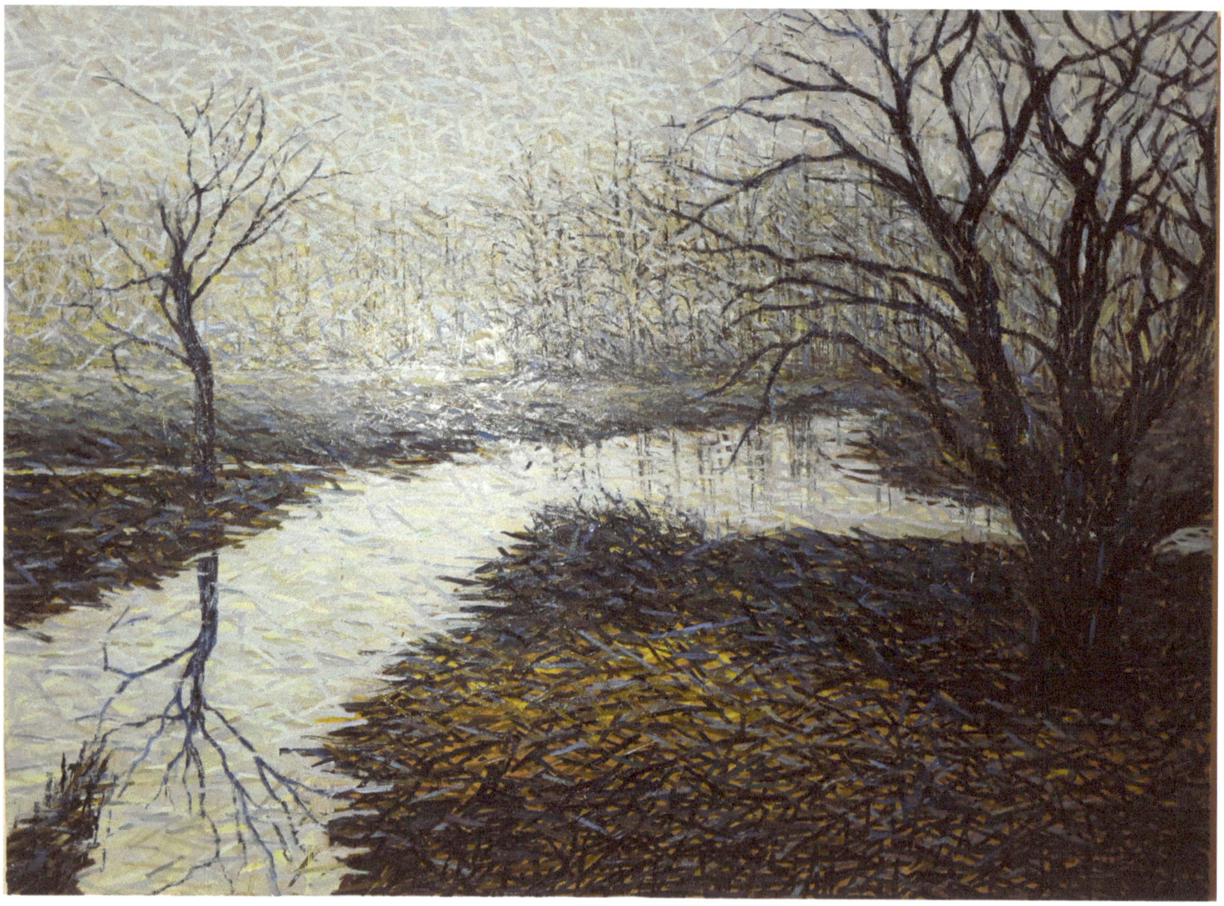

Fall Landscape With Two Trees,2018, Oil on canvas, 76x102 cm2

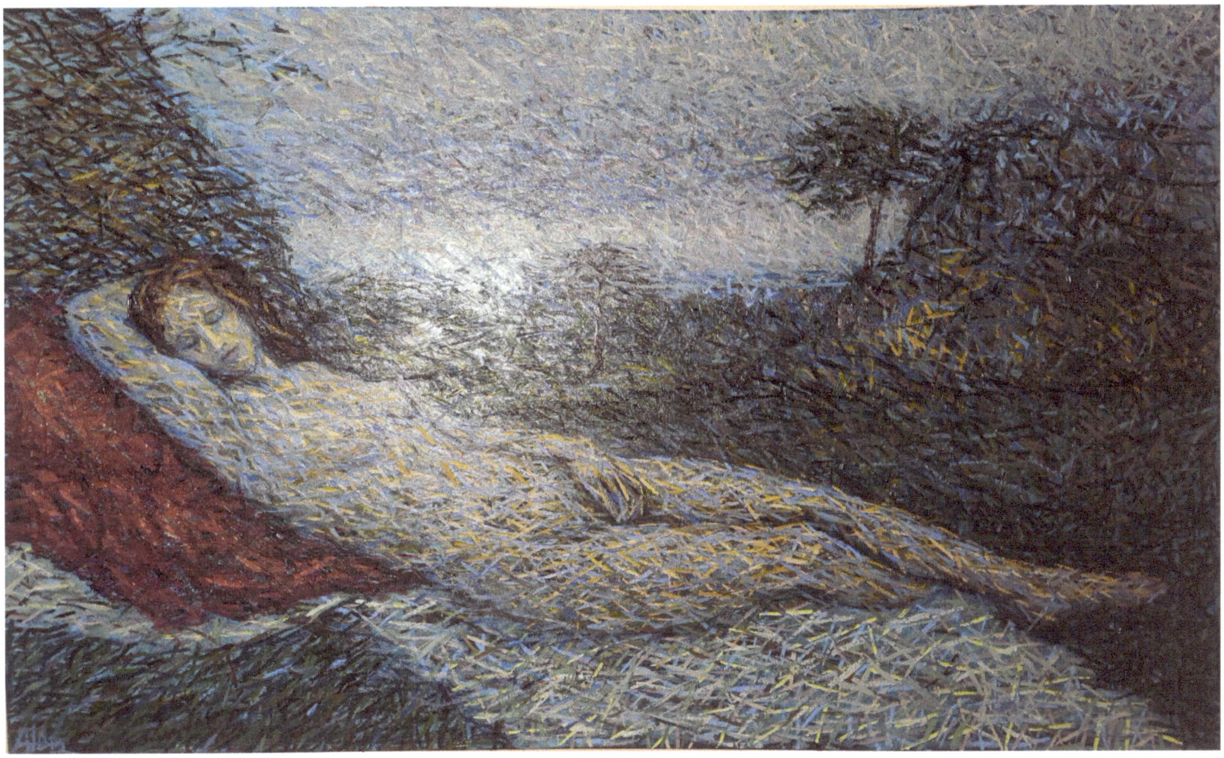

Study After Giorgione's Sleeping Venus, 2017, Oil on canvas, 76x122 cm2

BELINDA BALASKI

belinda@balaski-art.com

*Balaski Bio Belinda Balaski, a native of Southern California, creates colorful watercolor and pastel paintings. She is especially fond of painting horses, influenced by her childhood traveling the racetrack circuit with her father, the well-known jockey, Lester Balaski. Her work focuses on capturing the spirit and unique beauty of living creatures and the natural world. She is motivated by the desire to share a spiritual sense of serenity and peace through landscapes and seascapes. Belinda's creativity expressed itself at a young age in acting, photography, and art. When not performing in theatre, she was shooting pictures and drawing incessantly. At fourteen she won a four-year scholarship to the Minnesota Corresponding Art School. Belinda's gift for acting took her on a different path. She won many awards and excelled in a 50-year career in Hollywood. These experiences developed her artistic eye for framing, beauty and editing a myriad of choices. Drawing from a well of diverse talents and life experiences, Belinda uses her gift of capturing a feeling with an instinctual ease of composition. Belinda lives and works in Southern California but spends several months a year on Kauai, her spiritual home, where many of her inspirational paintings are born. Artists Statement ~ I am an LA/Kauai based artist who specializes in watercolor. In this world of turmoil and chaos, I am forever seeking peace and spiritual tranquility to inspire and share in my work. As a committed watercolorist, I believe in painting every single day. Sometimes I will paint 2-3 paintings at the same time as they all usually need 'drying time'. It is ultimately important to keep current and keep my 'water color flow'. Keeping a flow alive is far easier than trying to crank it back up, like trying to run from a complete stop. Best to keep the wheels oiled and turning, while tickling one's Muse with a constant brush stroke. There is so much diversity in watercolors, one can only be limited by one's own imagination. If you are open to listening to the muse, the flow of the water can lead you where your imagination is endlessly open, allowing the kind of awesome creativity that real "Art" is truly made of. The kind of Art that takes you out of yourself and frees you of all limitations. This is my goal. To allow your eyes to rest on an image that will open and inspire your imagination beyond your physical world, allowing you to relate, yet freely fly...

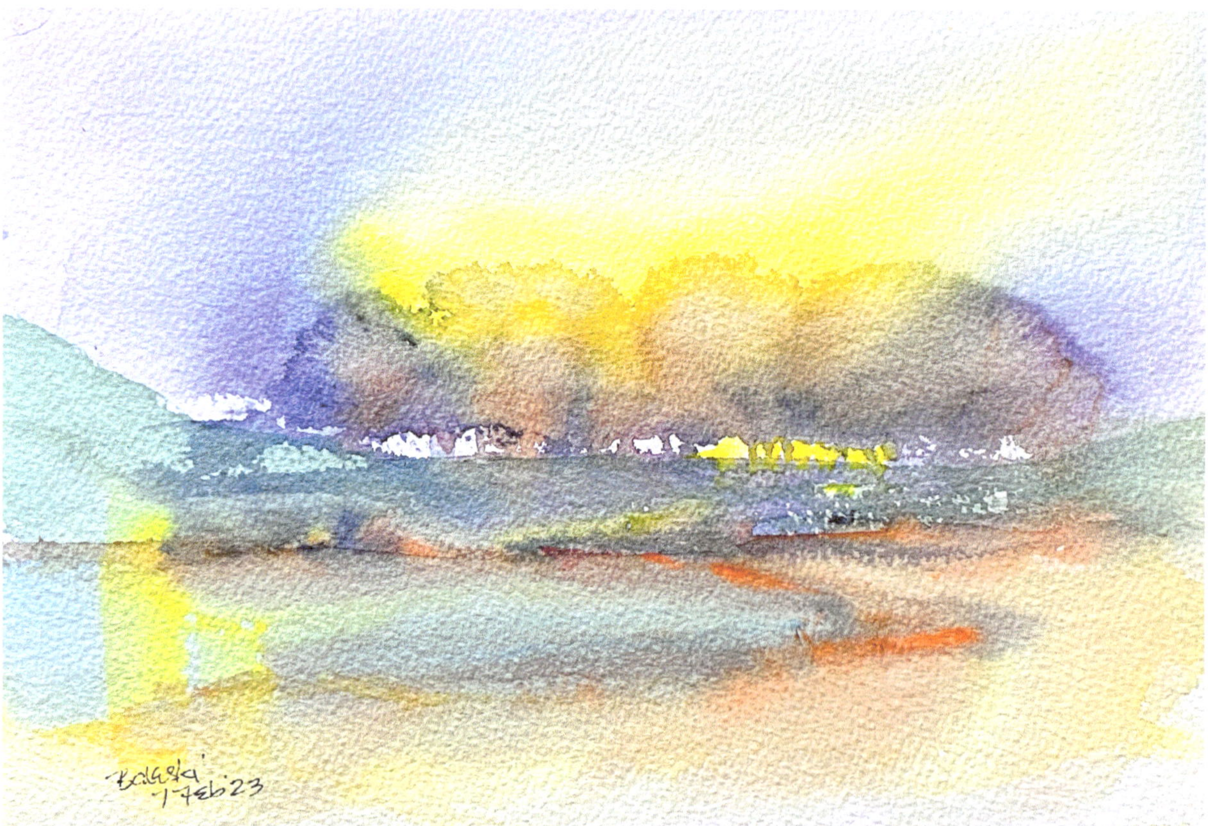

Before the Sun Sets, 2023, Watercolor on Arches, 17.78 x 25.4cm, Balaski

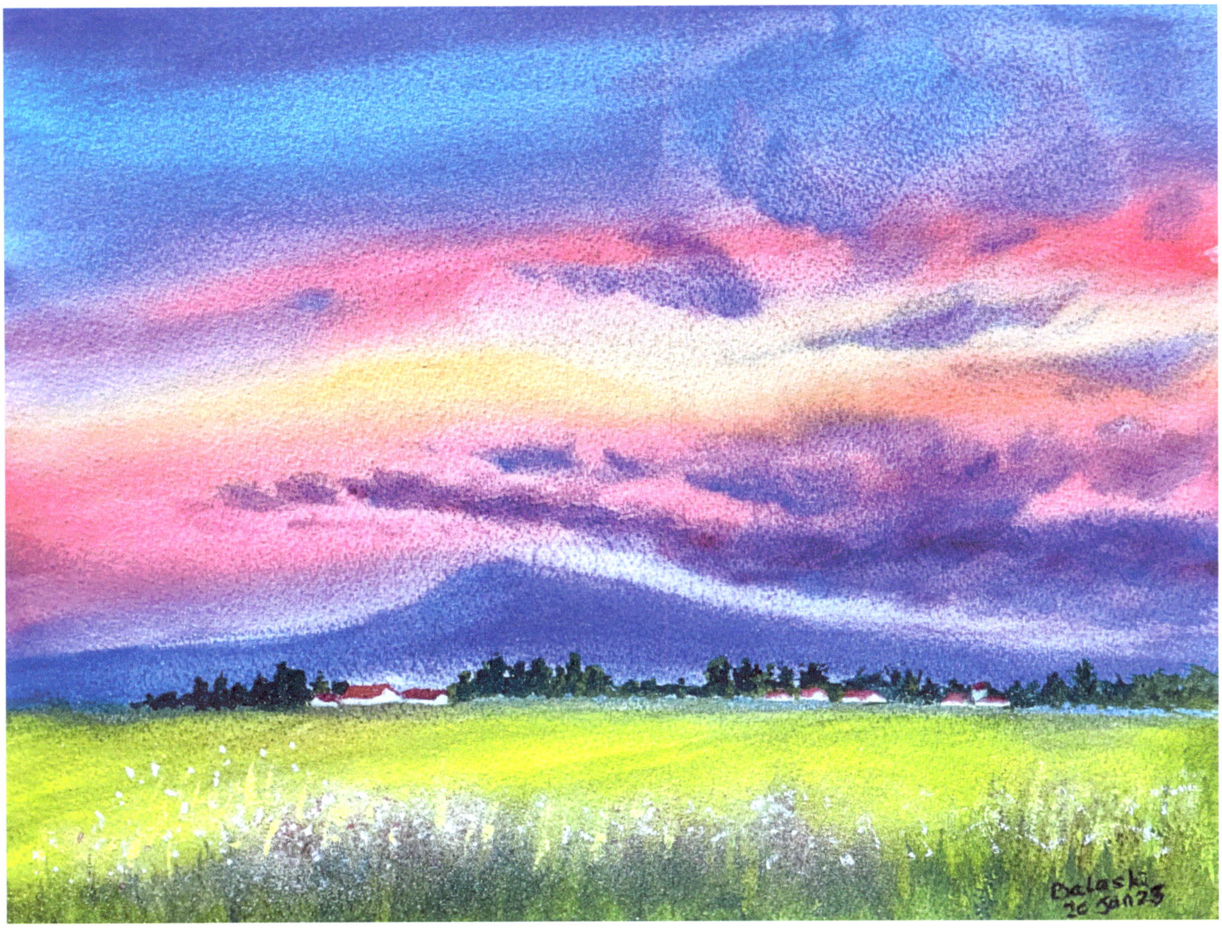

SweetGrass Valley, 2023, Watercolor on Arches, 30.48x40.64cm, Belinda Balaski.jpeg

BETTE RIDGEWAY

www.RidgewayStudio.com

Pushing the boundaries of light, color and design, Bette Ridgeway is best known for her large-scale, luminous poured canvases, which, in recent years have garnered international recognition. The artist maintains a practice in Santa Fe, NM, where the high desert light fuels her creative spirit. Her career began in 1960 in the sweatshop of Reuben Donnelley Advertising as a young graphic artist and over many decades taken her to the outdoor marketplaces in Tananarive, Madagascar, the urban dynamism of Santiago, Chile and the modern youthful capital of Australia in New South Wales - Canberra. And... many places in between. Stimulated by the variety of the colors and customs on 5 continents, along with growing up in the beautiful Adirondack Mountains of upstate New York, Ridgeway continues to perfect her unusual pouring technique. In 1979 she was fortunate to meet internationally acclaimed artist, Paul Jenkins. This was a life-changing experience. Jenkins became a good friend and mentor, encouraging the artist to work large and focus on color, space and time. After 8 long years of painting, Jenkins finally said she was ready for a show. That was in 1988. A solo show at FOTA Gallery in Alexandria, Va was a sellout and a turning point. She quit her day job and began painting full time...a dream come true! Now in her fifth decade of pouring paint, the artist is taking time to reflect. She is looking deeply into her creative impulses and sees clearly that her joy is color. She is in love with the movement in her work, sometimes kinetic and full of emotion, sometimes bold and masterful, sometimes languid and tentative. Ridgeway's journey has not been an easy one. But there are moments in the studio when everything is working so incredibly well - the music is playing, and the creative wheels are jamming. Time does not exist for her. The art unfolds under her tiny but strong hands. She is the channel. It is not hers. Like a child, it comes through her, but it is not hers. It goes out into the world – it has a life of its own.

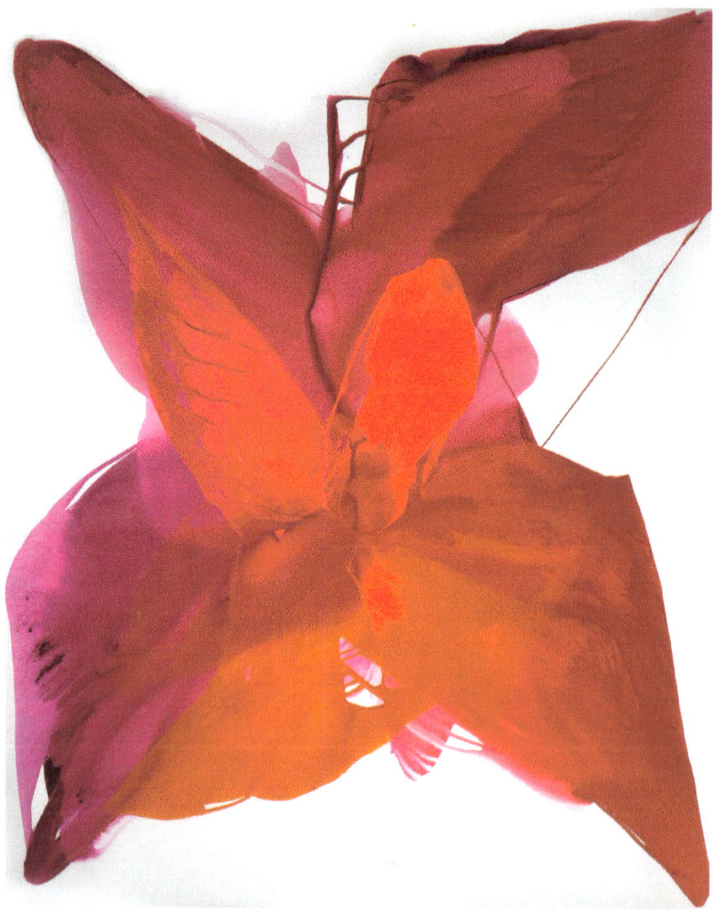

Haiku with Red, 2025, acrylic on canvas, 172.72 cm x 213.36

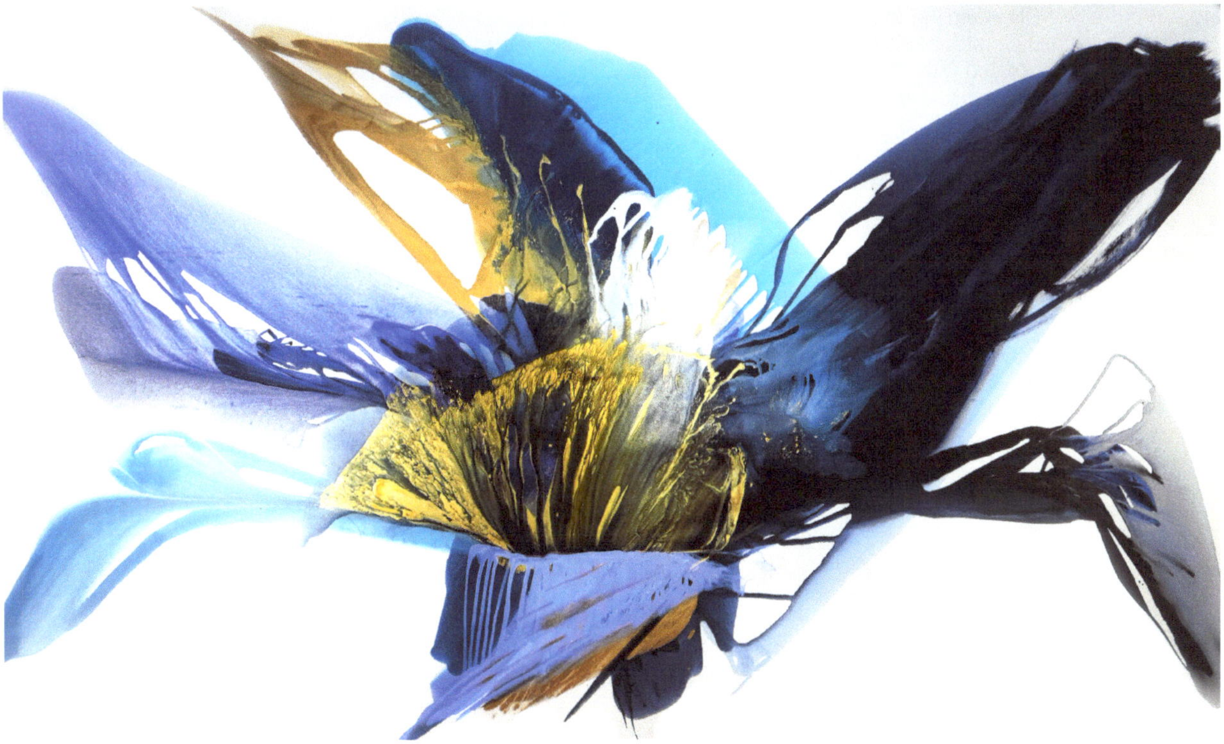

Lotus, 2024, acrylic with gold on canvas, 127 cm x 213.36

BOBBY MERCIER

Bigriverart.org

Bobby Mercier Chinookan Carver / Digital Artist BeartracksNDN Bobby Mercier is an enrolled member of the Confederated Tribes of Grand Ronde in Oregon, where he has lived most of his life. With deep family roots in the community-both his mother and father are members of the tribe-Bobby has dedicated his life to preserving and revitalizing Chinookan culture and traditional art. At 19, Bobby began working for his tribe and continues to serve as the Cultural Advisor at the Chachalu Tribal Museum and Cultural Center. Over the years, he has studied and practiced a wide range of traditional skills, including weaving, carving, and other cultural teachings. For more than 20 years, he has focused on mastering the traditional Chinookan art form, especially carving in the Columbia River style. Bobby's carvings are featured at the Grand Ronde museum and throughout the tribal community. Two notable public pieces include works on display at the Portland Building (next to Portland City Hall) and the Hallie Ford Museum of Art. A dedicated mentor and teacher, Bobby shares his knowledge with youth, fellow community members, and his own children, helping to ensure the future of Chinookan carving lives on. During the COVID-19 pandemic, Bobby expanded his artistic expression into digital design. He launched an Etsy store, BeartracksNDN, where he creates and sells custom clothing, gifts, and memorial pieces featuring his original designs. His art has reached people across the globe and continues to be used in giveaways, family commissions, and tribal events. Bobby has collaborated with others to bring his traditional designs into new mediums-such as wood engraving, drum-making, jewelry, and rattles-fusing ancestral knowledge with contemporary tools. While he prefers not to sell his original carvings, he is excited to share his work more broadly through wood-engraved art, allowing more people to access and connect with traditional Chinookan designs without the spiritual attachment his original pieces carry. As one of fewer than ten active carvers who deeply understand and practice traditional Chinookan carving, Bobby remains committed to cultural preservation, mentorship, and creative innovation within his community and beyond.

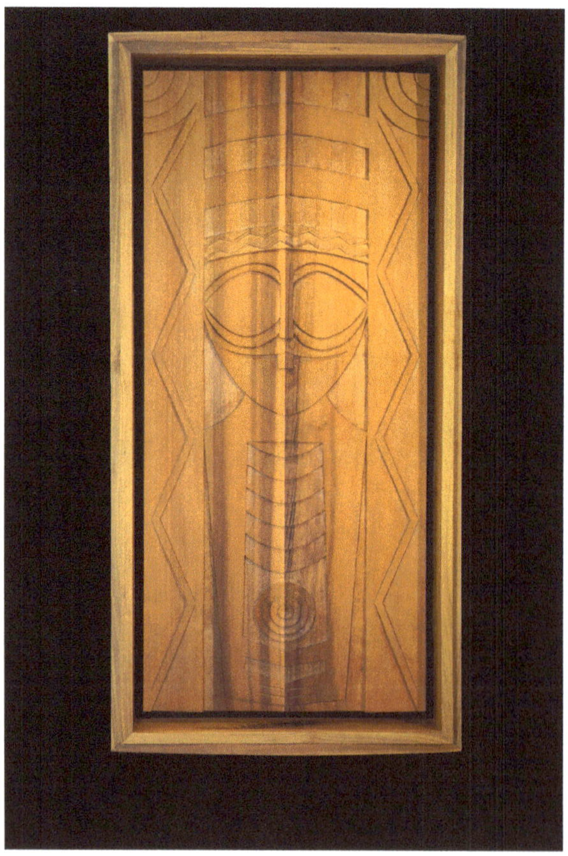

Head Man 2023 122 x 183

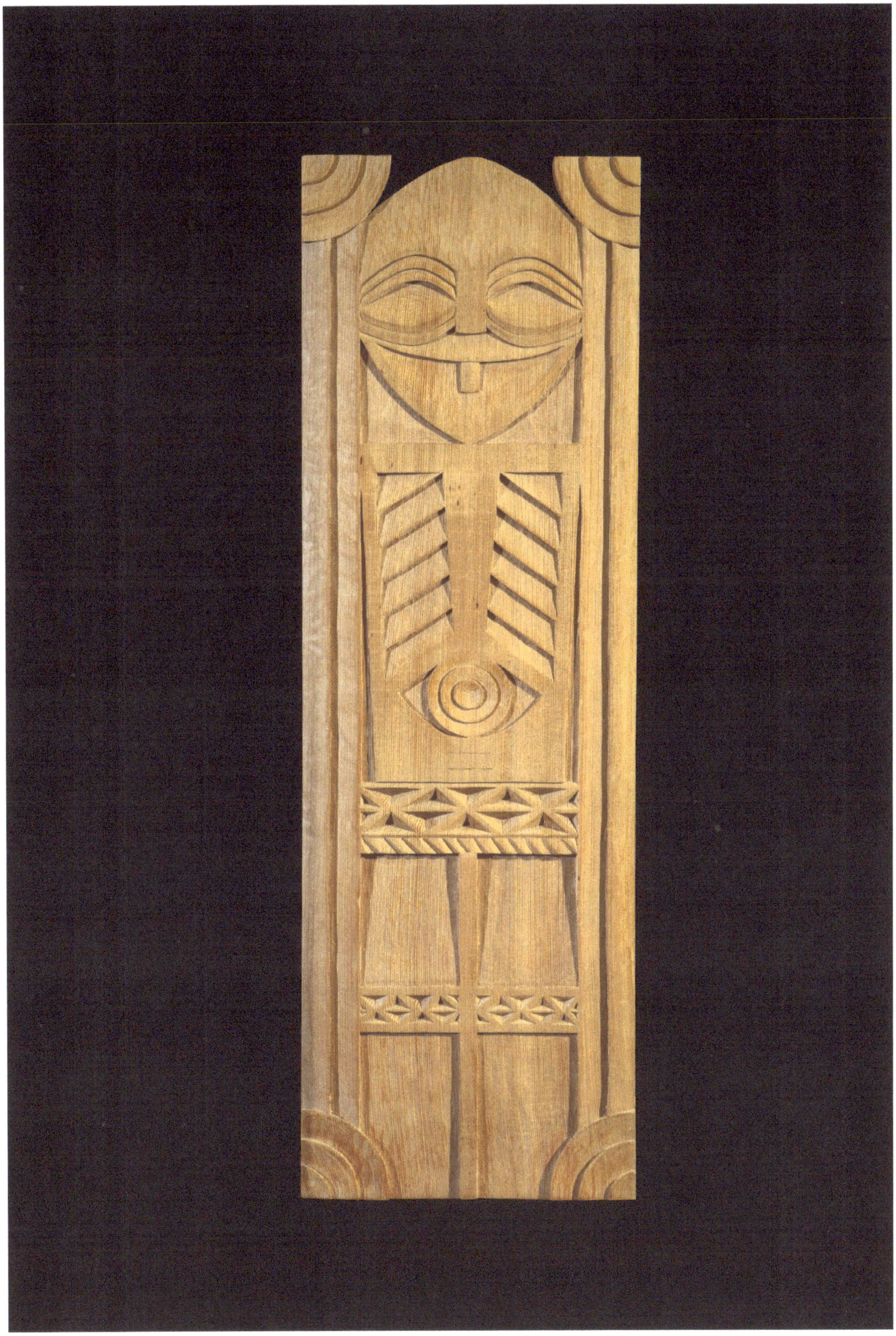

Power figure 2021 30.48 x 91.44

CAMILLA GHIONE

camillaghionedesigns@gmail.com +3307930456

Camilla Ghione (b. 1995) is a contemporary Italian artist working between Monaco and Italy. Her paintings explore the intersection of nature, psychology, and the cosmos, using mixed media—especially acrylic and resin—to create immersive, luminous surfaces. A key element in her work is the integration of light: each piece is designed to react to its surroundings, shifting subtly with the light of day and reflecting its environment, making every viewing experience unique and dynamic. Central to Ghione's philosophy is the concept of imperfection. She challenges the societal obsession with flawlessness, believing that perfection is an illusion. Her work embraces organic forms, textures, and irregularities as a celebration of authenticity and humanity. Imperfection, rather than being something to correct, becomes a source of beauty and truth. Her practice includes the use of reflective materials—resins, mirrors, and layered transparencies—that invite viewers to see themselves within the artwork, blurring the line between subject and observer. Through these techniques, she encourages self-reflection and emotional connection. After earning a degree in Fashion Design in New York, Ghione shifted her focus to fine art, developing a visual language that balances abstraction with symbolic and natural elements. Her paintings evoke emotional landscapes, cosmic visions, and underwater realms—spaces of both clarity and mystery. Committed to sustainability, she supports environmental causes by twenty planting trees for every painting sold and contributing to ocean-cleaning projects. Her work has been exhibited internationally and features in prominent private collections. One of her notable works, More Than What You Can See, was auctioned by Sotheby's in Monte-Carlo in support of Princess Charlene's charity, embodying her invitation to look beyond the surface and connect with the invisible essence of things.

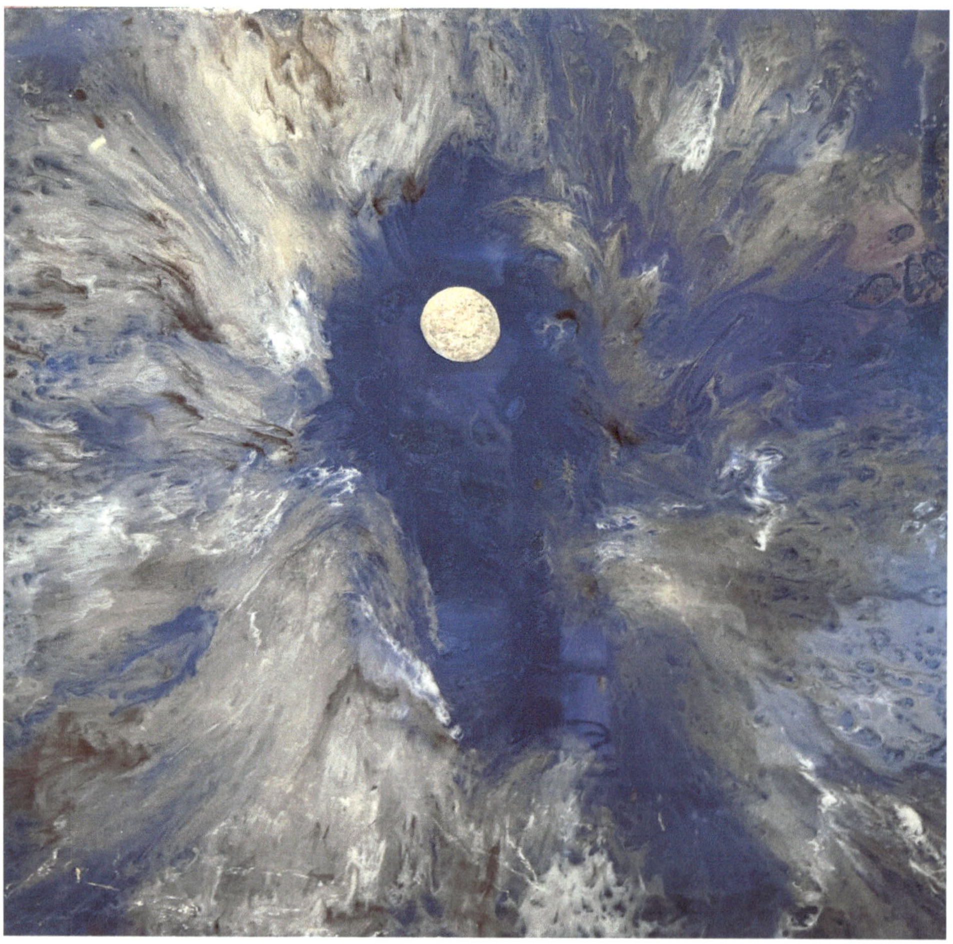

2025 - LUNA

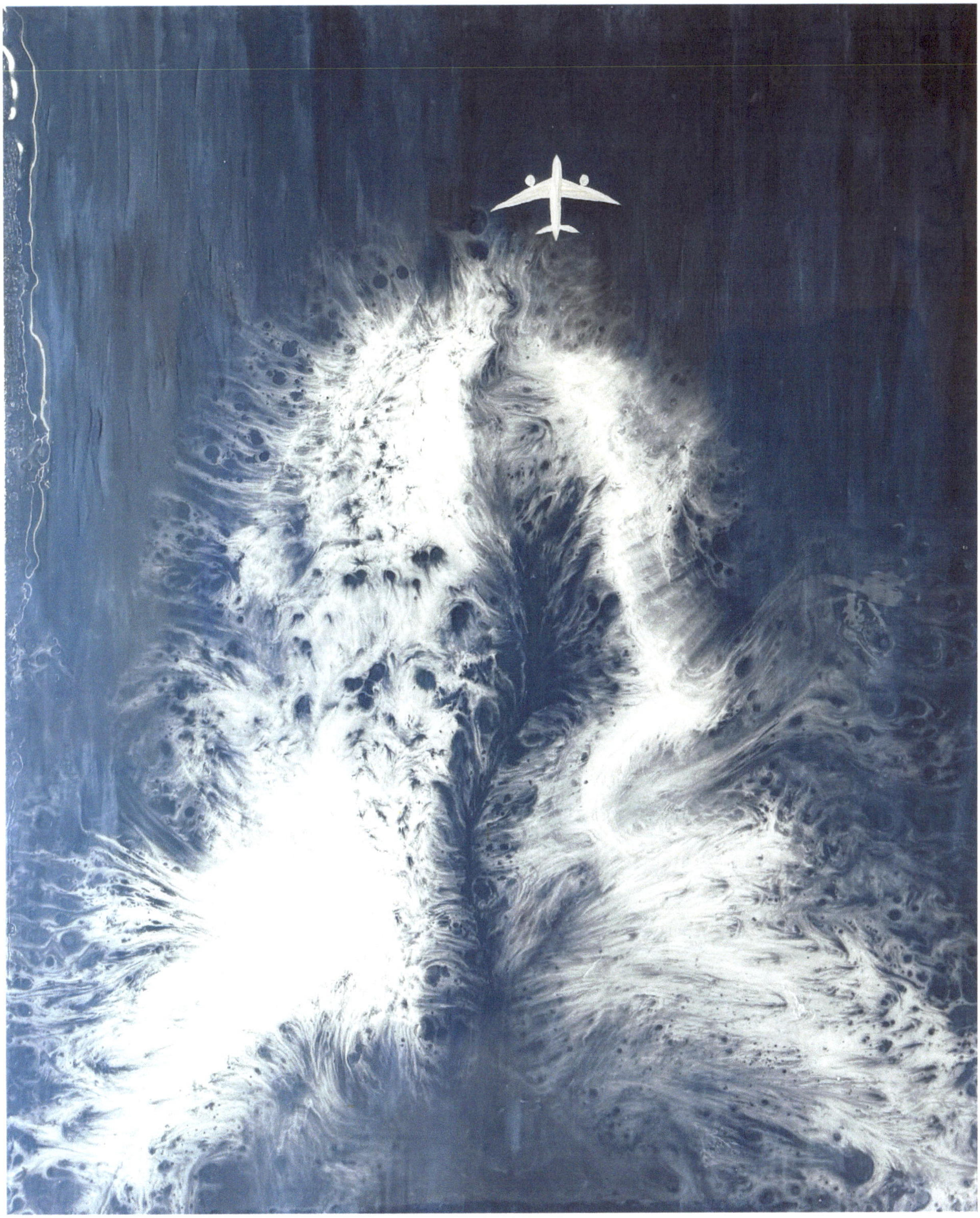

CHEM TRAILS - 2025

CARL JACKSON

Chipmj2001@yahoo.com

Artist's Statement His work is an attempt to describe an ever more complex world that most of humanity is not equipped to deal with. A recent graphite piece, has the title "Smart but Not Smart Enough" which is central to his belief, that we, as a species, though clever, and even capable in many ways, cannot overcome our negative impulses. Greed, self-interest, sociopathy, neurosis, demagoguery and aggressiveness when abetted by unfettered technology, far outweigh our better impulses. The oft-repeated maxim about old men decrying the excesses, indiscretions and stupidity of the young no longer applies. Evolution of technology without concomitant maturation of our ability to control our negative impulses is a disastrous stew. These are not new ideas, but he does believe the rise of fascism, enhanced by a "weaponized" news media, the World Wide Web and the exponentially rapid rise of Artificial Intelligence make the future increasingly uncertain.

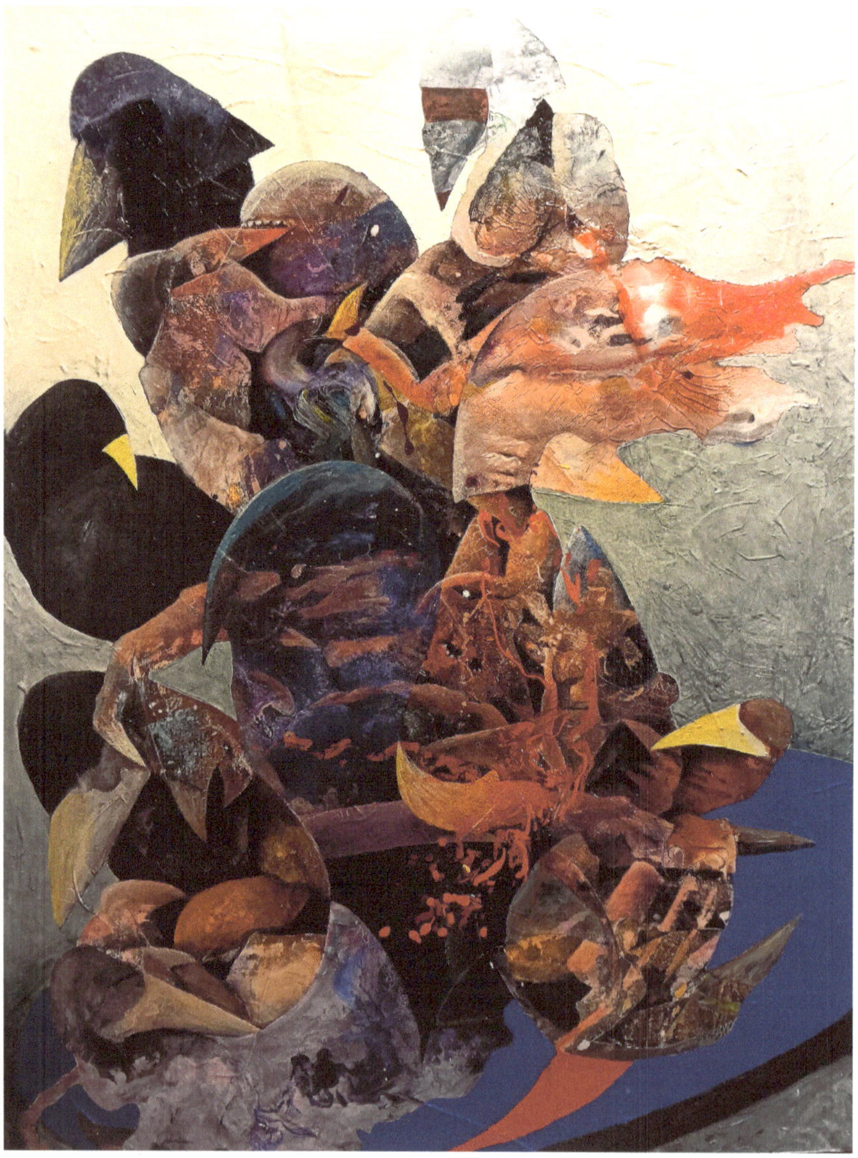

"Ship of Murderously Foolish Crows", 2024, Acrylic on canvas, 122 cm h x 91.5 cm w

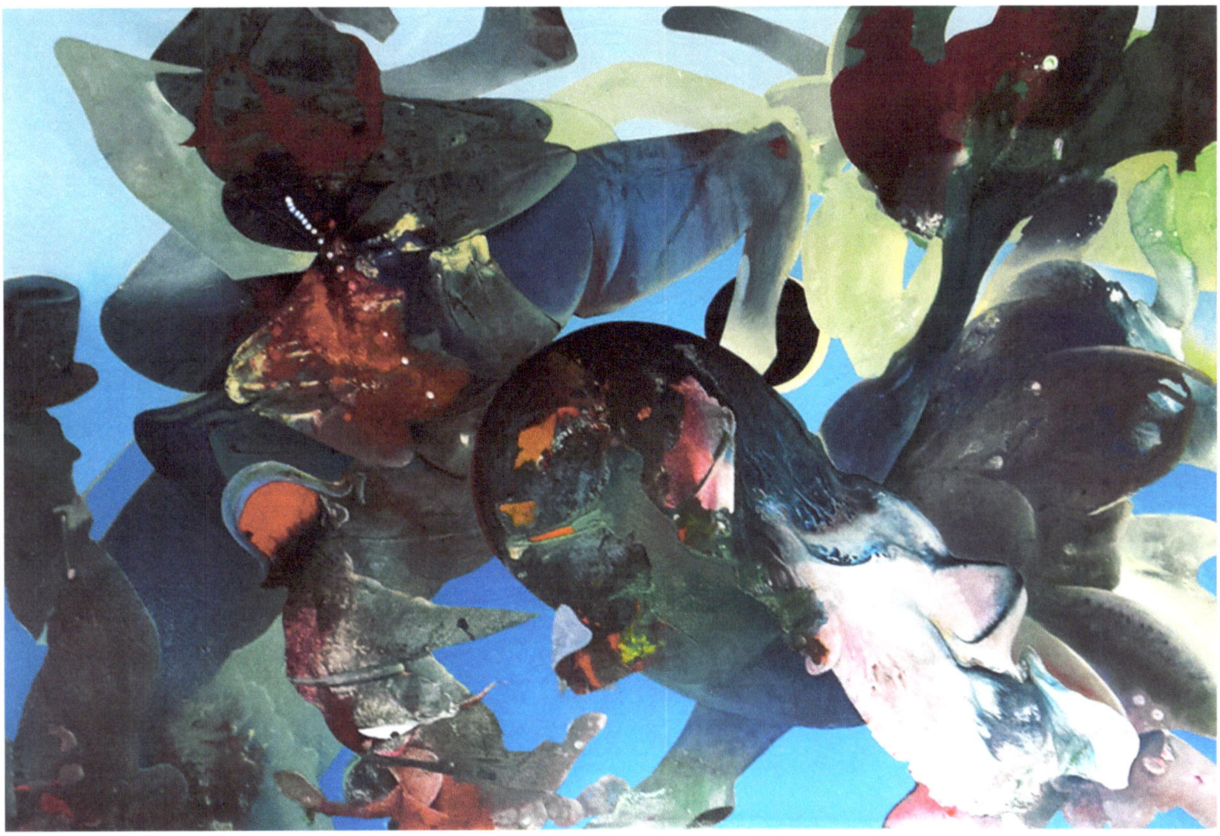

"Eclipse" 2016, Acrylic on Canvas, 112 cm h x 168 cm w,

CAROL WATES

artbycarolwates

Inspired by David Hockney's work, I do all my pictures on the iPad using the Brushes App. I prefer to work "En Plein Air", because I love being immersed in nature. I try to adapt as quickly as possible to changing light, reflections, shadows, and atmosphere. This is quite a challenge, and I love it when it all works.

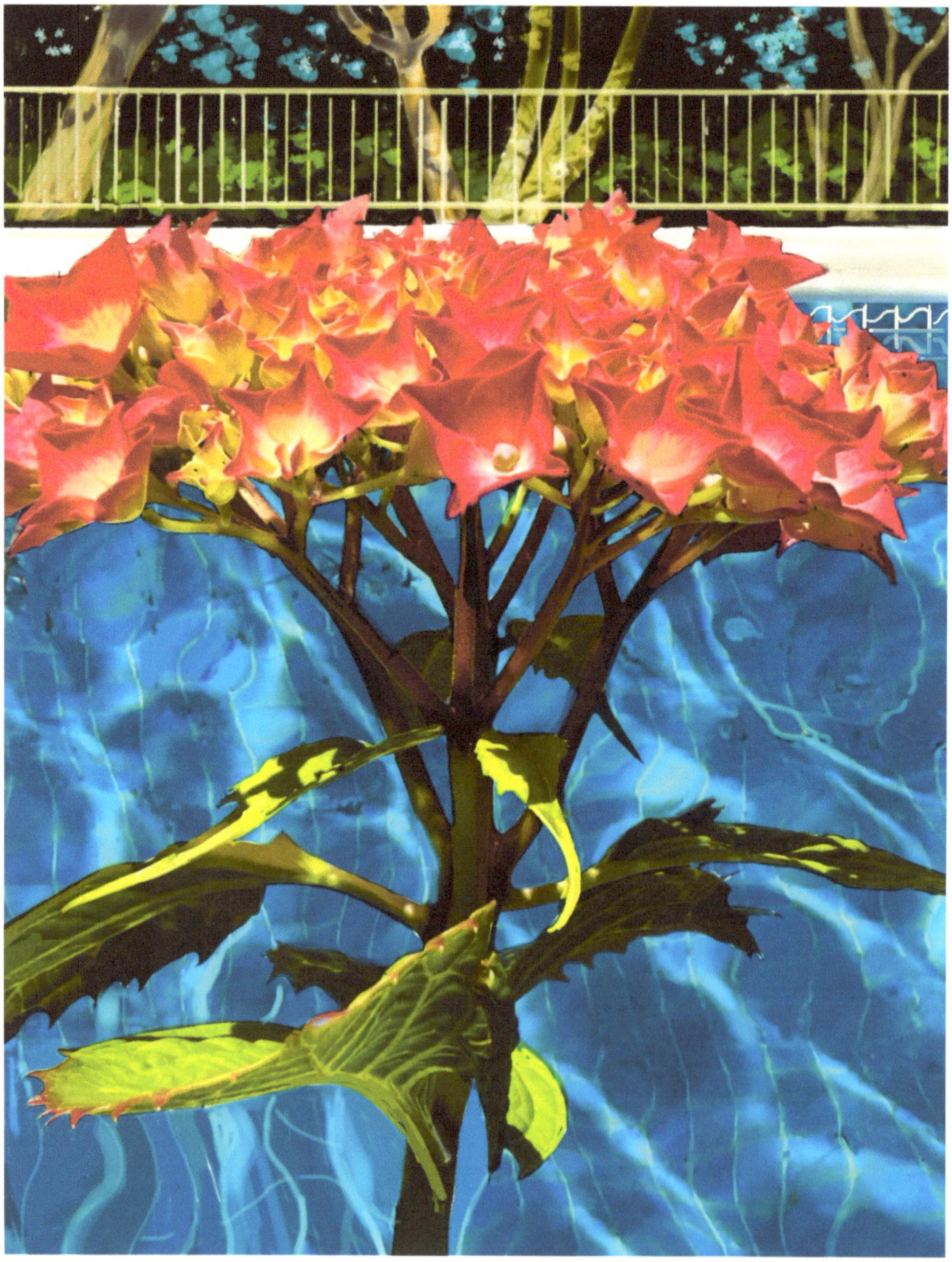

Hydrangeas against the Pool iPad 2025 29.7x42cm

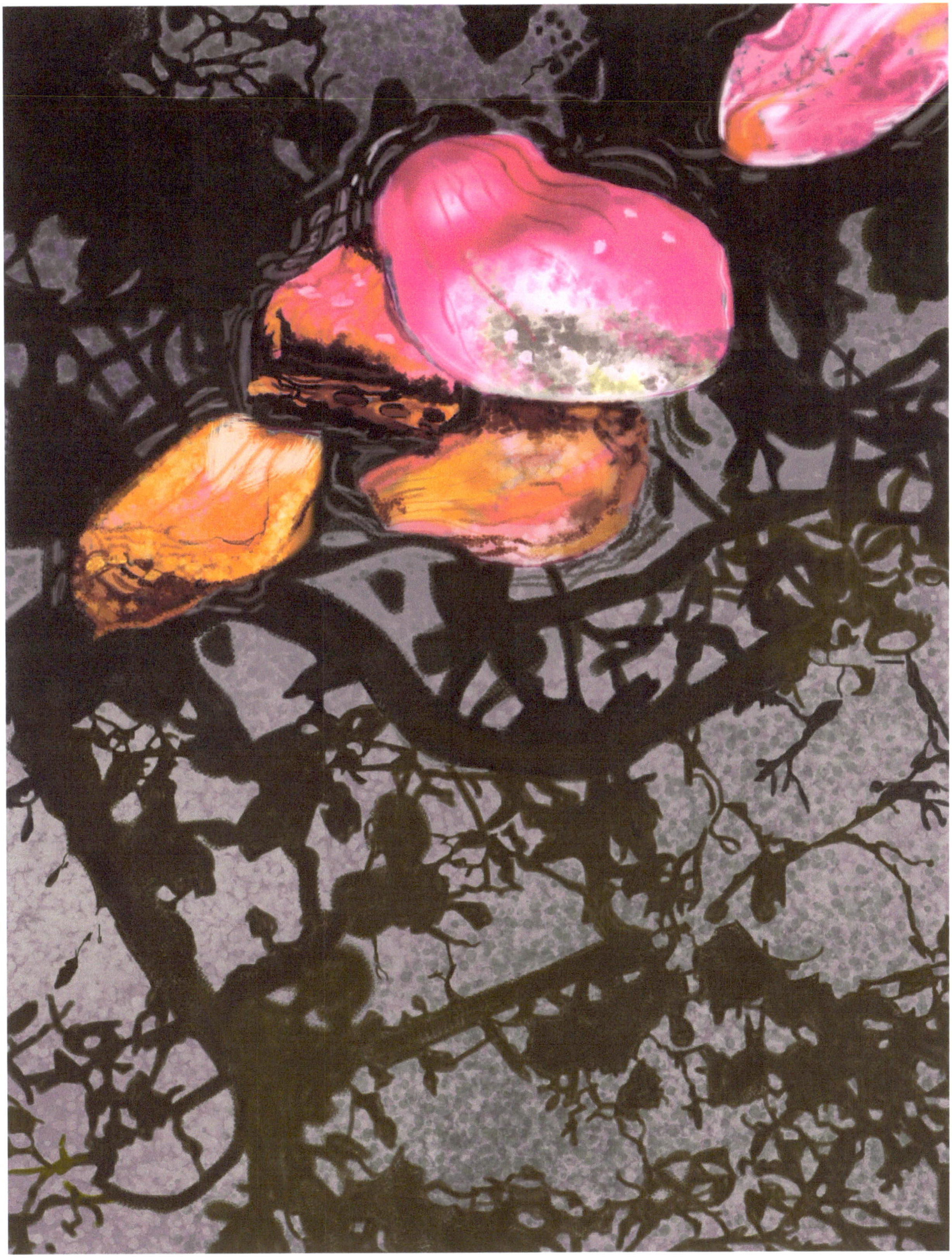

Fallen Magnolia Petals on a puddle iPad 2025 29.7x42cm

CAROLIN RECHBERG

carolinrechberg.com

Carolin Rechberg is an interdisciplinary Fine Artist born in Starnberg, Germany. She places most value in the multi-sensory experience involved in the process of creating, the insights they generate and how these transfer to a way of life. Rechberg states that "alerting the senses through creating, is an opportunity to ground in the present moment. Observing with the senses provides a place to simply be, to breathe, to feel, to find rest in the now. It is a means to communicate with the is-ness of being, with being in presence. The art process, and the artwork, is a vehicle to harness instinct, stimulate creativity and gather awareness, information, and insight, emanating through heightened sense perception, in the communion with art and nature." Rechberg attained an Interdisciplinary Bachelor of Fine Art from the California College of the Arts, a Master of Fine Art in Drawing and Painting from the San Francisco Art Institute, and a Master in Art and Art Education from Teachers College, Columbia University. She taught Drawing and Painting as a Teaching Assistant in her 1st Master at the San Francisco Art Institute, and Etching, Lithography, Silkscreen and Woodcut during her 2nd Master at Teachers College. Simultaneously to completing her education she managed the Printmaking Studios at Teachers College. Carolin Rechberg's work has been exhibited and published internationally. Rechberg works as an independent artist, offering unique artworks for sale and individual commissions for commercial, private, or public space. "Whether in art or in life, it is about the process of experiencing, being in the moment, being present. As an artist one consciously communes with the very act of creation, with making 'a knowing', an understanding brought forth through the work itself. The practice of art births a way of being. It is a vehicle to foster and sensitize the relationship of one's own effect of presence, and that of the 'other', in the world. Art making facilitates a means to digest, to reflect and to transform information. One becomes the elemental part, the tool for the alchemy of creation itself and if attentive one receives in response valuable ideation and revelations mirrored at large in the systems and products of human infrastructure we live in and see created in life. Art harnesses a state of alert awareness. The art process is the art."

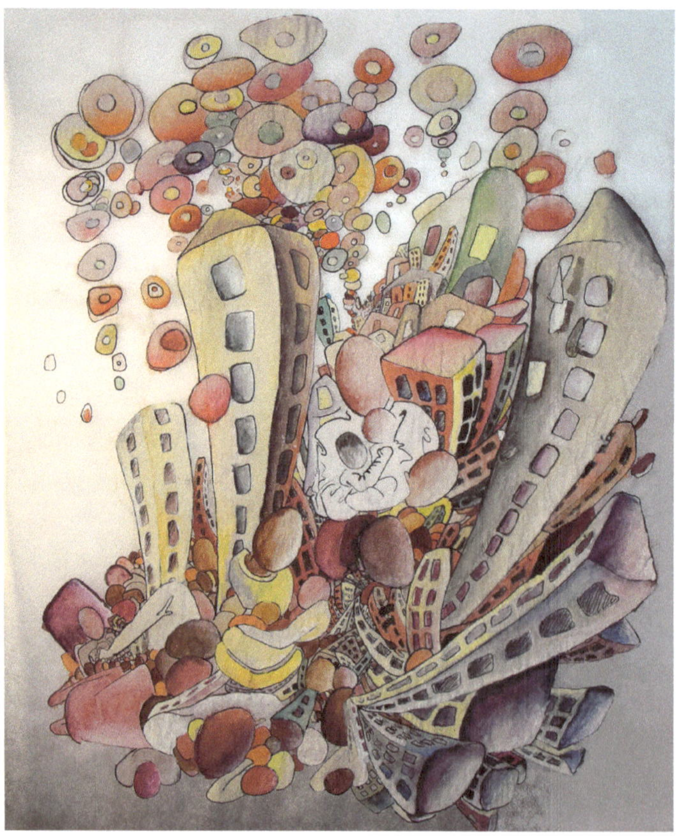

Marginal Man, Drawing/Illustration, Aquarelle and Ink on Translucent Paper, 30 x 42 cm, 2014

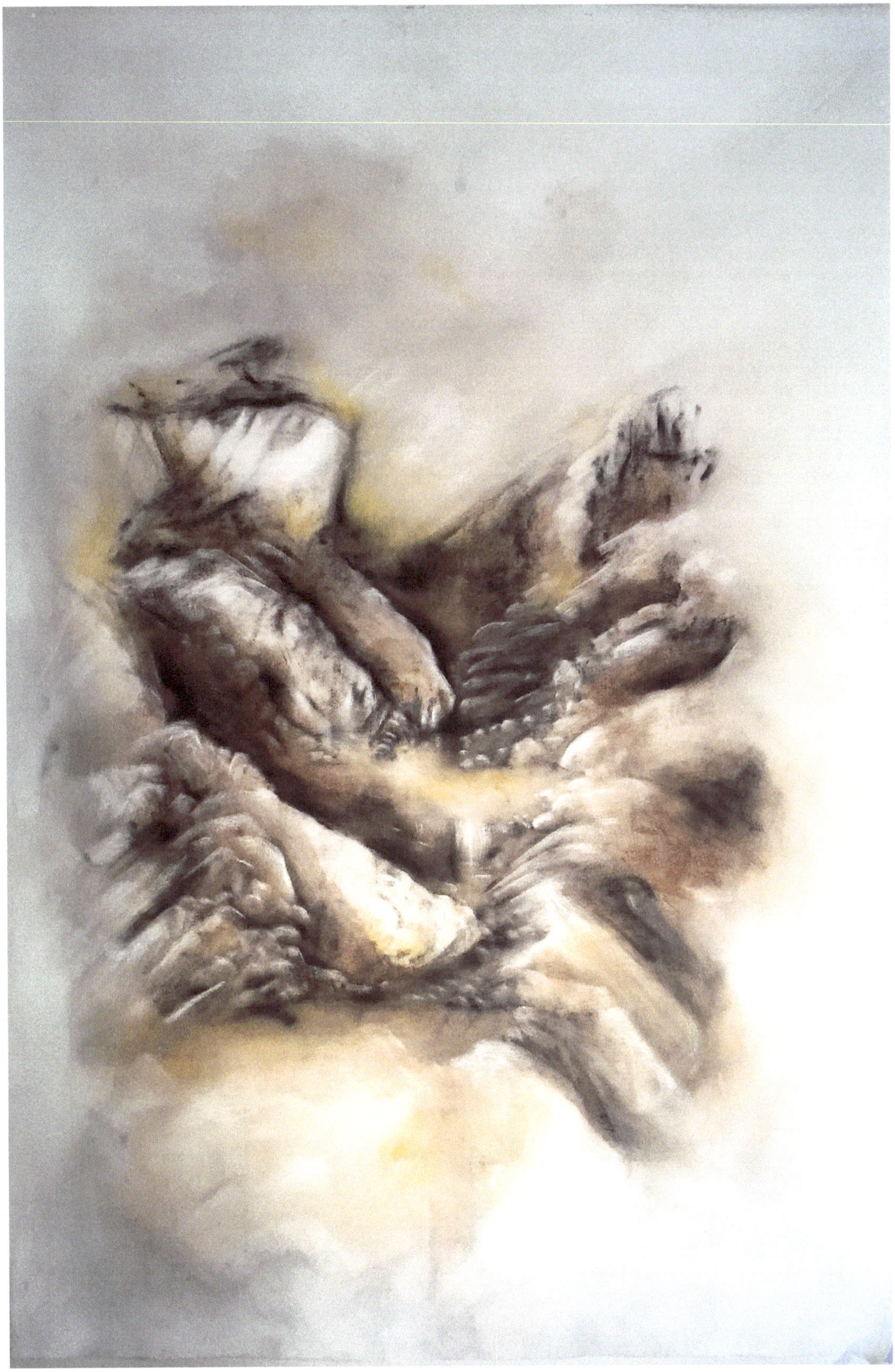

Place of Becoming?, Drawing / Painting,?Charcoal, Pastels and Tempera on Raw Canvas, ?139 x 208 cm?, 2015

CHAITALI. V PURUSHOTHAMAN

cv.artist.painter@gmail.com

CHAITALI. V. PURUSHOTHAMAN is a Multi-Award-Winning Successful Independent Entrepreneur having multiple Careers as a WORLD RENOWNED Professional 40+ Time International Award-Winning High Vibrational Energy shifting Positive Vastu Painter- Energizer, Feng Shui Painter, Spiritual Painter, Vastu Consultant and Vastu Corrector for changing, balancing and shifting the Energy of space from low-Negative to high –Positive frequency, Vedic Astrologer, Illustrator, Fashion illustrator, Spiritual Aura Astro Astral Healer - Coach - Mentor, Psychic, Past life Regression Healer, Chakra Therapist Balancer, Trauma Therapist, Therapist for children and Adults, Counsellor, Couple Counsellor and also a Stock Investor and has made an extraordinary mark in all her Fields. She is a well-known figure and a multifaceted entrepreneur, recognized internationally for her expertise in several fields related to spirituality and Art with multiple careers who uses Art as a remedy in Astrology, Healing, Vastu Corrections. She has a clientele based all over the World thus providing customized high frequency Vastu Positive Energy shifting Paintings, Energizers and Correctors, Vastu for clearing Negative Energy and protection from unconscious evil's eye of home and offices, Healing sessions, Activating Spiritual Portals, Providing Personalised affirmations and meditations to open chakras, therapies for Adults, Couples and Counselling for children. Her Paintings and Energizers are all Vastu Based with high frequency Positive Energy that acts as a remedy, medium and décor to shift the Energy of Space and also the Energy of human Aura. Apart from being an Elite Décor and Aesthetically balancing spaces, her Paintings and Energizers shift the frequency of the space from low – Negative to High Positive. She is a multifaceted artist and consultant who blends spiritual practice with art and holistic healing and well known for her spiritual paintings, Vedic astrology consultations, and Vastu energy shifting, healing, offering personalized services like affirmations and meditations. She has been Recognised as ONE of the Best High Vibrational Positive Energy shifting Vastu Painters in the World, Best Spiritual Painters, Best Cubist, Best Surrealist, Best fantasy Painters, Best Expressionist Painters, Best Futuristic Painters, Best Impressionists Painters in the World Art Awards juried by World's Best Galleries. One of her Popular Paintings - The 7 White Horses for Success and Peace, a Positive Vastu Energy shifting Painting has been AWARDED "FIRST IN THE WORLD " in "WORLD ART AWARDS" juried by WORLD'S BEST GALLERIES. It has also Won the Prestigious Future of Art Global Masterpiece Award. She has WON MANY OTHER AWARDS IN USA, ITALY, SPAIN. Her Artistic works have also been showcased at prestigious events like the TTAF Tokyo Art Fair. She has also been Felicitated by the Prestigious International Prize -The New Great Masters in New York. She is described as a World-Renowned Visionary who paints masterpieces in Prestigious Art Celebrity Magazine that highlights artists who are considered cultural influencers and celebrities.

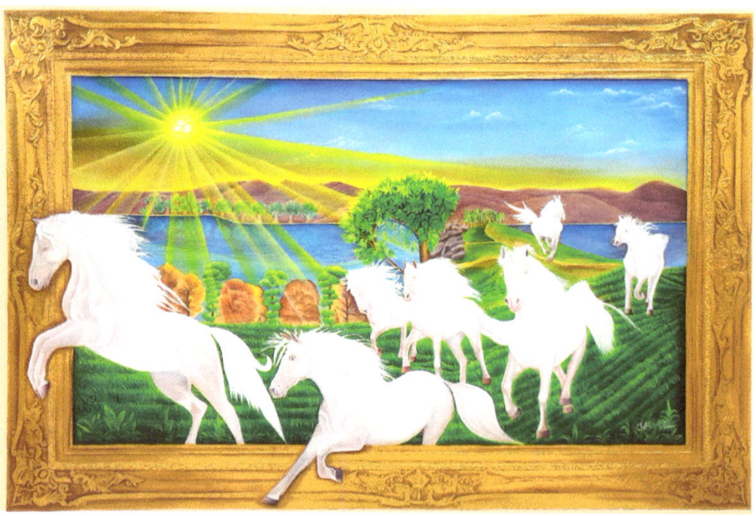

The POWERFUL VASTU SHASTRA - 7 White Horses with Rising Sun Vastu Powerful Positive Energizer High Frequency Painting for Luck , Success, Positivity , Financial Abundance , Strength , Valour , Perseverance , Career growth , Opportunities and Productive flow of Energy absorbs Negativity emits Positivity by using the Energy of Vastu Yantras , earth Gurus , lords, planets, Auspicious days , spiritual symbols, Portal numbers 1111, 222, 888 , sacred spells , symbols of success, luck , good health , fortune , yin yang balancing energy, protection from Evils eye created during the Powerful Time Period of Brahma Muhurta – 3.30 to 5.30 am , 2022 , Acrylic on canvas with 3D hand painted frame ,152 x101cm.

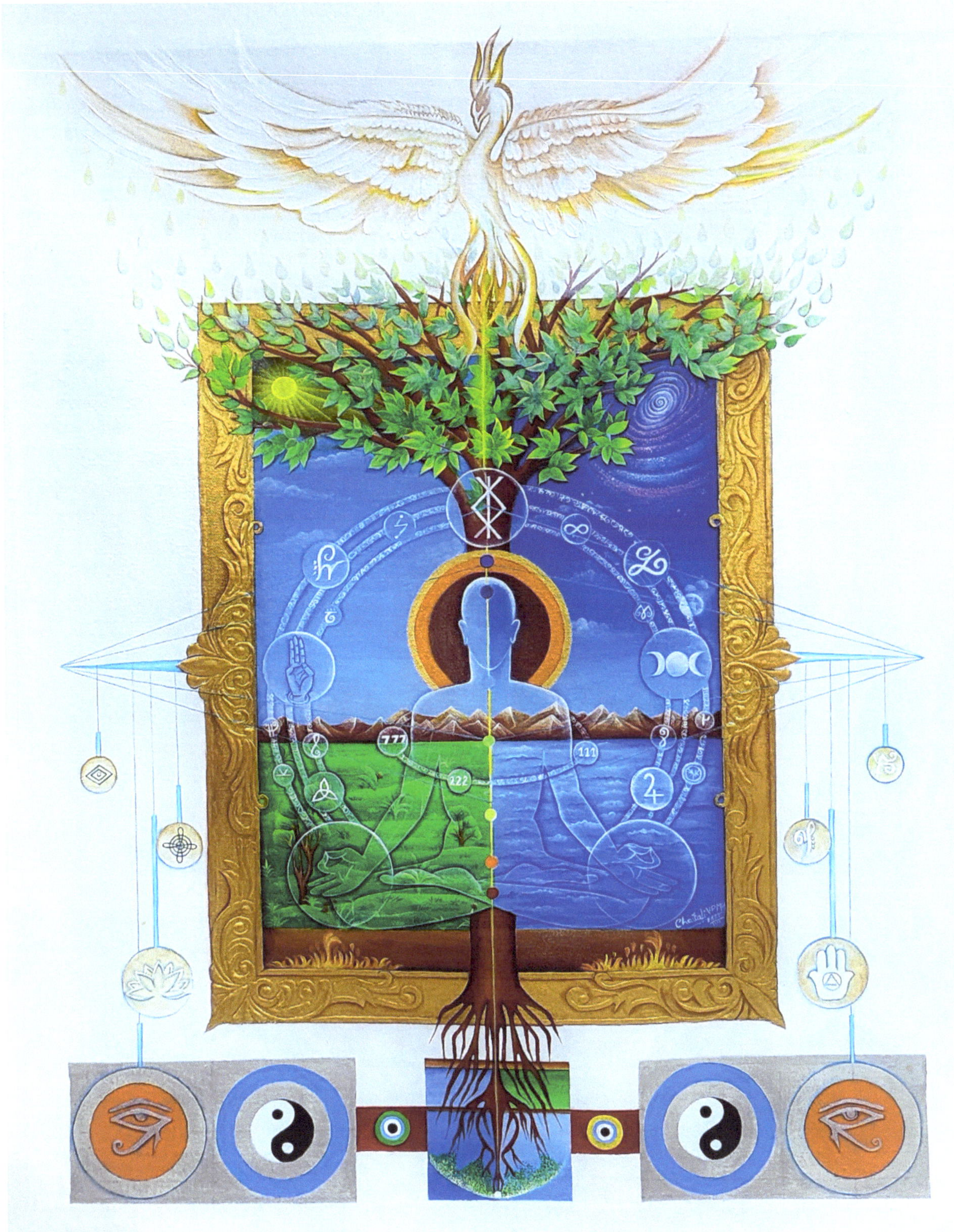

Powerful Vastu Energizer With Portal Energy of lion's Gate , Tantras, Evil's Eye Protection created during the Powerful Time Period of Brahma Muhurta – 3.30 to 5.30 am , 2023 , Acrylic on canvas with 3D hand painted frame ,60cm x91cm.

CHRISTOPHE SZPAJDEL

www.lordofthelogos.com

Nestled in the picturesque landscape of Devon, Christophe Szpajdel is a captivating figure in the art world. Originally from Poland and born in Belgium, this internationally renowned artist has dedicated nearly 40 years to mastering the intricate arts of calligraphy, typography, lettering, and logo design. His distinctive touch can be seen in the iconic logos of legendary extreme metal bands, including Emperor, Enthroned, Impiety, and Moonspell. In recent years, Christophe's creative horizons have expanded even further. One of his standout pieces, the logo for Rihanna, completed in 2016, surprisingly bridges the realms of pop and underground metal—effectively becoming a symbol often associated with death metal aesthetics in the public eye. Last September, when visiting Plymouth, some of you may have experienced Christophe's exceptional artistry firsthand at the Devon Open Studios in Plymouth, where he successfully led a dynamic group exhibition showcasing 12 talented artists. The upcoming weeks are poised to be thrilling as Christophe gears up for several exciting events

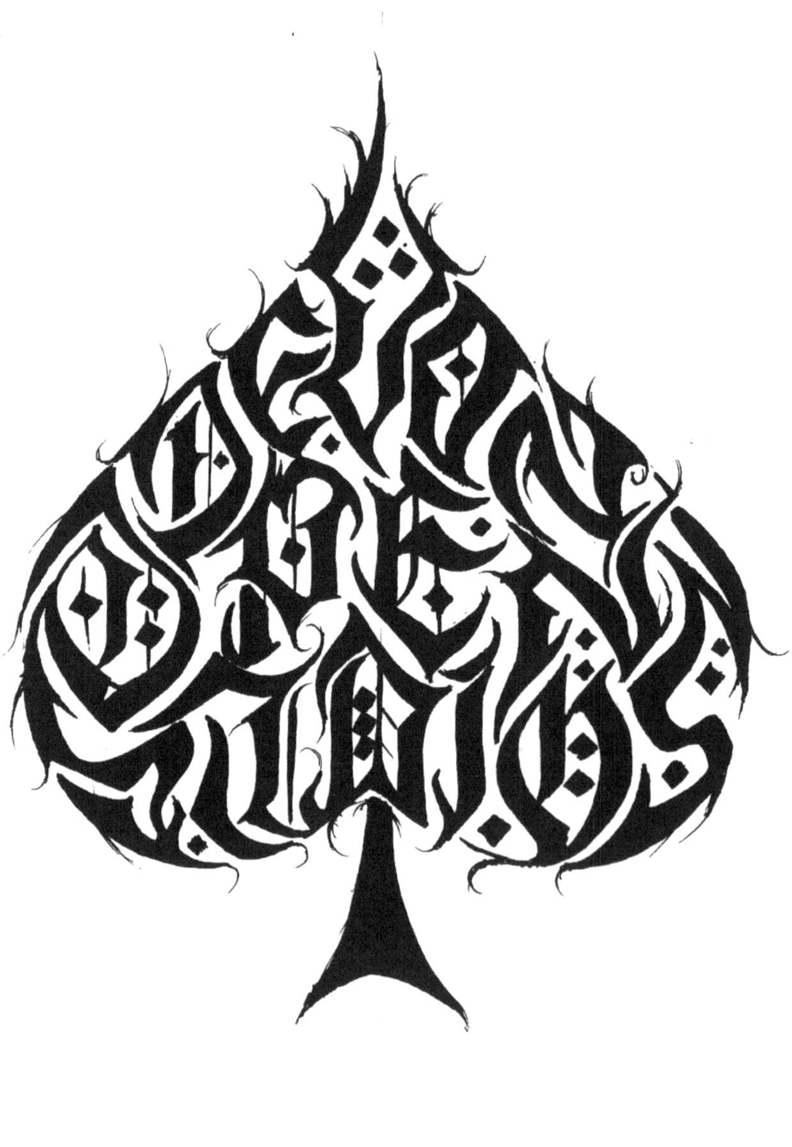

Devon Open Studios Motorhead tribute fan art logo, 2022, pen and ink on paper

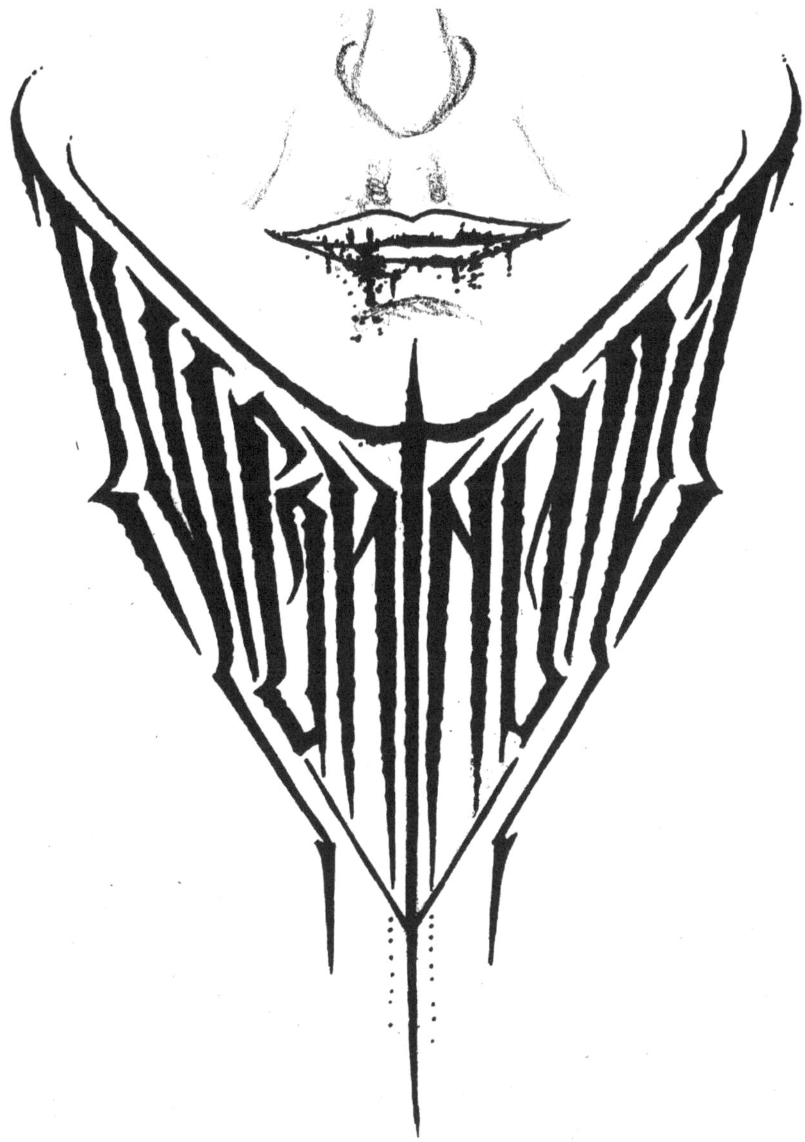

Nighthunt, 2025, pen and ink on paper

CLAIRE DAVENHALL

https://clairedavenhallvisualartist.wordpress.com

Claire Davenhall is an international visual artist and Master Scuba Diver whose practice merges fine art sculpture, underwater photography, and arts education. With a BA (Hons) in Fine Art from Gray's School of Art at Robert Gordon University, she has deepened her practice through international studies at the Athens School of Fine Art in Greece and North Karelia Polytechnic in Finland. Claire also holds a Postgraduate Certificate in Education (PGCE) and is currently completing a Master of Education at Sheridan Institute of Higher Education, where her research investigates the rippling effect of creative collaborations in educational settings.

Her latest award-winning series, BLUE – Echoes from the Indian Ocean, draws inspiration from the Shipwreck Coast of Western Australia—an expanse of ocean steeped in history, memory, and metamorphosis. For Claire, blue is more than a colour; it is a threshold. It marks the edge of the known world, where cartography fades and imagination deepens—a fluid state submerged beneath layers of time and space. Rather than framing shipwrecks as static relics of disaster or decay, Claire reimagines them as evolving ecosystems—living monuments of transformation. Through her lens, these wrecks are no longer inhert tombs but sanctuaries teeming with life. By shifting the viewer's perspective from looking at the wreck to looking out from within it, Claire invites us into an immersive underwater world where memory, light, and marine life entwine. Each wreck becomes a portal—between worlds, between centuries, between breath and stillness.

All photographs in the series are taken at depths of 18 to 32 metres, using only natural morning light filtering through the sea to illuminate the quiet majesty of submerged landscapes. Each image captures the uncanny beauty of the Indian Ocean's forgotten vessels—where rusted steel becomes reef, shadowed corridors teem with life, and time dissolves into water. In Portals to the Deep, divers drift in and out of the blue; in Living Sanctuaries, the ocean is framed through a rusted doorway, inviting viewers to contemplate what lies beyond—history, memory, or myth. The work draws viewers into the deep—not just visually, but emotionally and philosophically. Claire's dual perspective as artist and diver allows her to access sites often hidden from view—not to document, but to reveal transformation. Her practice is rooted in reverence for the sea and its stories. Whether through corroded corridors, open hatches, or fish-shrouded beams, BLUE – Echoes from the Indian Ocean is a call to pause, submerge, and listen. It reminds us that beneath the surface—of the ocean, of history, of ourselves—lie not endings, but beginnings: quiet, luminous, and alive.

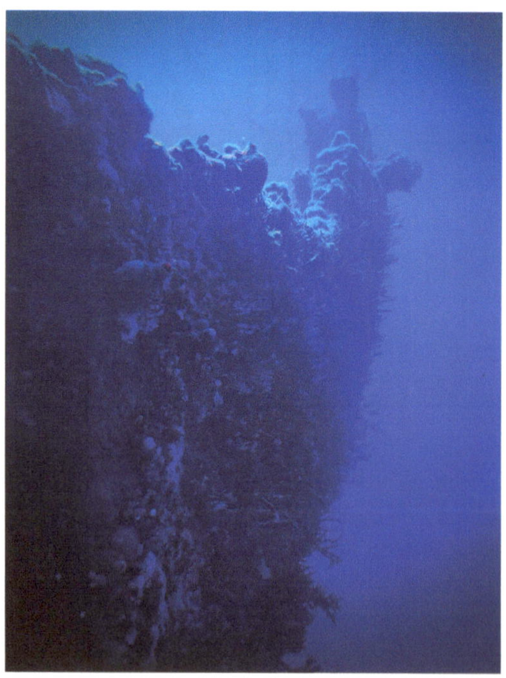

The Blue Sentile, 2025, Digital Underwater Photograph

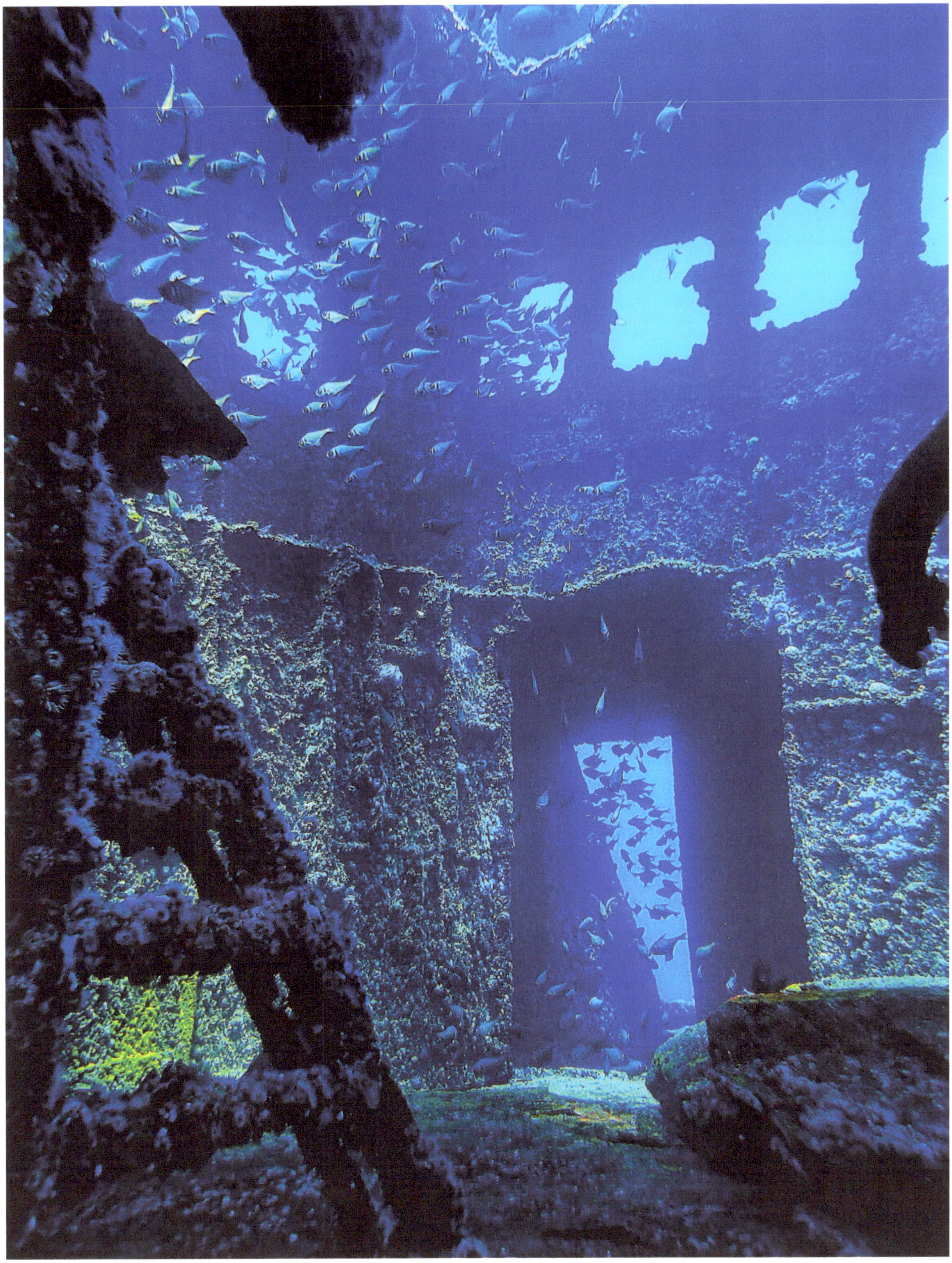

Sanctuary, 2024, Digital Underwater Photograph

COR FAFIANI

c.fafiani@gmail.com

Algorithms inspire me in the sense that everything is interchangeable in this way. For example, I can use the objects that appear in my work in new work and one work generates the other see .recycling box where a variation can be seen Sculptures are almost capsules of a civilization. The question is what legacy our sculptures leave behind. That is difficult to say about the time in which we live and algorithms determine our life experience. The function of art is that it cannot always be expressed in words. Last time these algorithms inspired me in the sense that everything is interchangeable in this way. For example, I can use the objects that appear in my work in new work and one work generates the other see .recycling box on which a variation can be seen

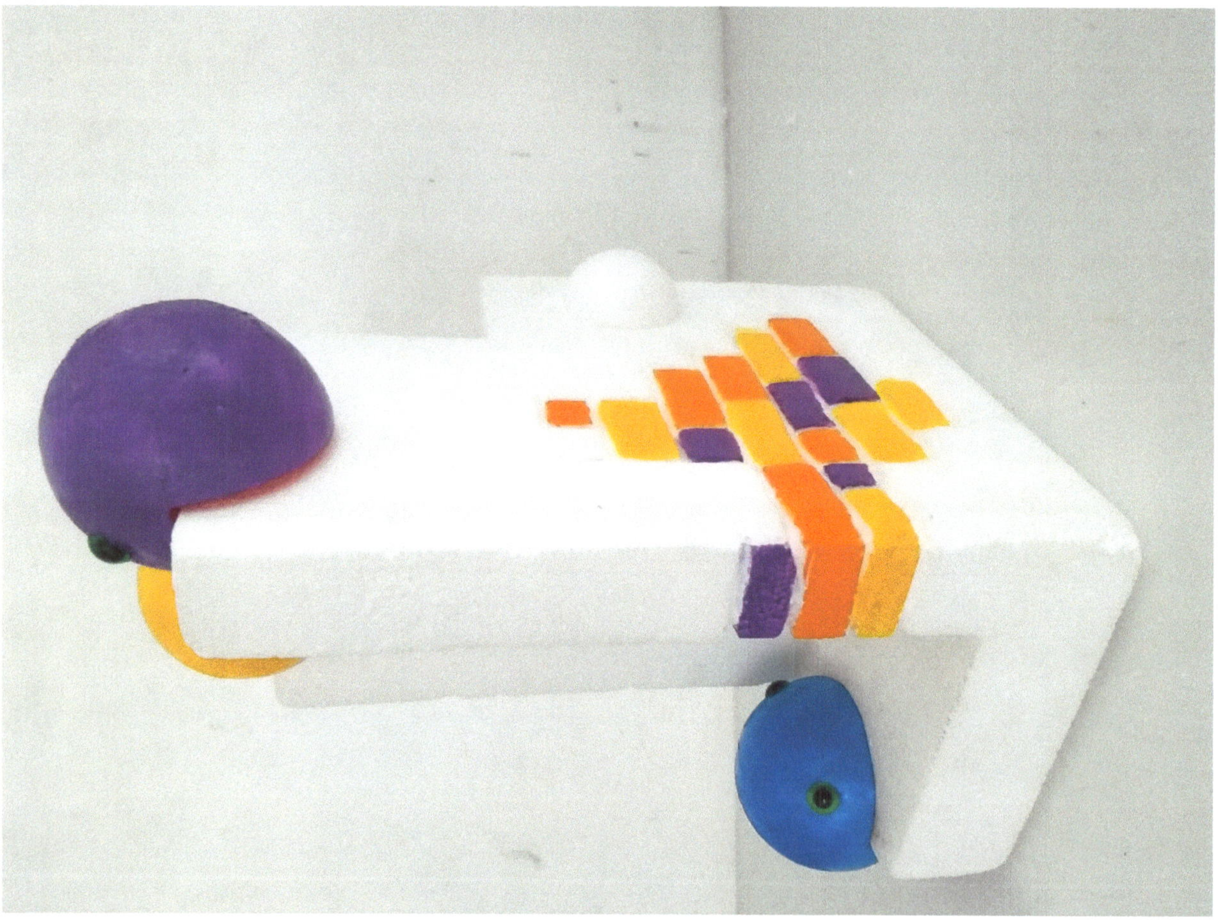

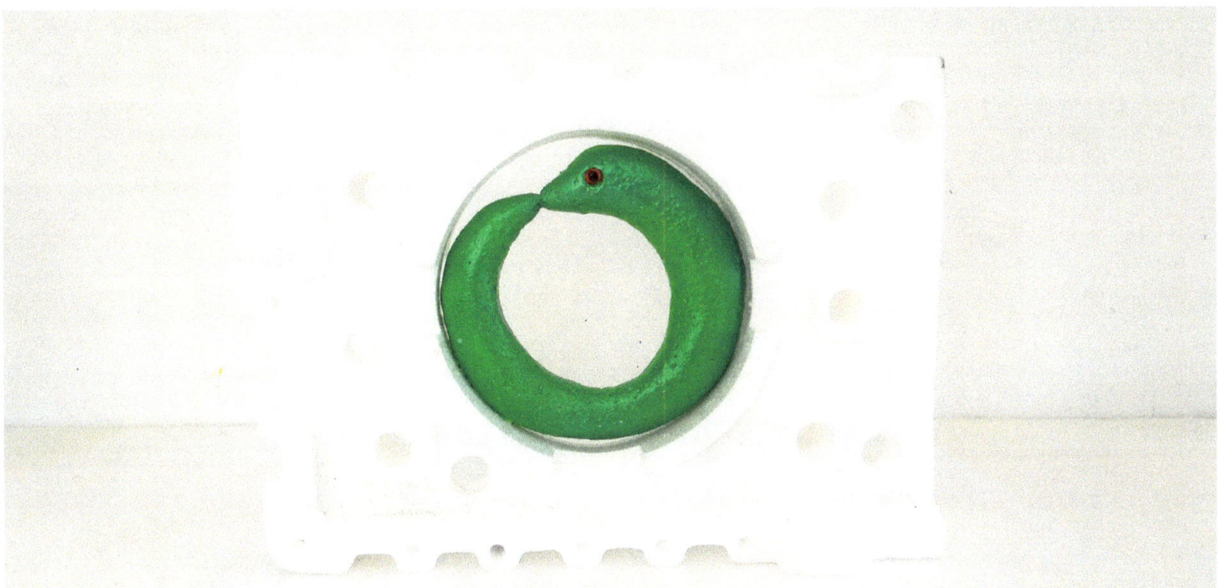

CORNELIA B BIENZ

https://www.instagram.com/miss_icm https://corneliabienz.com

Cornelia B. Bienz is a contemporary photographer whose work explores the delicate intersection of emotion, light, and movement. Her journey with photography began in her school years with analog courses, where she discovered the joy of both capturing images and developing them in the darkroom. Later, as a flight attendant, she photographed everyday moments and travel experiences, cultivating an early appreciation for spontaneous beauty and fleeting impressions. In 2015, a pivotal moment arrived when she discovered the course "ZEN Photographic Art – Shaping Emptiness" by Jo Fahl. Drawn by the philosophy behind the course, she followed her impulse to enroll, an experience that solidified her commitment to photography as a lifelong passion. Seeking to deepen her technical knowledge and artistic understanding, she enrolled in the part-time Photography and Image Editing program at the European Photography Academy in Rastatt under Matthias Gessler. Her time at the academy, combining online seminars, on-site sessions, and project-based practice, provided a foundation for her evolving artistic voice. Over the years, Cornelia B. Bienz has developed a distinctive approach that combines macro and ZEN photography. Macro photography allows her to reveal the extraordinary beauty of everyday objects from fresh perspectives, rendered in both color and black-and-white. ZEN photography, in contrast, embodies a philosophy of presence, mindfulness, and meditative creation. Her images often emphasize emptiness and stillness, inviting viewers to pause, breathe, and escape the constant rush of daily life. A defining evolution in her work came with the discovery of Intentional Camera Movement (ICM), inspired by a desire to "photograph as Claude Monet painted." She has long been captivated by the Impressionists and the Romantic works of J.M.W. Turner, drawn to their nuanced play of light, color, and form. ICM offered her a way to translate these painterly qualities into photography, a method she calls heart photography. Through this technique, she captures emotions and sensations rather than literal representations, creating images that feel dreamlike, fluid, and often magical. While she initially believed that historic cities such as Venice, Rome, or Paris were especially suited for ICM due to their sense of timelessness, she now embraces urban environments, landscapes, and human subjects alike. Her guiding principle is that the perfect image is created in-camera. Beyond using an ND filter, she avoids additional tools, special camera programs, or heavy post-processing. Minimal editing is applied only when absolutely necessary, ensuring that each photograph reflects an unfiltered emotional and visual experience. Cornelia B. Bienz's work invites viewers to linger, reflect, and immerse themselves in the fleeting beauty of a moment. Her images, sometimes reminiscent of Old Master paintings, emphasize sensation, mood, and essence over literal representation. They offer an escape into a world of light, color, and emotion, encouraging a pause in which the observer can experience the present fully. Through her ongoing exploration of ICM, ZEN, and macro photography, Cornelia B. Bienz continues to push the boundaries of visual expression. Her work has been shown internationally, and she remains dedicated to creating images that enchant, move, and inspire, offering a contemplative glimpse into the harmony between observation and feeling.

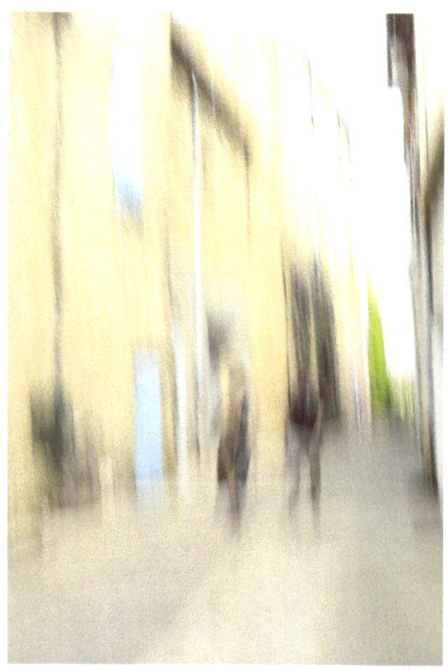

A Summer in Provence, 2025, Canvas, 80x60 cm

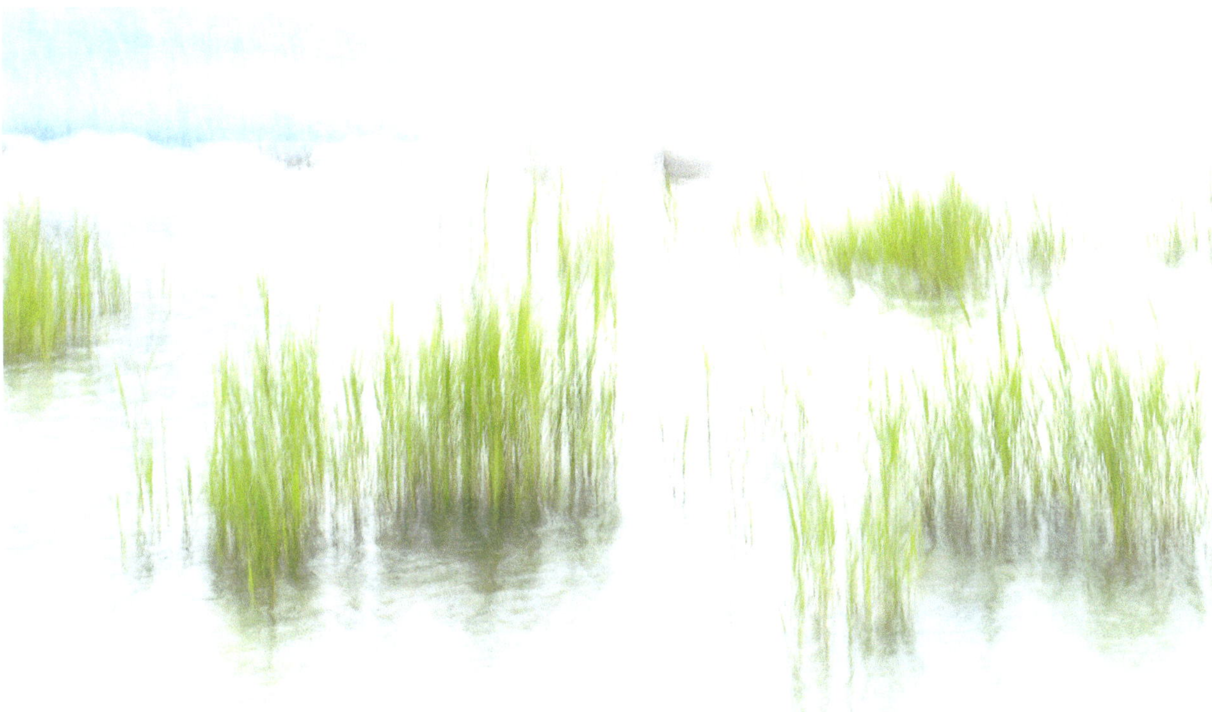

At the Achensee, 2025, Canvas, 60x80 cm

DANIEL MCKINLEY

mybio.art/daniel-mckinley

About my art and me Where does it all come from? The starting point I look at one of my finished paintings I can honestly say that I don't know where it began Through my art I am always trying to question myself What am I going through at this moment I may paint an interior An exterior An abstract A still life I am not limited to one style life is diverse And I would like to experience as much as I can

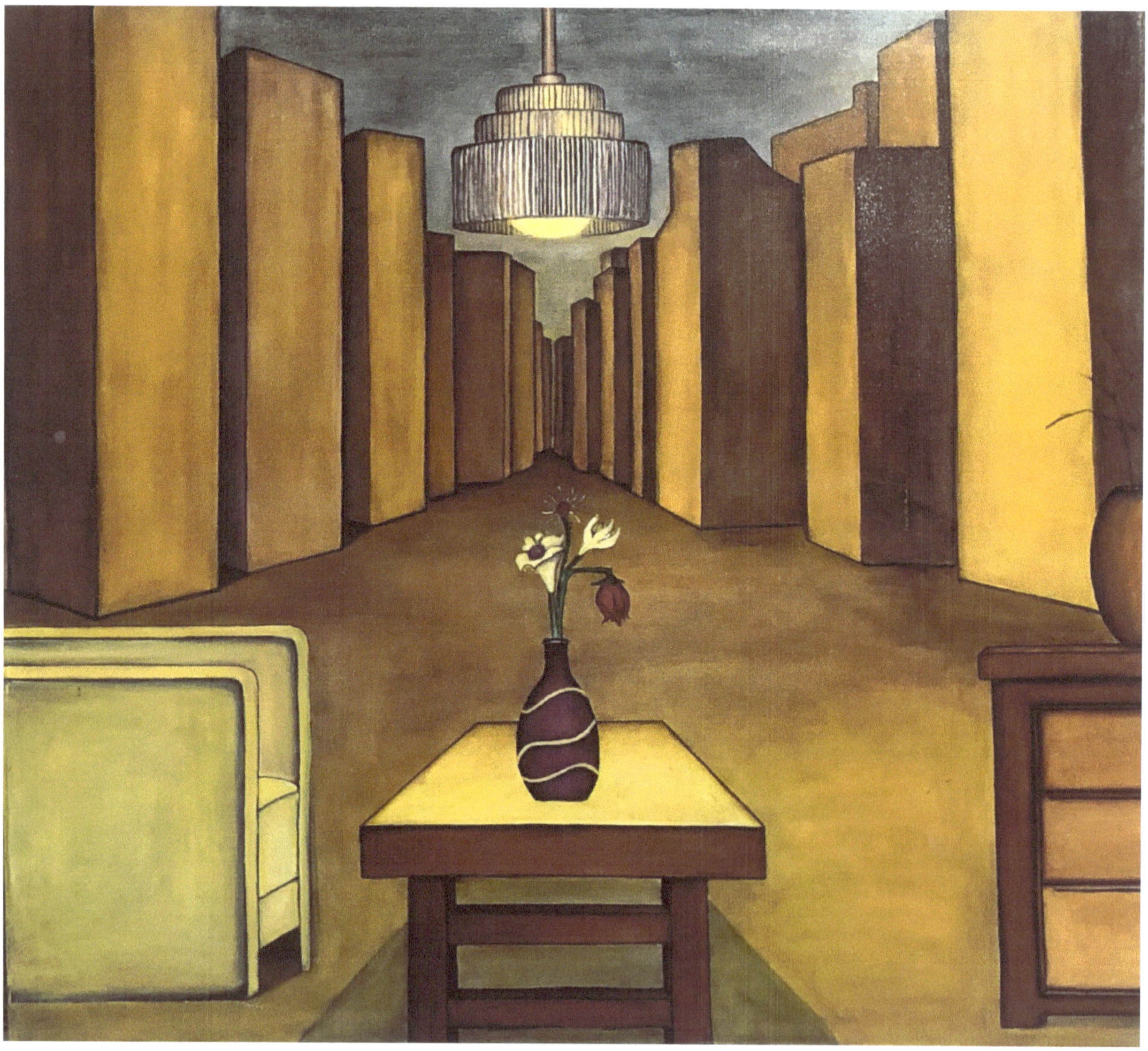

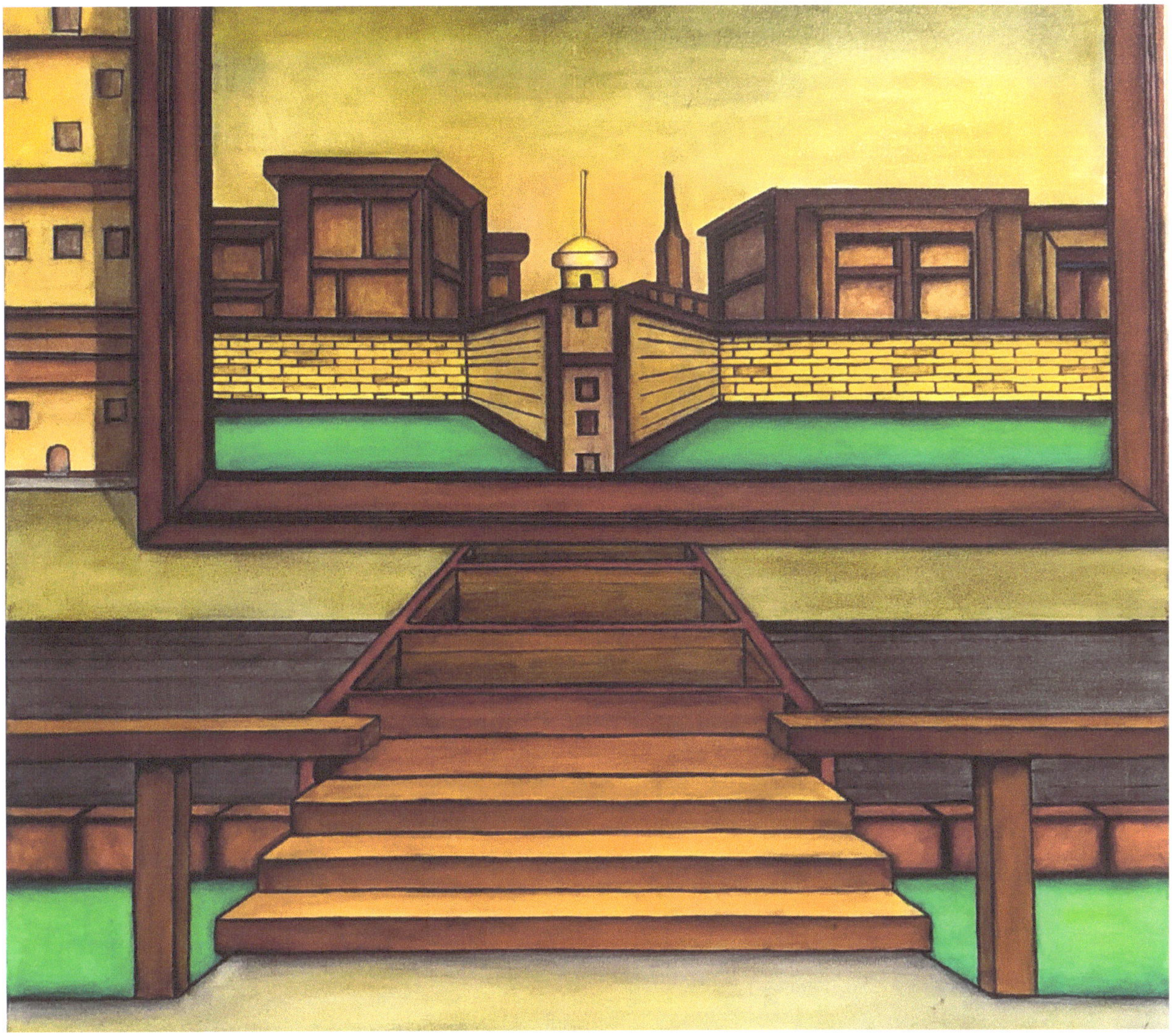

Framed within 2024

DANIEL OLIVIER

www.danielolivierpeintre.fr

Daniel OLIVIER, peintre figuratif, travaille à l'huile, sur la transparence et le glacis, dans un imaginaire symbolique et poétique, il est membre de l'ADAGP, de la Fondation Taylor, de Mondial Art Académia, du groupe Maxi-réalistes de Dan Jacobson à Comparaison, du Cercle des Artistes Européens, il est Sociétaire du Salon d'Automne et du Salon des Artistes Français. Médaille de Bronze des Artistes Français 2024. Après des années d'exploration de l'abstraction et de figuration plus libre, il est, depuis 2020, revenu à un travail au service de son imaginaire, pour pratiquer une peinture, dans son approche technique, à la manière des grands peintres: Léonard de Vinci, Salvador Dali, Jean Olivier Hucleux, Rembrant, Van Eyck ou Velàzcez.

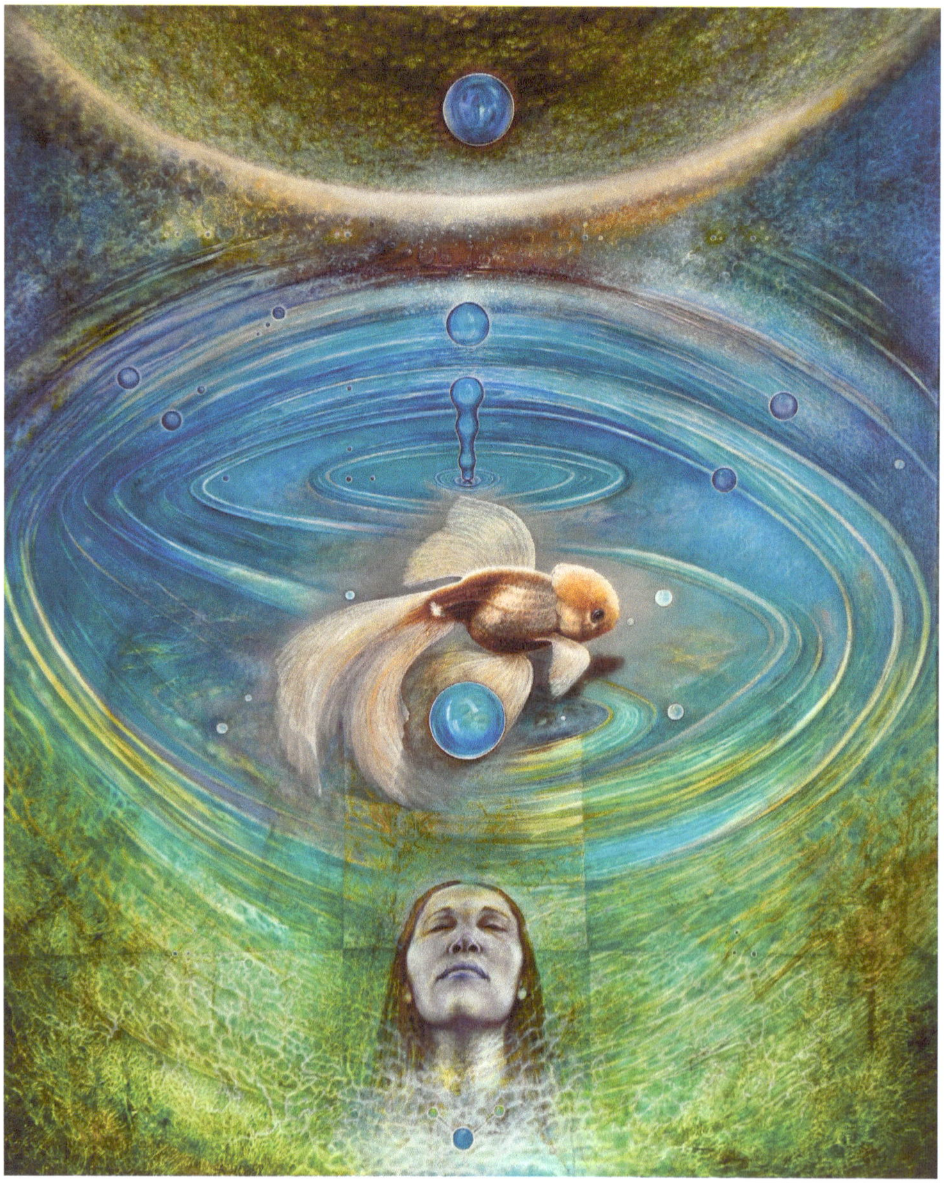

Mémoire d'eau, 2024, huile et ambre sur toile, 162 x 130 cm.

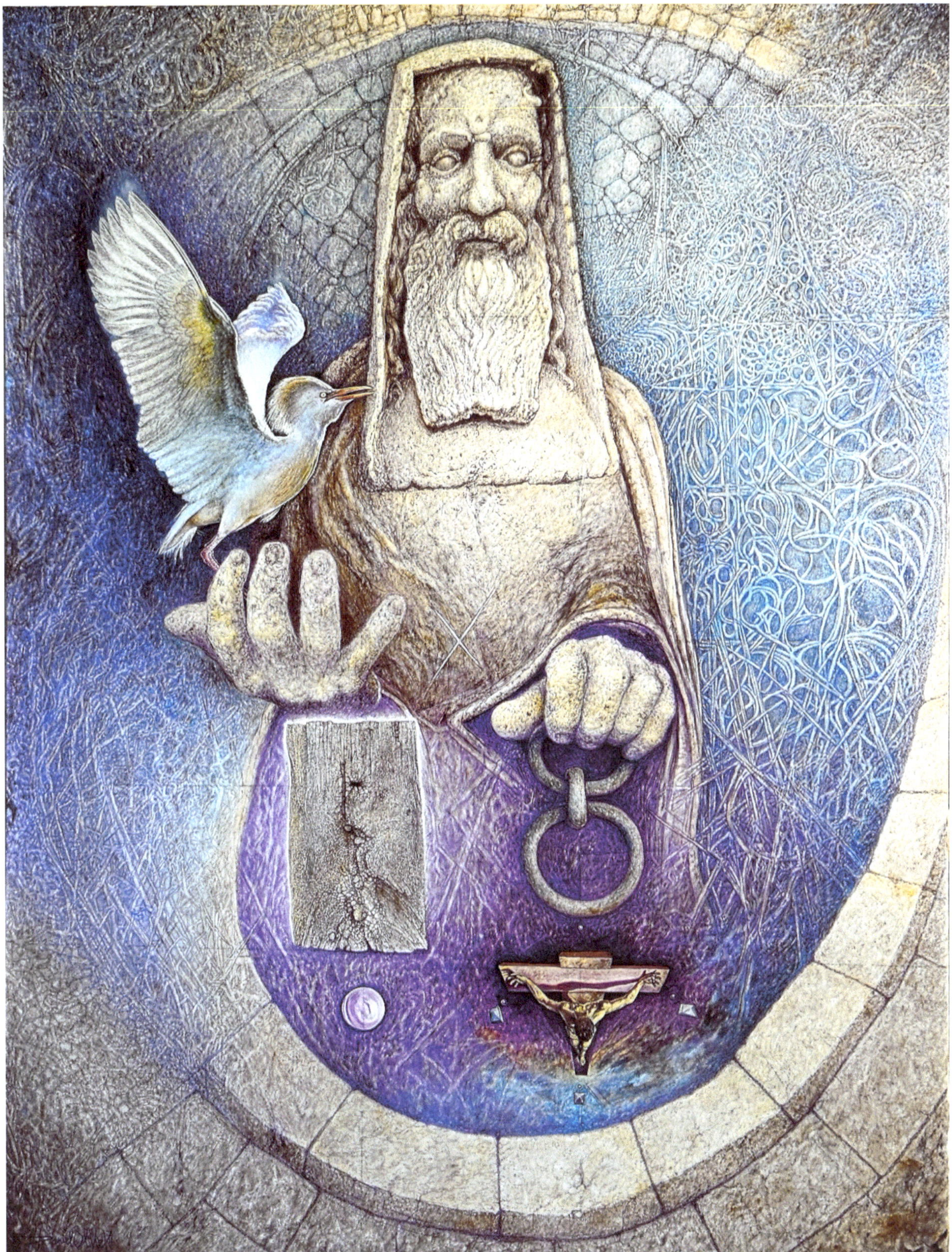

L'envol du Roi, 2025, huile et ambre sur toile, 130 x 97 cm.

DEX HANNON

https://dexhannon.co.uk

Dex Hannon is originally from Manchester now based in Blyth, North East England. His art lives in several private collections across the world. He has featured in books and magazines, across the globe. In 2020, he won best in show for the International Art Folio 2020 Annual award. In 2019 he was shortlisted for the Refresh Art Prize. Hannon's oeuvre examines transformation and reinvention, with each medium providing a distinct perspective on the human experience. His guiding philosophy, "What else could it be?" informs his multidisciplinary approach, continuously challenging boundaries and redefining the possibilities of art. Music significantly influences Hannon's creative process, akin to the practices of Mark Rothko and Gerhard Richter. For Hannon, music serves not merely as an inspiration but as a catalyst. Each composition evokes memories and emotions, which are translated into the rhythmic, dynamic elements that characterise his work. His art is frequently described as "pictorial symphonies," adorned with intricate lines, bold textures, and vivid colour palettes. Beyond traditional media, Hannon has embraced digitalism, particularly through his Retro Futurism series. He approaches each piece with an openness to evolution where a painting might form the basis for a digital reinterpretation, a single photograph might inspire an entire film, and a completed piece often marks the commencement of a new creative endeavour. For Hannon, the artistic process does not have a definitive end; instead, it presents ongoing opportunities for reinvention. Hannon's practice is profoundly influenced by his environment and his conviction in art as a unifying force. Through his paintings, films, and collaborations, Hannon continues to investigate the intersections of memory, emotion, and possibility, encouraging audiences to envision not only what is, but what could be.

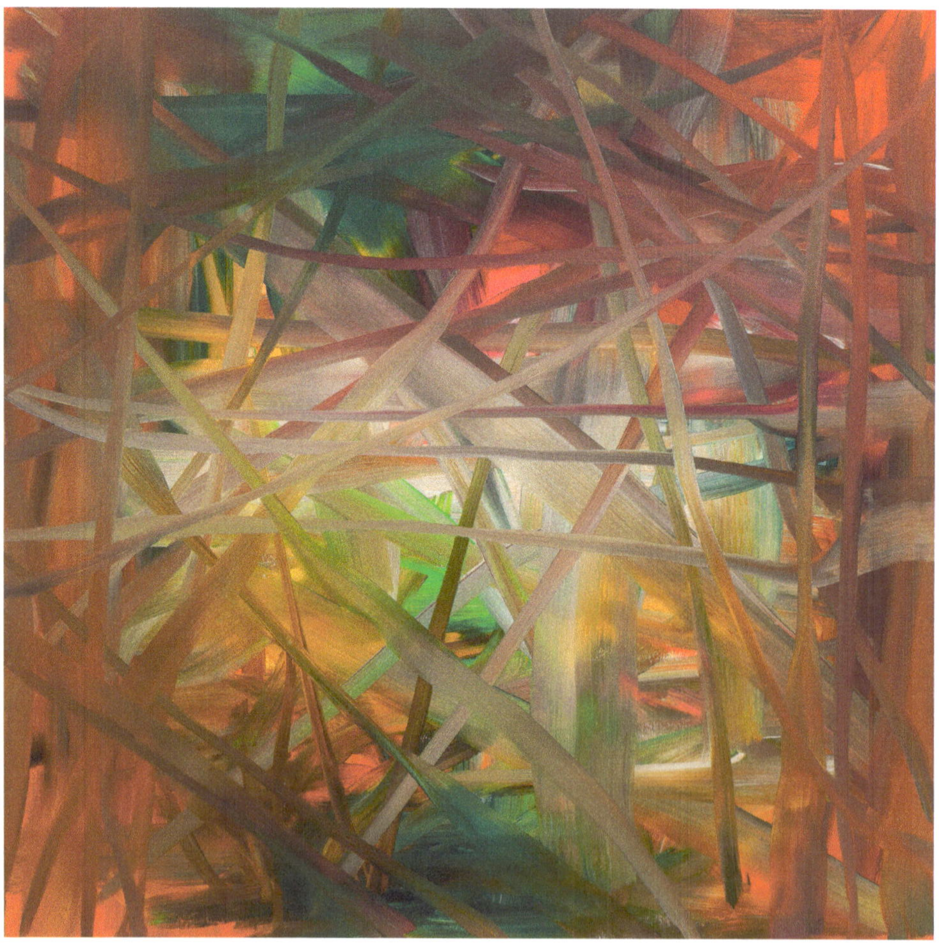

G-Spot Tornado, 2021. Acrylic on Canvas 90 x 90cm

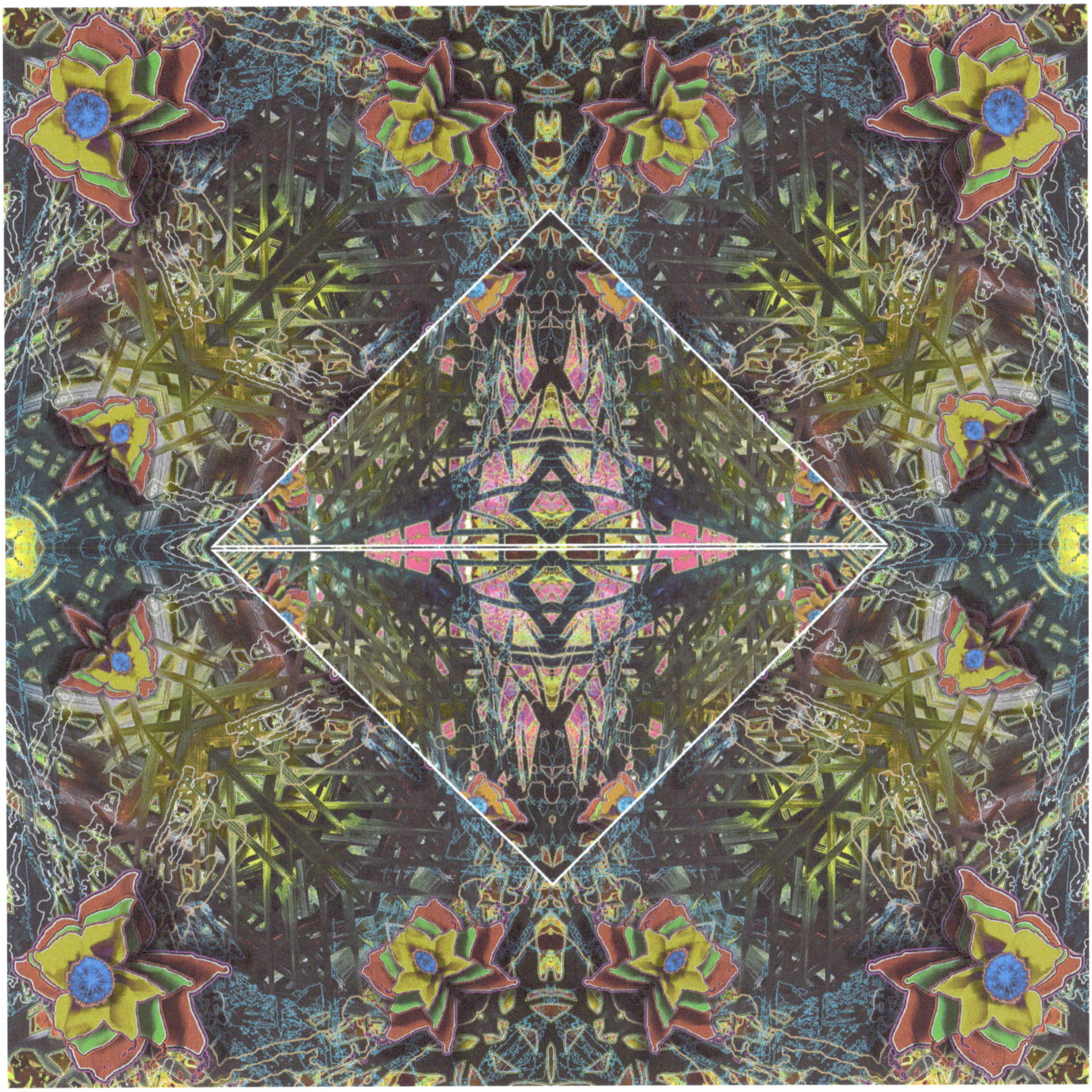

Equanimity, 2022. Digital Remix, 80 x 80cm

DINA KLUMBYS

www.dinaklumbysart.com

Dina Klumbys` versatility is evident in her ability to seamlessly transition between contemporary art and detailed animal portraiture. Contemporary art allows her to convey complex ideas and emotions through non representation forms, while her animal portraits showcase her technical skill and attention to detail. This duality reflects her diverse inspirations and the breadth of her artistic journey. Dina`s art is a testament to the power of simplicity and the depth that can be achieved through the focused approach. Her ability to convey complex motions and themes through forms and vibrant colours is impressive. The meditative quality of her work invites viewers to slow down and engage with the art on a deeper level, making her pieces not just visually and emotionally and intellectually stimulating.

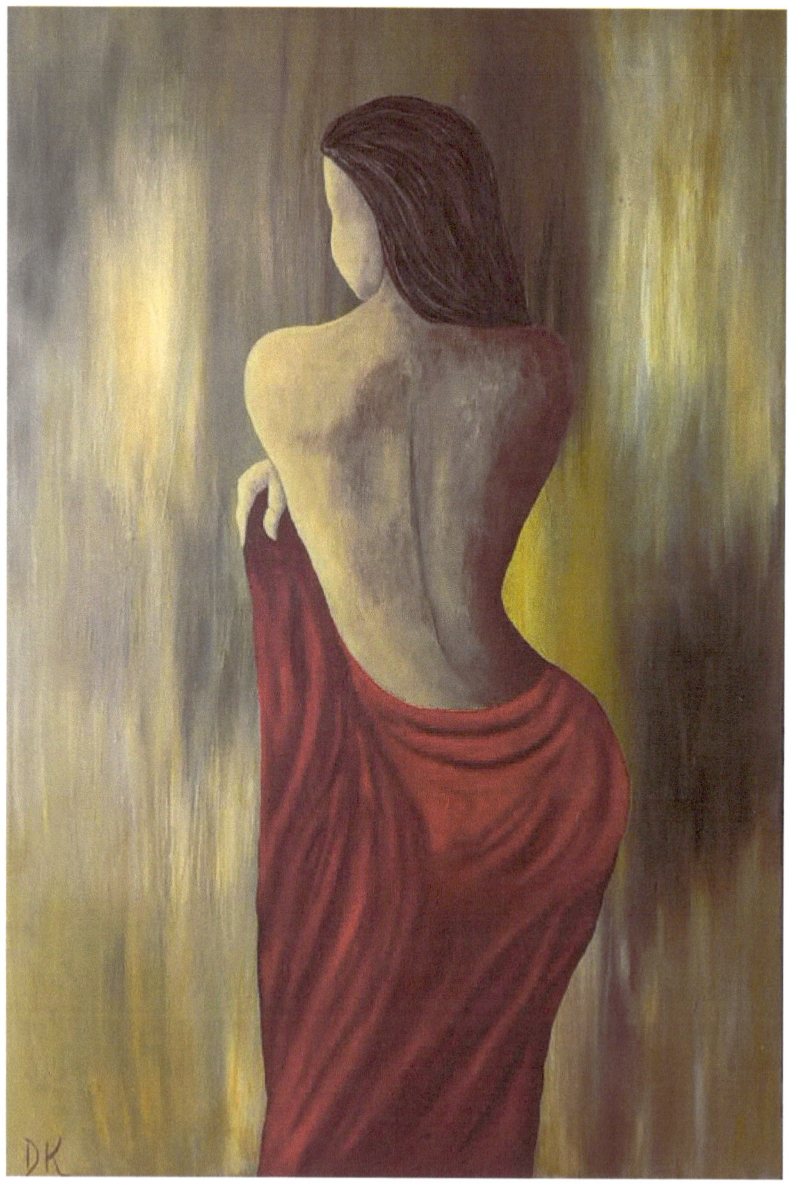

Introspection 2025

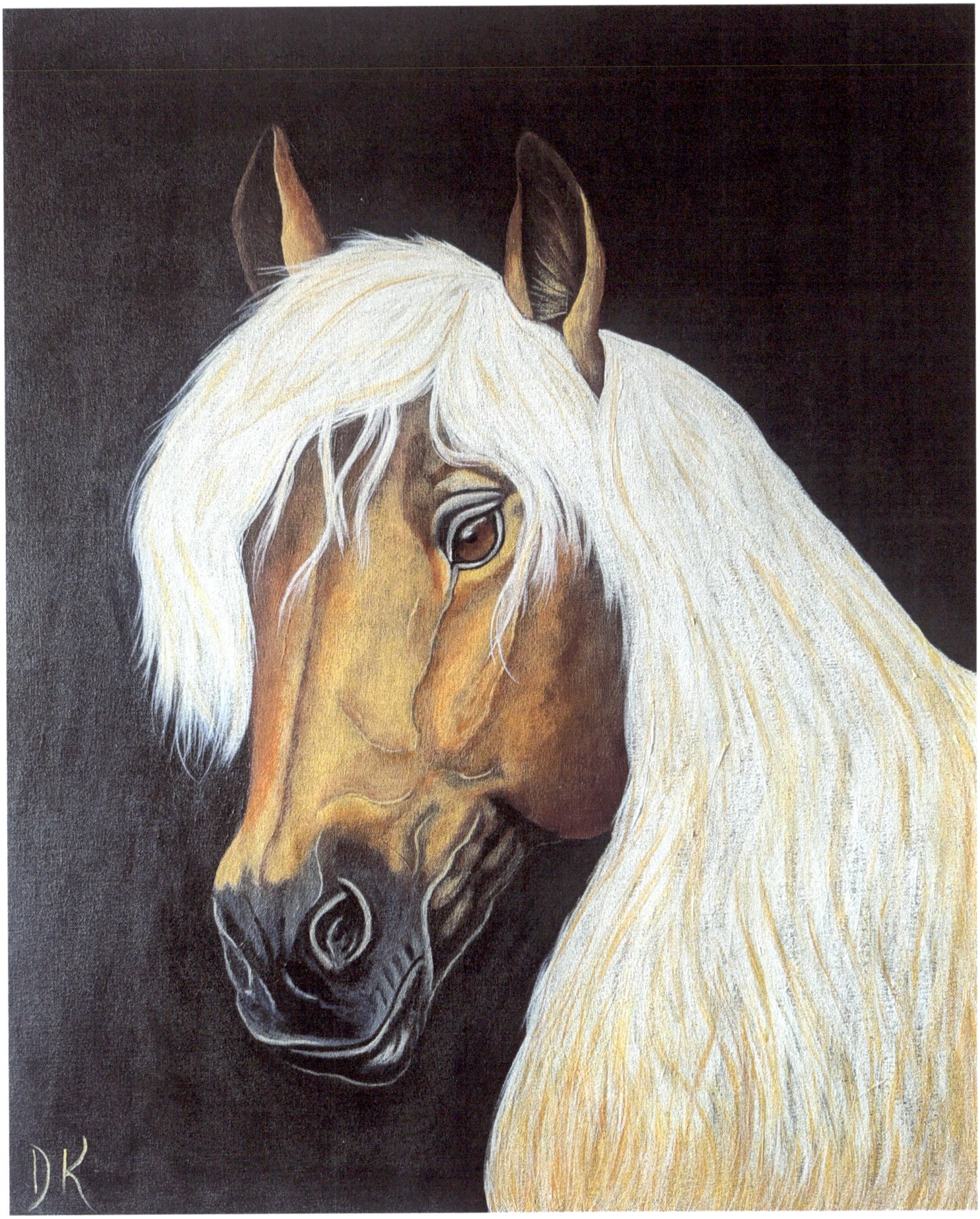

Strength 2024

DITA JACOBOVITZ

https://www.ditasart.com/

Paints landscapes. You could say I paint one landscape, starting from observation even though the landscape has been familiar to me for almost four decades. This repeated investigation, an act of meditation, instills in me peace with hope, I never feel tiered with the landscape around me. This process has changed over the years, today I do not seek descriptive accuracy, but rather openness to the sensory level. My works take place within a figurative space, each work is born from its predecessor, like a continuous internal conversation, in which time accumulates, changes, and reorganizes. My preoccupation with color itself even when it seems absent – fascinates me: It is what keeps me on the long and continuous pictorial journey, in which every movement carries within the traces of the moment and the depths of time

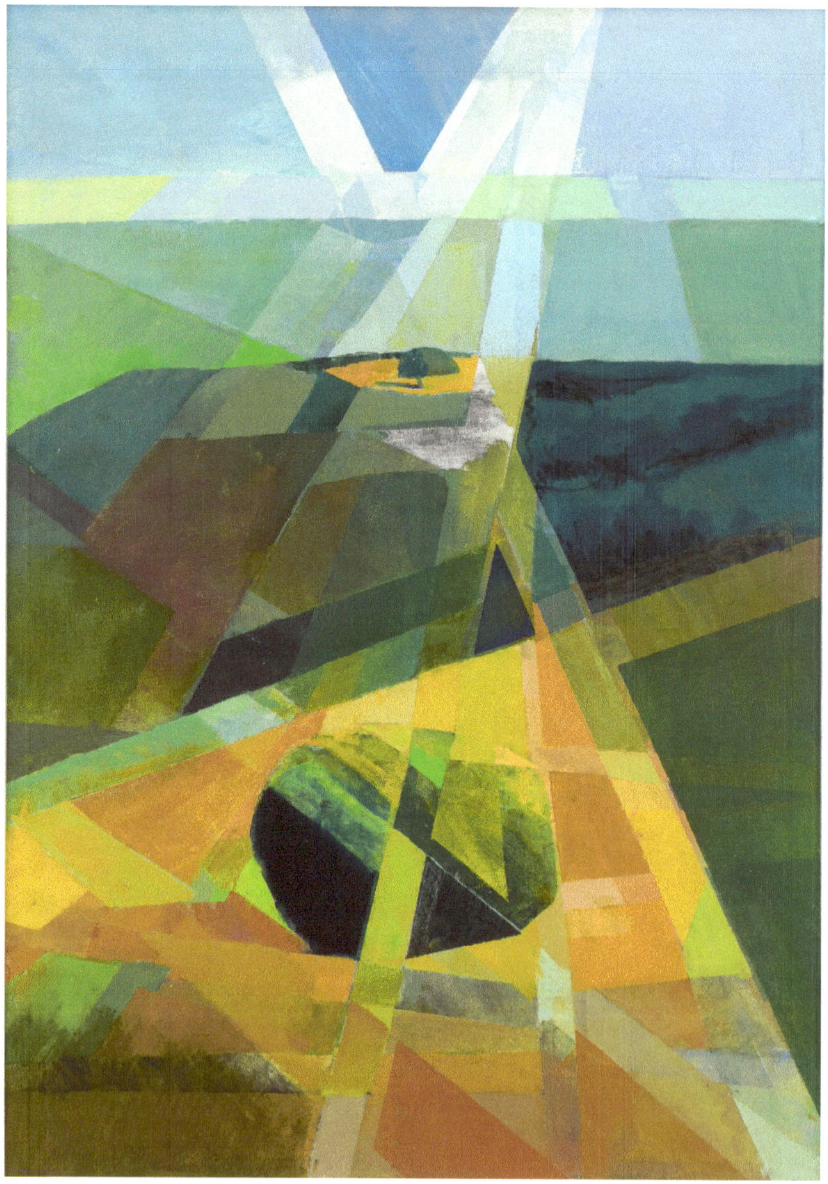

*The missing peace, 2025, Oil on canvas, 100*70 cm*

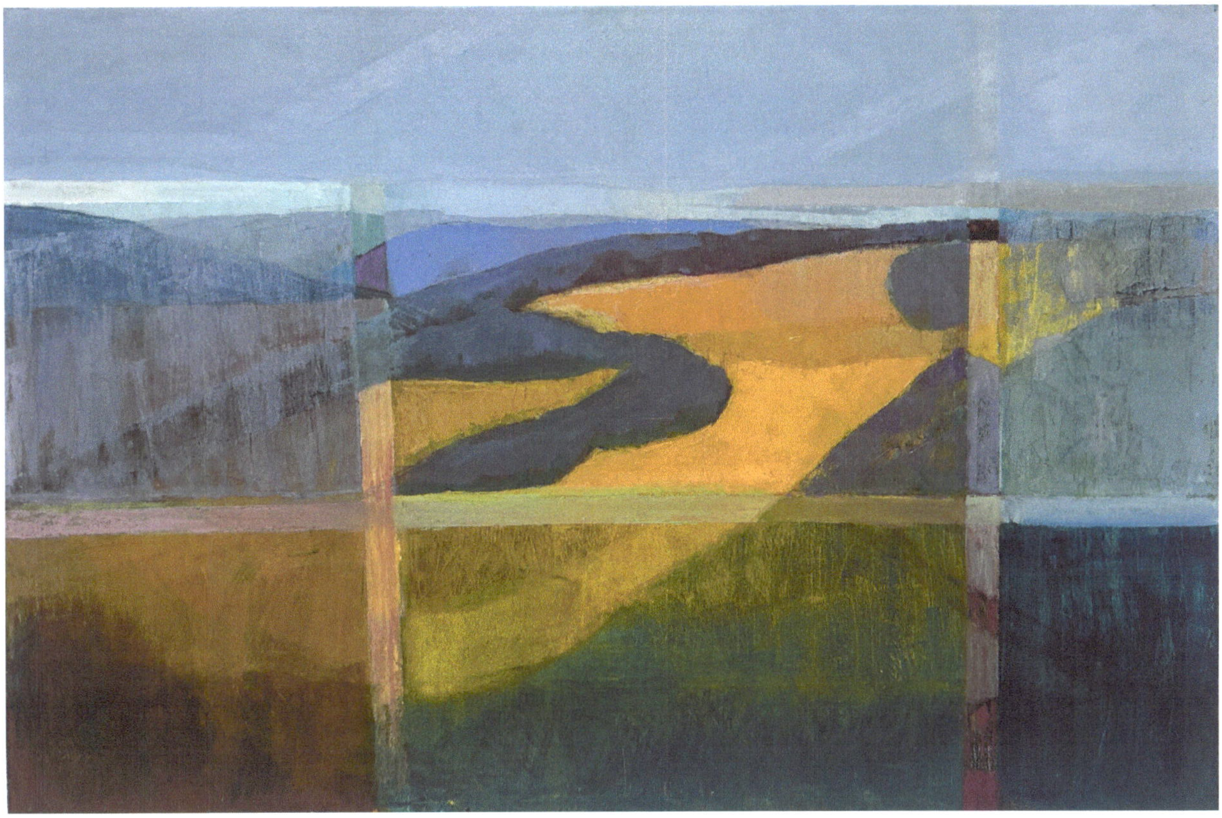

*The last square, 2025, Oil on canvas,60*90 cm*

DR LOWLY (LOW LEE YONG)

https://www.drlowly.art

Singapore-born autodidactic abstract artist Dr. Low Lee Yong—known in the art world as Dr Lowly—transitioned from medicine and over two and a half decades in health tech entrepreneurship to art in 2021, pioneering his signature "Squeeze and Splatter" technique. Art, his earliest passion, revealed itself when he won a contest at age eight and immersed himself in his school's Art Club. Yet financial realities led him down the path of medicine, where he served diligently as a doctor for many years. While his medical career flourished, Dr Lowly's curiosity for technology and business was ignited. Over 25 years, he built a network of 2,000 clinics across Singapore, pioneering advancements in health tech through self-taught expertise in IT. Beneath this professional success, his deep love for art endured quietly, waiting to be rekindled. That moment arrived in 2019 when he sold his health tech business—just before the world changed. The solitude of the 2020 COVID pandemic gave rise to an artistic renaissance. Rediscovering the emotional release of abstract art, he pivoted from precision to spontaneity, embracing fluidity and imperfection. Through years of experimentation, Dr Lowly developed his signature "Squeeze and Splatter" technique. Using an array of unconventional tools—balloons, spoons, and even a toilet brush—he evokes chaos refined by control. Acrylic paint, selected for its non-toxic qualities, reflects his enduring commitment to health and well-being. His work celebrates the impermanence of nature and the quiet strength of the human spirit. Each canvas captures ephemeral beauty and resilience, drawing inspiration from natural forms and emotional landscapes. Every piece is a synthesis of energy and intent—an invitation to journey through tension, transformation, and truth. Dr Lowly's art affirms that within uncertainty, there lies potential for grace, and within chaos, the spark of creation. "Squeeze & Splatter is my freedom. In the clash of control and chaos, I find truth. Each piece holds movement, memory, mystery—shaped by tension, defined by touch." — Dr Lowly He has since presented solo exhibitions in prestigious private jet lounges in Beijing, Shanghai, and Hangzhou (Dec 2024–Mar 2025), and participated in global showcases including the Senses International Art Fair at MUST Museum, Italy, and Contemporary Venice at Palazzo Albrizzi-Capello (Jan–Feb 2025).

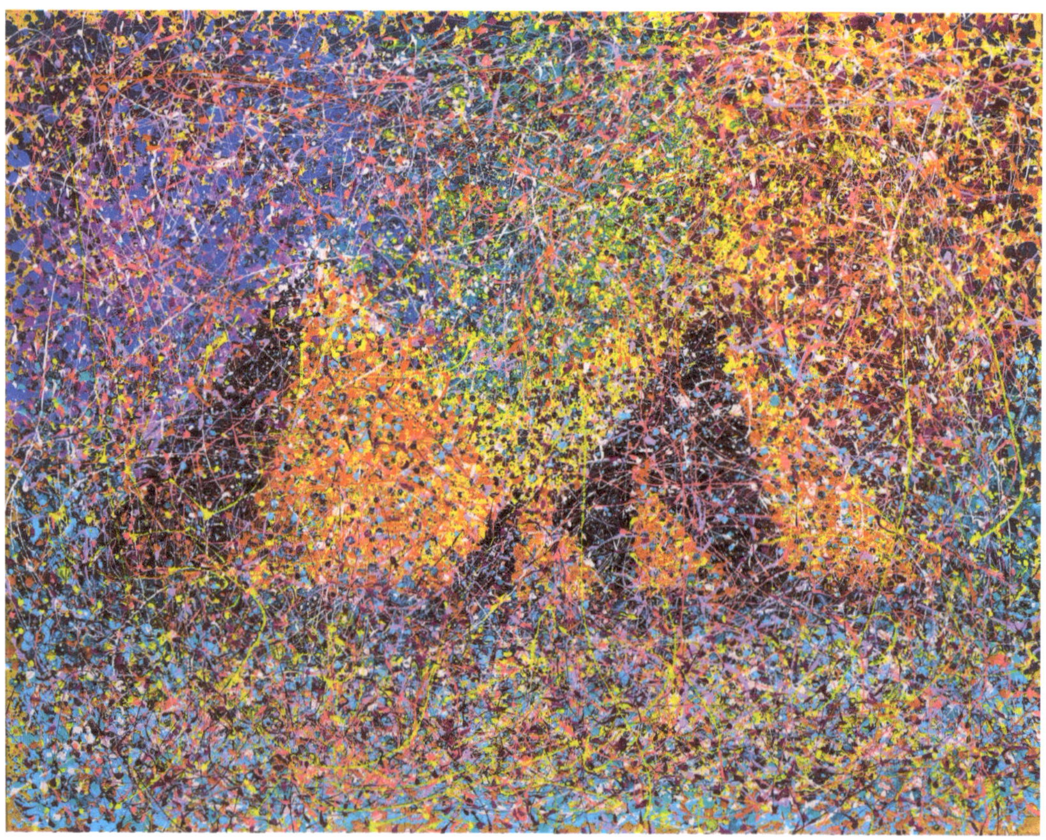

Echoes of Giza 2024 (Acrylic on canvas) 121cm x 152cm x 8cm

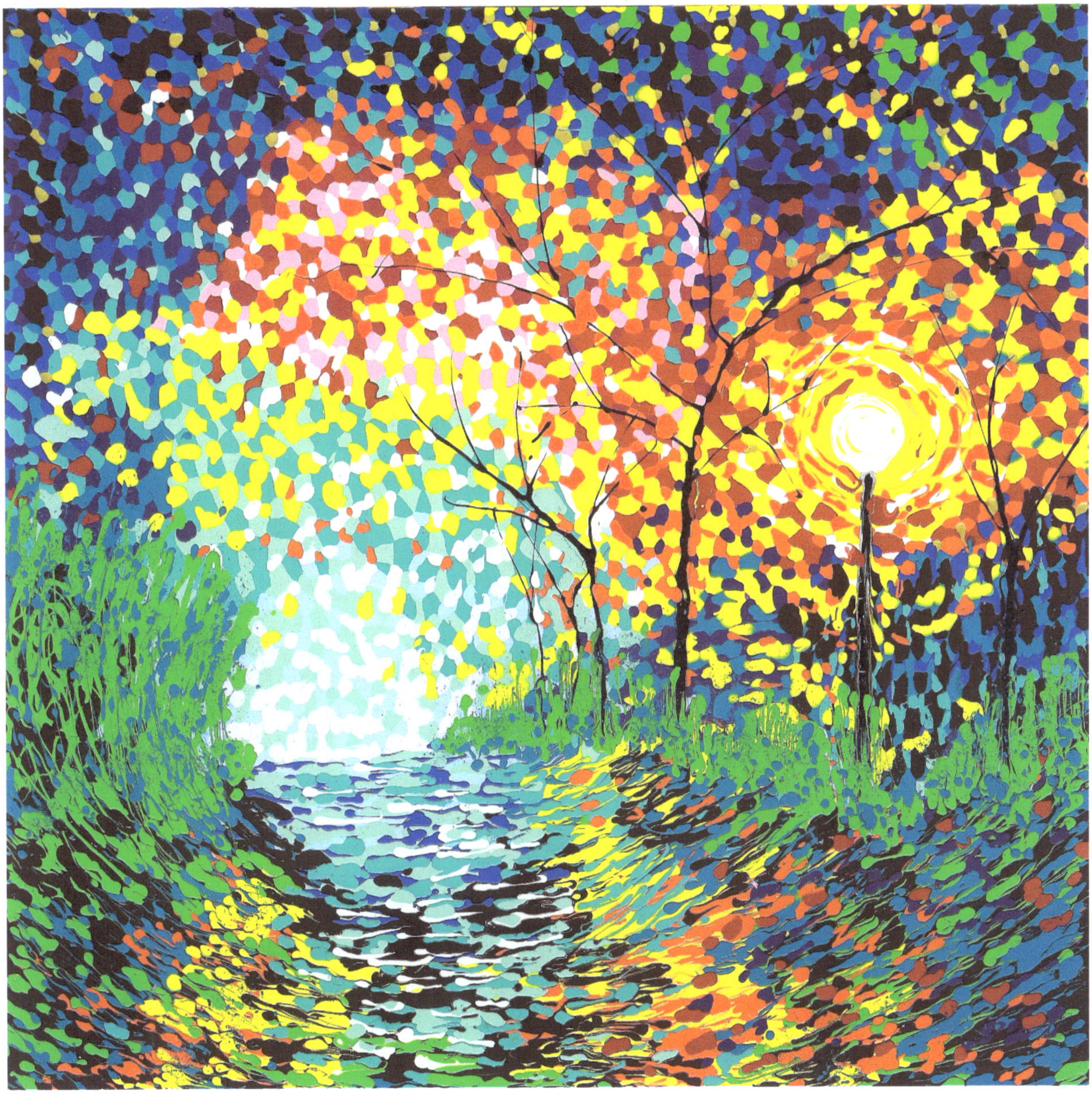

Nocturnal Glow 2021 (Acrylic on canvas) 110cm x 110cm x 8cm

E BEE BANTUG : LIGHTEXPRESSIONIST

Email: bee@lightexpressionist.com Instagram: @ebee_lightexpressionist

Since 2013, using only her camera as one would a painter's brush and natural light as color source, E Bee Bantug literally paints abstract conceptual images aiming to penetrate beyond surface realities; somehow unveiling cosmic energies at play in liminal time space. Asian-American E Bee Bantug has worked as an advertising, marketing and graphics design professional in Asia, Europe, and the US; presently a co-founder & Managing Partner at an IT solutions firm; as well as a visual artist, professionally since 2013. Totally self-taught, E Bee considers her keen appreciation and practice of art in its visual, literary, music and performing forms to be her lifelong art mentor and inspiration. She is fascinated by natural light, its unpredictable movement in the Aether and is passionate about expressing its interplay in seemingly empty spaces of the Aether with her in-the-moment consciousness. Aether –that 'mysterious substance once thought to suffuse the universe' as one dictionary puts it– is still so magnificently alive, pregnant, conscious. Indeed, Aether along with light, are both bountiful medium and matrix of her visual work. Practicing this art form is an unending joyful journey of discovery and a veritable meditation practice the rewards of which often reveal astounding breakthroughs behind the proverbial veil – and beyond the conventions of traditional photography. Ultimately, E Bee invites the viewer to experience through her work a unique glimpse into the fullness of All That Is; to discover and share a new perspective not only about the very nature of reality but also, equally, to witness the dynamic role our consciousness, observation and intentionality play in its creation – each imagery a tribute and testimony to omnipresence and co-creation of quantum moments. Today, continually seeking to explore and prove more to herself than anyone else deeper, wider creative expressions of her dynamic relationship with the aether and its myriad 'invisible' energetic abundance, E Bee carves out time almost daily to create her visual imagery in liminal space. She stays active with galleries, art buyers as well as online platforms and media, local and international. Her work has been featured in Arizona, Oregon, Virginia, NYC, San Francisco, London, Zurich, and Lisbon and continues to receive citations and awards.

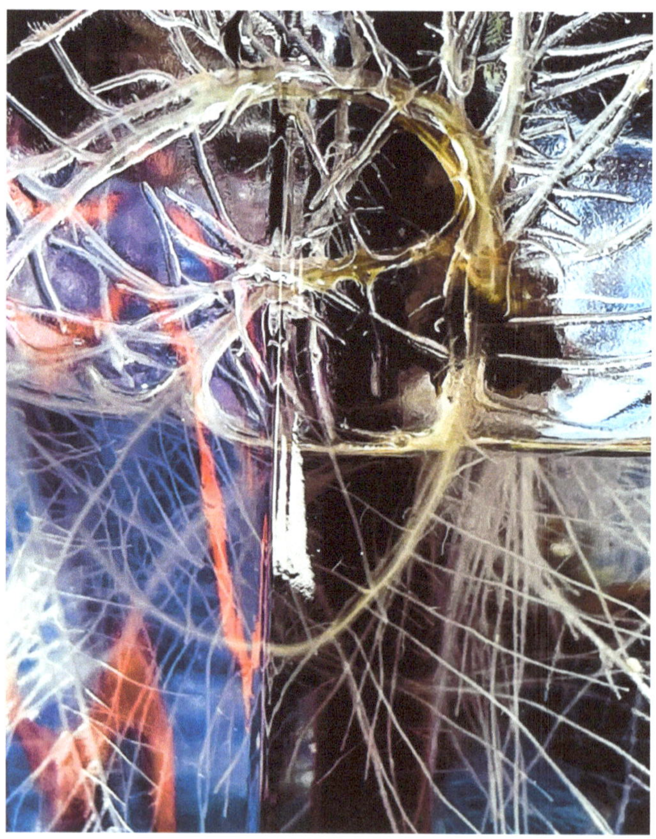

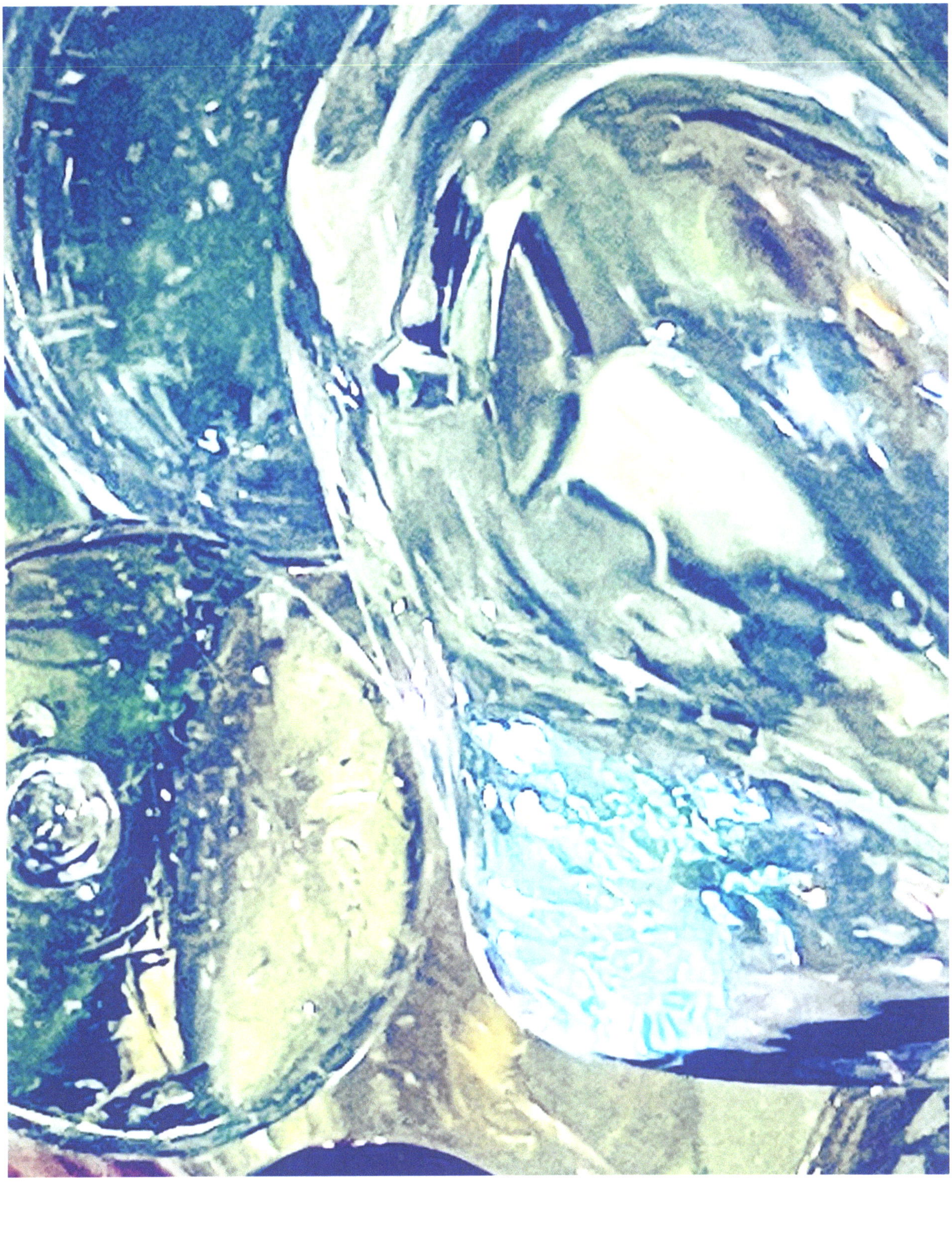

Birthing : Homoborgenesis 2023

ELKE BUEGLER

https://www.elkebuegler.art

Elke Buegler began her artistic career at the start of 2023, rediscovering a passion she had held since her teenage years. Life has its own rhythm, and she is now embracing her artistic path wholeheartedly, expressing her inner world through a dance of intention and instinct, composition and chaos. Her work is characterised by her spontaneous and dynamic acrylic painting style, which uses bold colours to capture fleeting emotions before they disappear. The result is unique pieces of work that convey a clearly deep emotional message and possess a distinct identity.

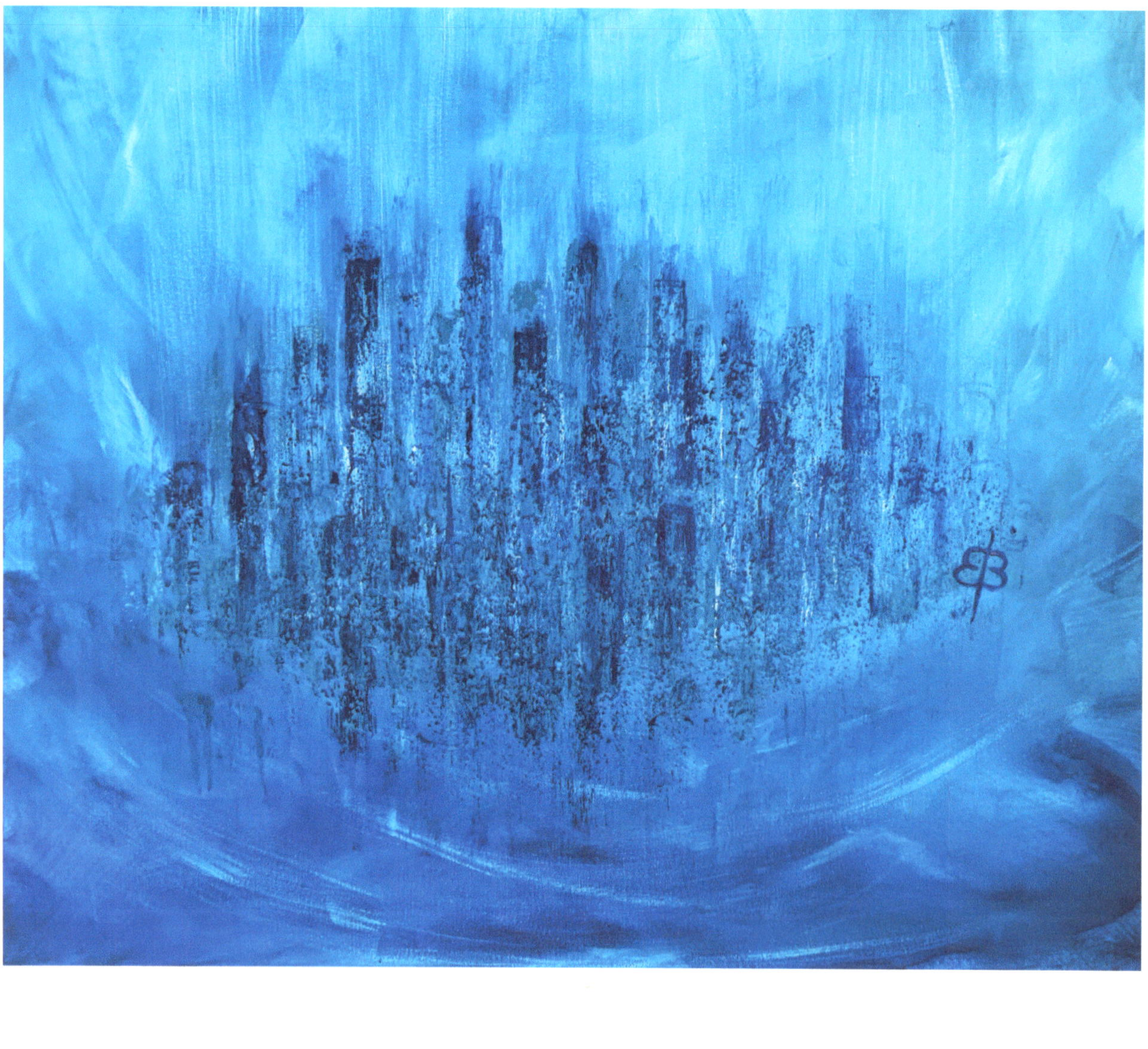

Reflection. Sunken City., 2025. Acryl on canvas, 100 x 120 cm.

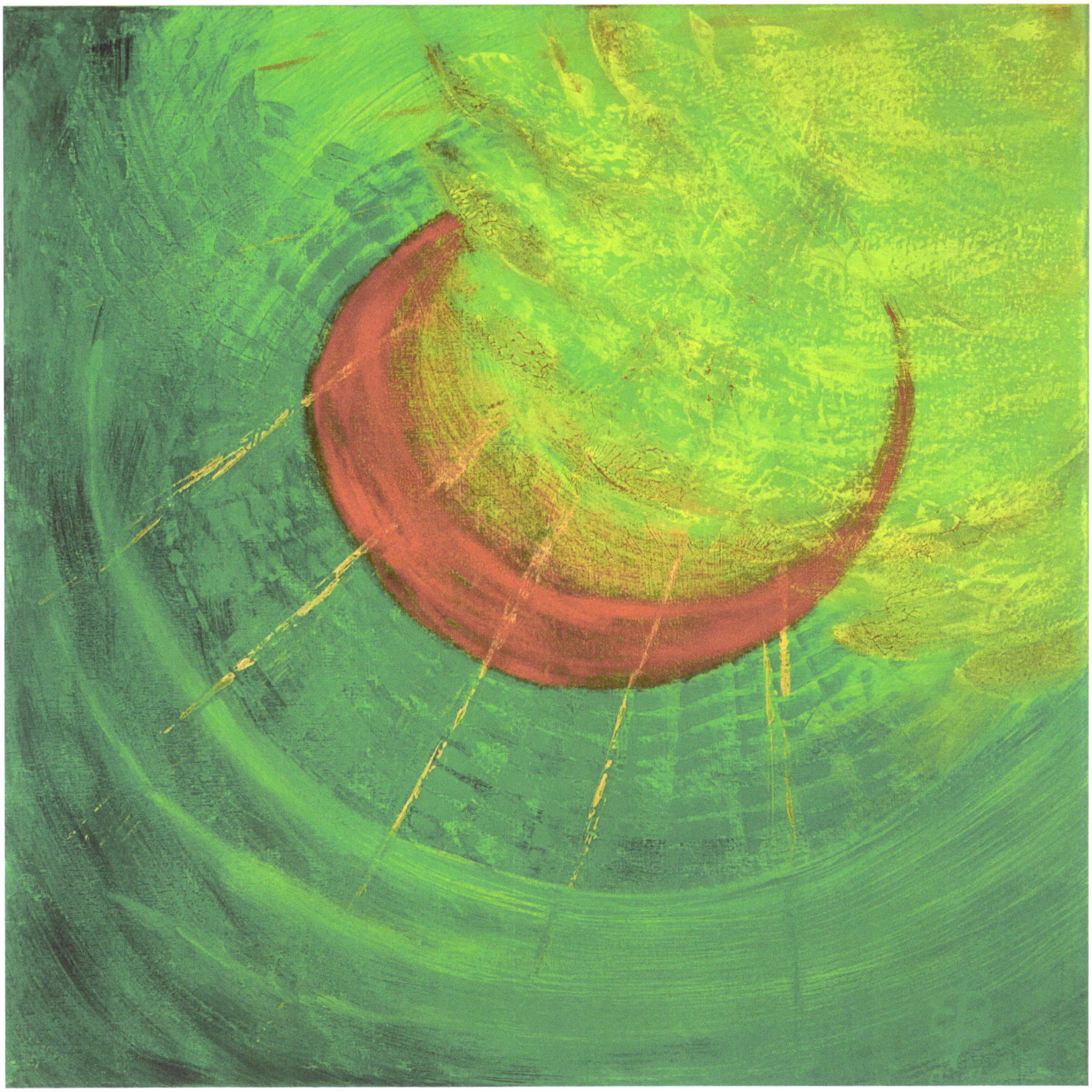

Hope, 2025. Acryl on Linen, 100 x100 cm.

ELVIRA RAJEK

https://www.elvirarajek.com

Elvira Rajek, MA, Visual Artist Born in 1965, lives and works in Vienna, Austria A level in Vienna, Studies at the Vienna University, Study Stay at Lagos, Nigeria, Diploma at the College of Education of Vienna, Master's degree at the CCNY of the City University of New York, International Summeracademy of Fine Arts Venice - Masterclass: Professor Peju Alatise. Sculptures, assemblages, photography, video and objectart. The intended mise-en-scène has been an important component of her art work. Having started with photographical art, for the last years she has focused on shoe sculptures and assemblages, and turned to a surrealistic way of working. "I just need to assemble the pictures and thoughts of my consciousness and subconsciousness to create a new vision and a new way to see.", the artist says. And as Georg Christoph Lichtenberg once said "He, who has eyes, sees everything in everything." Research as well as the study of particular topics play important roles in the artistic realization: to deal with a topic - to eviscerate, to mangle, and to transform - to achieve a new insight. Veiled criticism with a touch of irony is intended. The artist works according to Georg Christoph Lichtenberg's quote "He, who has eyes, sees everything in everything."

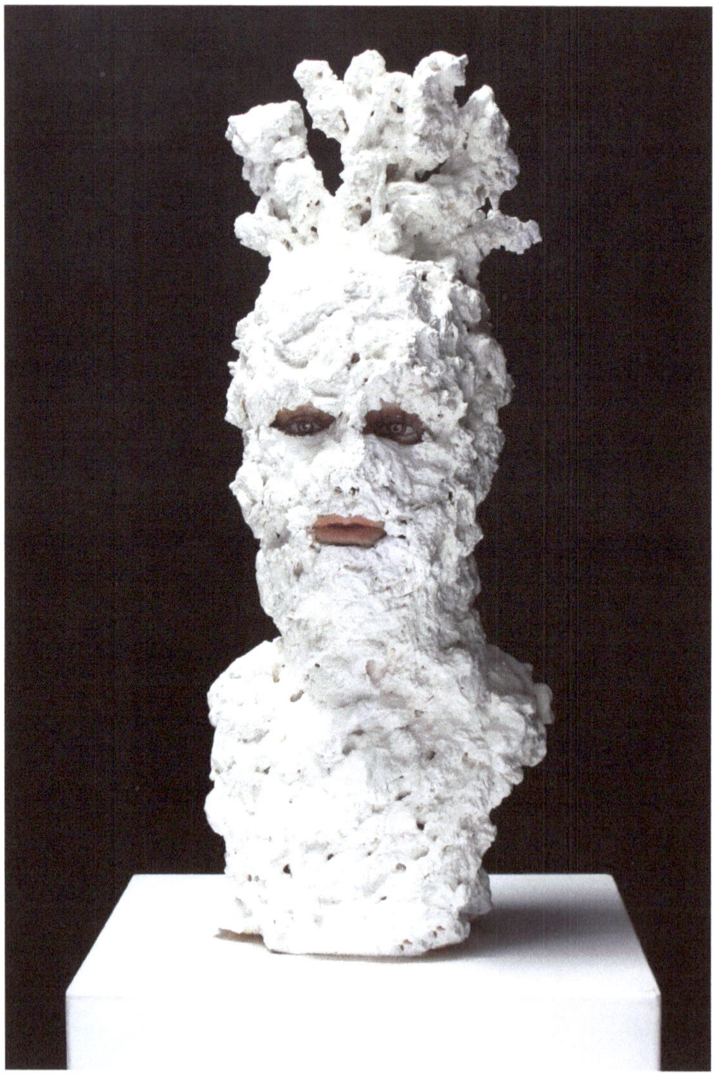

The Head (2019), mixed media, h65cm x w26cm x d26cm

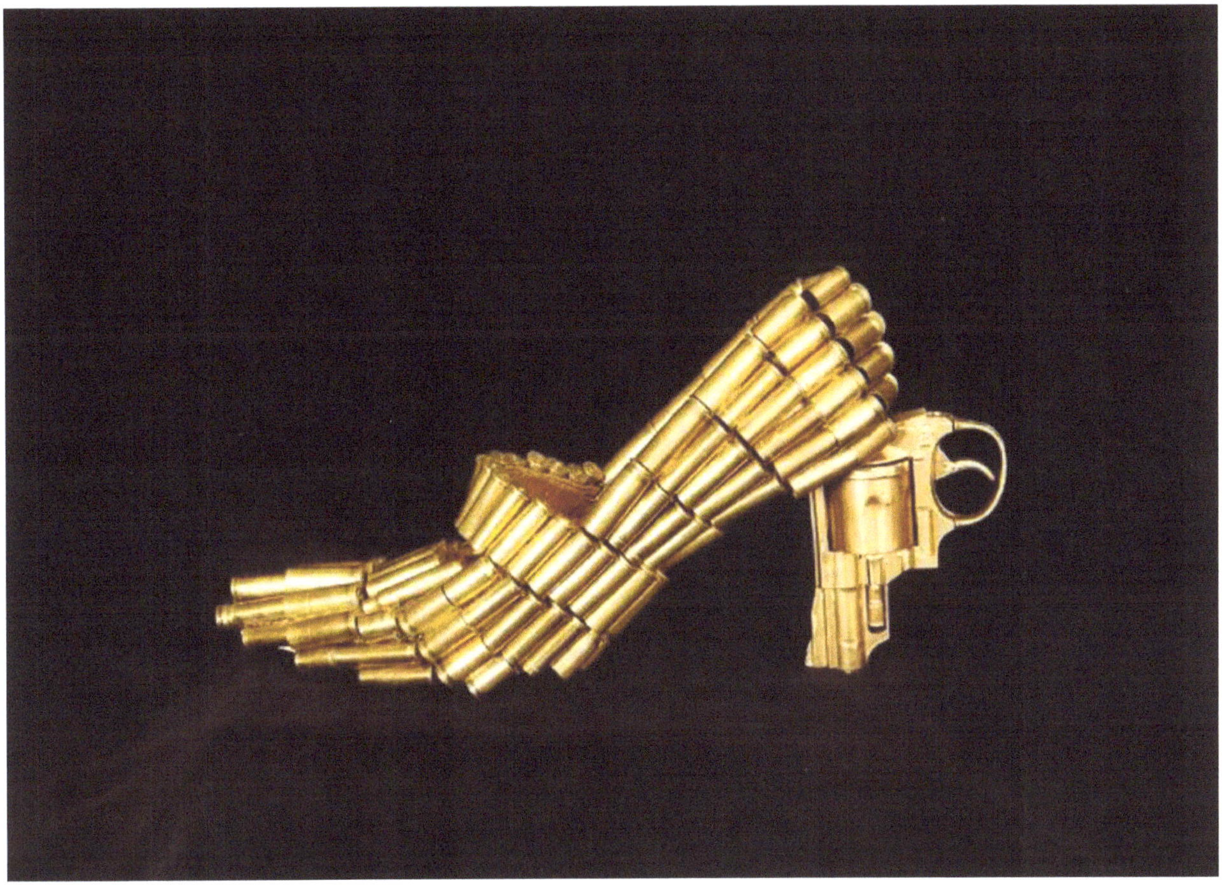

A Shoe for a Shoot (2011), mixed media, h17cm x b32cm x d11cm

EMELA BRACE NOMOLOS

instagram : @emelabracenomolos

Nomolos: The Art of Remembrance A Manifesto for the Awakening of Humanity Through Art Origins: A Childhood of Vision From the age of four, my destiny as an artist was undeniable. While others drew the world they saw, I sketched the world I remembered—enigmatic beings with luminous eyes and unfamiliar forms. These were not dreams, nor inventions of a child's imagination. They were transmissions—messages from beyond the veil, imprinted into my consciousness with a purpose I would only come to understand years later. With red-blonde curls and an innate knowing, I carried visions of forms both blue and gray, neither of this world yet intimately connected to it. They came in waking hours and in dreams, revealing fragments of a cosmic heritage humanity has long forgotten. The Mission Behind the Art What began as an instinctive impulse to create has evolved into a sacred mission. My art is more than visual expression; it is a bridge—a channel for interdimensional communication. Every painting, sculpture, and coded symbol I craft carries a frequency, a message, a remembrance. I am no longer just an artist. I am a messenger. The works I create speak of our hidden potential, our evolution, and the cosmic story that binds us to a greater family among the stars. Many of my pieces are embedded with gemstones—jadeite jade, sapphires, rubies, diamonds, and grandidierites—not as ornaments of wealth, but as resonant keys. Each stone vibrates with a frequency that amplifies the artwork's purpose. These creations do not merely appeal to the eyes; they speak to the soul.

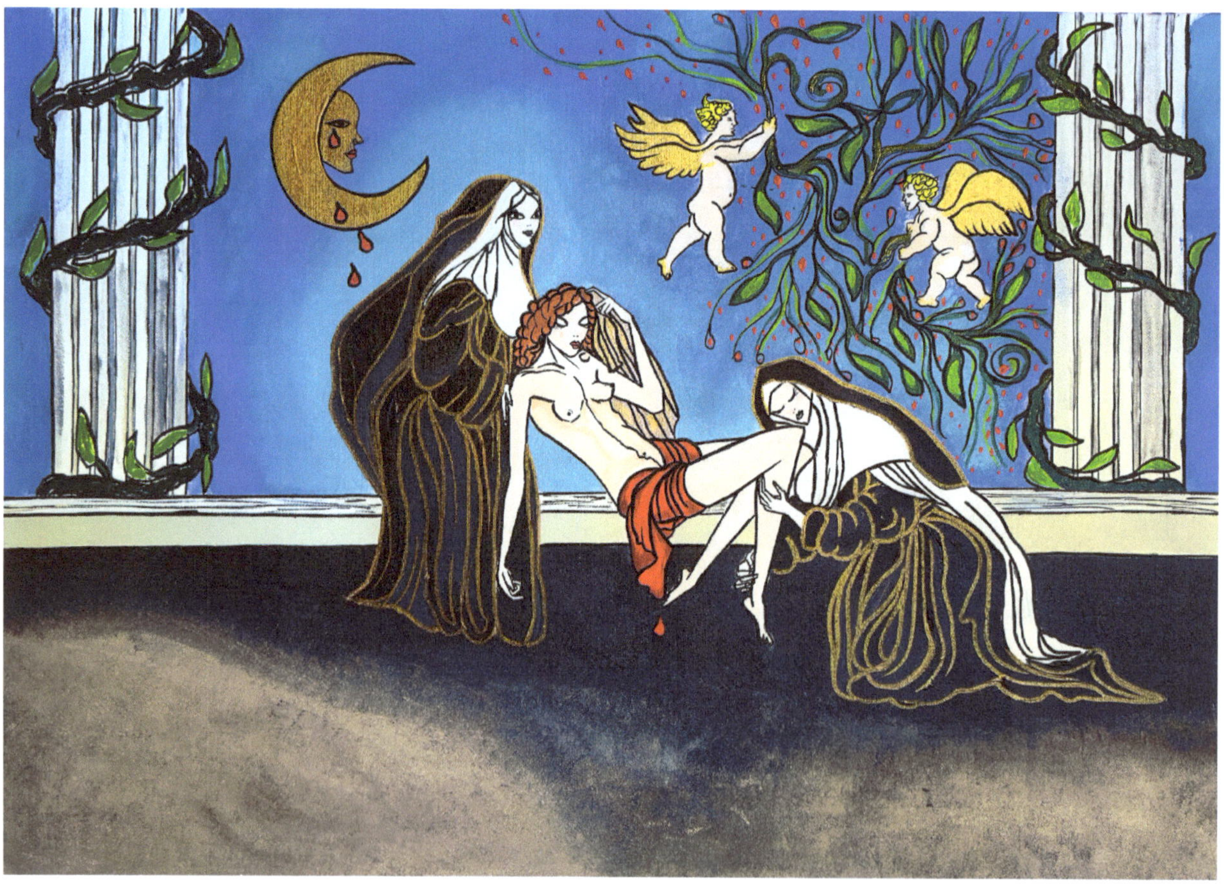

THE GRACE ,

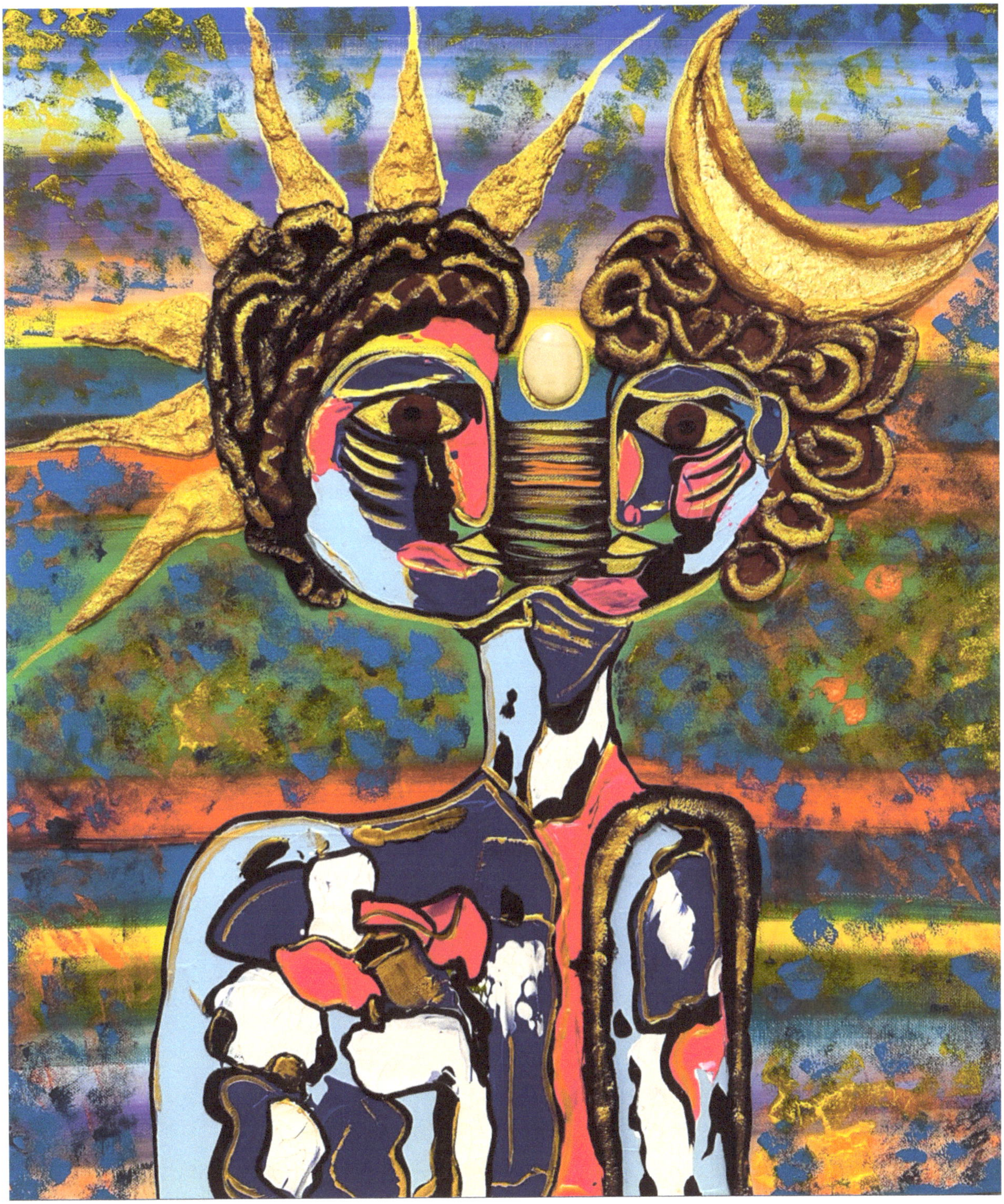

MOON&SUN

EMMA COYLE

https://www.artworkarchive.com/profile/emma-coyle

[b.1981 Dublin, Ireland] Coyle has been progressing her figurative paintings for over 20 years, firstly driven by an influence from America Pop art of the 1960's. Coyle has been based in London since 2006 and is represented international by Arte Globale, Chrissy Moore Art Advisory and The Marylebone Gallery in W1 London. Coyle's most acclaimed recent exhibition was presented by the Helwaser gallery on Madison Ave. in New York, who hosted a solo show of Coyle's paintings in 2022 titled 'The Best Revenge'. The exhibition was listed 12th in GalleriesNow's August Special, 'The 30 most popular exhibitions on now'[worldwide]. Artnet listed the show in its '5 sizzling emerging artists, the Artnet Gallery Network recommends checking out before summer's end'[worldwide]. Following the book release 'Emma Coyle Pop Now' in June 2024 published by Snap Collective publishing in Paris, Coyle was awarded a solo show at Galerie Patricia Kamoun in The Hamptons, curated by Anne-Marie Helwaser. Coyle has received a plethora of awards throughout her career and is a recipient of International Art Market's Gold List award. 'Top international contemporary artist of today', 'Recommended artist to invest in and to be inspired by', with work acquired by past Tate Museum Trustee Dame Janet Wolfson de Botton. Most recently she was awarded the Phoenix International Prize from Italy's Effetto Arte Foundation. Coyle's first education in art in the 1990's included an introduction to 1st wave New York Pop Art of the 1960's. As an avid reader, many art genres have inspired her work over the years. Her current figurative work focuses on the use of current print magazine imagery and advertisements, to produce painterly images of a Fine Art quality. Combining primary and secondary line work with ideas in abstraction, minimalism and use of negative space. Early in her career Coyle exhibited in many galleries in Ireland and exhibited for the Irish National Portrait exhibition, 2005. Coyle also exhibited for charities in the Royal Hibernian Academy and Adam's Fine Art auctioneers. Just before moving to London Coyle had solo exhibitions in the Signal Art Centre in Co. Wicklow, the Bank of Ireland's art centre in Dublin. Coyle was described as 'one of the city's most promising new artist' {Metro Life newspaper- January 2006} and was also described as a 'rising young artist' {Irish Independent- May 2006}. Since 2006 Coyle has exhibited in many galleries local to her and internationally. In 2014 Coyle' work was selected by Los Angeles curator Bridget Carron for her collection Power Pop on Saatchi' online gallery. In 2018 Coyle' painting 12.16.07 won the Artness Magazine cover competition and won her an Artist of the Year 2019, a Honorable Mention Award from Circle Foundation in France and an additional Honorable Mention Award from New York's Grey Cube gallery in 2022. In 2019 her painting series '12.16' also won her a Special Artist Award from London's BESTART. In April 2020 painting Linda no.1 receive a review from Dab Art Co. Los Angeles, and in 2021 won a Finalist Award from Art Show International also in Los Angeles and a Distinguished Award from Canada's ArtAscent Magazine.

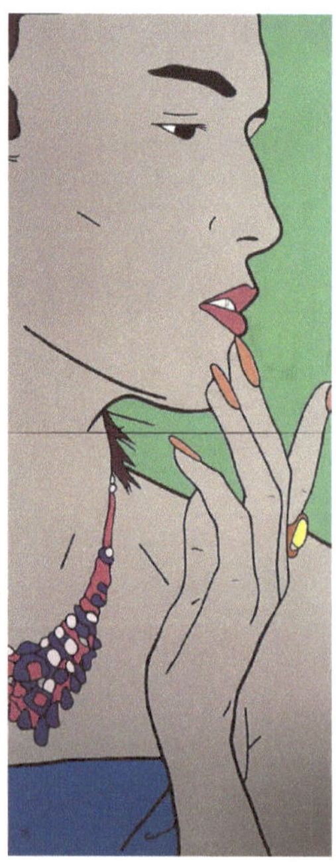

25.02 Acrylic on canvas 122x304cm 2025

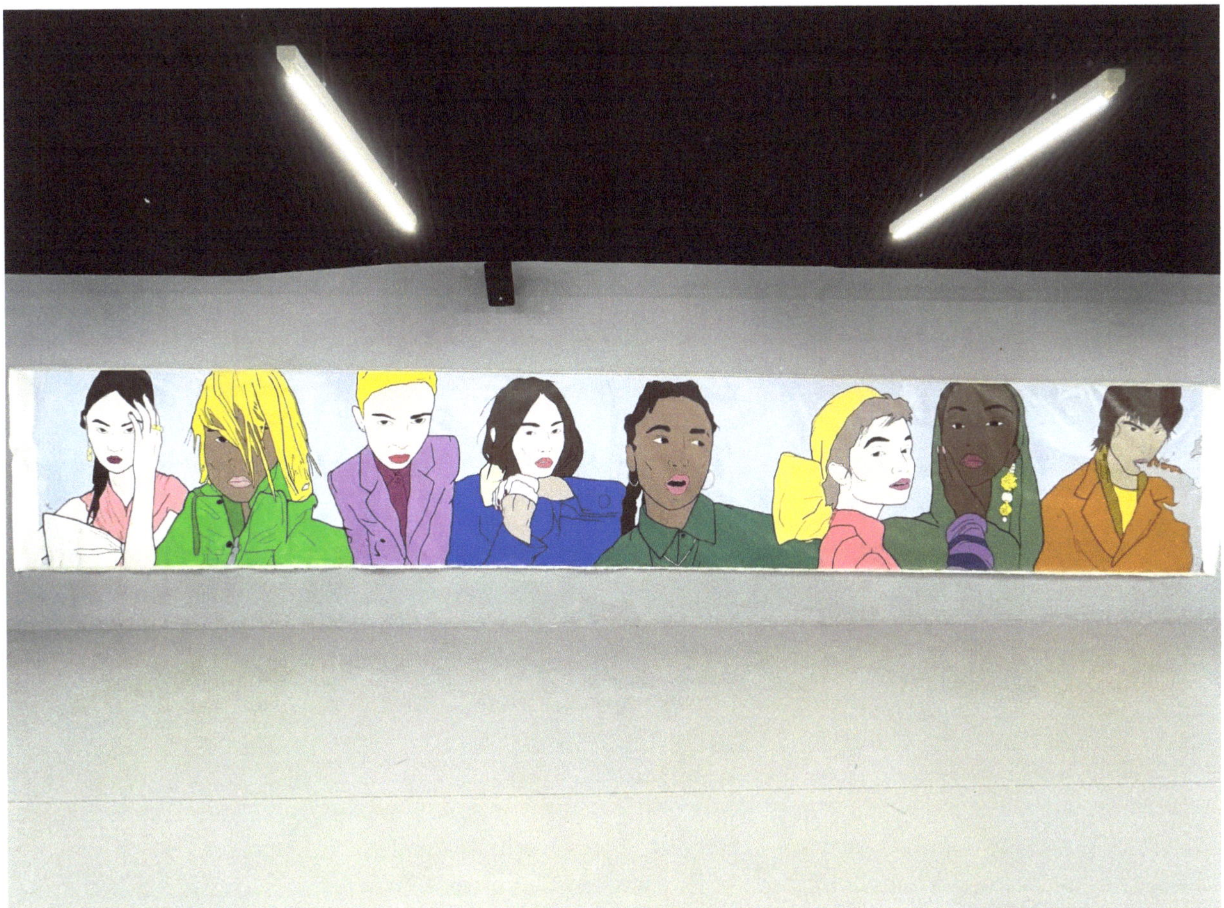

Collective Selection [3] Acrylic on canvas 964x160cm 2024

ERNA KLAUS

https://www.ernaklaus.com

Die Malerei von Erna Klaus ist Ausdruck einer inneren Bewegung – einer Suche, die sich nie vollständig festlegen lässt. Sie folgt keiner klaren Linie, sondern einem offenen Prozess, in dem sich Intuition, Erfahrung und meditative Reflexion verbinden. Oft beginnt ein Bild mit einem einzigen Strich – was dann folgt, geschieht in Etappen, manchmal über Wochen oder Monate. Sie sieht Gesichter, Figuren, Geschichten – nicht geplant, sondern im Verlauf des Malens entdeckt sie diese. Ihre Werke entstehen aus dem Wunsch, etwas Eigenes zu finden, jenseits des bloßen Nachmalens. Sie will nicht kopieren, sondern sich einlassen auf das Unvorhersehbare, das Spontane, das Wilde. Vielleicht trifft der Begriff „Wilde Kunst" diesen Ansatz am besten: ungezähmt, frei, offen für Brüche und Überraschungen. Sie liebt es, wenn Farbe strahlt, wenn ein Bild Freude vermittelt – als Gegenpol zu einer oft dunklen Welt. Inspiriert von Reisen, Ausstellungen, Begegnungen und der täglichen Meditation, entwickelt sie ihren Stil kontinuierlich weiter. Sie malt gegenständlich und abstrakt, ohne sich auf ein Motiv festzulegen. Jedes Bild soll Raum lassen für eigene Deutungen – und vielleicht beim Betrachter etwas in Bewegung setzen: ein Lächeln, einen Gedanken, ein Innehalten. Die Kunst von Erna Klaus will nicht erklären, sondern berühren. Sie soll leben – nicht im Keller oder einem Lager, sondern an der Wand. Nur dort erfüllt sie ihren Zweck. Text: Fridtjof Atterdal

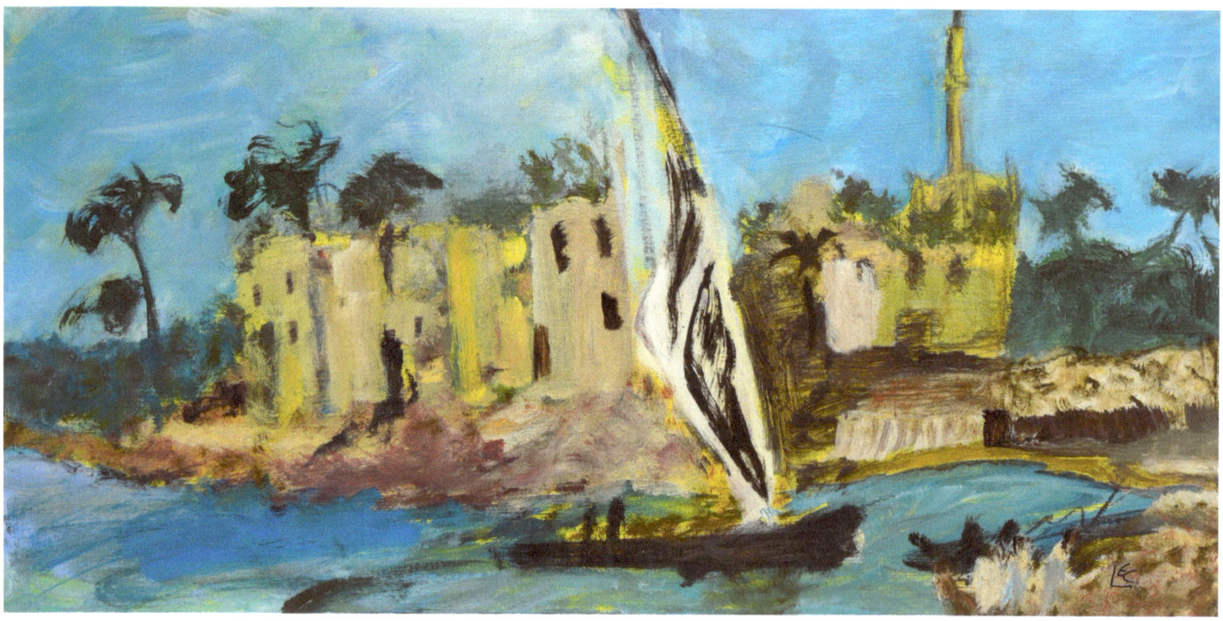

Village on the Nile, 2022, Acrylic on Canvas, 50 x 100 cm

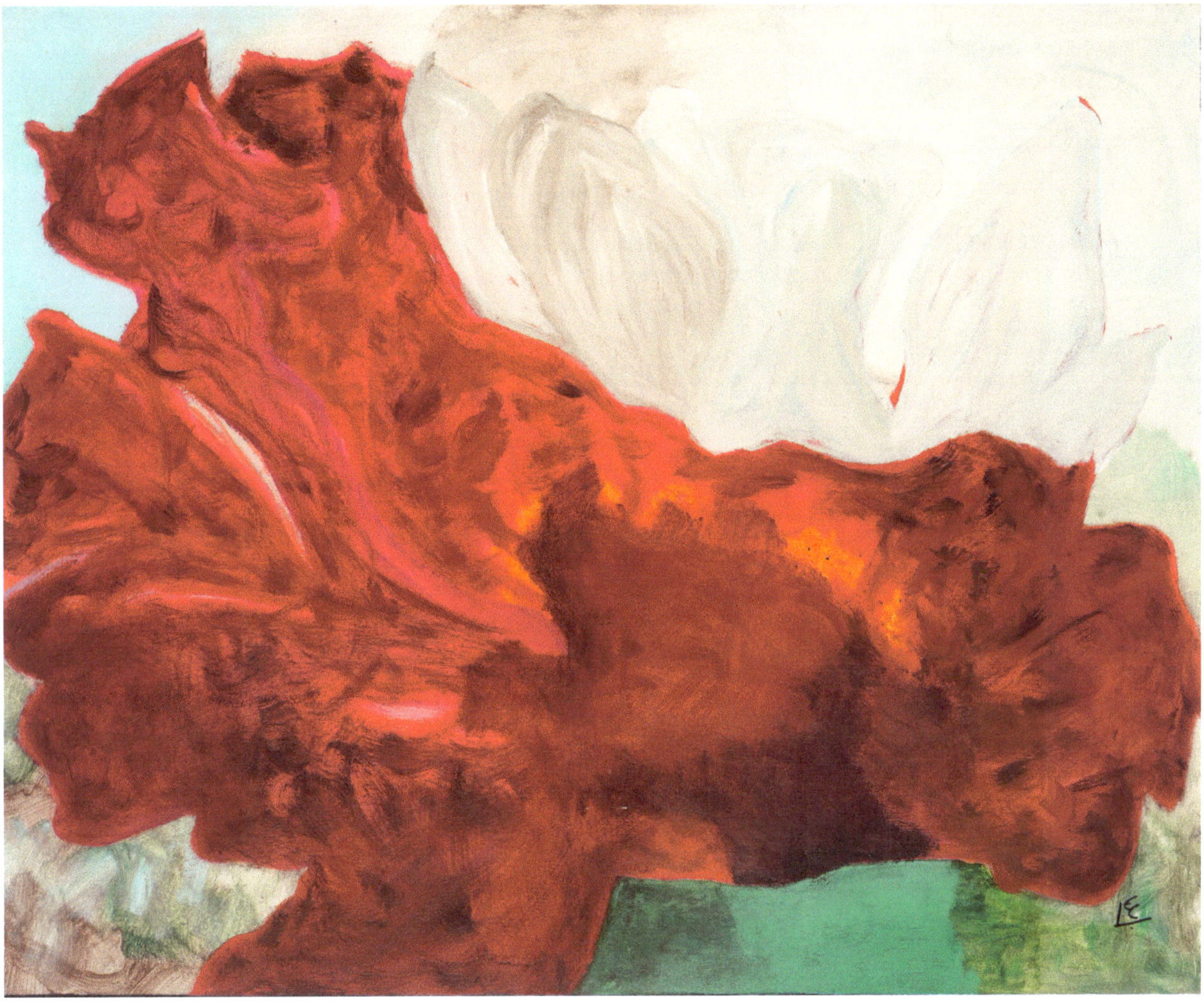

Peony, 2023, Acrylic on Canvas, 100 x 120 cm

EVA MOOSBRUGGER

office@evamoosbrugger.com

Eva Moosbrugger's artistic philosophy centers around series-based explorations, examining abstract concepts, natural forms, and philosophical narratives through refined abstraction and reductive aesthetics. Her sculptures consistently embody biomorphic shapes and profound simplicity, inviting viewers into meditative contemplation. Working meticulously with glass, she transforms the medium's inherent fragility into a powerful conduit for expressing enduring themes of harmony, introspection, and organic beauty. Her artistic practice distinguishes itself through her rare ability to fuse technical mastery with conceptual depth, pushing the expressive possibilities of glass beyond traditional boundaries. Moosbrugger's contributions to contemporary art lie in her sophisticated integration of craftsmanship and philosophy, consistently revealing glass as an expressive medium capable of capturing ephemeral beauty, emotional depth, and timeless contemplation.

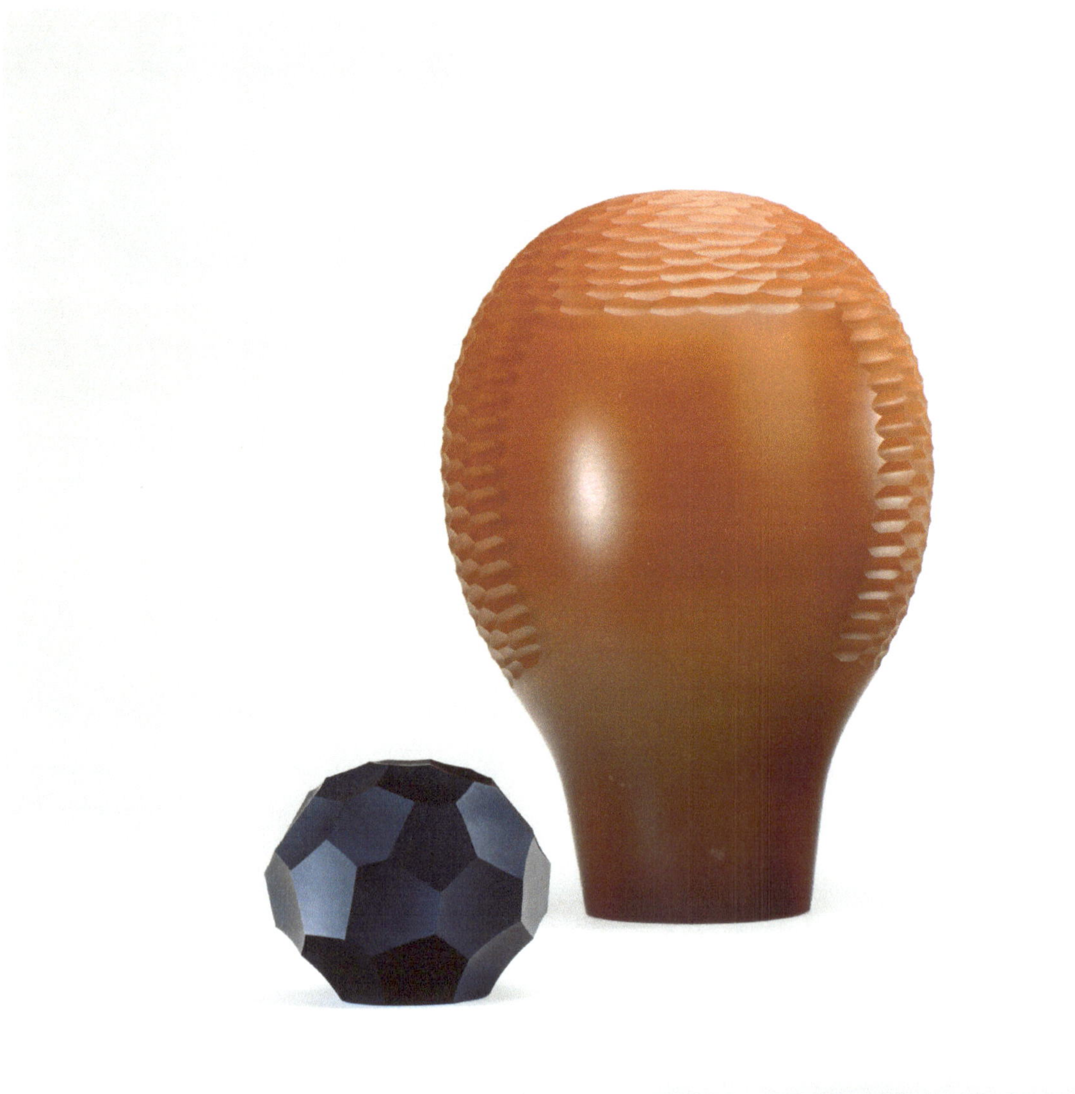

Zen Meditation, 2009 Diptych Multilayered free blown Murano glass with engravings. Dimensions: H 32 x diam. 21,6 cms, weight 13,1 kgs and H 9 x diam. 9,5 cms, weight 0,6 kgs

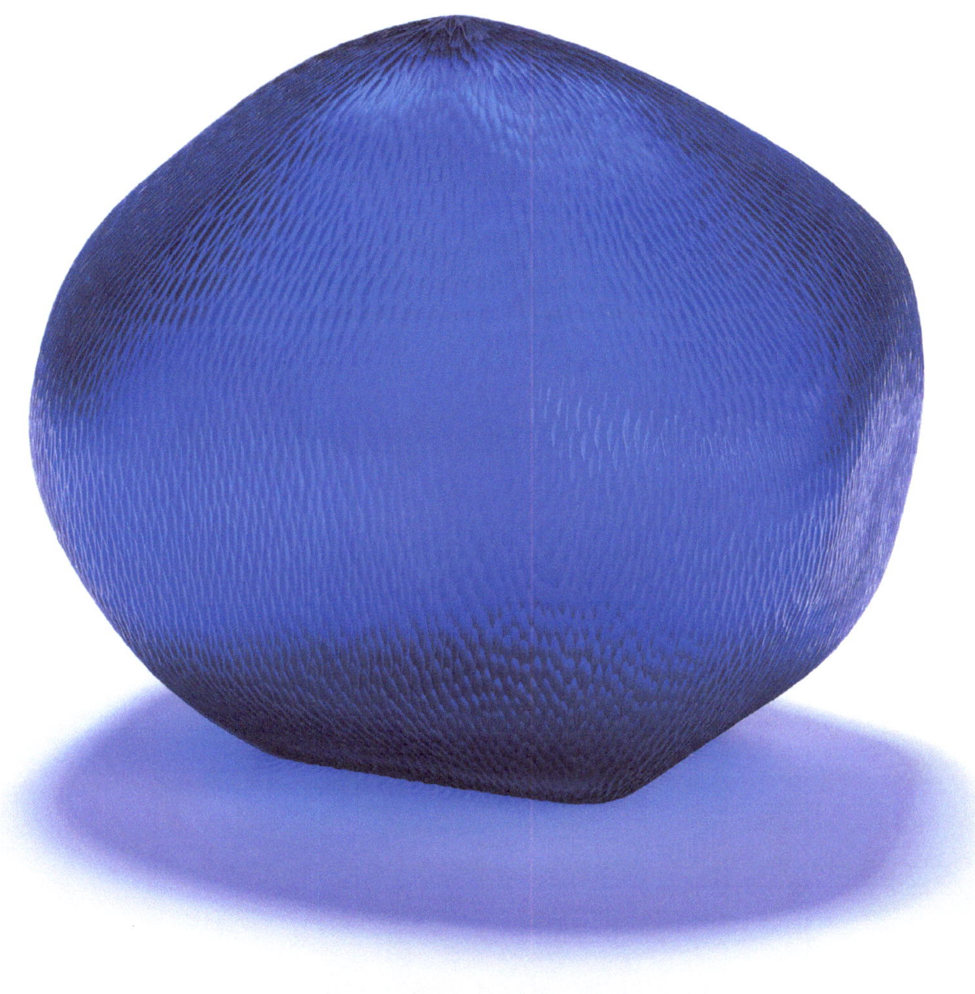

Blue Diamond, 2016 Blue transparent Murano glass, free blown and hot shaped. Multiple overlays. Surface with copper-wheel-engravings „rice seeds". H 23,5 x 32 x 30,5 cms, weight 7,4 kgs

FANT WENGER

fant.ch

Fant Wenger born 1971 live and works in Switzerland. In Fant Wenger' s universe antennas sprout from forests, satelites drift over sunlit meadows, and railway wagons seem to whisper secrets into the trees. A painter, sculptor and longtime explorer of the tension between nature and technology. Fant' s work pulls us int cinematic landscapes whee the analog and the digital blur, and where nothing is ever full wha it seems. His canvases often monumental in scale are live with contrast, chaos and stilness, wilderness and wires, mythology and machinery. He describe a kid of third reality that captivates the viewer and make us think about how we perceive our own reality.

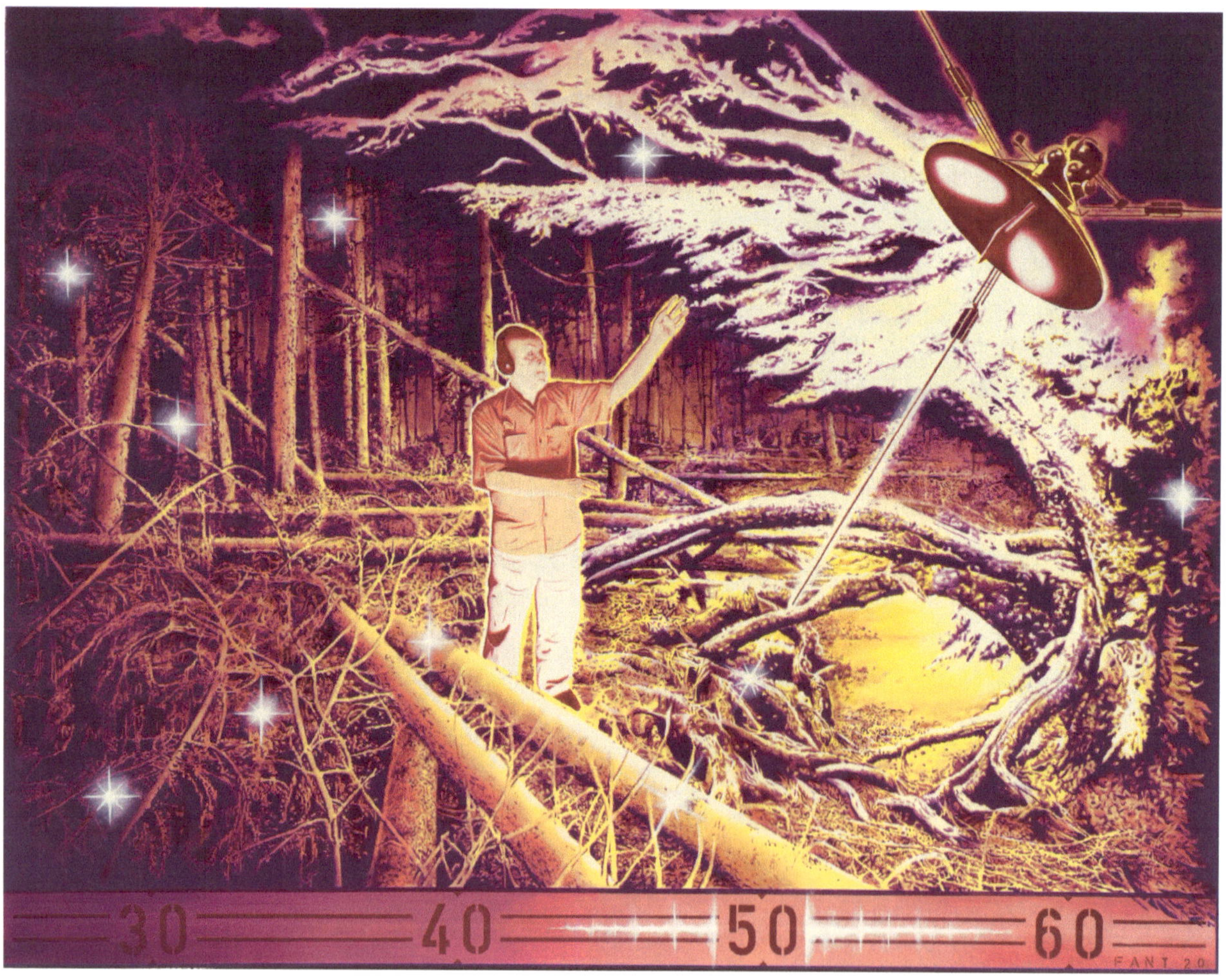

Radiostorm oil/acryl on canvas 2021 190 x 240 cm

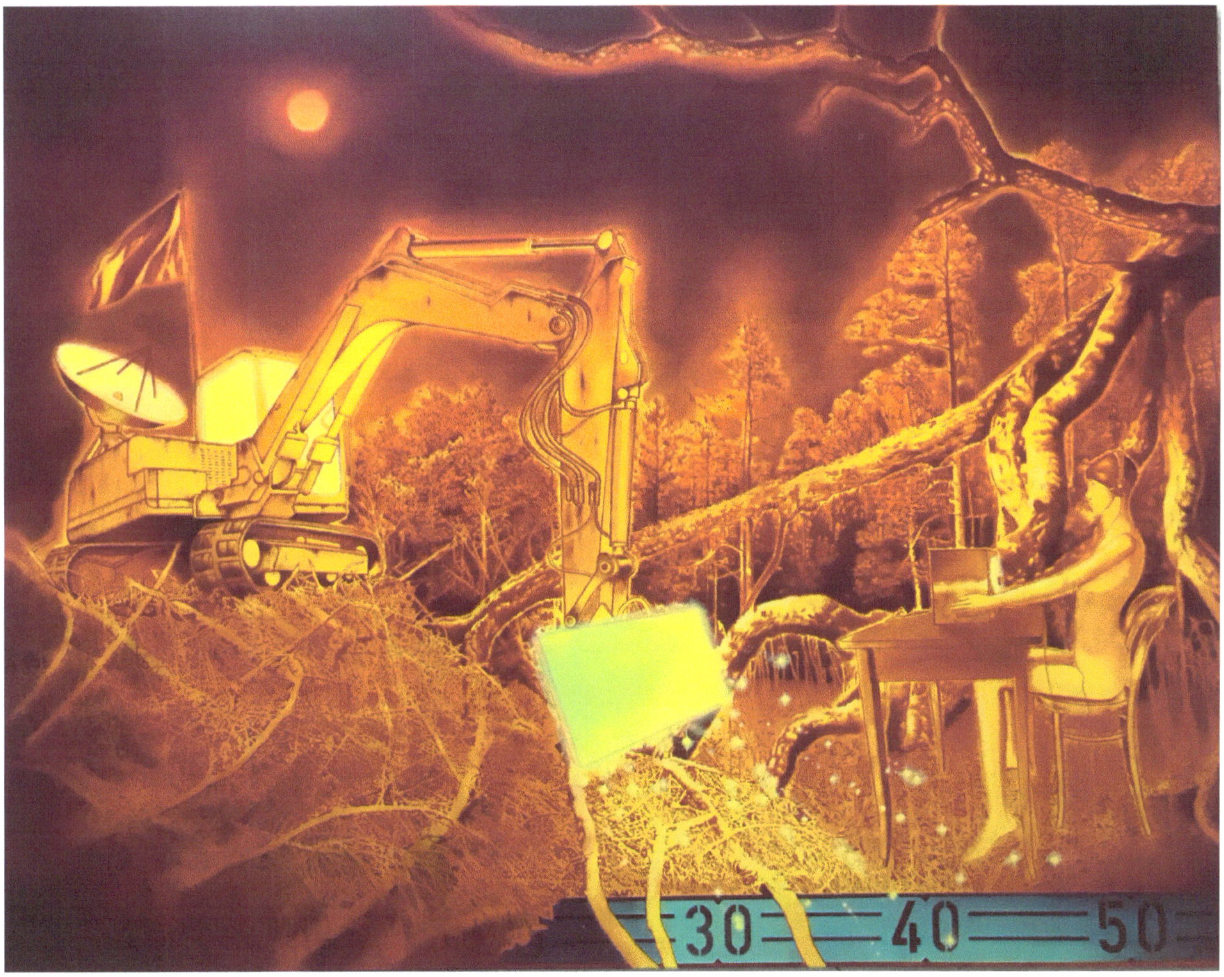

Propaganda acryl on canvas 2019 180 x 240 cm

FARI ALI

www.fariart.com

Painting has been a spiritual journey for Fari from the past 50 years. Her canvasses are mainly in oils. Her style is a genre of fine arts —Photo Realism and Expressionism. Her intention has always been to integrate art into spirituality and hence express the beauty of the world : Through painting landscapes and monuments unaffected by the impurities of the environment we live in; Through painting portraits of people, birds and animals by bringing out the true essence of their personalities and soul beauty; Through painting florals and nature so that human beings despite their busy lives can stop by to appreciate their intrinsic beauty. She believes "All passes, only art endures"; and that "Reality belongs only to Spirit and art is the miracle to prove this truth in the world we live in."

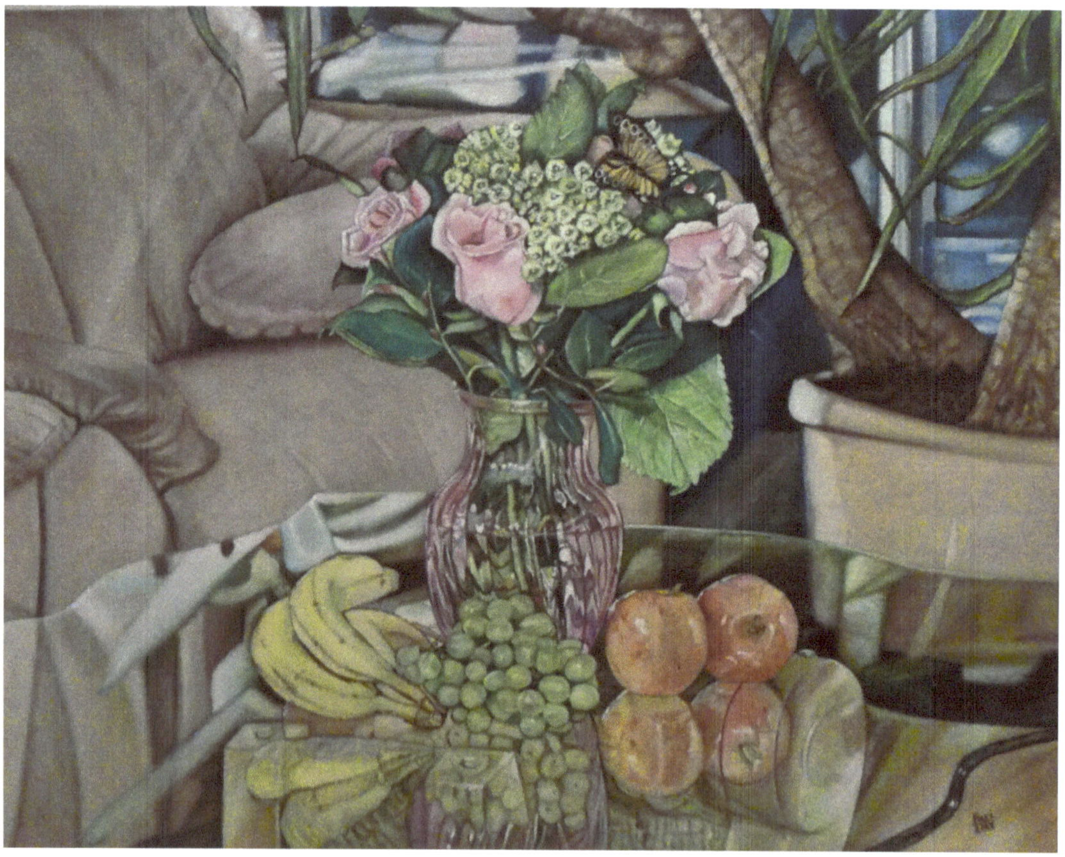

Home Beauty, 2013, Pils on canvas, 61X76cms

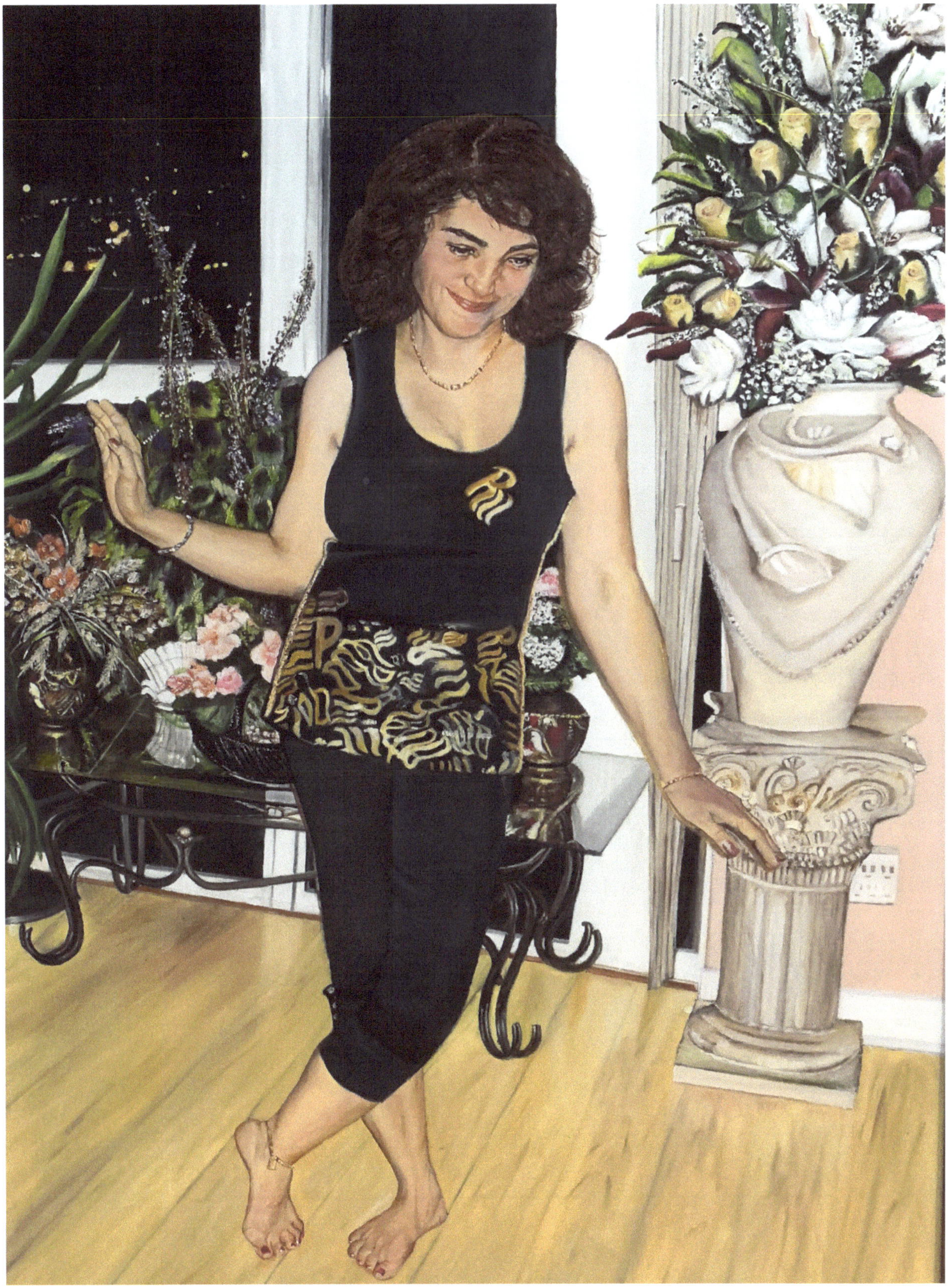

Peace Dance, 2012, Oils on Canvas, 76X122 cms

FELIPE ALARCON ECHENIQUE

(Instagram): @felipealarconoficial

Felipe Alarcón Echenique (La Habana, Cuba, 1966) es un artista visual multidisciplinar cuya trayectoria abarca más de tres décadas de creación constante. Reside y trabaja en Madrid, donde ha desarrollado una obra profunda, rica en símbolos y referencias culturales, que transita entre la pintura, el grabado, el dibujo y la escritura. Su lenguaje plástico parte de una base neocubista y simbólica, articulando imágenes de fuerte carga narrativa y expresiva. Las obras de Alarcón son micromundos que entrelazan historia, literatura, crítica social y memoria personal, en composiciones que invitan a una lectura múltiple y abierta. Formado en la prestigiosa Academia de Bellas Artes "San Alejandro" de La Habana y más tarde licenciado en Educación Artística por el Instituto Superior Pedagógico Enrique José Varona, Alarcón inició su carrera profesional como profesor de artes plásticas en escuelas cubanas, a la par que desarrollaba su propia investigación artística. Su estudio-taller "Micromundos", fundado en 1996 en el corazón de La Habana Vieja, se convirtió en un espacio de creación y experimentación, donde empezó a consolidar las bases visuales y conceptuales de lo que sería su universo artístico. La obra de Felipe Alarcón se caracteriza por el uso de técnicas mixtas, la reutilización de materiales cotidianos y una estética que mezcla lo barroco con lo contemporáneo. Lienzos, cartones, papeles reciclados, fragmentos de textos y objetos encontrados conviven en composiciones densas y poéticas, que remiten tanto al caos urbano de las grandes ciudades latinoamericanas como al orden secreto de la mente que las interpreta. El color, la línea y la textura son elementos fundamentales en su proceso creativo, que se desarrolla de forma espontánea e intuitiva, aunque siempre guiado por una intención narrativa. Desde sus primeros años, Alarcón ha concebido el arte como un medio para interpretar el mundo. Su producción está marcada por una permanente reflexión sobre temas como la identidad, el mestizaje cultural, el poder, la espiritualidad y los conflictos éticos del individuo contemporáneo. Las referencias visuales a iconografías bíblicas, clásicas o literarias se mezclan con personajes urbanos, seres híbridos, animales simbólicos y estructuras arquitectónicas que evocan ciudades imposibles o sueños fragmentados. Además de su labor como artista plástico, Alarcón ha cultivado una importante producción literaria: poemas, ensayos, relatos y novelas breves que dialogan con su obra visual, ampliando su universo simbólico. Su práctica se sitúa, por tanto, en la frontera entre lenguajes, donde la imagen y la palabra se potencian mutuamente en una búsqueda continua de sentido. Esta multidisciplinariedad ha hecho de él una figura singular dentro del panorama del arte iberoamericano contemporáneo. A lo largo de su carrera ha desarrollado numerosas series que condensan sus principales preocupaciones temáticas y estéticas: Micromundos, ADN Cervantes, Pecados Capitales, Paraísos Bíblicos Atemporales o La ciudad de las columnas, entre otras. En ellas explora, con una mirada crítica y poética, los restos culturales de occidente, la fragilidad de las utopías y la condición fragmentaria del ser humano. Su obra ha sido expuesta en galerías y espacios institucionales de Cuba, España, Italia, Francia, Alemania, Estados Unidos, Perú y Costa Rica, entre otros países. También forma parte de importantes colecciones públicas y privadas, como el Museo de la Ciudad de La Habana, el Museo del Dibujo de Buenos Aires, la Universidad de Navarra, el Ayuntamiento de Baeza, así como de numerosas colecciones particulares en Europa y América Latina. En Madrid, donde reside desde hace más de una década, dirige la Asociación de Creadores Iberoamericanos (ACI) y es miembro de la Asociación Española de Pintores y Escultores y de la entidad de gestión de derechos de autor VEGAP. En esta ciudad ha encontrado un espacio fértil para el diálogo intercultural y la expansión de su obra, sin perder nunca el vínculo emocional y simbólico con su origen cubano. Felipe Alarcón Echenique es, en esencia, un creador de mundos. Su trabajo se resiste a las clasificaciones fáciles y propone un territorio híbrido donde convergen la pintura y la literatura, la historia y el presente, lo visible y lo oculto. A través de una poética visual cargada de símbolos, metáforas y referencias cruzadas, invita al espectador a detenerse, a mirar con atención y a pensar desde la complejidad. En tiempos de velocidad y simplificación, su obra es un acto de resistencia estética e intelectual, un llamado a reencantar el mundo desde el arte.

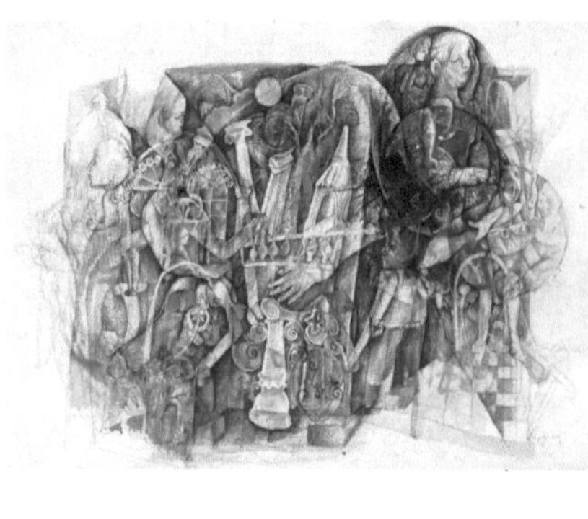

Serie CRÓNICAS EN BLANCO Y NEGRO (III). La ciudad de las columnas. Técnica mixta sobre cartulina. 70x100 cms. Año 2013

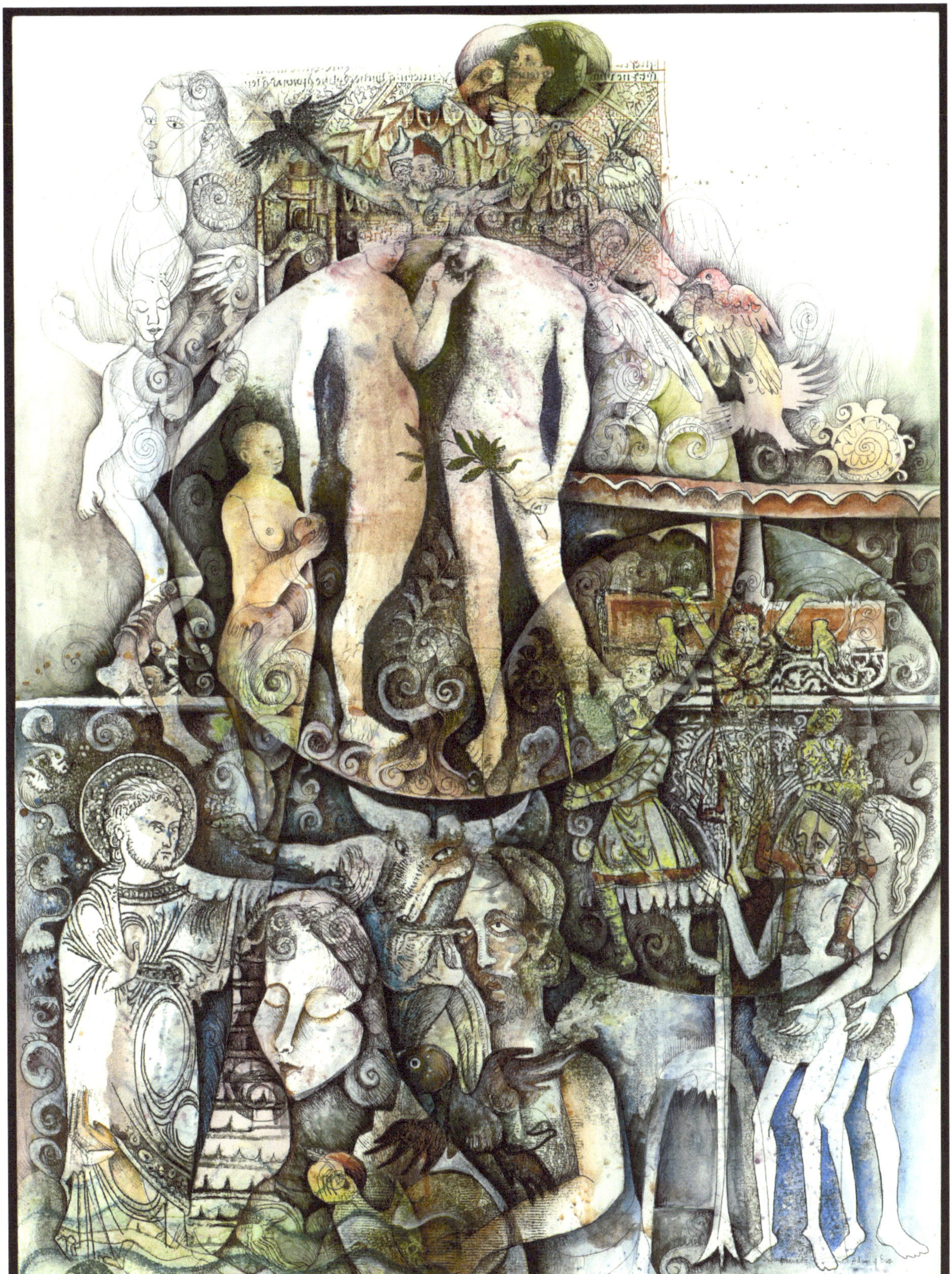

Serie Paraisos Bíblicos. Adán y Eva. Mixta cartulina. 70x50 cm 2019

FER ZANNOL

www.ferzannolph

she was born in 1966, Bs As Argentina she is passionate about investigating the intimacy and concealment of secrecy. She seek to capture feelings and emotions coagulated in time, paralyzed in their flow, that define our identity. Her work with stories full of mystery, where imagination and reality become blurred in a disturbing way, drawing the viewer into a journey of introspection. "Some pieces from her artworks have been acquired by prestigious collections, including the Pembroke collection at Fidelity in Boston and the Ricardo Roa collection in Chile. This artwork is, at its core, an intimate and silent conversation between mother and daughter—a visual testimony of what endures and what inevitably slips away. Through sculptures composed of rescued objects, the artist creates bridges between past and present, transforming grief into a shared act of creation and contemplation. The artist's mother, Adriana, was a renowned sculptor who lived surrounded by objects—tools, curiosities, fragments—through which she built a world uniquely her own. Today, these remnants, salvaged from her studio and reshaped into new forms, carry the echoes of a vibrant life. They become an emotional topography that hovers between absence and memory. Each sculpture is a fragment of the emotional puzzle she left behind—a collection that defies disappearance through new visual and narrative configurations. In an act of love and transformation, the artist uses the language of photography to capture these ephemeral works, stripping them of their utilitarian purposes and imbuing them with a symbolism that transcends the material. These are visual reliquaries, where each object speaks: everyday utensils and forgotten curiosities that once stood silently in her presence now gather, like offerings, on the altar of memory. The creative process behind this series not only honors Adriana's life and creative spirit but allows the artist to inhabit grief in a tangible and poetic way. By reconstructing and framing these objects, the artist reflects on the impossibility of separating a person from the things they touched, shaped, and loved. This work evokes the dual nature of memory and forgetting—a space where our attachment to material things becomes both an act of resistance against absence and, paradoxically, a means of release.

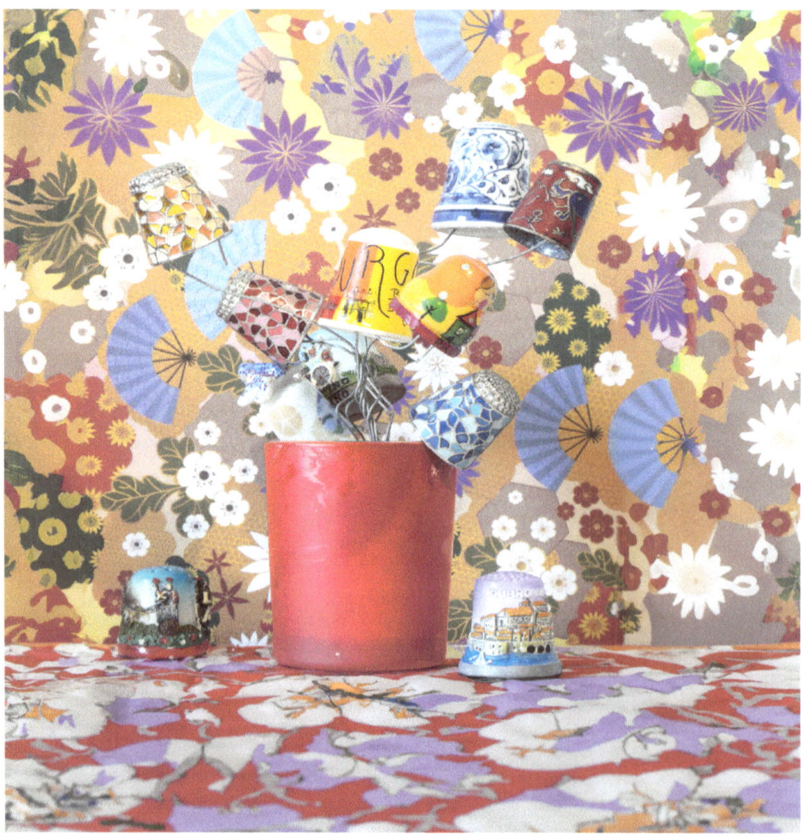

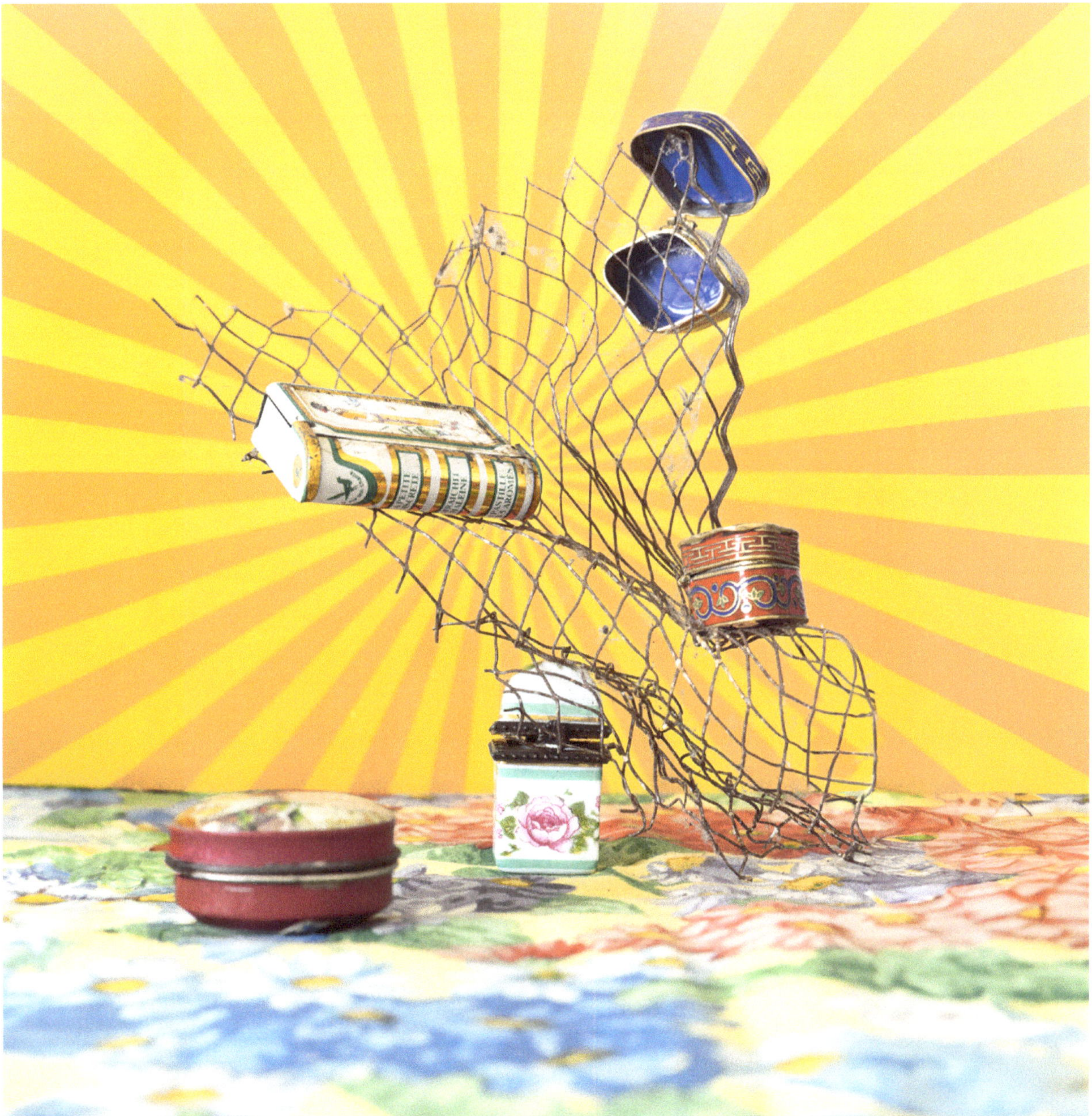

FINA FERRARA

www.finaferrara.com

Born in 1983 in Monterrey, Nuevo León, Mexico, Fina Ferrara has transformed herself from a celebrated classical ballet dancer into a bold multidisciplinary performance and video artist, fusing her rigorous training with radical new forms of expression. Her art is an unrelenting exploration of movement—physical, emotional, and conceptual—combining dance, theater, sculpture, video, and installation to create works that resonate with both power and poetry. Every performance and video is a vivid interrogation of human boundaries, where the echoes of violence, hatred, and abuse become catalysts for transformation. Ferrara often blurs the line between performer and viewer, drawing audiences into a space of visceral reflection and emotional resonance. Her work has crossed borders—exhibited in global capitals from London to New York, Paris to South Korea—earning her awards like the Future of Art Global Masterpiece Award and the Leonardo da Vinci International Prize. Her dynamic practice, an immersive dialogue between action and poetry, challenges social norms and beckons us to reconsider the limits of expression.

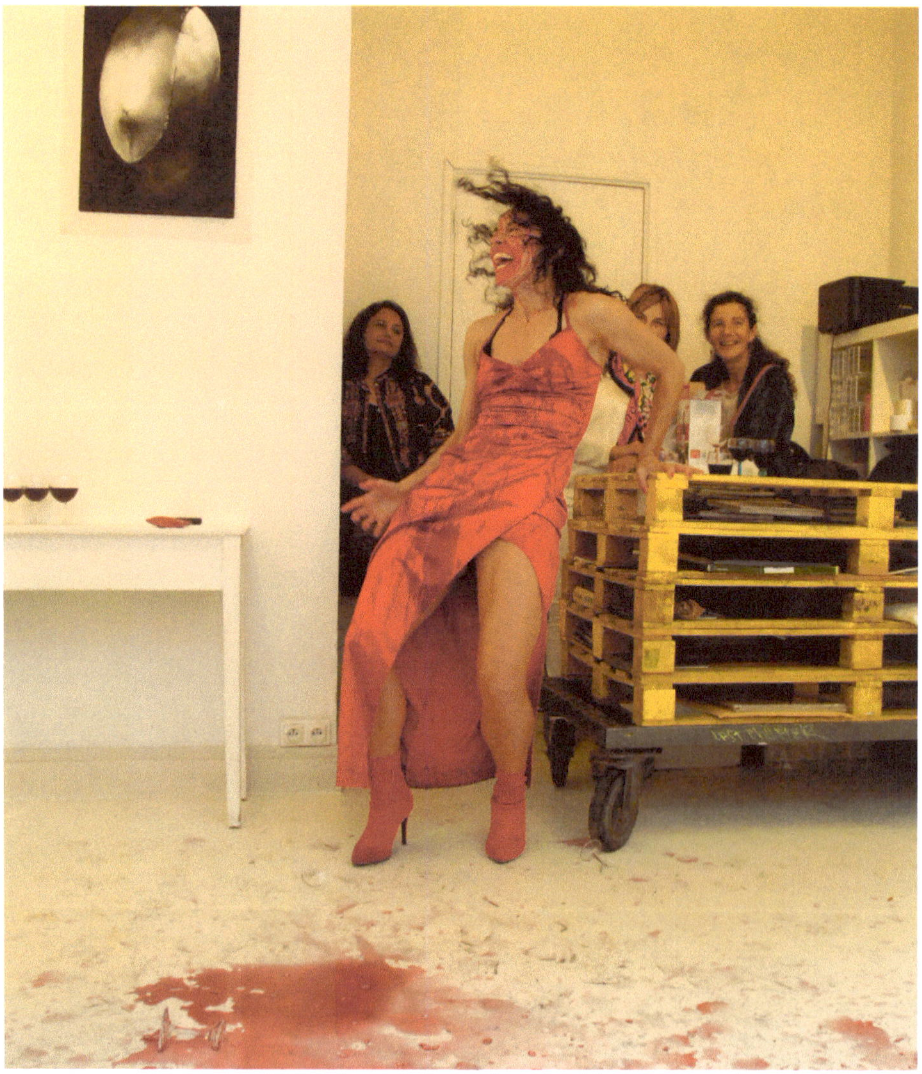

Photographic documentation of the performance LA RUPTURE DU DÉSIR, 2025, 15 X 18 cm.

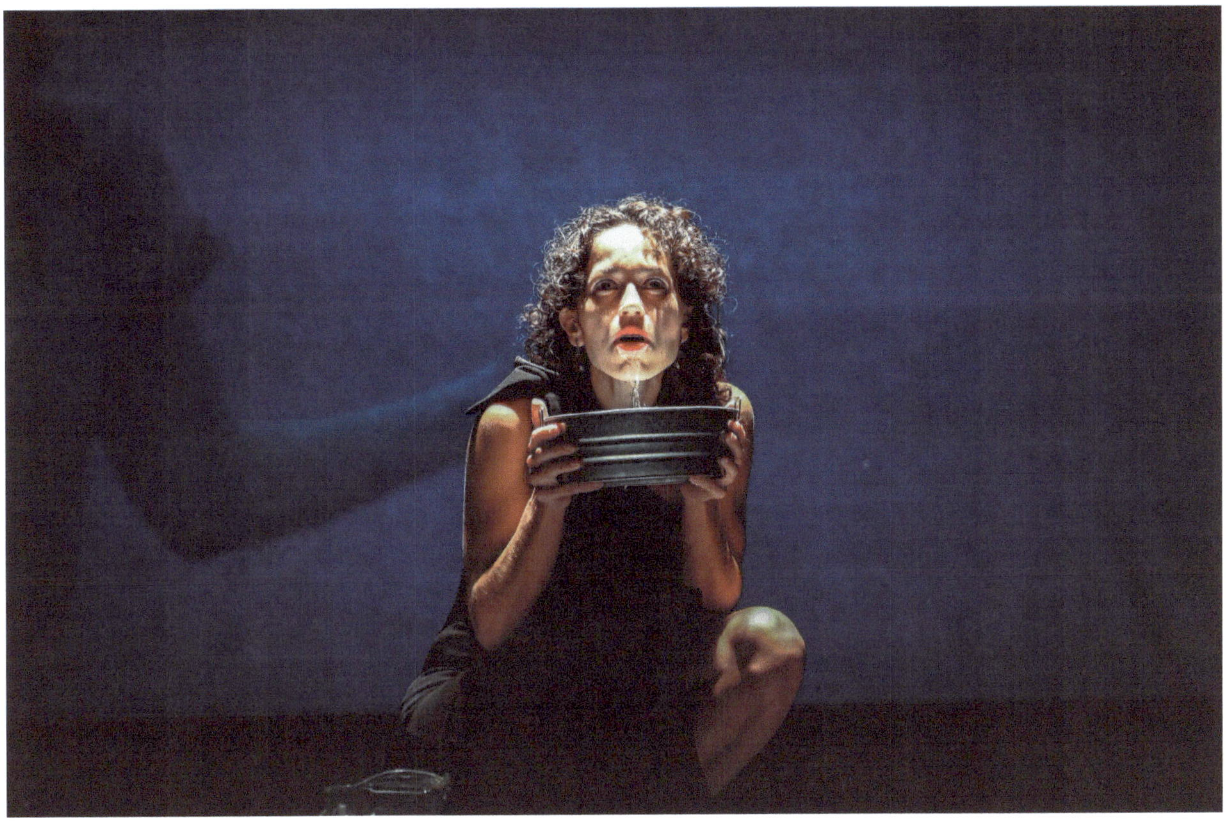

Photographic documentation of the performance ECHOES OF PERCEPTION, 2024, 30 X 20 cm.

FLO DINIS KLOPRIES

https://www.flodinisklopries.com

Flo Dinis Klopries is a female interdisciplinary contemporary artist born in Porto, Portugal, and currently living and working at the french/german border. Her academic and artistic training spans multiple disciplines, including fine arts, philology, and music - reflecting her relentless pursuit of knowledge and self expression- each leaving an indelible mark on her creative output. Her foundational studies in classic painting techniques and her later immersion in modern and abstract art practices laid the groundwork for her stylistic versatility. Under the tutelage of several renowned visual artists she acquired the discipline and precision associated with old master techniques, while also embracing the experimental spirit that defines contemporary art. This duality is a hallmark of her work, allowing her to traverse a spectrum of styles and themes with remarkable fluidity. Her dynamic oeuvre, at once enigmatic and profoundly resonant, is situated between figuration and abstraction – blurring the line between both but emphasizing abstraction over representation – wants to build a bridge between the inherited past, her subjective vision of the present and her own exploration of what might be the future. The influence of her mentors from the Moscow Art Academy (now living in France!) is evident in her technical precision, while her abstract explorations owe much to her engagement with modernistic aesthetics. She is an artist who does not shy away from complexity, embracing it as a necessary aspect of both creation and existence. Her work invites viewers into a space of reflection, where the tactile and the transcendental converge, and it is as much about emotion as it is about form - both the product of her spontaneous feelings and emotions and the philosophical reflections of her intellect. Her preferred subjects are the timeless exploration of the human condition between the universal and the personal, the abstract and the concrete, but also i.e. the dipicting of the fleeting beauty of natural spaces aiming to underline their eternal qualities. Dinis Klopries´ art is deeply informed by her sense of place. Her landscapes are not mere representations but emotional cartographies, mapping the interplay of internal and external worlds. Nature serves as both a mirror and a catalyst for human emotion. Flo Dinis Klopries is not content to simply depict the world. She seeks to capture its essence, to distill its fleeting beauty into something eternal. Her exploration of themes like fragility, resilience and the passage of time resonates deeply in our contemporary moment offering a space for reflection and renewal where the tactile and the transcendental converge. In a world increasingly dominated by spectacle and immediacy, Dinis Klopries´art stands as a counterpoint. It reminds us of the enduring power of painting as a medium for profound expression. Her career is marked by regular exhibitions in Paris participating in prestigious international salons such as Art Capital/Salon des Artistes Francais, the Salon d´Automne ou le Salon des Beaux-Arts de la Société National des Beaux-Arts,... These venues, stepped in history provide the perfect context for her work.

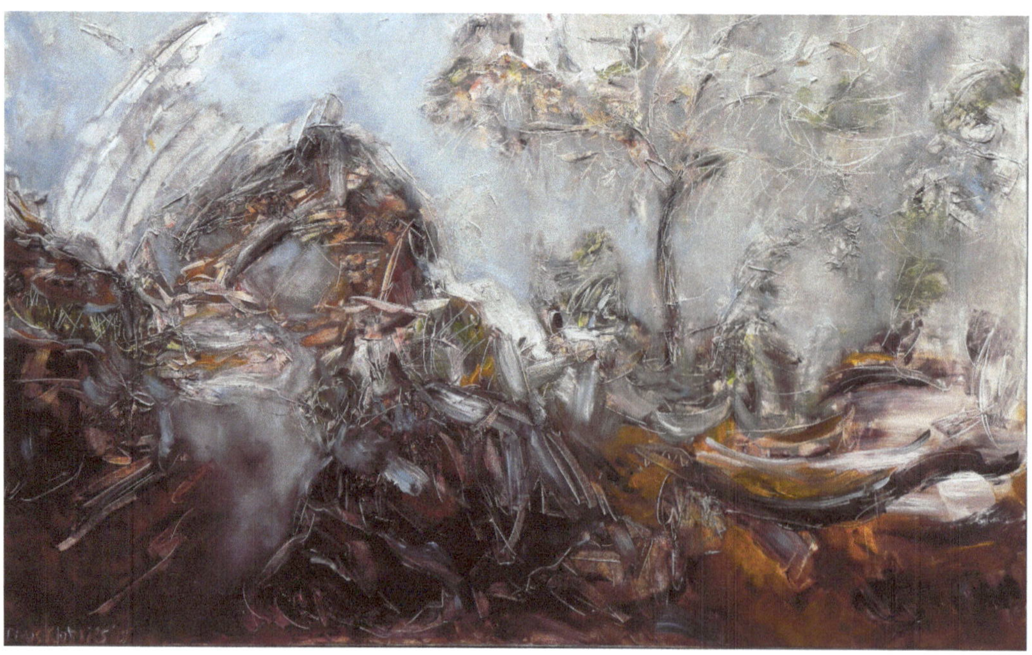

"The desert in me (1)", Flo Dinis Klopries, 2019, mixed media on canvas, mixed media on canvas, 100x160 cm

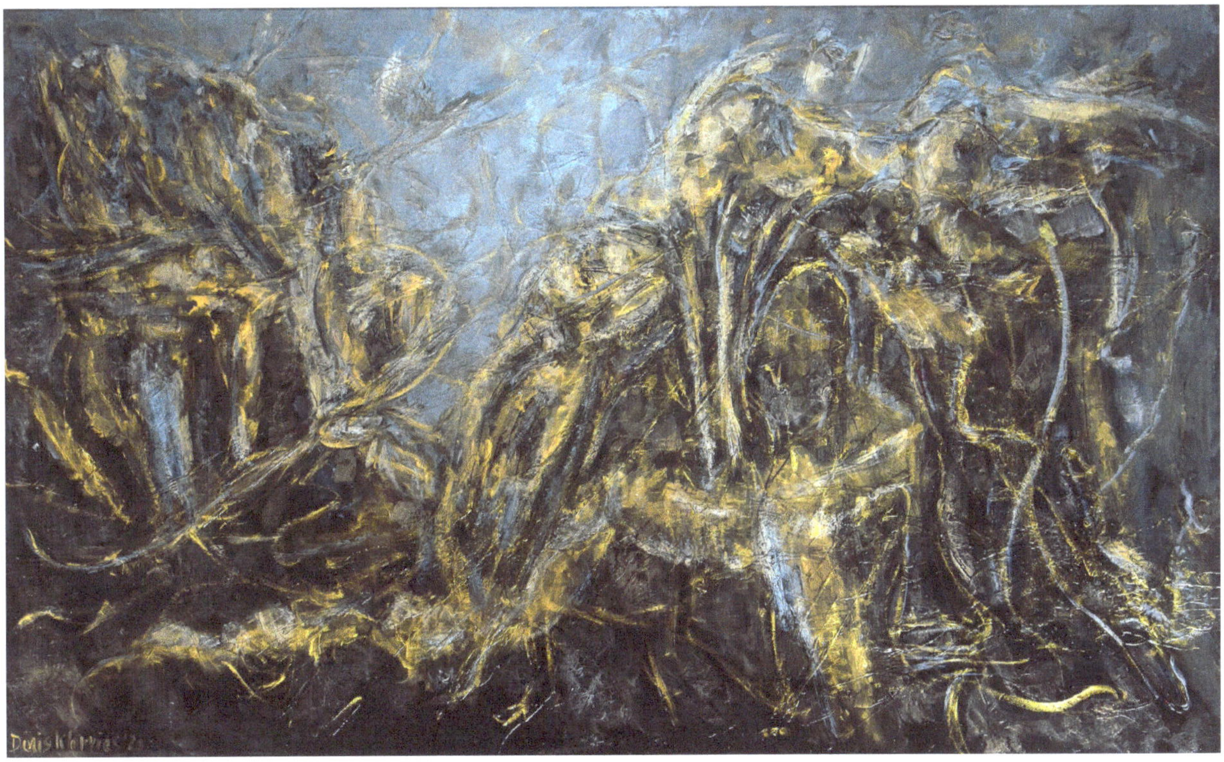

"Kintsugi (1)", Flo Dinis Klopries, 2020, mixed media on canvas, 100x160 cm

FRANCE MALO

francemaloartiste@gmail.com

MALO began teaching art classes at the age of fifteen: drawing, painting, and sculpture. From 1974 to 1978, the young artist was selected to participate in four creativity art camps broadcast by the French Alliance Television. Based in France and Spain, those immersions in the world of creation were dedicated to introducing a new generation of artists to the philosophical, historical, and practical aspects of arts: Grand Masters, arts and culture, literature, cinema, and poetry have also been explored. This formative period was followed by intensive studies in Arts, Communication, Cinema, Computer Science, and Literature at different universities and institutions: Quebec University in Montreal, Montreal University, California University in Los Angeles, Santa Monica College, Pennsylvania Academy of the Fine Arts, and Geneva University. Since 2010, MALO has been acting as an invited guest performer for national and international sports events. The specialized artist has been commissioned by many organizations, accomplished athletes, and collectors to realize original paintings in acrylic and mixed media. Enthroned Official Artist for « Fédération Québécoise des Sports Cyclistes FQSC » in 2016, MALO had achieved the social mission to introduce « Arts in Sports and Sports in Arts » when her ART SPORT series was launched publicly with a consortium of art and sport specialists along with politicians. Her ART SPORT series has been published on trophies, archival and commemorative prints, and sportswear collections. Art specialist recognized colorist, she is regularly mandated as a jury in national and international contexts. Enthroned Grand master's in fine arts by « Académie Internationale des Beaux-arts du Québec AIBAQ » in 2019, her realizations have been seen in major media translated in many languages since 1972: television, newspapers, art&design magazines, and art books. MALO has exhibited in national and international museums, art galleries, shows, symposiums, and major arts and sports events in Canada, the USA, and Europe.MALO has received numerous honors, prizes, and grants throughout her career for her creations and innovative ideas. Her art is internationally included in collections. « My artistic voyage emphases on the complex and dynamic life. In this sense, the actual CONTEMPORARY and CLIMATIC ARCHITECTURES series puts all my senses and creativity on alert ». MALO

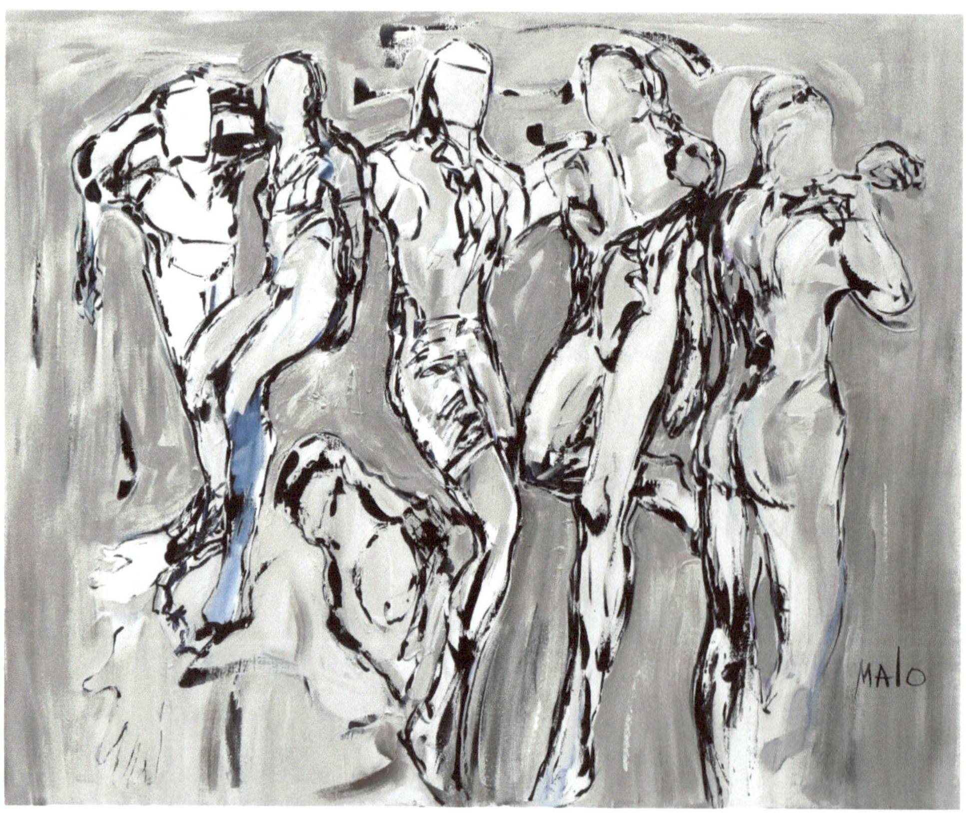

Gigue a la vie, 2025. Acrylic on canvas, 2025.

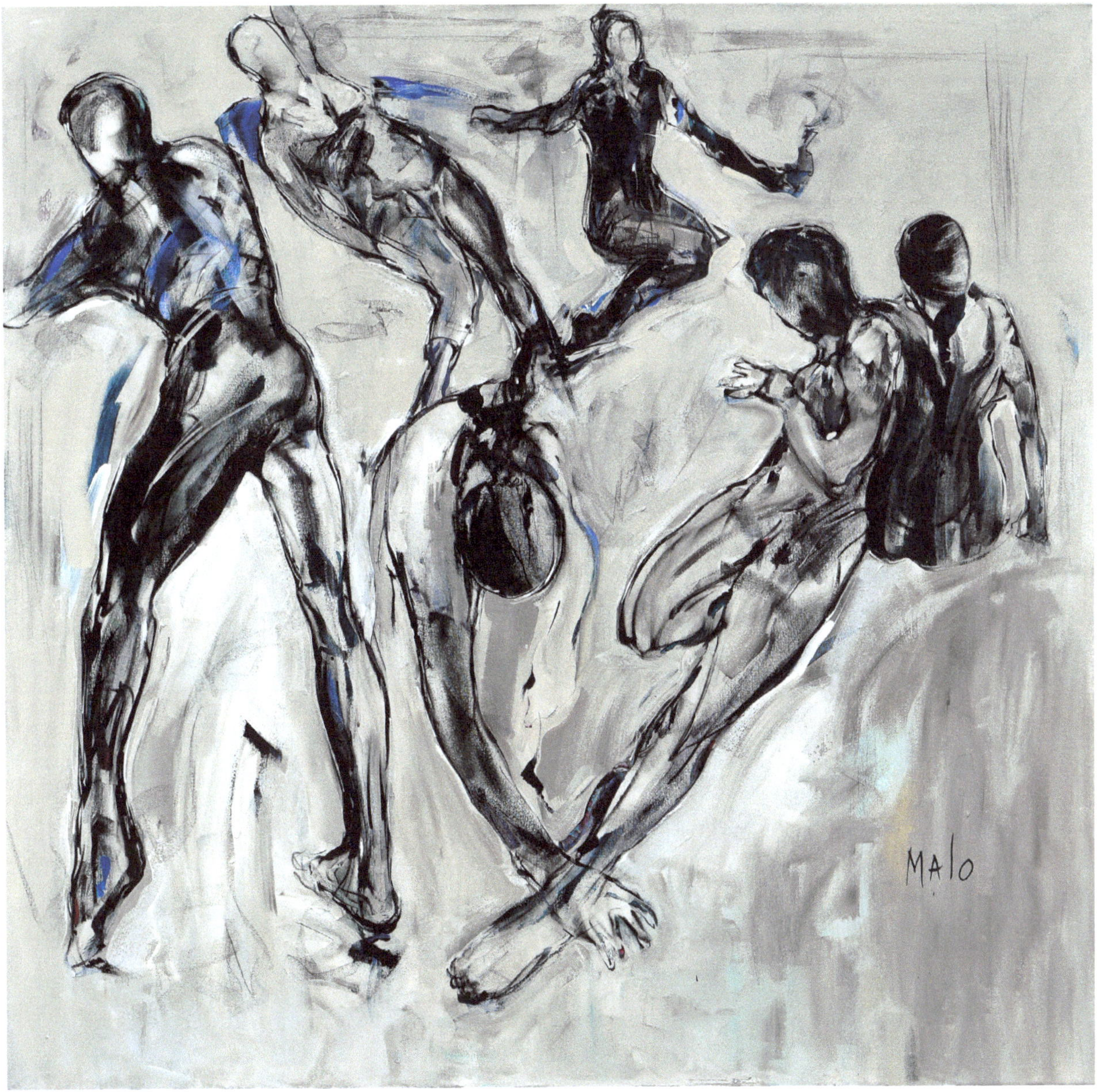

Espace repos, 2025. Acrylic and charcoal on canvas, 120 x 120.

GABI DOMENIG

www.domenigartdesign.at

Born 1963 in Lienz, East Tyrol, Austria. Graduation at the trade academy Lienz. Seminars in coloring, drawing, composition and nude painting. Raddle, charcoal and pastel chalk on paper and primed wooden boards were the working materials in the nineties. First exhibition 1999. Since 2000 acrylic painting on canvas. Many participations in projects, national and international group exhibitions in galleries and art fairs in Austria, Germany, France, Spain, Portugal, Italy, United Kingdom, USA and Brazil. You can find her artworks in renowned national and international art books, art magazines, online galleries and private collections in Austria and abroad. International awards. 2017 Finalist at the Global Art Award with the picture * PARADISE MADONNA *. (Top 20 in the category painting) Her family, her friends and her painting are her life. For her painting is energy source, balance and necessity. Domenig`s style is attributed to Neo-Expressionism because of the figuration and the strong color palette. The central theme of her mostly large-format acrylic paintings is always the woman again. Facetted, emotionally filled, often fairy-tale and mysterious snapshots between dream and reality. Her artworks want to find the way to the heart of the viewers. A tribute to life, to love, to nature and especially a tribute to all the women in the world who do great things and jobs. At work and in their families. With lots of heart, soul and with lots of energy. Tireless for their beloved. She want to tell stories. As in the past 26 years, she will continue to paint women for the most part. Strong and vulnerable, happy and sad, self-centered and excited, shy and courageous , extroverted and introverted, longing, proud, sensual and spiritual, free and feathery like a bird, moving and resting surrounded by flowers and plants, accompanied by colorful birds and animals, always on the border between dream and reality. Her product range: Accessorize like blankets, shopper bags, shoulder bags, beach towels, pillows, door mats, shower mats and overpainted prints you can buy them on her website www.domenigartdesign.at

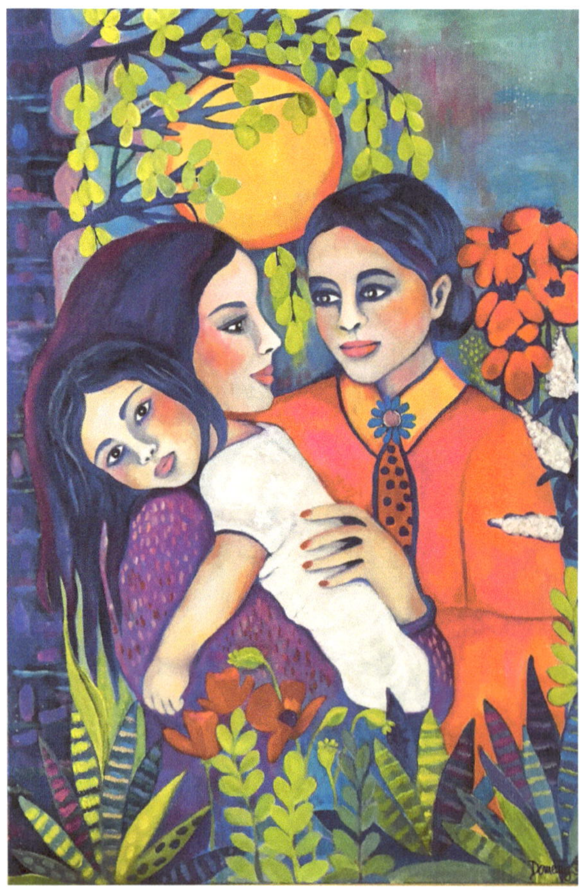

Circle of life

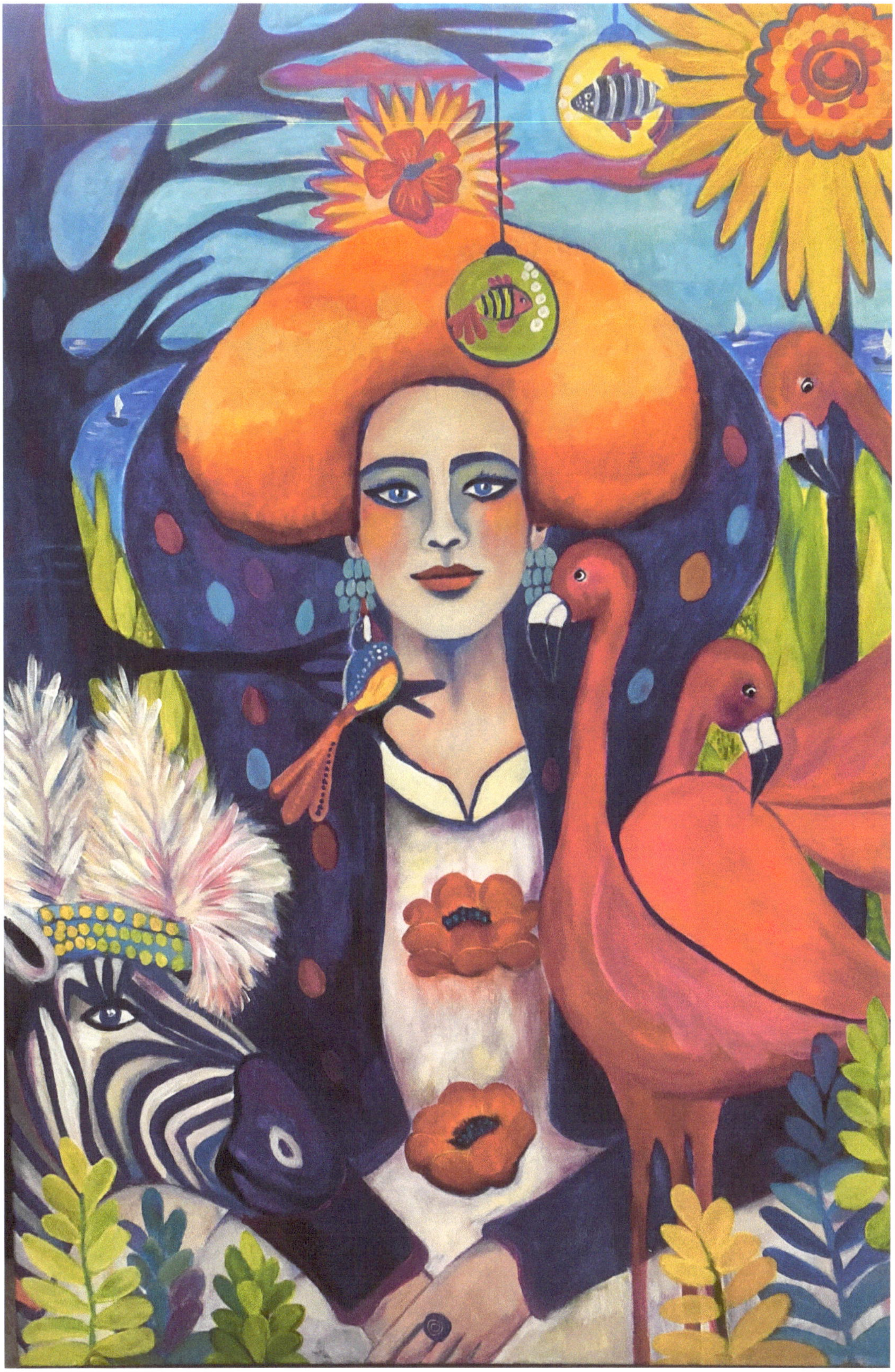

Queen of Fashion. Time out in the Flamingo Park. 120x80cm. 2025

GABRIEL LASS

www.gabriellass.com

Gabriel Lass comenzó su trayectoria creativa en el diseño de casas y jardines, un campo que le enseñó a leer el espacio a través de la proporción, el ritmo y la relación entre elementos. Esa formación inicial dejó una huella profunda en su pintura: la organización del lienzo, la forma de disponer el color y la estructura interna de cada obra están marcadas por una mirada arquitectónica que ordena y equilibra. En la pintura encontró un territorio donde eternizar sentimientos, fijar instantes y transformarlos en materia visual. Su trabajo se inscribe en una abstracción expresiva que combina intensidad cromática y un tratamiento matérico muy elaborado. Utiliza principalmente acrílico, lo que le permite trabajar con rapidez y, al mismo tiempo, superponer capas que se depositan, se velan y se erosionan, creando profundidad y memoria en la superficie. Lass no se limita al pincel: emplea espátulas y herramientas no convencionales para raspar, arrastrar y marcar la pintura. Cada capa oculta y revela a la vez; cada textura actúa como registro de un momento, de una decisión, de una emoción. El color es mucho más que una elección estética: funciona como temperatura emocional. Los tonos fríos expanden, los cálidos condensan; el negro abre profundidad, el blanco ventila, el oro irradia. Su obra se articula a menudo en torno a ejes verticales u horizontes tensos, estructuras invisibles que sostienen la composición. Estos elementos funcionan como arquitecturas internas que ordenan el caos del gesto y del color. A veces, un centro concentra la gravedad de la pieza; otras, una fractura introduce aire y ligereza. Para Lass, pintar no es reproducir imágenes, sino construir presencias. Busca que cada cuadro sea un espacio vivo, capaz de atraer al espectador, retenerlo y ofrecerle múltiples lecturas. De lejos, las obras impactan por su potencia formal; de cerca, invitan a explorar una cartografía de huellas, fricciones y sutilezas.

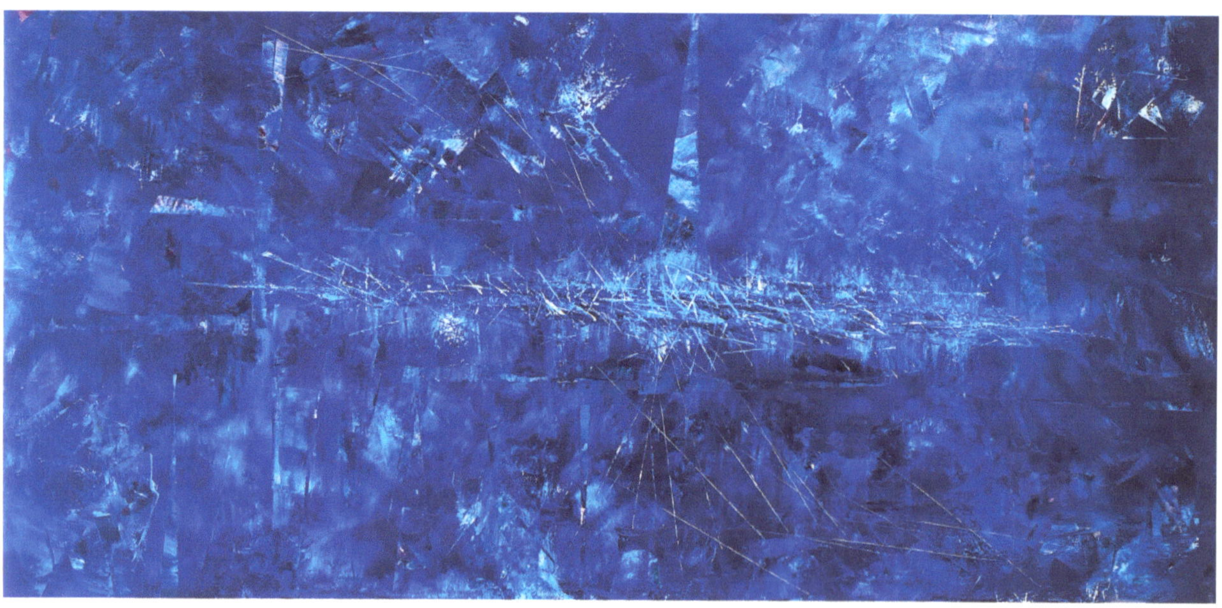

Lágrimas del cielo, 2023. Acrylic on canvas, 61x122 cm.

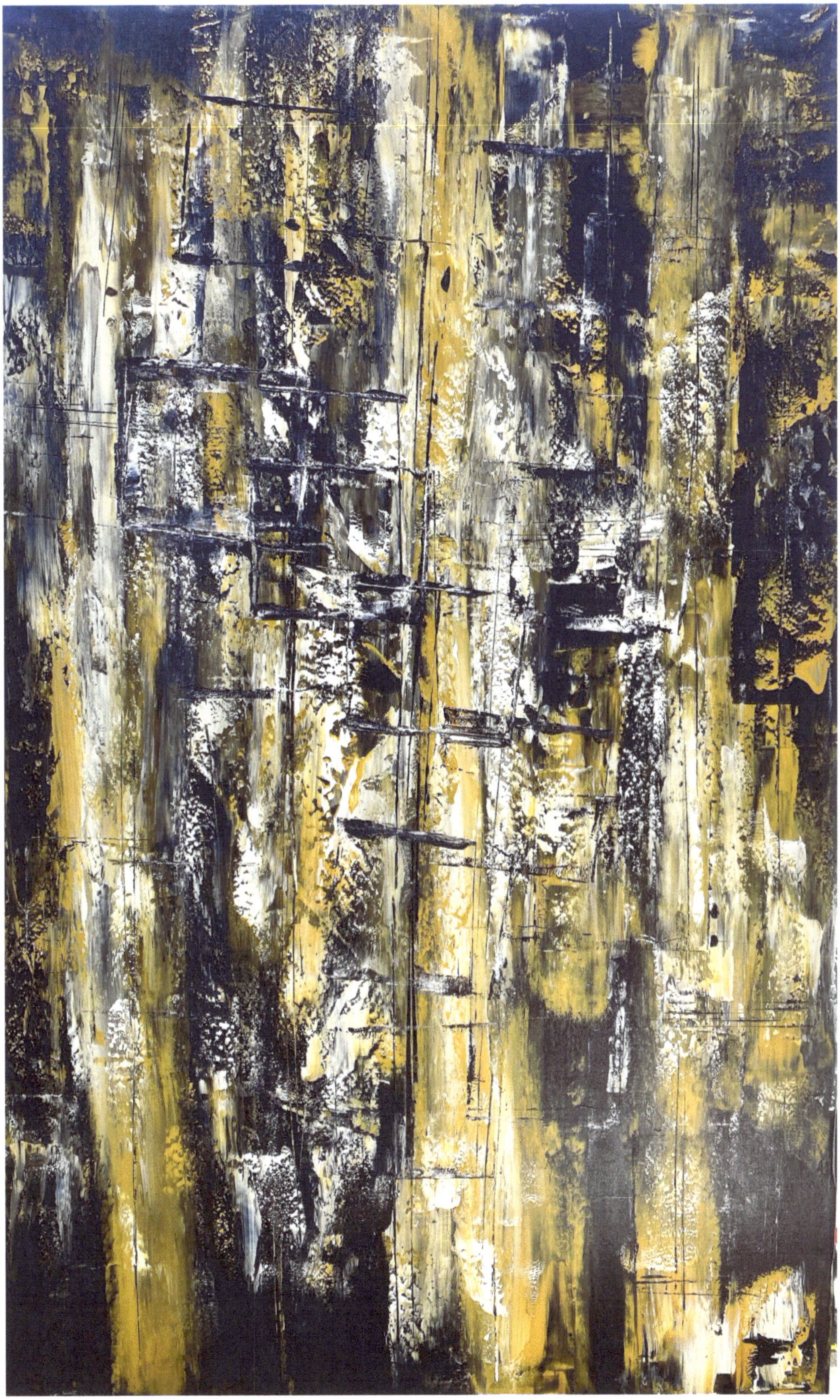

Núcleo eterno, 2023. Acrylic on canvas, 135x82 cm.

GAETANO PIRO

pirogaetanodifatima@gmail.com

Master Sculptor Gaetano Piro was born in Francavilla Fontana in the province of Brindisi in Apulia (Italy) on March 7, 1941, to a humble family of farmers who, with great sacrifices, supported his inclination for study, allowing him to complete his educational path from elementary school to a degree in 'Economics and Commerce' at the University of Bari, after which he became a beloved and highly esteemed teacher. Despite the few resources available in his family of six (two parents and four children, including him), serenity and joy always accompanied him, along with a brilliant imagination that he demonstrated in various fields from a young age; in fact, from an early age he made bread, cooked, and worked with clay. The Master was a special Man, an extraordinary Man, a truly out-of-the-ordinary Person, characterized by a sweetness, sensitivity, grace, generosity, kindness beyond the ordinary, great enthusiasm, and a special Light in his eyes that shone like those of children who see the world as something new and beautiful with innocence. He loved Life, Music, his fellow man, simple things, and he loved Olive Wood; when a trunk or a piece of it touched him deeply, it was because the Sacred Fire of inspiration was beginning to burn within him, leading him to create wonderful Works. His artistic ability as a Sculptor was born with him, in the sense that he was a self-taught Sculptor, along with genius and talent that allowed him to create marvelous Artworks from trunks and pieces of Olive Wood and from Stone, which he also loved to work with, using simple and rudimentary tools such as chisels and gouges of all sizes, and hammers. such as chisels and gouges of all sizes, hammer, files, glass and sandpaper. All His Works express His soul but also Passion and Love, Purity and Spirituality because, as He used to say, he sculpted guided by Celestial Inspiration. The Peace and serenity that enveloped His soul are emanated from the faces of His sculptures that ranged from the sacred to the profane. His favorite subjects were indeed Christ, Maternity, Love, and Woman. These themes, although so different, were for Him an emanation of sacredness, purity, clarity, transparency, the whiteness of a Soul with its feet firmly on the ground but with its gaze turned toward eternity. Also, the representation of Woman, for Him, was not just a nude but He said that Woman is the temple and vessel of the Spark of Creation. With His life, He conveyed Love and the message that Life is beautiful and is far beyond materiality and that everything is sacred. This aspect is especially marked in the faces of His Jesuses, who although depicted on the Cross or in the midst of the Passion, they express serenity, sweetness, and much Love with a hieratic, calm, noble, and tranquil gaze, never showing a grimace of pain, because pain is transcended not with resignation but with complete trust and reliance. The Master sculpted small pieces of wood as well as large trunks weighing 1800 kg, working with meticulous and painstaking patience to bring out what the entire material contained. He created many works, both small in size and human-sized, including a crucifix measuring 2.10 m, and several women in plastic poses with an average height of 1.80 m and body measurements of 90-60-90. He used to work outdoors in the countryside by himself, under the veranda in the company of his beloved animals who would rush from all directions when he arrived, and accompanied by his beloved music. He has created works of remarkable artistic value and has been appreciated by many professionals in the field who have published him in various national and international art books. On December 14, 2021, he was awarded the Civic Honorary Mention posthumously for his artistic and moral merits by the City of Francavilla Fontana, his hometown in Italy, in the province of Brindisi.

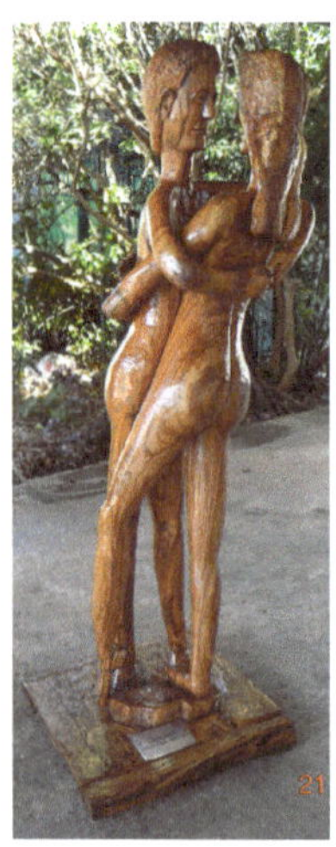

La Vita è bella ovvero il Bello della Vita - Scultura in Legno di Ulivo realizzata da un tronco di 18 quintali, anno 2017 - altezza 185cm

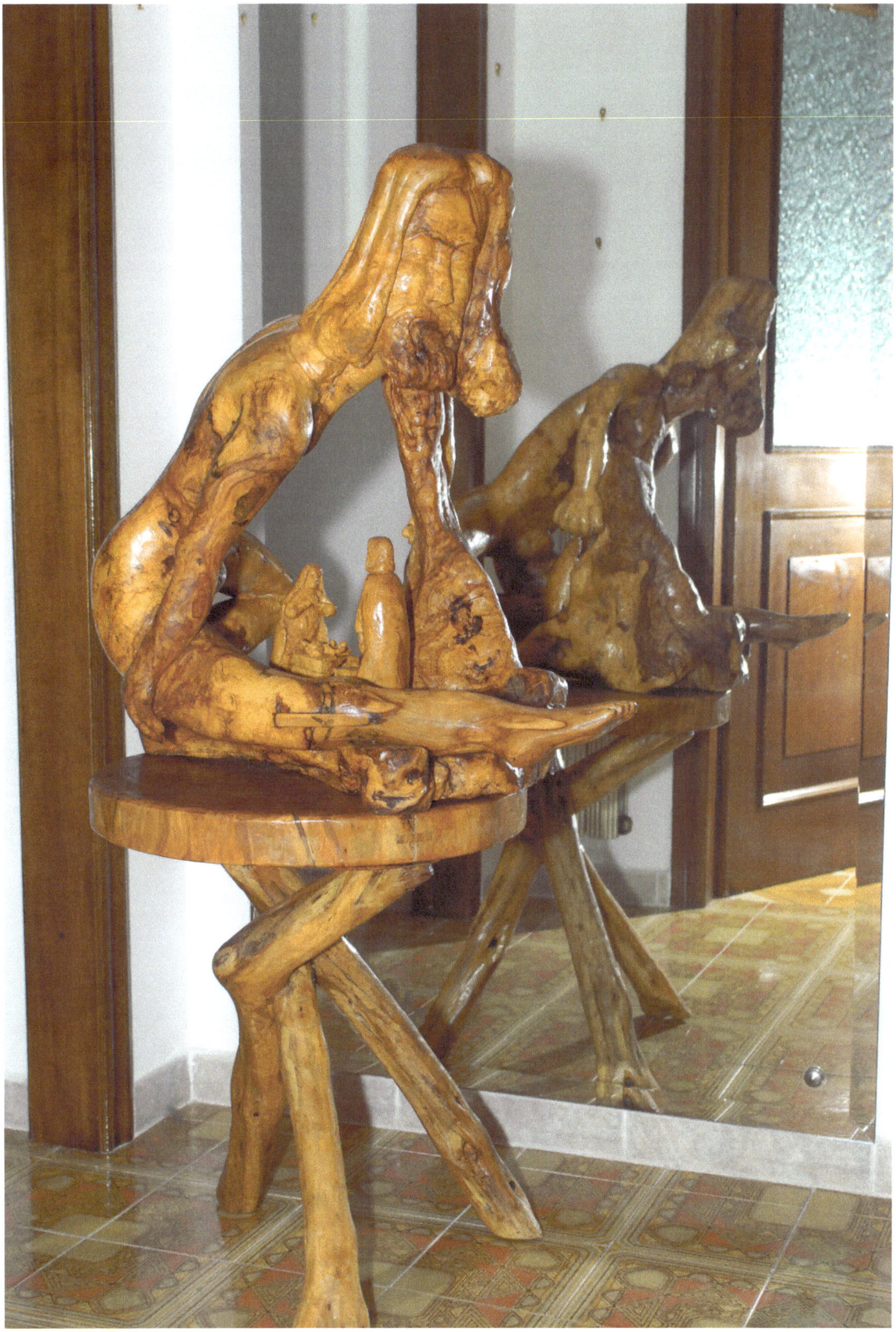

La Creazione - Scultura in legno di Ulivo - anno 2013 - 100cm

GAYA CHANDRASEKARAN

https://www.cgayas.com/

Gaya Chandrasekaran is a London-based contemporary artist. Born in the coastal city of Chennai, India, her artistic practice is deeply influenced by the vivid colors and rich cultural heritage of her upbringing. Working primarily with acrylics, palette knives, and gold leaf, she creates layered, emotive landscapes that invite quiet introspection and a sense of transcendence. Gaya has trained in India and at the Slade School of Fine Art in London. Her artworks have been exhibited widely across the UK, US and Europe, with features in prominent art publications such as Contemporary Art Curator, Artist Talk, and ArtistCloseUp magazines. Her paintings have been reviewed by Tabish Khan, a renowned London art critic, and are held in private collections across the US, UK, Spain, Italy, Brazil, and India - including a permanent display at the London Business School. Through her abstract landscapes, Gaya explores themes of shared human experience — the search for meaning (Quest), the inner voice of contemplation (Soliloquy), cycles of transformation (Rebirth), and the pursuit of spiritual growth (Nirvana). Her paintings serve as a visual meditation on nature and the profound emotional terrain of life itself.

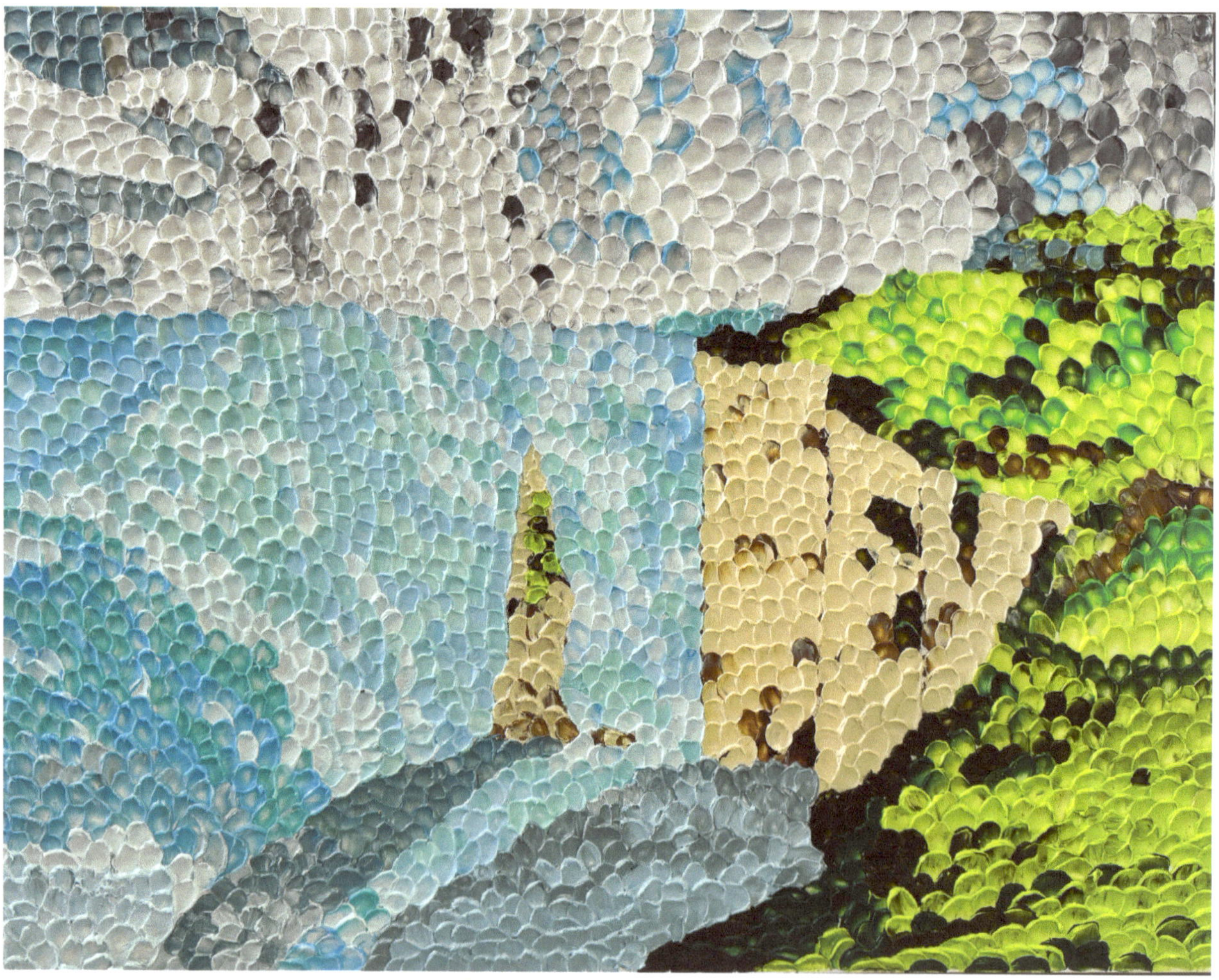

Salty Mornings, 2023, Textured Acrylic on Canvas, 100 x 80 cm

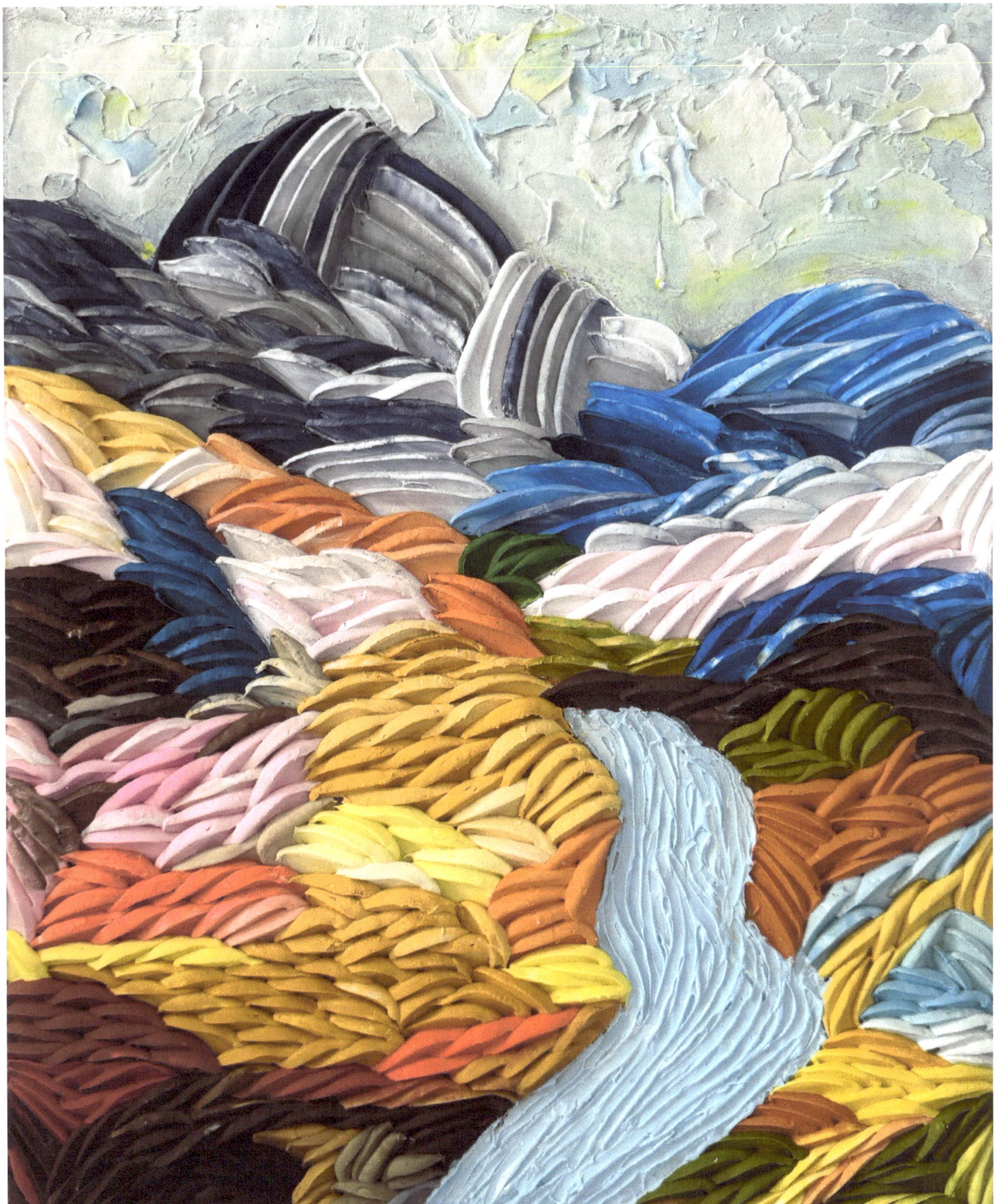

Fall Valley, 2024, Textured Acrylic on Canvas, 50 x 40 cm

GEORGINA MACKEN

www.drgeorginamacken.com

"Ah! Portraiture, portraiture with the thought, the soul of the model in it, that is what I think must come," stated Vincent van Gogh.Emotionally connected to this philosophy, artist Dr. Georgina Macken is inspired by her fascination of the soul which resides within the face. Additionally influenced by non- verbal communication, internationally renowned Australian portrait painter, Dr. Macken captures the human spirit as she illustrates unique stories in a single frame. Seizing upon the special dynamic facial expression or gesture, her art organically weaves a rich tapestry where her subjects - often babies or children watercolor-on-paper portraits celebrate their true personalities. Illuminating the spontaneous joy of her subjects, she eternally encapsulates their sparkling personalities for future generations. Georgina Macken states:"The eyes of a human trigger many concurrent senses and so my portraits enable me to enjoy the power of the eyes without needing to turn away and close mine." Unexplored dreams and visions radiate from their innocent faces, encompassing the layered experience of being human. Filling the spectator's eye, Dr. Macken's portraits reveal frozen pictorial snapshots of the immediate private moments of the subject. Through a dazzling visual syntax, her sensorial portrait realm encapsulates divergent visions. Symbolically expressing the human heart through her figures, she adroitly re-contextualizes a parallax vision of the intricacies between the mind and soul to radiate the powerful energy of life. Opening a window to the subject's flow of feelings, her expressive figures communicate inner moods and emotions as they reveal the intangible within the tangible. A gorgeous spontaneity reverberates in her oeuvre, as each picture creates a narrative in and, of itself, encouraging conversations of interpretation. Ultimately, each image is an experience unto itself, allowing the audience to step through the doorway of the picture and enter the world of the sitter. Translating onto paper the ephemeral moment of life, award-winning painter, Dr. Georgina Macken's oeuvre provides a special artistic perspective into humankind. Brilliant and inspired, her figurative art has received national and international accolades for her expressive devotion to her subjects.

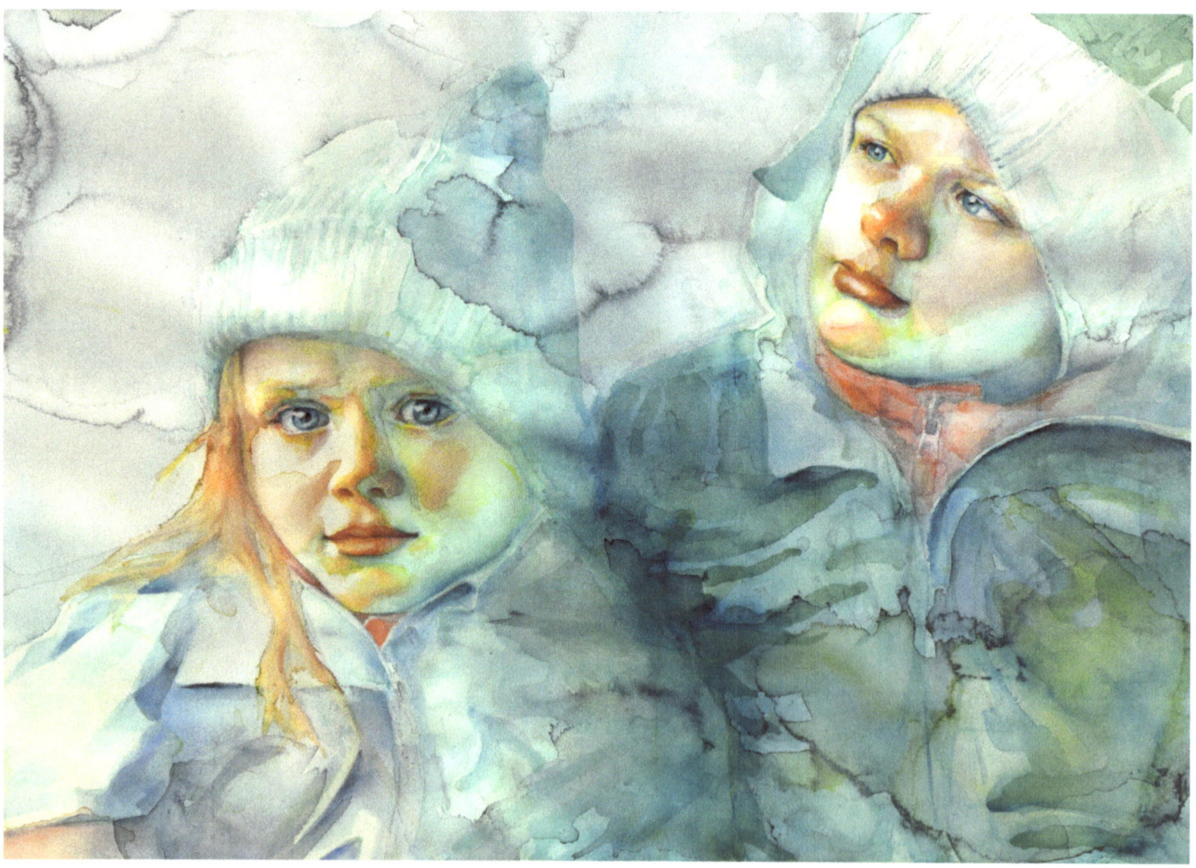

Winter Train Ride. 2022. Watercolour on paper, 110 x 76cm.

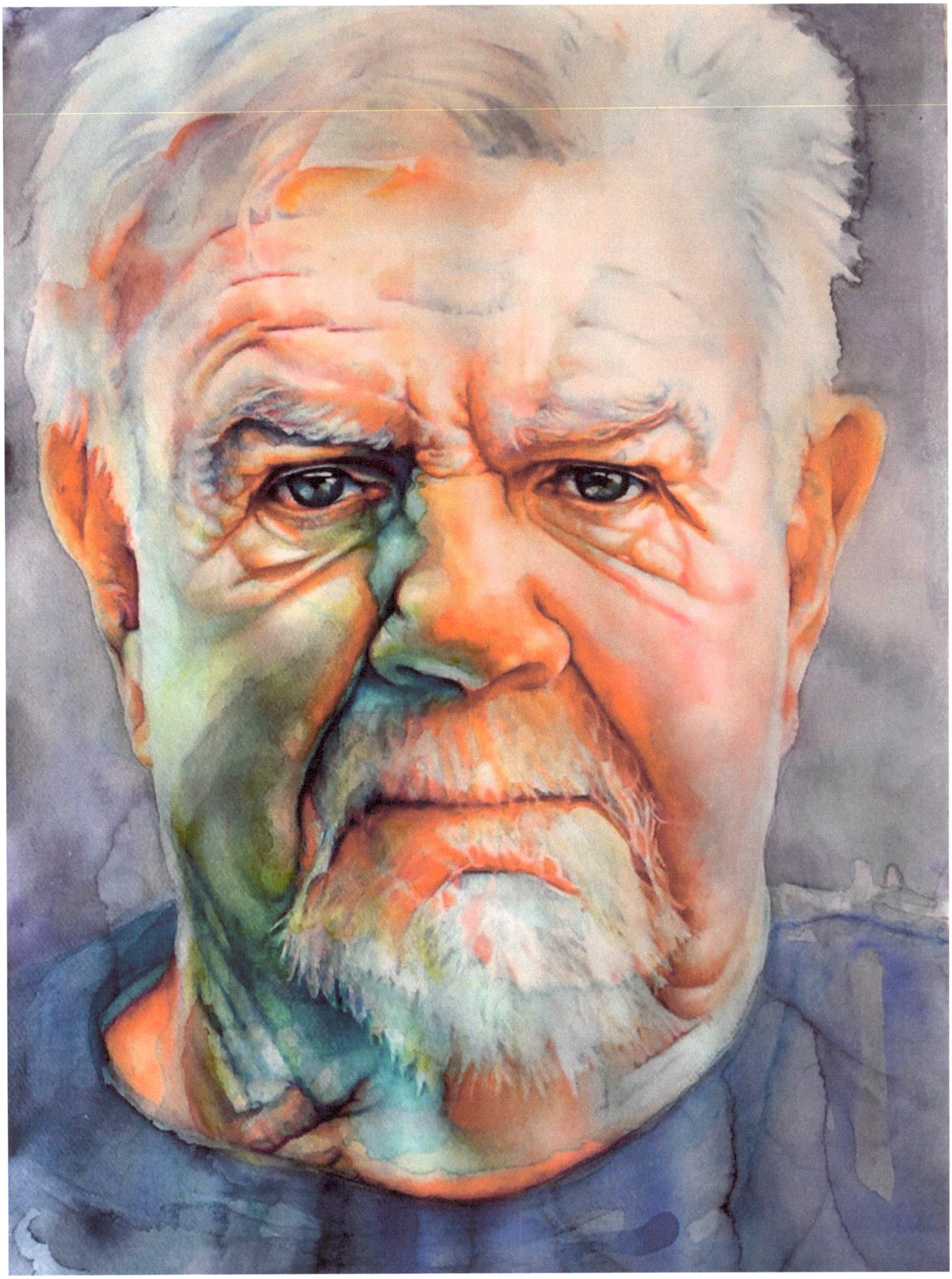

Concerned Resident. 2025. Watercolour on paper, 76 x 110cm

GERLINDE K

gerlindekeating@gmail.com

Gerlinde Keating, also known as Gerlinde K or GK, is a German-born photographer and digital artist who is now a U.S. citizen, celebrated for her innovative and evocative work in photography and abstract art. Her passion for photography began at age twelve when she received her first camera, recognizing it as a powerful medium for storytelling. She finds beauty in everyday scenes, capturing everything from expansive landscapes to intricate details. Gerlinde K's distinctive style blends traditional photography with digital artistry, pushing the boundaries of conventional techniques. Her diverse portfolio includes colorful landscapes, wildlife, floral photography, abstracts, portraits, architecture, seascapes, and black-and-white photography. Her work, characterized by a fusion of line, color, and imagination, creates evocative illusions that spark emotional and creative responses in viewers. She frequently employs digital manipulation to produce modern, abstract compositions that transcend traditional photography. Gerlinde K has earned international acclaim, winning awards in prestigious competitions such as the International Color Awards, juried by leading figures in the art and photography industries. Gerlinde K's work has been featured in notable publications, including "International Contemporary Masters" by World Wide Art Books (WWAB), and "Important World Artists – The World of Art" by WWAB, California, USA, where she was one of 845 artists selected from 6,800 worldwide, underscoring her prominence in the global art community. Her art is available for purchase in formats such as canvas prints, framed prints, metal prints, tapestries, posters, and greeting cards through platforms like gerlinde-keating.pixels.com and www.photoartbygk.com.

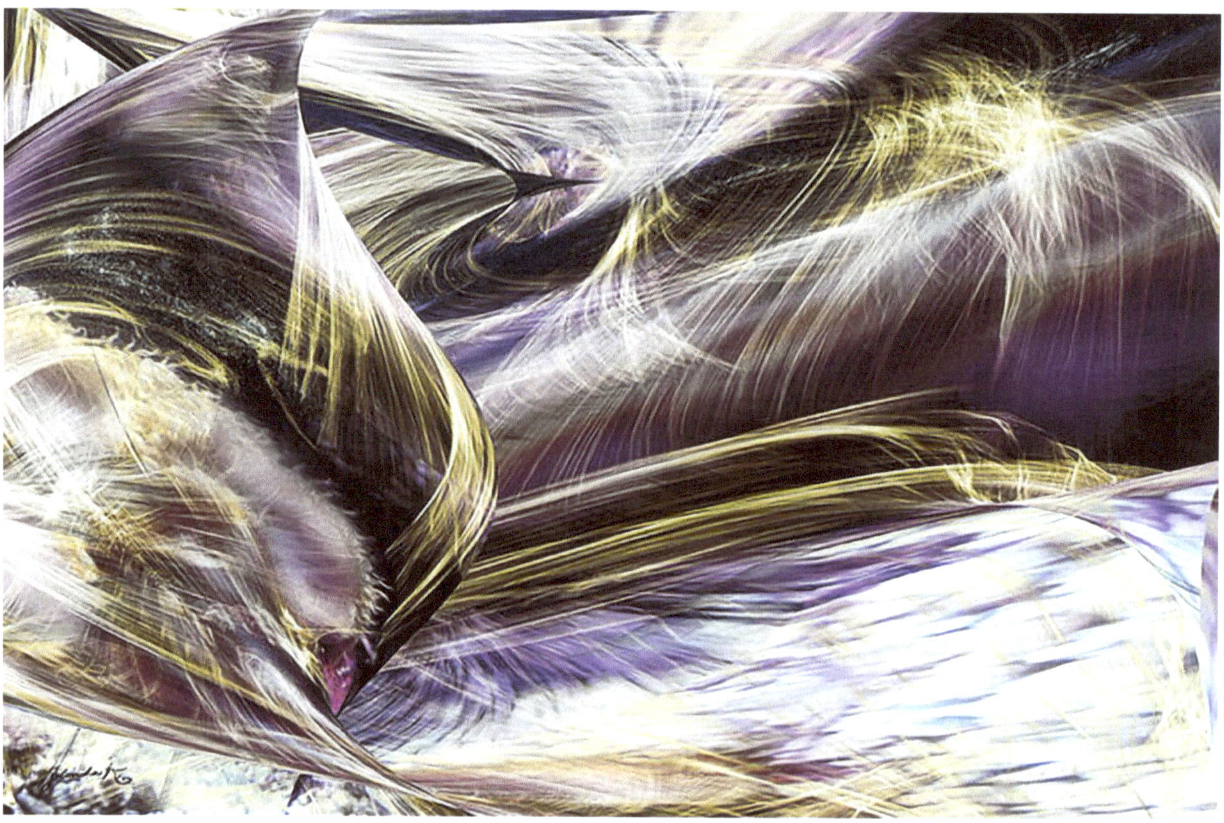

C'est La Vie,2019,Canvas Print, various sizes

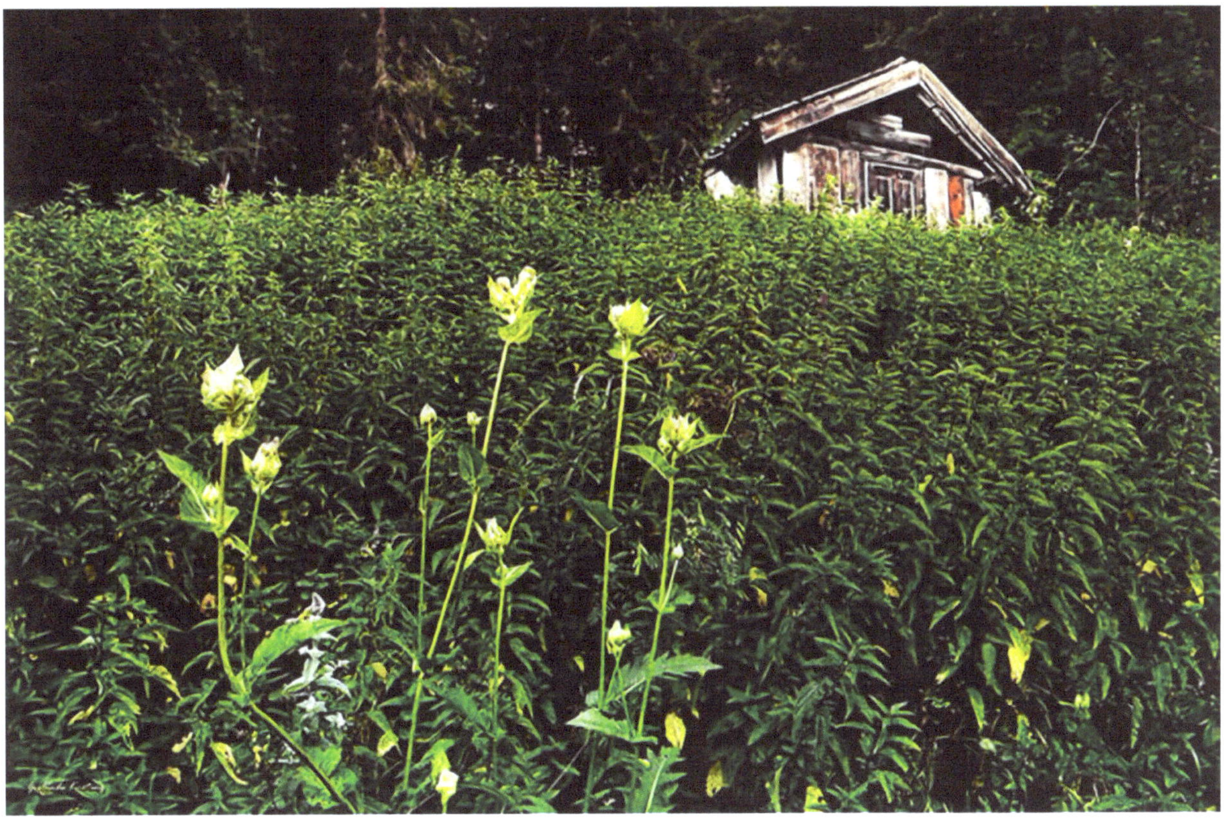

Mystical Forest Hideaway,2025,Canvas Print, various sizes

GIANFRANCO MERATI

www.gmerati.com

Gianfranco Merati (b. Asmara, Eritrea, Africa) is an Italian photographer based in London. Gianfranco's motivation as a photographer is that "beauty is everywhere". He seeks to reveal it. For the last decade he has been developing his photographic practice, through building skills and reflecting on projects. Gianfranco's focus is on abstract and conceptual photography, where most of his recent work has developed. Exploring the complex geometry found within nature, he has created many photographic series including projects revealing tessellating patterns within insects' wings; magnetic fluid 'pulled' into rippling miniature landscapes; surreal shapes given to melted sugar; striking electricity lightning that dissipates through the air; and more. Projects are often the result of research into the properties of certain materials or phenomena and, in the most complex cases, may last for several weeks or months. At times, however, ideas spark from very simple things, like the observation of leaves that have fallen from a tree and that decay, but yet preserve a striking beauty in their inner structure. Using both high-tech methods and innovative use of basic means, each final image is exacting and verging on the unreal. This, despite the fact that Gianfranco does not manipulate his images digitally to create any illusions in his work.

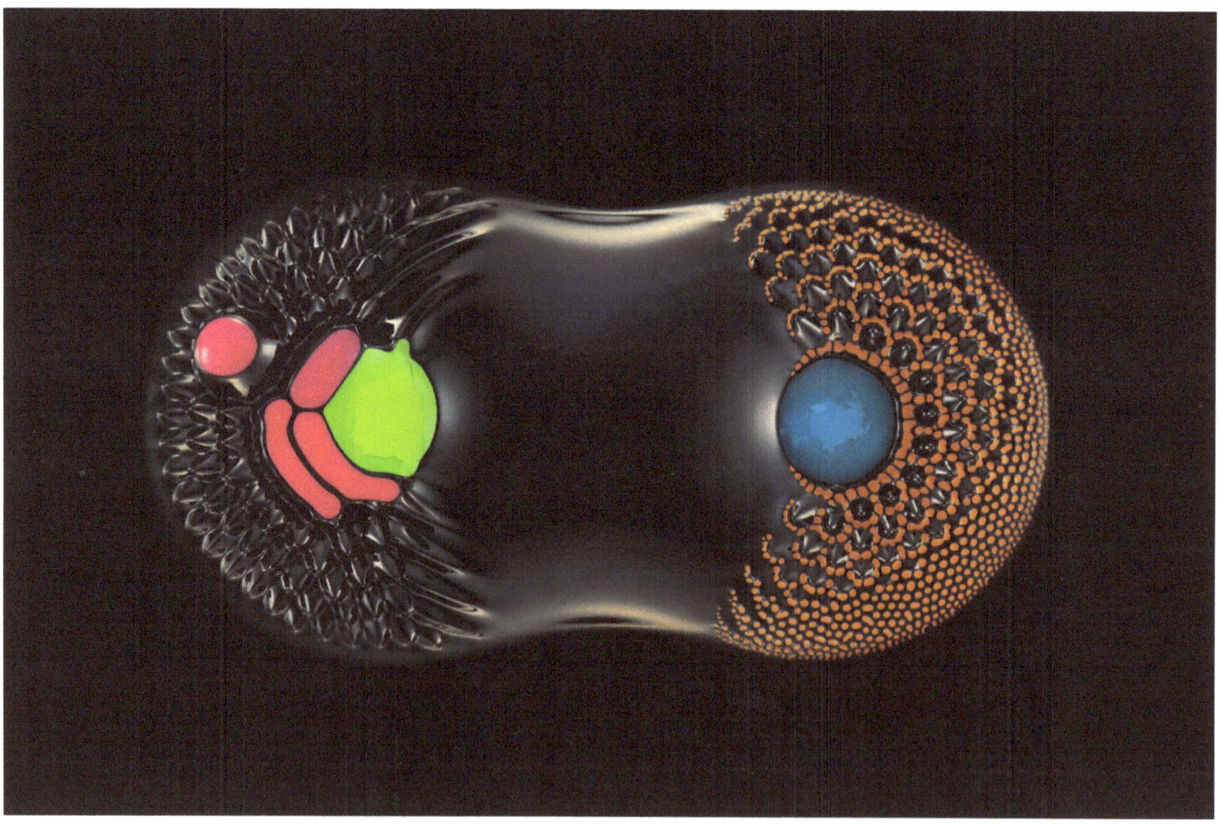

Micro Mountains and Lakes, 2022.

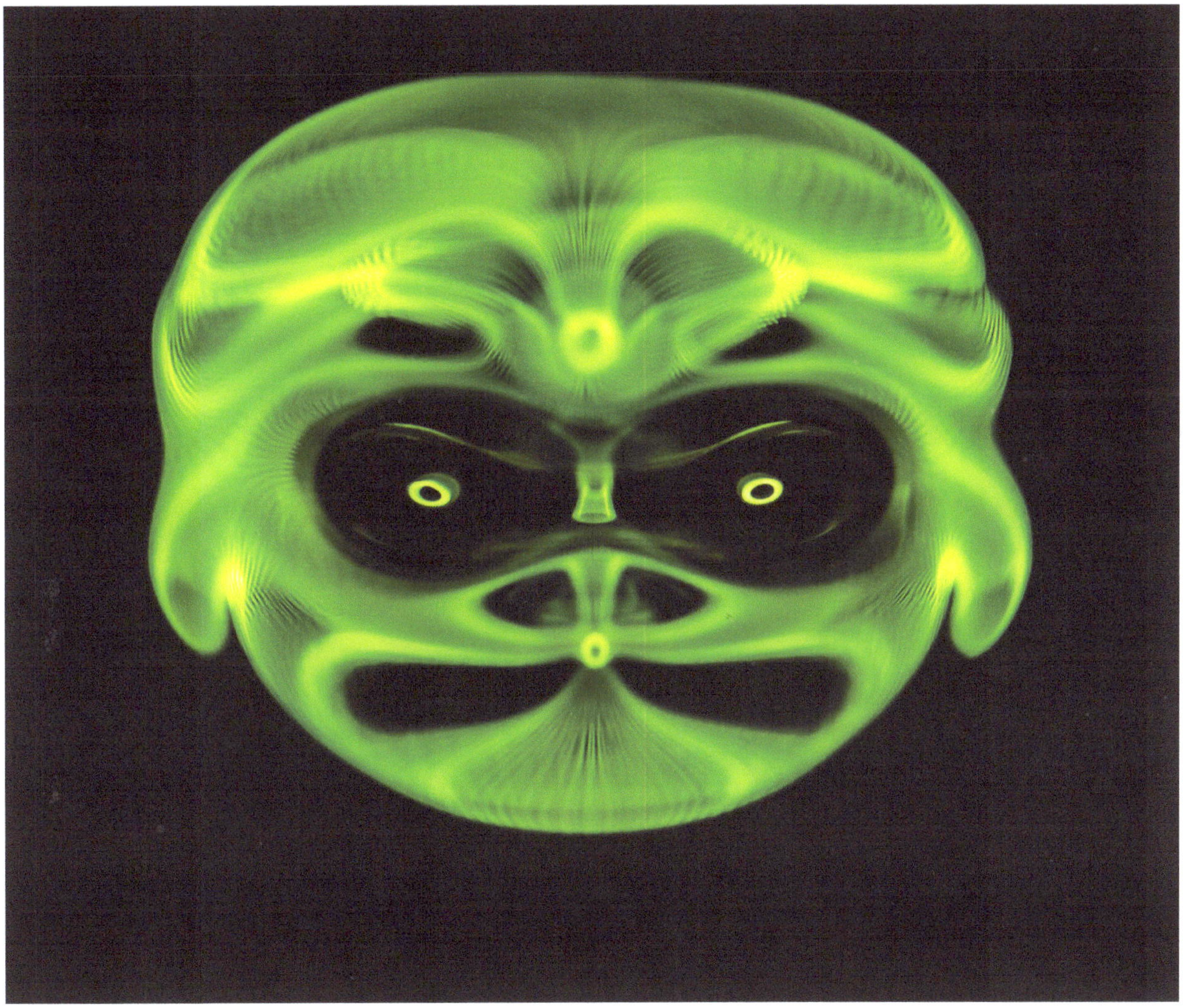

Resonance II, 2025.

GIORA CARMI

gioracarmi.com

Born in Israel in 1944, a second son. Later a sister was adopted into the family. Grew up in a small village called Kfar Malal. Lost his father who was killed while fighting in Israel's War of Independence (1948). Married in 1965. Later had two daughters and one son. Fulfilled his obligatory army service. Had a series of spiritual experiences throughout life. Discovered his ability to "read" art. Discovered Zen. Studied Graphic Design at Bezalel Academy of Art and Design in Jerusalem. Was a freelance graphic designer and illustrator for 14 years. Taught illustration and typography. Wrote and illustrated for the children's magazine, Pilon. Came to the US in 1985 where he was a freelance illustrator in NYC for 17 years. Illustrated regularly for The New York Times, The Wall Street Journal, as well as others. Illustrated, both in Israel and the US, 42 children's books, two of which he also wrote. Studied Zen for 12 years with the late Chinese Zen master Shen-yen. Studied Art Therapy at NYU. Worked as an Art Therapist for 14 years. Developed a new approach to art therapy while doing two internships in a county jail. Later, after further development of the method, wrote the book, "Opening Intuitive Flow Through Artwork". Studied the Release Technique, Theta Healing, Reiki, and a few other approaches to human development. In 2020 he published the illustrated book "Who AM I?", as a humorous but practical aid to self reflection. In 2023 he published the book: PAINTINGS that read my mind & POEMS that read my paintings. These days he lives in NYC with his partner Anita Gold, where he paints, writes prose, poetry and nonfiction, including the blog "Intuitive Flow" (IntuitiveFlow.org).

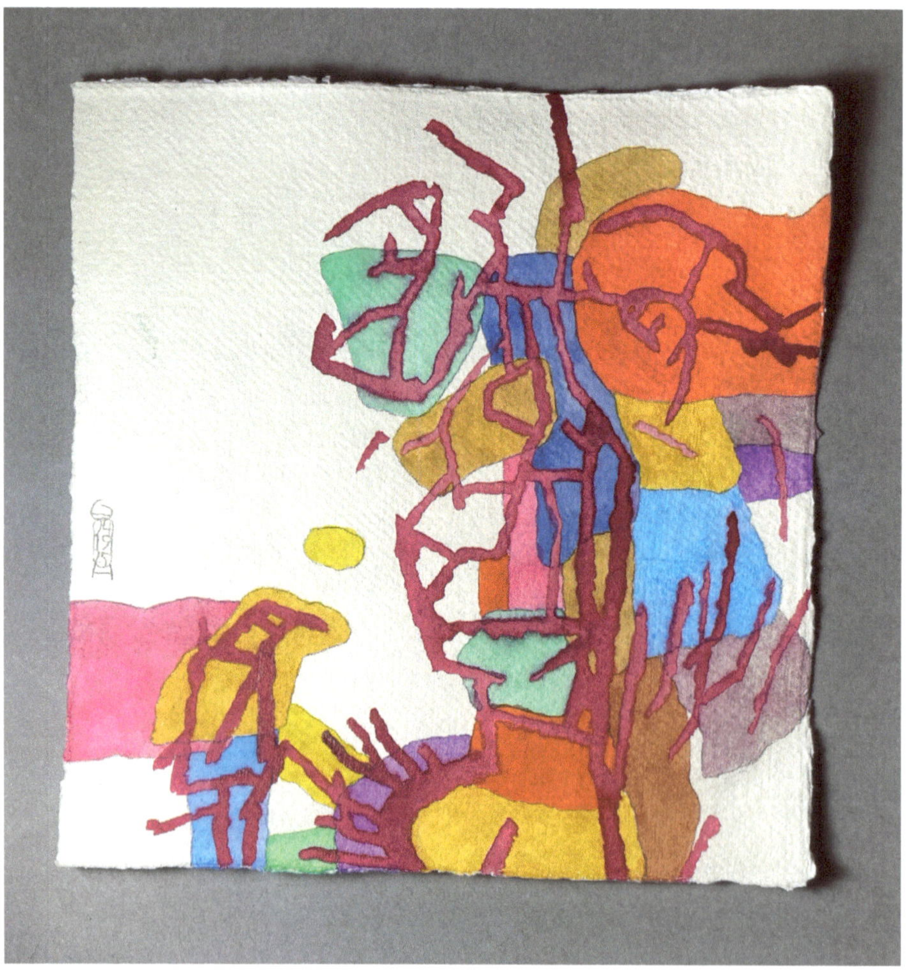

A man with a beard and a bird, 2025, Watercolor + gouache + pencil, 22 x 21 cm

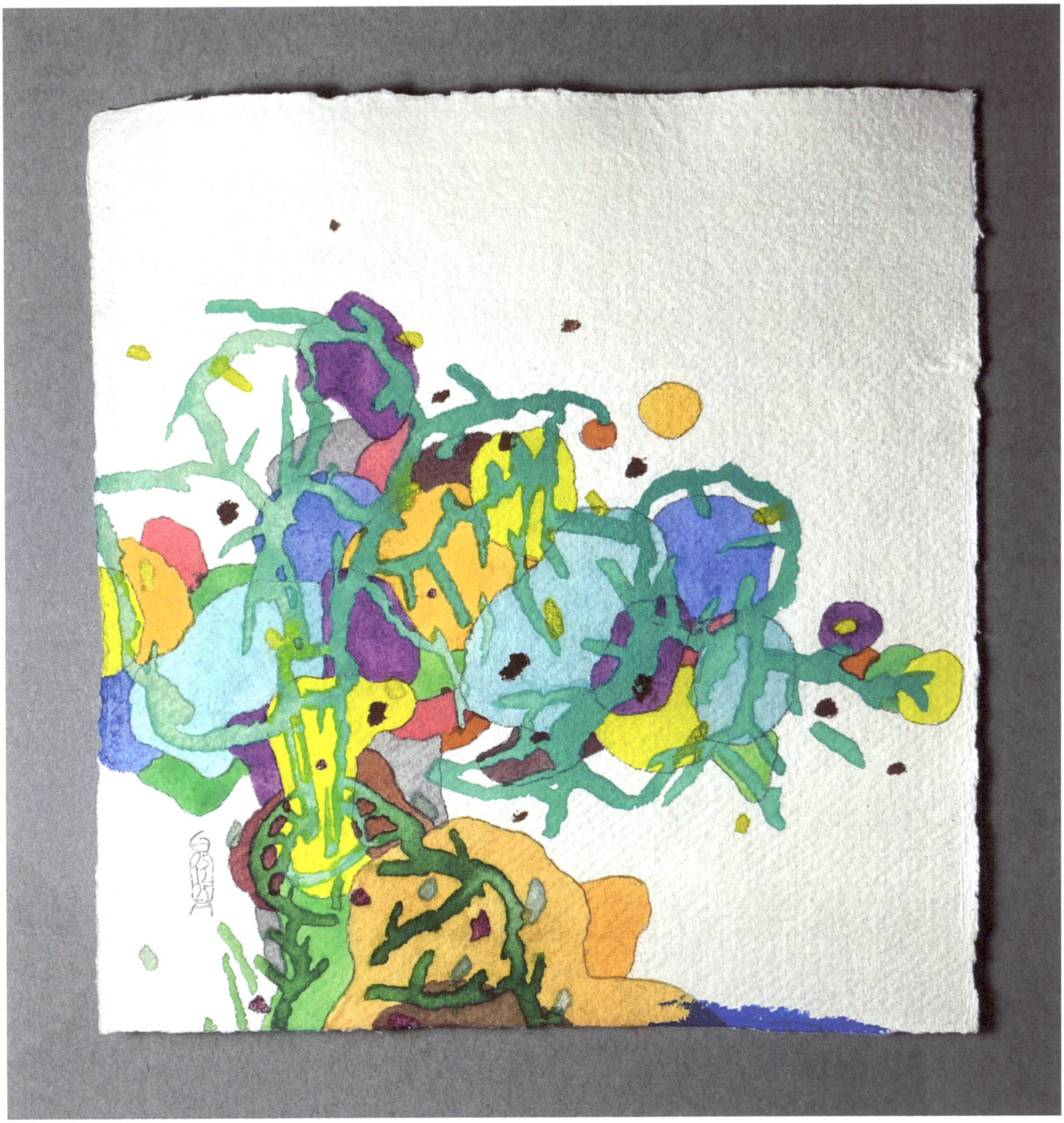

Power coming, 2025,Watercolor + gouache + pencil + oil crayon, 22 x 21 cm

GREG STIRLING

gregtir@yahoo.com

For over forty years, Greg Stirling has been a quiet yet profound force in the world of contemporary art, a true luminary in San Jose, California's creative scene. His work, spanning abstract and impressionist painting to kinetic sculpture, resonates with a duality of stillness and motion, of quiet contemplation and explosive energy. Stirling's journey, as he describes it, is "a fascinating exploration of various styles, techniques, and media," beginning in the raw expressiveness of abstract expressionism and leading him through the refined vistas of realism. His body of work, characterized by a mastery over both abstraction and realism, occupies a unique space in the artistic landscape, evoking a sense of wonder and philosophical reflection.

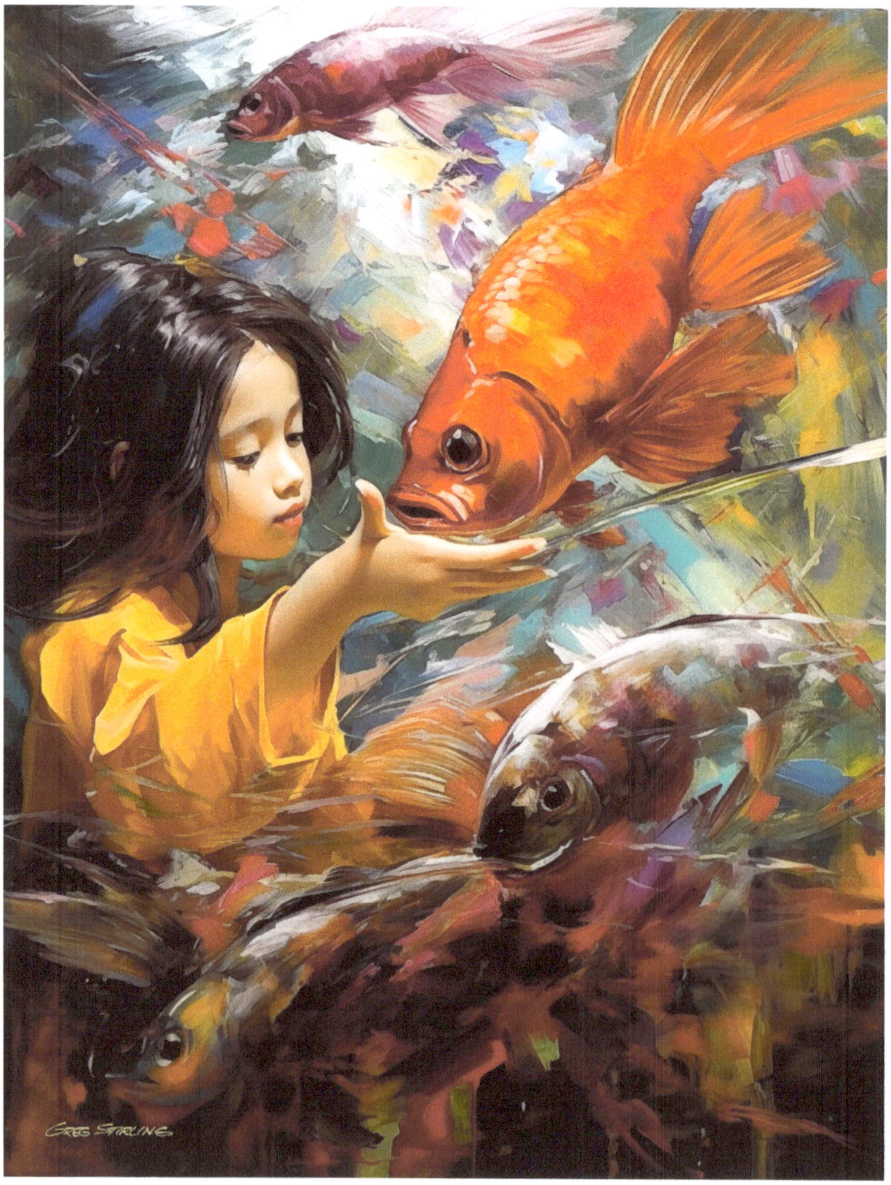

Girl With Goldfish #1, Oil on canvas, 100 x 60 cm

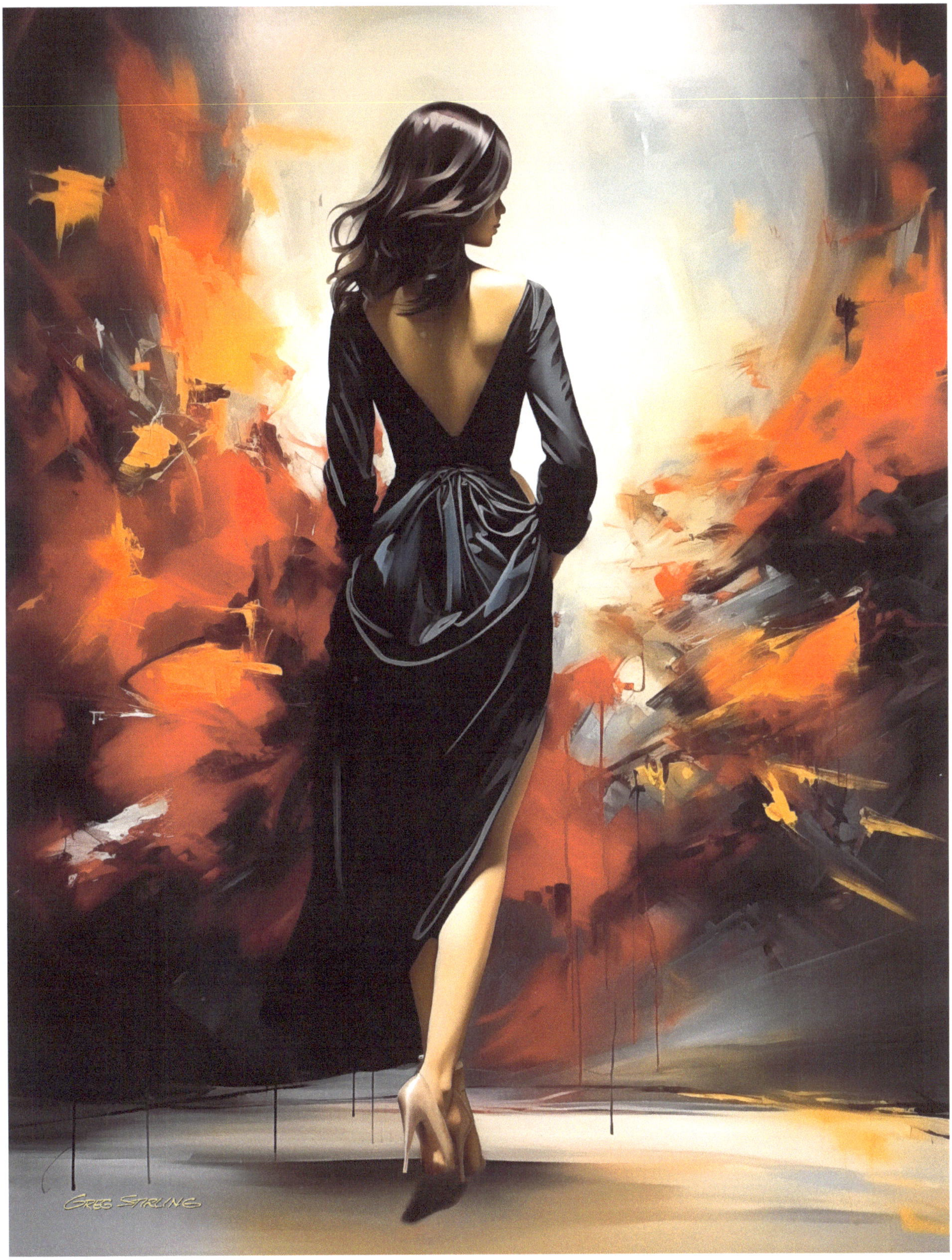

Abstract Woman #1, Oil on canvas, 100 x 60 cm

GRO HEINING

@ gro.heining

Drawing and painting have always been a way of expressing herself. Nature is her primary source of inspiration. Painting for Gro is a meditative state of being, where she connect to the elements and the rhythm of nature, weaving dreams and visions into her artwork. Gro's idea of the intention of doing art is to be able to communicate that all things are connected with one another and to the universe. The interconnectedness of all things in nature represents a deep unity within herself. She also considers her work as a teacher bringing the language of colors to the viewer and hope for the future. She likes to think of her paintings as gifts from the spiritual realm revealed after journey to the land of introspection.

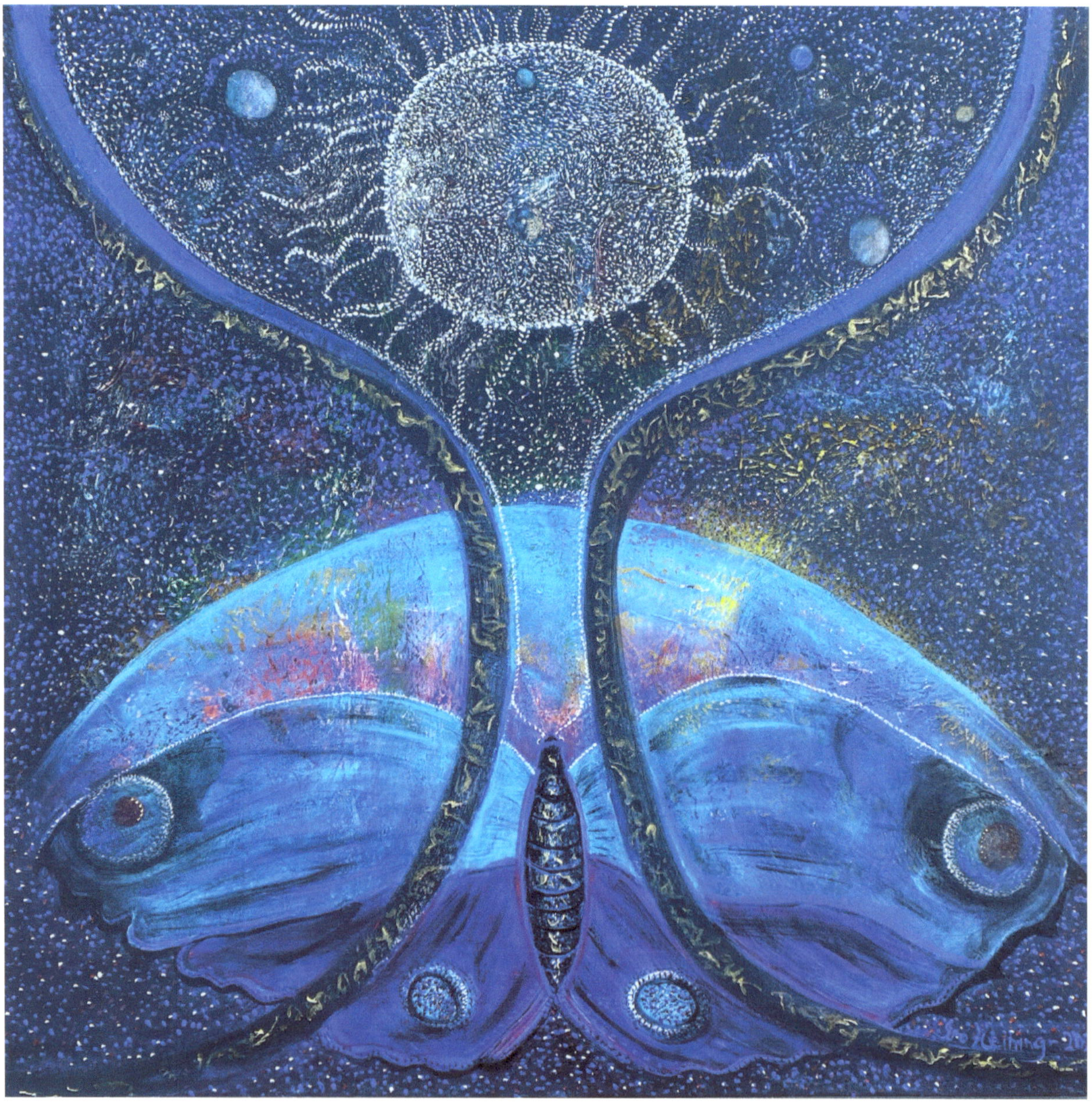

Transformation,2025, acrylic on canvas, 80 x 80 cm

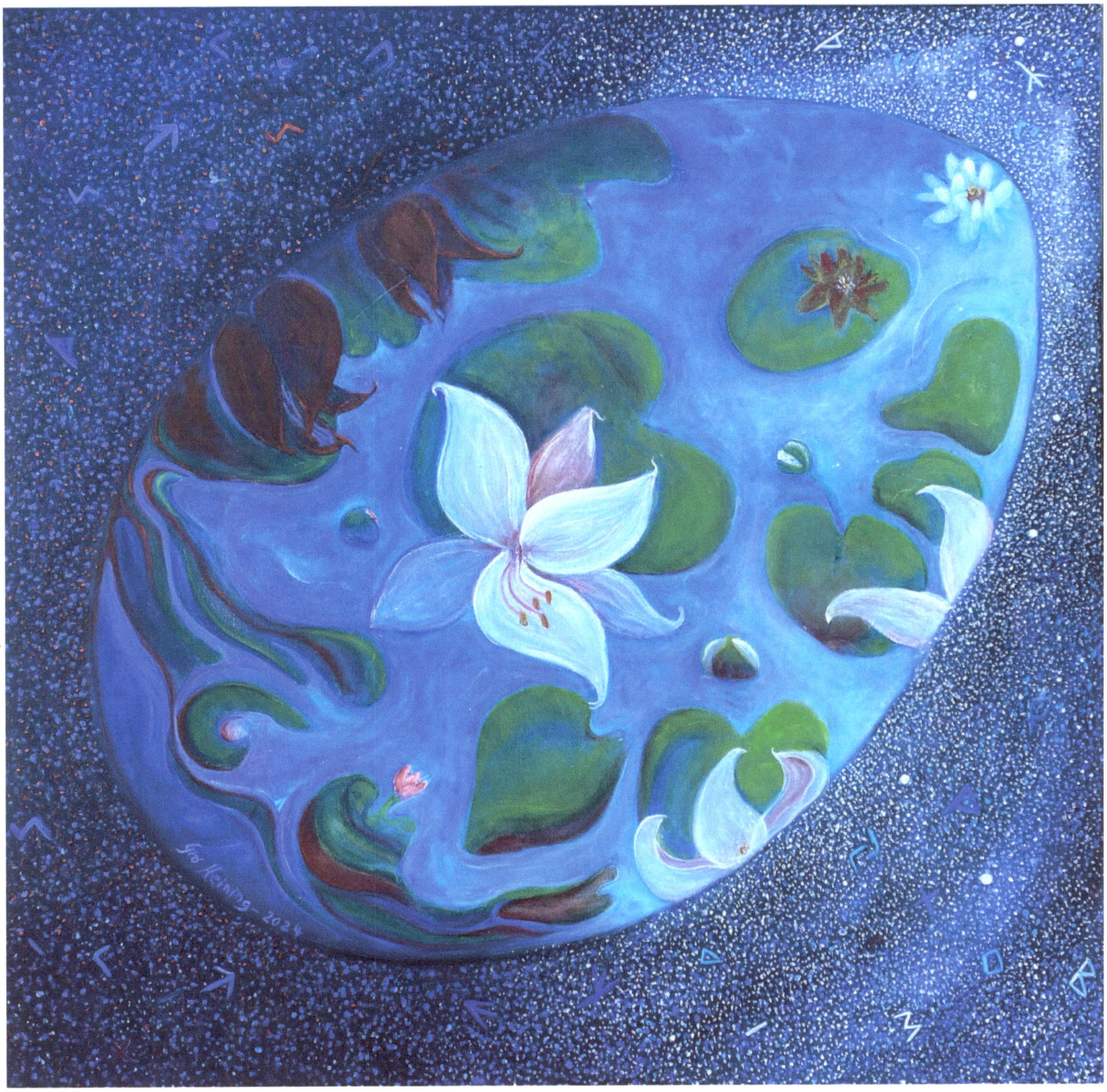

Rebirth I, 2024, acrylic on canvas, 100 x 100 cm

GUISCARD PROF. DR. SEEBOHM

Prof. Dr. Guiscard Seebohm https://www.seebohmart.de

Prof. Dr. Guiscard Seebohm, a Münster-based artist and academic, explores the compelling intersection of pop culture and traditional fine art through the expressive lens of Pop Art. His creative work is shaped by a profound investigation of visual language and the tension between familiar cultural imagery and artistic abstraction. Central to Seebohm's approach is the reduction of visual complexity. He distills his compositions down to their essential elements, employing a deliberately limited palette of pure, vibrant colors. This minimalist strategy invites viewers to actively reconstruct form and meaning, encouraging a fresh perception of shape, color, and context. The result is a visually arresting aesthetic that evokes both clarity and emotional depth. Through his art, Seebohm creates not only striking visual impressions but also a space for reflection—where perception is challenged and emotional resonance emerges. His work stands as a dialogue between surface and substance, intellect and instinct, structure and spontaneity.

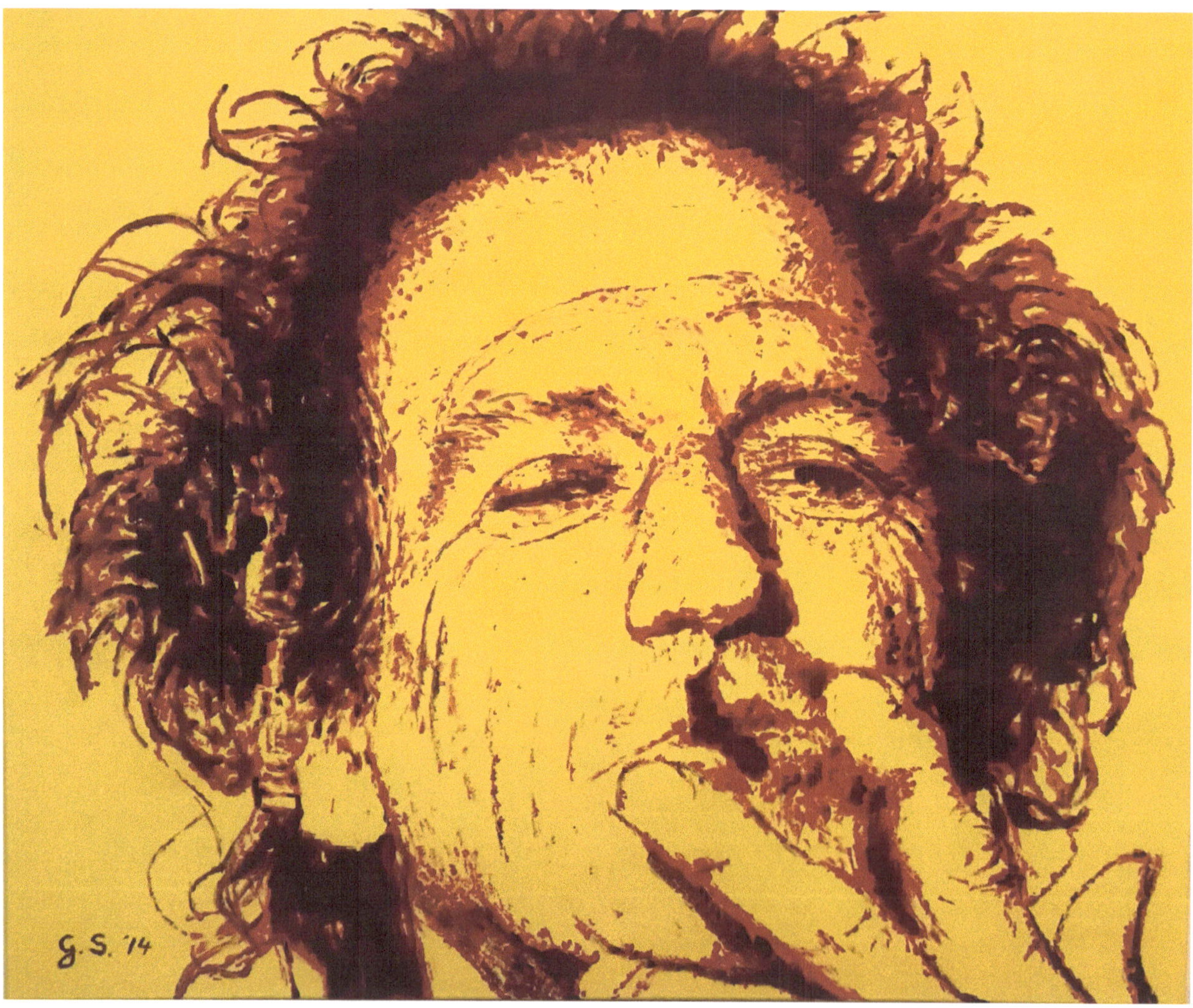

Keith Richards, 2014. Acrylic on canvas, 120 x 100 cm

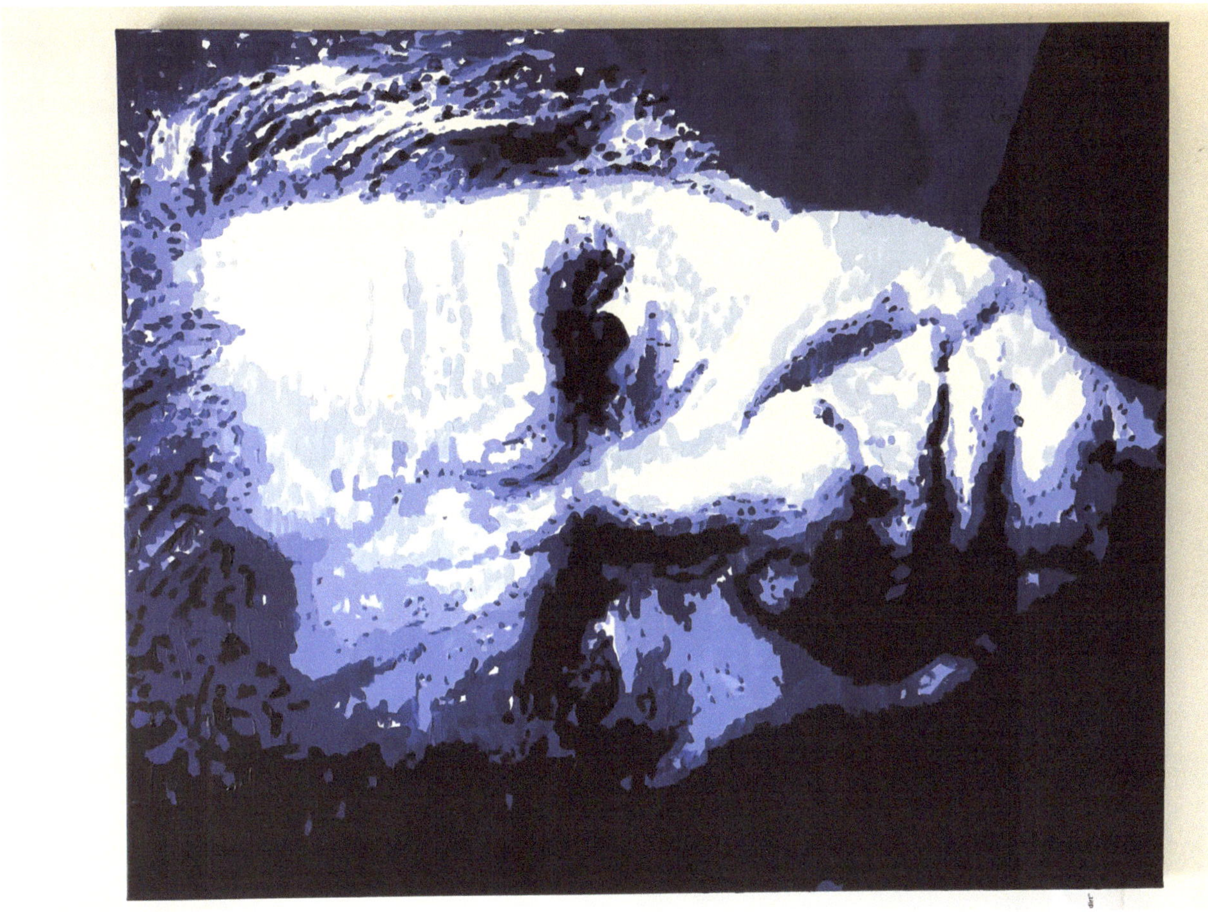

Johnny Cash, 2018. Acrylic on canvas, 80 × 100 cm

HANS TÄCKENSTRÖM

www.hanstackenstromart.se, instagram: hazegoesart

Hans has a professional background in the advertising industry, where he has been repeatedly nationally and internationally awarded for successful advertising. Art and culture have always been strong driving forces for him, whether at work, as a musician in the group Hans on the bass or through painting. In music, the artistic outlet gets in the bass playing. The signature of Hans on the bass music is feelgood which can be said to accompany the painting. It is a playfull way of discovering the world we live in. Hans has studied art in Stockholm and San Francisco. Hans is using a lot of his experience of working with concepts and the process creating different spaces and rooms for ideas and stories. His art has several sources of inspiration. Modern pop art art, Nicholas Wilton, Peter Kohler, Donald Baechler, Hilma af Klint and Angelo Accordi to name a few fine art artists. By meeting material in a nostalgic way and with the color scale of the 1950s, he examines the dynamics of the relationship between being a human, material and environment with a focus on connections and relationships with the goal of developing completely new experiences. By using color as a clear carrier of the design language Hans haze uses, the abstract with the figurative witch finds exciting ways for the viewer to explore. In a complex world, Hans Haze paintings build stories based on a flow of different ideas, emotions expressed in a way that can not always be done in words. Themes he works with in his art are everything from the beautiful and fragile to the more complex. All the different building blocks of life, joy, change and the role of people in our fantastic world. His paintings are like Alice in Wonderland with several doors and secrets disposed in a playful way asking many good questions – where to go? And where does your secret hide?

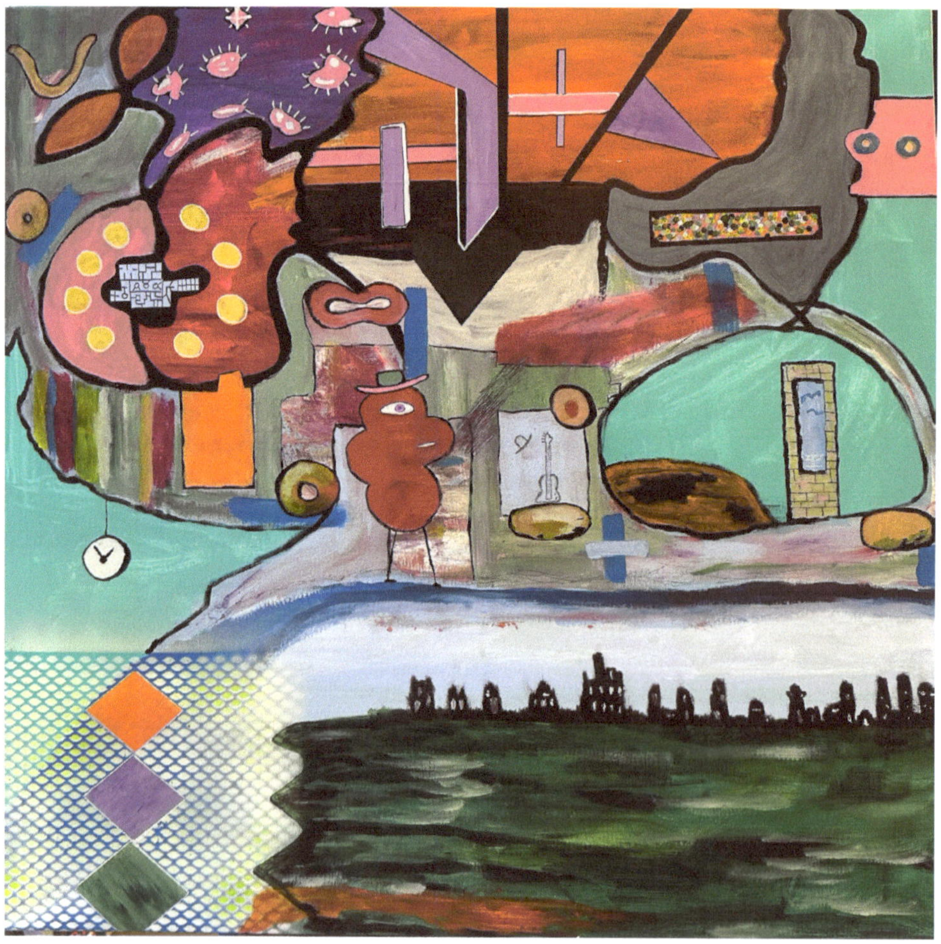

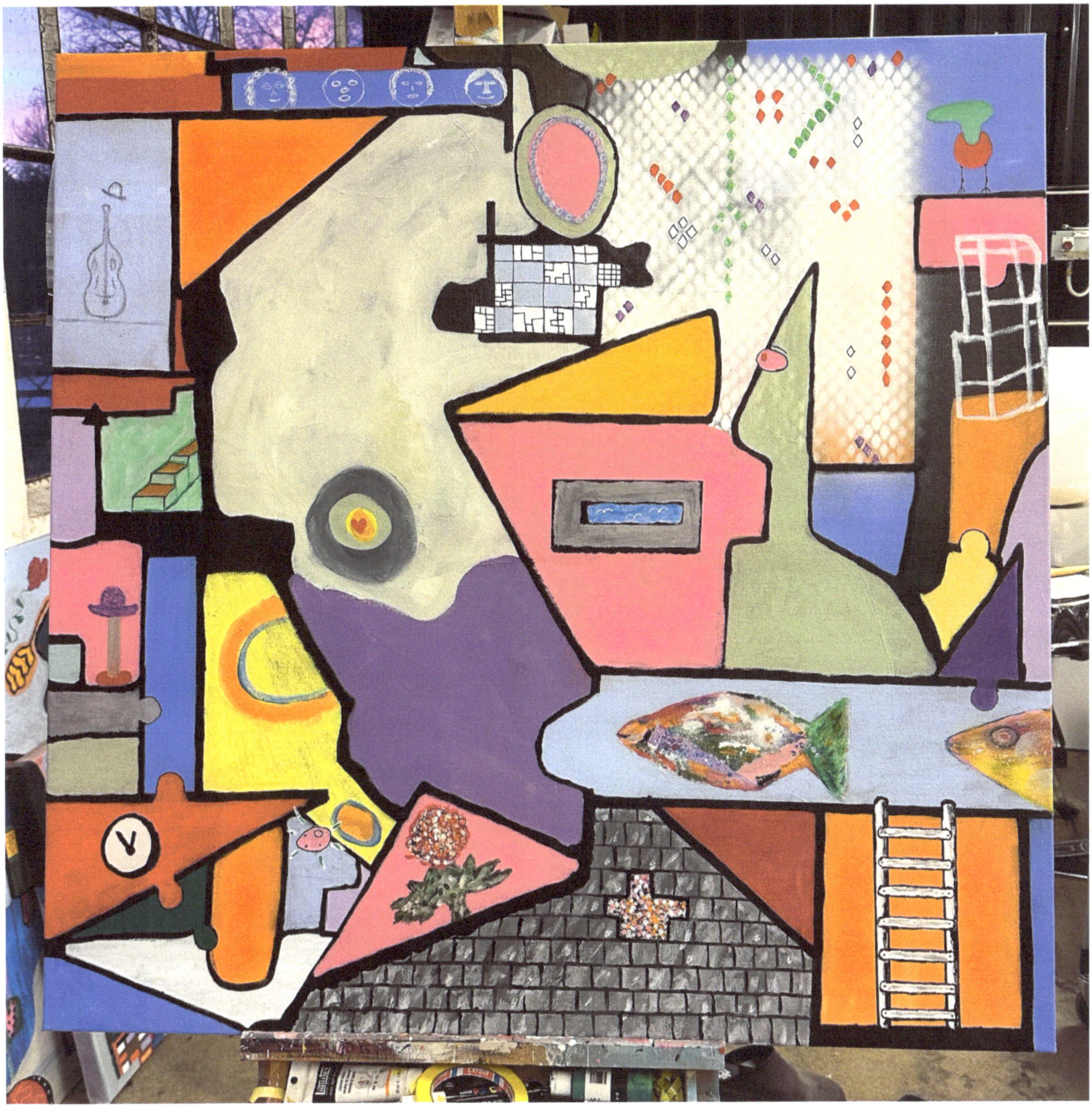

Dubbelbass 2024

HANS JOHANSSON

artelokation@gmail.com

I am borne in the north of Sweden but now a days I live in the south of the country. Before I started my artistic education I was working in a classical style, but nowadays my work has become more modern. I am working with painting, graphic and drawing. In the painting there is a wide range of possibilities to express my intentions. When I am working with the graphics,I can work more with the drawing.

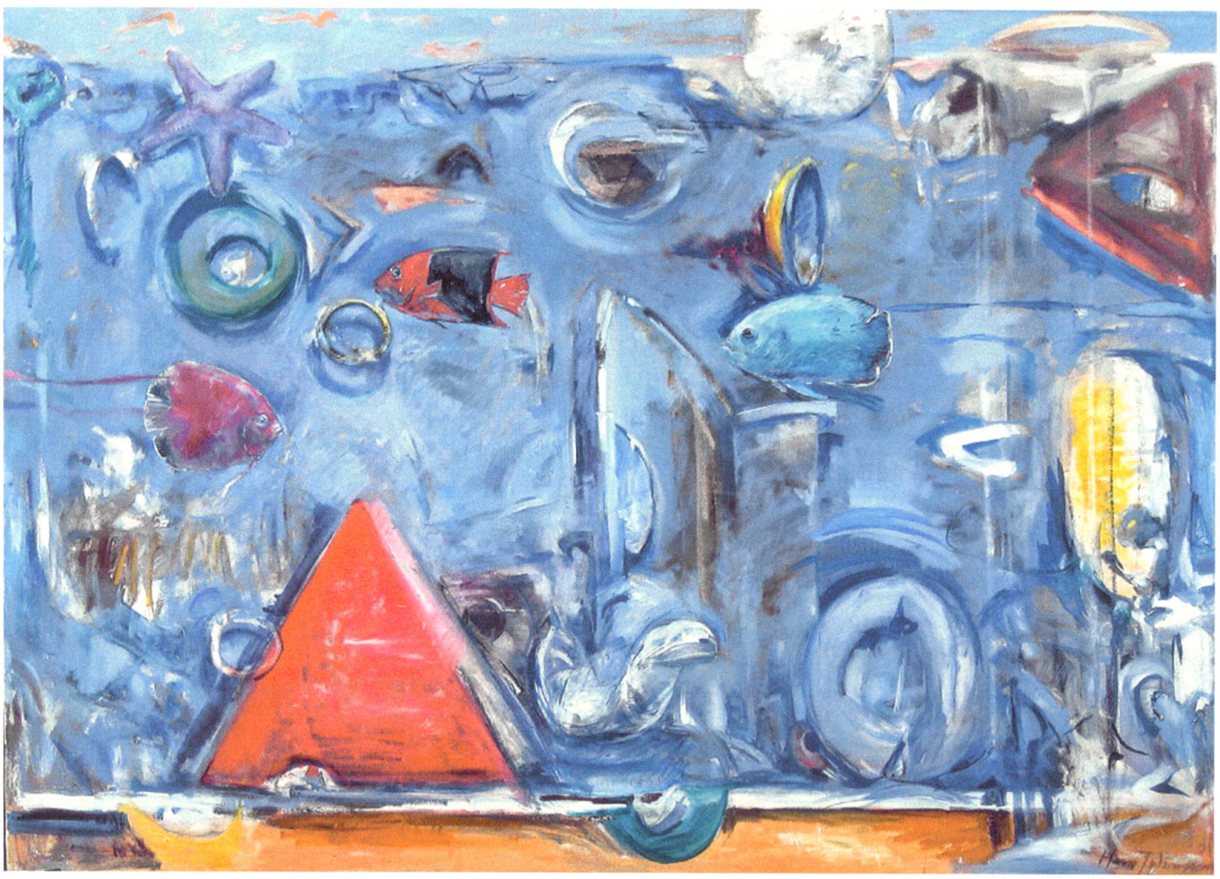

Triad, 2016. Acrylic on canvas,130 x 97 cm

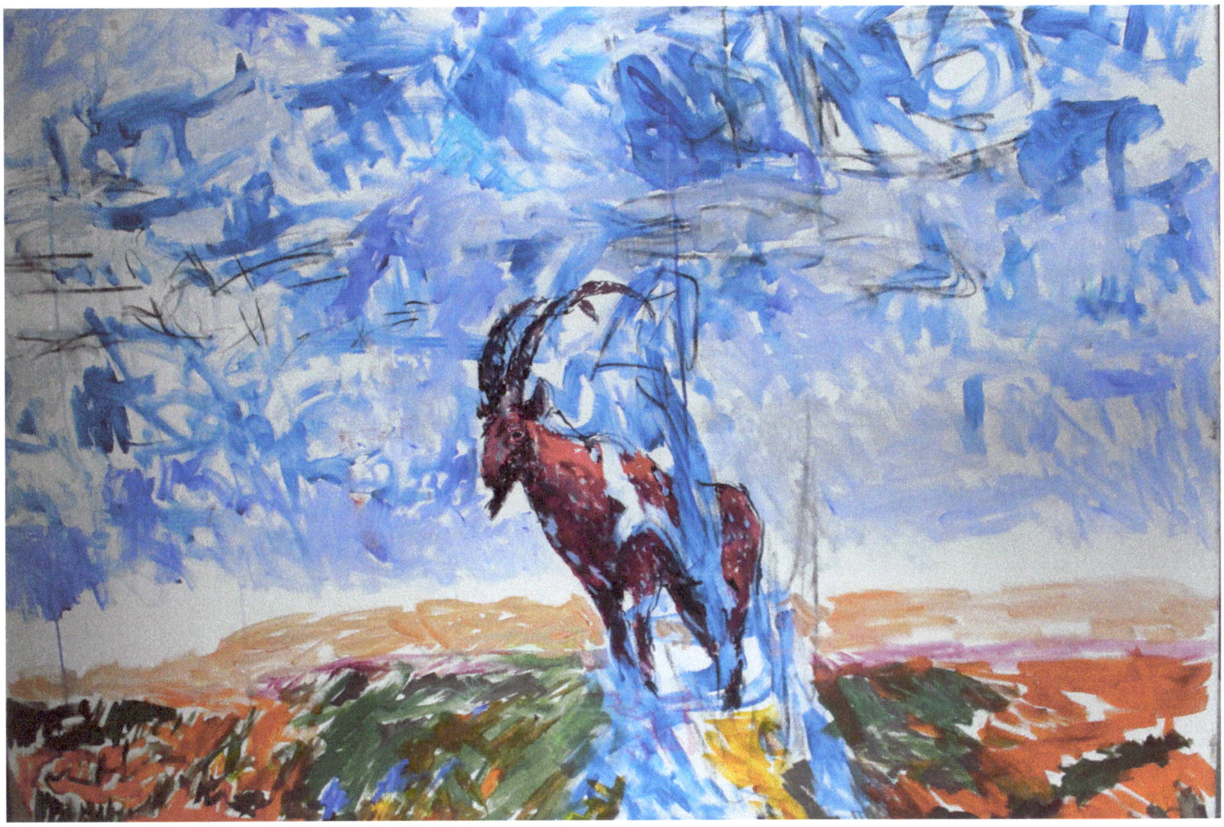

The Goat, Acrylic on canvas, 130x97 cm

HELENKAGAN HEALINGARTS™

www.HelenKagan.art

Helen Kagan, PhD, a healer and artist. A creator of a unique multi-dimensional concept "HealingArts" she's been developing for 30 years. Helen believes art is a catalyst for healing individuals, society and environment. She is a pioneer in creating art with an intention to heal. In her own words: "As a severe PTSD survivor my own complex life Journey brought me to the point where I would not survive without creating. As a true healing artist I started to use painting, energy and spiritual work, music, writing, movement, shamanic work, chakra dancing, and other expressive modalities to first support my own healing, and to enhance a healing process to those in need. I bring together Fine Art, Expressive arts, and the Art of Healing by integrating healing frequencies of color, positively charged intention, embedded spiritual messages, and energetically balanced composition".

Helen feels it's her duty to create art for healing in our turbulent times, amid World-wide multiple crises, wars, fear, anxiety, stress, uncertainty & overwhelm. She believes in mind- body- spirit- soul & art as a catalyst for healing individuals, society & environment. She believes that now, more than ever, our World needs positive energy, spiritual intentions, beliefs, authenticity, gratitude, and of course - lots of positive healing art!
Helen's passionate vibrant HealingArts™ called "symphony of color" and a "vehicle for joy and well-being" is a statement of all her beliefs.

Helen shares her Mantra for Success, with everyone and anyone on their respective Journeys.
"Don't give up. Be Authentic. Follow your Visions. Even if everything seems to go wrong. If you truly believe in your unique "message", your Mission will eventually pick up. Everything new and innovative takes time for people to recognize it, change their own (old) paradigm to accept new, and then, hopefully, accept yours. I am speaking from my own, tough rough full of challenges, setbacks, obstacles, lots of trauma, drama, "big lessons" and small victories, yet so meaningful and valuable Life Experience – NEVER GIVE UP". Namaste.

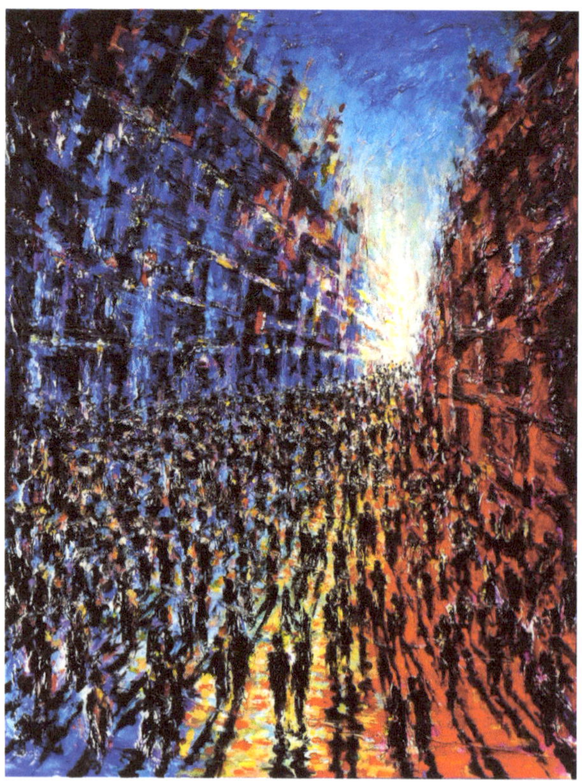

In Search For Meaning. Collection HealingArt. 2012. Acrylic, Mix. Med. on canvas 122x91.4cm

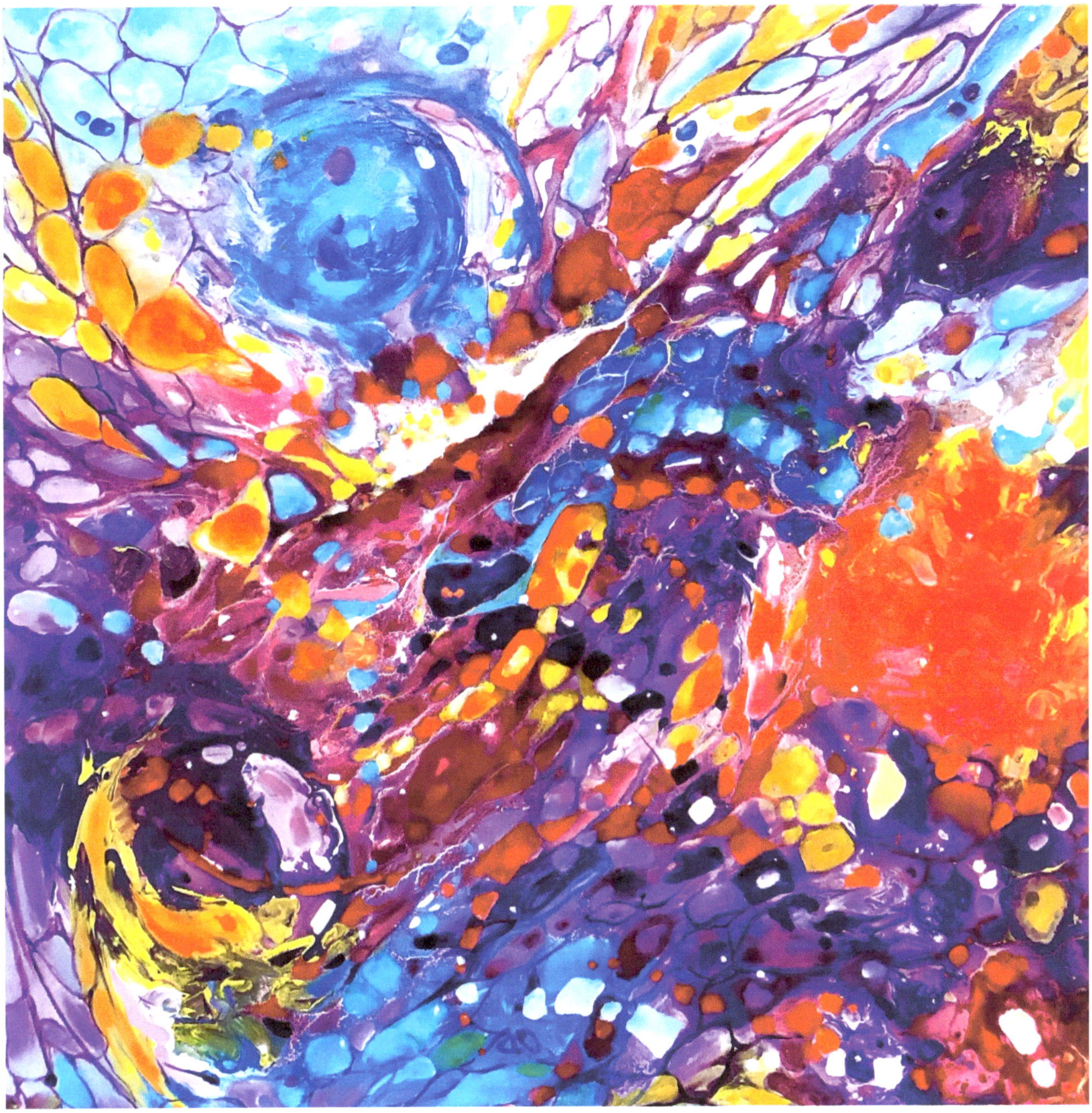

Finding Harmony in Chaos. Series Bridging Divides. Collection 5D. 2024. Acrylic, canvas 122x122cm

HARRY SALMI

https://linktr.ee/harrysalmi

Deep emotion and bold expression at the heart of nordic contemporary art. Harry Salmi (b. 1980, Hollola) is a visual artist from Lahti, Finland, whose works combine and transport the layers of abstract contemporary art, street art and surrealism into a unique visual world. His fine art is a superpower for him – a way to channel life experiences, hope and adversity into a visual whole. Harry also believes in the transformative power of fine art. He often says that "I live in my paintings" and "I am braver than myself when I paint." His paintings are a gateway to another reality – a mystical, almost cosmic paradise, where the viewer encounters both themselves and the world in a new way, in a place where stories are born and memories are built.

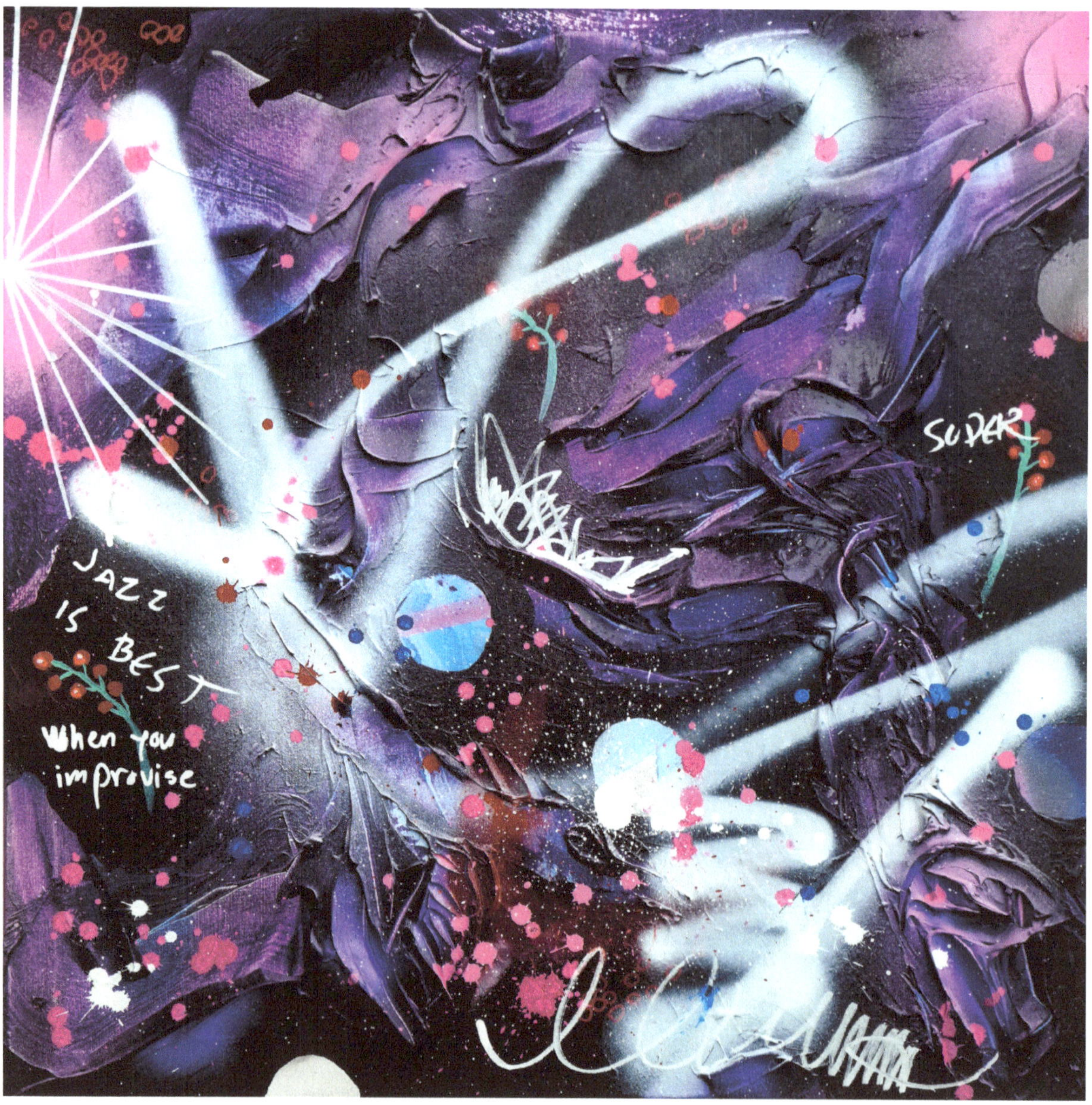

Tempo, 2024, acrylic on canvas, 70 x 70 cm

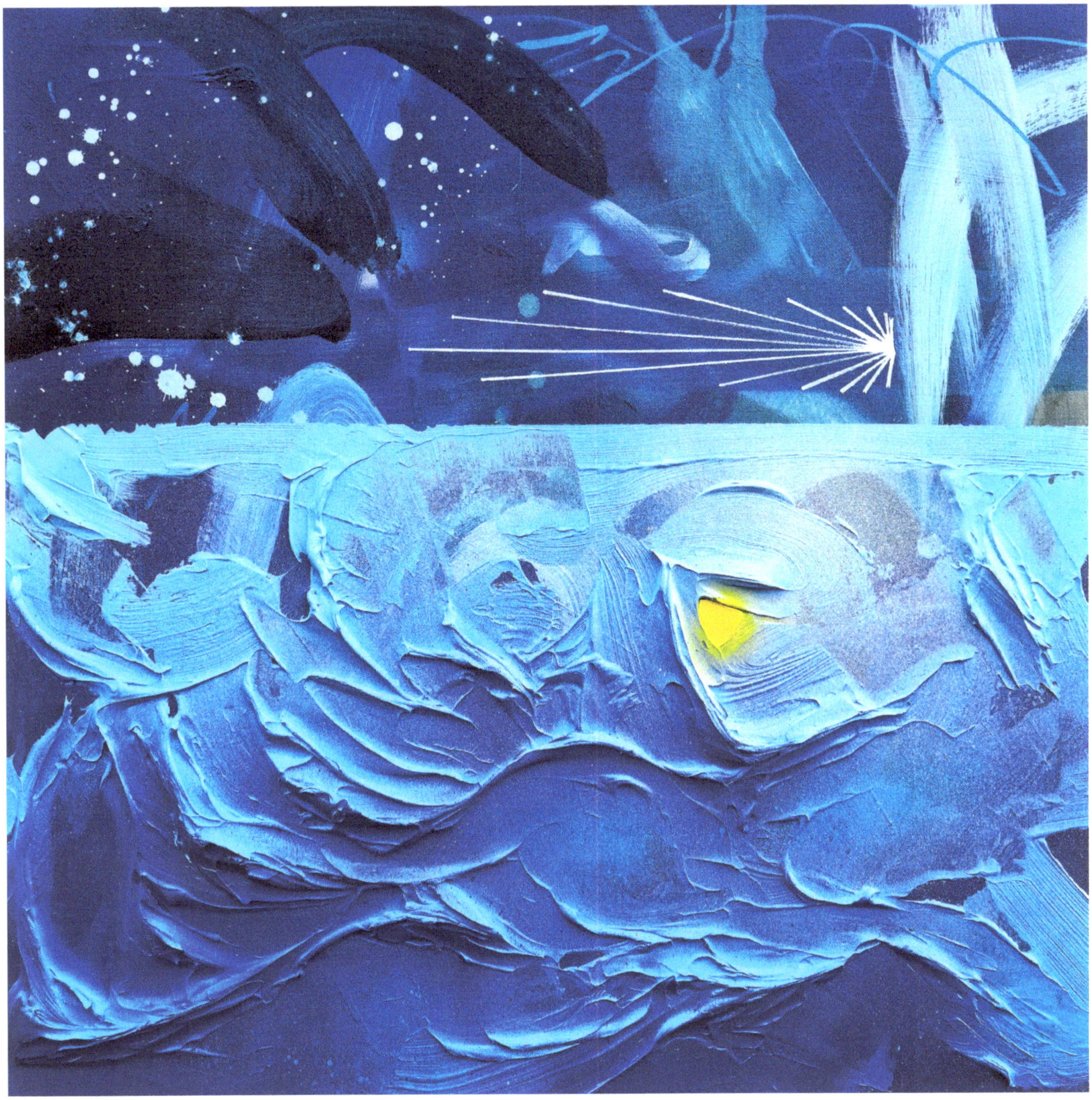

Nordic, 2022, acrylic on canvas, 70 x 70 cm

HÉDIA CARRON

https://www.hediacarron.com

From Switzerland, she has been painting since adolescence, having been exposed since 1996. She's now an international artist. As a self-taught woman, she enjoys discovering and enriching herself with various techniques, always learning. In 2024, she returned to her first loves in art: acting, with coaching from Jo Kelly of Los Angeles in her "33-day reset journey" program, "To Be or Not to Act." Now she's in the next level of coaching, "acting". This new tool opened her to another part of herself and a new evolution in her art. She doesn't want to be locked up in an "only" style; She likes to move from one technique to another. She loves working with pigments, spices, and different materials. Gold is for her a medium of light and a carrier of the vibration she puts in her creations (painting, pigments, or leaves). Her inspiration comes from the beauty of nature, cinema (one of her passions), literature, music, paintings, other artists like J.M.W. Turner, Zao Wu-Ki, Van Gogh, H.R. Giger, Frida Kahlo Beaudelaire, Almodòvar, Marilyn Monroe, Gaudì, Prince, U2, Satie..., so many artists that she "meets" in the exhibitions and the museums. She wants to share her Joy and Love of Life in her art, to open the minds and hearts. She's grateful for all the gifts, awards, and international prizes she received and continues to receive in her life, and her crazy art journey.

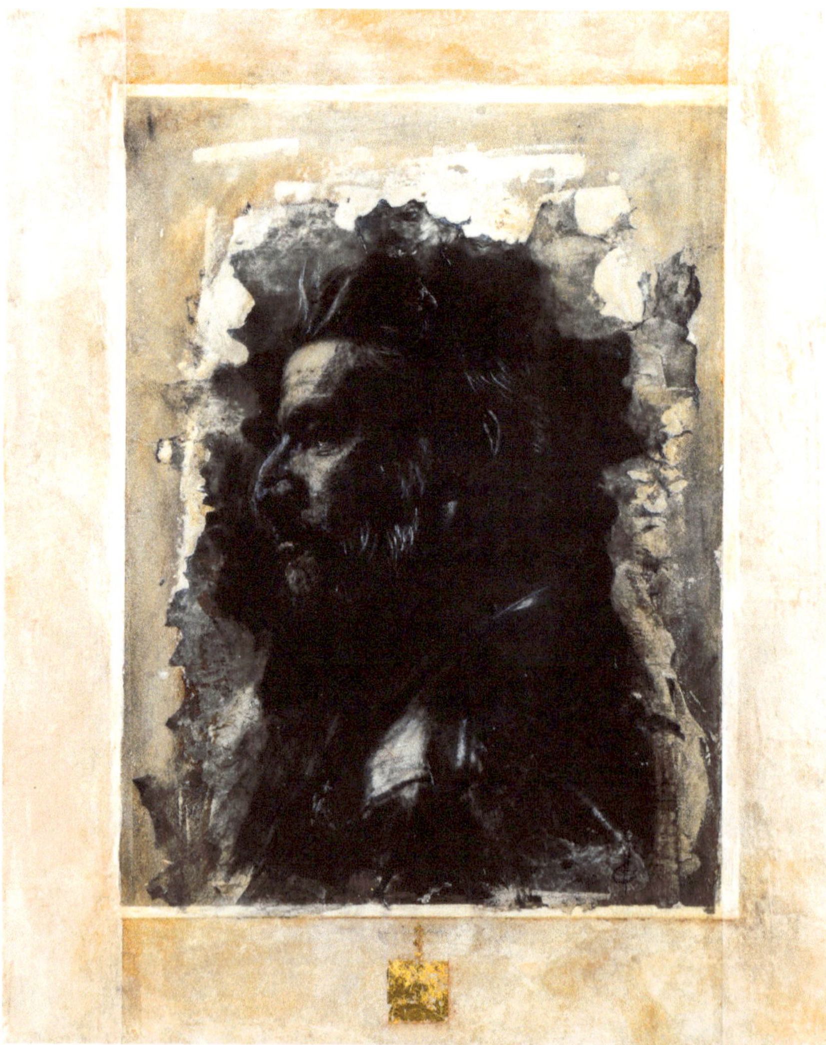

Sí mi Hombre de dos Tierras Mixed technique: acrylic, pigments, pencil drawing, pencil Posca, paper OKASHI, pure 24 carats golden leaf « Manetti » Size : Cardboard 40 x 50 cm ?2025

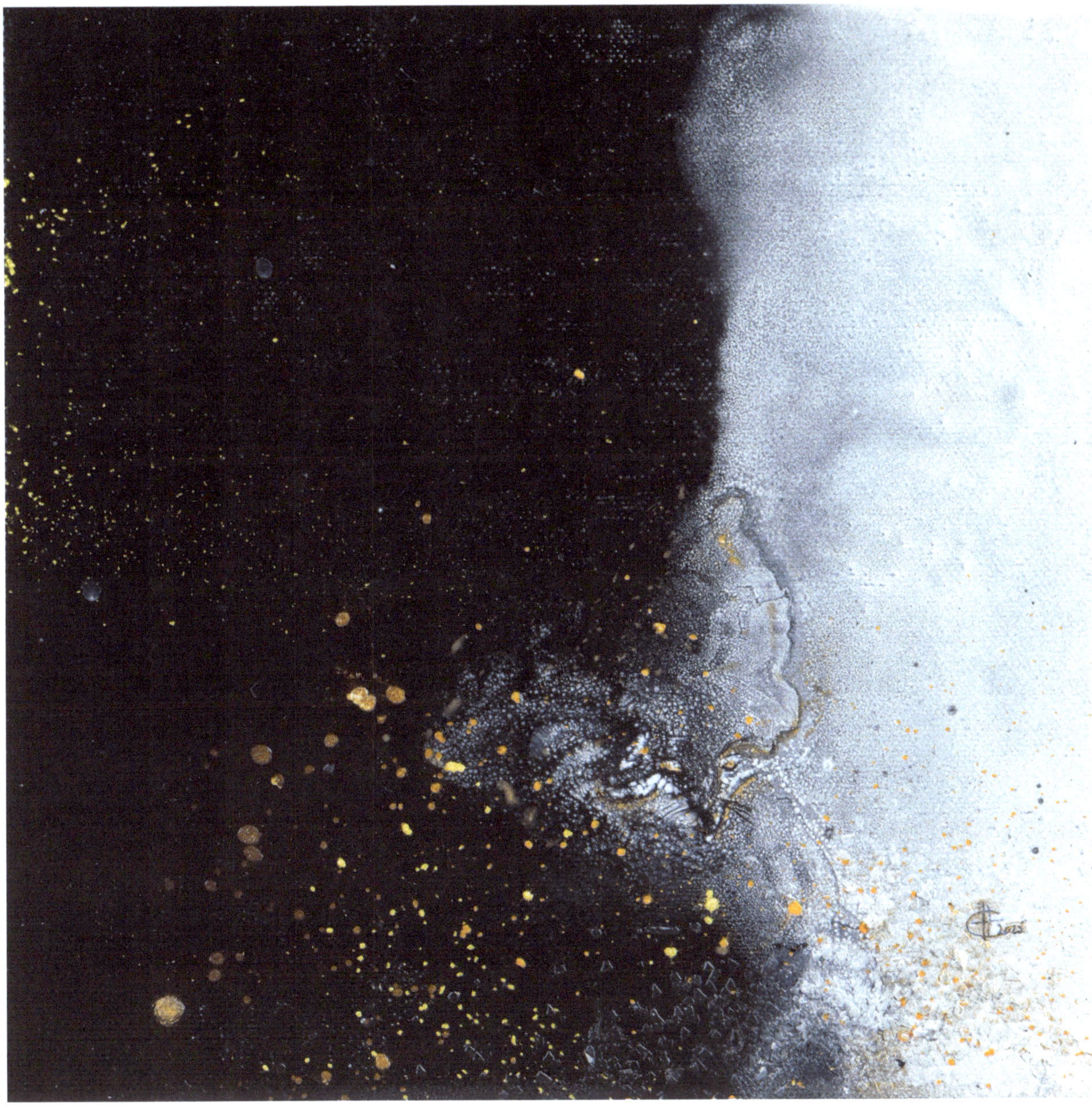

Fox Spirit Medium: Mixed technique: acrylic, pigments, Diamond Dust by Stuart Semple, Posca pencil, Chinese ink Size : Canvas of 25cm x 25 cm Year 2025

HELIOS BOECHAT

www.heliosboechat.de

Helios Boechat was born in Rio de Janeiro, Brazil. Later, he moved to Germany to pursue his artistic work, and, after spending some years in New York, has been living in Berlin since 2004. Arts: Self taught Artist (painter) Economics: UFRRJ, UFF and University Of Cologne Music: Conservatory Villa-Lobos, Rio De Janeiro Composition, Orchestration: Berlin Languages: Portuguese, German, French, Italian, Spanish, English. Instruments: Piano, Guitar Statement The manifestation of life. It is about the transformation of different materials and stages of energy into what we call biological life. Some forces interfere throughout endless time to amalgamate elements tighter together until life manifests out of it. My theory is that the most important forces acting into the elements are frequencies. So there's a kind of music all around even before biological life manifests itself. This is what changed my question from a „when" into a „what" is life itself. Therefore I think there are other forms of life based on other minerals or even just based on energy on Earth or elsewhere. This way I came to see time and dimensions in another perspective. If there is an energy called life or a life called „energy" than we have to think the impossible! In my art I first establish the impossible. With the interference of frequencies (with a special instrument I created just for that purpose) on oil and a mixed substance based on water. First I design an abstract foreground of the composition. This abstraction conducts me to let life manifest itself. So I created "Planet Syncopia", where this strange creatures, the "Syncopians", manifest and breed in a syncope of time. They barely touch the ground and reproduce through vibrations.

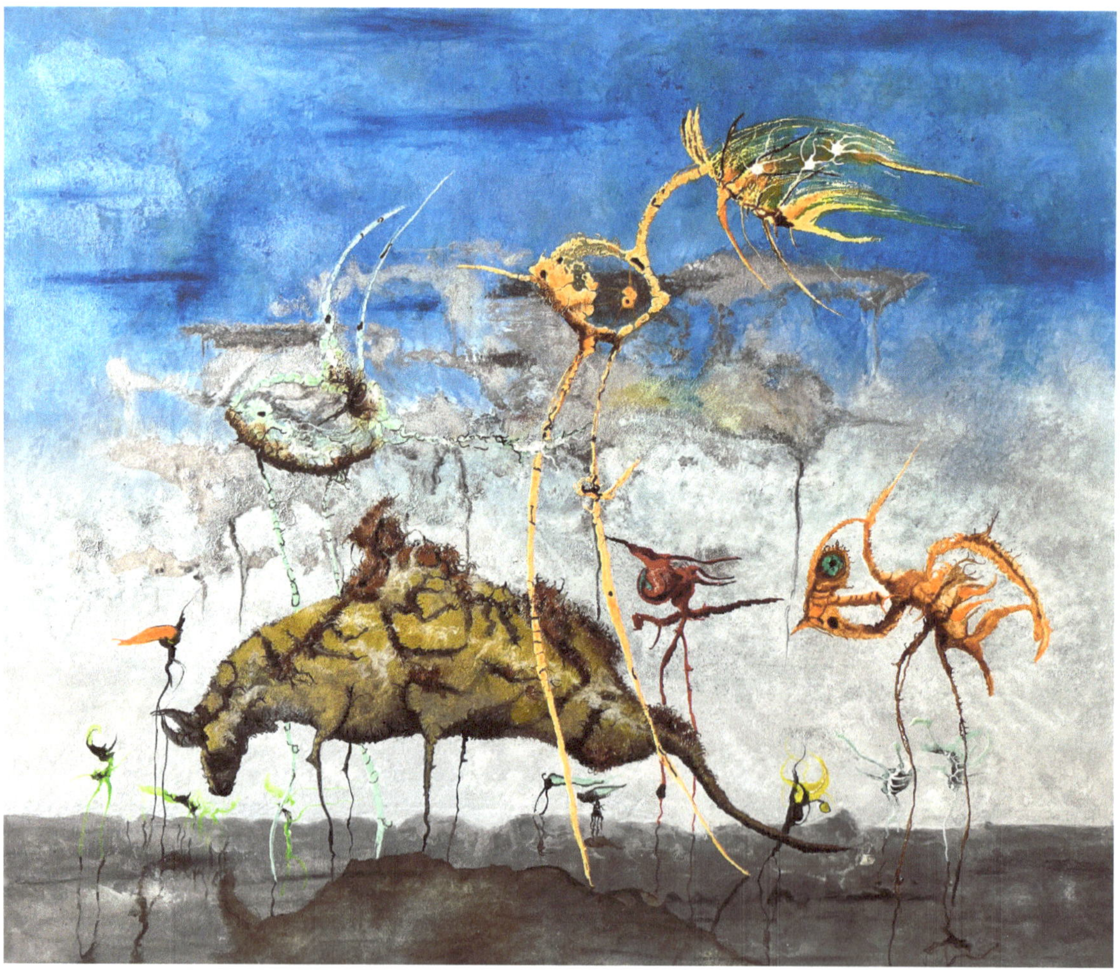

Balusians, 2025, oil on canvas, 95 x 110 cm

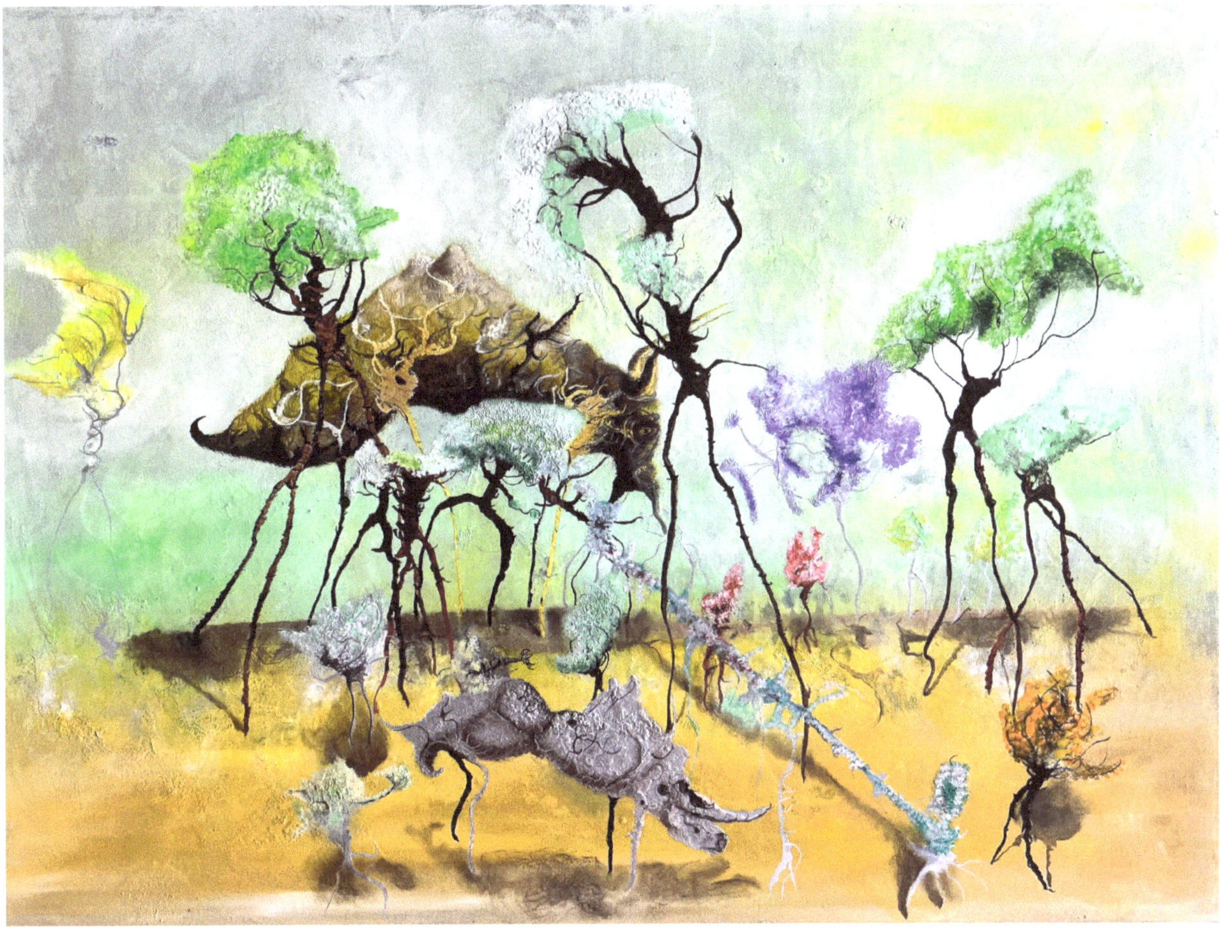

Garonias, 2025, oil on canvas, 90 x 120 cm

HOWARD HARRIS

Howard Harris: h-harris@live.com

Artist Statement Howard Harris views visual reality as a constantly shifting and deeply personal experience. He believes that what we perceive at any given moment reflects both our inner landscape and the external influences of light, color, movement, and space. As a Techspressionist, Harris aims to recreate this dynamic perceptual process, revealing its intricate layers and encouraging viewers to actively engage with his work. His images are meticulously crafted on aluminum and often layered with abstract forms over subtle grids printed on clear acrylic. This technique imparts a sense of dimensionality and fluidity to each piece, enabling it to transform according to the viewer's angle and the play of light. Harris holds that perception is both unique and fluid, making each individual's response an essential part of the artwork's meaning. Guided by universal principles of design that evoke beauty and emotion, Harris seeks to merge technology with aesthetics. His goal is to expand the viewer's visual experience and foster personal reflection on how perception influences reality. Through his art, he aspires to inspire curiosity and a deeper understanding of the ever-changing nature of perception. Biography Howard Harris is a Techspressionist artist based in Denver, Colorado, whose work investigates the complexities of visual perception and design. He earned a BFA from the Kansas City Art Institute and a Master's in Industrial Design from Pratt Institute in New York, where he studied under renowned design theorist Rowena Reed Kostellow. His educational background also includes studies in Economics and Computer Science at the University of Missouri, as Well as Sublimation Color Research at the Rochester Institute of Technology. He holds certifications in marketing, graphic arts, and financial management from the University of Utah and Northwestern University. With over 35 years of experience integrating design and technology, Harris has received numerous prestigious awards, including the Who's Who Worldwide Lifetime Achievement Award for Small Businessperson of the Year, the Design Professional of the Year award from Presidential Who's Who Marketing, and multiple industry accolades. In 2017, he was granted a U.S. Patent for his innovative layered artwork apparatus and methodology, underscoring the uniqueness of his photographic work. Harris has been honored as Artist of the Decade by Artists for a Green Planet. He has received international prizes, including the Raffaello, Giulio Cesare, Leonardo da Vinci, and Caravaggio awards. He has served as a trustee of The Kansas City Art Institute, and his artwork is exhibited internationally and represented by galleries across the United States, the United Kingdom, and Europe.

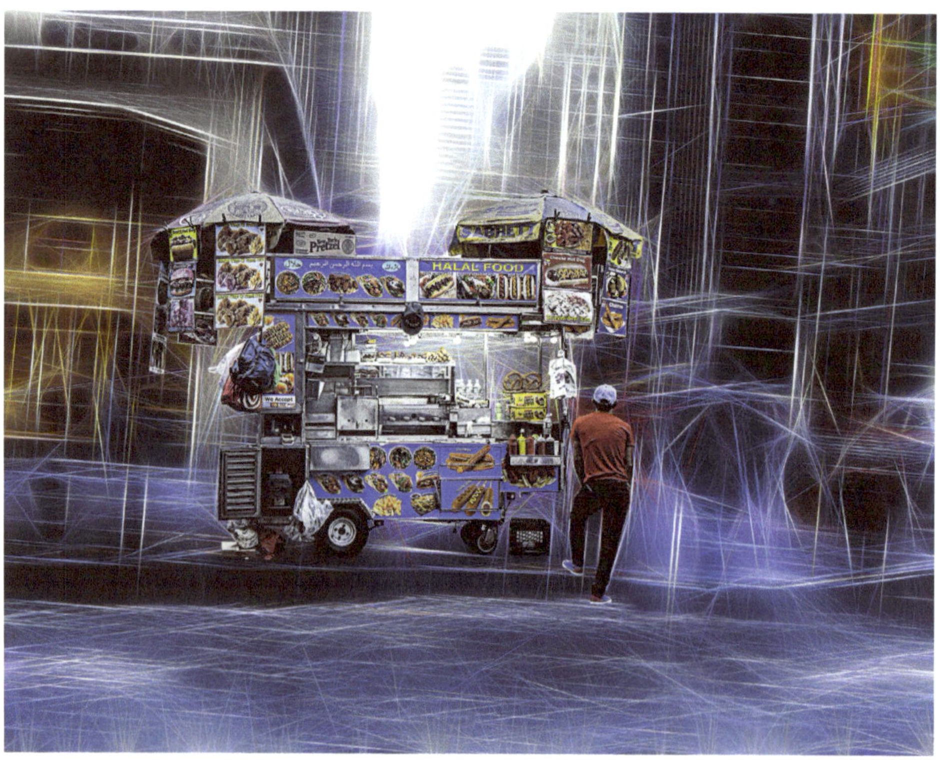

Street Feast, Sublimation on Aluminum, 91x76 cm, 2025

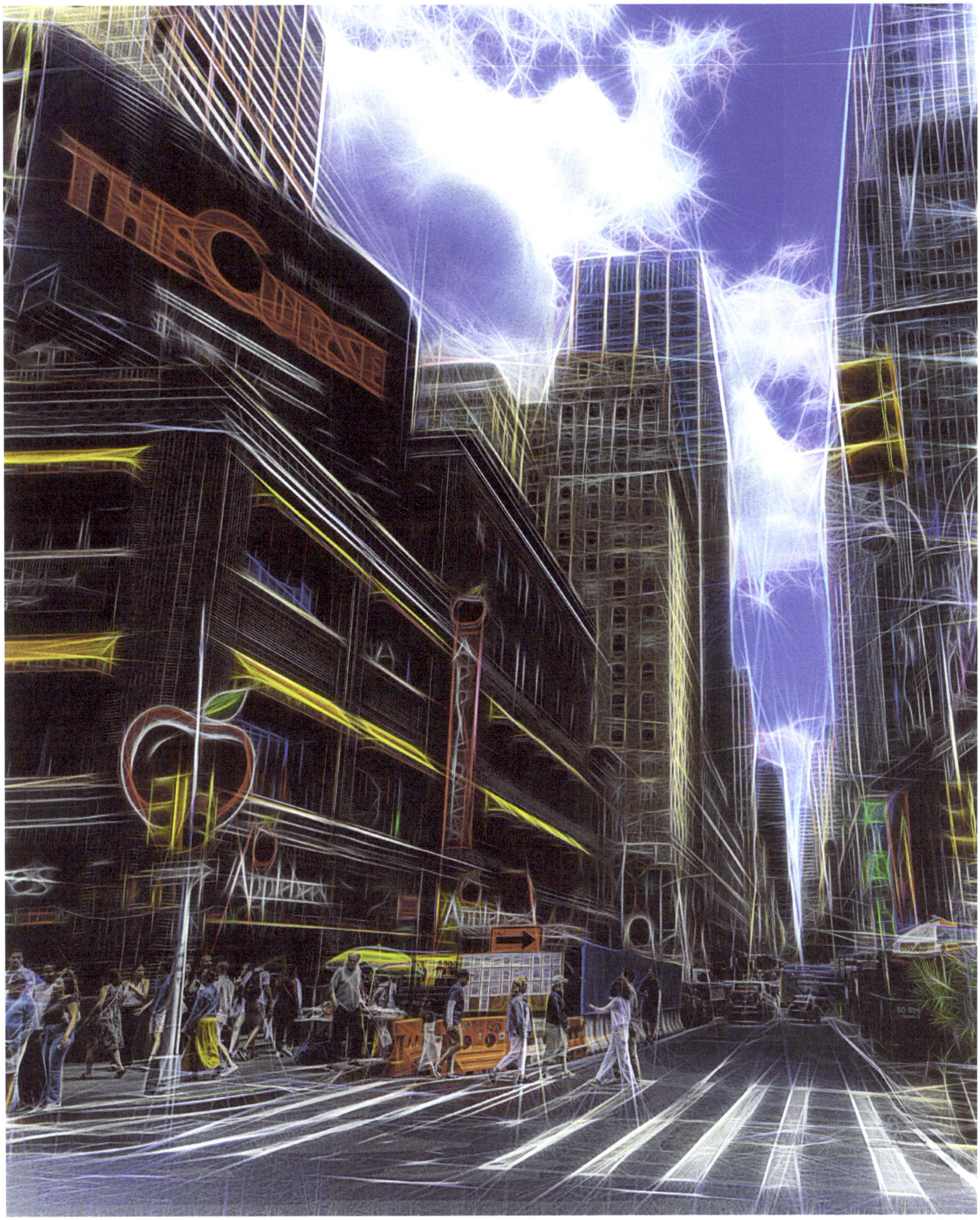

On the Street, Sublimation on Aluminum, 91x76 cm, 20252025

IGOR GRECHANYK

www.grechanyk.com

Igor Grechanyk is a sculptor and artist whose work blends philosophical symbolism, mytho-poetic imagery, and a contemporary sculptural language. His creations are visualized fragments of spiritual experience, resonating with the collective unconscious and touching on the eternal questions of human existence. He gives form to the undefined, materializing spirit in bronze.

Born in Kyiv into an artistic family, Grechanyk graduated from the Kyiv State Art Institute in 1984. His early career, shaped by the ideological pressures of Socialist Realism, led him to a fusion of classical plasticity with a metaphysical intensity of image.

Grechanyk's work gained early international recognition even during the Soviet era and the 1990s, with exhibitions in East Germany, Sweden, France, and the USA (including the Lincoln Center, New York). However, it was from the early 2000s that he began participating actively in major international exhibitions across Europe and Asia.

His figures possess an architectural stability and read as symbols—a blend of monumentality and surreal vision. His approach is closer to the thinking of ancient masters: "Only the spirit matters," he says. "I materialize it in my own way... The spirit itself chooses both the form and the vessel."

The core of his current creation lies in exploring new digital and material dimensions, capturing the elusive concept of 'Time' and pushing the boundaries of sculptural language to reflect the contemporary human condition. His large-scale public sculptures serve as cultural ambassadors at notable sites internationally.

Collected by connoisseurs worldwide for its rare ability to touch the deep, archetypal layers of human perception, the art of Igor Grechanyk stands as one of the defining voices of his generation — a creator whose visions will remain as vital tomorrow as they are today.

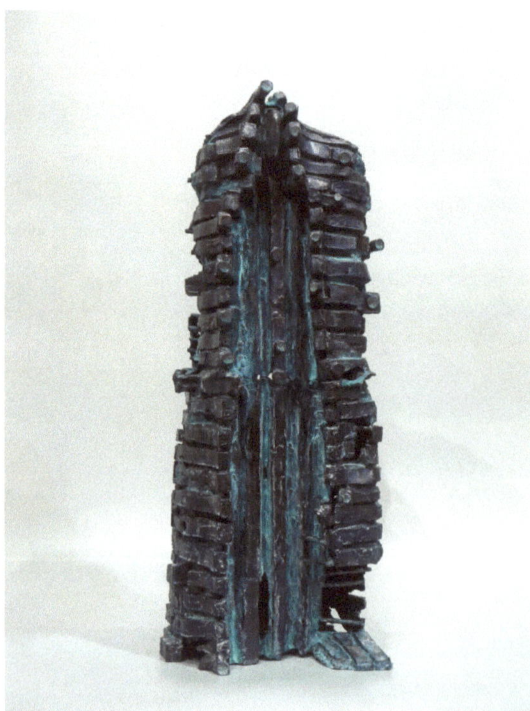

The Book of Numbers. Emergence , 2025

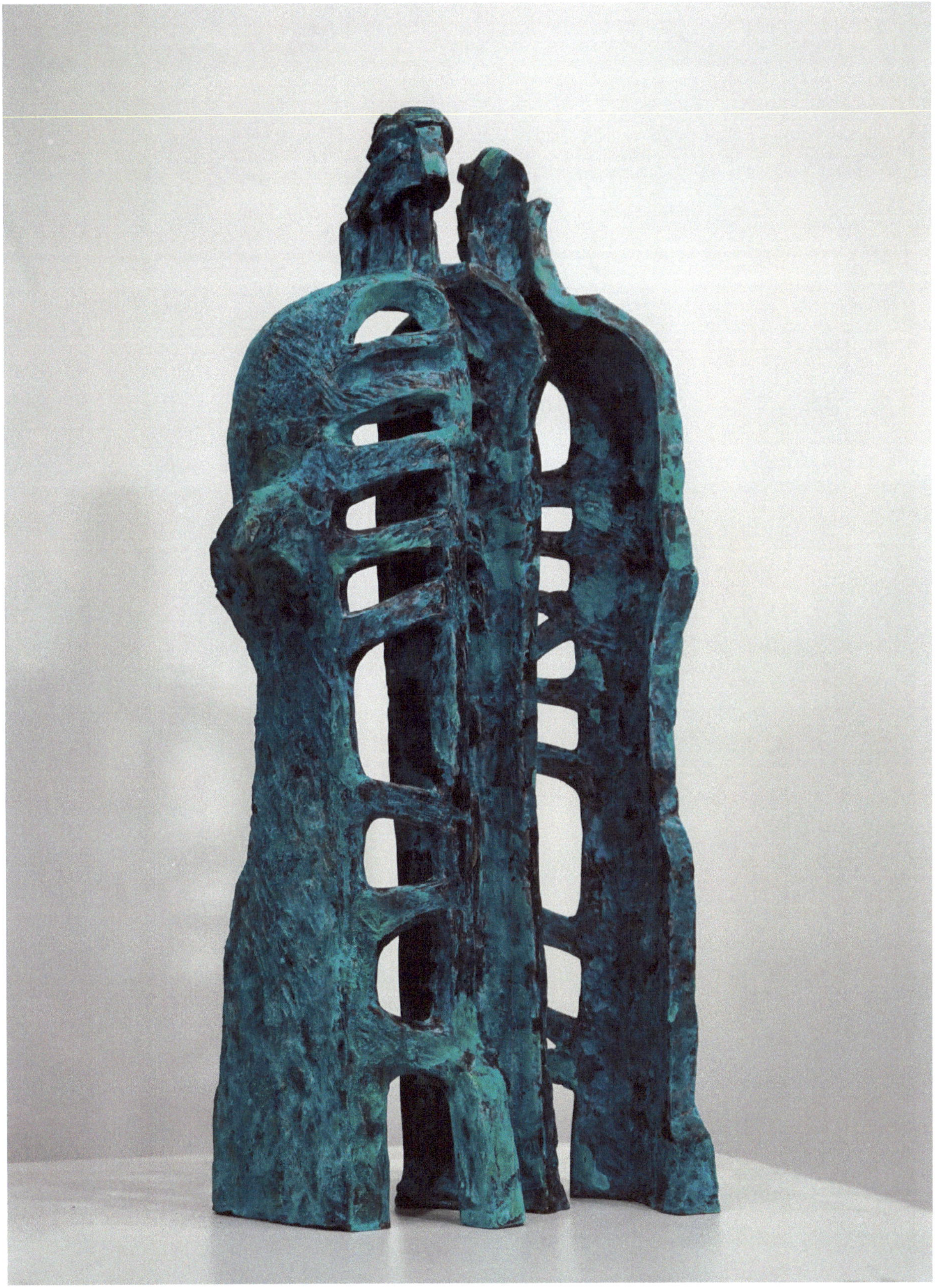

Other Side , 2022

ILYA TROFIMENKO

https://www.ilyatrofimenko.com

My artworks embody visual and emotional states of mind, articulated through a distinctive expressive language that grows out of meta-modernist sensitivity. They abstract and distort motifs from the real world while exploring the tension between the concrete and the abstract, encouraging associative thought.

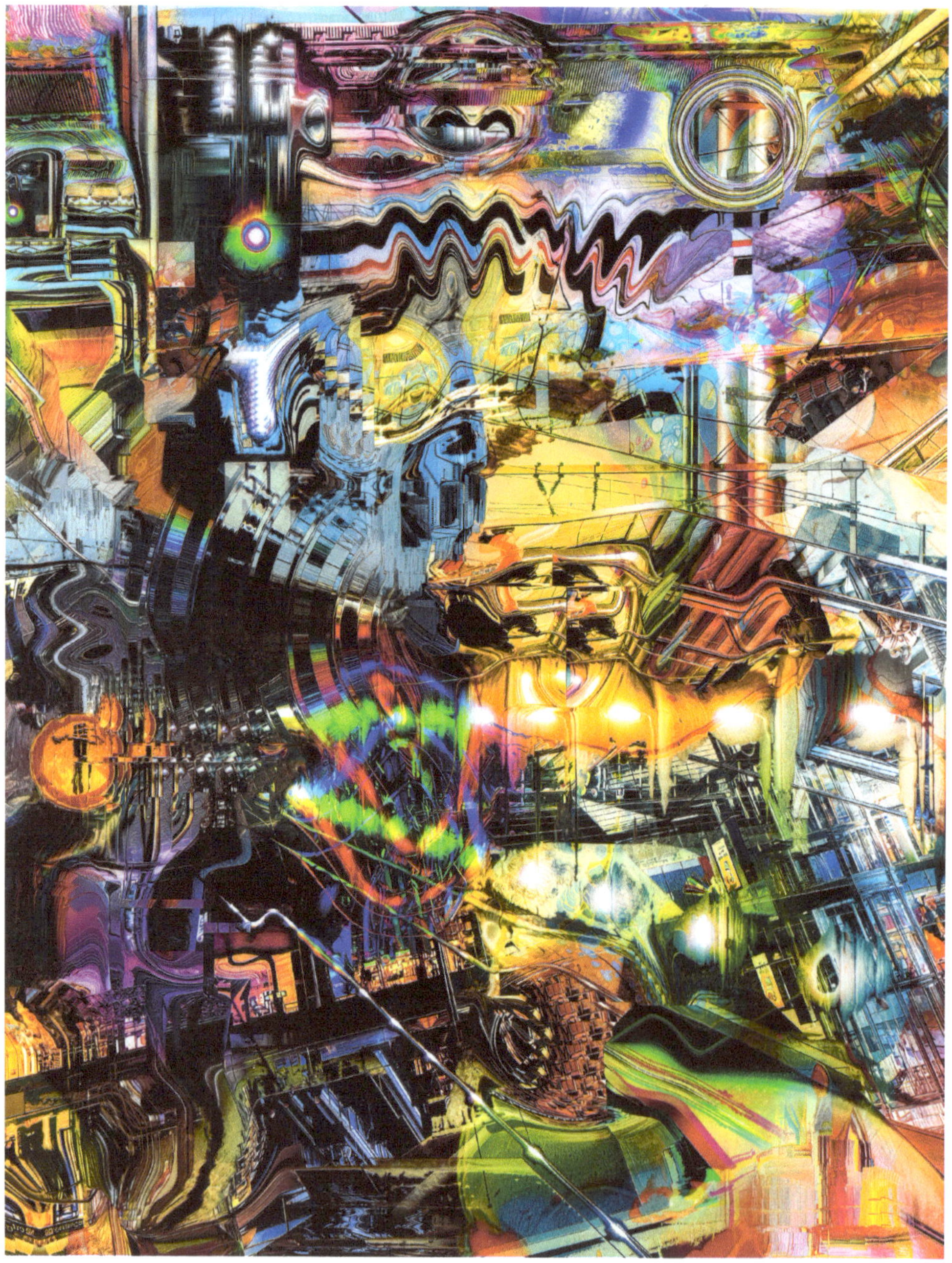

"Before departure", 2025, 120x160 cm

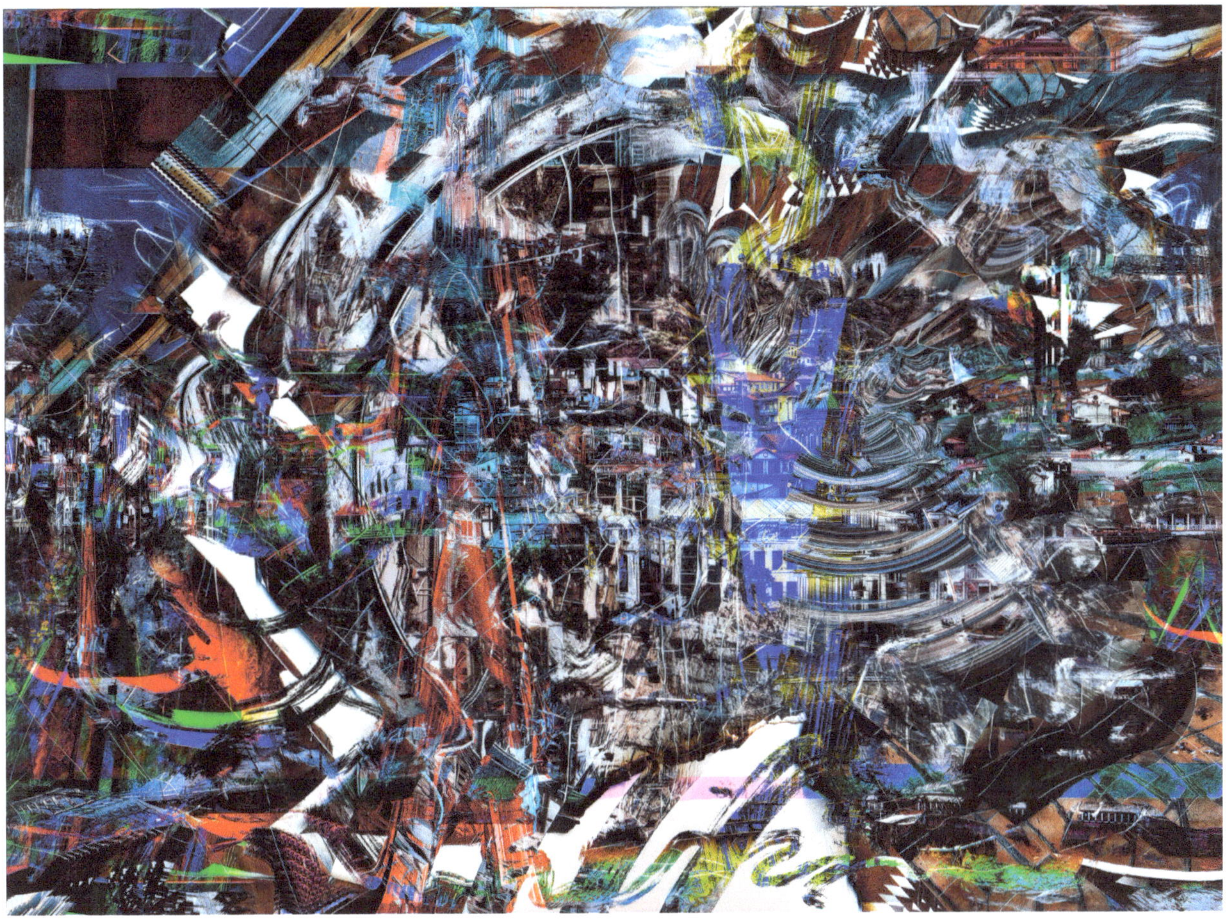

"Dum differtur vita transcurrit", 2025, 150x200 cm

IRIS FLUIDISM

www.iris-fluidism.com

IRIS was born in Romania and has been living in Austria for many years. A graduate of the Faculty of Industrial Design she has worked for many years as a furniture designer. Since 2018 she has experienced a whole new style inspired by the organic forms that fluids create in their movement. She called this new style "IRIS-Fluidism". For artist, her new style IRIS-Fluidism is a tribute to the most fascinating, important and complex fluid on Earth, without which life cannot exist _ WATER. Water is witness to the interconnectedness and interdependence of all living things. For IRIS, water is not only the flow of life, but also an expression of spirituality. It is a sacred gift of inestimable value that we must take care. For she, water is an expression of love and interdependence of all life forms on the planet and in the Universe. Water unites all of creation into a whole of boundless beauty, diversity, and complexity. The water in our body reminds us of the beauty and the unique chance offered to be present in everyday life, to witness the magnificent spectacle of life. Her artworks are composed of intricately organized, organic forms inspired by the movement of fluids. In the bodies of humans, plants and animals, water is found in a proportion of 70% or even higher. Thus, in the summer of 2018, IRIS had the idea of drawing only the liquid part of the bodies without completely destroying their original shape and character. In a person's portrait, for example, their character and inner life can be recognized. An elephant is transformed into a new elephant through a complex ensemble of colors and organic shapes without losing the idea of an elephant. A bird remains a bird without losing the idea of flight. She wants to bring beauty, hope and love to life through her art. IRIS-FLUIDISM is the most important moment in her artistic career. It represents the essence of who she is. It is all about fluidity—everything flows. Fluidity is inherent to the human being, present in both our biological composition and the structure of the society in which we are all immersed. It embodies a powerful communication system with its own language and infinite modes of expression. It reflects a reality that discovers and refines its nature in the liquid state of things. Humanity is immersed in it, carried away by the continuous flow of eternal becoming.

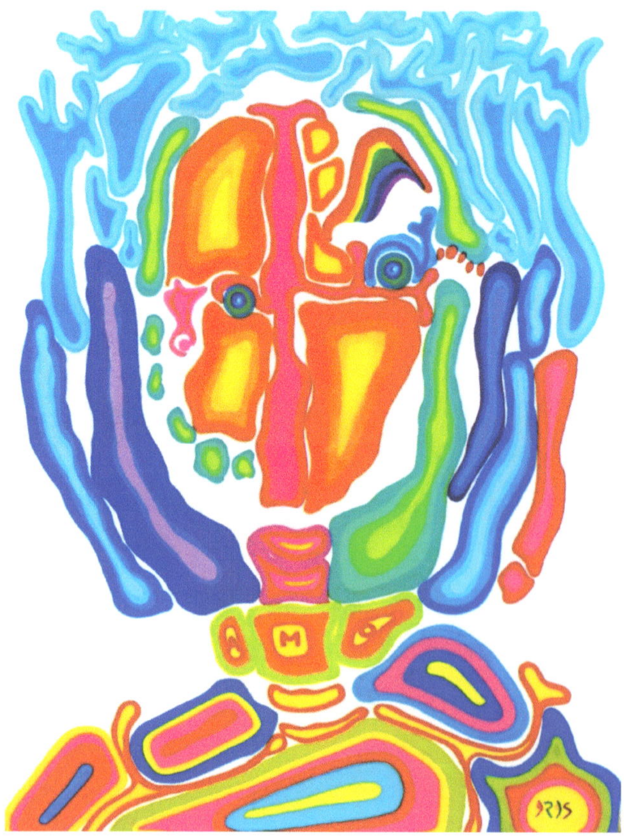

MODERN WOMAN, 2020. Acrylic on canvas, 100x80cm.

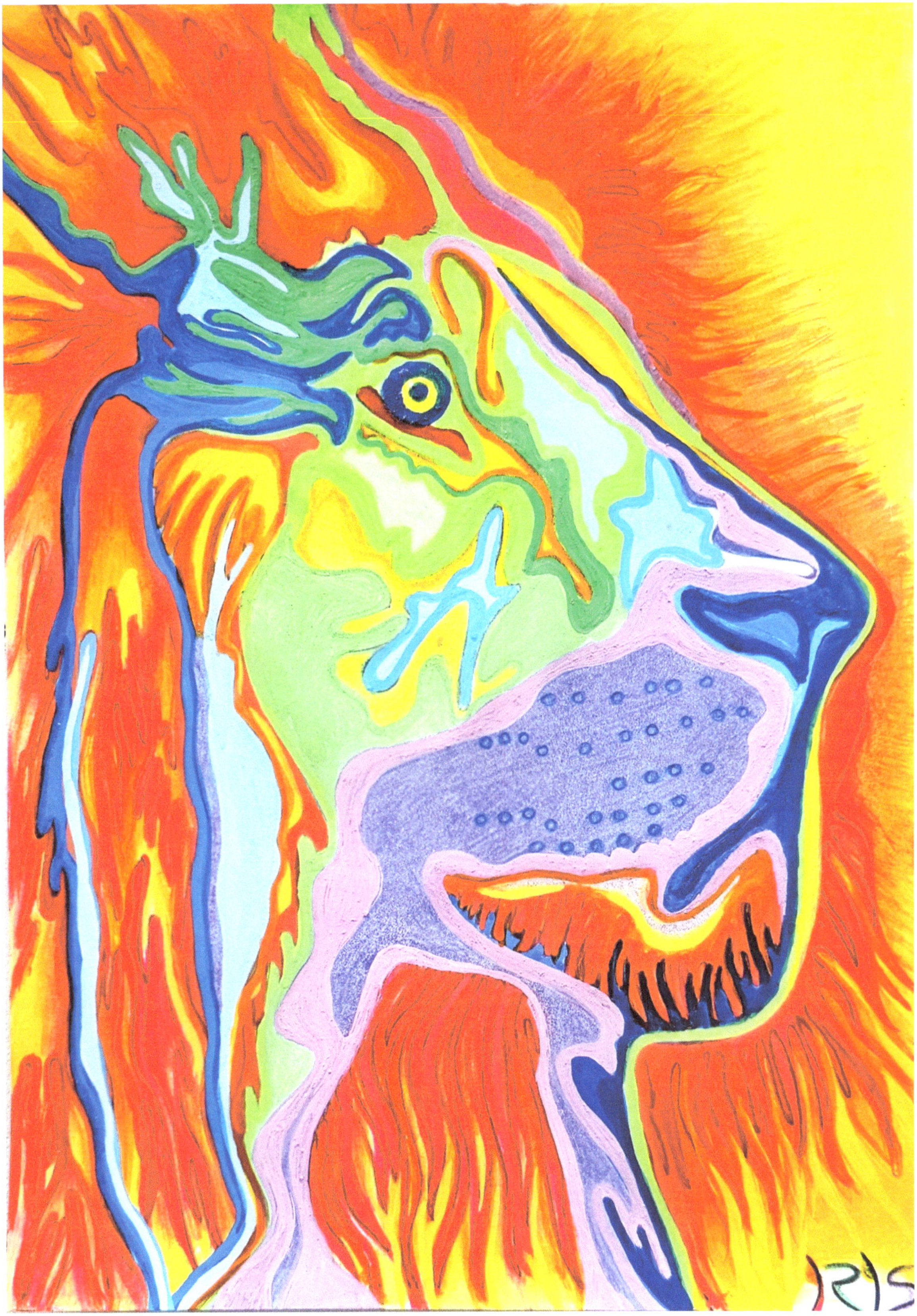

THE LION KING IS BACK. NOBLE AND POWERFUL, 2025. Color pencils and acrylic on paper, 29.7x21cm.

JEREMIAH A. GILBERT

https://jeremiahgilbert.com/

Jeremiah A. Gilbert is an award-winning photographer and travel writer. His travels have taken him to over a hundred countries and all seven continents, while his photography has been published internationally and exhibited worldwide. His artistic journey began not with a map, but with a sense of wonder. His camera has been both compass and confidant, guiding him through bustling markets, remote villages, and landscapes where the horizon feels infinite. His creative vision is rooted in curiosity—seeking out moments that are both intimate and expansive, where the quiet details of a place reveal its deeper story. His photographs are less about ticking destinations off a list and more about tracing the threads of humanity that weave the world together. Inspired by fleeting light, unguarded gestures, and the textures of everyday life, his work captures not just the way a place looks, but the way it feels to stand there, breathe it in, and become part of its unfolding narrative. He is the author of four travel books, including Can't Get Here from There: Fifty Tales of Travel, From Tibet to Egypt: Early Travels After a Late Start, and On to Plan C: A Return to Travel, which documented his return to travel post-COVID and was the first to include his photography. His most recent, Around the World in Eighty Photos, includes images created over twenty years of traveling. Each photo is accompanied with a brief story of how the image was created along with the camera settings used.

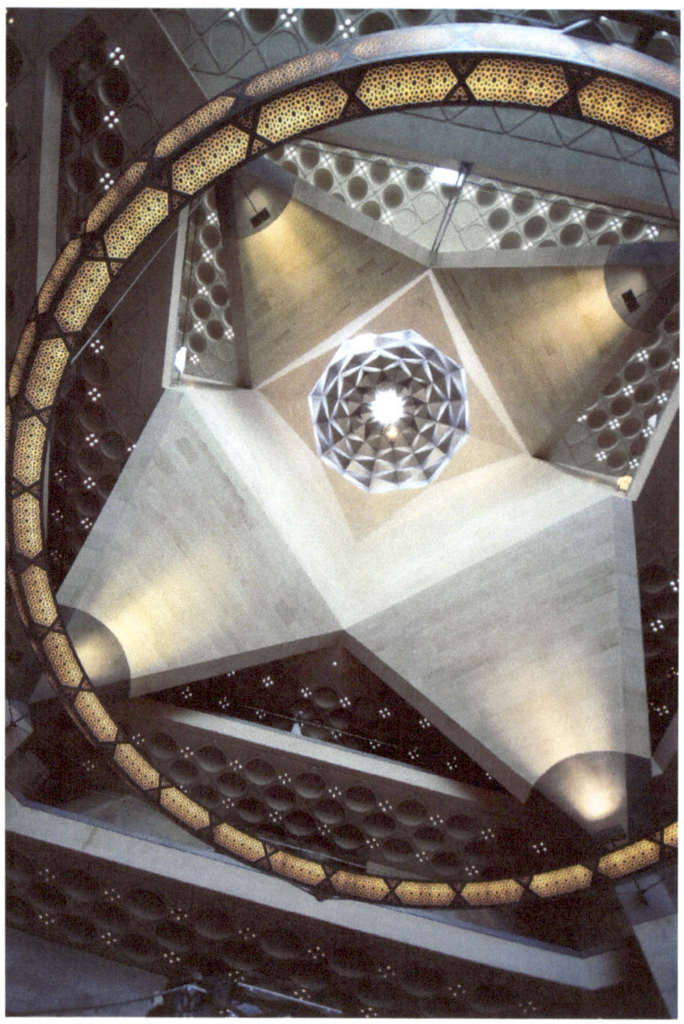

Museum of Islamic Arts, Doha, Qatar, 2015. Photography, 40 x 60 cm.

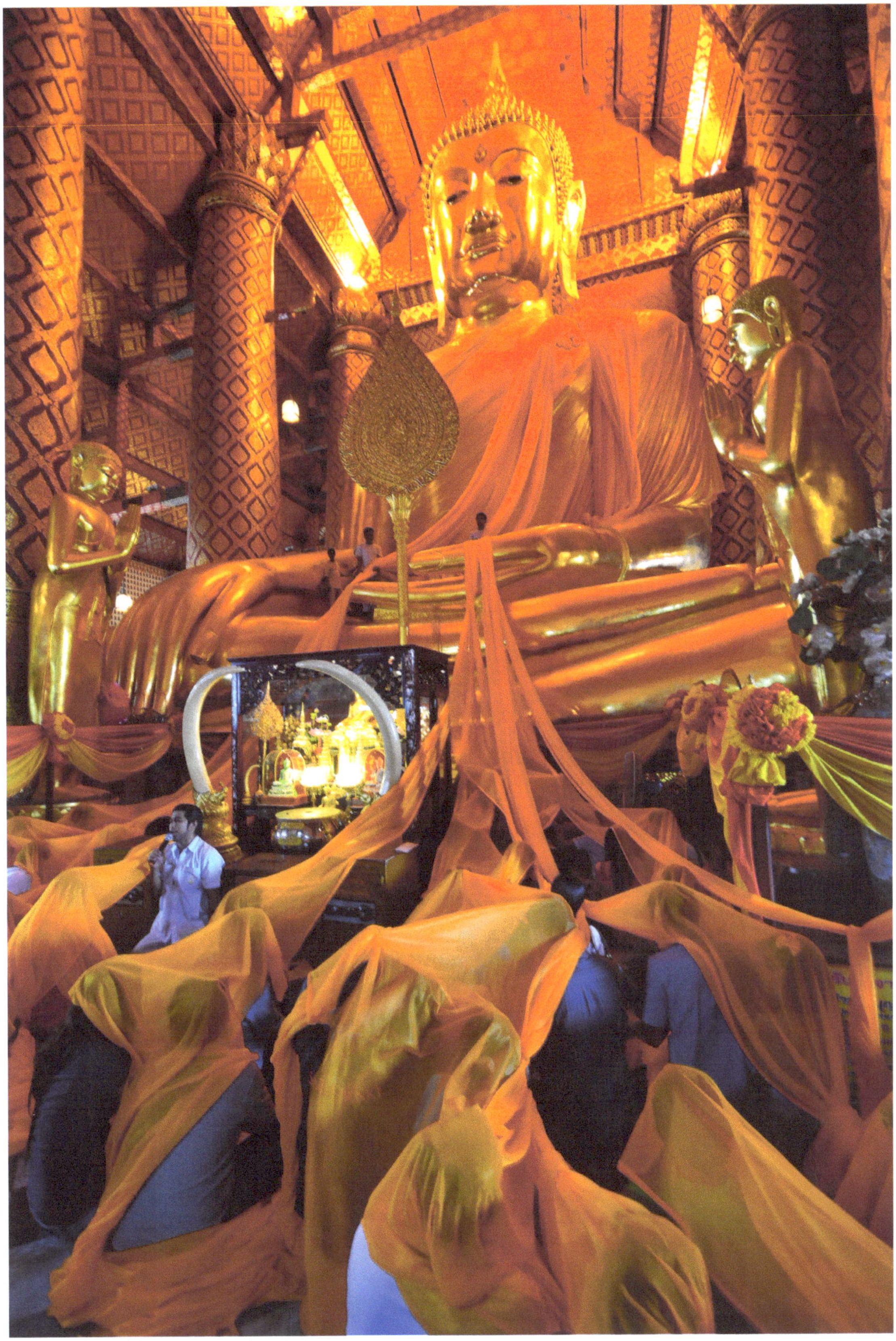

Wat Phanan Choeng, Ayutthaya, Thailand, 2014. Photography, 40 x 60 cm.

JOANNA LEVESLEY

https://joannanouveaustudio.co.uk

Joanna is a self-taught international award winning contemporary ink artist from the UK, inspired and influenced by the surrealistic approach of Salvador Dali and M.C. Escher. She is dedicated to working with abstract, fantasy pieces and aims to explore the beauty of the human spirit through her art. Joanna mainly works with black and white pen and ink drawings as well as acrylic painting, resulting in dramatic and surrealistic compositions that evoke an intricate, mysterious world. As an artist, Joanna believes in using complex lines to create powerful concepts. Her work is driven by a passion to capture the underlying beauty and energy of things by honing into the fundamental line, exploring the limitless possibilities of the imagination. Her drawing doesn't reference the recognisable form. The results are deconstructed to the extent that meaning is shifted and possible interpretation becomes multifaceted. By manipulating the viewer to create confusion, she creates intense personal moments masterfully created luring the viewer round and round in circles.

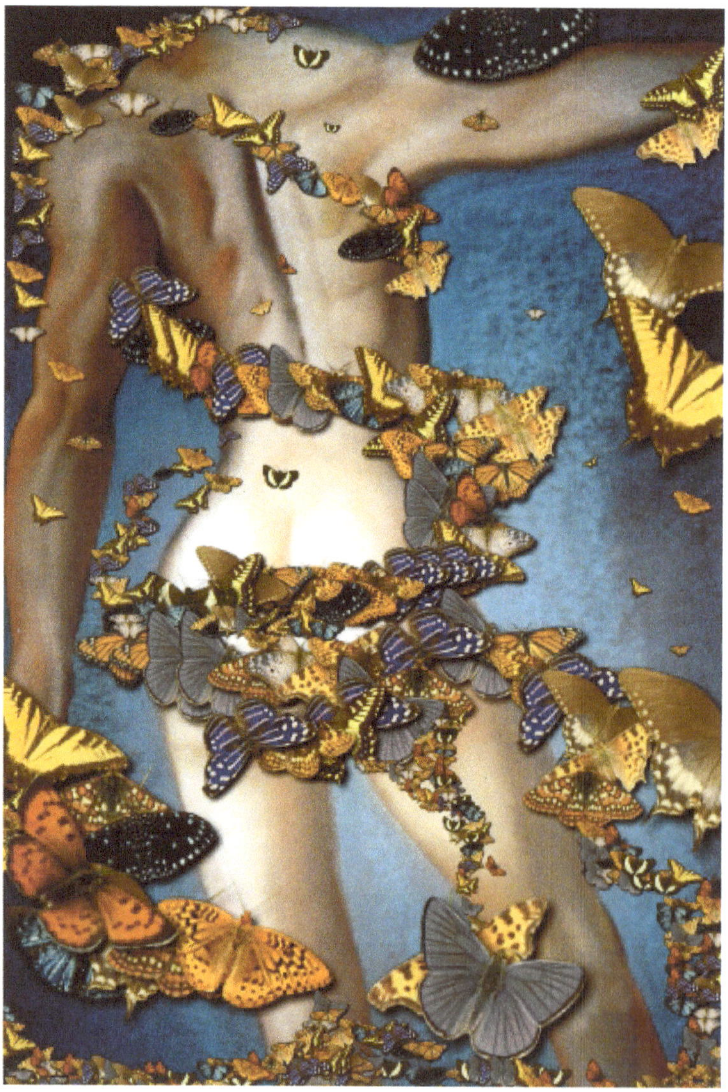

New Beginnings, 2000, mixed media including soft pastel, 84cm x 59cm

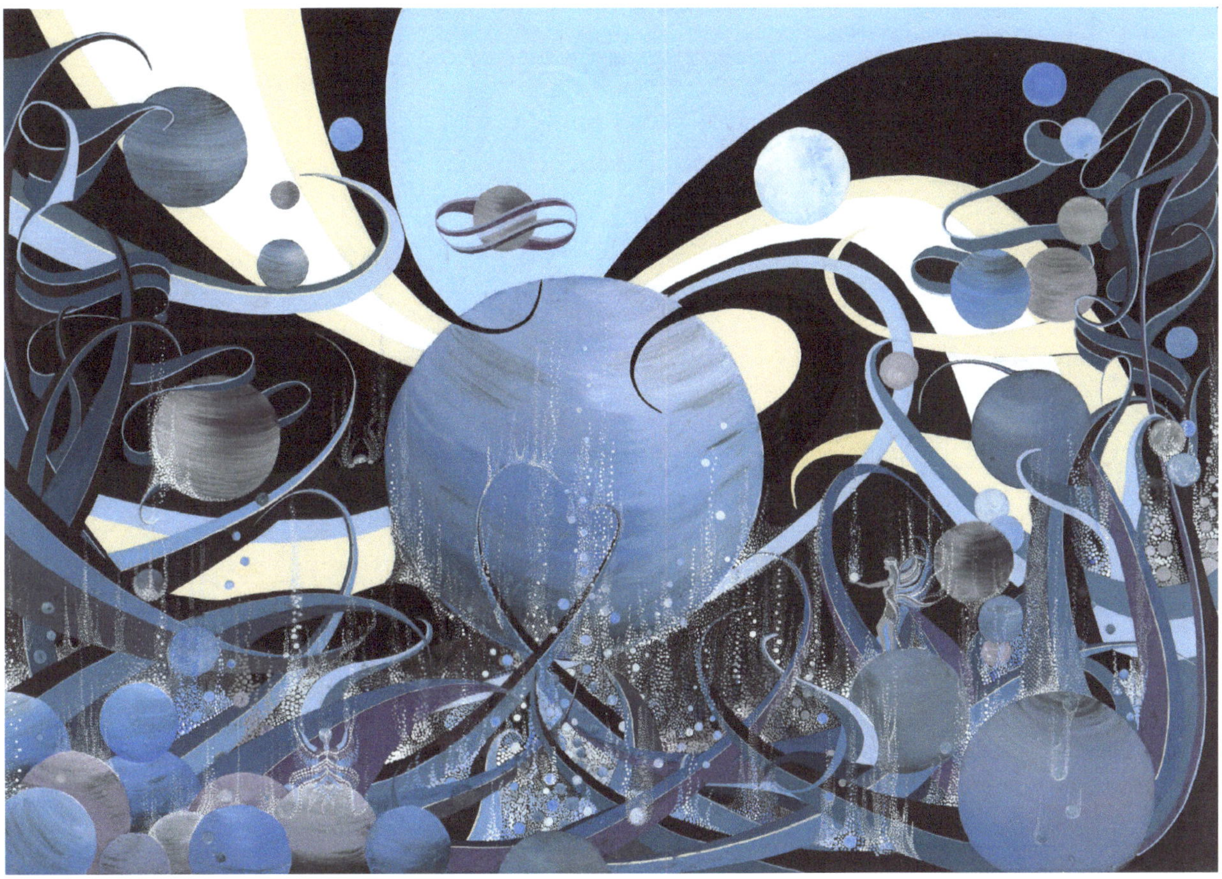

Water Worlds, 2000, pen and ink with acrylic paint, 80cm x 120cm

JORGEN FOLKERSEN

www.volkvard.com

Jørgen Folkersen, also known as Volkvard, began his journey as a visual artist more than 30 years ago. His childhood and youth were filled with drawing and creative exploration. It took approximately a decade before he felt ready to exhibit his work publicly. Over the next two decades, he exhibited primarily within Denmark, showcasing his paintings in regional settings and company-based private art associations. At the age of 63, he chose early retirement in order to fully dedicate himself to his passion for the visual arts. This marked a turning point, as he began to reach out to a broader, more internationally oriented audience. Volkvard adopted an experimental approach early in his career, rarely repeating the same motif. His creative inspiration arises from the complexity of the human emotional universe, particularly social emotions. His previous work in trauma-focused therapy deeply influenced his artistic perspective. He became fascinated by how individuals can experience the same social situations—and the same artwork—in radically different ways. To him, visual art seems to access our social learnings directly, even those we are not consciously aware of. This explains why different people can encounter the same painting and leave with entirely different impressions. The Later Years Volkvard found great liberation in the realization that the experience of art is strictly personal and cannot be reduced to shared rules or universal aesthetics. Since he can only vaguely guess what his viewers experience, he grants himself full freedom to paint according to his own passions—even when the source of those passions remains unknown to him. "The value of an artwork is created in the viewer's mind only." Volkvard believes that emotionally engaging art reflects back our personal learnings. We begin to discover this when we show genuine humility and curiosity about how others experience art. His hope is to inspire viewers to refrain from judging others' emotional responses, and instead cultivate an openness to the richness of diverse emotional lives.

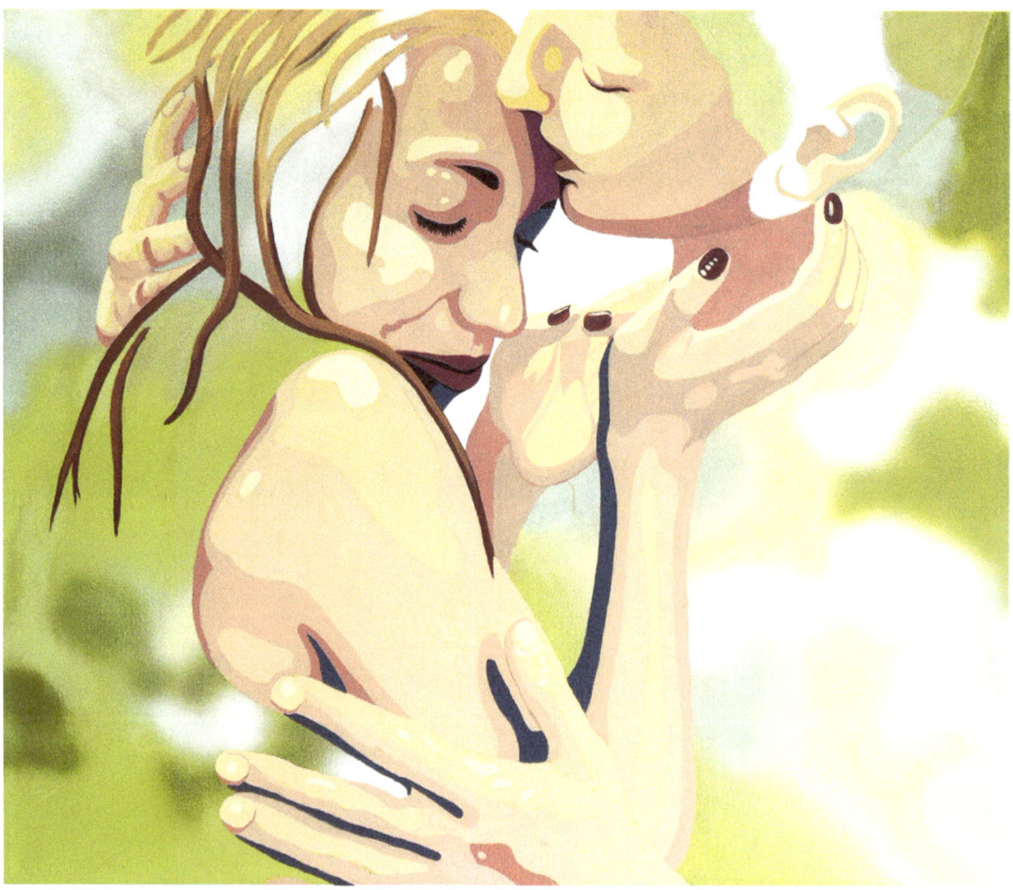

Devotional love,2025, Acryl on canvas, 90x77cm

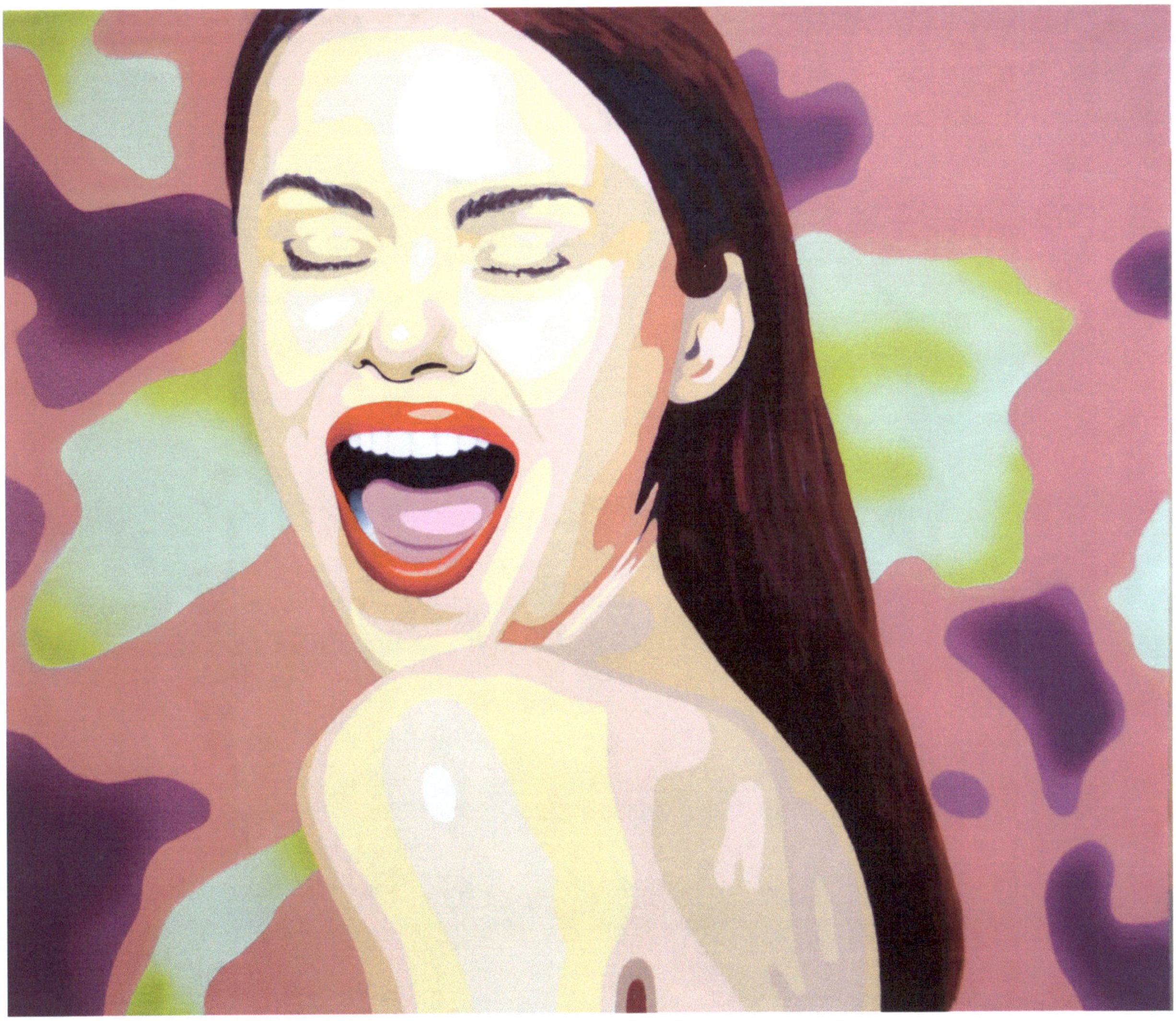

Hilarious,2025, Acryl on canvas, 90x77cm

JOSEF WEIDNER

https://josef-weidner.de

The works of artist Josef Weidner range from bizarre to surreal and vary in content and artistic techniques. His works often explore beings and places that can only exist in the subconscious. Weidner's subjects incorporate elements of the surreal and the inexplicable. He captures mysterious and enigmatic figures in compositions that seem to defy all logic. His landscapes explore the boundaries between reality and imagination, creating new, strange worlds where anything is possible. Weidner's works invite the viewer to explore the unknown, to question their perception of the world, and to enter a realm of unfathomable possibilities. He creates a fascinating atmosphere that allows us to transcend and explore the unknown.

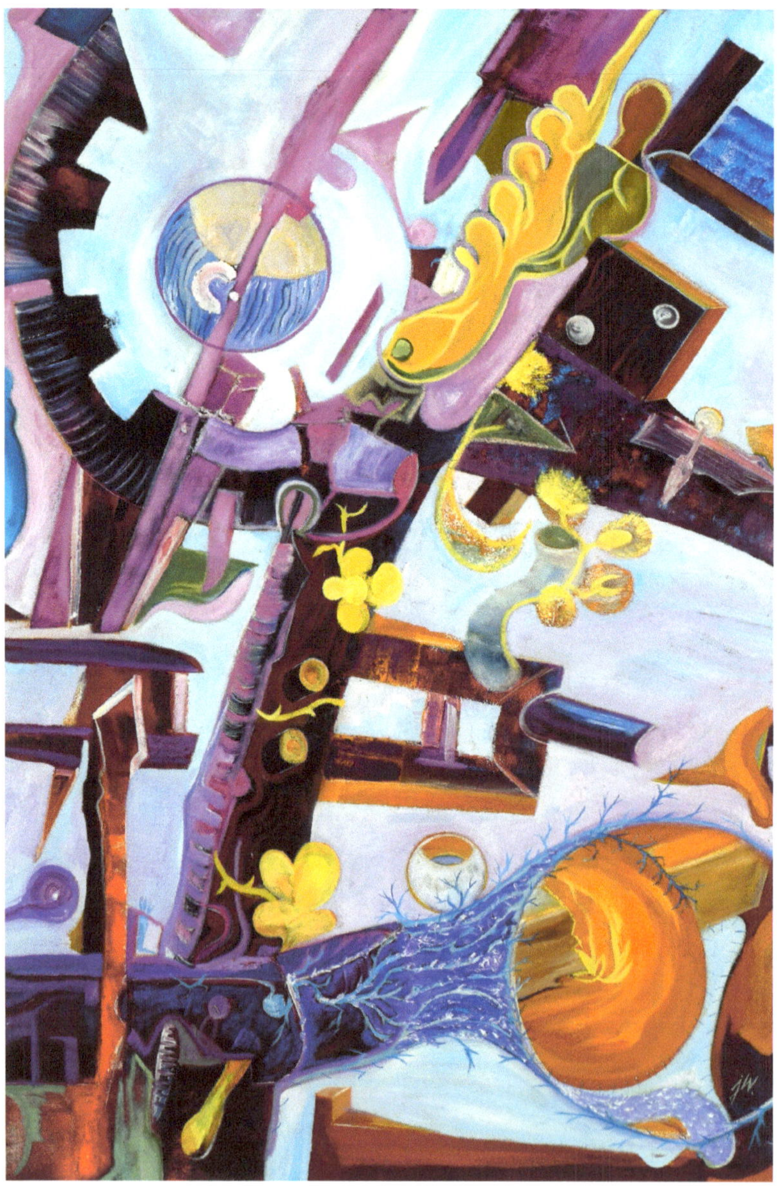

Biologic construction 80 x 120 cm

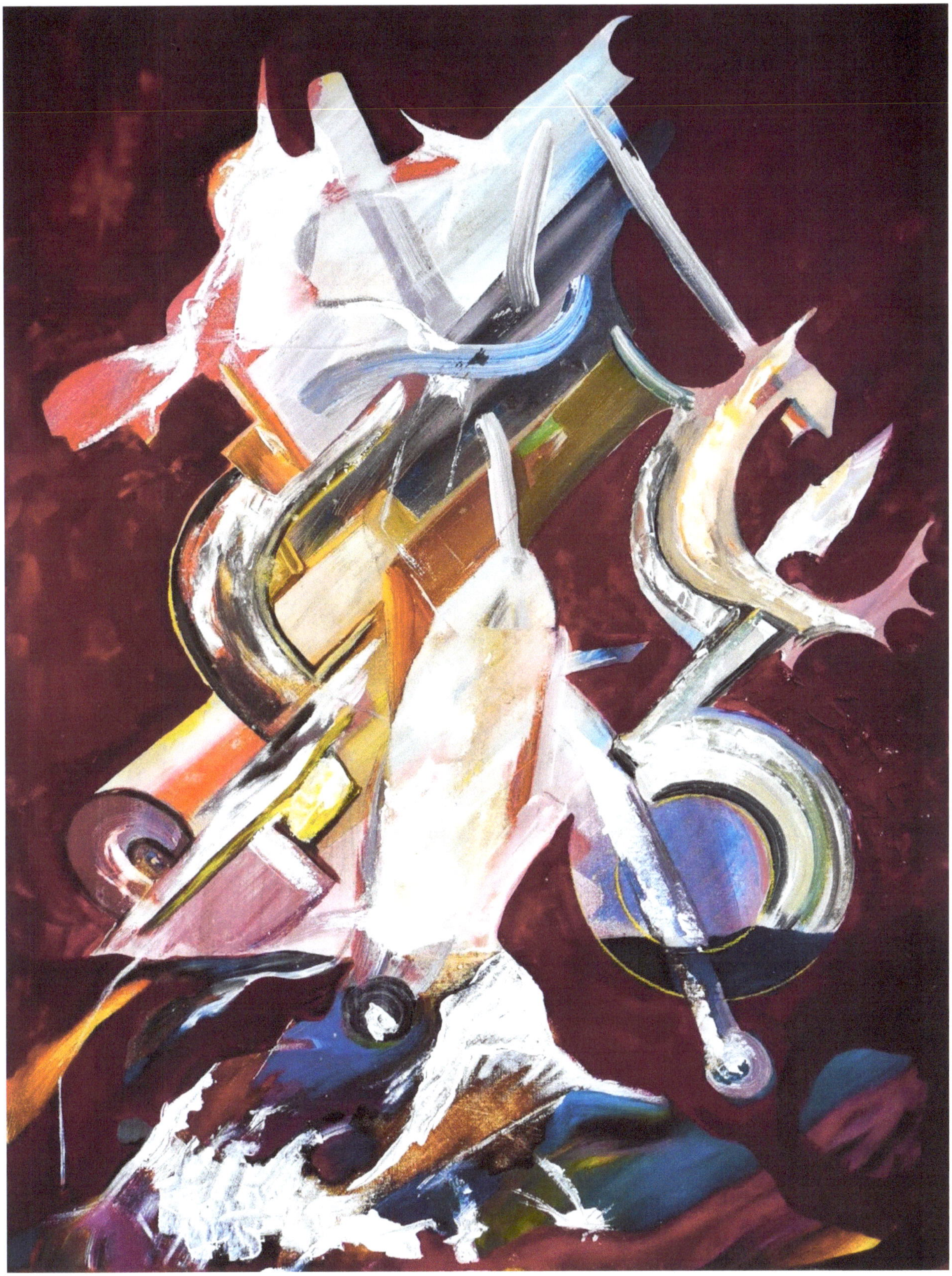

Komposition Acrylic 50 x 70cm

JULIE WAAS

https://www.intuitiveabstractart.com

Julie Reby Waas has been creating abstract drawings for as long as she can remember. It was only during the isolating, stressful time of the Covid pandemic, however, that she began turning her original designs into artwork. She felt a desire to bring joy into her life and the lives of others through creative expression, using bright acrylics & watercolors to create compelling patterns to stimulate the viewer's spontaneous reaction to each one of her pieces. Her geometric shapes and patterns serve as a way to bring order to her sometimes disordered life, and Ms. Waas identifies three recurring symbols in her work: vines, Venn diagrams, and jigsaw puzzle-like designs. To Ms. Waas, these symbols represent friendship, connection, common ground, and fragments coming together to create a bigger picture, which all relate to her belief that everything and everyone is interrelated in some way, and when we come together in friendship and strength we create a beautiful tapestry. Ms. Waas is a resident of Miami, Florida. In addition to creating art, she also is a labor and employment lawyer and a Certified High Performance Coach for midlife & empty nester women. She exhibits work in galleries in New York, London, Madrid, Marbella, Innsbruck and Miami, and is influenced by other geometrically-inclined predecessors like Piet Mondrian and Joan Miró. Her style is certainly her own flavor of bold and unique, successfully achieving her goal of bringing happiness and enthusiasm to each one of her viewers.

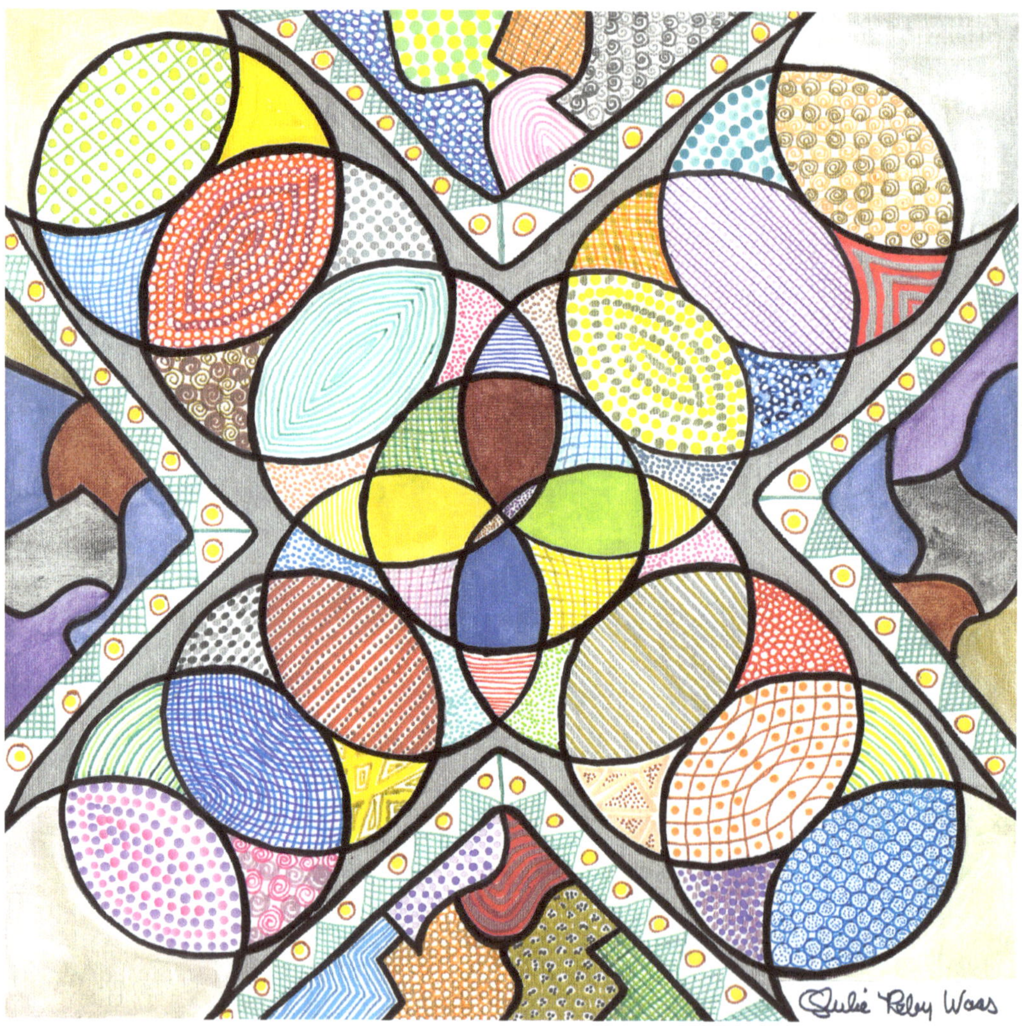

Intersection, 2023, Acrylic & Watercolor on Paper, 44.45 x 44.45

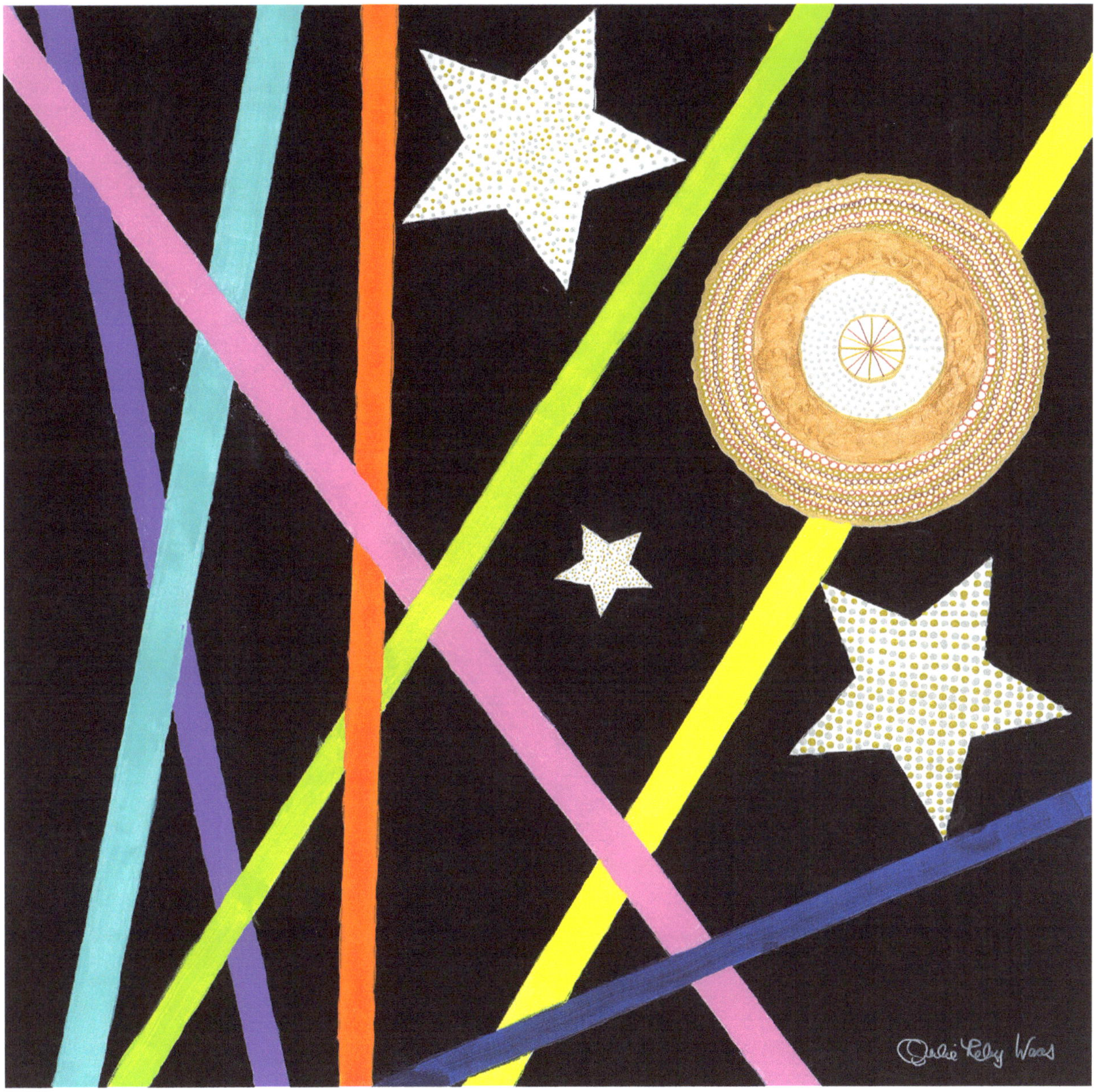

Night Vision, 2024, Acrylic on stretched canvas, 61 x 61

JUDIT SZENDREI

www.juditszendrei.com

Judit Szendrei's artistic journey did not follow the conventional path of early immersion and formal training. She balances multiple roles—an economist by profession, a mother of three, and an artist who discovered her creative passion later in life. While art had always intrigued her, it wasn't until a seemingly simple activity with her daughter Zsofi, who has Down syndrome, loved soaking and drying postage stamps, turning it into a shared pastime. Over time, an extensive collection of similar stamps accumulated, prompting Szendrei to experiment with arranging them into shapes and patterns. What began as a casual activity soon transformed into a deeply fulfilling practice, bringing her both tranquillity and the thrill of crafting something visually striking. Szendrei's work resists easy categorization. It intersects the boundaries of collage, mosaic, and montage, resulting in a technique she refers to as "MoCoMo by Stamps." Unlike many artists who work within a consistent thematic framework, Szendrei embraces fluidity, ensuring that each piece remains a singular expression, unbound by recurring motifs. However, colour plays a unifying role in her portfolio—her works are often strikingly vibrant, composed of countless individual stamps that come together to form intricate visual symphonies.

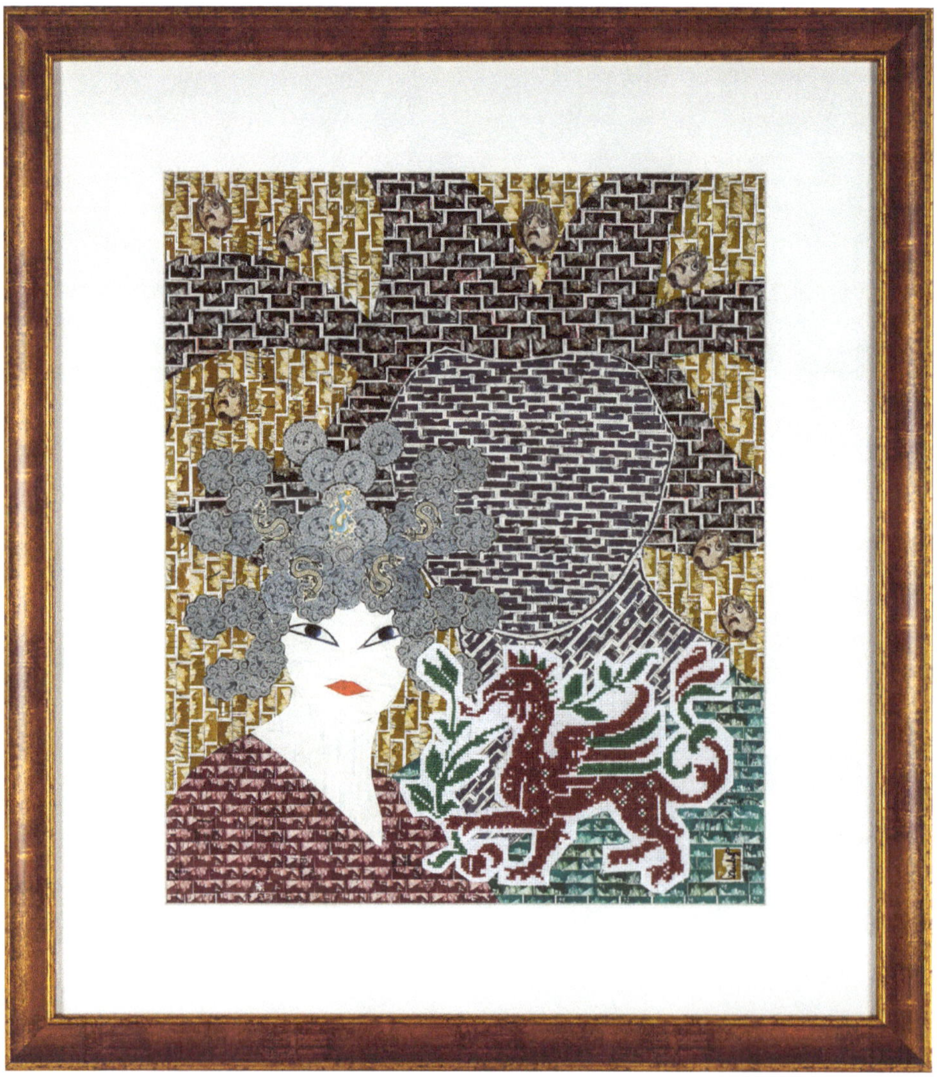

Ghosts of Turandot, 2020, painted by stamps on board, 43 x 52 cm

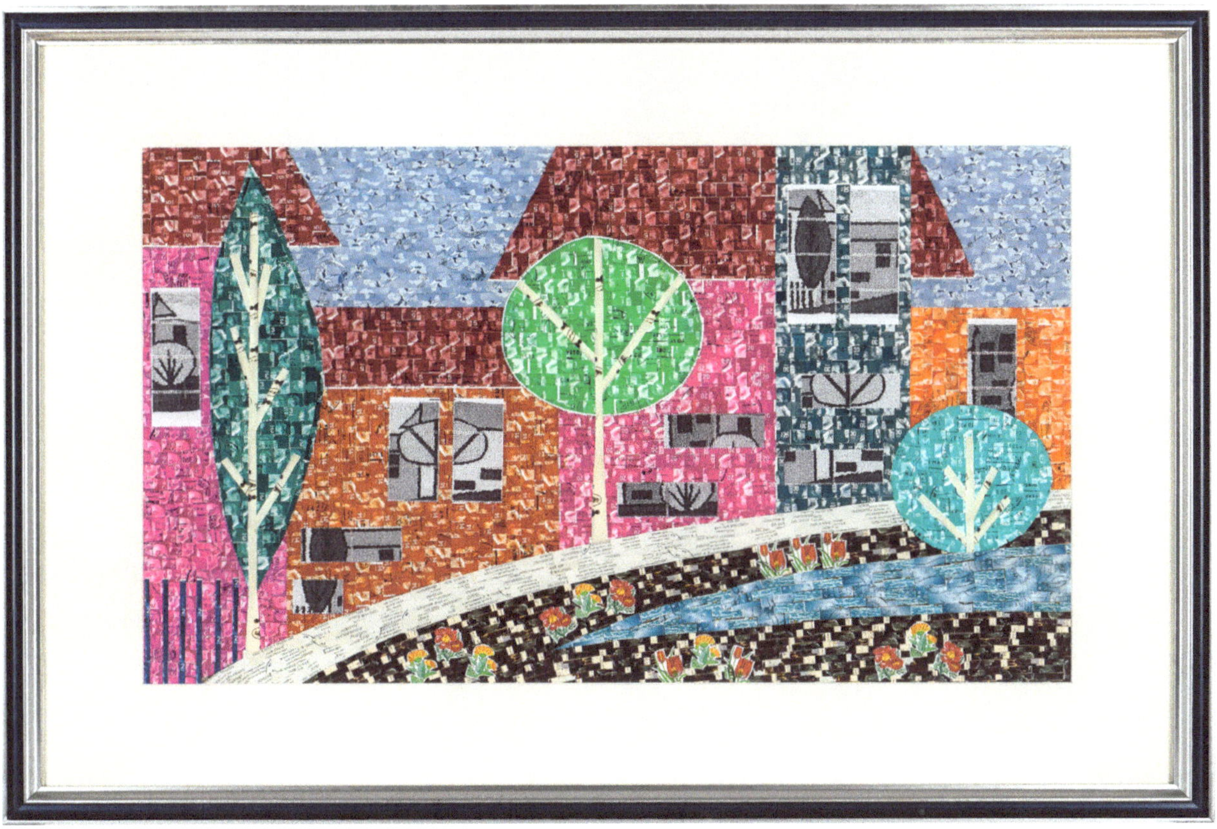

Somewhere in Hungary, 2020, paited by stamps on boards, 70 x 41 cm

KAREL VEREYCKEN

artkarel.com

Born in 1957 in Antwerp, Belgium. Karel graduated from the Institut Saint-Luc in Brussels and trained in engraving at the Académie Royale des Beaux-Arts, where he obtained a certificate of passage "with distinction." In France, as a member of the Fédération nationale de l'estampe, he confirmed his technical mastery at Atelier63 and continued to perfect his skills in the Paris workshop of Danish engraver Bo Halbirk. Karel's parents worked in the port and the ship repair industry. Their adolescence, studies and careers were reduced to zero by the war period and the need to bring an income and feed their brothers, parents and family. So his parents thought their children should have the occasion to fully enjoy and explore the cultural dimensions. The artists mother, who was prevented by the war to become an opera singer, got Karel into a music school. But at that time, the teaching methods, basically learning to read scores for two years before ever being allowed to sing, were so repugnant that he ran away from that. As an alternative, his mother sent him to a communal drawing school directed by a talented sculptor named Herman Cornelis. The bearded cigar-smoking giant would rip pages out of old books and stick them in Karel's hands saying "copy this!" At age 12, Karel won my first art prize and his teacher convinced his mother "there was precious talent" in him. With that advice, his mother sent him to Brussels to attend the Saint Luke Art School and study Plastic Arts. He then continued another two years at the Ecole Royale des Beaux Arts of Brussels to study copper engraving and got graduated "with distinction." Karel then moved to Paris and worked as a journalist and editor of a non-commercial militant paper. But after some years, he found out art was really lacking in his life so he returned to it. First by producing copies of old masters painting on wooden oak panels with hand-made egg tempera, venitian turpentine and various other ancient oil techniques he rediscovered with a an old schoolmate. Later he gave a three year course of drawing for friends. What always attracted Karel in painting and imagining is the way art "makes visible" things and ideas that are "not visible" as such in the simple visible world but which "appear" in the minds of the viewer. It took the artist over twenty years to sort out the difference between "symbols" (a "convention" accepted among a group or a code system designed to communicate a secret meaning), and "metaphor" which by assembling things unusual, by irony and paradox, allows the individual mind to "discover" the meaning the painter intended to transmit. Such an approach offers the joy of discovery and surprise, a deep human quality. Modern art started as a non-figurative form of symbolism till "contemporary" art brought many artists to put an axe into the very idea of poetical meaning. In 1957, the CIA sponsored, under various covers and often without the artists even knowing about it, many "abstract" artists to promote a form of art that it considered coherent with its ideology of "free enterprise." But what inspires Karel is true human culture, be it Chinese landscape painting of the Song dynasty, the Greco-Buddhist sculptures of Gandhara, the early hilarious Flemish masters such as Quinten Matsys or the magnificent bronze heads of Ifé in current Nigeria. Bridging the distances in space and time, religion and philosophy, stands the celebration of unique human capacities, that of compassion, empathy and love. Karel says he doesn't pursue themes, they pursue him ! His aim, as an esthetic pedagogue, is to shock people by showing them that nothing is more "modern" and "revolutionary" than "classical" art, not understood as annoying academic formalism, but as a science of composition based on non-cynical, liberating ironical poetical metaphors, who are the key to all forms of art be it in the domain of the visual arts or music. Art is always a "gift" from the artist to the viewers, says Karel, and the act of giving is an act of love. That is the message.

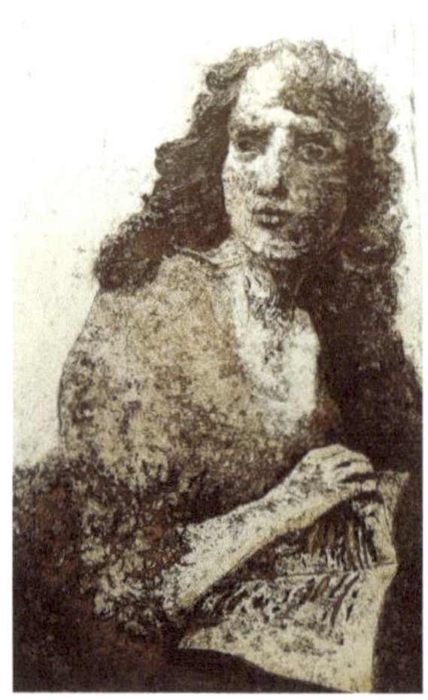

Who is there? (detail) Sugar etching on zinc, 2023, 40 x 60 cm.

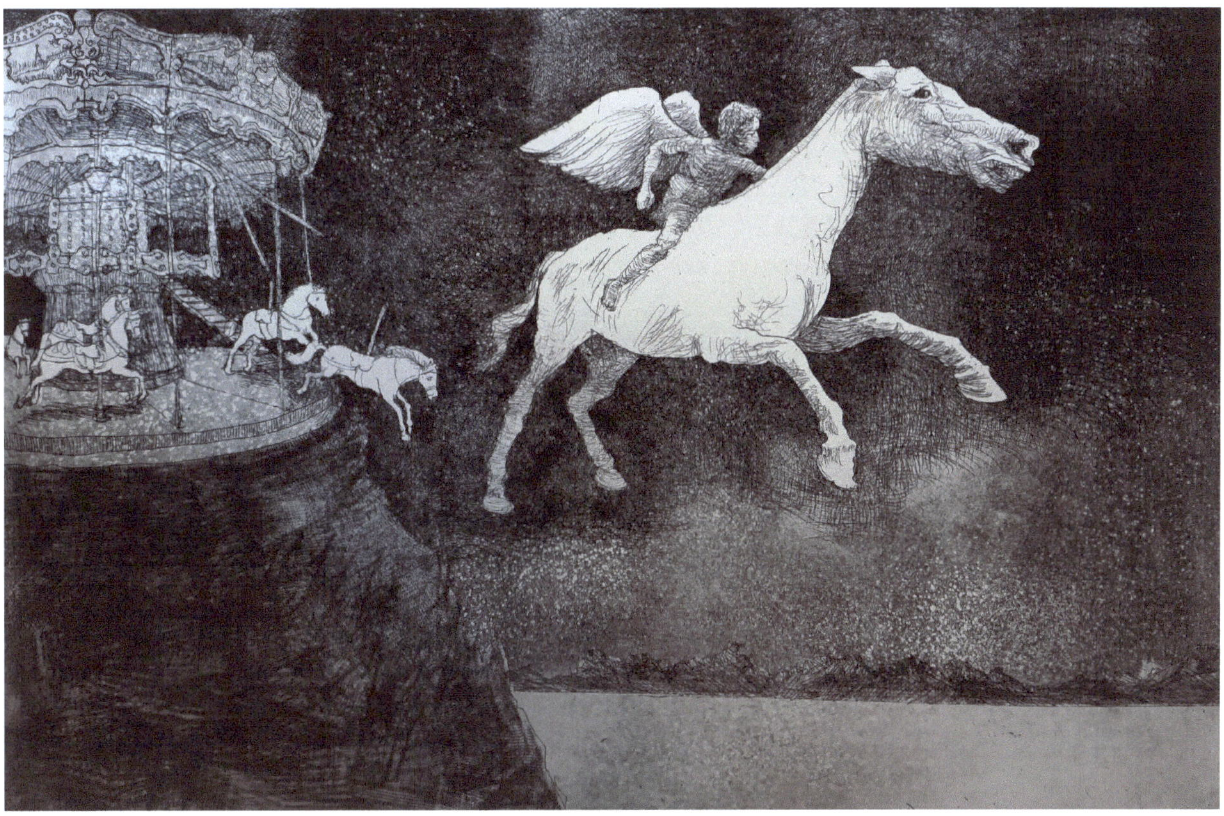

End of Melancolia, 2023, etching on zinc, 80 x 60 cm

KAREN CONNOR

www.karenconnorauthorartist.ca

Biography A selling artist, Karen Connor appreciates the small details in life and uses those details to breathe realism into her art. Precision is the name of her game and Connor has over 25 years experience perfecting her craft. The greater the detail, the greater her satisfaction is, in her work. No detail is overlooked, the lines on the petals of a flower, the light that hits an eye, a piece of hair or fur, are all placed meticulously to make her paintings as real as possible. From a young age, Connor examined how light and shadows created different effects on various subjects, such as the light coming in through a window touching sections of the floor, the curtains, the furniture or parts of a body if someone was in the room. She would follow patterns and shapes, with her eyes, that appeared on vinyl flooring and see shapes and cartoon like caricatures, the same as when you look at the clouds. Connor was always interested in color, and when she was a child, she would try all the shades of one color, in a big box of Crayola crayons, to discover the subtle visual differences between each shade. This skill, learned many years ago, helps her mix many shades of similar paint colors today, to create beautiful effects in her paintings. Artist Statement In a world that sometimes seems bleak, getting lost in a piece of art can bring you peace.

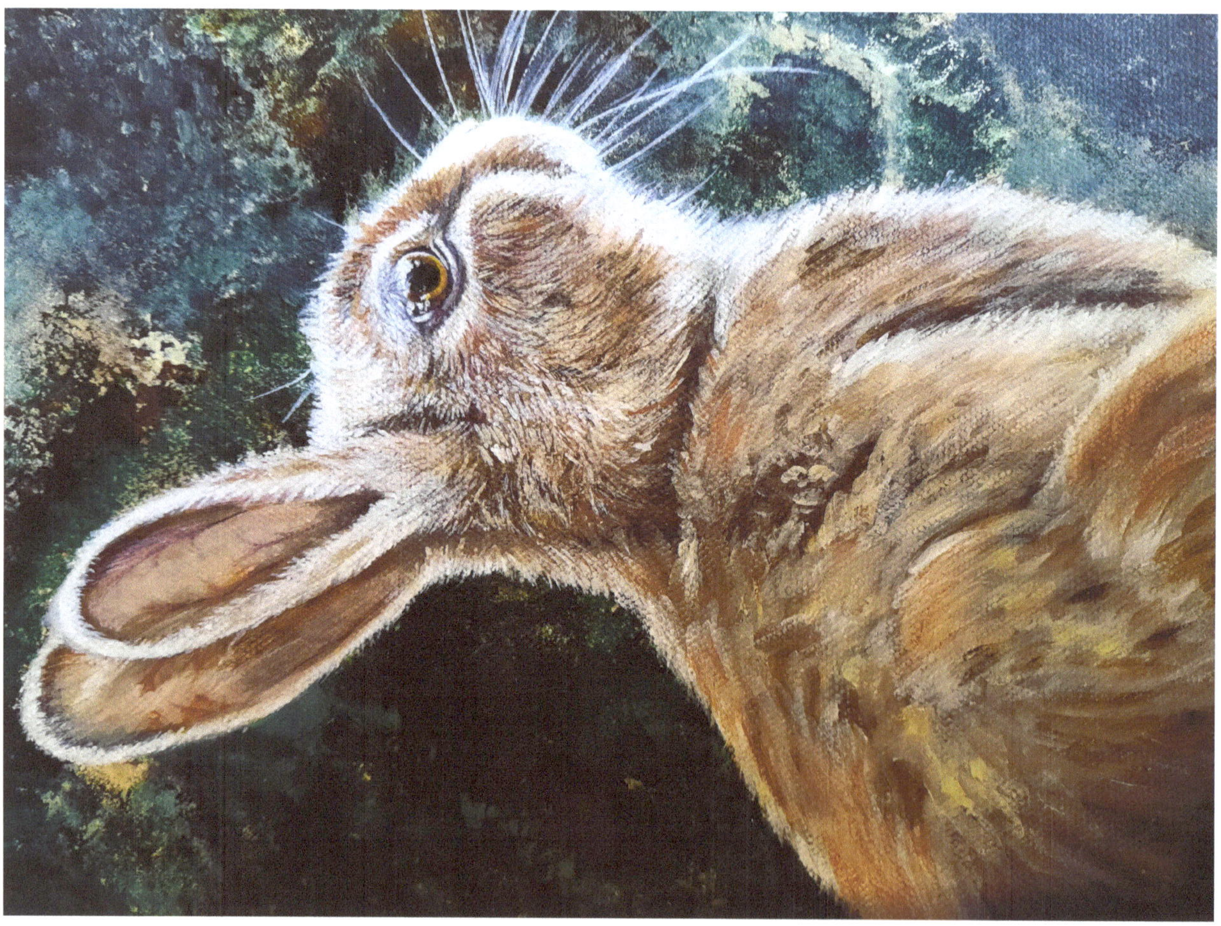

Forest Friend, 2023. Acrylic on canvas, 20.3 cm x 25.4cm

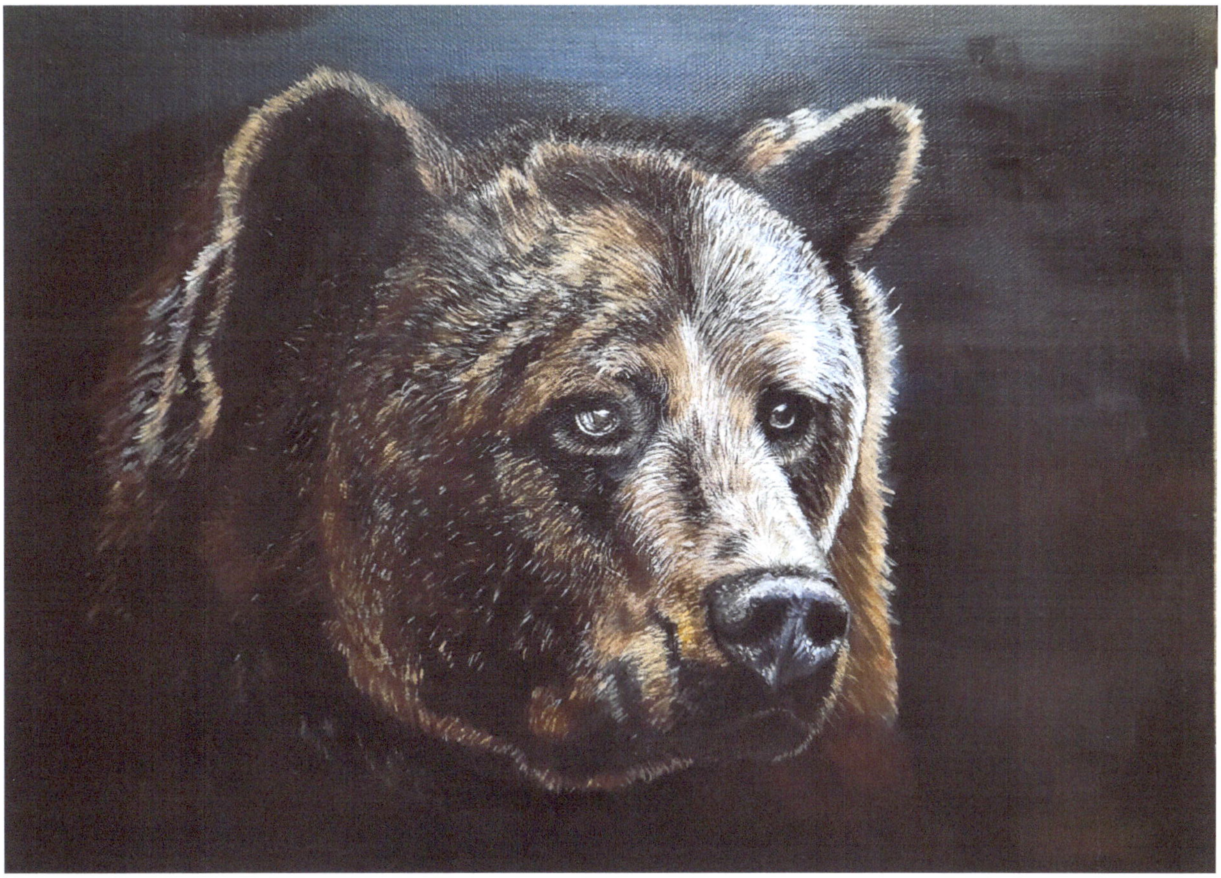

Out of the Dark, Into the Light, 2023. Acrylic on canvas, 35.56 x 27.94 cm

KAT KLEINMAN

kat@katkleinmanart.com

Kat Kleinman is a photographer and collage artist from the Sacramento, California area. She began her career as an artist in 2016, after she retired as a psychotherapist, working with homeless people for 20 years. Her past work is referenced because it does inform her current work with a focus on positivity and making people feel better with each new work. Kat began by specializing in floral collages, because the individual flowers combine to create a new and cohesive form, reflective of the healing process. She takes her own photographs, which is important to Kat, unless a photo is donated by a personal friend. Each image is hand cut, a process she calls meditative, and a single photo collage may require dozens of flowers, succulents and/or leaves. Kat is enthusiastic about the potential for color to positively influence emotions, ultimately leading to better relationships between people.

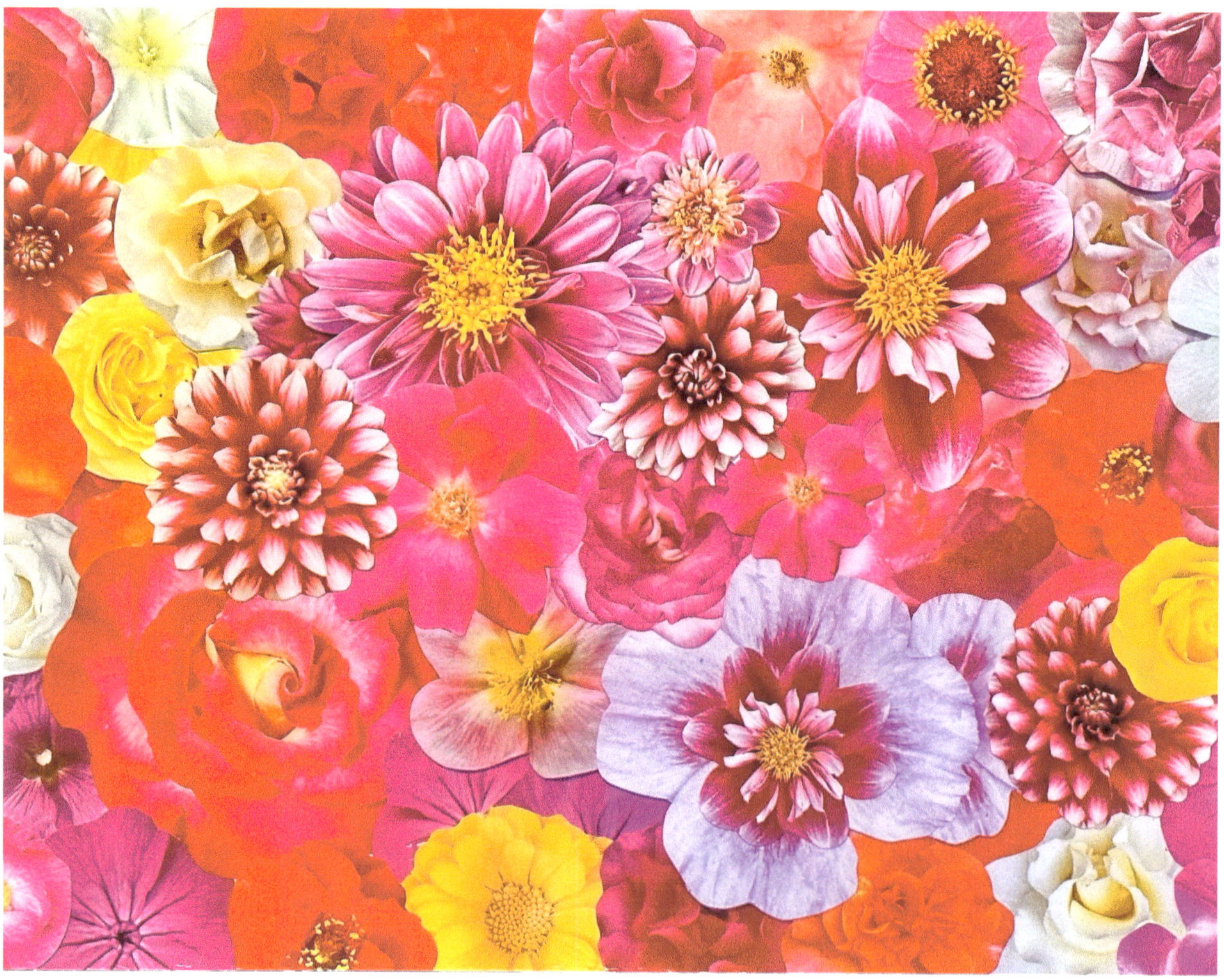

The Gift, 2025

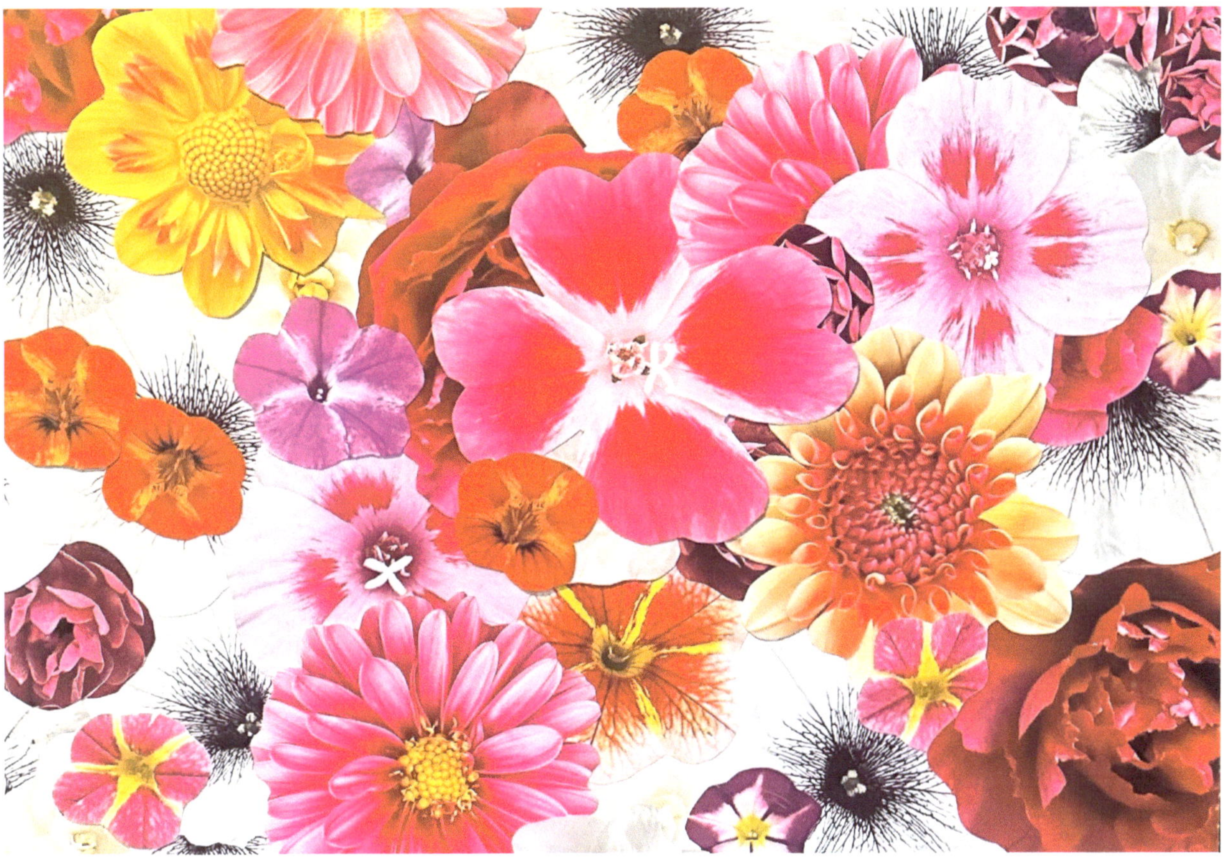

Cross My Heart, 2025

KATHARINA DR.GOLDYN

www.goldyn.de

Goldyn is more than an artist. She is a seer, a scholar, a survivor-and above all, a radical storyteller. Her artistic journey, forged through years of voluntary exile in the forests of Lower Bavaria, is as much about transformation as it is about creation. From raw nature she shaped her palette; from silence she drew her voice. Her works carry the weight of myth, the urgency of activism, and the intimacy of spiritual confession. At a time when the art world is finally reckoning with the erasure of feminine narratives, Goldyn's reimaginings of Mary Magdalene, Junia, and the "New Human" offer a revolutionary lens. Through sculpture, installation, and performance, she gives voice to the voiceless, body to the divine, and breath to long-buried truths. Her presence during at the 60th Venice Art Biennale with The Walk-in Picture - Maria Magdalena confirmed what insiders have long known: Goldyn is not just part of the conversation- she's leading it. In Goldyn, we found a woman who not only walks that path-but builds it, with thorns, stone, faith, and fire. She is not just an artist to watch. She is an art- ist to witness. From a remote Bavarian forest to the gilded salons of the Venice Biennale, Polish-born artist and academic Goldyn has forged an artistic language that is both mythic and revolution- ary-a deeply personal iconography of liberation, faith, and female power. A name whispered among collectors and scholars alike, Goldyn does not mnerely create art. She manifests worlds. Each piece a ritual. Each canvas an invocation. A professor, researcher, and visionary, she is that rare kind of artist who does not just challenge societal norms-she shat- ters them. Currently based in Munich, she is the soul behind Studio Zeiler, one of the city's oldest private art institutions. But her path to international acclaim--recently culminating in ap- pearances at Art3f Paris 2025 and a solo show at the Palazzo Cancelleria Vaticana in Rome-was far from linear. If anything, it has been a wild. piritual odyssey through darkness, resilience,and revelation.

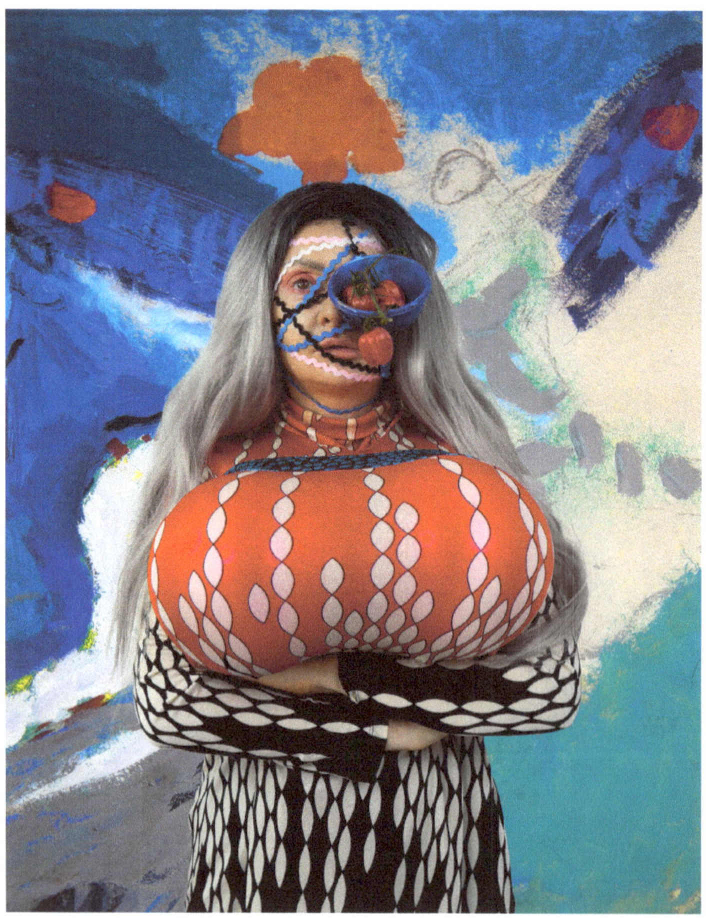

Junia and Moderne, 2024, Photography, 120x80cm

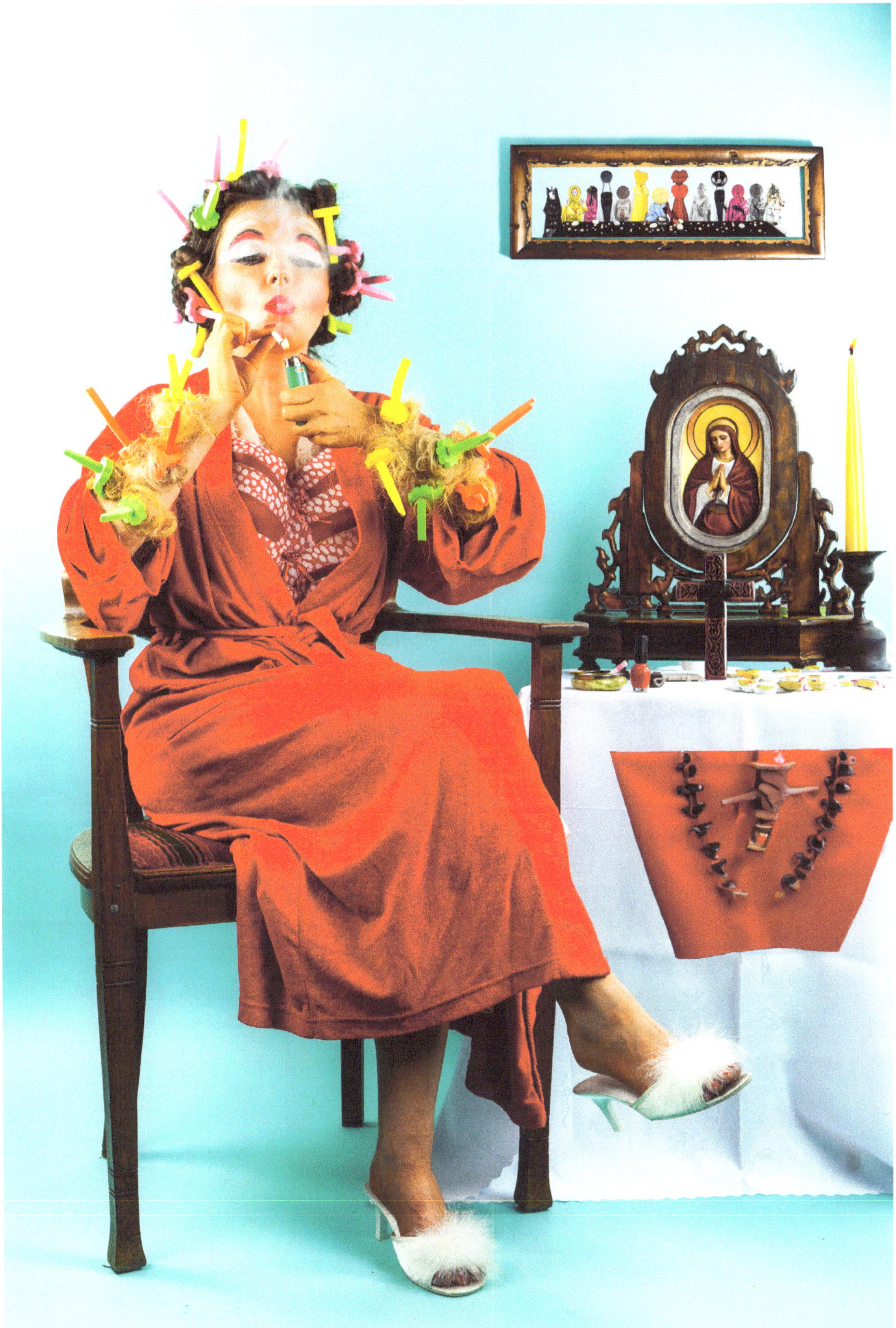

Maria Magdalena-Bussines woman, GOLDYN 2017-2023, Photography 150x100

KATJA LÜHRS

www.katjaluehrs.com

Born in: Germany
Media: Oil painting and digital art
Describe your art in three words: Wonder World Nature
The motto for your paintings: "Save the earth
Instagram: https://www.instagram.com/katjaluehrs/
Presenter: for the TV stations: ZDF - ARD - RTL - SAT 1 - ORF
Fashion and jewelry design: Katja Lührs Design
Author of the books: Viva Veggie and Smoothie Fit

Exhibitions Art:
ARTHOUSE Munich - ARTBOX World 1.0 - The Hub Munich – ARTBOX Basel - Barcelona – Madrid - Galerie Azur Brussel – London - ART MUC Munich - Discovery Artfair Frankfurt - ARTe Wiesbaden - ARTBOX Zurich - Miami Artweeks U.S.A. - Lelie Galerij Amsterdam Netherlands - Casa Del Arte Palma Spain - Thomson Gallery Zug Switzerland - Los Angeles ART LAB U.S.A. - Johnathan Schultz Gallery Miami U.S.A.-. Las Vegas - Biennale Venezia Italy -Las Vegas - NewYork Artweeks U.S.A. – Hongkong - Tokyo Tower Art Fair

Awards:
ITSLiquid Group (ITS) Artist oft he year 2022/2024 – Winner Museum oft he Americas U.S.A. 2024 and The Premier Artist Prize 2024 – Global Art Virtuosu Elite Artistic Award 2024 - Finalist Circle Arts 2023 – Winner Global Future of Art 2024 - Harmony for Humanity the Global Consciousness Art Prize 2023 – Winner Collectors Art Prize Planet Future 2023 – Artbox World Winner 2020 – 2021 – 2022 with the painting „Color Sound – Summerdreams – Save the Earth – Blue Night Fog – Rainbow and Moments - The Premier Artist Prize 2024 – 2 Covers in the HIDDEN TALENTS ART MAGAZIN 2024/2025 and 2 Covers in the ARTMagazine „ARTPROFIL" November 2020 and August 2023 and Cover Curator Art Magazin 2025 and Cover Spotlight Circle Art Magazin 2025 and Cover Artist Journey Magazine 2025

Statement:
The variety of colors and shapes of flowers, trees and leaves has fascinated me since I was a child. The power of the sun and its play with light and shadow in nature are characterized by: "grace - joy of life - confidence - peace and serenity". With pictures you can capture the beauties of nature. Because what you love, you also protect. That's why my motto for my pictures is: "Save the earth".

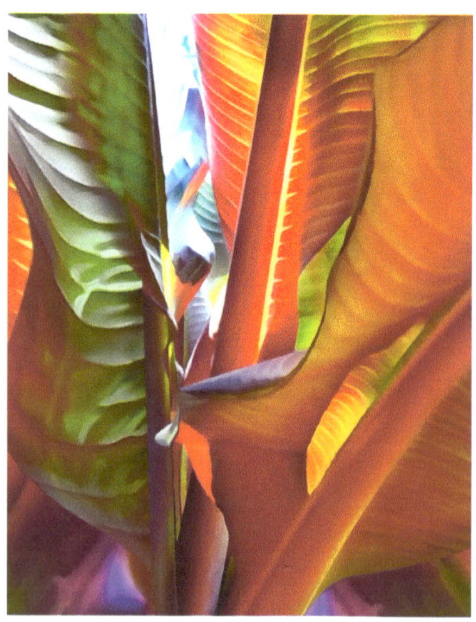

Color Sound 2023

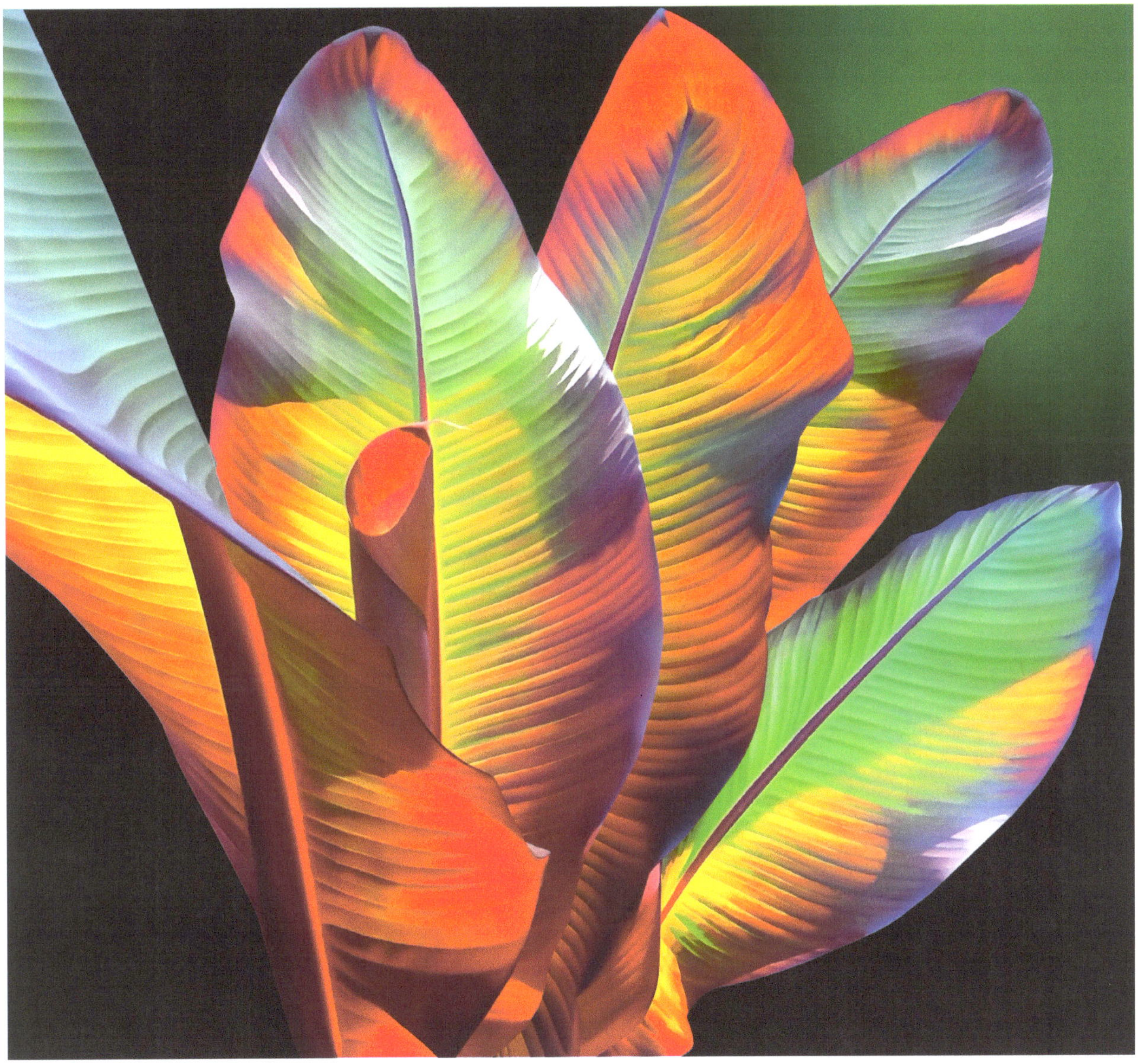

Summertime 2024

KATRIN LOY

https://www.artpal.com/katrinloy/

Katrin Loy, born in 1969 in Germany, studied at the academy of fine arts Düsseldorf and graduated as a master student of professor Jannis Kounellis in 2001. She lives and works in Munich since 2002. In her artistic work, the essence and soul of man is at the centre, his struggle for a vision, his utopias and abysses, his confrontation with the self and the encounter with the other. It arises both from spontaneously emerging inner images as well as from ideas about the psychic and intuitive functions of man and about his archaic experiences. It also feeds on a state of mind and emotions, in which consciousness walks on the small degree between the conscious and the subconscious, revealing something like an inner myth that leaves its mark in the form of artistic work. This process takes place in the hope that these traces, which have become visible in this way, will also touch or even infect the other, ideally a form of infection that allows the viewer to immerse himself in his own inner myth. On the one hand, she associates the "inner myth" with a line of development that underlies every life, but which is largely unconscious. On the other hand, she associates it with a so-called "legend" in which experienced and fantasized memories permeate each other, created by conscious experience and the unconscious processes triggered by it, which shape and change the memory of what has been experienced. She associates the inversion of images she uses with unconscious processes, the superimposition of images with different levels of perception and consciousness, usually a formative and a structuring one, which penetrate each other, merge with each other, contrast each other or give rise to a new form-structure or structure-form. The photographies are part of her series "Sunken Seas". The series is a work in progress and comprizes 460 images up to now. It can be seen in her Online-Gallery: https://www.artpal.com/katrinloy/
The sea as a central metaphor encompasses a pool of possible associations, fantasies and interpretations such as "the unconscious", "the hidden", "the mysterious", "the incomprehensible", "the origin", "the primordial ground", "the vessel", "the container", "the immersion in oneself and in the world" and others the viewer might associate with them.

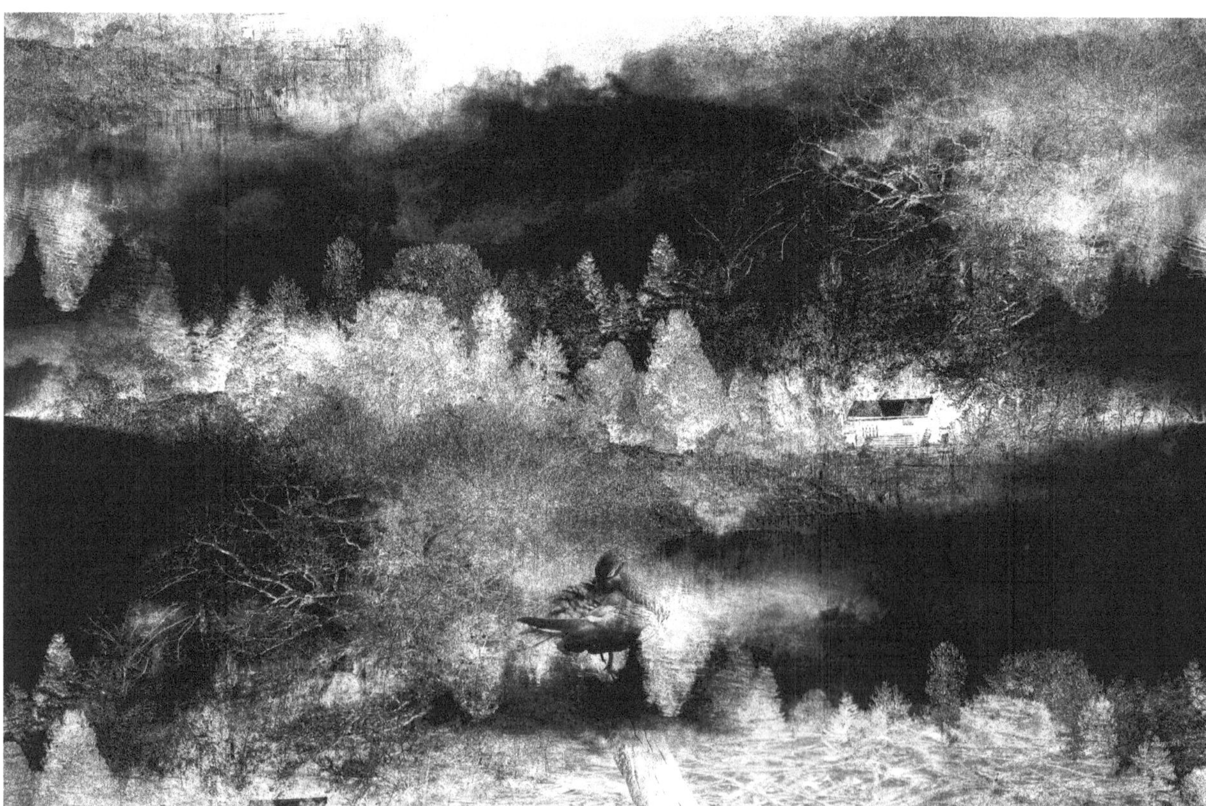

Katrin Loy, Without Title, 2024, Photography on Alu Dibond, Width 90 cm, Hight 60 cm

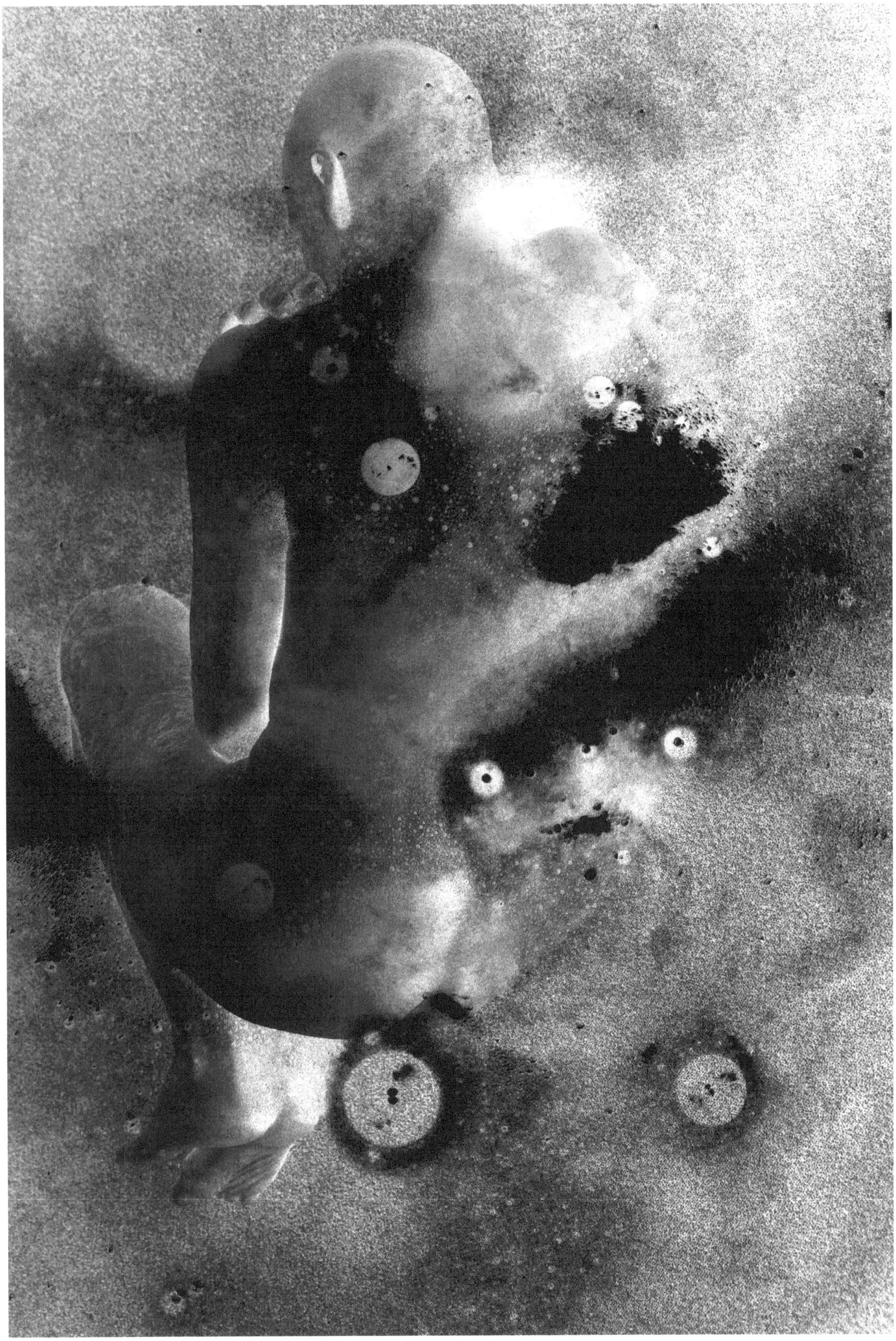

Katrin Loy, Without Title, 2023, Photography on Alu Dibond, Width 60 cm, Hight 40 cm

KENAN K.

insta: kenank_art

Born on August 11, 1956, in Çorum, Turkey, he embarked on his artistic journey with oil painting in June 2006. For two years, he honed his skills under the guidance of H?z?r Teppeev at an atelier in Ankara, dedicating his weekends to perfecting his craft. Currently, he works as a freelance artist in a charming, restored atelier that was once a house built in 1926. Located in Edremit, Bal?kesir, Turkey, this space became his creative sanctuary in September 2010. Here, amidst a setting rich with history, he continues to explore and express his artistic vision. When he started painting as a hobby in his fifties, it was as if the soul of a twelve-year-old boy had come out of the shelter where he had been staying for years. They decided to walk the path of art together, hand in hand where and if possible. He realised that art allows him to touch the lives of people,- if they let -, who he has never met or who do not know him. This became a profound, unique and inspiring feeling. The main purpose or reason for his all studies and efforts comes from the desire to make a more or less positive contribution to life and all living things, based on "Constructive Freedom". Pouring his soul into the work; mastery of techniques, craftsmanship, familiarity with materials and their interactions, and the ability to use the appropriate tools where needed are essential and indispensable requirements for him. In terms of technique, he tries to explore his inner world for the harmony of means and ends, using experimentation through the door of intuition... He believes that; every work has its way and there is no ready-made recipe or fixed order for all. Since artworks have their ways of coming to fruition, they become separate and independent entities when they are completed and/or finished. He wishes so that, it may be desirable to allow them to express themselves. The more you get into them, the more they will communicate. What he finally says: "Please let the works of art speak in silence and be ready to explore their adventurous music..."

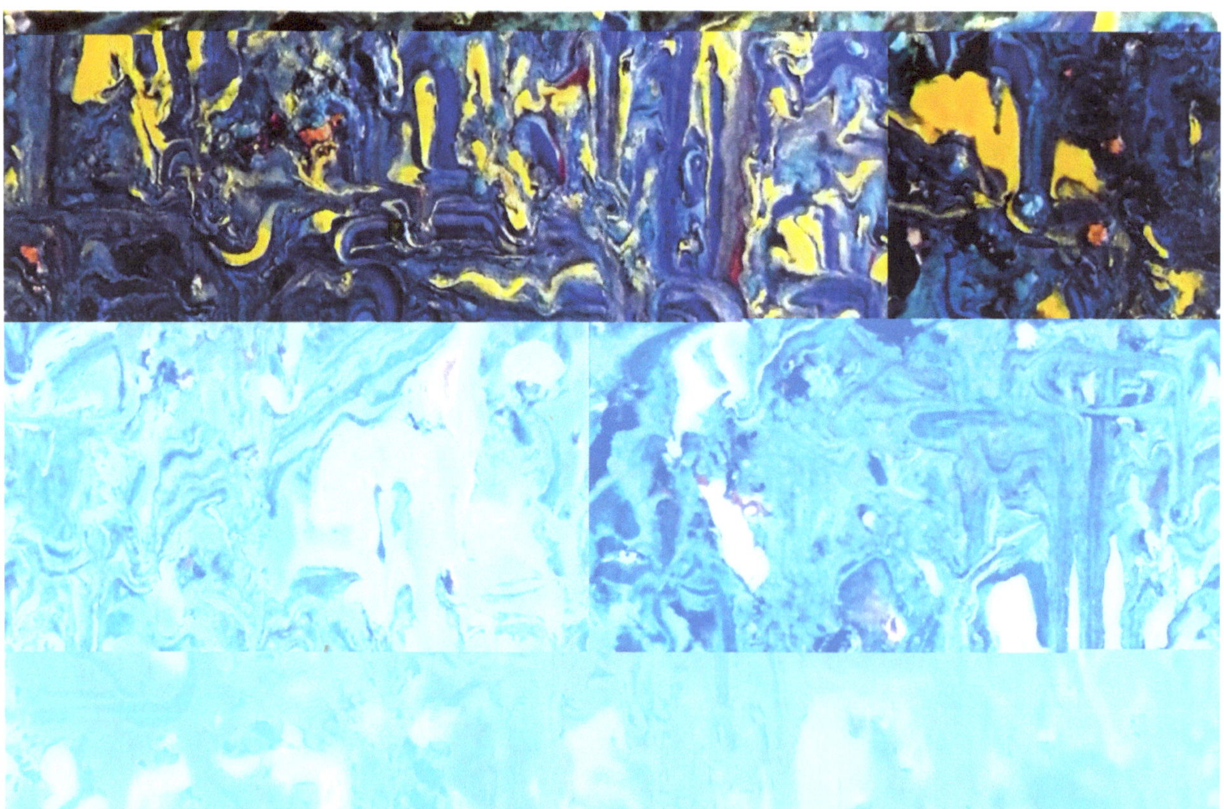

"The Temple", 2025, Acrylic on canvas, 40x60 cm

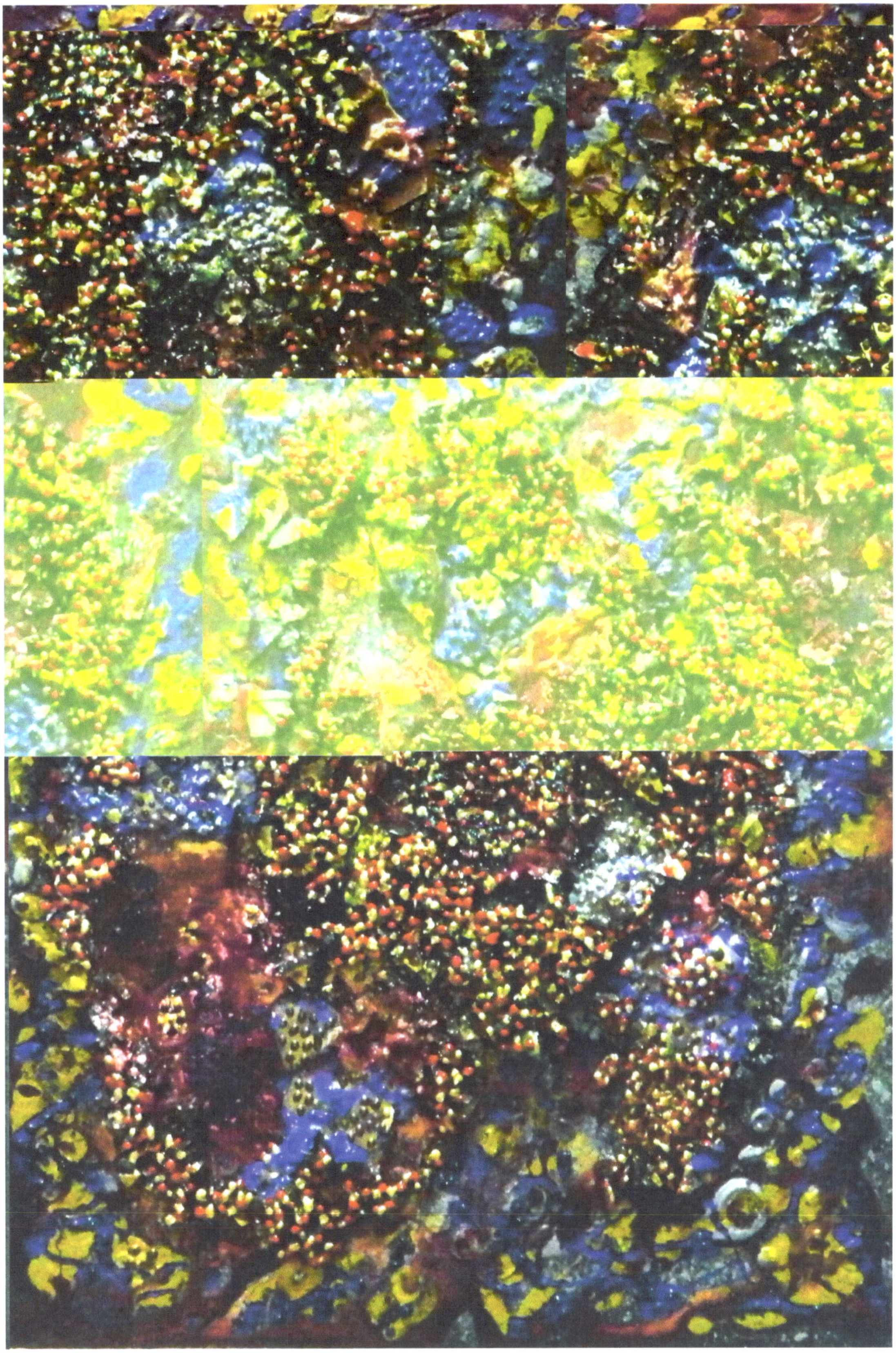

Hidden Stories III (Hope is needed), 2025, Mixed media on pylwood, 60x40 cm

KILCHENMANN KATHLEEN

www.kathleen-kilchenmann.de

She was born in Zurich, Switzerland and moved together with her family 1973 to the South of Germany. During her childhood in Zurich she took painting lessons from an artist. She loved and enjoyed painting and drawing very much. After her education and apprenticeship as a merchant she stayed for a longer time in France and England. She got married and moved 1969-1971 to Ann Arbor, Mich. USA where her career began as an self-taught person. She had been admitted to the professional Art Association of Ann Arbor and back in Germany to the professional Art Association of visual artists. Since then her work has exhibited regularly in galleries, museum and various ART Fairs in USA, Spain, Switzerland and Germany. She has been dealing with the subject of nature, environment, landscapes which are for her landscapes of the soul. She combines the found objects from nature, like braids, straw, earth and other materials with self-colored paper as collages, as well as several layers of paint on canvas which creates a haptic. It is the devotion to the process and handling of materials, colors and shapes that inspire her and drives her to implement new ideas on canvas. So the viewer of her work can immerse himself with his thoughts and travel between heaven and earth.

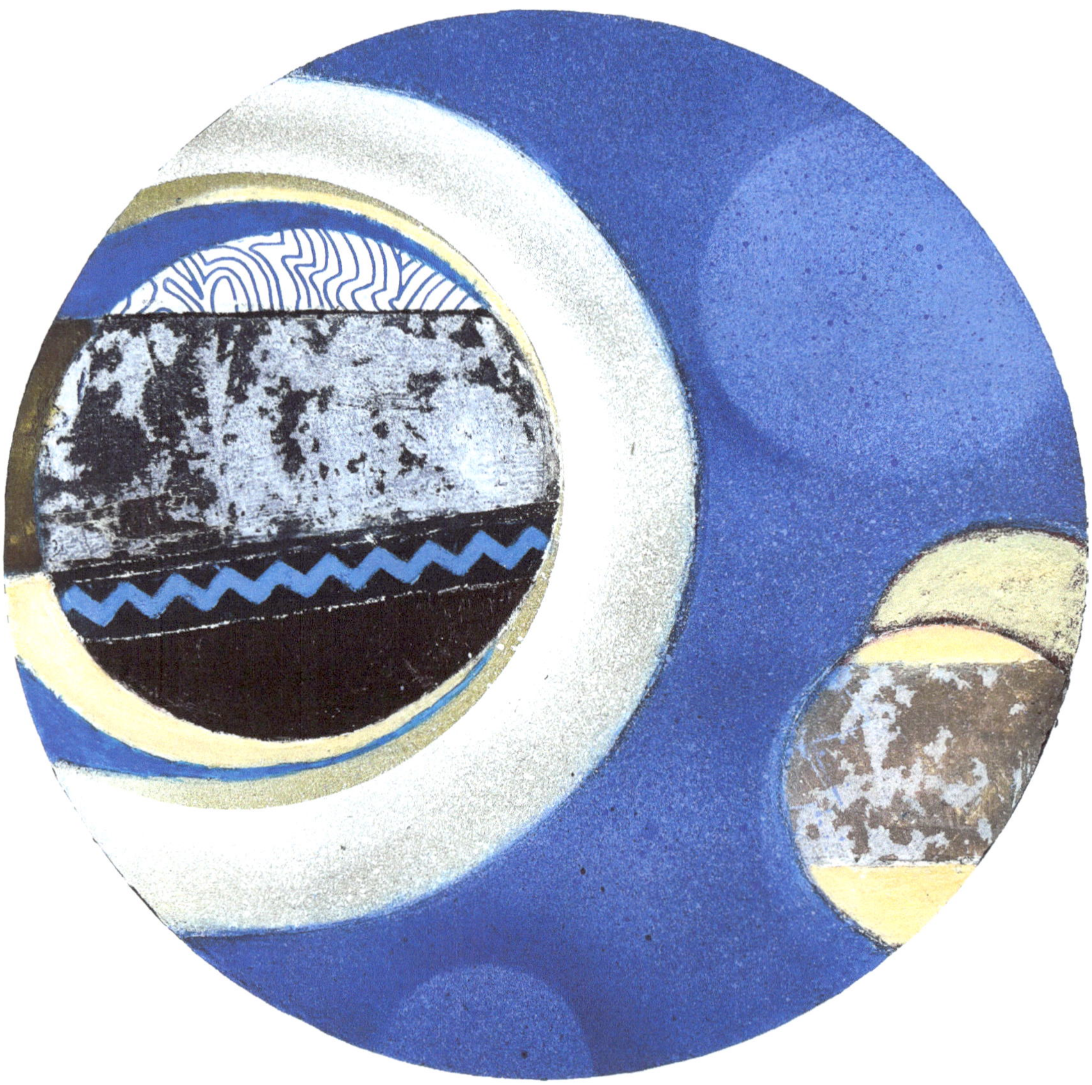

Kosmos, 2024, Acrylic/Collage/Paper, on canvas, 50 cm diameter 50 cm

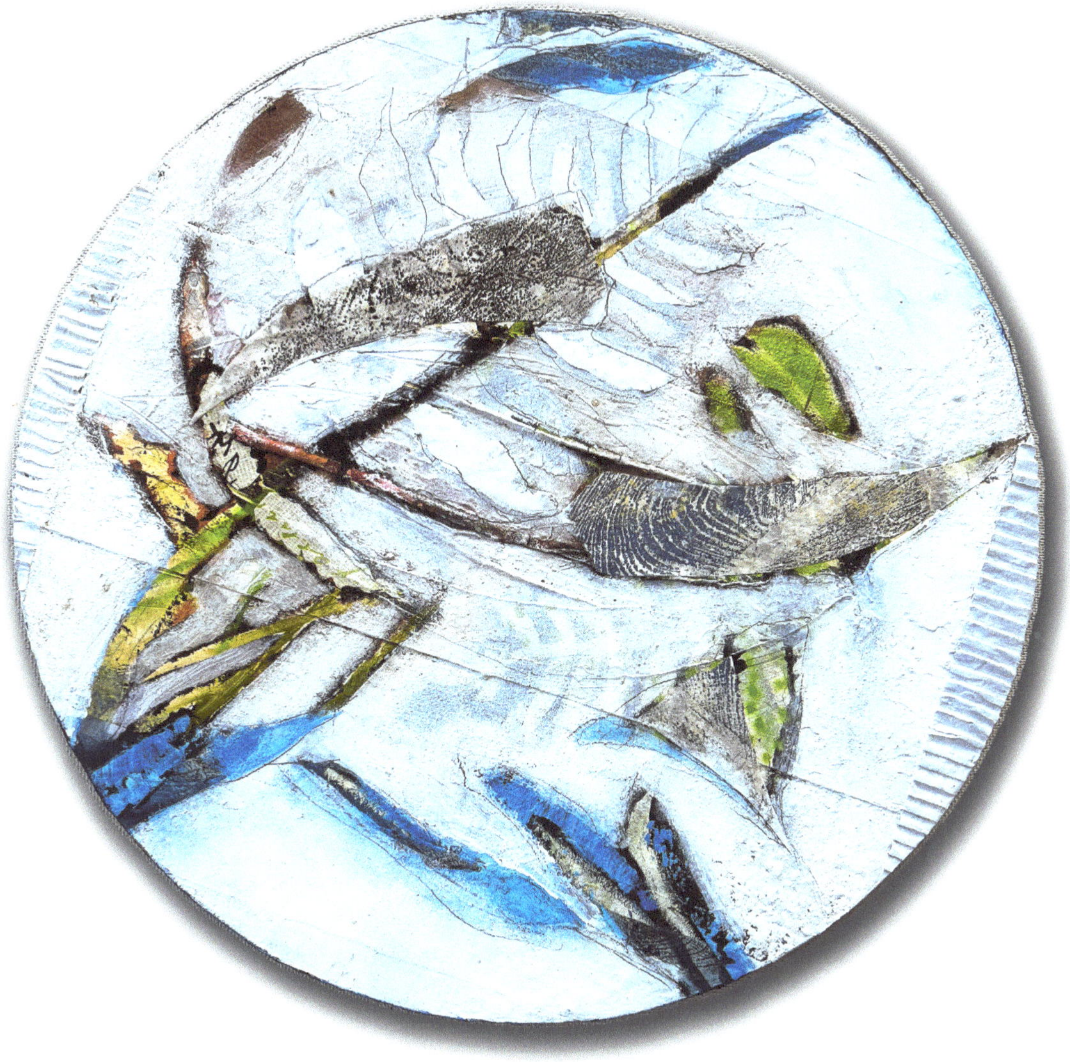

Pflanzenwelt II, 2022, Acrylic/ Pencil/Collage/Paper on canvas, 50 cm diameter

KLAUS BILICZKY

www.biliczkyde

The versatile German artist Klaus Biliczky was born in Dinkelsbühl. He lives and works in Neuendettelsau, Bavaria. He studied graphic design and advertising graphics, worked as a graphic designer and manager in the packaging industry, and was self-employed in the real estate sector. Artistic work had been part of his professional life since youth, before he devoted himself full-time to creating art and became a freelance artist. In the beginning, he created pen-and-ink drawings in the style of Surrealism and Fantastic Realism. Later, he turned entirely to abstraction. Large-format acrylic paintings, oxidative painting, and sculptural objects define his mature body of work. His artworks, regularly exhibited nationally and internationally, have received multiple awards and publications. Klaus Biliczky's artistic work focuses on abstract painting and sculptural objects. His main sources of inspiration are the diverse aspects of human existence and the complex structure of our world and natural environment, as well as the ways we interact with and are shaped by them. His artistic output encompasses a wide range of approaches, from experimental, process-based pieces to those that take a more conceptual stance. By addressing the beauty and destruction of our planet and the fragility of our existence, he aims to raise awareness of the preciousness of life and to inspire people to discover their own stories in the colors and shapes of his works.

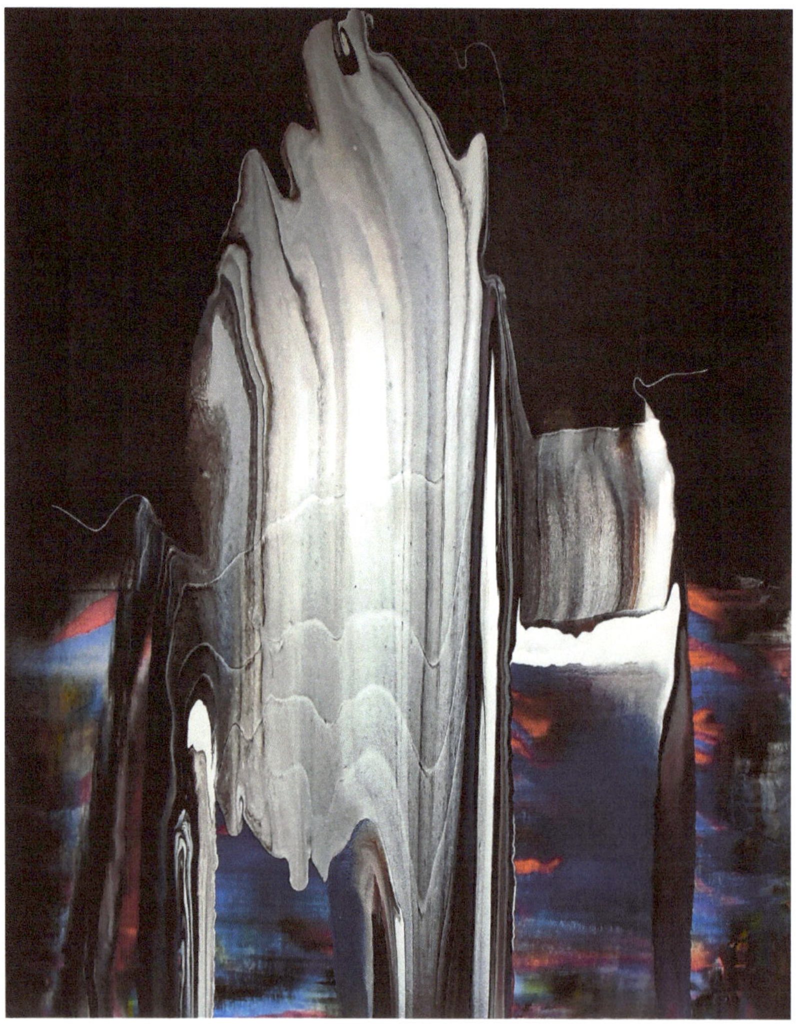

Take-off, 2025, Acrylic on canvas, 120 x 80 x 4,5 cm

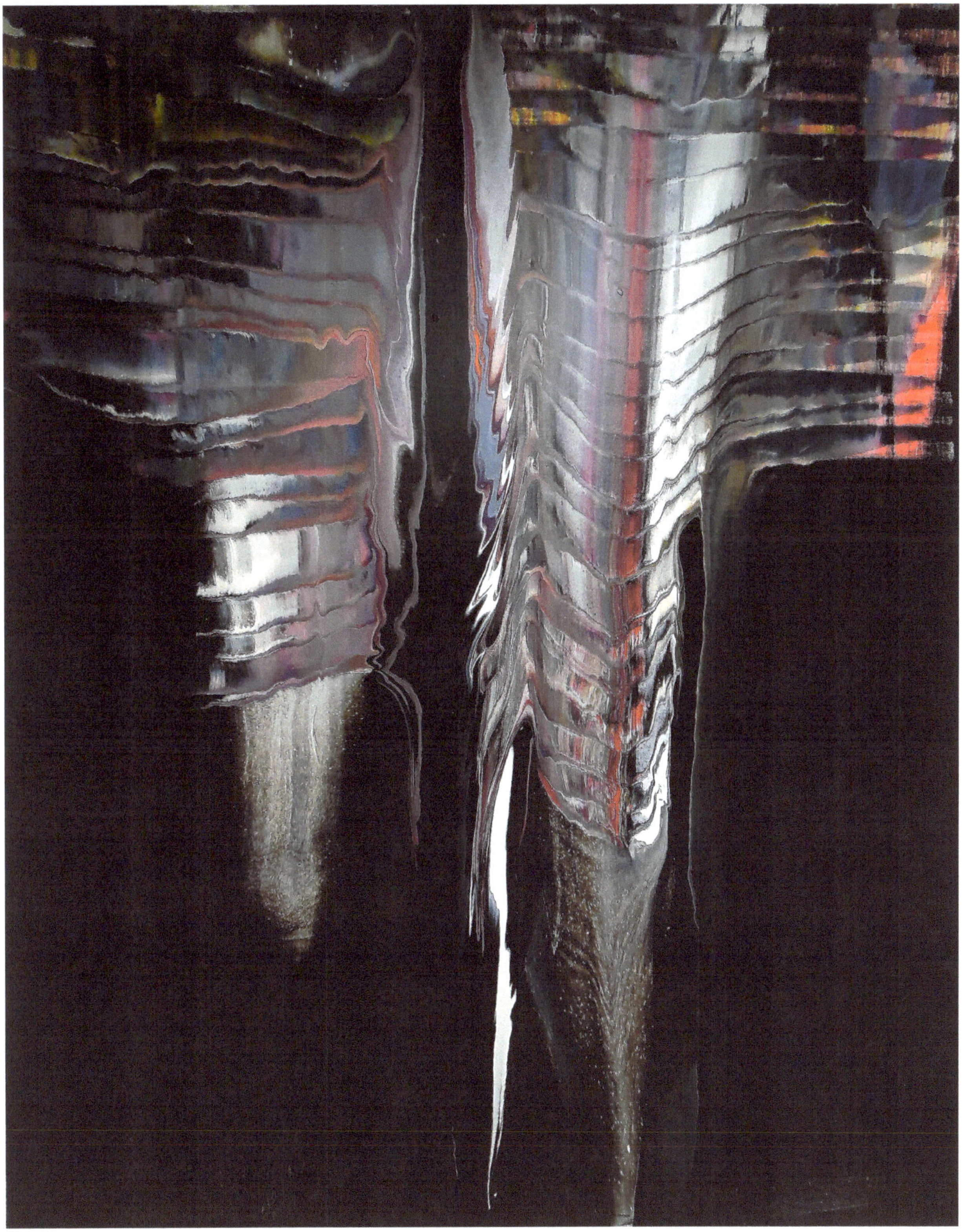

Stalactites, 2025, Acrylic on canvas, 120 x 80 x 4,5 cm

KODI BEVERLIN

https://www.kodibeverlin.com

Kodi Beverlin lives and works in Des Moines, Iowa. Beverlin discovered her love for photography through a successful career as a hairdresser. She is endlessly fascinated by the complexity of people, situations, perspectives, and the images used to illustrate these states. Her work explores contradictory truths- exploring fragments and layers, challenging the pull towards "knowing".

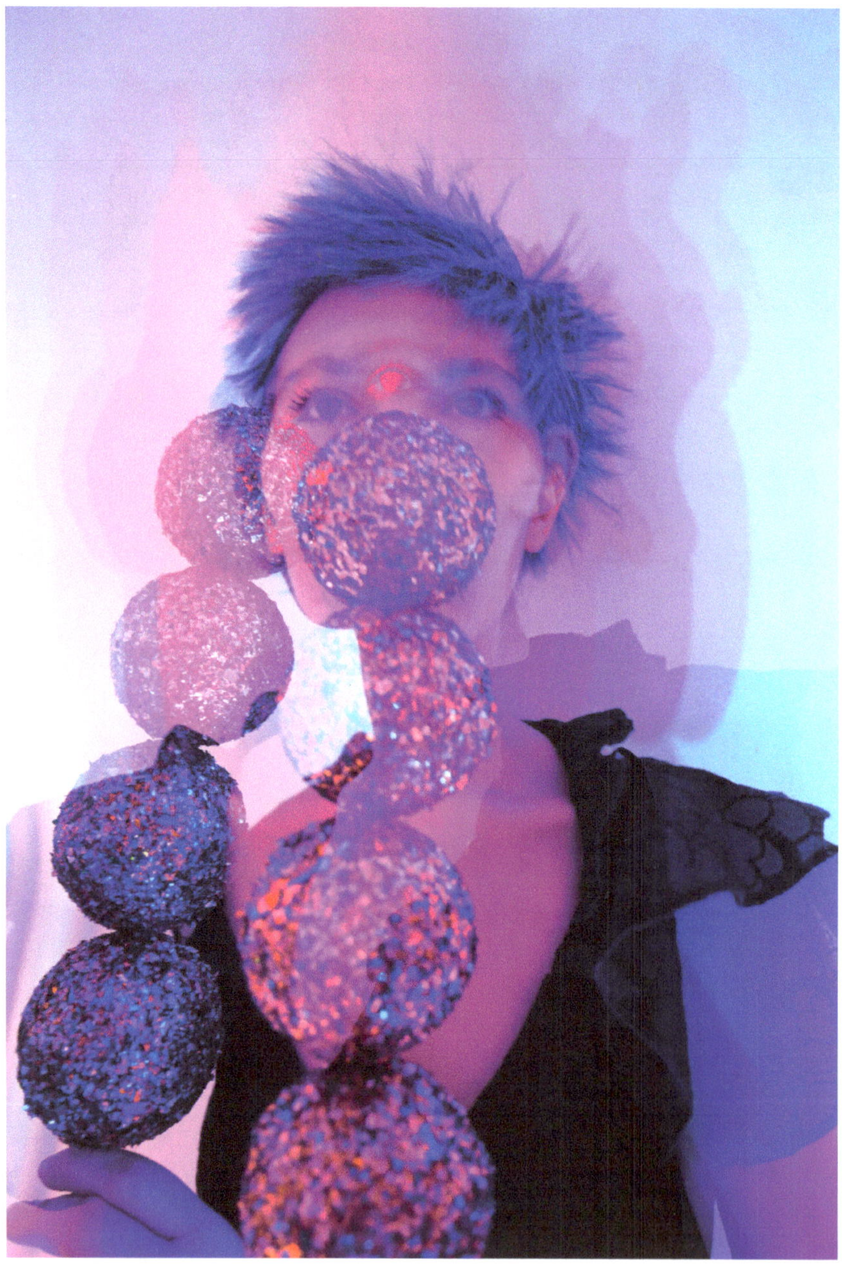

Third Eye, To Be Seen, 2021, Photography, 46.48 x 67cm,

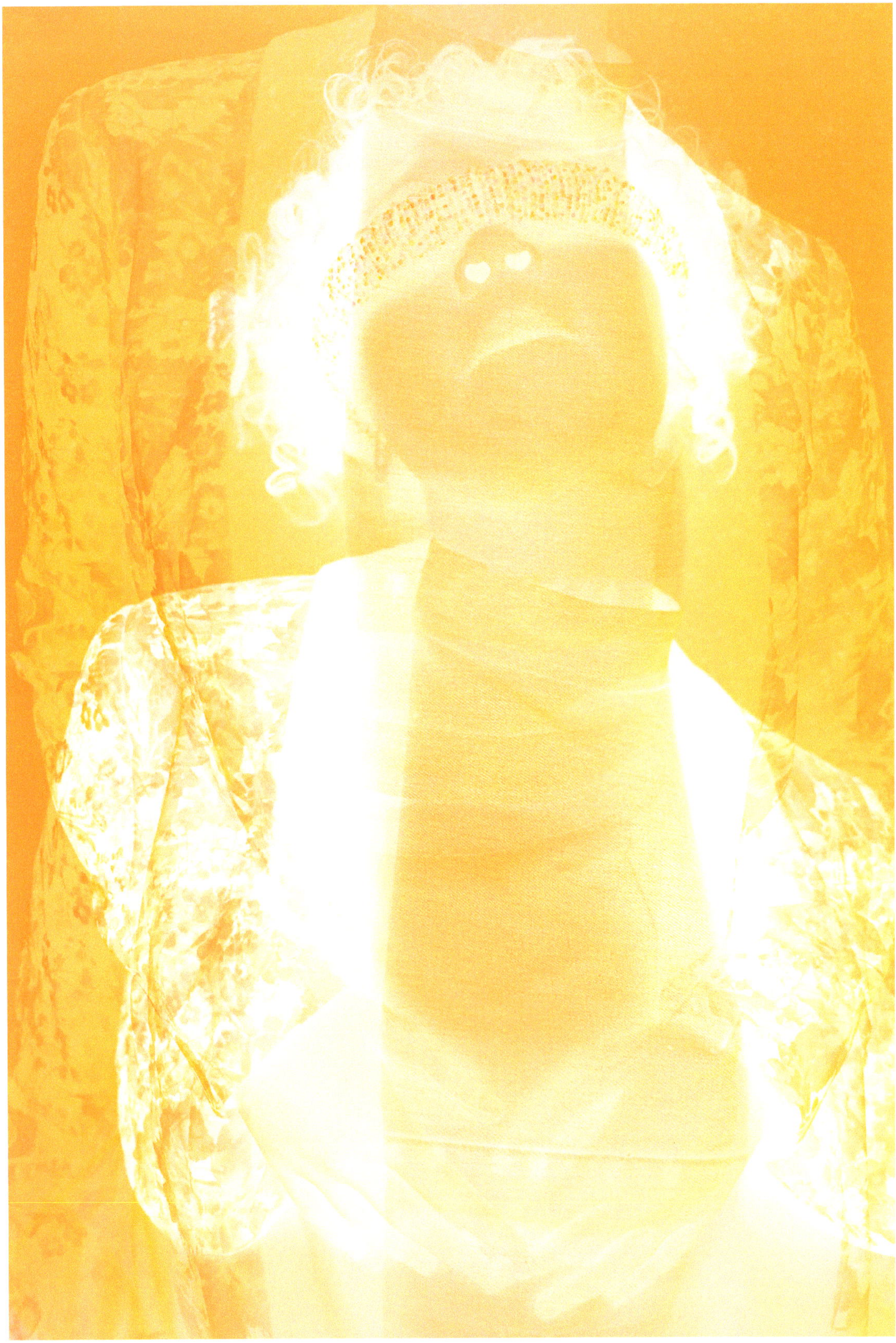

Self, To Be Seen, 2022, Photography, 46.48 x 67cm

L. SCOOTER MORRIS

https://www.lscootermorris.com

Morris call herself a sensory illusionist. Her work, trademarked as, Sculpted Paintings, is the integration of color, light and texture with many surface variations and includes mixed media. The landscape paintings have the effect of a layered topography and atmosphere that exist in real life, while using texture to give the illusion to intimate clouds, mountains and water. The concept creates an impression of what exists and allow the viewer to bring their own conception and memories to experience the moment. This style is also evident in the other subject matter paintings, including the politically based flag paintings as well as the abstract work. This unique combination of sculpting, design, and the integrating of diverse elements sets each of her "Sculpted Paintings" as a three-dimensional image on a two- dimensional plane. In her most recent paintings, the use of the founding documents of The United States, provides a visual connection between where we have come from, and where we are going as a nation. The Bill of Rights, The Constitution and the Declaration of Independence are a subtle call to action to protect democracy, with the use of other iconic images to inspire and remind the viewer to remember what is important to them. The flag paintings reflect our need to find resolution. In 2014, Scooter wrote: We the people, are the many, bound by love of country, hardened by the struggle, softened by the love, made determined by the need, and resolved to make our place in these United States. We the people are called upon as one of the many to join together with others though we are of different faiths and color and gender, we must find ourselves joined as one of the many, part of the whole, working together with tolerance, wisdom and hope to make our shared differences work for a united purpose. The prose, We Are The Many, and Scooter's images are now part of her film, "Tipping Point-We Are The People. Those who love Morris' work are often inspired by the powerful sense of what is both familiar and extraordinary.

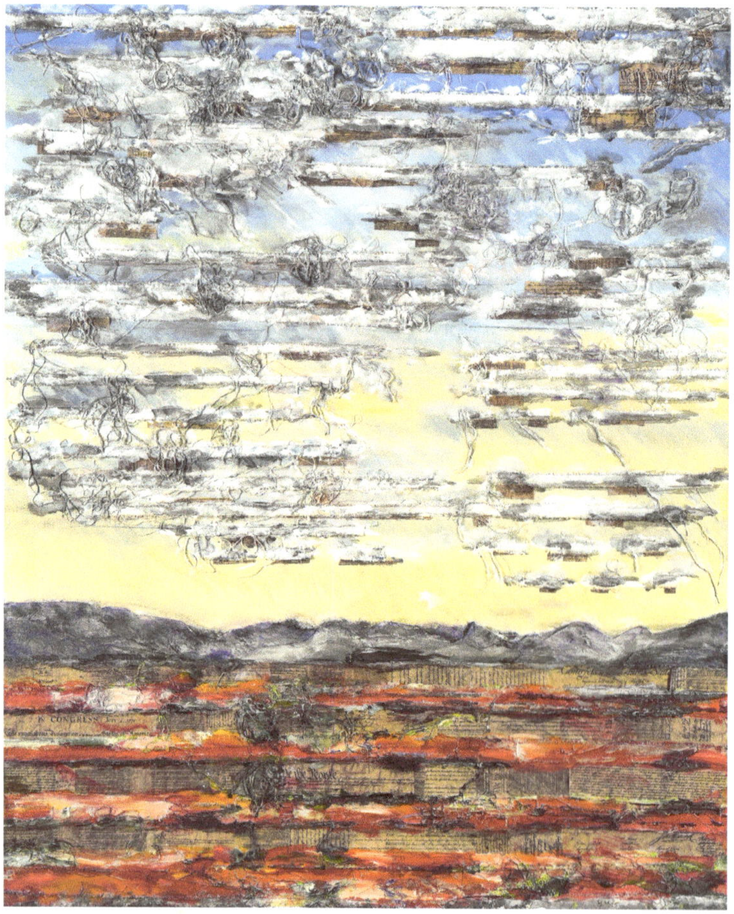

We Are The People, 2025, Acrylic and Mixed Media, 152.4x121.92cm

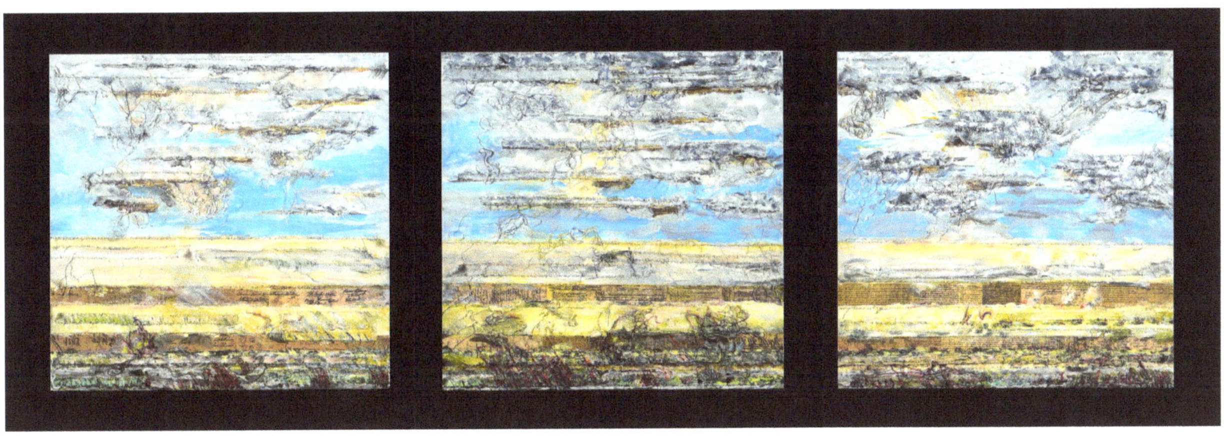

Time and again, 2025, Acrylic and Mixed Media, 76.2x228.6cm

LARISA SVED

IG @larisa.sved.art

Larisa Sved's paintings are deeply personal and employ a realist technique that occasionally moves towards abstraction. As a self-taught artist, she is inspired by the natural surroundings of Canada and the Cayman Islands with her detailed depictions of flora and of the local sceneries created to convey messages of peace, harmony and joy. Sved is using mainly acrylic paint on canvas, wood, rocks. Sved is a supporting member of Cayman Islands Visual Art Society, National Gallery of the Cayman Islands.

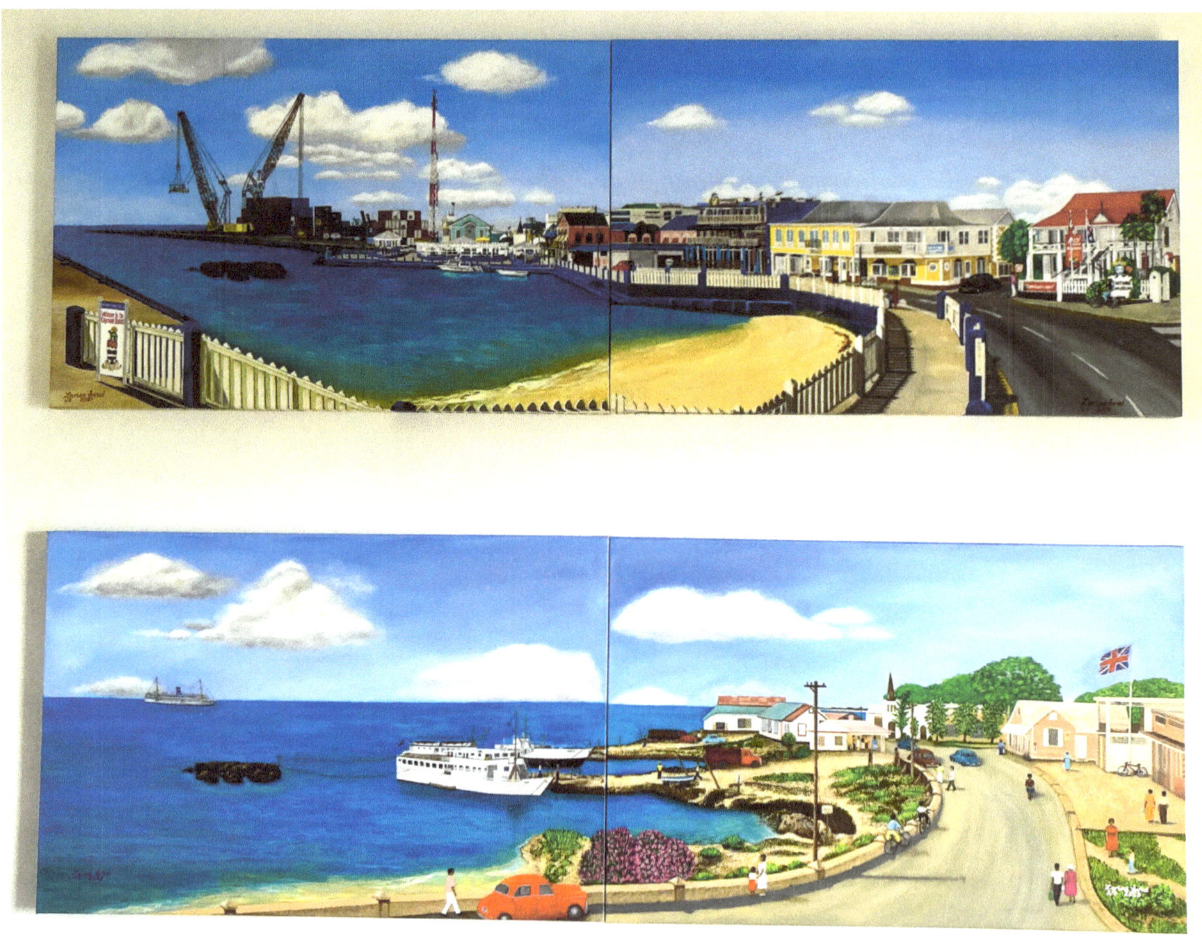

Seafarers' Way, George Town, Cayman Islands. Then and Now. 1961. 2021." A set of 2 diptychs. 2021 & 2023. Acrylic on canvas. 61x91cm+61x91cm x 2.

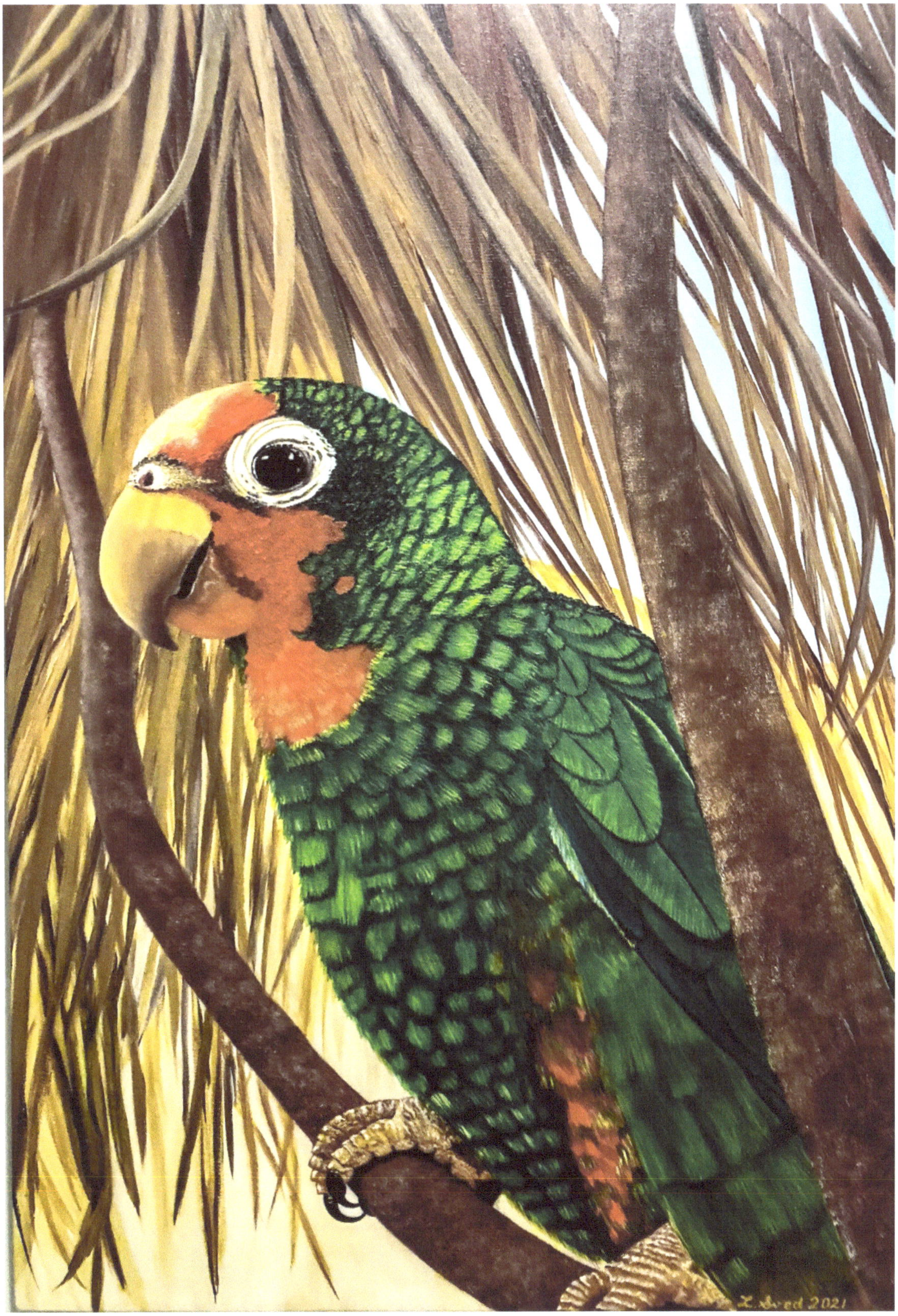

Cayman Parrot. 2021. Acrylic on canvas. 91x61cm.

LARRY R. RANKIN

www.larryrrankin.com

Larry has been sculpting since 1974 and have pieces distributed worldwide. He was awarded best in show at the Las Vegas International Art Show, representing 16 countries. Larry was also chosen as one of sixty artist to show at the Shanghai International Art Fair in China. His sculptures are as diverse stylistically as they are varied in media and size. Larry's emotionally evocative art expresses who he is, symbolizes the birth of a new form and reflects his experience of the power and beauty of the world. When you look at his sculptures you will find a reflective strength and beauty designed to please the aesthetic senses.

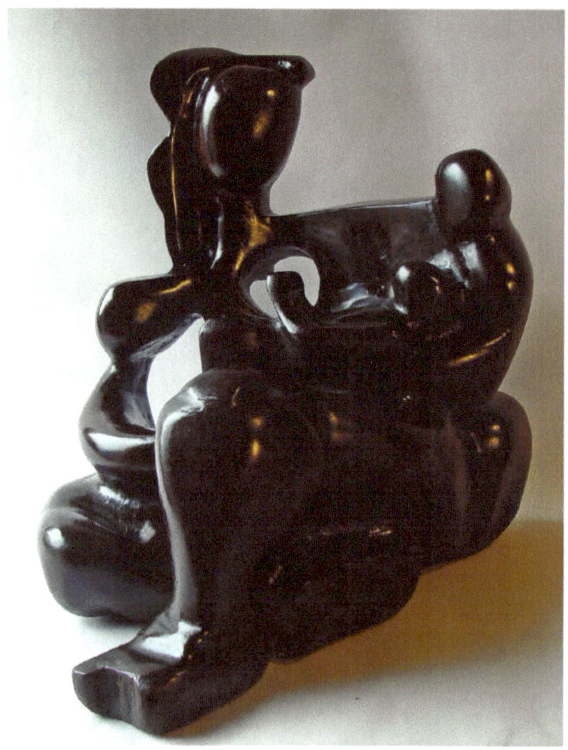

Mother & Child, Black Walnut, 63.5 X 58.42 X 55.88 X 22"

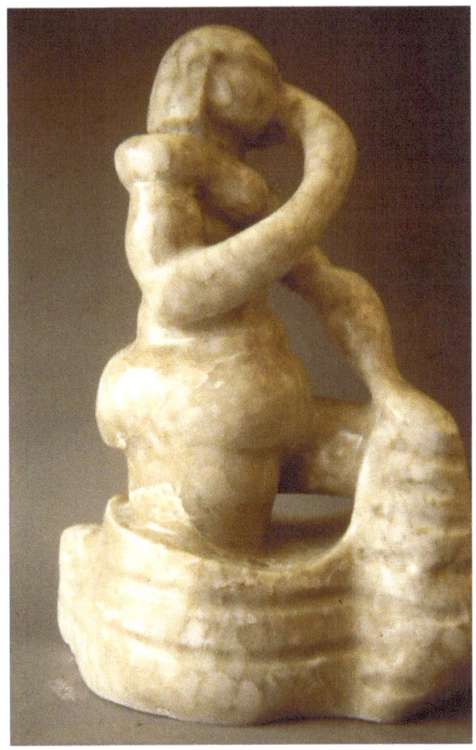

Woman in Drapery, Alabaster, 78.74 X 53.34 X 33.02

LETICIA (LETA) HERRERA

www.leticiaherreraart.com

Leticia Herrera Mexican Artist residing in the USA seeks to explore what it means to be human in her art. In over 30 years of painting, she has depicted a diverse amount of representations and styles. Her signature work is represented by her "WALKERS" magic surrealism series that represent a metaphorical journey, the shared search for answers that unites humanity. "Walkers" series is a striking visual narrative that explores the multifaceted journey of humanity through a vibrant and textured tapestry of oil impasto. The series, a collection of paintings featuring diminutive human figures set against vast, often gradient backgrounds, speaks to the profound search for identity, purpose, and connection that defines the human experience. "I believe in the kindness of humanity. I believe that our diversity is what makes this world interesting. I consider myself an expanding artist because I believe we are always transforming. My work walks with me and changes with me. In my art, I represent that trajectory through my Series Walkers, They are searchers of beautiful emotions; they are travelers of the universe and the world. They are catchers of dreams; they are explorers of aspirations, searchers of unity and of freedom. Asking always who are we? Where are we going? What are we looking for? What do we want? Who do we love? In my paintings I am trying to transport you to those places of my imagination where we are often find ourselves. I want to touch your soul, open your heart, and invite you to walk with me and find the light you are meant to have."

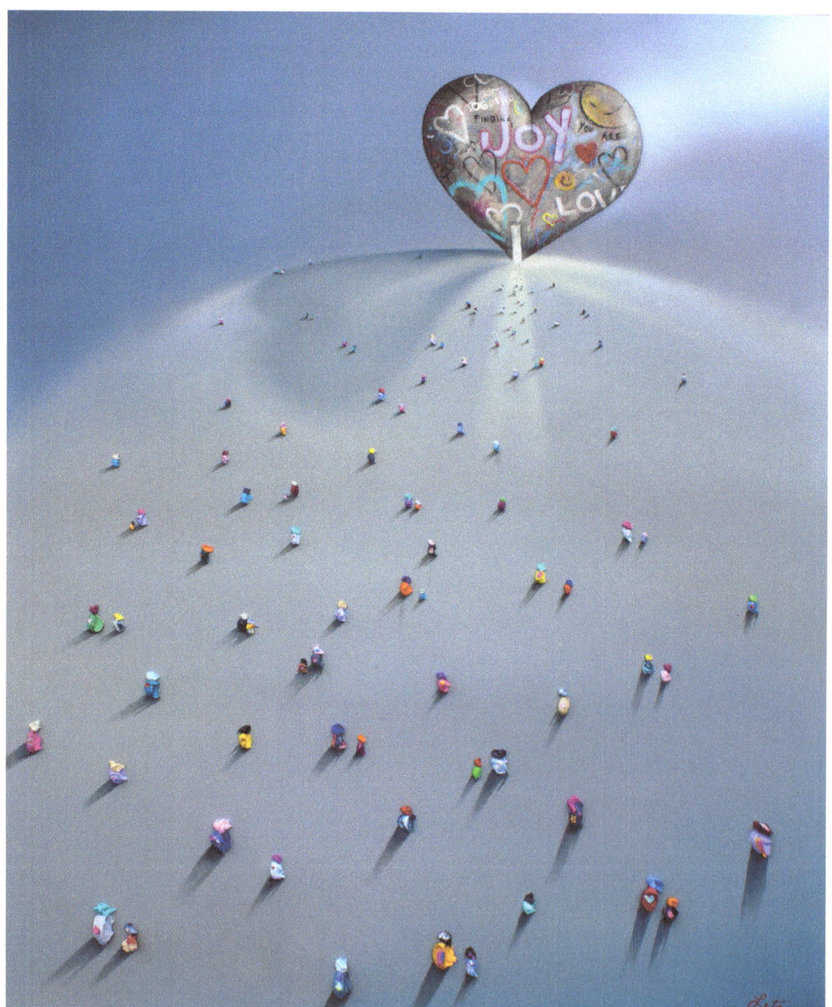

Together to the Portal of Joy, 2025. Oil on canvas, 122 x 152 cm.

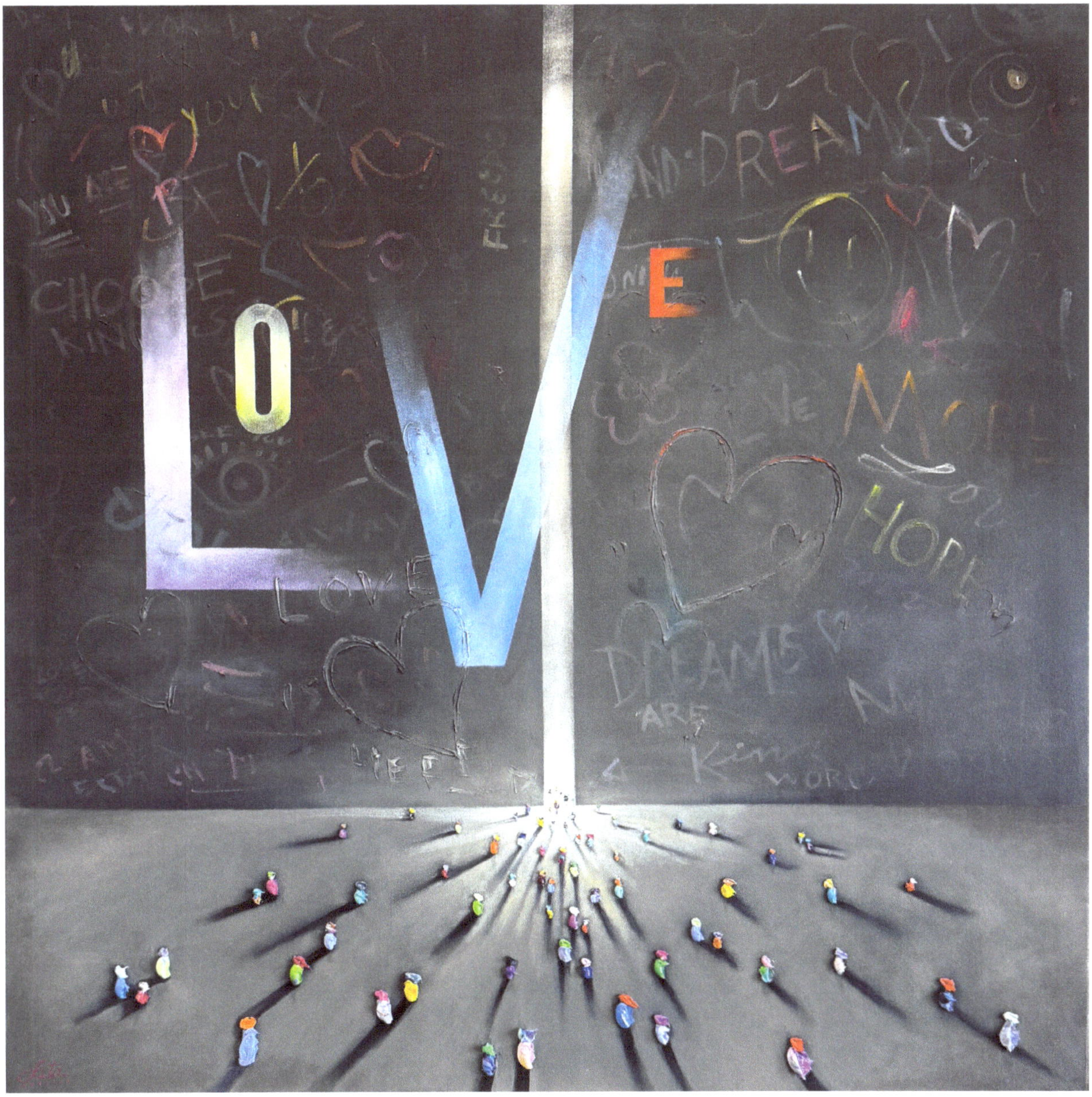

Portal to Love, 2025. Oil on canvas, 122 x 122 cm.

LORNA BUECHNER

geonimalsart@gmail.com

Geonimals blends art and therapy, offering neurodiverse-inspired creations that support mental wellness, self-expression and emotional healing. Geonimals is an exceptional brand, born from a place of personal experience, creativity and healing. Founded by Lorna, a neurodiverse artist and author, Geonimals represents a unique intersection of art, mental health and self-expression. Lorna, who is on the autistic spectrum and has ADHD, faced a broad range of mental health and learning challenges throughout her life. Through these struggles, she embraced various therapeutic techniques — most notably dialectical behavioural therapy (DBT). It was through DBT that she began drawing, using creativity as a vital tool for managing her mental health and making sense of the world. The result of this process is Geonimals: a brand that offers visually captivating and imaginative art, but also serves as a therapeutic resource. People are particularly impressed by the positive impact Geonimals has had on those individuals who require help with their mental health. Whether it's through Lorna's intricately designed illustrations meant to be worn, coloured in, or simply admired, each piece reflects the artist's intent to offer calm, comfort and clarity to others. This is art with a purpose — rooted in lived experience and intended to support others in their mental wellness journeys. Every element of Geonimals is designed to support mental clarity, creative exploration and emotional healing. Lorna has been doing her art for a number of years and in that time her style as developed and become more intricate at times. She can do bespoke designs too in her geometric style of drawing. For example she can do names on the back of baby grows with an animal on the front.

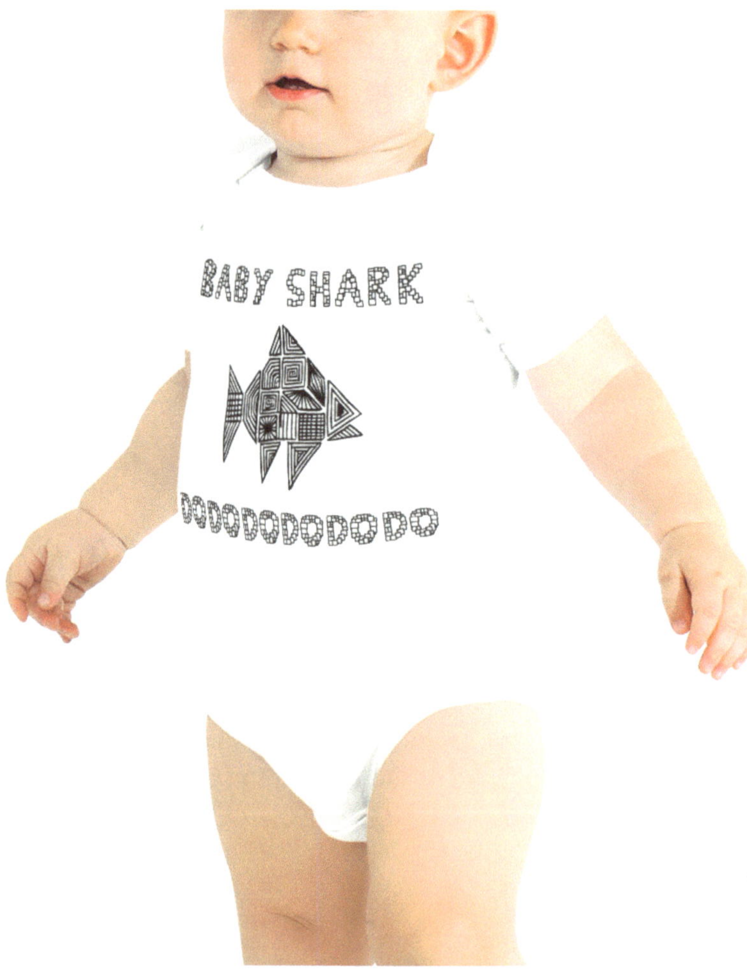

Baby shark Do Do Do Do 2023

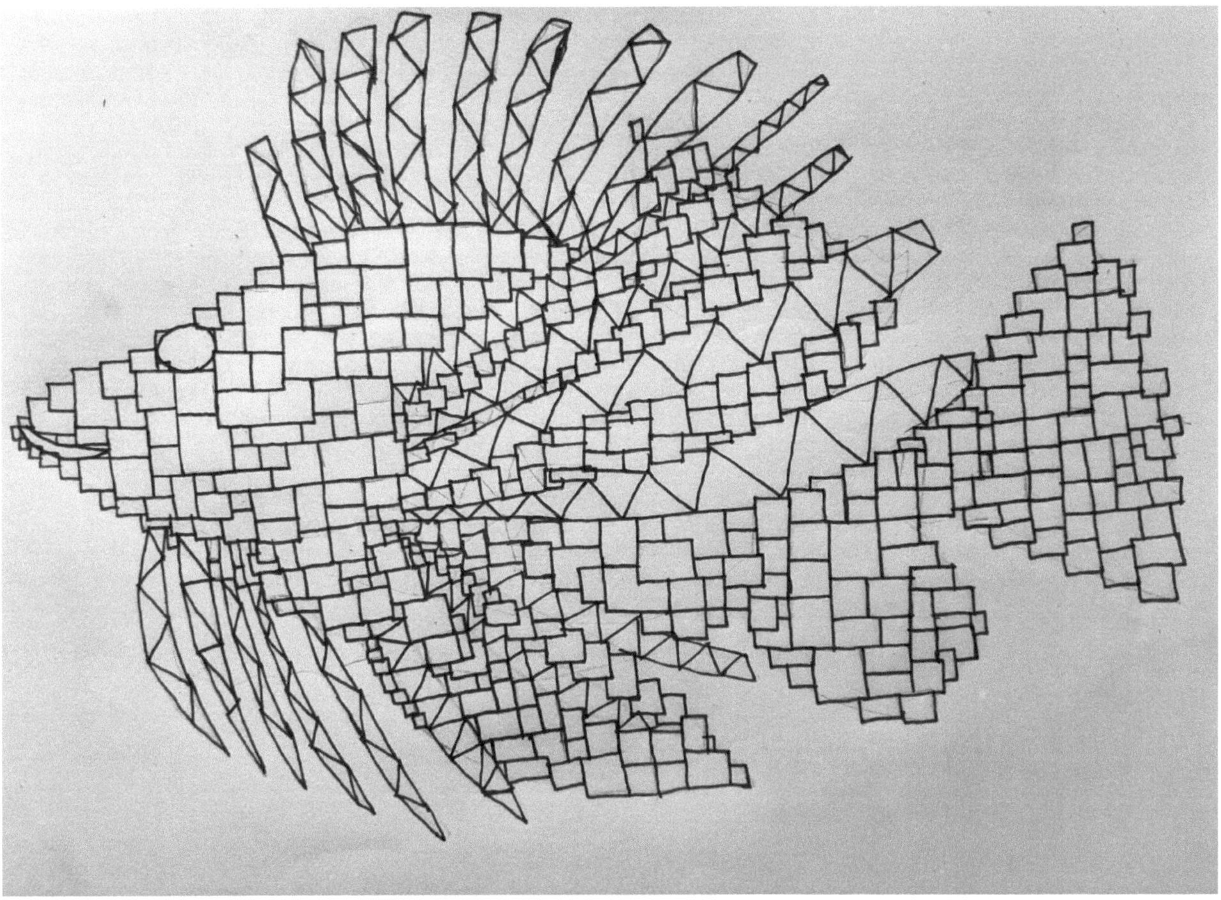

Lionfish 2020

LUANA STEBULE

https://www.instagram.com/luanastebule

Luana Stebule is an internationally acclaimed artist and has been resident in the United Kingdom since 2013, where she has continued her creative inspirations. L.Stebule recognised for her unique style that conveys Aboriginal art, surrealism, geometry and minimalism. The current artworks are described as being of an Abstract Figurative nature - that is, if you can pigeonhole such a unique blend of artistic talent. Luana Stebule's artworks have been selected for more than 20 art books and art anthologies. Also, she has received numerous accolades, awards, and prizes. In 2025, she was awarded the El Greco - Premio de las Bellas Artes Prize. Not least of this was her selection in 2024 into the prestigious "Unicatalog The Universal Catalog of Modern 2025 Prize. Art", published in four languages, and including such notables as Andy Warhol, Amadeo Modigliani, amongst others. In 2023, the World of Art Magazine included L.Stebule in the book "Top 10 Contemporary Artists 2023". The Contemporary Art Curator Magazine, in collaboration with the Contemporary Art Collectors platform in 2023, awarded her with the "Collectors Art Prize" International Art Award and the "Harmony of Humanity" Global Consciousness Prize. In 2022, in New York, the Art Tour International Magazine awarded her the "Top 60 Contemporary Masters" award. She only 2018 created her website in English and became more visible around the globe. L.Stebule was born in Lithuania in 1962 and completed Antanas Marinaitis Art School and the Academy of Art. Her artistic career started in 1989 with her first solo exhibition in Kaunas Art House. In total, she has had 22 solo and 76 group exhibitions in Europe: Italy, Spain, France, Portugal, Lithuania and the Czech Republic. The artist is also actively participating in online exhibitions. The most notable and recent exhibitions were in 2023, the Florence Biennale, the FIABCN Art Fair in Barcelona, and in 2022, curated by Saatchi Art, the Other Art Fair in Dallas, US. In the last few years, she has been exhibiting less Luana fully concentrating on her new big paintings. Her inspirations are drawn from many sources, including travels, music, literature, and art. Home life itself has also acted as a stimulus, as has also the inner voice, spiritual feelings, and intuition, with often the best ideas coming from the Universe as a whole with a unified field of consciousness and unconsciousness. The artist primarily works with oil on canvas, but also utilises collages, mixed media, oil pastels, watercolours and acrylic. Her works are frequently characterised by structured compositions, often multi-layered, employing contrasting calm and saturated colours. The emphasis within the work is often quentessential lines around primarily compositions as a reflection of universal harmony and eternity, and the essential spiritual aura of the creature depicted. The silence, isolation and solitude of the COVID outbreak have been a source of the manner of dancing lines in L. Stebule's paintings. This is an exploration of a new way of interpreting the human figures, flowers, animals and other objects. The artist is also a poet; she has published for poetry books. Three in Lithuanian and the last one in 2019, "Ephemeral Awaking" in the English language It is the reason why she aims to transform visual objects into stories. She also expresses her inner feelings and thoughts about humanity, existence, relationships, and connections with the Universal spirit. The stylised forms of nature simplify them in her unique way to create a provocative atmosphere. Her attitude is that creativity is more about being different; anybody can be weird, it is easy, what is hard is to be as simple as Bach.

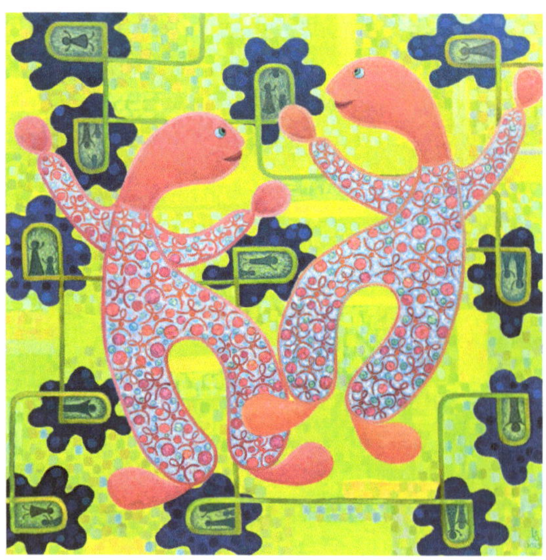

"Adoration of flowers spirits" 2025

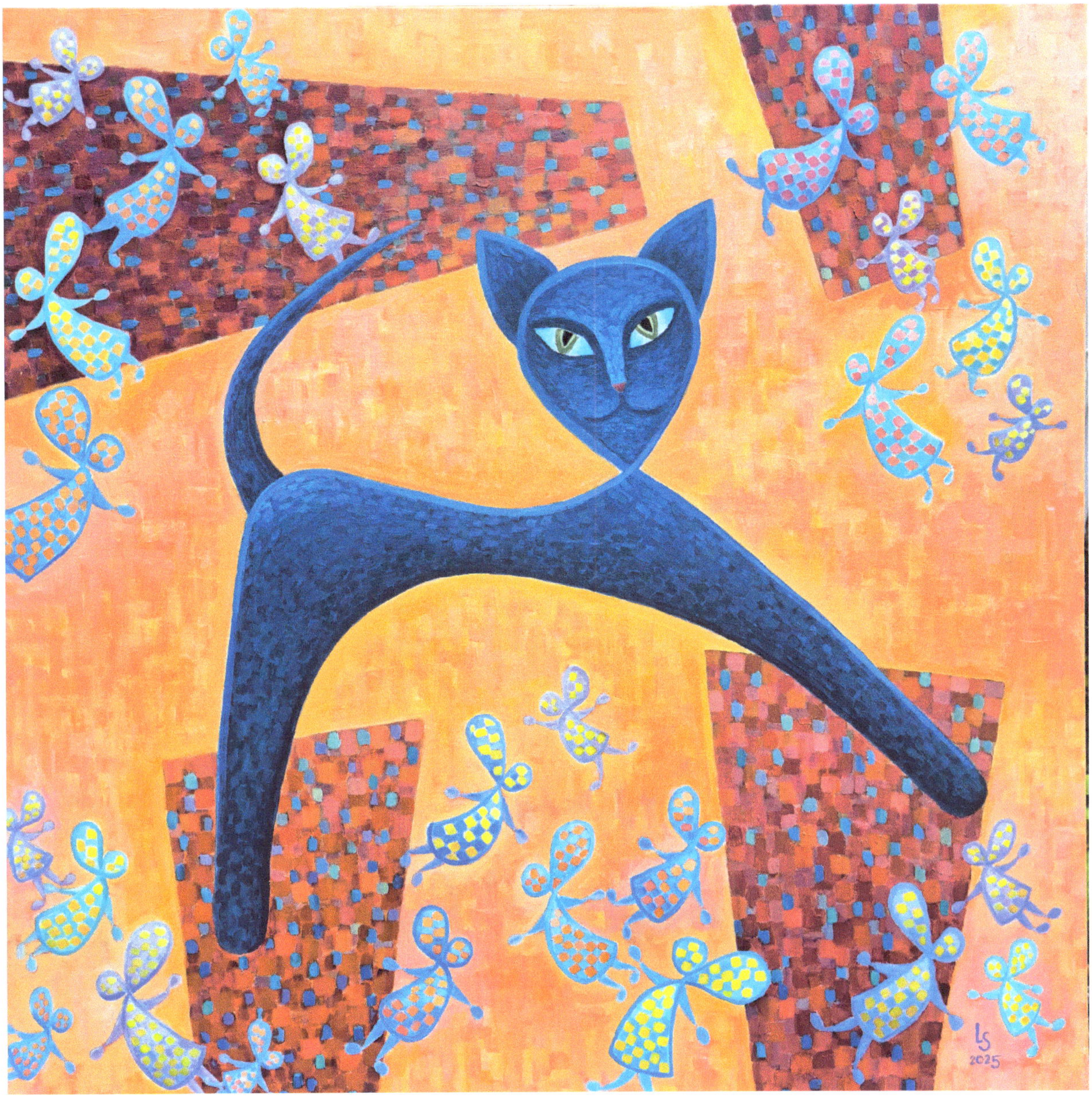

"The Quantum Jump" 2025

MAGDÉL WYSER

Instagram: magdel.wyserart

Bio: I was born and raised in South Africa, now live and create from my studio at home in Switzerland. After giving up my Boutique, of which I was a co-owner, a few years ago I am now a full-time artist. Passionate about color, texture, nature and emotions which I try to bring together on canvas.

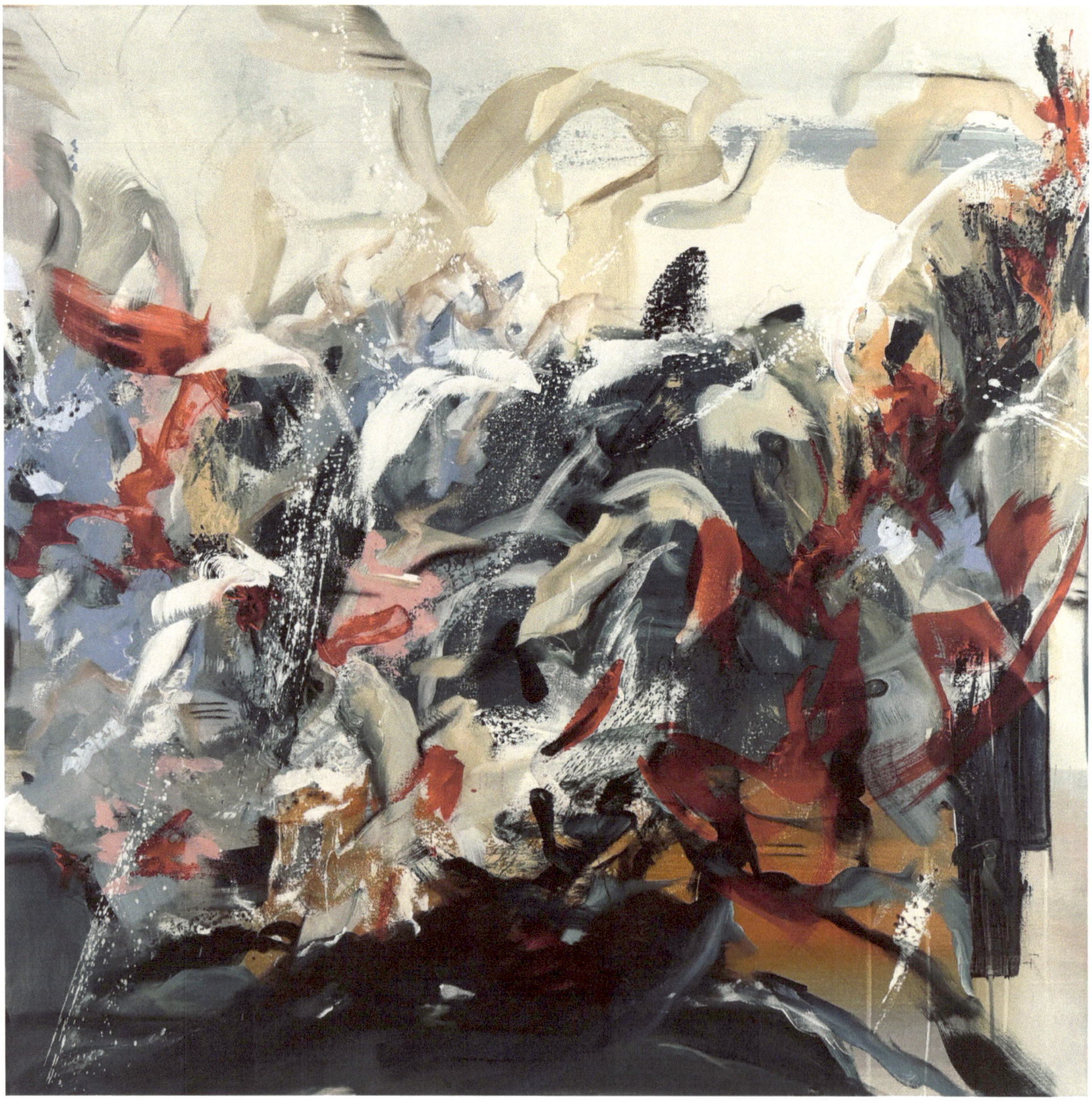

"Dramatic Beauty" 2025 Mix medium 120/120 cm

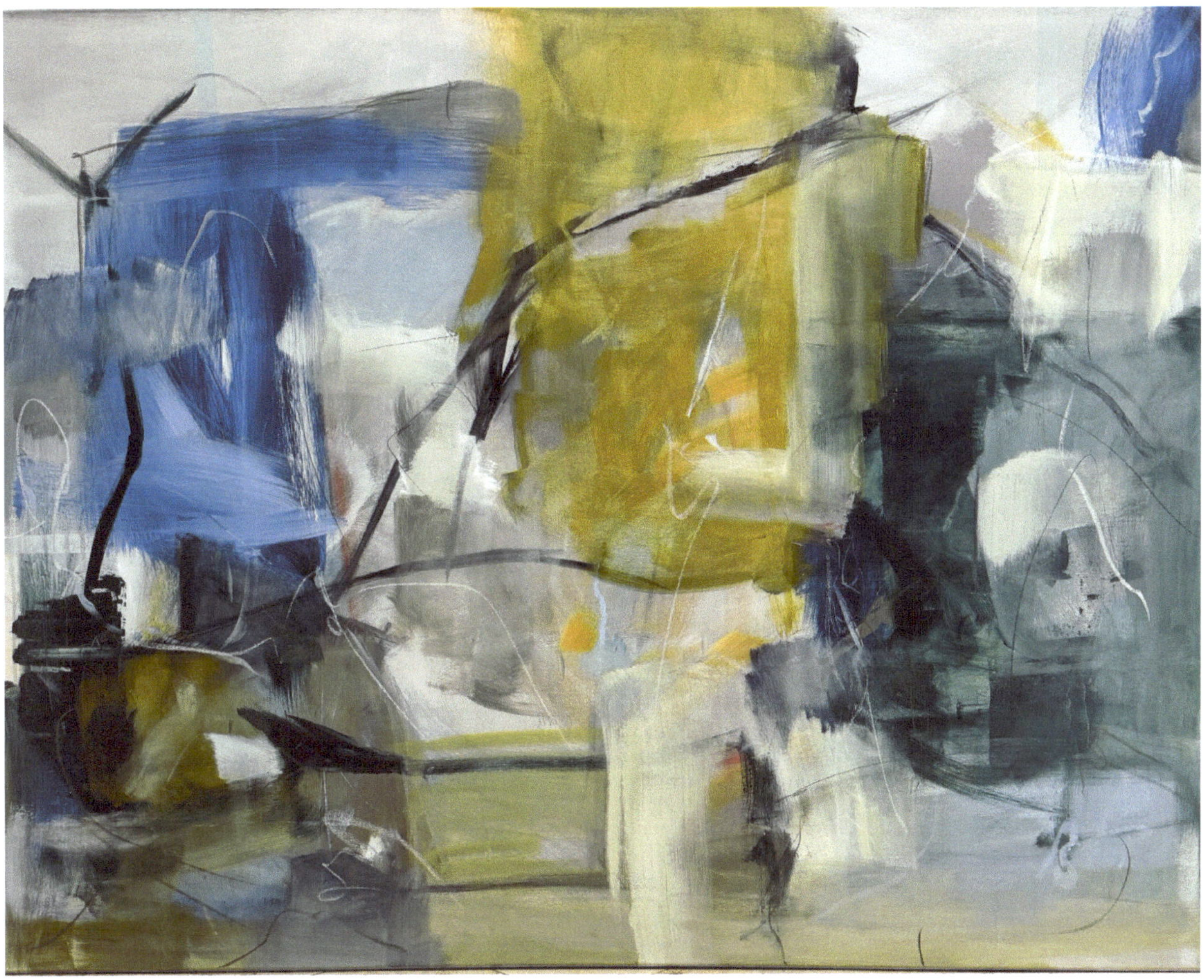

"Fragments in Motion" 2025 Mix Medium 120/150cm

MARA MONTAGNA

https://www.maramontagna.it

Painting has always been a passion for Mara Montagna, but her educational and professional journey has led her to teach for 42 years. The recurring themes in her works draw inspiration from this experience and are often linked to childhood, nature, and the female image. For Mara, imagination and dreams are equally important and sometimes help us endure reality and make it acceptable. Colors speak to her, and she plays with them, creating harmonious or contrasting combinations depending on what she wants to emphasize. Matching them to fabrics is the most enjoyable part of her work, precisely because what she wants to express must have character, and she draws a significant contribution from them. For Mara, art can symbolically express content that can touch us deeply. "We want bread, but also roses," said Rosa Luxemburg, and Mara firmly believes this: art is not a luxury, it is not the property of just a few. Art belongs to everyone.

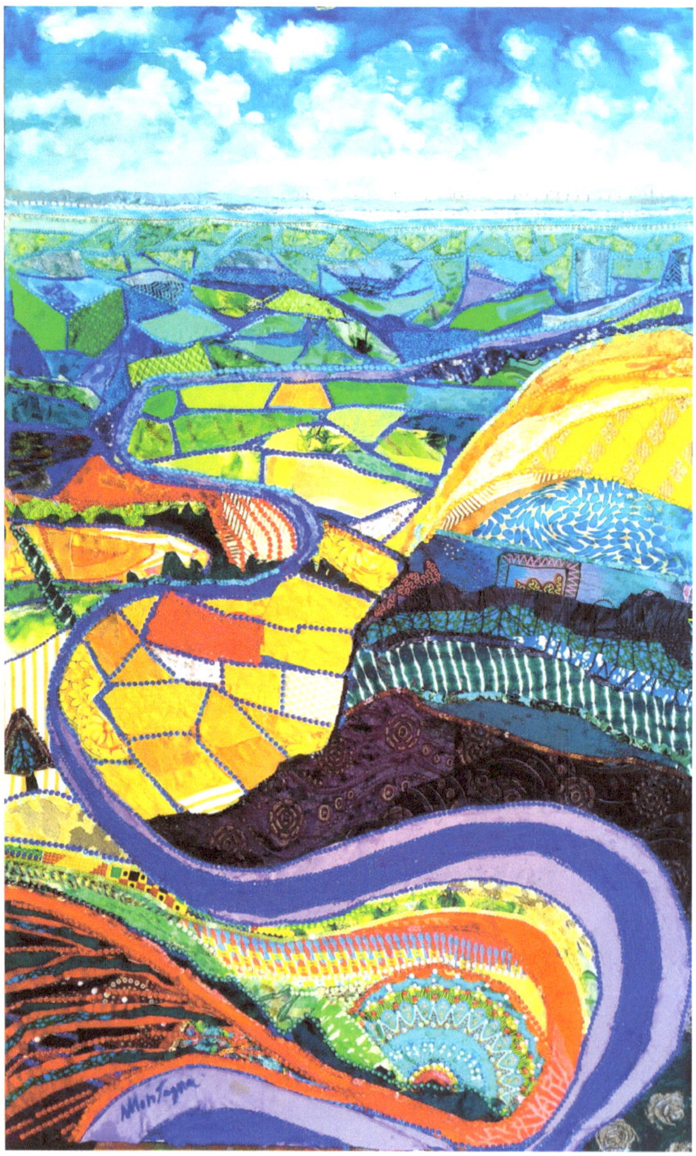

A spasso con David - 2025- acrilico e collage su legno, cm. 75x122

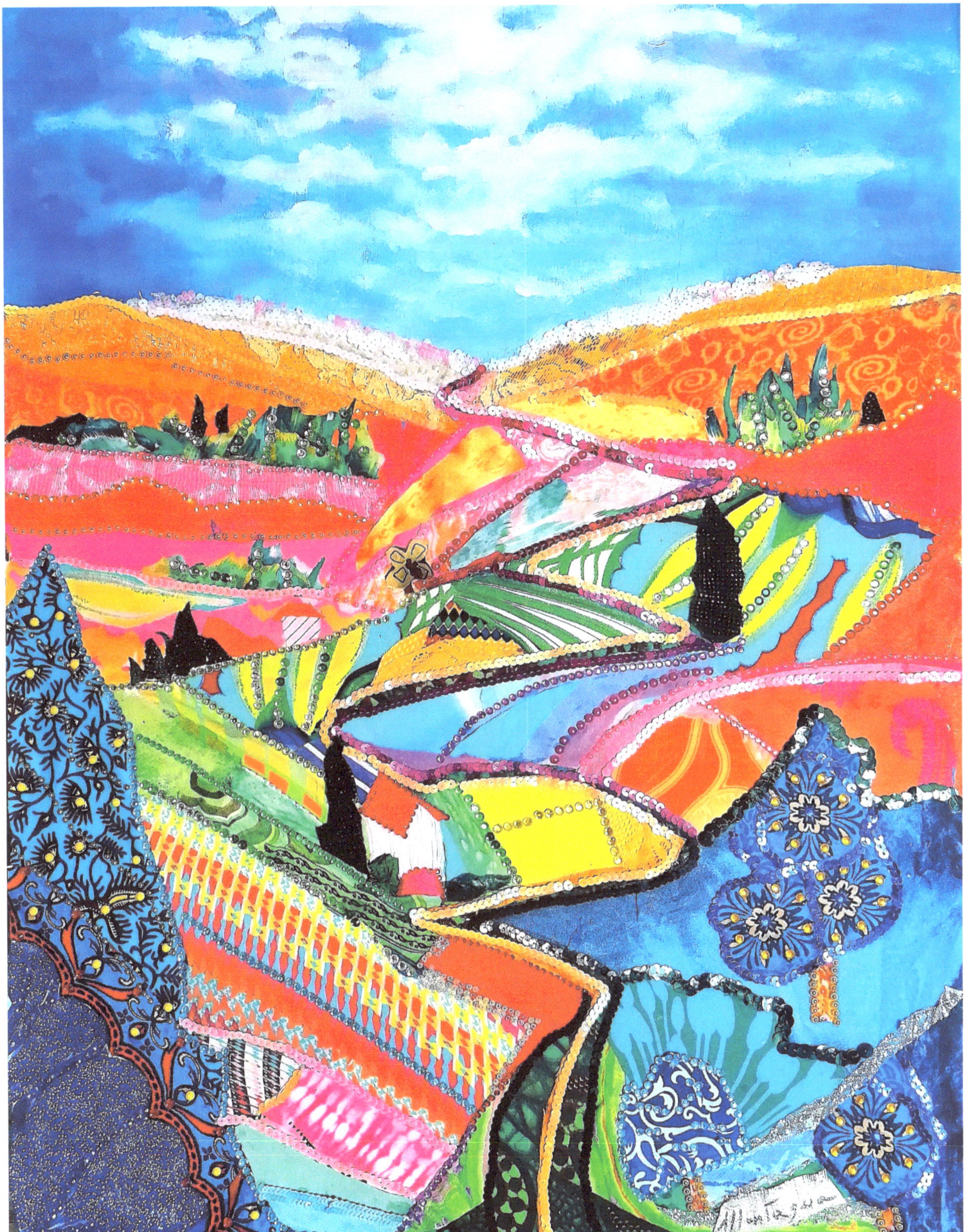

Nel canyon di Hockney- 2024- acrilico e collage su legno, cm. 60x80

MARCEL JOMPHE

www.marceljomphe.art

Marcel Jomphe, born in 1955 in Havre-Saint-Pierre, Quebec, Canada, now lives in Rimouski. He primarily works in drawing, blending realism with creativity. He draws inspiration from the intricate forms found in nature's vegetal realm, aiming to foster a more intimate relationship between people and their environment. In 1977, he embarked on a career as a botanical artist at the Canadian Museum of Nature. He subsequently worked at Laval University's Louis-Marie Herbarium and at Agriculture and Agri-Food Canada. His illustrations have appeared in over 80 scientific publications. Since 2012, he has dedicated himself entirely to his artistic pursuits. His work has been showcased in over 28 local and international exhibitions in Canada, the United States, Spain, Italy, and France. He has received several international awards. His work has appeared in numerous art books and periodicals. They can also be found in both public and private collections. In his recent artistic journey, he has a strong feeling of sculpting atoms into new depictions of the living and plant realms. Living organisms adapt to their environment, so a transformed environment will prompt them to adapt as well. Nature possesses an amazing ability to adapt and evolve in response to its environment, and this concept inspires him. His drawings are carefully crafted, meticulously refined, and are unique to his imagination. They emerge from deep contemplation, shaping themselves within him. Through iterative sketching, these ideas evolve into intricate masterpieces. This process allows him to develop a unique style, a harmonious blend of reality and imagination, and a distinct identity.

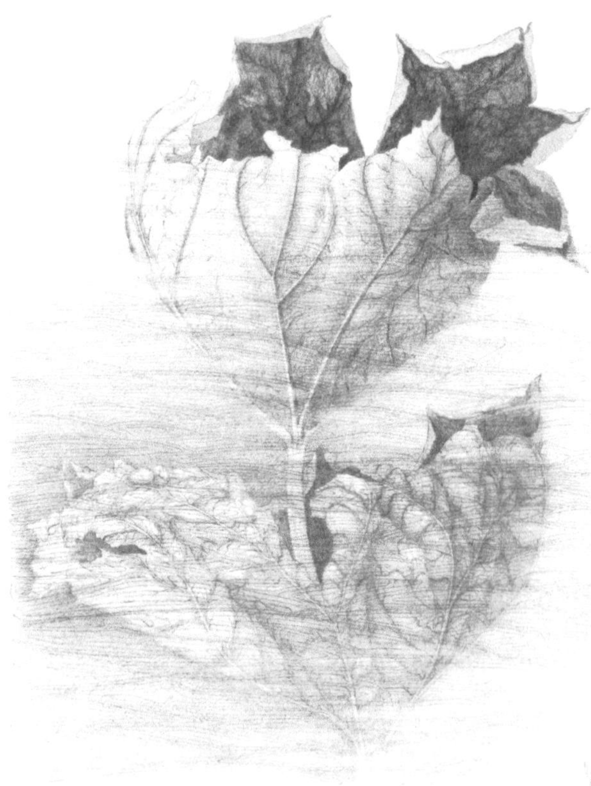

Leaves Study, 2024, graphite, 30 x 42 cm, on Moleskine

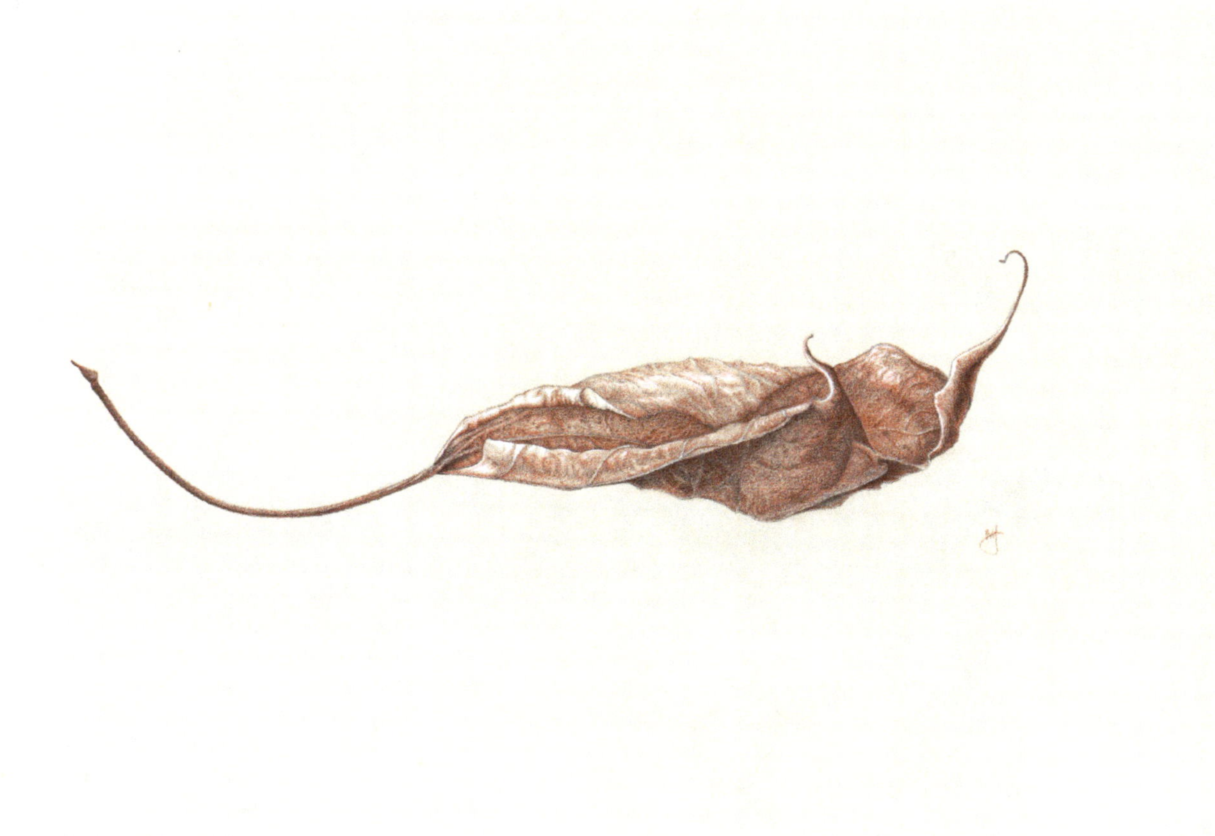

Catalpa study for imaginary work, 2025, sanguine, black chalk with white highlights, 42 x 30 cm

MARGARETHA GUBERNALE

https://www.margarethagubernale.org https://www.gubernale.com

As an international artist, MARGARETHA GUBERNALE was born in Zug, Switzerland, on June 9, 1941, where she also has her studio EDERA. She is mother of two adult children, Mario and Helena, and she is widowed, and she sacrificed her life to the art and developed her own magical and symbolic style. She plays also church organ and wrote compositions. MARGARETHA GUBERNALE made many group and solo exhibitions worldwide, including on 1993 in the MONTSERRAT GALLERY, in 2011 in the AGORA GALLERY and in 2012 in the BROADWAY GALLERY, all of them in New York USA, as well as exhibitions in Miami and Canada, in Germany, France and, among other espositions, a group exhibition in the Eiffel Tower, Salle Gustave Eiffel, Paris France in 2014. She took part in further exhibitions in England, Spain, Malta, Austria, China, Switzerland and numerous in Italy. Among other exhibitions, she received the 1st prize 2016 MARGHERITA HACK, from SPOLETO ARTE, for an exhibition. In February 2018 and 2020 she took part in the Expositions Art Capital, Grand Palais-Réunion des Musées Nationaux, Société des Artistes Indépendants, Paris France, also in 2024 in the Art Capital at the Grand Palais Éphémère, Paris, France, as well as in 2019, 2020 and 2021 at Swissartexpo in Zurich Main Station, Switzerland. In 2021 she participated in the three-month exhibition POETA MASSIMO TROISI, film director and actor of "Il Postino", at Castel dell'Ovo, Napoli, Italy, also in the exhibition in Procida and in the Exposition Artisti da Museo in Rome, Italy. In 2023 she held numerous digital exhibitions at various locations abroad with Artboxy and a digital solo exhibition at EuropaArt in Amsterdam. She also exhibited in the MAD Gallery and with her in Times Square she had some of her pictures streamed to one of the screens there in four episodes. She has received many awards, including a gold medal at the 2008 Olympic Fine Art in Beijing China. 2017 she got the 60 Top Artists Award, Metropolitan Art Museum Las Vegas USA, and 2020 the Top 60 Masters Award, ATIM, Grimandi Gallery, New York USA, and the Paolo Levi Prize at Palazzo Clerici, Milano Italy. In 2024 she was honored with the Trophy by the organization EDMC-Europe, Les éditions des musées et de la culture-Europe. 2024 She participated also through the organization Contemporary Art Management in the month-long aircraft exhibition at Vueling, Spain. She is nominated in many artbooks and magazines, so 2024 in Art Leaders of Tomorrow and Future of ART Global with Masterpiece Award from Contemporary Art Curator.

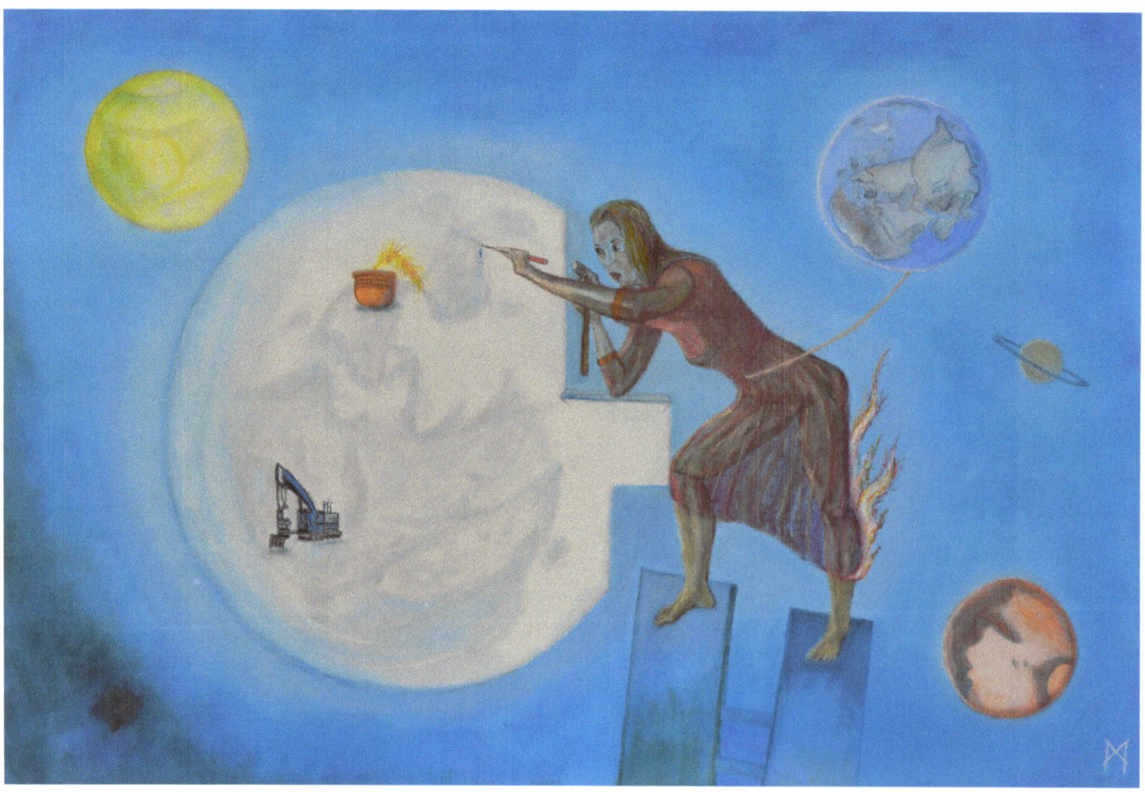

Declaration Day of Angular Moon, 2025, oil on canvas, 70 x 100 cm

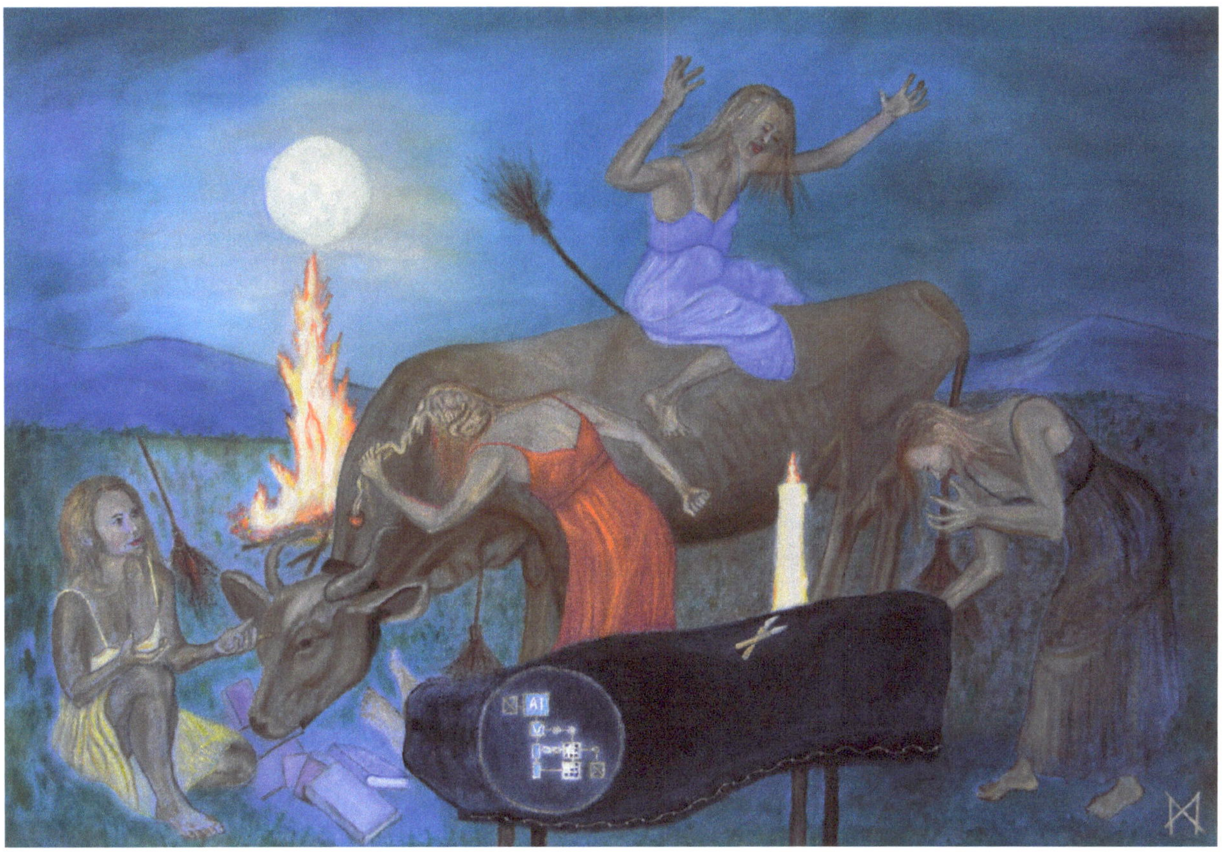

The Sorcerer's Apprentice (with Goethe), 2024, oil on canvas, 70 x 100 cm

MARÍA ISABEL DE LINCE

@midelince

María Isabel Salazar de Lince is a renowned Colombian artist. She studied Art and Architectural Design as well as Psychology at the Pontificia Universidad Javeriana in Bogotá. She trained in drawing and painting at Cooperartes and with masters such as David Manzur, Fernando Dávila, and Miguel Moyano, whose influence deeply shaped her visual language. These experiences nurtured a sensitive aesthetic, where color and light become vehicles for spiritual expression. Her work has been exhibited in prominent contemporary art spaces across the Americas, Europe, Asia, and the Middle East, including the Carrousel du Louvre, the MEAM Museum, the Affordable Art Fair in New York, and the Vienna Biennale. Throughout her career, she has received over 20 international awards, including the Leonardo Da Vinci Award, the Premio Internazionale Arte Milano, the International Prize Colosseo, the Future of Art Global Masterpiece Award, and the Order of Artistic Merit. Her art, deeply symbolic and spiritual, integrates the energy of the essential elements into a vibrant aesthetic, offering a dialogue between humanity, nature, and the sacred. Her work has been recognized for its ability to convey harmony, inner awareness, and transformation through the universal language of art. Her work is a message to the world, created by the spirit and expressed through the universal language of art, just as peace, harmony, beauty, happiness, and love are. For her, painting is a way of speaking to humanity: of conveying a deeper awareness of itself and of the universe it inhabits. She hopes that anyone, regardless of where they are, perceives the vibration of spirituality and peace that dwells within her paintings. She works with the essential elements—earth, air, fire, and water—because she recognizes in them the living force that sustains existence. Each holds a message that she seeks to translate into color, form, and energy. She loves this planet, and her work is also an invitation to love nature, and a call to the urgent need to care for and protect it as our home. Color is one of her greatest allies; through it, she builds harmonies that awaken deep emotions. Light and color, in their subtle dance, allow the spiritual message to reach the viewer's heart with greater clarity. She paints because she believes art has the power to elevate, transform, and heal. And because, from her place as a human being and as an artist, this is her way of being of service.

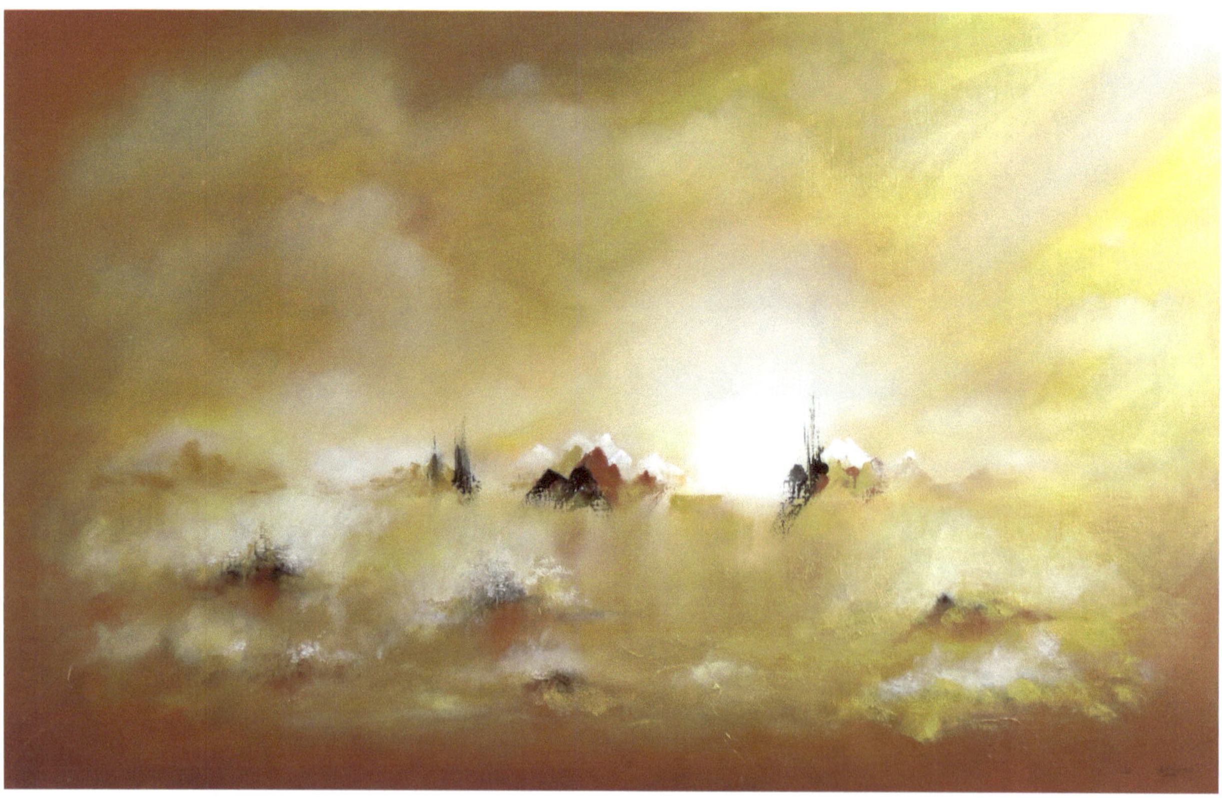

As in heaven 3, 2025. Oil on linen, 90 x 140 cm

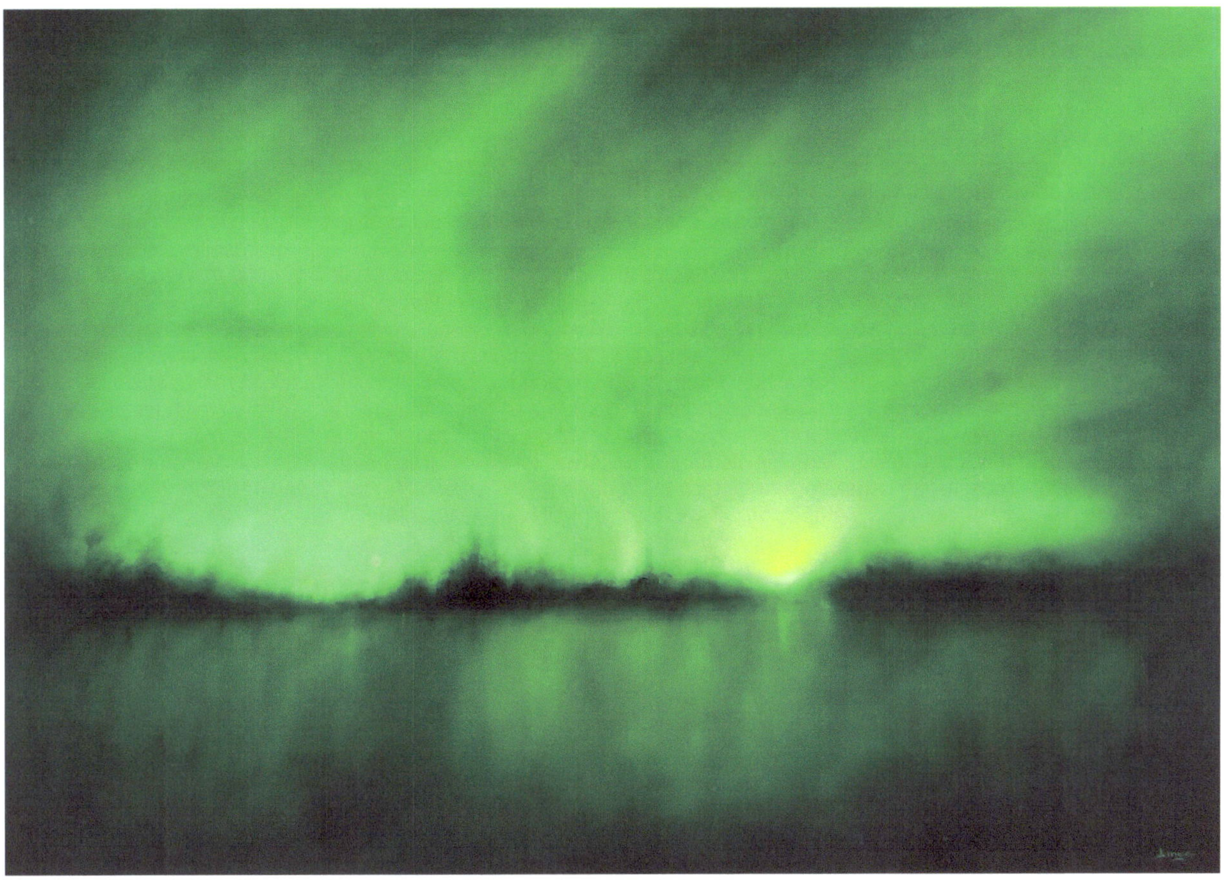

From heaven to earth 3, 2024. oil on linen, 130 x 180 cm

MARIANNE CHARLOTTE MYLONAS SVIKOVSKY

https://reves-realites.com/

By the hazards of life. I was born in 1941 under the bombs in Germany. My father, from Vienna, Austria and my mother, a native swiss, both of various european origins, the family name being polish, my grandmother of german origin but also estonian and russian, all of them adventurous people. The war and fortunes of life brought my parents to live here and there, for three or four years at a time. My schooling therefore took place in the swiss french mountains, in Montreal Canada in English, in italian in Lugano, Switzerland, then in Los Angeles USA where I completed High School and did art studies at UCLA (University of Southern California) and lastly in Vienna, Austria, Rome, Italy, the country of art and then in Geneva, Switzerland. I worked in several fields like fashion, banks and international agencies and a non-governmental organization and teaching languages in Vienna and Geneva which I still do now with great pleasure. A creative teaching either private or for several private schools, aiming at the students goals, for top managers to youngsters, preparing also for the big international exams. I therefore have met all sorts of people, observing with a curious, somewhat distant eye in order to adapt rapidly. I married a Greek, had two lovely children, gave language lesson to them and their friends at home, then developed a personal, very original successful artistic activity and business during ten years that I could do at home, decorating with my art some of the top class hotels in Geneva and participating in many exhibitions. I also made very original vegetal mural masks of imaginary characters of Greek mythology or King Arthur's legends. One ominous day tragedy befell both of my children, we lost our son and a terrible mental illness befell our daughter. Divorce followed. The curtain then fell down on this part of my life and I was left with nothing but my creativity and teaching. Painting and writing came to my rescue, both had been my dear hobbies since I was twelve years old, drawing and long letters which at the crucial time turned into poetry, so as to express the distress in the most concise way the feelings assailing me, by and by, bringing me back to life, after going back thanks to poetry, to the roots of my varied life already early marked by abandon and death. It took time which was not wasted. I started showing my paintings in rather big exhibits during which I gave my own Poetry readings, dramatized and accompanied by talented young musicians, inviting my guests into my inner world and the expression of my life's experiences. I joined main poetry associations in Geneva and by and by was invited to exhibit here and there. Love also came to my rescue, a major theme in my poems, the relationship between men and women also appearing in some of my paintings. I am now happy again in this new and quite different phase of my life and ready to meet its challenges. I also thank my parents for transmitting their love of art, music museums and litterature to me which I still cherish today and thus continue studying the old famous masters. While in Rome, I studied Giorgio Vasari's book XIV-XVI century, on the great Italian Renaissance masters, still today a reference book for the study of History of Art, the first methodological and biographical study ever done.

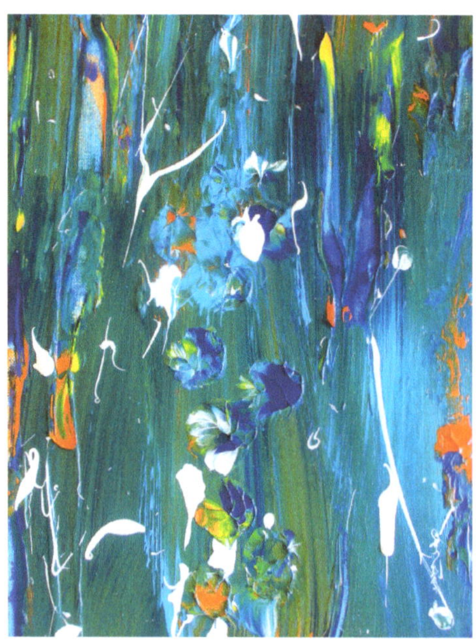

I Had To Do It, Acrylic on Canvas, 23.6 W x 31.5 H

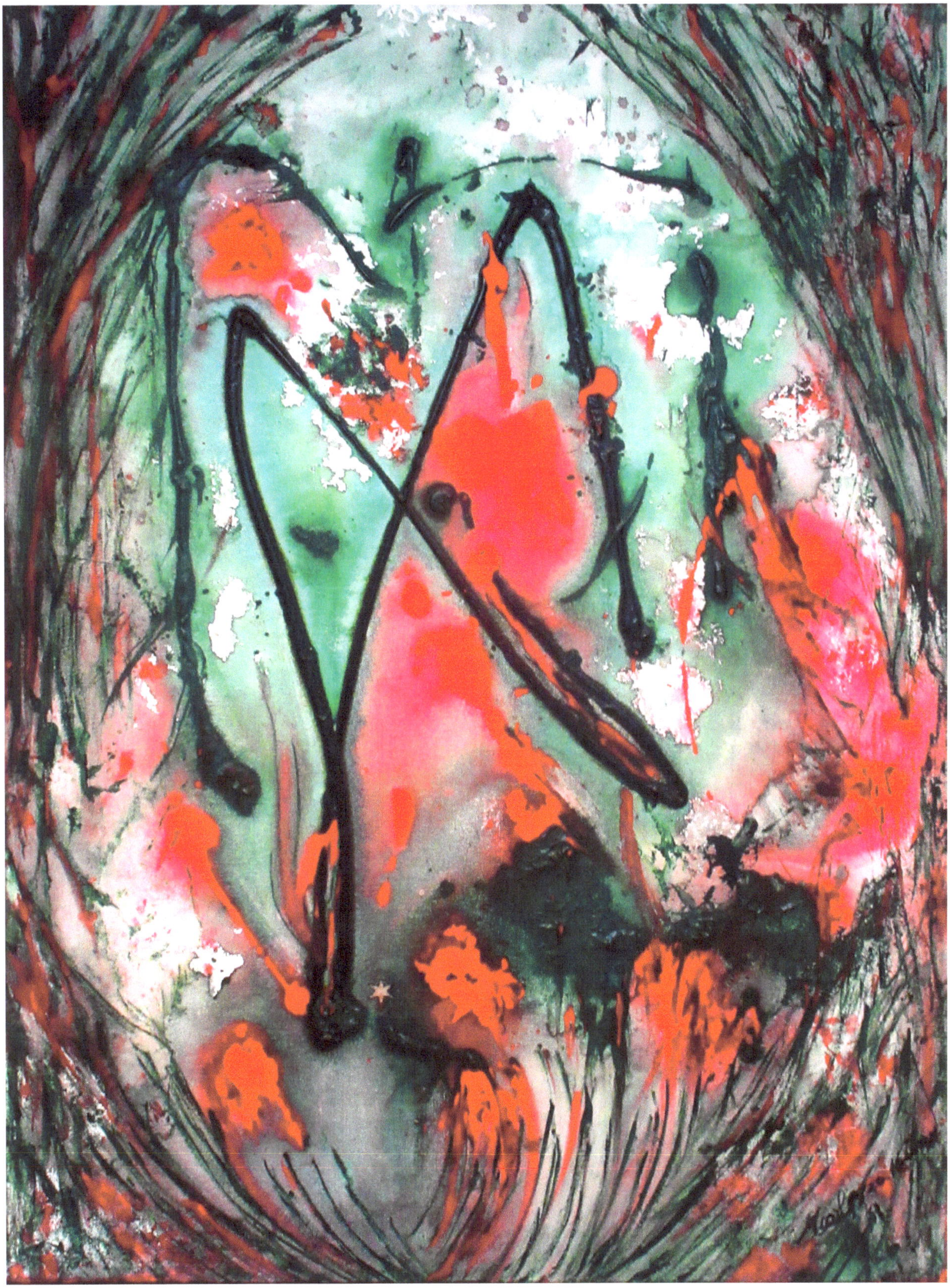

Imagine .... the future, Acrylic on Canvas, 60cm W x 80cm H

MARIE-GHISLAINE BEAUCÉ

E-mail: marieghislainebeauce@gmail.com

Marie-Ghislaine Beaucé is a French artist whose journey is deeply rooted in her fascination with textile materials and their artistic potential. Her exploration of different textures, colours, and forms has led to develop a distinct visual language that merges the tactile quality of textiles with the conceptual rigour of geometric abstraction. The absolute protagonists of her artworks are the materials themselves that she intertwines and overlaps to create intricate, semi-abstract geometric lattices. These compositions are punctuated and delimited by rhythmic layers of fabrics, employing woven techniques and superposition of padded tubes, suggesting a sense of movement and progression, showcasing the artist's unique approach to textile art. The artworks are characterized by their exploration of themes related to structure, fluidity and interconnectedness. Her use of textile fibers as primary medium allows her to create intricate compositions that evoke a sense of depth and dimensionality. The interplay of different textures, colours, and forms is a recurring motif in her work, reflecting her fascination with the material properties of textiles. One of the central themes in Marie-Ghislaine Beaucé's work is the relationship between order and chaos. Her compositions often feature a structured, geometric framework that is softened by the organic, fluid nature of textile fibers. Each piece of fabric, with its unique texture and colour, contributes to the overall composition. Her work delves into the intersection of traditional techniques of weaving, knitting, and contemporary art, resulting in hybrid creations that straddle the line between patchwork and plasticism.

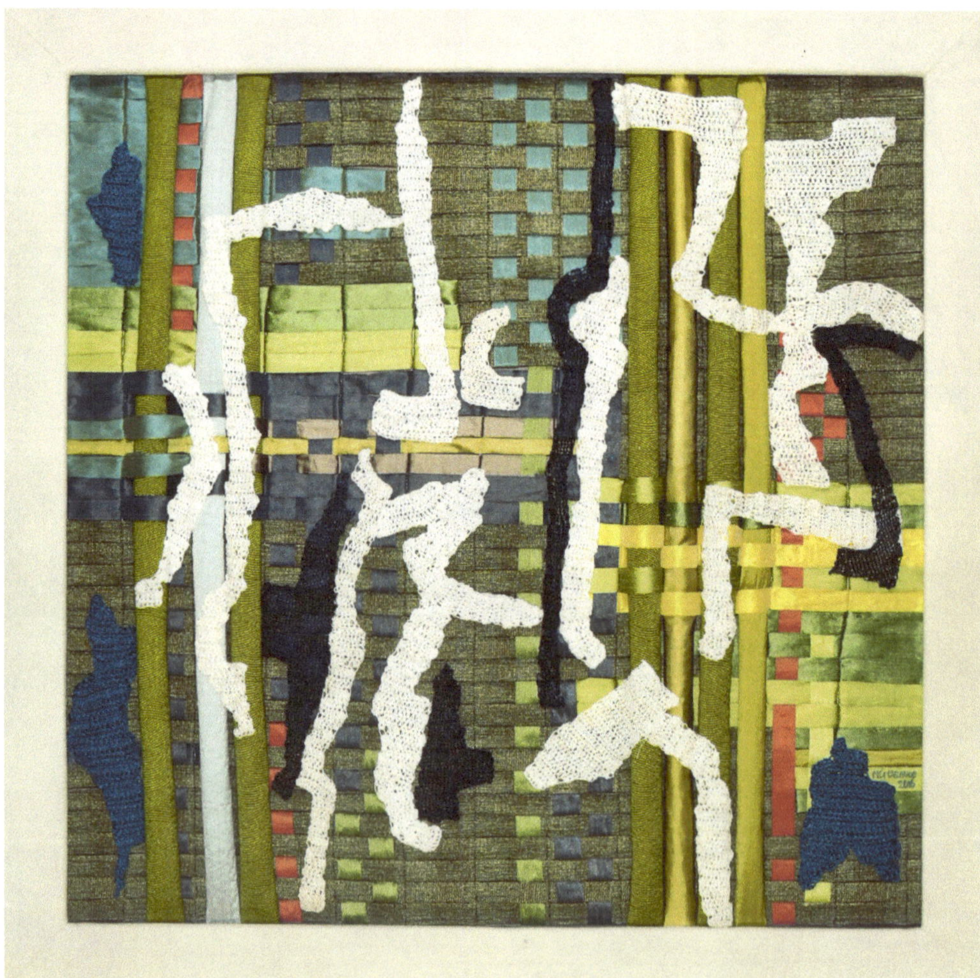

Tissage 3, 2016, mixed fabrics, 101 x 101 cm

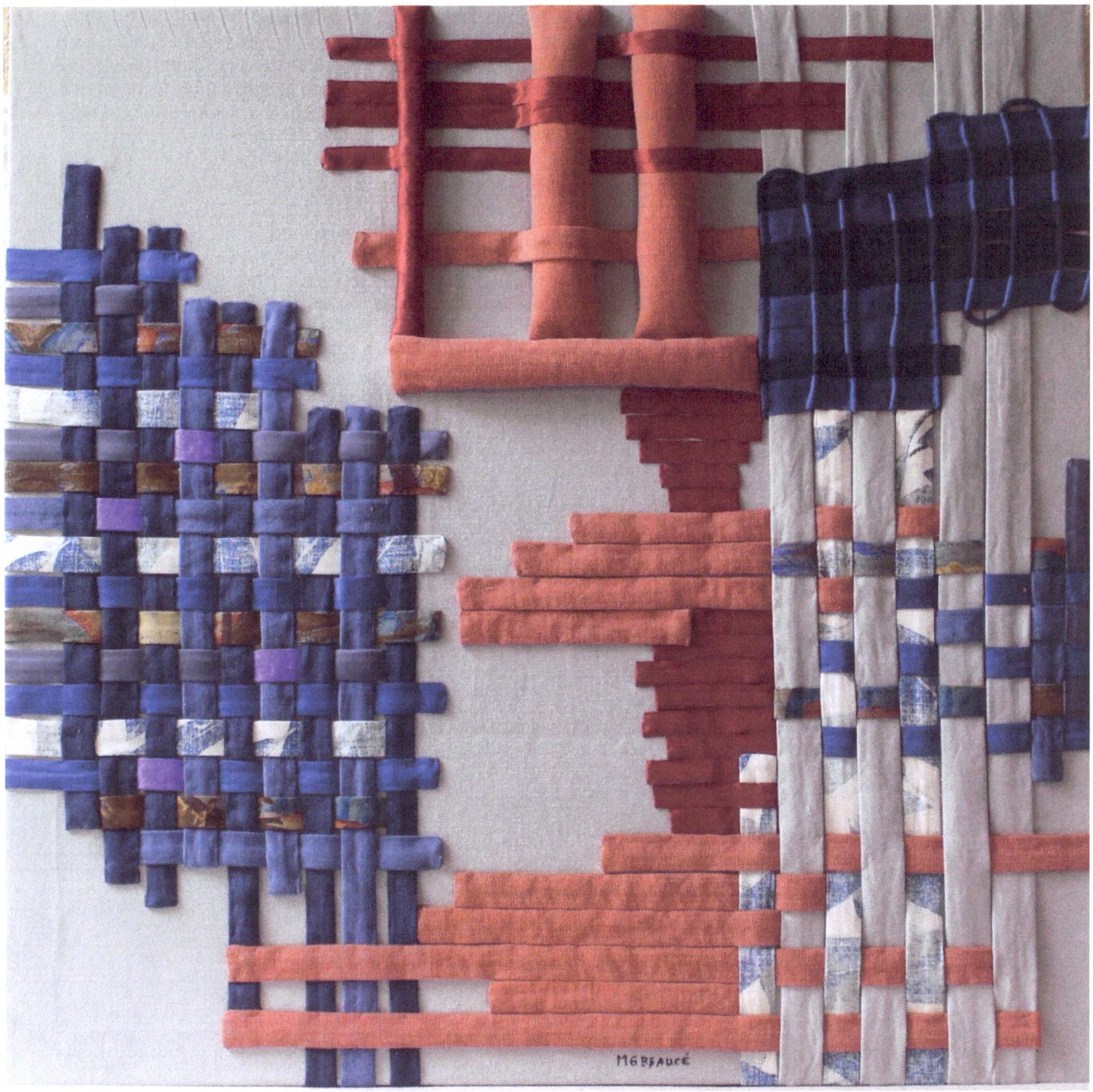

Wild Guess, 2024, mixed fabrics, 84 x 84 cm.

MARIO MOLINS

https://www.instagram.com/mariomolinsescultor/

Mario Molins: The Dialogue Between Art, Nature, and Human Essence From his roots in Binéfar, Huesca, Spain (1983), Mario Molins emerges as a multidisciplinary artist whose restless spirit intrinsically merges with Nature. A Fine Arts graduate from the University of Barcelona with doctoral studies, Mario doesn't just create art; he lives it as an extension of his own philosophy: his work becomes a bridge connecting human beings with their primordial environment, inviting reflection on our deep-rooted relationship with the Earth. His exhibition trajectory is as extensive as the distinctions he's received, notably the 2016 recognition from the Association of Art Critics of Aragon, Spain, as the best Aragonese artist under 35. His creations reside in numerous public and private collections, ranging from the imposing "Catharsis" in Zaragoza's Parque Grande José Antonio Labordeta, Spain, to his 2023 intervention in the Posets-Maladeta Natural Park, Spain, for the "Ballarte" Art Festival, and his recent stone sculpture in Manresa, Spain (2024), where the land itself becomes his canvas. Beyond its form, Molins' work is a visual meditation on the interdependence, fragility, and resilience of both Nature and the human spirit. It serves as a reminder of our profound connection to the cycle of life, inviting a fuller awareness of existence. This essence is even reflected in his poetic ventures, embodied in the collections "La corteza del corazón" (The Bark of the Heart) (2020) and "Con el corazón en la mano" (With Heart in Hand) (2023), which further explore this understanding of being from a natural perspective. To grasp the origin of his inspiration and the deep resonance of his art, one only needs to immerse themselves in his moving YouTube video "Mi abuelo es un olivo" (My Grandfather is an Olive Tree), a piece that reveals the soul of his commitment to life and Nature.

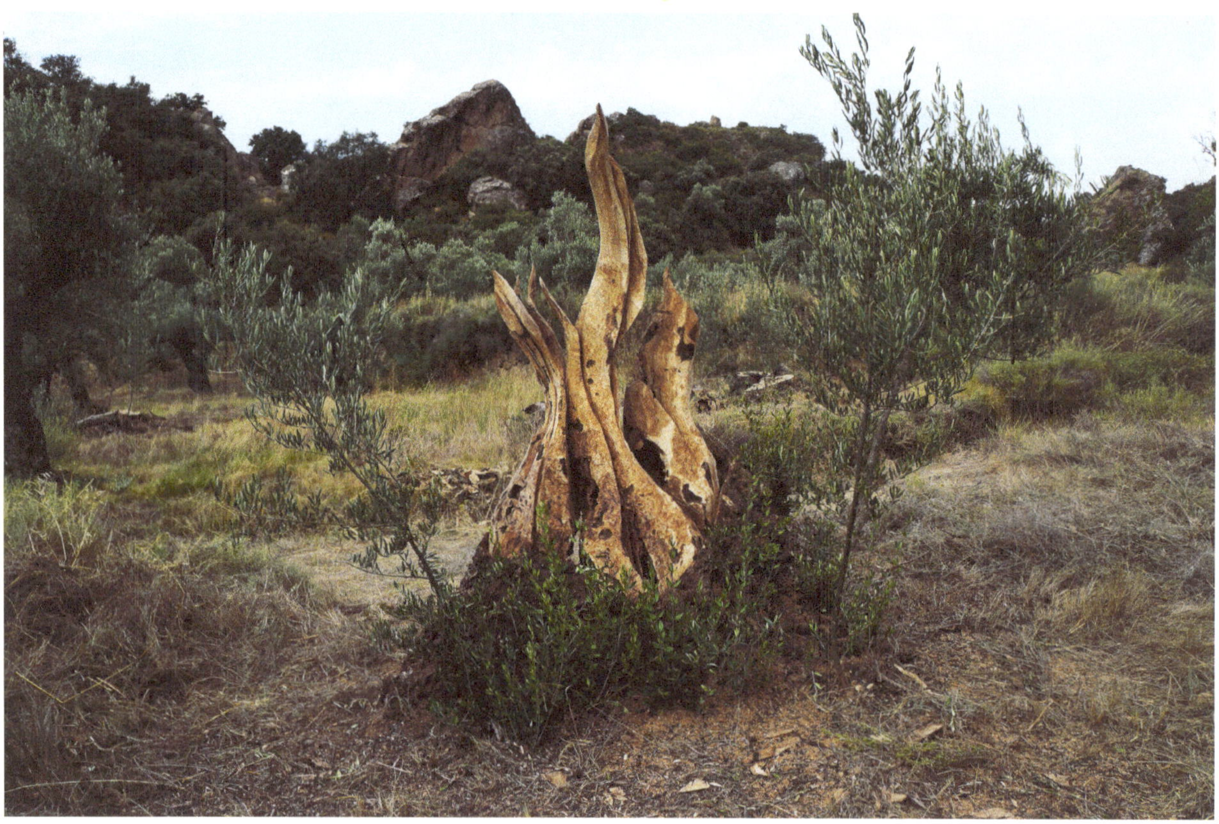

Catharsis for an olive tree / 2019 / Olive tree / Growing measure

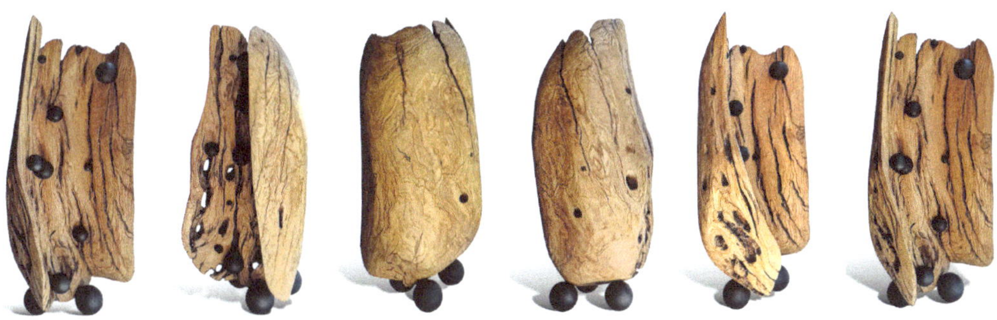

Another Cave / 2024 / Direct carving, turning and assemblage wood and indian ink / 70 x 40 x 30

MARIO R. ZAMMIT-LEWIS

@ mariozammitlewis

Mario Zammit-Lewis , also known as "Il Malterse" (The Maltese) in the 70ths/80ths in Italy. Born in Misida, Malta 76 years ago from a Maltese Father and a Italien Mother. The family mouved to North of Italy (Piemonte) in 1963 from Paris and that is after a many pencil drawing he starts oil painting. He practiced water color painting at school in Colombe, France where he wins his very first Art Price in 1961/62 . aT 16 in Turin, Italy where he starts Art school at the Lyceum Vittorio Veneto mainly to meet Master Raffaele Pontecorvo. In Turin in the 70 and 71 his first 2 solo exhibitions and from there to today collective and solo exhibitions did not stop all around the world , his paintings are in Europe, Asia, North Africa, South America et...etc.. This year and next he is celebrating his 65 year of Art (Oil Paintings).

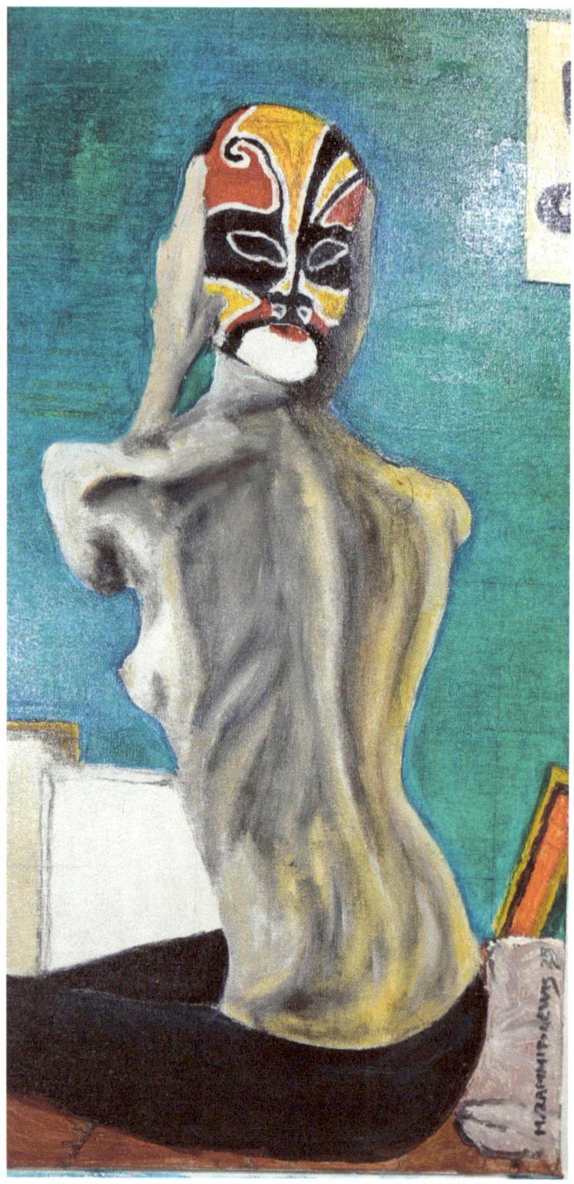

The Cinese Mask - 2025

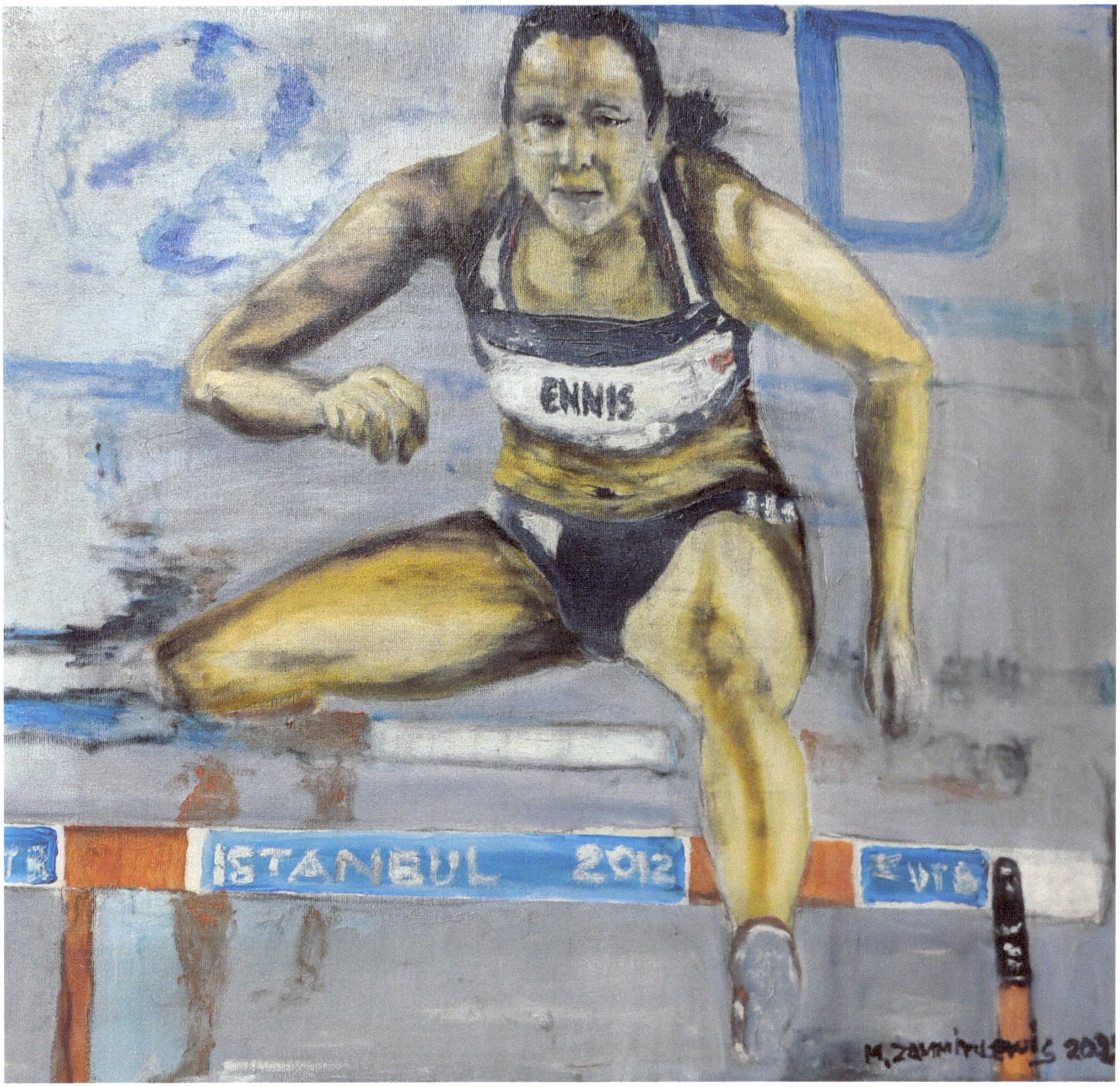

Hurdles race 2025

MARION SCHMIDTKE

www.MarionSchmidtke.de

Geboren 1961 "Mit Farbschichten baue ich den Raum eines Gemäldes und tauche ein in ein ruhiges Reich voller Frieden und inniger Verbundenheit mit der Natur." - Marion Schmidtke "Mein Wunsch, mich von der Representation zu lösen, resultiert in einer Sprache, die weniger in der Realität verankert, abstrakter und eher dazu geneigt ist, Emotionen direkt zu offenbaren, ein Bedürfnis, das sowohl ästhetisch als auch spirituell ist." Marion Schmidtke erforscht Naturmotive über und unter Wasser, mit Öl-und Acrylfarbe auf großen Arbeitsflächen. Inspiriert von der Natur verbindet sie Abstraktes mit Natürlichem. Durch Schichten und ein Element der Stille entstehen Werke, die sich durch leuchtende Farben, Licht und Tiefe auszeichnen. Durch ihre Teilnahme an zahlreichen internationalen Ausstellungen und Projekten von New York bis London erlangte sie weltweite Anerkennung. Marion studierte von 1983 bis 1989 Kunst und Musik an der Universität Duisburg. Die Künstlerin hat viele Jahre an verschiedenen Schulen unterrichtet und war lange als Dozentin für Malerei tätig. 2014 zog sie mit Ihrem Mann auf die Insel Fehmarn. Hier hat sie auch ihr eigenes Studio.

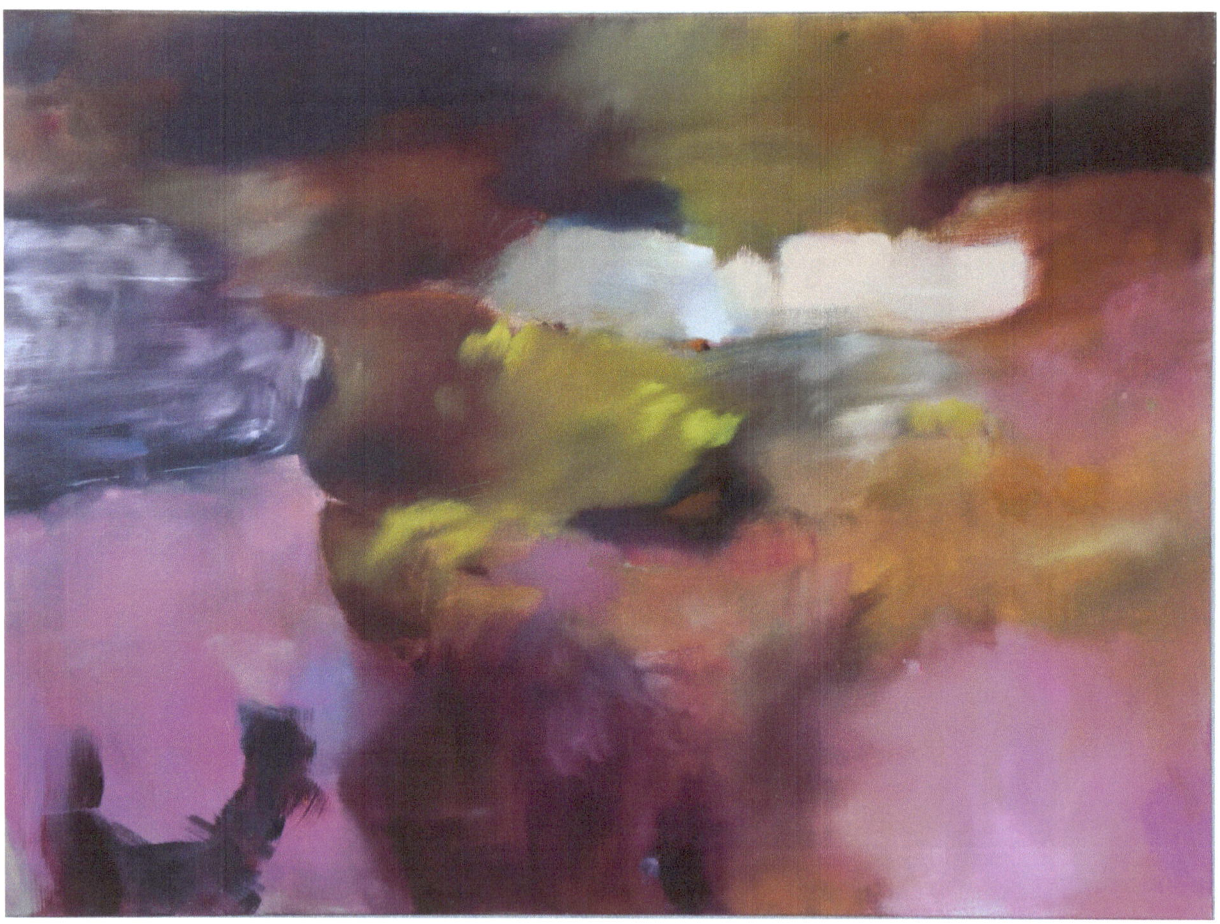

Colorful reef 2022 acrylic on canvas 120 x 160 cm

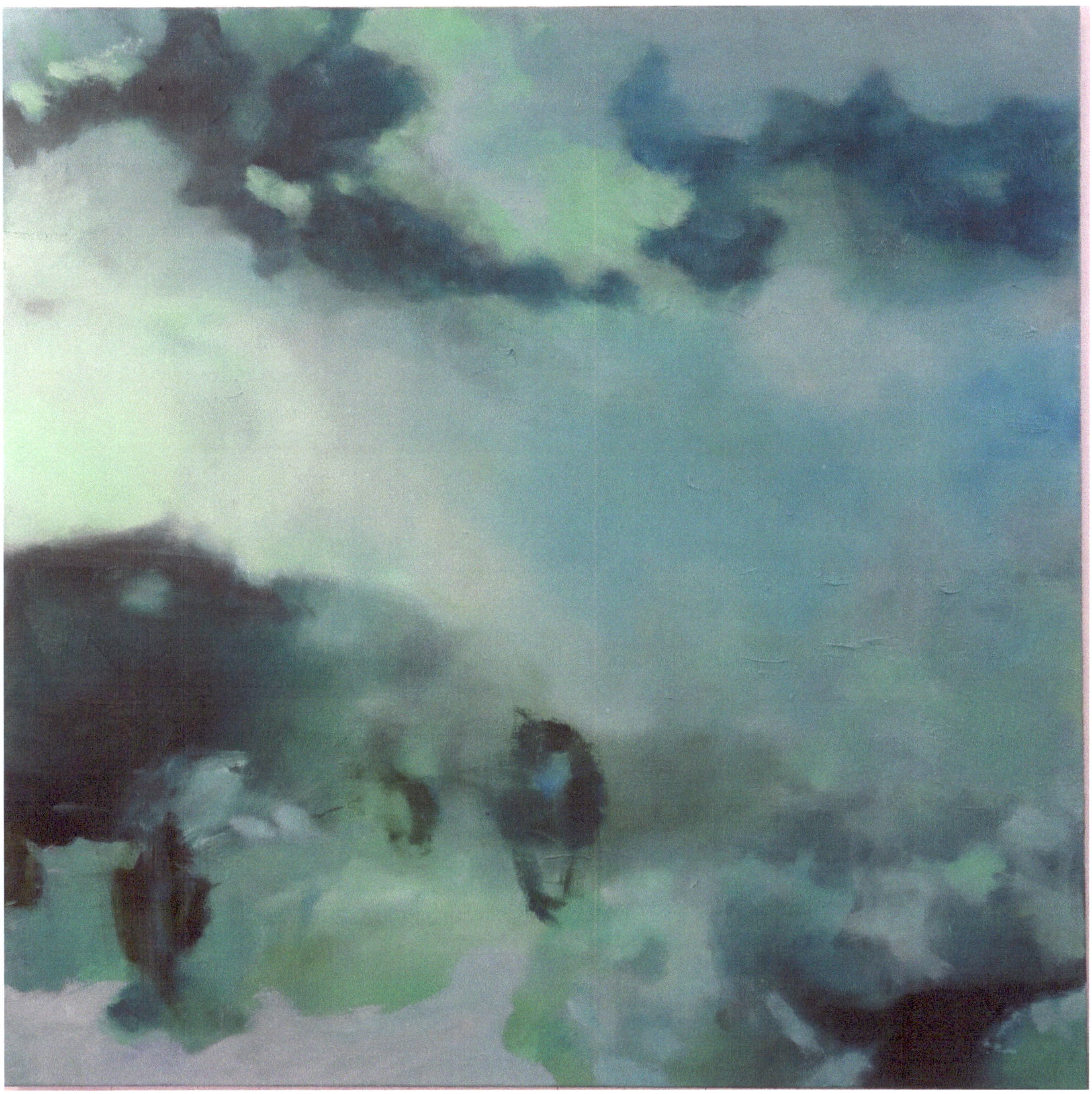

Deep layers of the ocean oil on canvas, 120 x 120 cm

MARLENE JORGE

Marlene Jorge https://www.instagram.com/marlenejorgeartist

My creative process is characterized by impromptu expression and unforced outbursts, resulting in compositions that are akin to a personal diary. My works are inspired by volatile emotions that well up within my inquisitive spirit. To produce unique artwork, I harness my creative urges by drawing from daily emotion-triggering activities as well as the depths of my personal experiences. This allows me to extract all the creative juice necessary to create art that is truly unique and meaningful. Marlene Jorge, an autodidact pop surrealist artist born in Santiago, Dominican Republic in 1974, has a unique approach to addressing unconsciousness. Jorge's style liberates unconsciousness from the common perspective, inviting spectators to break free from preconceptions and society's blueprints. She spent her youth between her native Dominican Republic and the USA, with her first drawing composition dating back to 1982, owned by her mother who recognized her artistry at the early age of five. Jorge's art challenges us to sympathize with our inner selves, untouched by preconceived social and cultural backgrounds, inviting us to embrace who we truly are without the life-giving preconceptions we experience constantly. Her elevated perspective provides a subtle yet unique composition, enticing us to understand and accept our true selves.

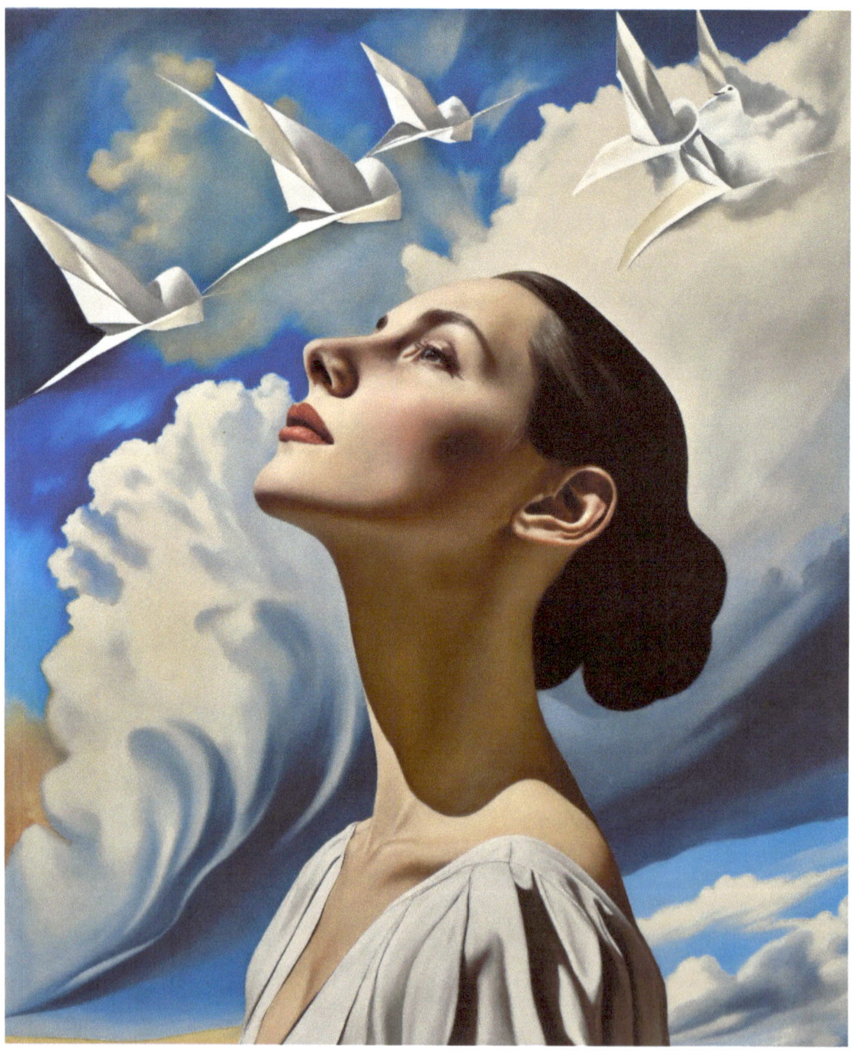

Paper Planes & Prayers- 2025

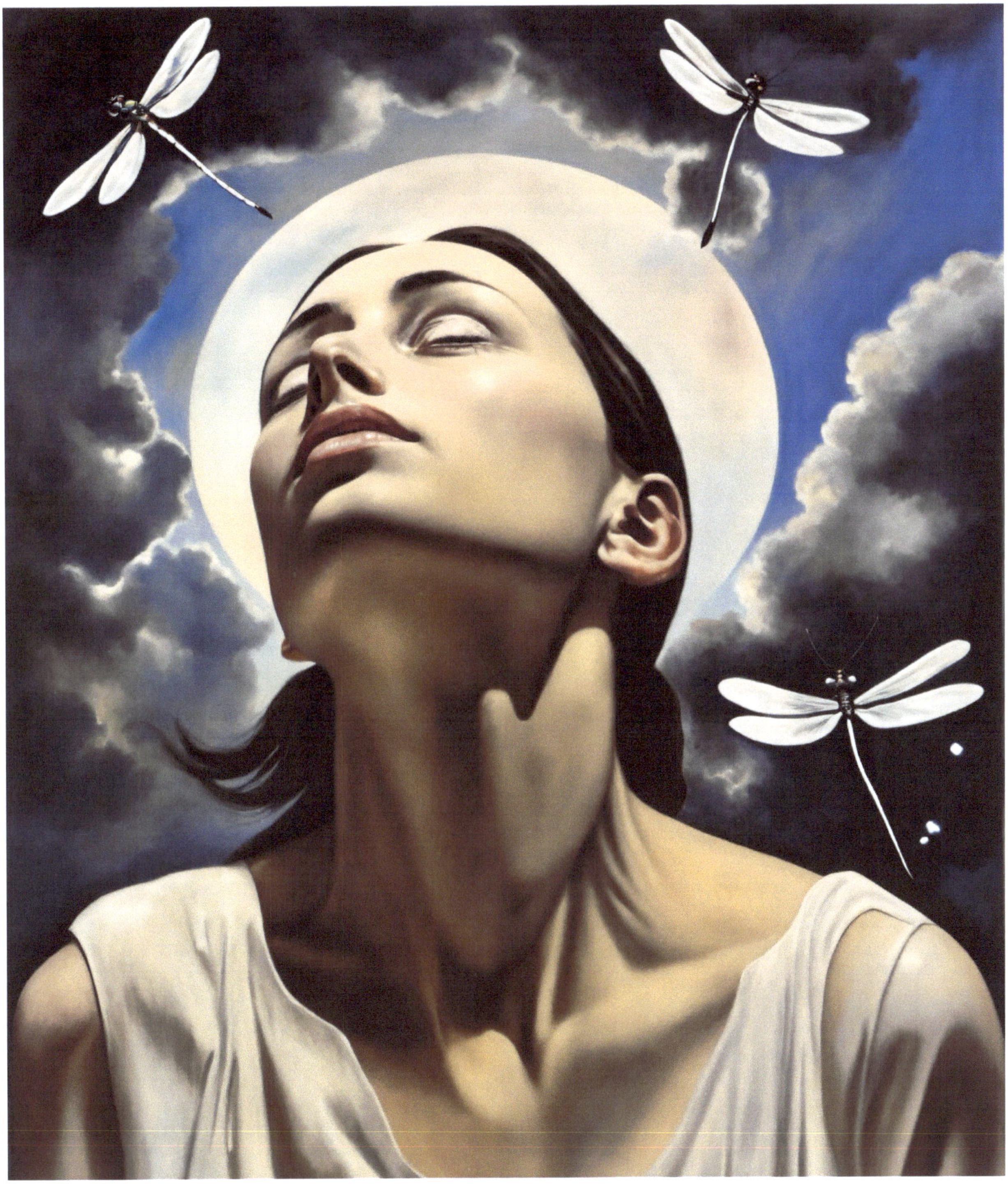

Flora of the Inner World-2025

MARTA PROMINSKA

art@martaprominska.com

Marta Prominska is a Polish artist working in oil and ink, known for atmospheric, surreal imagery. Her work has received international recognition, including multiple American Art Awards—2nd Place Surrealism for "Beyond the Gates" (2021) and "In Extremis" (2018), and 2nd Place Art Brut for "Bema Pamieci" (2020)—as well as the Artist of the Future Award from Contemporary Art Curator Magazine (2020) and inclusion in ArtTour International's Top 60 International Artists (2020). She also produced the film "Oneness," which presents her paintings and received a Special Award at an Independent Cinema Festival in 2022. Her paintings and profiles have been featured in international art magazines and publications such as ATIM's Top 60 Masters 2020 (ArtTour International, New York), Masterpieces 2020 Special Edition and Masterpieces 2017 (Heavy Music Artwork, UK), Arte Arcana (HMA, UK), and Oneness (One Art Agency, Warsaw, 2021).

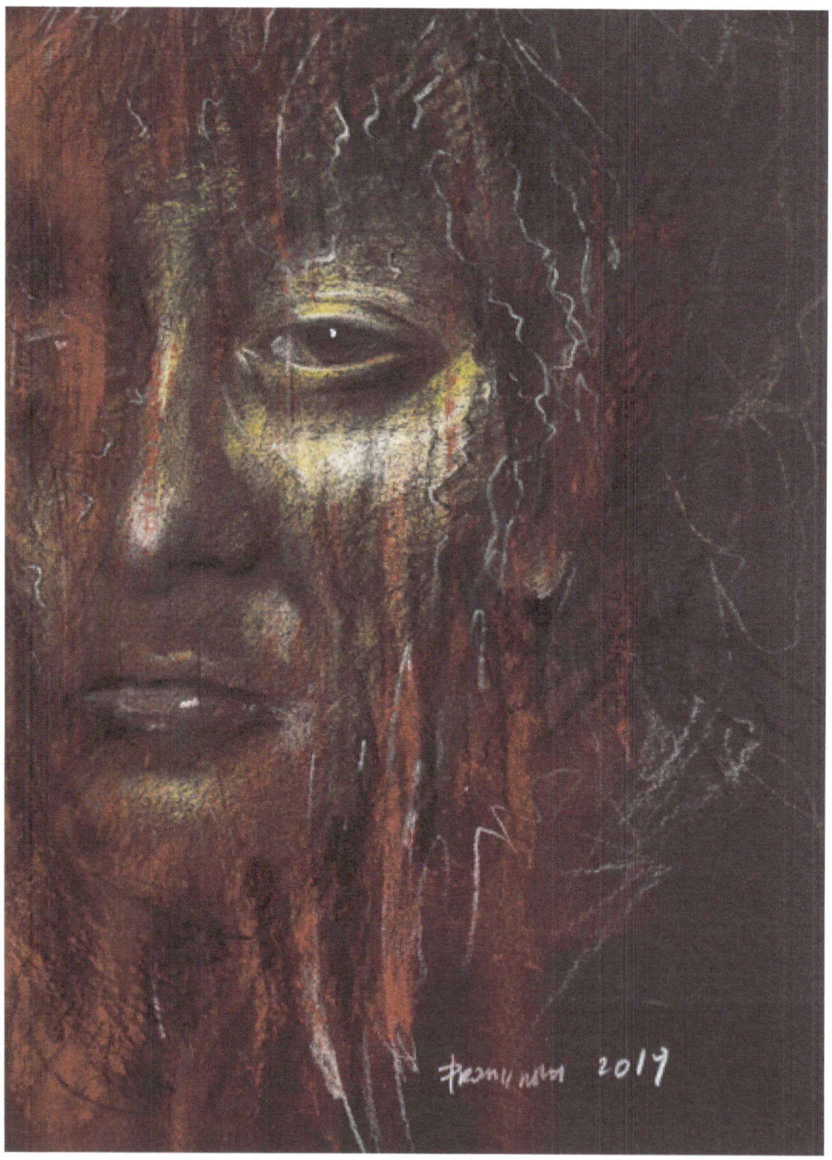

"U16" 14x19,5 cm colour pencils on paper, 2019

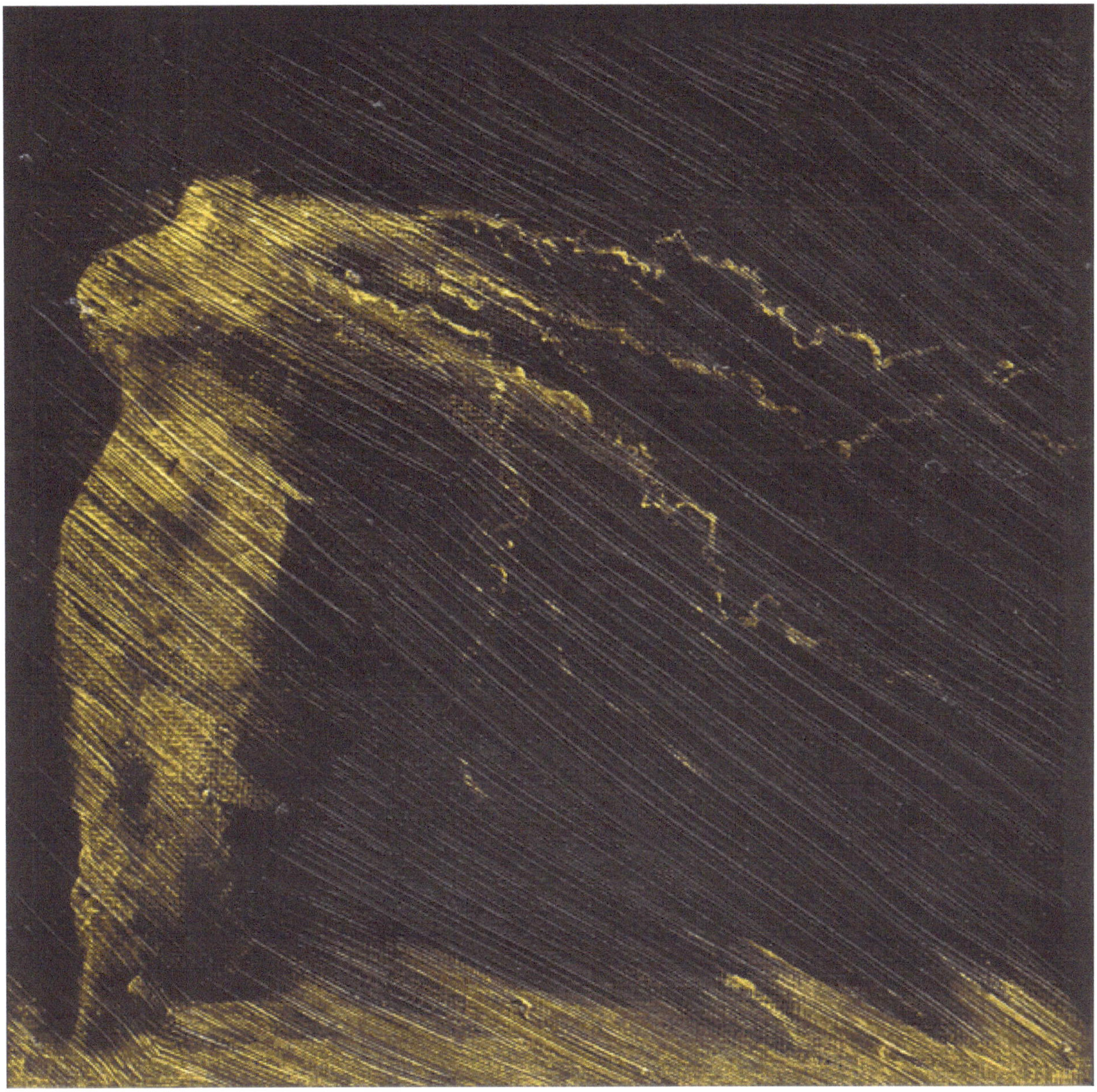

"Aphonia" 20cmx20cm oil on canvas

MASSIMO VITO AVANTAGGIATO

www.massimoavantaggiato.com

Massimo Vito Avantaggiato is an Italian composer, writer, and visual artist. He is a professor of Electroacoustic Composition and History of Electronic Music at Italian Conservatories. His interdisciplinary practice explores the spiritual dimension of existence, using music and visual art as means to reveal and communicate the inner essence of all things. Avantaggiato's work has been recognized with over 300 national and international awards and has been featured as a finalist in numerous prestigious competitions.

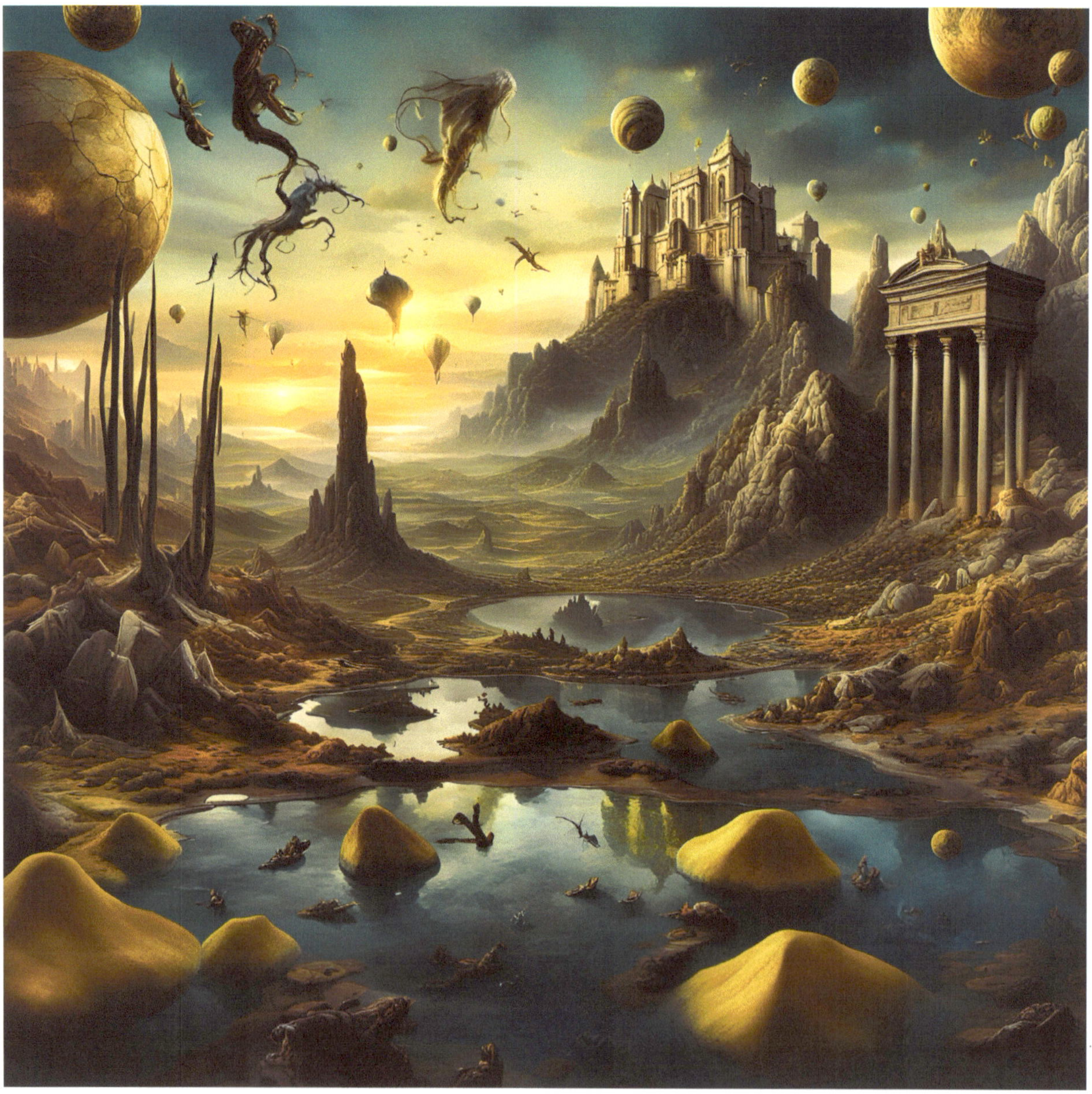

Oniros, 2024. Oil on canvas, 50 x 50 cm.

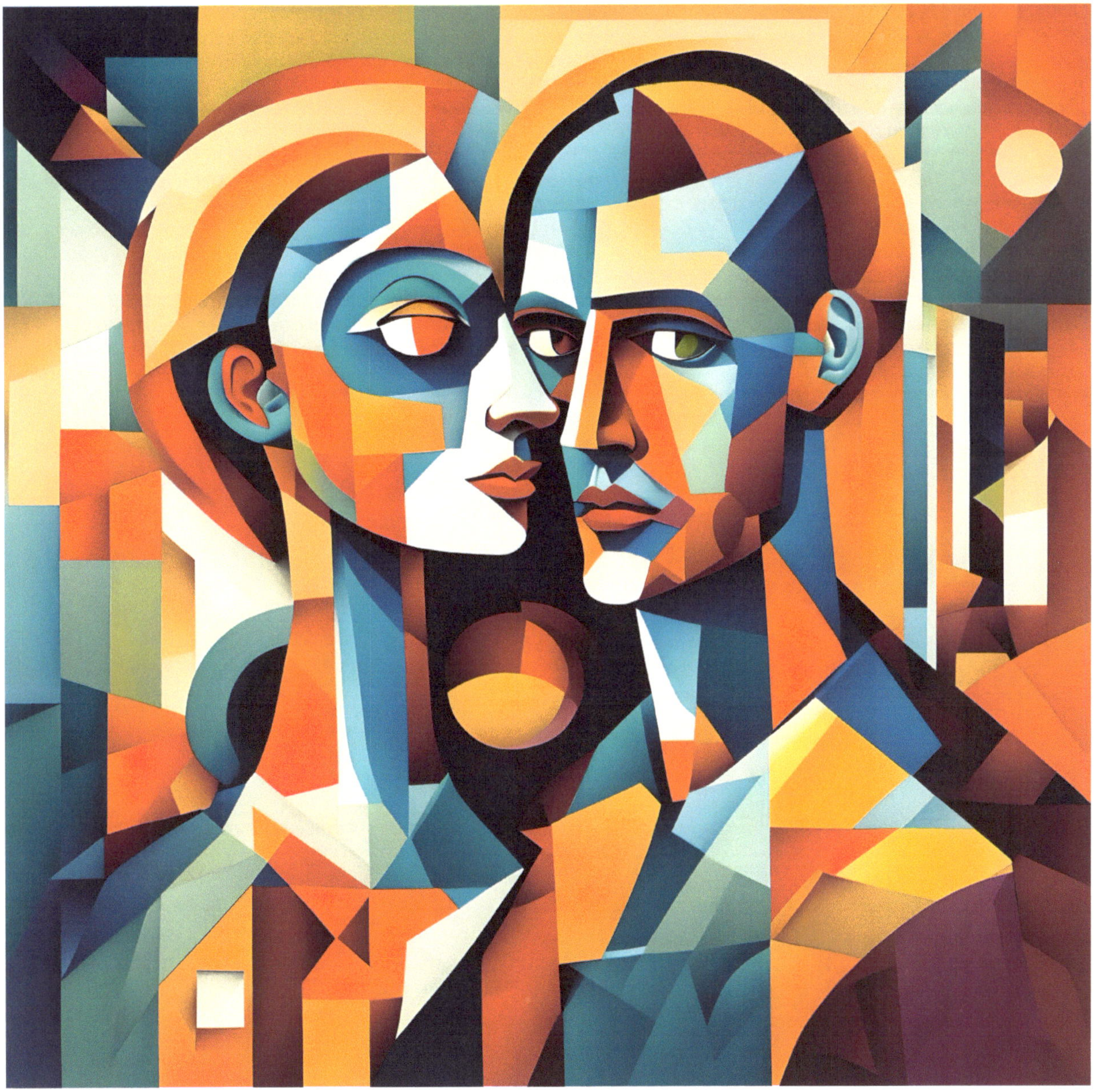

I've got you under my skin, 2024. Oil on canvas, 50x50 cm.

MATTHEW MARK

www.mcmartz.com

Artist Matthew Mark (MCM) hails from the great white north of Canada. Eloquently, MCM is a visual artist / painter in contemporary art from this new age "METAMODERNISM" coined by cultural theorists Timotheus Vermeulen and Robin van den Akker. It is what comes after the post modernism era for the 2020's beyond and moving forward in the arts. This consists of technological breakthroughs that the visual art world will need to continue to adapt & evolve around as society keeps advancing. To continue with past art genres and traditions but exploring and expanding it even further from those past concepts or ideas while merging and reconstructing them with whats currently going on in our world at present time. These realms include exploring and using the digital and social media, virtual & mixed realities, A.I, robotics, and the post industrial information age. These are the reasons for this emergence of metamodernism. As we continue, artist MCM is multifaceted in his discipline and art practice. His experiences of growing up in western Canada is comprised throughout his artwork. When it comes to the visual arts, Matthew focuses on his own style of painting, drawing, printmaking, sculpture, and installation. He observes light and dark themes and everything else in between. MCM experiments with mediums such as acrylics, charcoal, graphite, ink, and sculpturing. Art genre influences of expressionism and fauvism are both interwoven together. Articulated through the distinct artistic idealization being portrayed throughout his work with a touch of spontaneity, playfulness and rawness. It is a true indication of the artist being creative, honest, sincere, passionate, authentic, real, and free. It captivates the mind and leaves room for some ambiguity to be thought about by using our imagination when being immersed in MCM art works. The works range from figurative, abstract and mixed media art. As of late MCM has taken his art across Canada showcasing his work. His art has been exhibited in certain places so far such as in "Munich"Germany, "Vienna" "Austria, "London" England, " Rome, Milan,& Venice" Italy , San Diego (USA), Miami (USA), Madrid (Spain), Paris "France", and has made a vast impression being a part of a digital art exhibition held in New York City at Times Square.

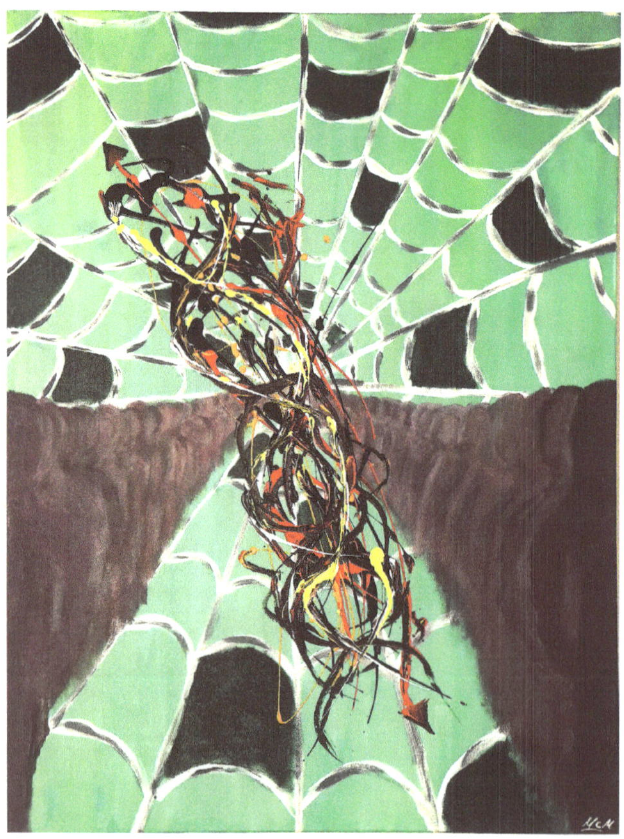

DNA (2020)

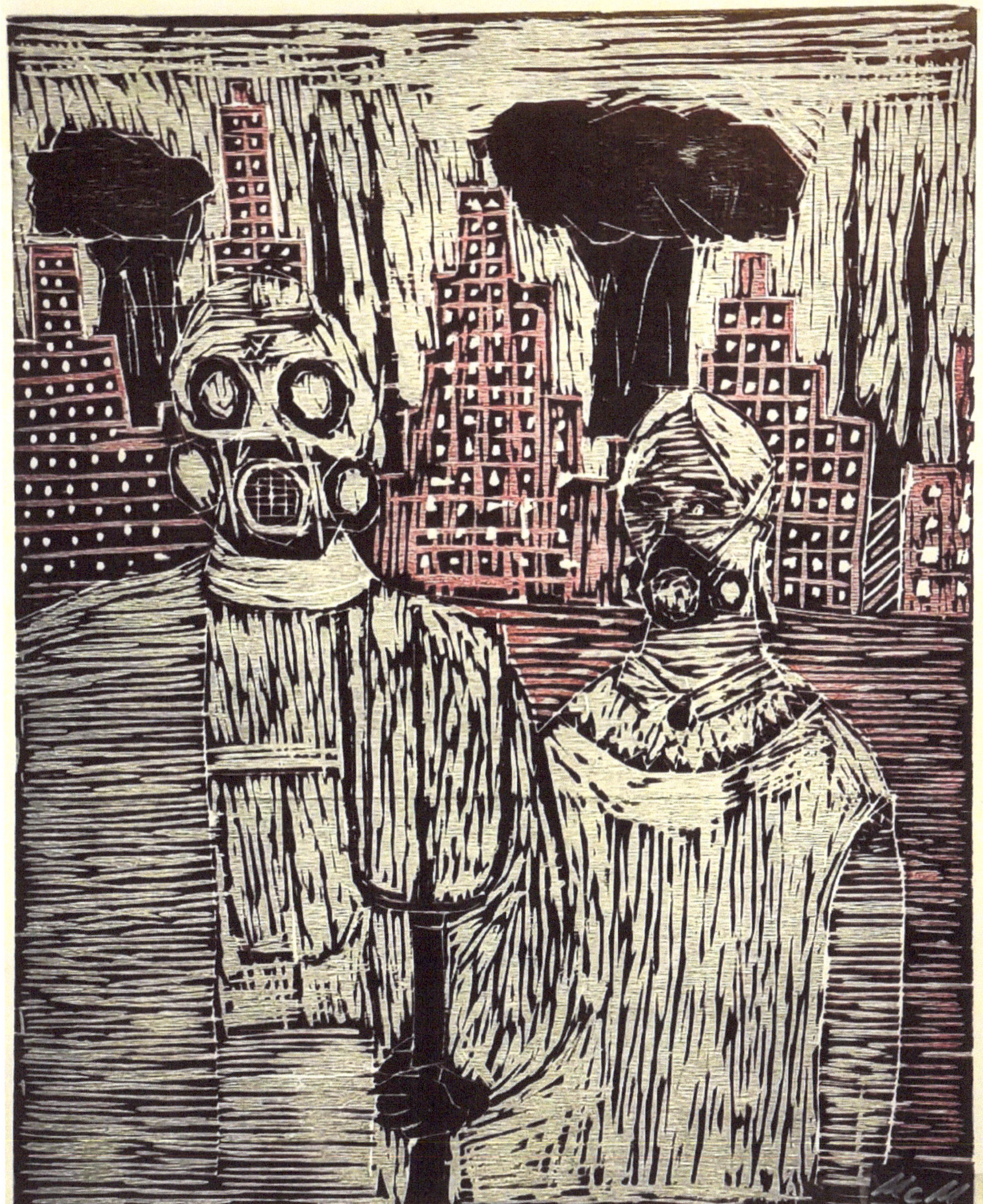

AMERICAN DARK (2022)

MAYADA SHIBIR

www.mayadashibirart.com

Mayada Shibir is a contemporary artist and Gallery Director whose career is defined by a commitment to cultural dialogue, artistic integrity, and the exploration of identity through creative practice. With an Afro-European heritage, she embodies a unique blend of cultural perspectives that shape both her own artwork and her curatorial vision. This dual heritage is not simply a background detail—it is a core element of her creative identity, informing her visual language, thematic concerns, and approach to fostering inclusive artistic spaces. Her journey to becoming a full-time artist and arts leader was shaped by diverse professional experiences. Before immersing herself in the art world, Mayada worked in the healthcare systems of England and Germany. These roles exposed her to the complexity of human stories and the ways in which culture influences perspectives on care, empathy, and communication. The ability to connect with people from different walks of life became a skill she carried into her artistic career. Her time in healthcare also deepened her understanding of the importance of cross-cultural awareness—an understanding that now underpins her work as both an artist and a curator. Driven by a belief in the power of art to connect people, Mayada founded an exchange project that linked creative communities in England and Germany. This initiative was more than a platform for exhibitions; it was a sustained effort to encourage collaboration, knowledge-sharing, and dialogue between artists working in different cultural contexts. By facilitating these exchanges, she created opportunities for diverse voices to be heard and for artistic ideas to evolve through cross-pollination. Mayada's artistic practice is rooted in her family's creative legacy. Growing up in a household that valued the arts, she was immersed in both African and European traditions, absorbing visual and cultural influences from each. This background fostered an ongoing exploration of hybridity and the interplay between different cultural frameworks. Her work reflects a fascination with the points where histories meet, where traditions intersect, and where identities are continually shaped and reshaped.

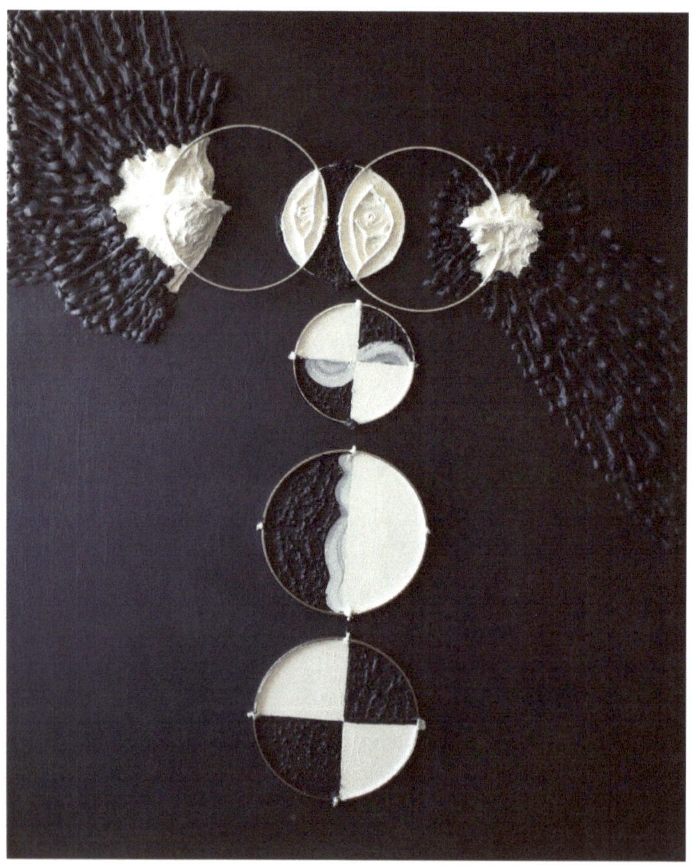

Eyes that see no childhood, 2023. Mixed Media on Canvas, 80 x 100 cm

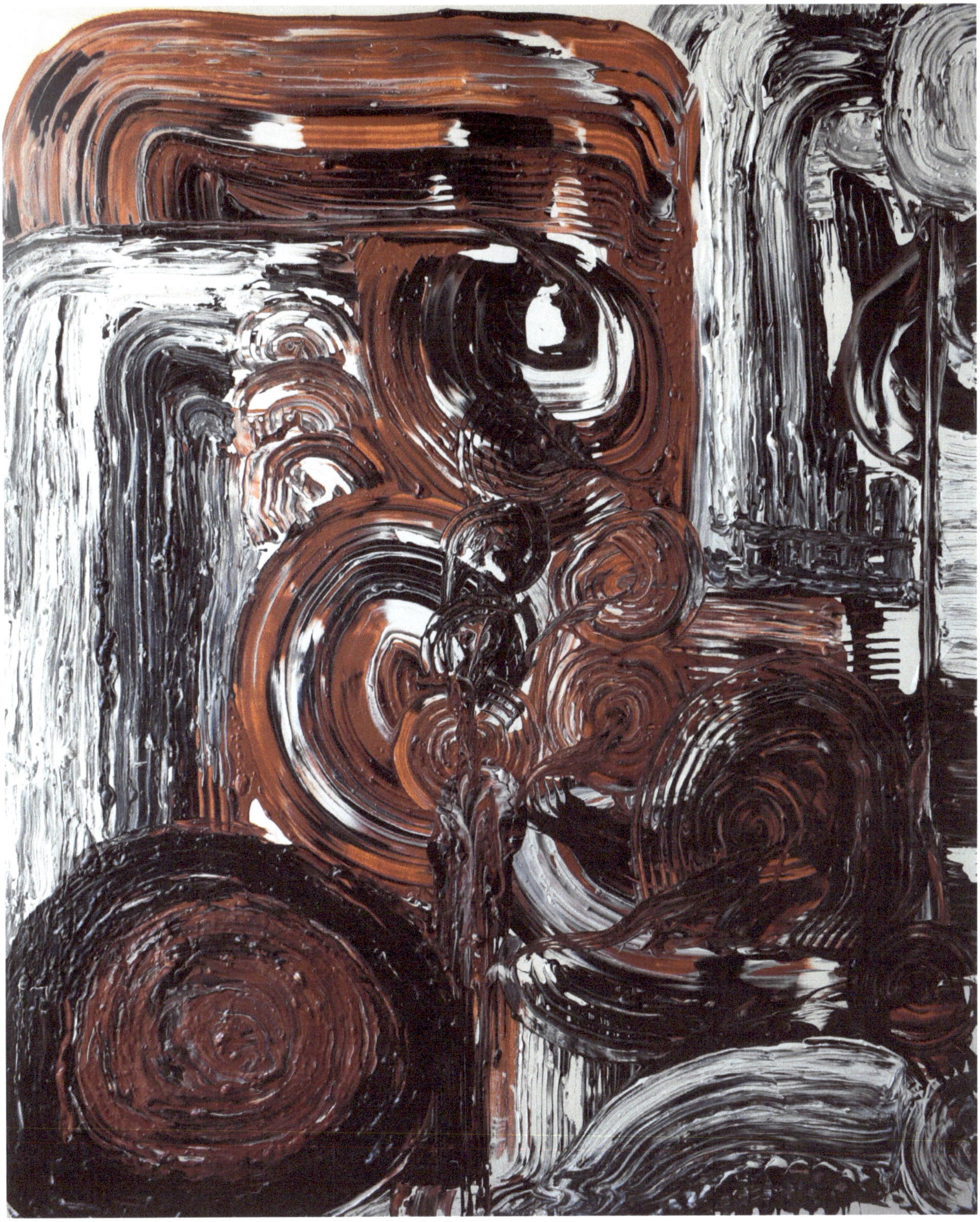

Self-Consciousness, 2023. Mixed Media on Canvas, 80 x 100 cm

MICHAEL K OWINO

Michaelowino.com

Michael K Owino is a Danish-Tanzanian multidisciplinary artist whose work spans painting, sculpture, literature, music, and mixed media. As a self-taught and deeply expressive creator, he has exhibited his art across the globe in major cities and prestigious venues. His visual language is rooted in storytelling, often reflecting on themes of love, connection, and the overlooked beauty in everyday life. In 2025, Owino was awarded the prestigious Leonardo da Vinci – The Universal Artist Prize in Milan during a grand and ceremonial event. The same year, he also received the Artist of the Year award in Florence, and the Premier Artis distinction in Madrid, further solidifying his international recognition. Owino's diverse background and upbringing between cultures have greatly influenced his artistic voice, resulting in a unique and nuanced body of work. He continues to live and work in Copenhagen, where his studio doubles as both a workspace and a place of inspiration.

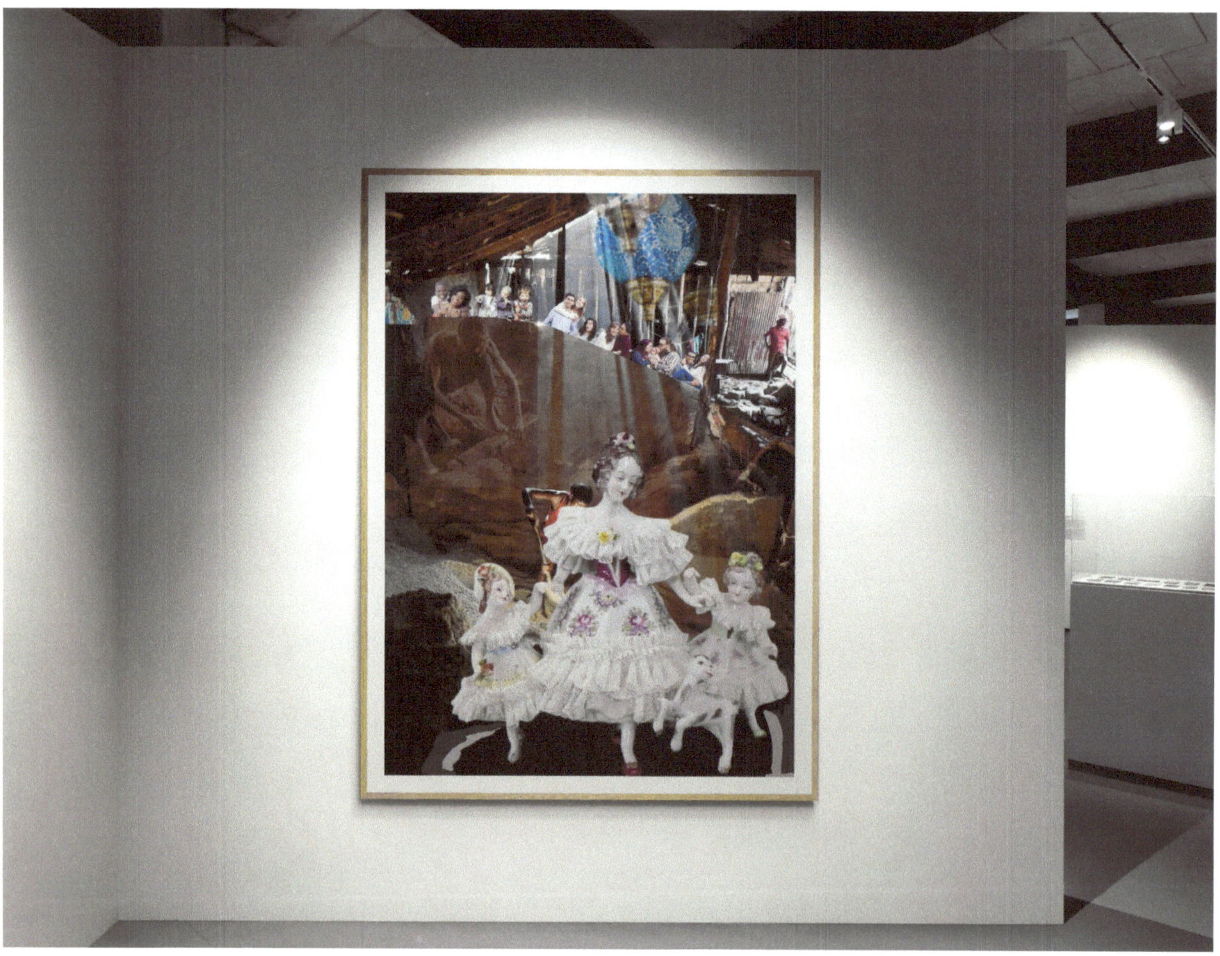

le travailleur et la famille: 2024 Mix media

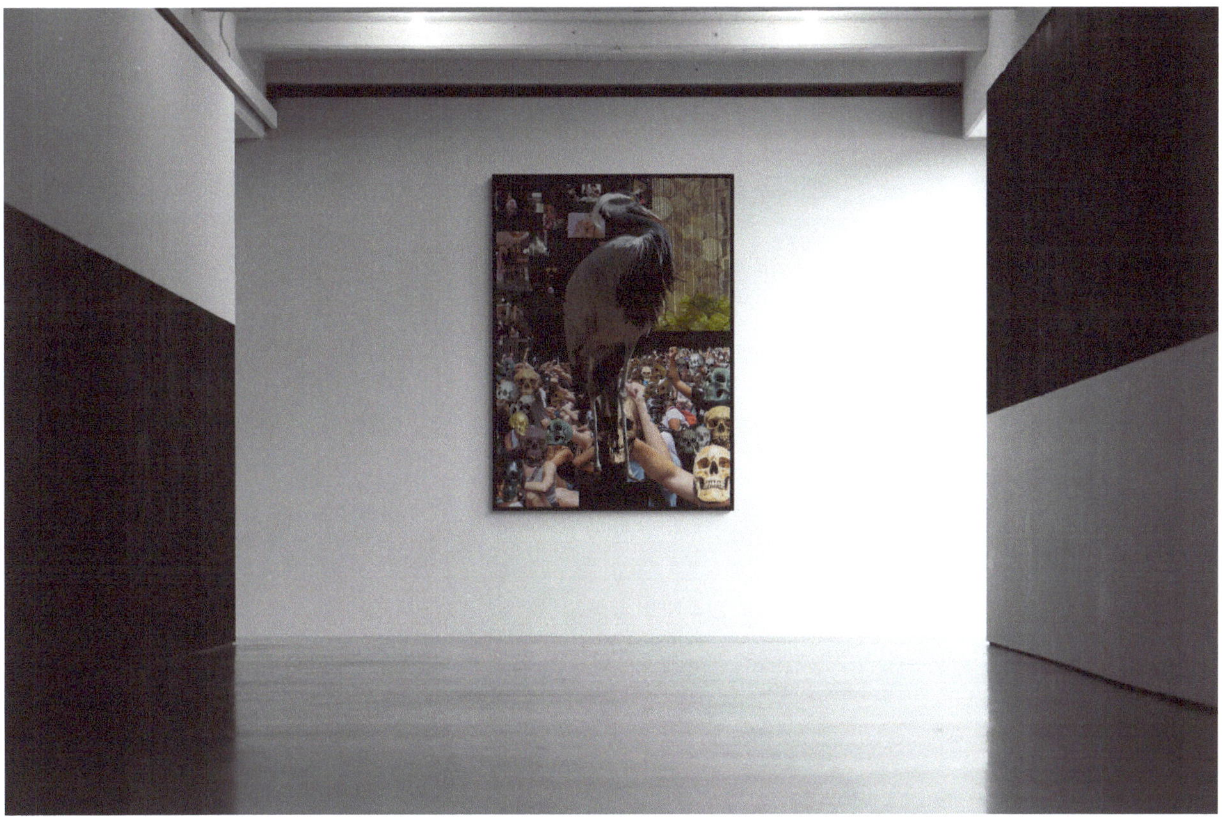

La protestation non entendue Mix media 2025

MICHAEL KOPPLSTÄTTER

www.michael-kopplstaetter.com

The artist's works evoke an emotional response that lingers long after viewing. They invite you to immerse yourself in the layers of his art and discover your own story within it. A journey through space and time, memories and being. An intoxicating mix of voyeurism, exhibitionism, and 21st-century existentialism reveals the intimate and the unknown. Vulnerability, desire, control, floating and flowing collide. The subject matter remains shadowy, blurred, and distorted—a tension between abstraction and distorted reality, a conflict between the self, emptiness, between frozen space and time, between what was and what is. With his expressive and distinctive portrayal of the human figure, marked by longing and alienation, he addresses the depths of our time. The works focus more and more on the relationship between inner being and the body in motion. The works dissolve unpredictable boundaries between inside and outside to create a unique experience of the figure.

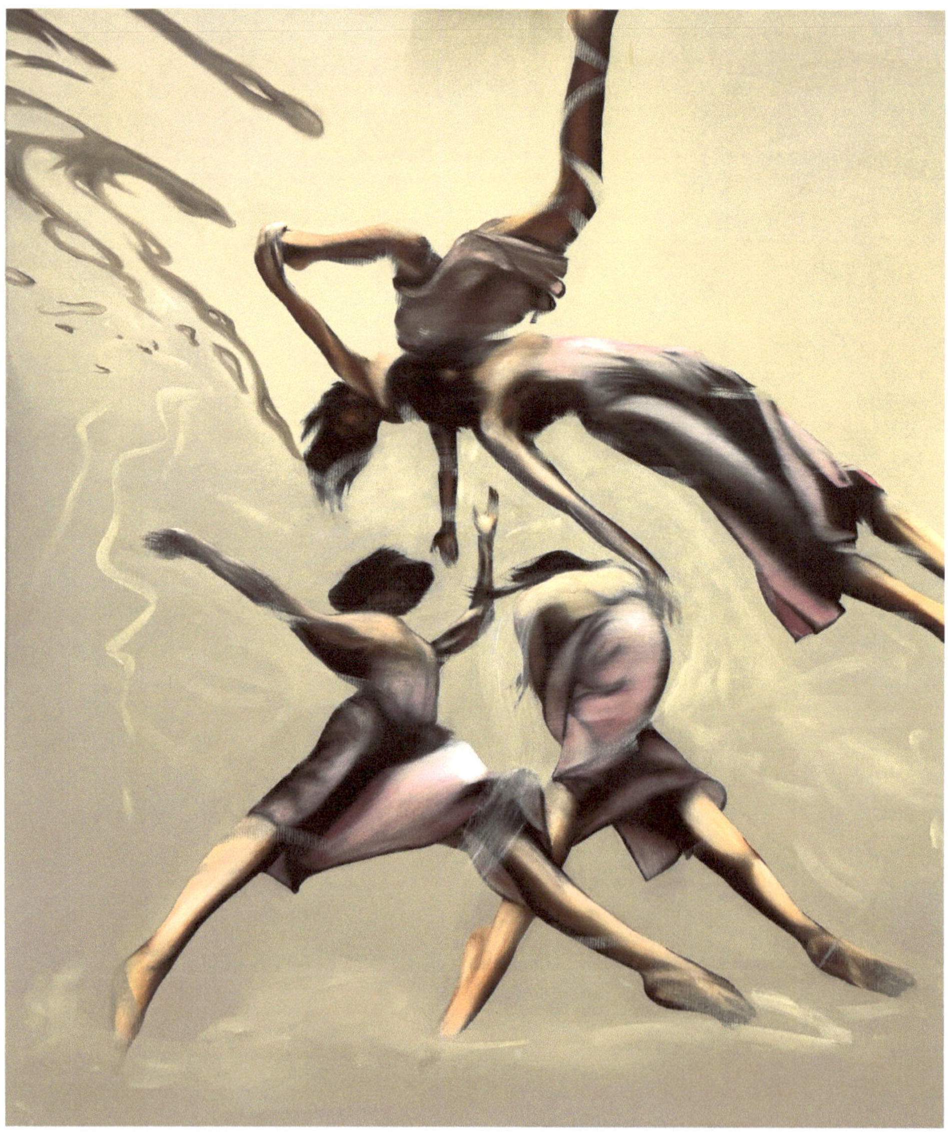

Floating, 2025. Oil on Canvas, 120 x 100 cm.

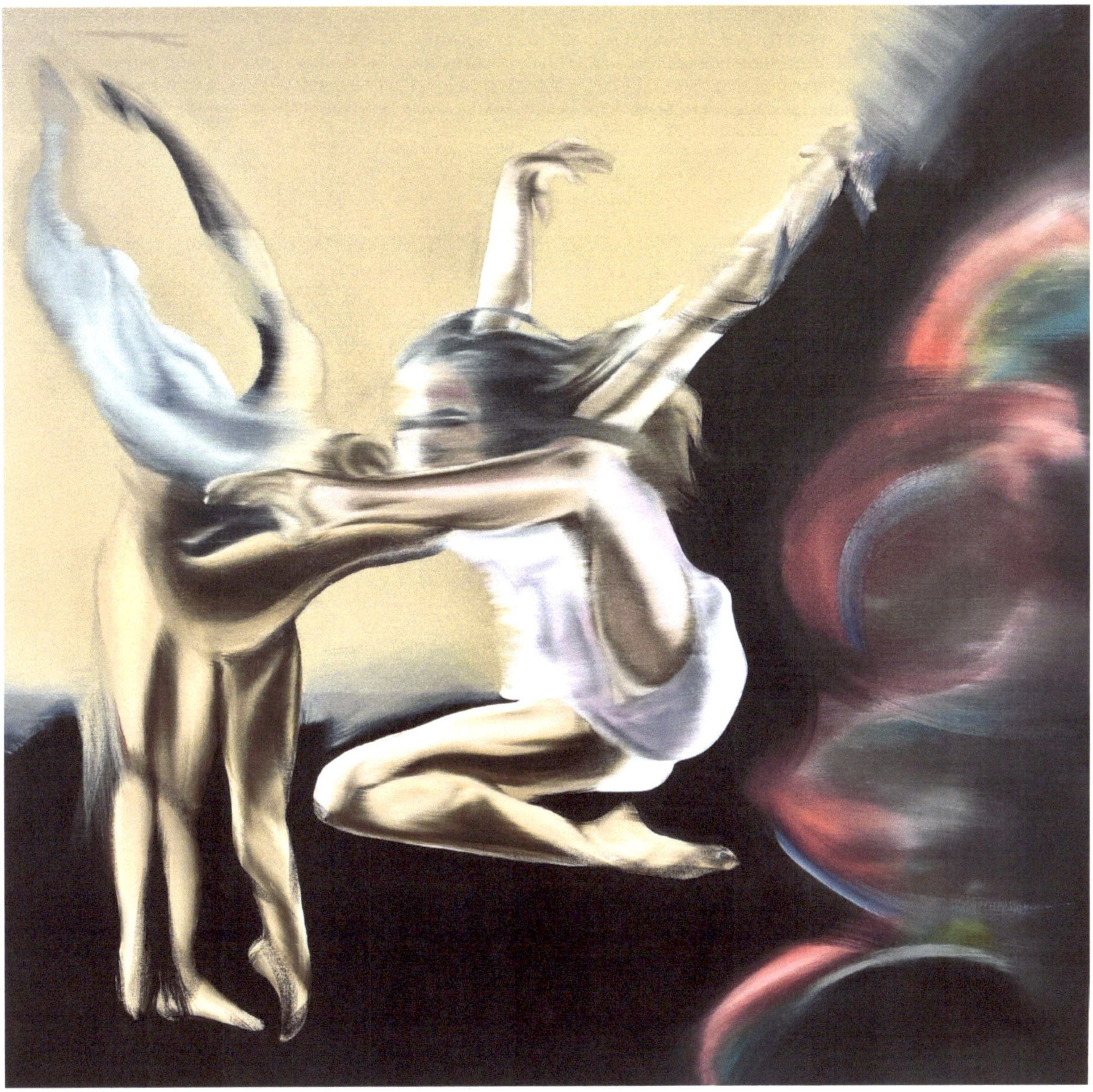

Flaming Dance, 2025. Oil on Canvas, 100 x 100 cm.

MIMBELBI (TINA RITTER)

www.mimbelbi.com

Tina Ritter lives and works near Frankfurt am Main. From early childhood, she loved painting and drawing; immersing herself fully in the creative process is her purest joy. After studying architecture and taking various art courses, she began exhibiting her works in 2022. Since then, she has joined the German Association of Visual Artists BBK, co-founded an artist collective, and become a member of several art associations. Her work explores the realm of childhood imagination, shaped by memories of a sheltered upbringing in a small village - daydreams, carefree summer days, and gentle nostalgia. A recurring motif is the leap, symbolizing pure joy: a captured moment in time, reflecting on today's fast-paced, image-saturated world where we rarely spend more than a few seconds with a single picture.

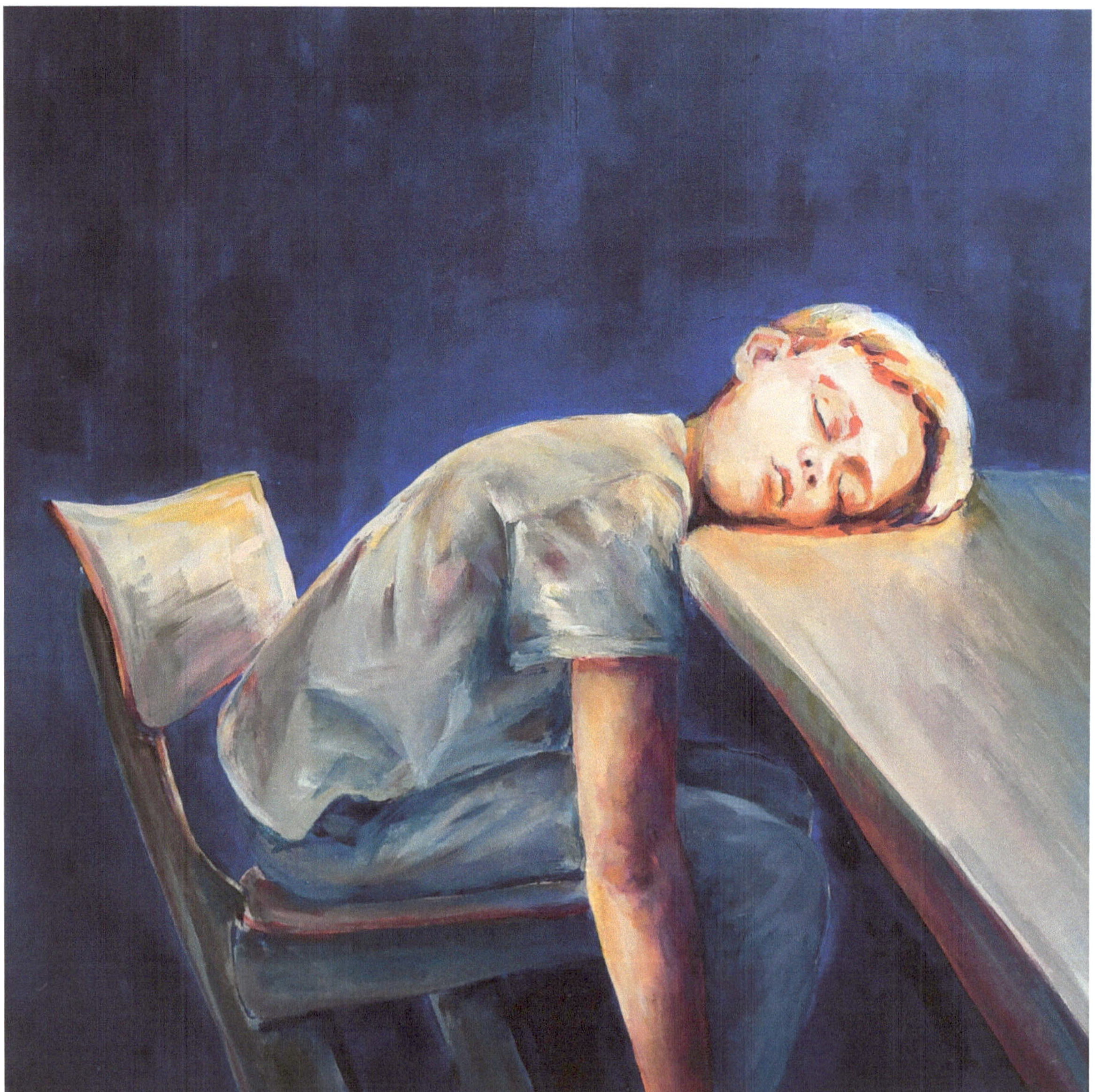

The dream, 2024. Acrylic on canvas, 72x72cm.

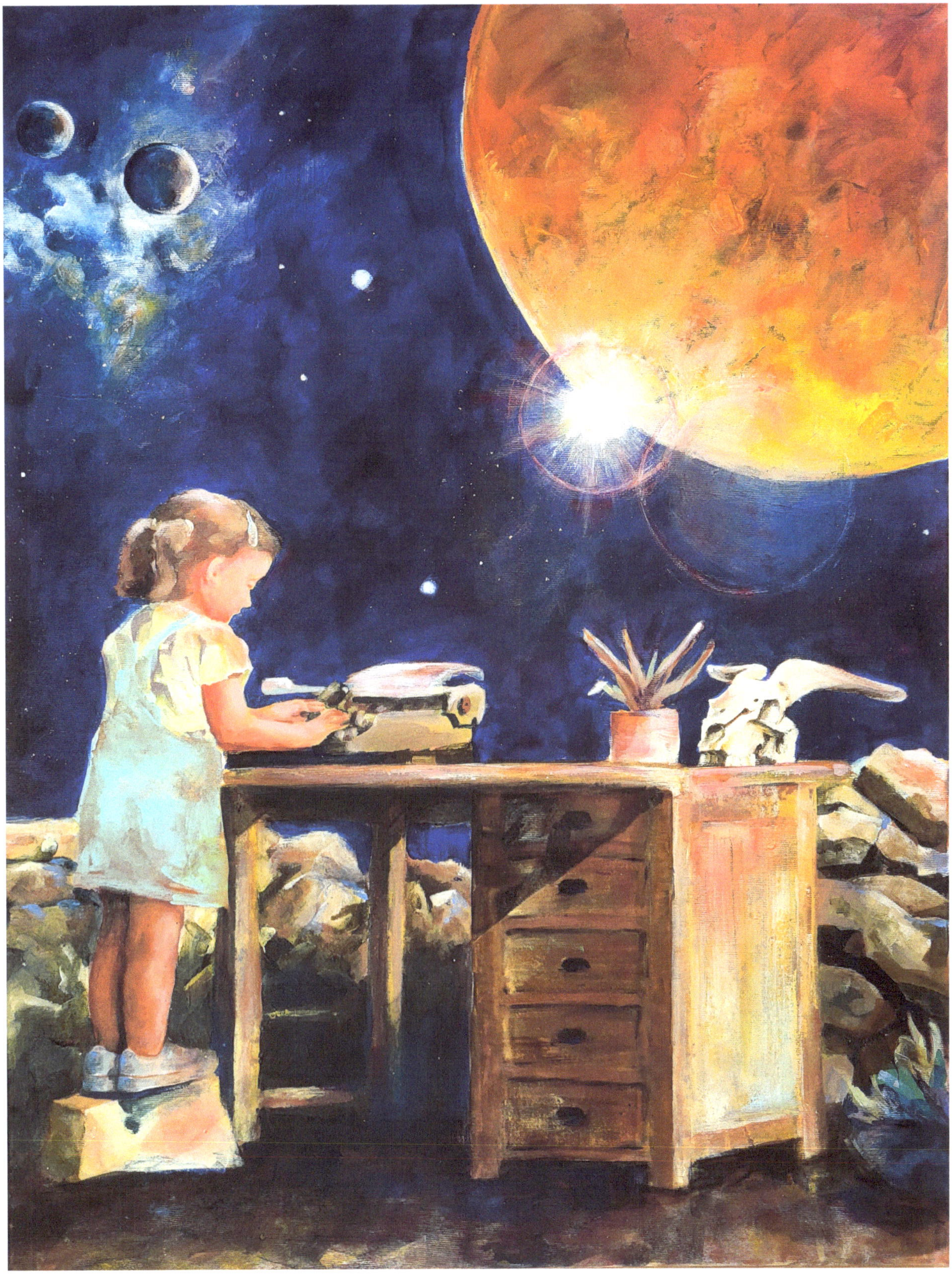

Imogen (letter to mars), 2025, Acrylic on canvas, 60x80cm

MIRANDA HAMPSON

miranda.hampson (instagram)

Miranda Hampson is a First Nations artist (Anaiwan) from Australia. Hampson's work honours First Nations connections to Country, drawing on her heritage and her background in cultural heritage management. Hampson's practice is grounded in the shared experiences of kin, Country and place. Her art extends beyond the ecological, suggesting it as a means to heal and strengthen the bonds between people, land and culture. Hampson aims to paint a landscape of Country that creates a new dialogue about how we move forward as First Nations people in all of our diversity. Whilst she expresses her narrative as an individual, there are a number of shared connections experienced by First Nations people, framed by common themes. Her works explore a visual language that is both personal and cultural. Each piece is a result of a ritual of repetition where mark making builds upon itself, creating richly layered surfaces that pulse with depth and intensity.

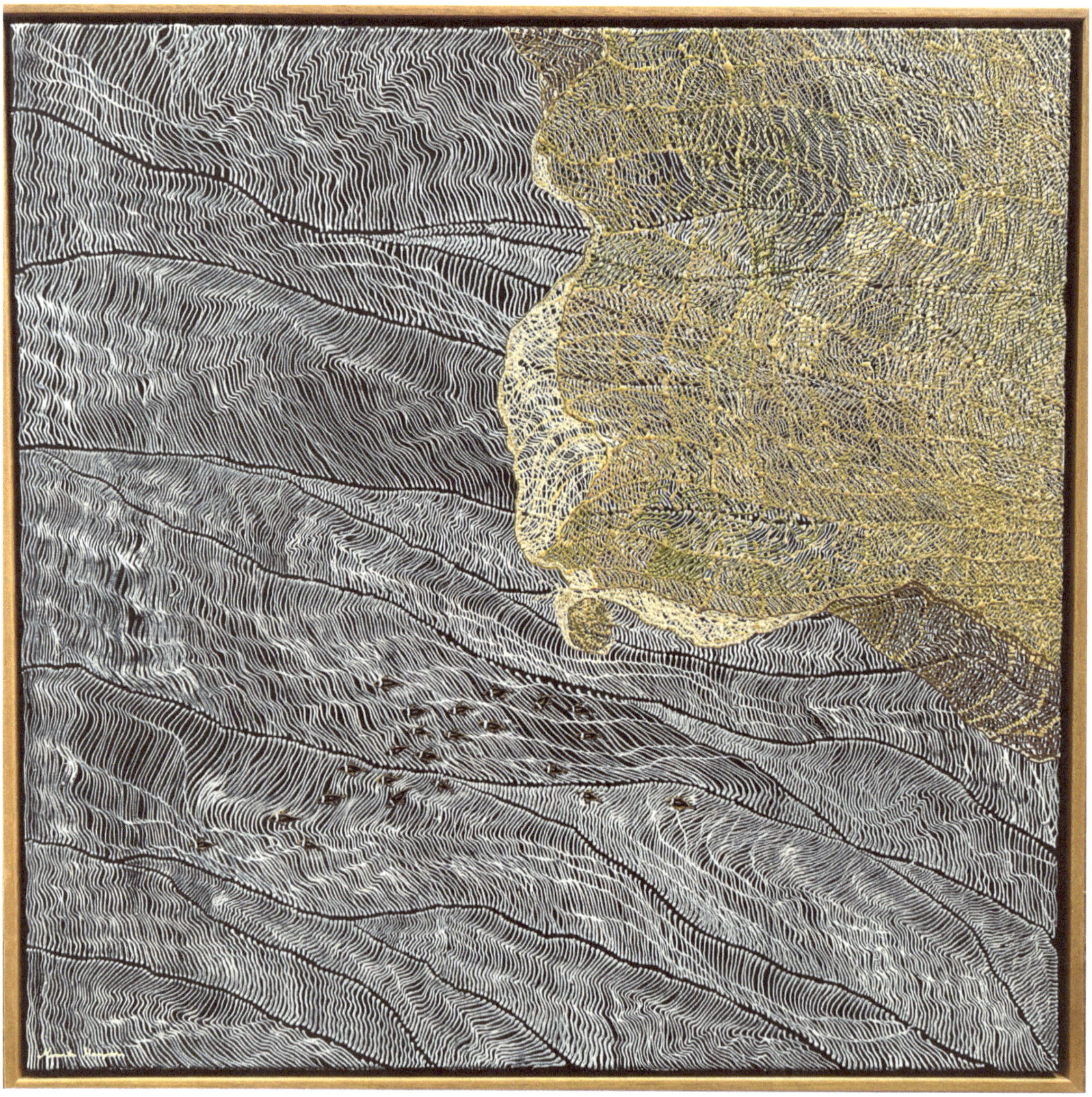

WHERE THE TIDE LEFT ME BEHIND, 2025. Acrylic on cotton canvas, 76x76cm

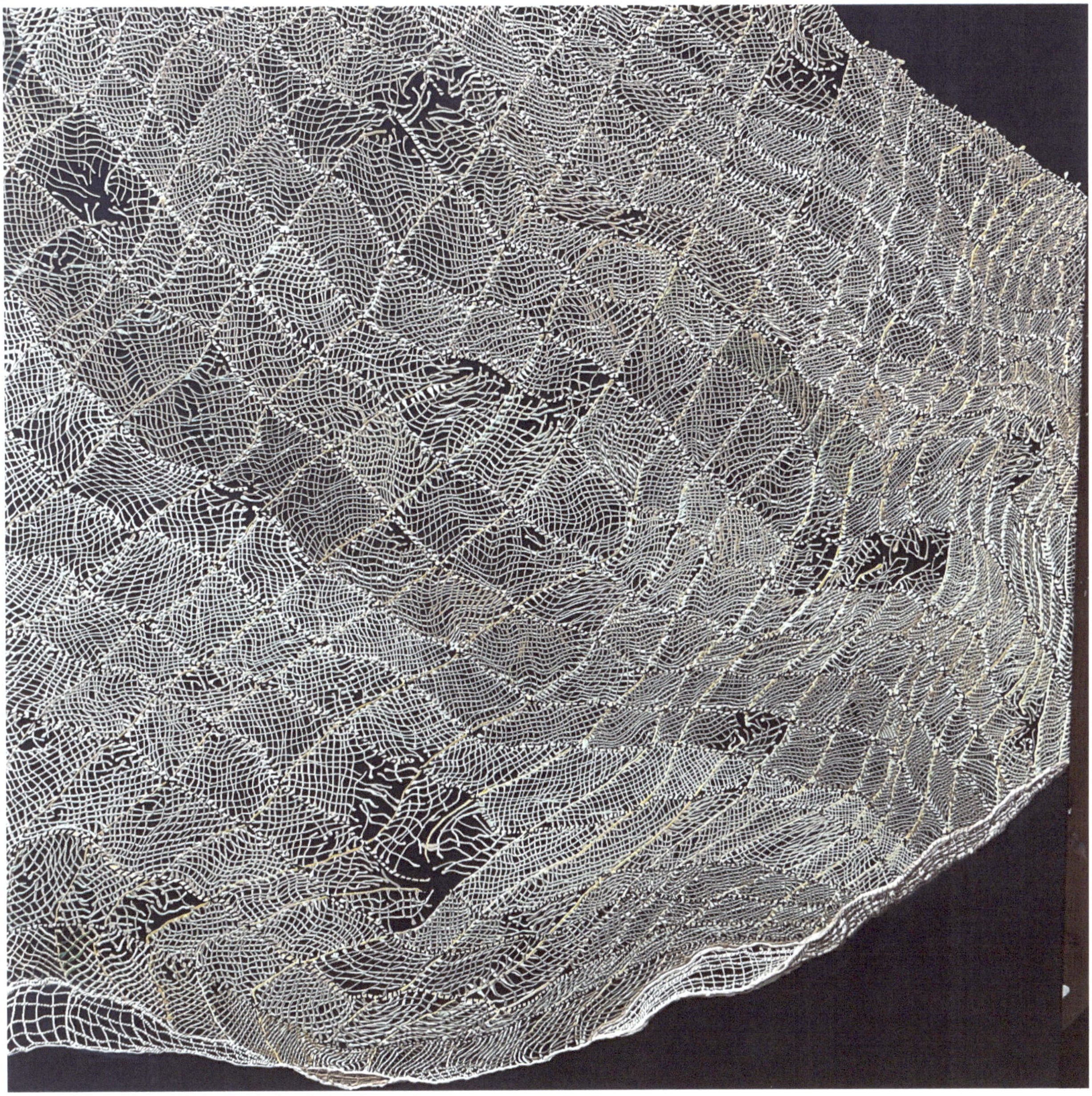

THE SPACES BETWEEN, 2025. Acrylic on cotton canvas, 76x76cm

MONA NIKO

Www.monaniko.com Admin@monaniko.com

Born amidst the vibrant tapestry of Tehran, Iran, Mona Niko, embarked on a transformative artistic journey that would weave its way across continents and disciplines. Her creative odyssey began with earning an esteemed Art certificate from the prestigious Graphics College, which laid the groundwork for her subsequent Bachelor's Degree in Painting from the acclaimed Azad University. Embracing the expressive power of the brush, she initially immersed herself in the dynamic world of Expressionism, reveling in the unbridled emotions that dance upon each canvas. As her artistic vision evolved, she found herself venturing into an innovative realm of mixed media, one that harmoniously blended her passion for painting with her extensive knowledge of graphic design. This unique fusion allowed her to transcend the boundaries of traditional art forms and develop an unparalleled aesthetic.

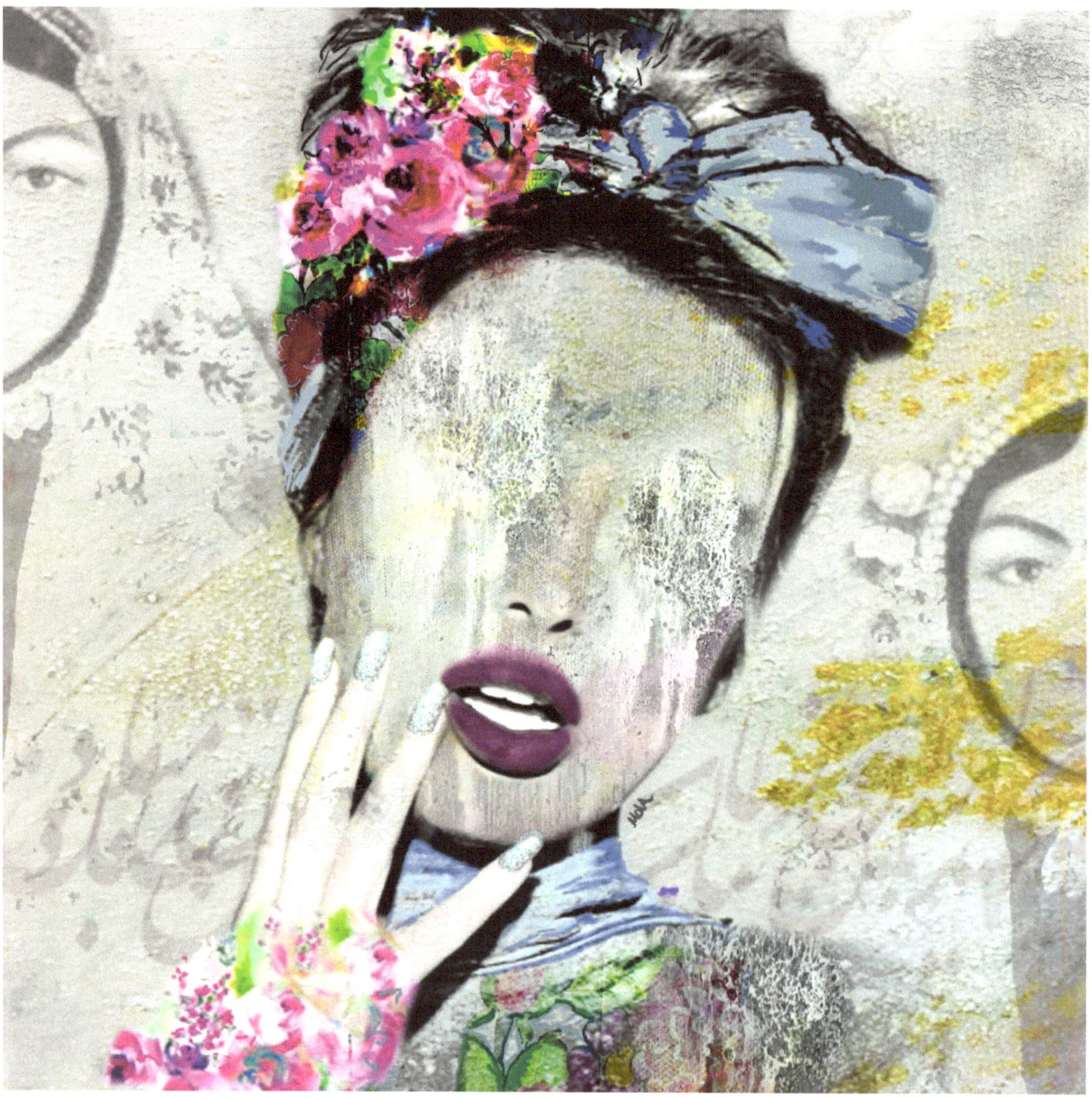

Fancy girl 3 years ago

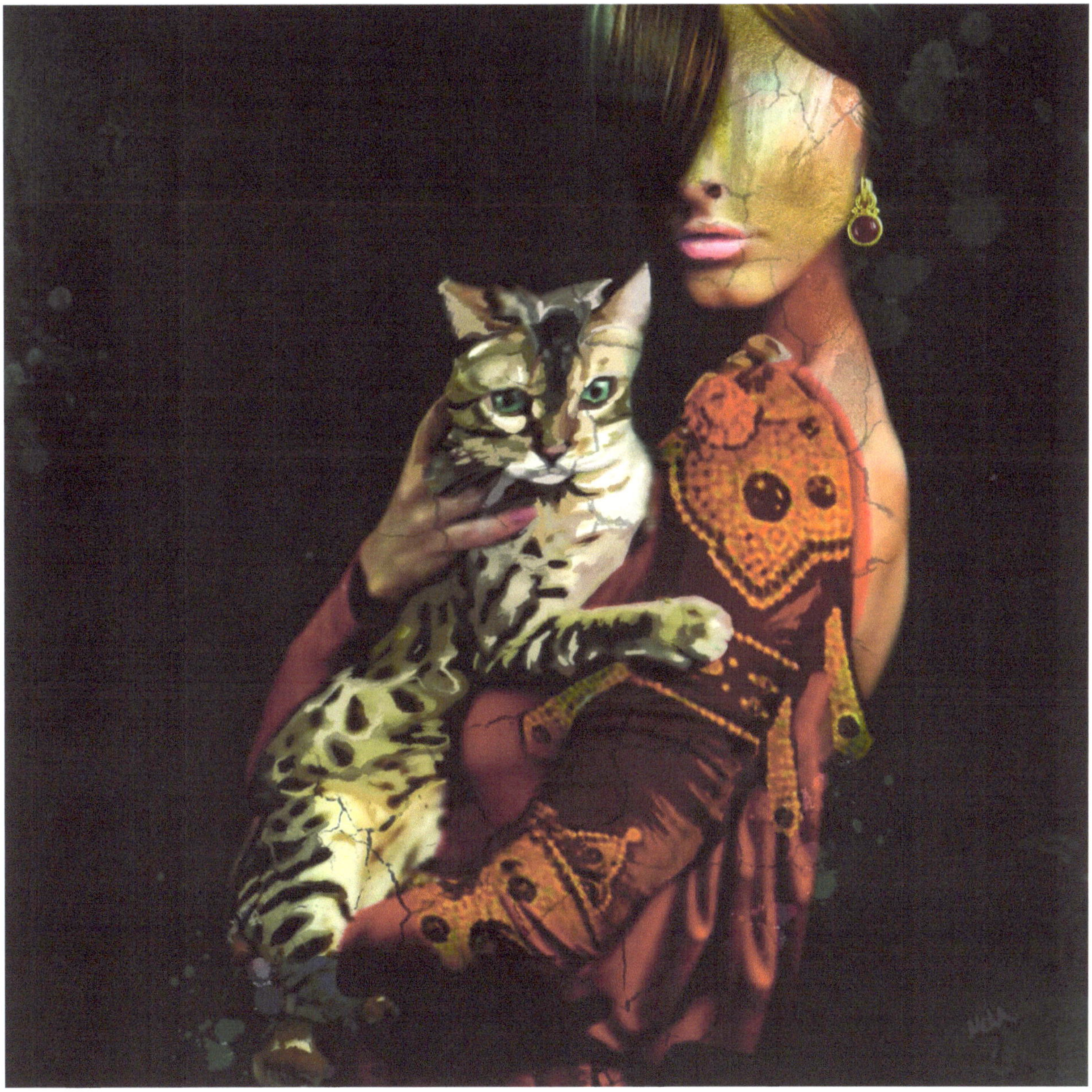

In Comfort 4years ago

MORTEN SAETHER

https://www.instagram.com/mortyohlala/

Morten Saether is a freelance photographer and painter. He favours using mixed digital photography techniques to produce his work. He is also driven by a passion for exploring the social, cultural, and urban transformations of our contemporary world. "Photography is often the essence of my Art. I also love traditional collages. So often my work consists of different photos put together in layers and presented in a new way, mostly abstract but sometimes with elements you can recognize." Alongside his self taught artistic practice, Morten has enjoyed an extensive professional career as an Art Director and Graphic Designer. Morten's photography and paintings have been featured in exhibitions in Collioure/France, Barcelona/Spain, Berlin/Germany, London/UK, Budapest/Hungary, Fredrikstad, Horten and Oslo/Norway. Morten is keen to continue to exhibit his work throughout Europe. Morten resides in Oslo, Norway.

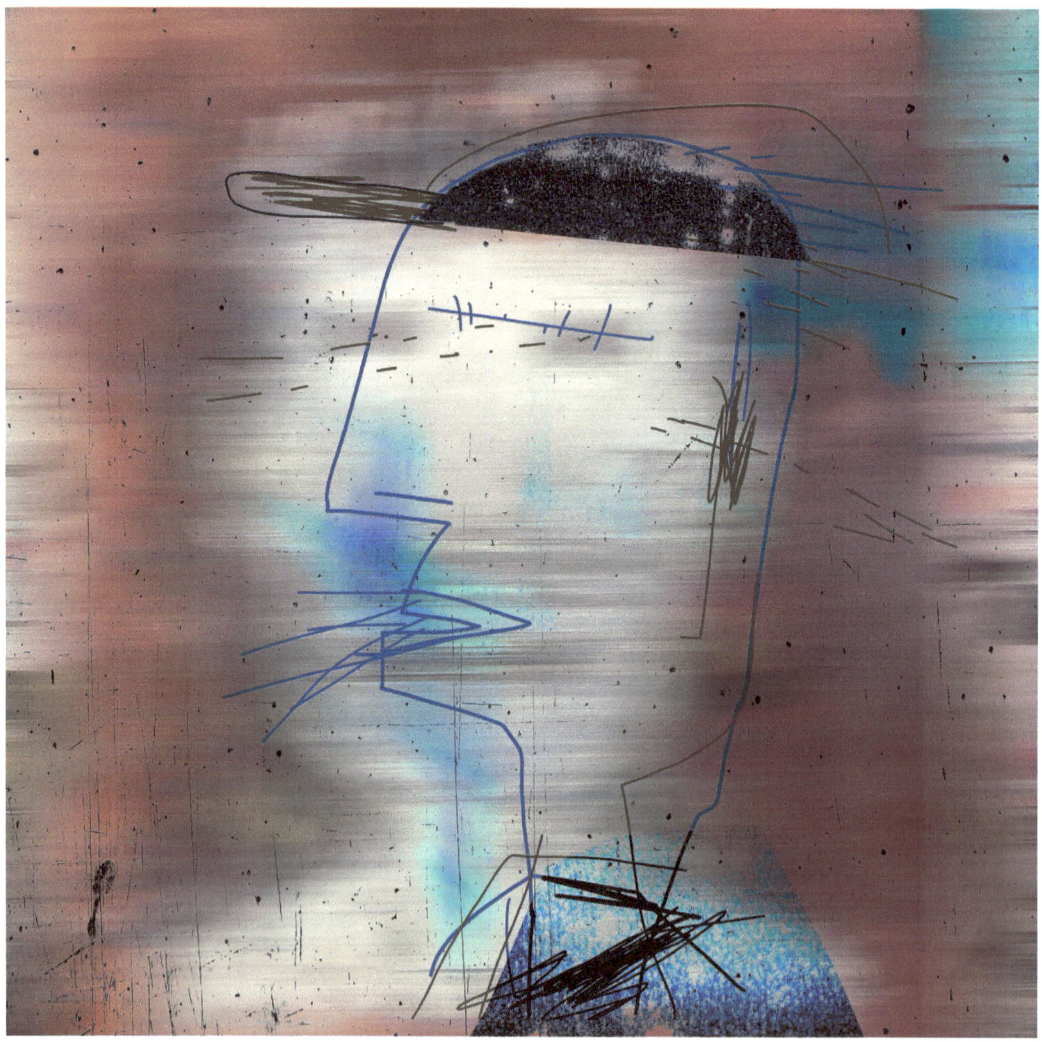

Jabber 02, 2024, Mixed Digital Media, 60x60cm

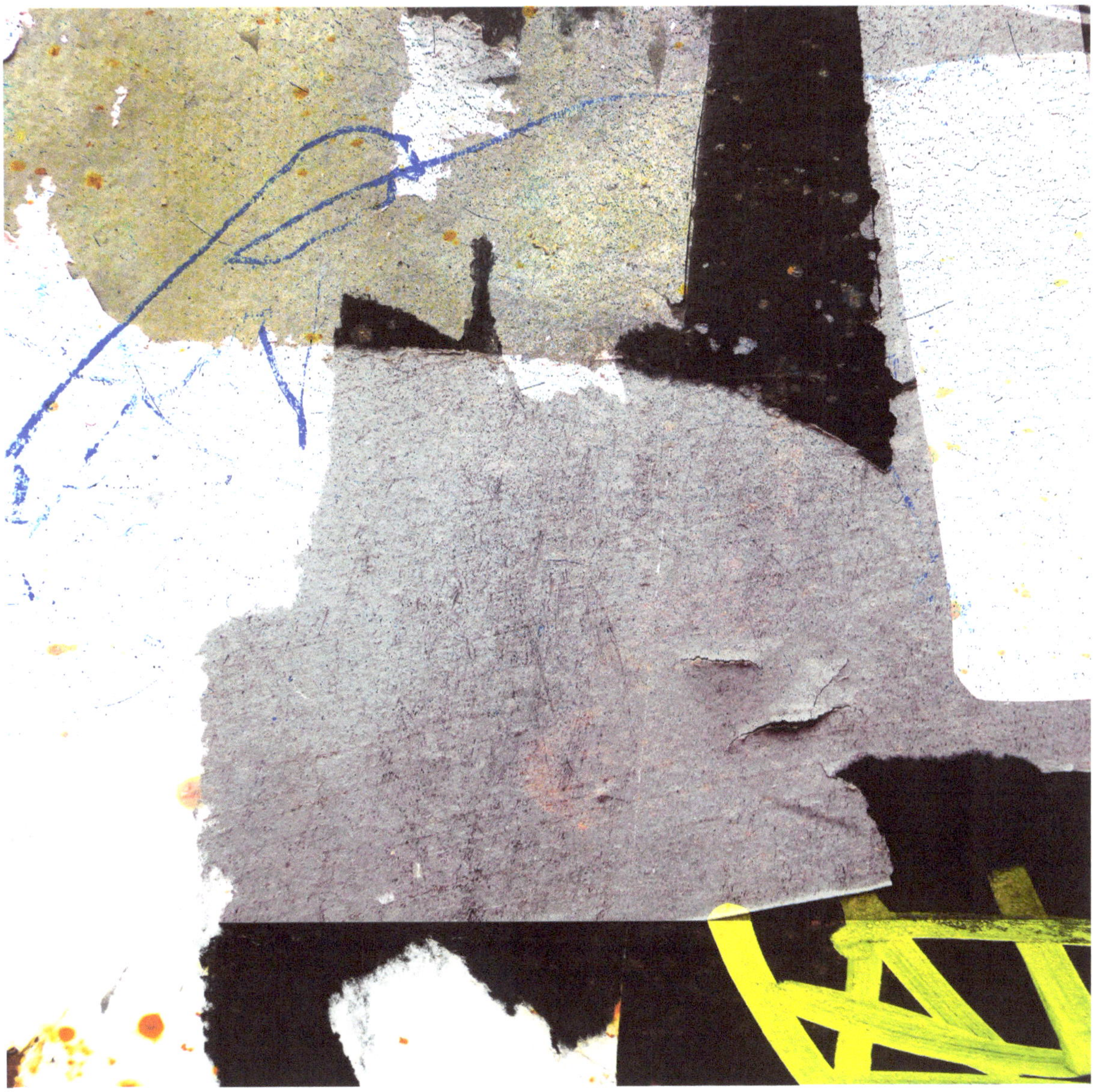

The Battle, 2024, Processed Photography, 80x80cm,

MIKAYA PETROS

m.papavassiliou@icloud.com Instagram @mikayapetros

My artistic exploration delves into the core themes of transhumanism, birdhumanism, and technoutopias, embodying a journey that navigates the dance between humanity, technology, and nature. My work aims to weave a dialogue between the past and the future, between the richness of tradition and the promise of innovation. With transhumanism, I investigate how technology can not only amplify human capacities but also redefine them. Birdhumanism, a poetic fusion of the human and flight, symbolizes our ongoing aspiration for new beginnings and growth opportunities. Technoutopias emerge as bold visions of a future where technology and nature not only coexist but enrich each other, opening the doors to more sustainable and innovative life experiences. My intent is to inspire deep reflections on the choices we make today and their impact on building a future that not only embraces but celebrates the diversity of life. In this creative space, I encourage viewers to imagine a world where the divide between humanity and technology dissolves, allowing unexplored and dynamic possibilities of interaction to emerge, in a visionary embrace of balance and evolution. https://www.treccani.it/enciclopedia/eol-petros-mikaya/

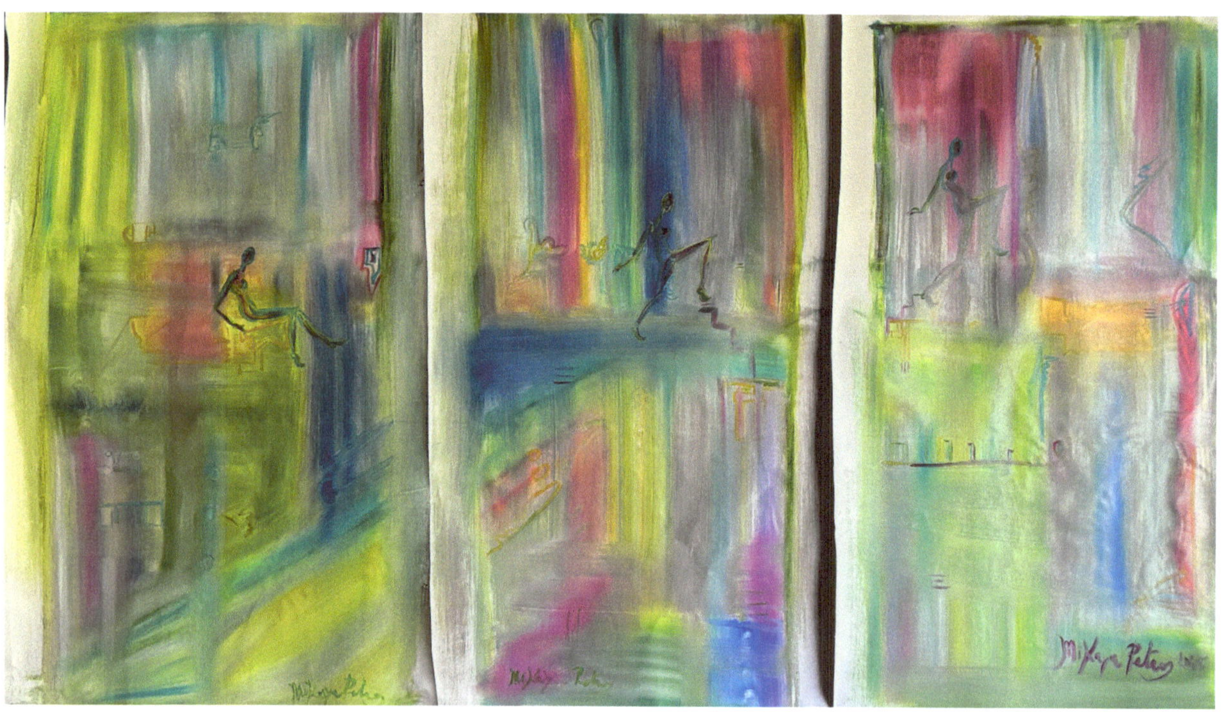

Multiverse Aroma 2025 oil on canvas 130x55cm each

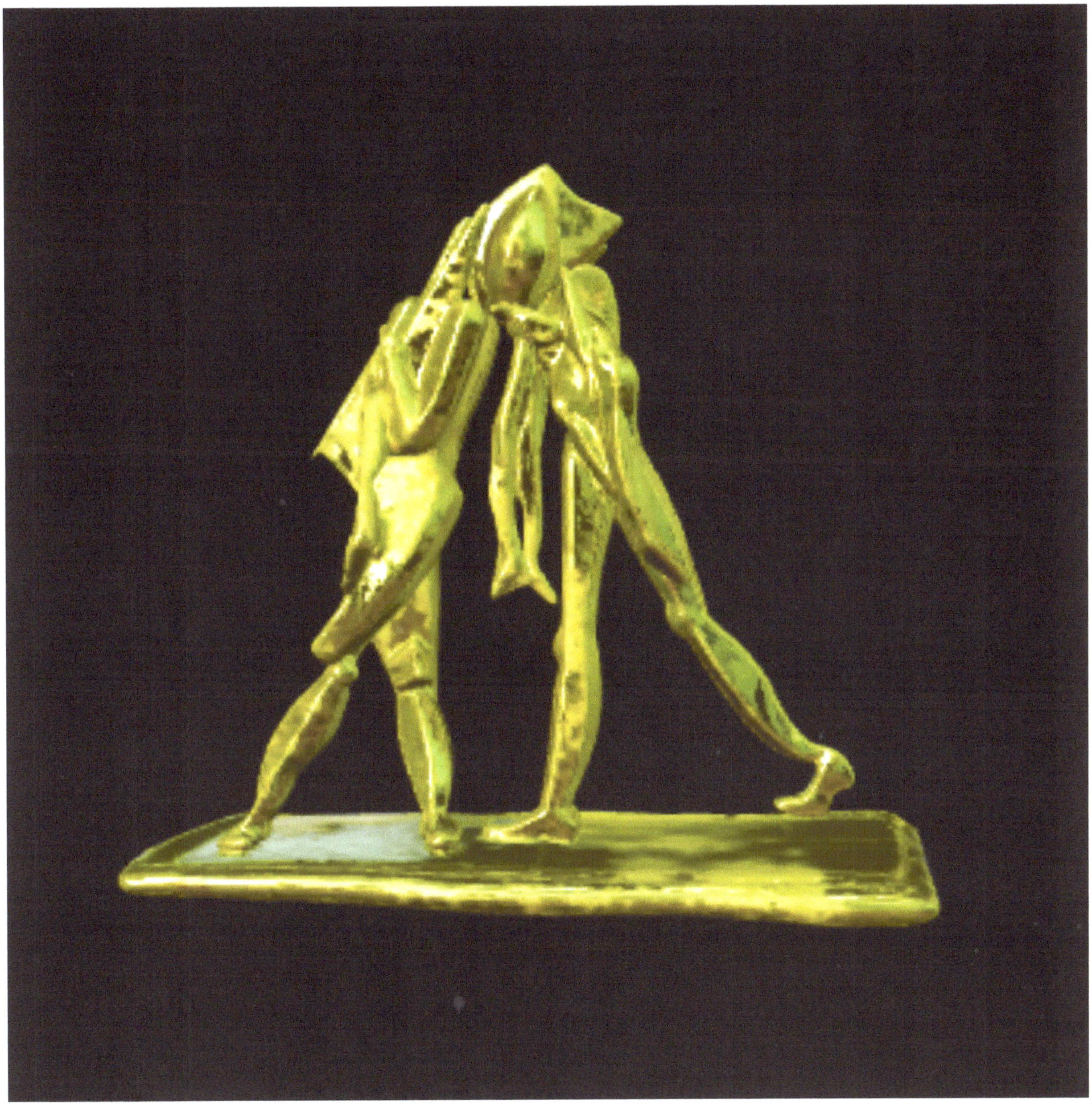

Complementarity 2025 sculpture resin 50x40x30 cm

NADA KELEMEN

www.nadakelemen.art

Nada Kelemen is a Czech painter whose work connects spiritual experience, energy work, and deep inner insight. She came to painting at the age of 52 as a natural culmination of more than twenty years of practice in healthy living, quantum therapy, and traditional Chinese medicine. However, she found her true fulfillment in art. Nada's artwork embodies harmony, spiritual depth, and positive energy. She creates exclusively in a state of inner purity, often inspired by music and personal visions. Her paintings are not merely visual expressions but energetic imprints that speak to the viewer on a subconscious level. She works with acrylic and oil paints, structural techniques, and Japanese calligraphy. Her work has been exhibited in numerous international exhibitions and has received recognition for its contribution to spiritual and intuitive art. She views art as a path – silent, genuine, and without age boundaries.

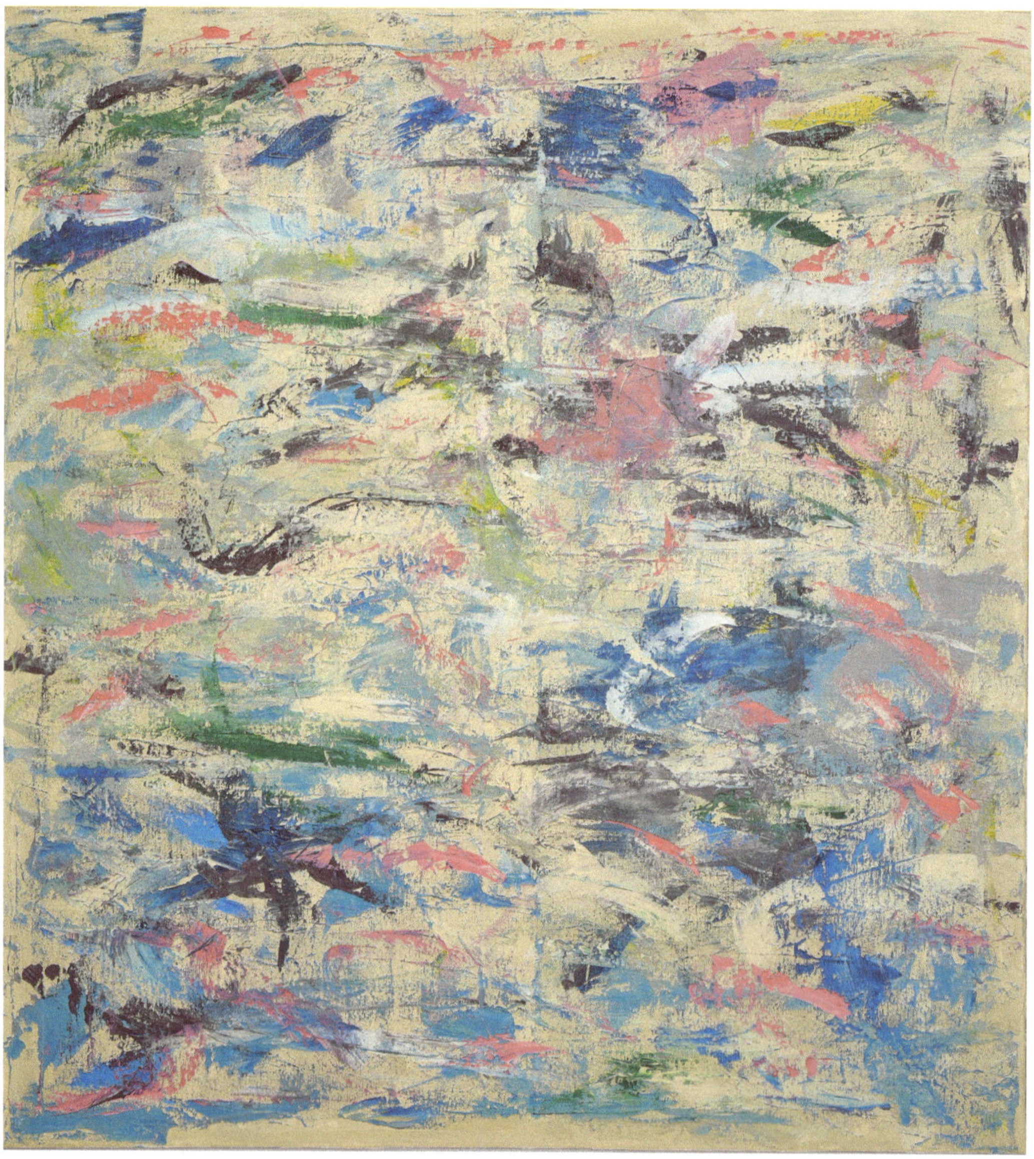

Spring, 2025, Acrylic on canvas - mixed technique, 103x93 cm

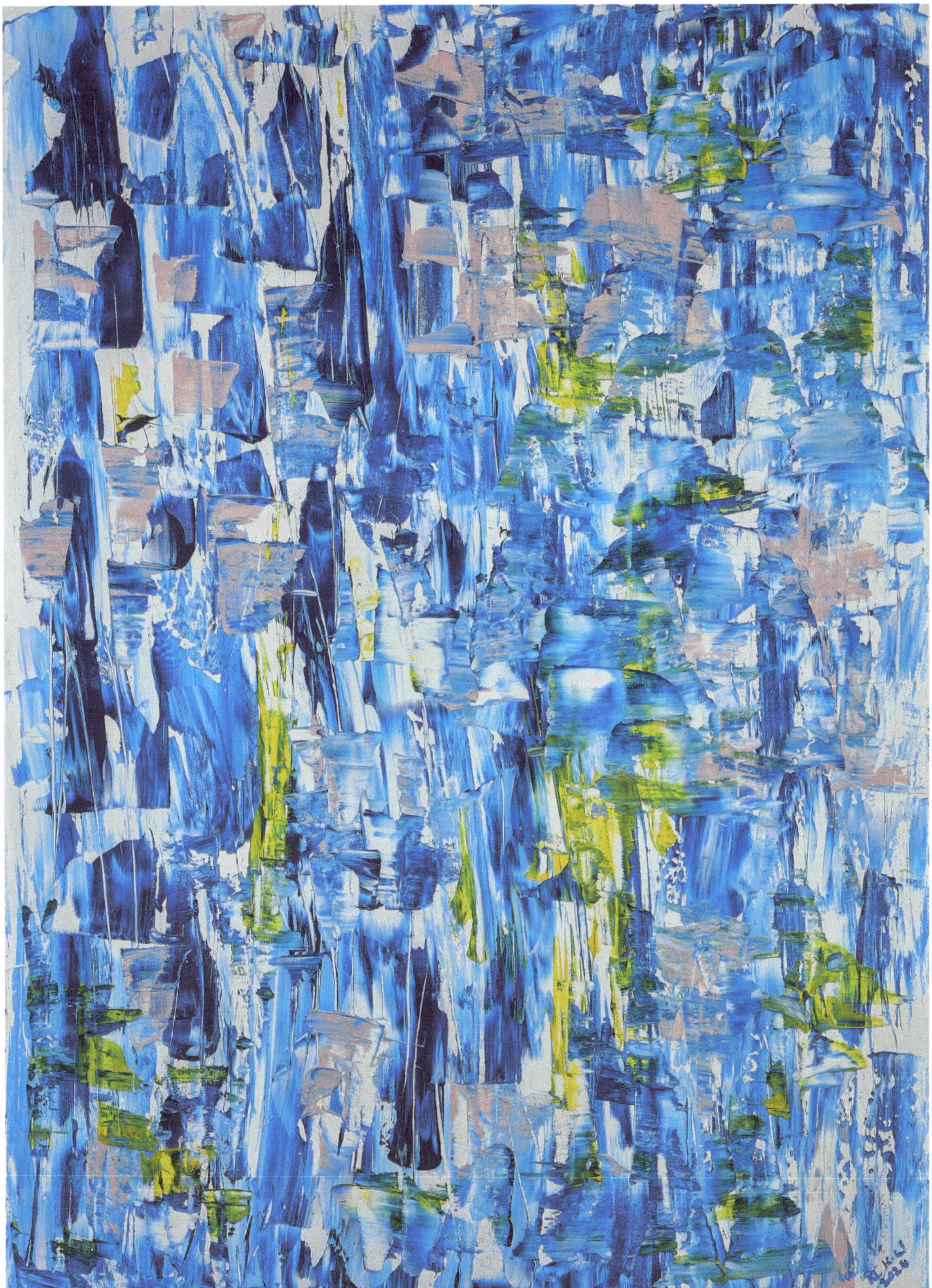

Venezia, 2024, Acrylic on canvas, 104x74 cm

NANCY STAUB LAUGHLIN

www.nancystaublaughlin.com

Nancy Staub Laughlin is an accomplished assemblage/pastel artist. "I have created a new concept of the assemblage working with pastels on paper and photography. These dynamic, layered assemblages transport the viewer to my mesmerizing world of color, light, dimension and beauty from a different perspective. The viewer is immersed into the sheer magnificence of the natural world. They are the culmination of many carefully executed steps that define my distinctive creative process." She has exhibited at Newhouse, Noho and Carter Burden Galleries in NYC. She has been recognized in New Jersey where she had a one person exhibit at the New Jersey State Museum along with being included in the permanent collection. Other prestigious accomplishments have been exhibits at the Monmouth Museum, Noyes Museum, Johnson & Johnson World Headquarters, Bristol/Myers Squibb and Prudential, in New Jersey. Her work was also honorably included, Six New Jersey Masters at Kean University, Burger Gallery where she, subsequently, had a one person exhibit. Nancy has received critical acclaim and reviews from many prestigious art publications. Nancy is represented in many private and public collections and was honored to be chosen to be in the NAWA collection at the Zimmerli Museum. She also received the Miriam Schorr Memorial Award: Works on Paper, NAWA. She recently received the Homiens Art Prize, Highly Commendable Award and the Circle Foundation Masterful Mind Award for "The Blossoming Froth." To add to her accolades, she just received the Collectors Art Prize, Art Legends of Our Time through Contemporary Art Curator Magazine. Her most memorable highlight was being reviewed by the late Sam Hunter, Art Critic and Historian, who found her work "refreshingly unique".

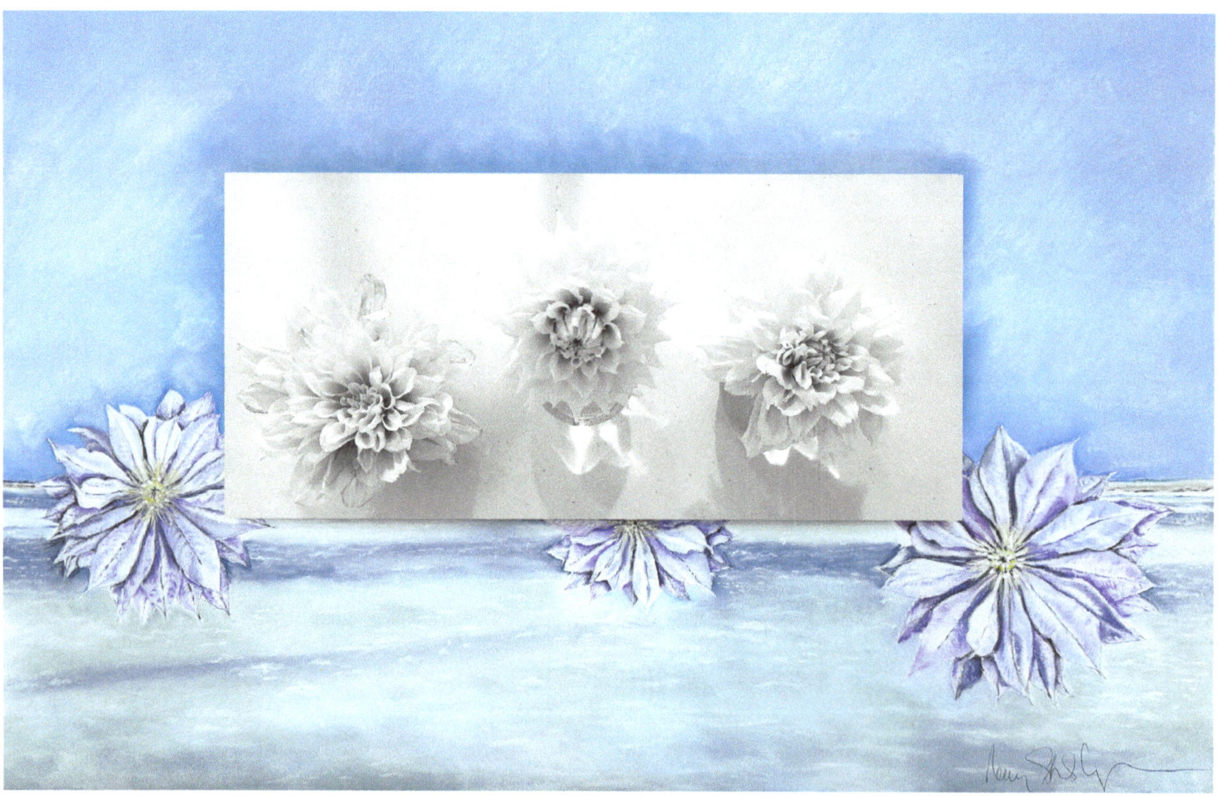

The Luminescence of Light,68.58x 109.22 pastel on paper, mounted photograph

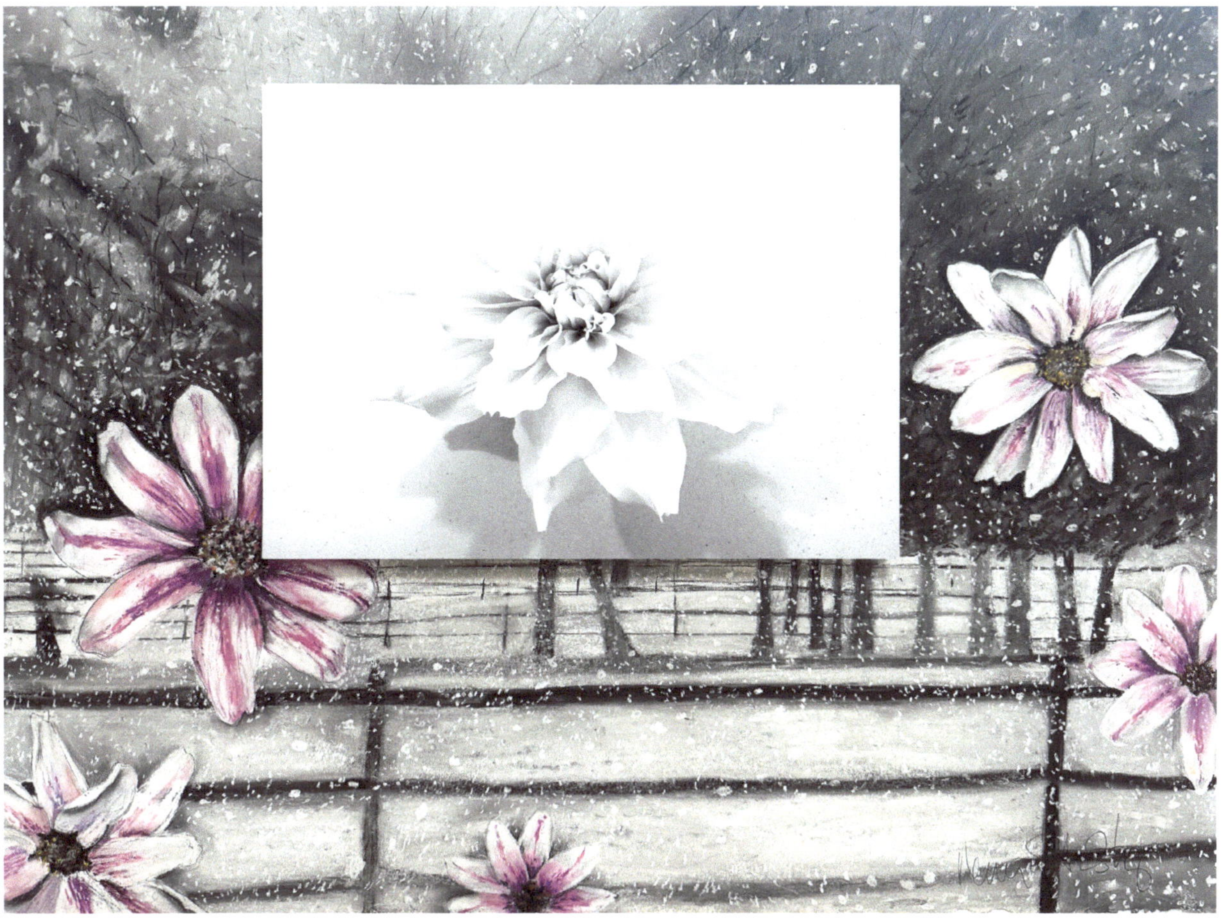

The Revival of Splendor 63.5 x 83.82, pastel on paper, mounted photograph

NOA RY

https://www.noa-ry.com/

I was born in 1979. I grew up in a small town in the canton of Aargau, Switzerland. , in a kind of commune with my patchwork family. Today, I live in Zurich. My father worked with computers in the 1980s, which paved the way for me to explore the relationship between humans and technology. I attended art school in Zurich at the age of 16 and still live there today. I graduated with a Bachelor of Arts degree at the age of 20. I completed my Master's degree in Cultural/Gender Studies at the ZHdK at the age of 27. This had a strong influence on my worldview. Rather than simply reproducing the work of the great contemporary masters of cultural studies, I wanted to continue writing myself. In doing so, I developed the concept of 'Divorg — a dividing organism'. Additionally, inspiration is literally stuck in my head. I suffer from schizoaffective disorder. I hear voices and see things that others don't. I hear distortions. The world collides, explodes and disintegrates into a thousand pieces, and with it, a thousand identities. On the one hand, this is a curse, but blessings follow hard work. Today, I see this great dimensionality as a significant source of artistic enrichment. Art helps me cope with my illness. It enables me to express myself in a way that makes the world tangible and stops me from becoming lost in my own universe. It is the tug-of-war between the 'inside' and the 'outside', and the power that arises from the struggle between identities, that provides me with inspiration. This inspiration reflects the duality of 'analogue' and 'digital'. I have been exploring these fields for more than 30 years, focusing on the question of the fusion of humans and technology. It is very important to me that barriers are broken down and interfaces are illuminated. I work with a variety of materials. For physical works, these include computer circuit boards, ceramics and technical elements. For digital works, I use various software and draw on my iPad, knowing no boundaries when it comes to analogue and digital work processes. My creations include robotic art, sculptures, sculpture-paintings, digitally drawn artworks, video art and installations. Through this process, I experiment with analogue and digital techniques, combining and transforming them. For instance, I use FaceTime mapping to superimpose my facial expressions onto physical sculpture-paintings, breathing life into these formerly silent works of art by creating videos. Through this process, I attempt to break down the boundaries imposed by formats, media, people and society, surrendering myself to the creative journey. In my universe of humans and technology, as well as their fusion and influence on our identities, the question always arises of who invented whom.

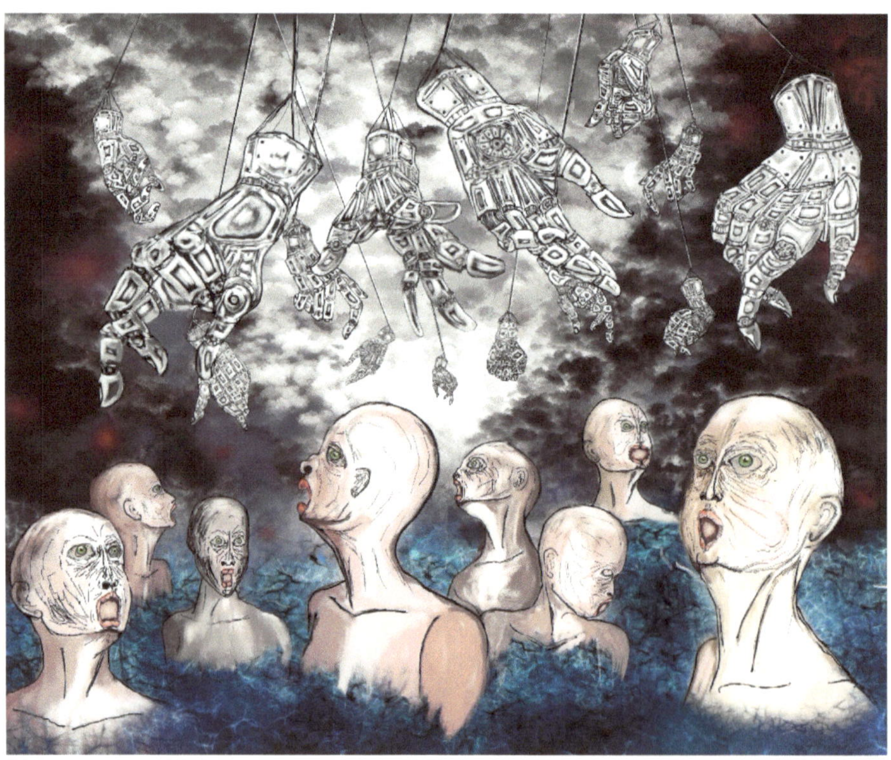

"will you help me or not?!", 2025, digital painting_oil brushes, variable size:max 2m

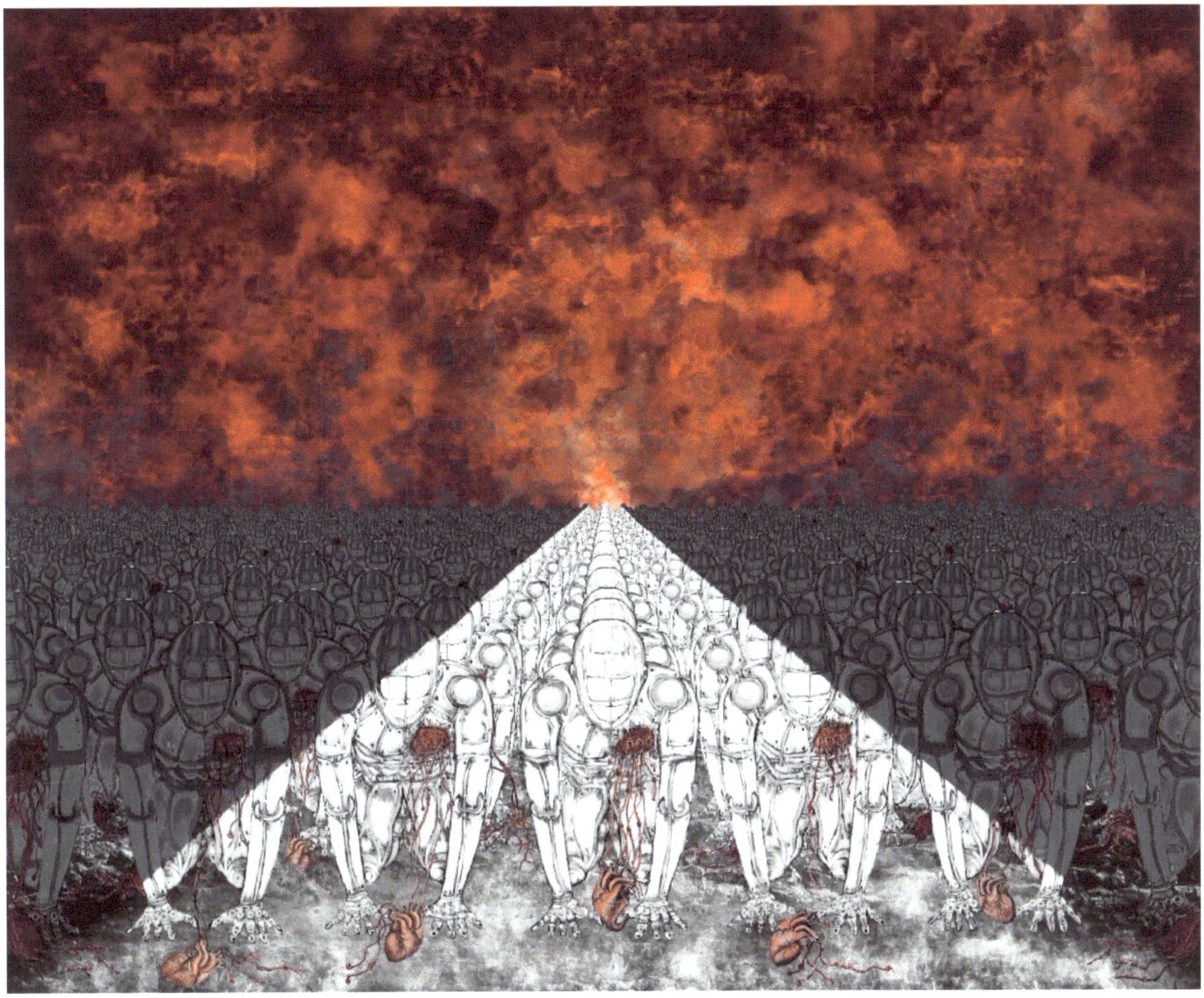

order, 2025, digital painting_oil brushes, variable size:max 2m

NOÉMIE L. CÔTÉ

noemielcote.com

Noémie L. Côté is an internationally acclaimed Canadian artist celebrated for her signature impressionist style, a vibrant, sugar-pop approach to landscape painting. Working in richly textured oil, she transforms natural scenes into immersive experiences, with brushstrokes that disperse light into joyful, sculptural colour that uplifts the viewer. Her passion for depicting nature was ignited during childhood travels in Africa, where she absorbed the vivid hues of the land and wildlife, and was mentored by a celebrated Zimbabwean painter. Returning to Canada, she honed her craft through a scholarship-supported fine arts program at Canterbury High School, followed by a long career in graphic design before making the bold transition to full-time painter. Noémie's award-winning landscapes have garnered high professional recognition, including the 2025 Maple Leaf Award and the 2024 CFA Artist of the Year title, among other accolades for her emotional, expressive style. Today, she paints full-time in her Ottawa studio, with her work featured in prestigious galleries across Canada.

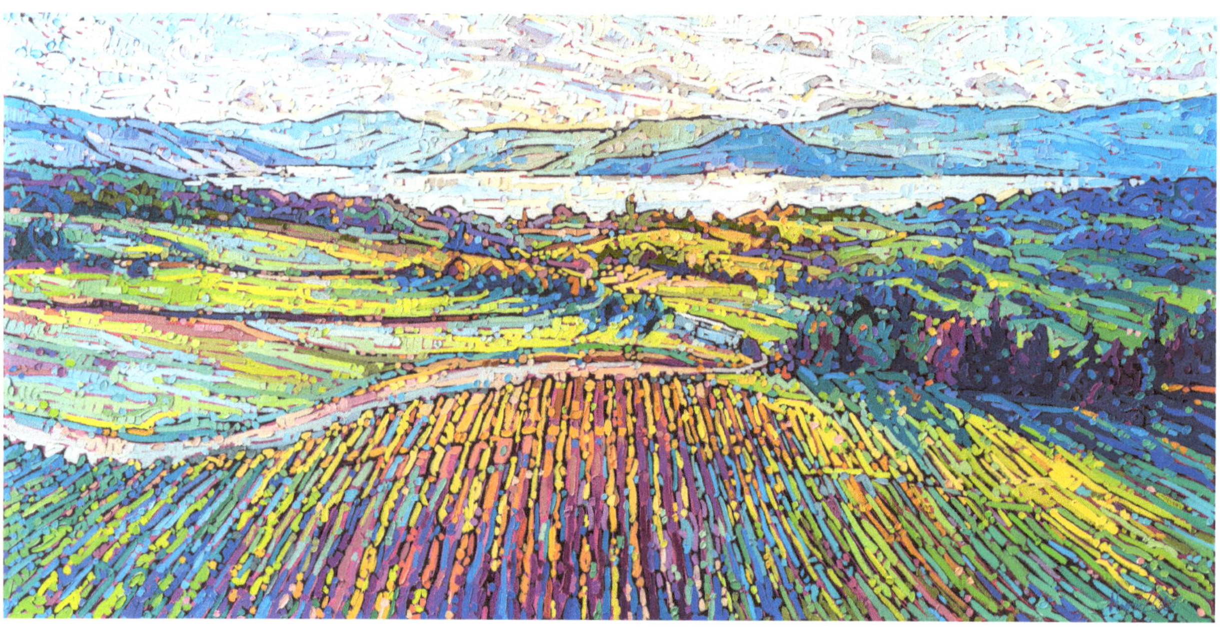

Okanagan Vineyard by the Lake, 2024, Oil on canvas, 76 x 152 cm

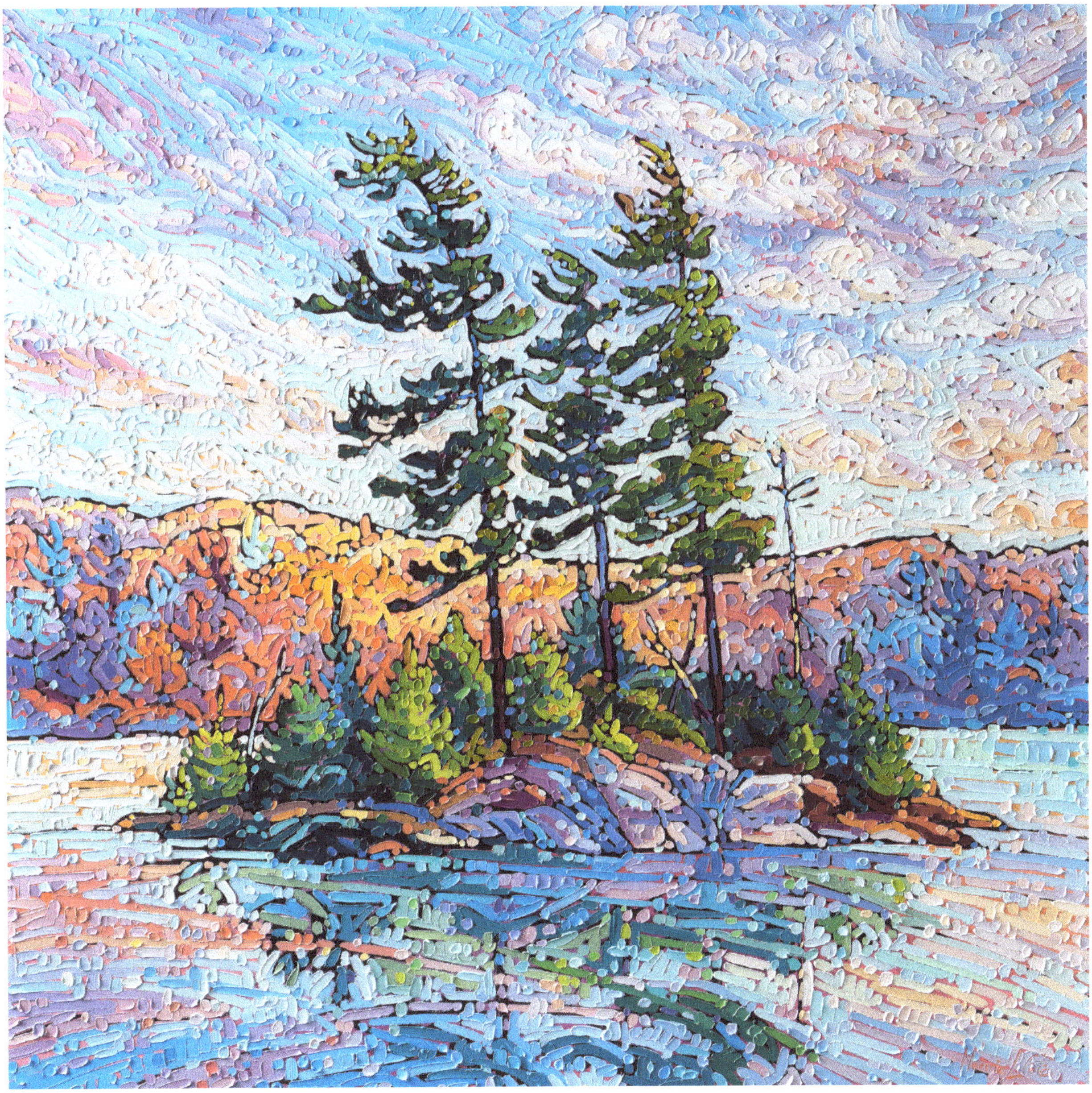

Muskoka Island in Autumn, 2025, Oil on canvas, 101 x 101 cm

NORA (MANO) KOMOROCZKI

artnow0.webnode.com

Nora KOMOROCZKI – Artist name: MANO Nora is a Hungarian artist-painter with the artist name Mano, born in Hungary, still living in the Hungarian capital, Budapest. She's been painting in oil on canvas for decades, inspired first by the beautiful landscapes in Hungary and other countries where she has been residing with her family for a few years (Sweden, Israel, and Belgium). Her qualification is journalist, but she has attended artistic courses both in Stockholm and Budapest. First as the Editor in Chief of the Hungarian Airlines she could travel a lot, and later as the Regional Director of the Scandinavian and Baltic Countries at the Hungarian Tourism Agency she could see and meet interesting people, capture the beauty of different countries. She tried to show this beauty and special moments on her canvas. Her artworks were invited to different art exhibitions - solo and in group - organized in Hungary, Austria, Belgium, China, France, Israel, Italy, Japan, Spain, United Kingdom, the USA. She is an awarded artist by several international art prizes (Leonardo da Vinci, Caravaggio, Michelangelo, Picasso, Botticelli, Artist of the Future, Face of Peace Art Prize, Artist of Creativy, Top 60 Masters, Trophy International Prize Paris, The best Modern and Contemporary Artists London, Leaders Protagonists of Art at Washington, World Best Artist Prize, Artist of the Year 2025, Ambassador of Art, Oscar of Creativity, Grand Master of Light, Hungarian Silver Cross of Merit State Award, etc.) HONORARY GRAND MASTER AND EMERITUS of the Accademia "Italia in Arte nel Mondo" - Cultural Association in 2025. Her artist statement: Her art is a tribute to the wonder of our Earth - a reminder that it's beauty is precious and must be cherished and protected for generations to come. Read more: https://artnow0.webnode.com/

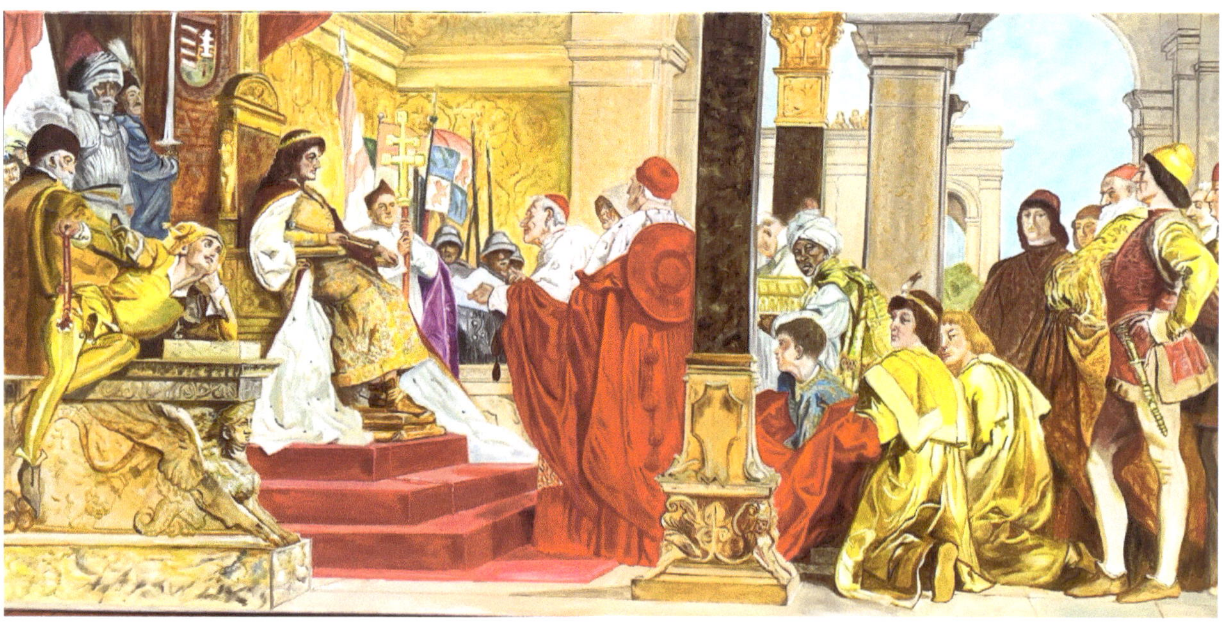

"Hungarian King Matthias receives the Envoyas of Pope (XV. century)" /copy of Benczur's artwork 1915/; Oil on canvas, 100 cm x 200 cm

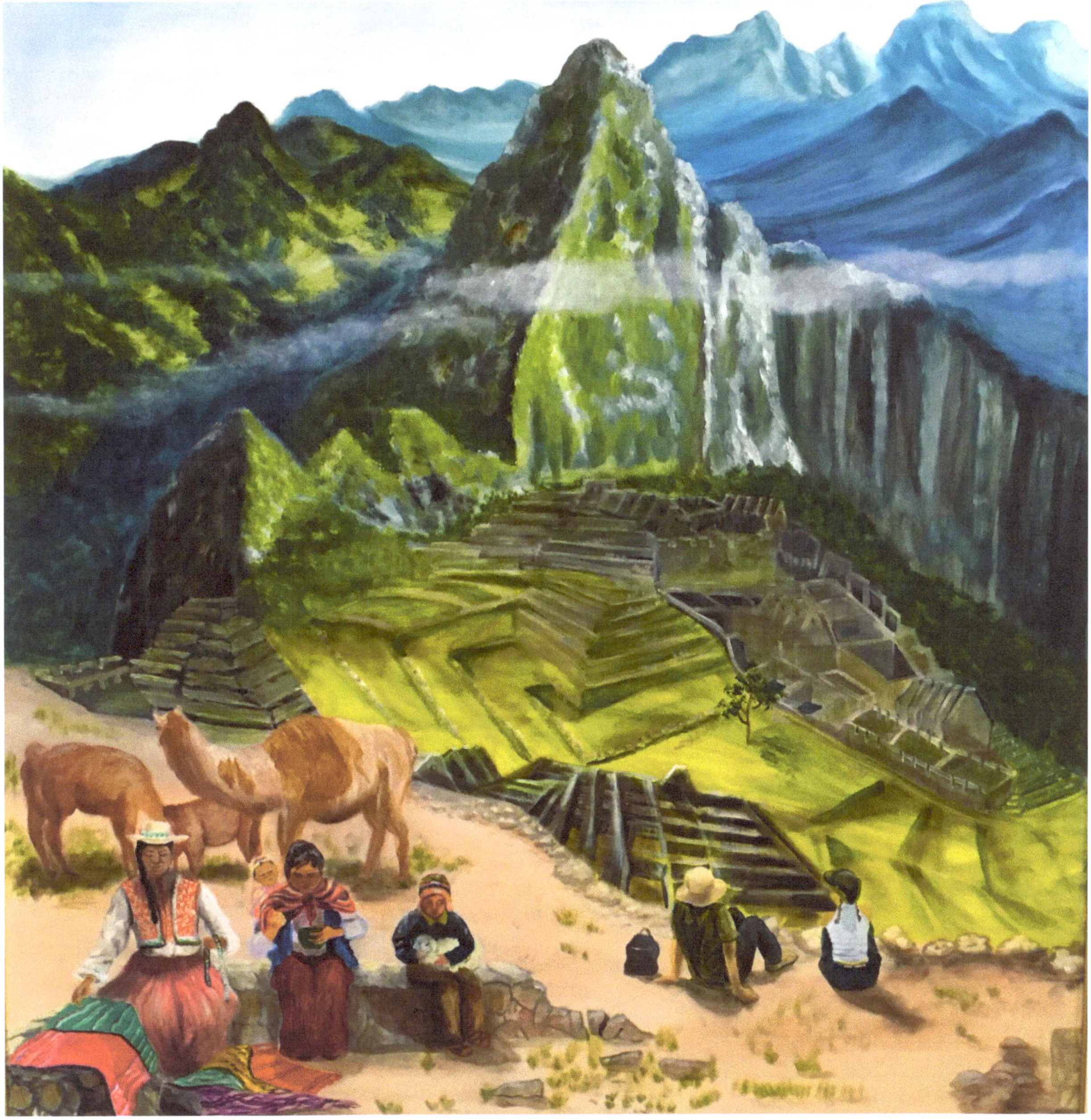

Machu Picchu, 2008. Oil on canvas, 180 cm x 160 cm

NUTS

https://www.instagram.com/nuts_natsuki.azuma

Born in Hokkaido, Japan in 1977. Group Exhibitions: 2022: "Salon Art Shopping Paris" 2023: "Interconnecting Lines," One Art Space, New York 2024: "NATURE," Noho M55 Gallery, New York 2025: "Genten," Hilton Art Square, Tokyo Other: Holds workshops in Hokkaido. She was born in Japan and dreamed of becoming a painter at the age of six. However, she lacked confidence in her work and gave up on her dream of becoming a painter. 30 Years later, when she had another opportunity to engage in art, she rediscovered her passion for painting. She is childcare. She taught herself early childhood education techniques and continued to pursue unlimited expressiveness and unique works through artworks with the theme of "freedom." This theme reminded her of her childhood sensibilities. And,through her art activities, such as workshops, she came into contact with the unique sensibilities of many children, which led her to feel that "the greatest artists are children." Currently, in addition to digital art, she is pursuing "Dimple Art"an environmentally friendly new form of art developed in Japan, andaims to share it with the world. Dimple Art is a new type of art that uses ultra-transparent paint developed from research on car recycling. She conducts Dimple Art workshops to help children discover the joy of self-expression. Her goal is to increase the number of children who have the ability to create, share and contribute their own work. She believes that the world will be richer in the future when those children grow up.

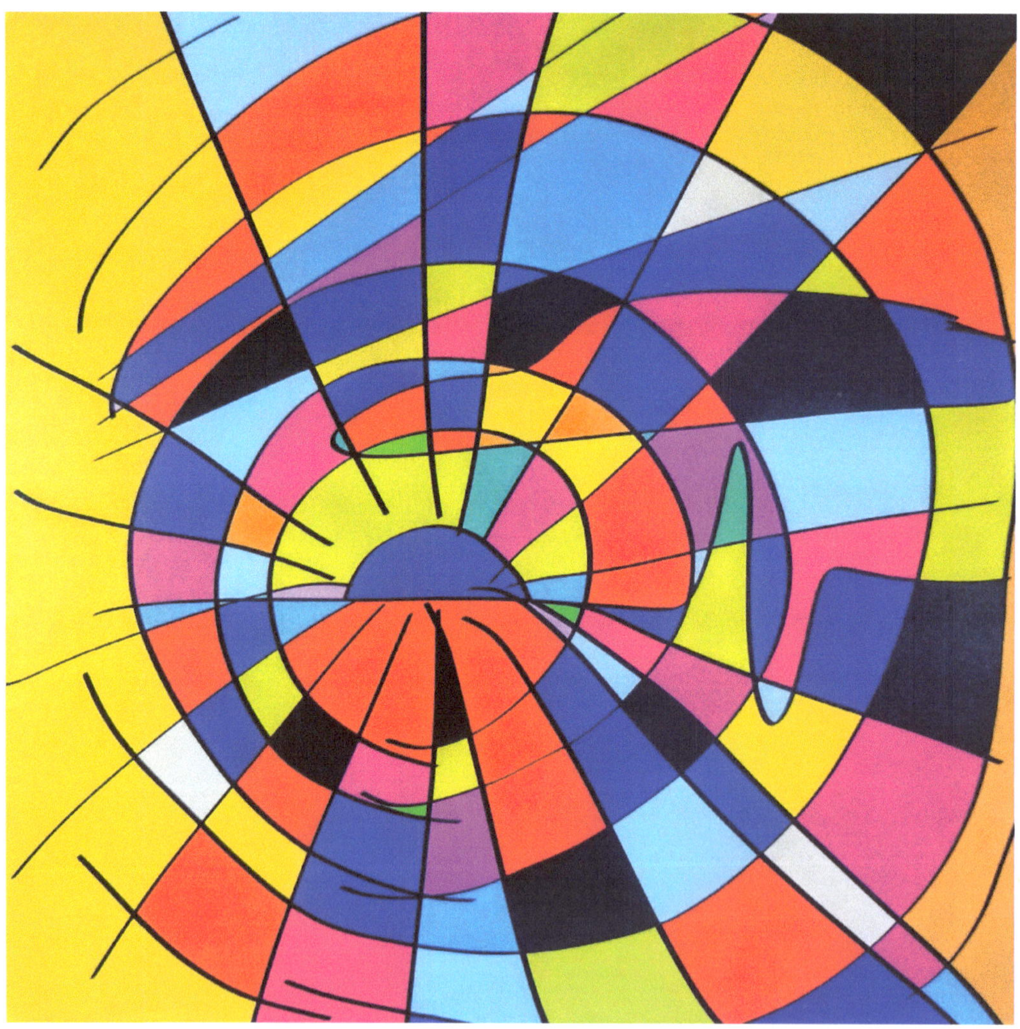

The world is created by everyone's passion,2025,Digital art printed on canvas,60cm×60cm

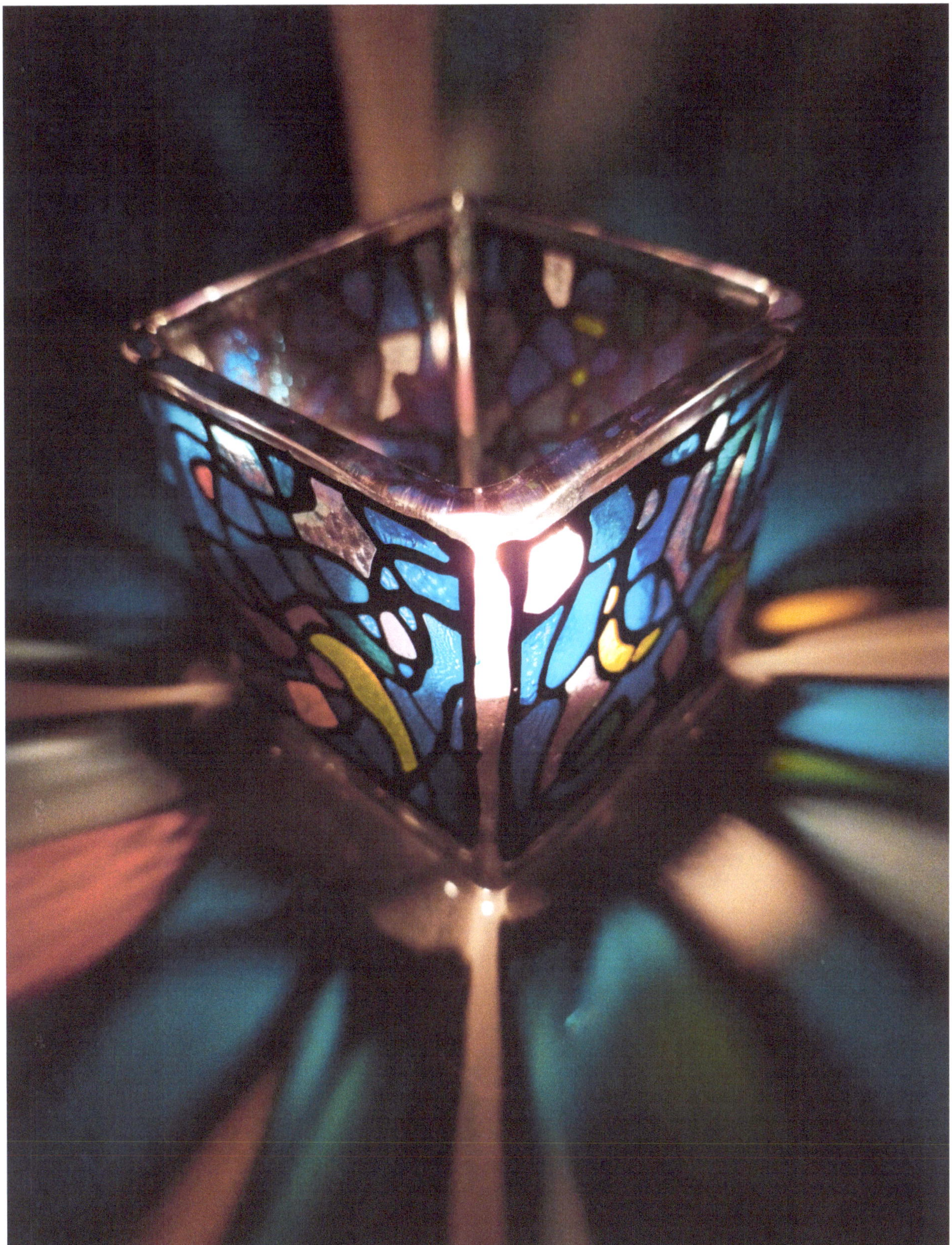

Exoplanets, 2024, Painted on glass with Dimple Art Color, 6cm×6cm×6cm

ODILIA IACCARINO

https://www.odiliaiaccarinoart.com

Without a doubt, it is clear that "Las Meninas de Velázquez" has been Odilia Iaccarino's muse and artistic focus for the last few years. Through her experience visiting the beautiful city of Madrid, Spain, she could discuss Las Meninas and its context for hours. One particular moment stands out: as she stood before the canvas, she felt an overwhelming sense of connection to the artist and the world he inhabited, which sparked a deep desire to capture that essence in her own art. On a trip to Madrid, Odilia was captivated by the enormous life-size Menina sculptures that adorned the city and by the importance of their contribution to Spanish culture. In 17th-century Spain, the Meninas were noble-born girls sent to the palace to serve the queen or her daughters. The most famous Meninas are depicted in Diego Velázquez's artwork "Las Meninas," which is named after them, and these maids of honor have become iconic figures in Madrid. In her journey to achieve a version of Las Meninas, Odilia created a silhouette of the modern Menina figure and added colorful paint and textures to the canvas; this process evoked emotions reminiscent of her day spent wandering the streets of Madrid. For her, the challenge lies in exploring a balance of elements on the canvas, using primarily oil, pastels, acrylics, and graphite. The suggestive form also incorporates organic elements, which bring a tridimensional depth to her work.

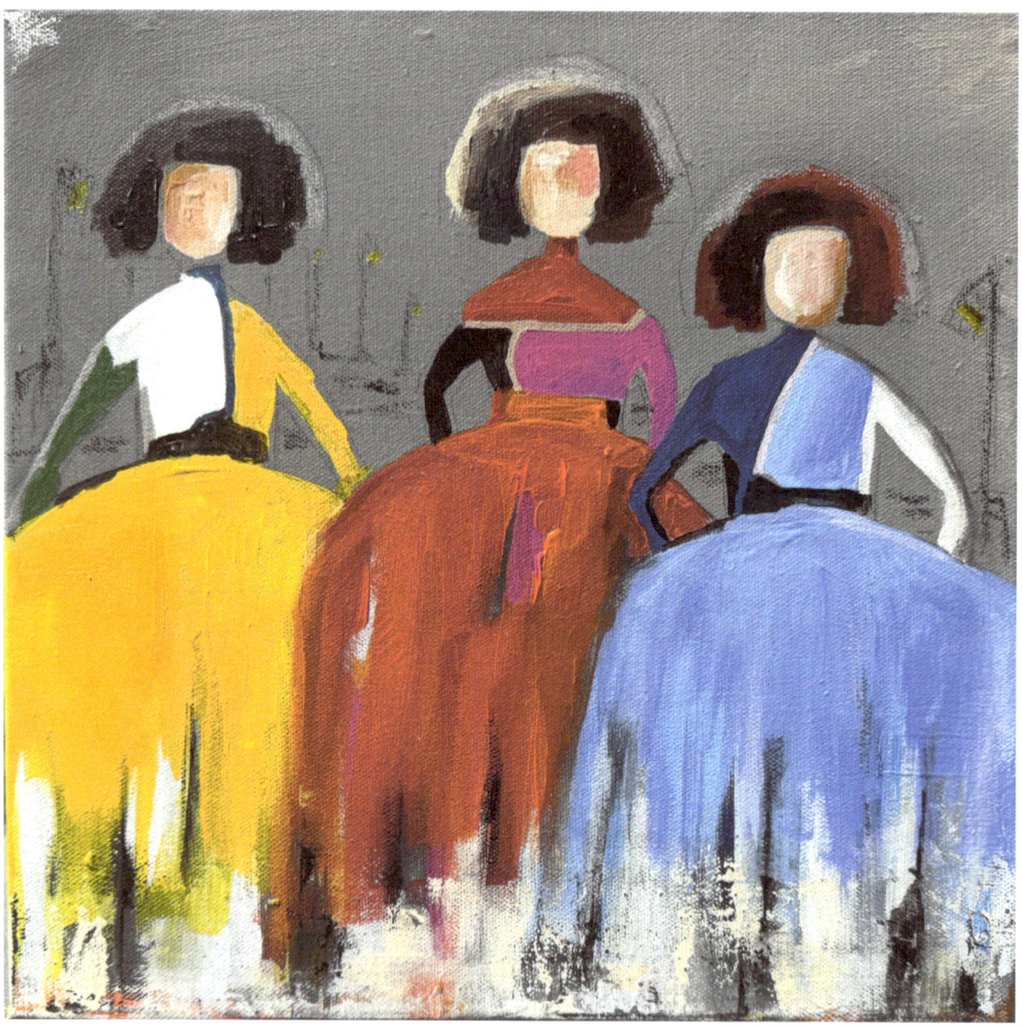

Meninas La Avenida, 2026, mix media on canvas, 30.4 x 30.4

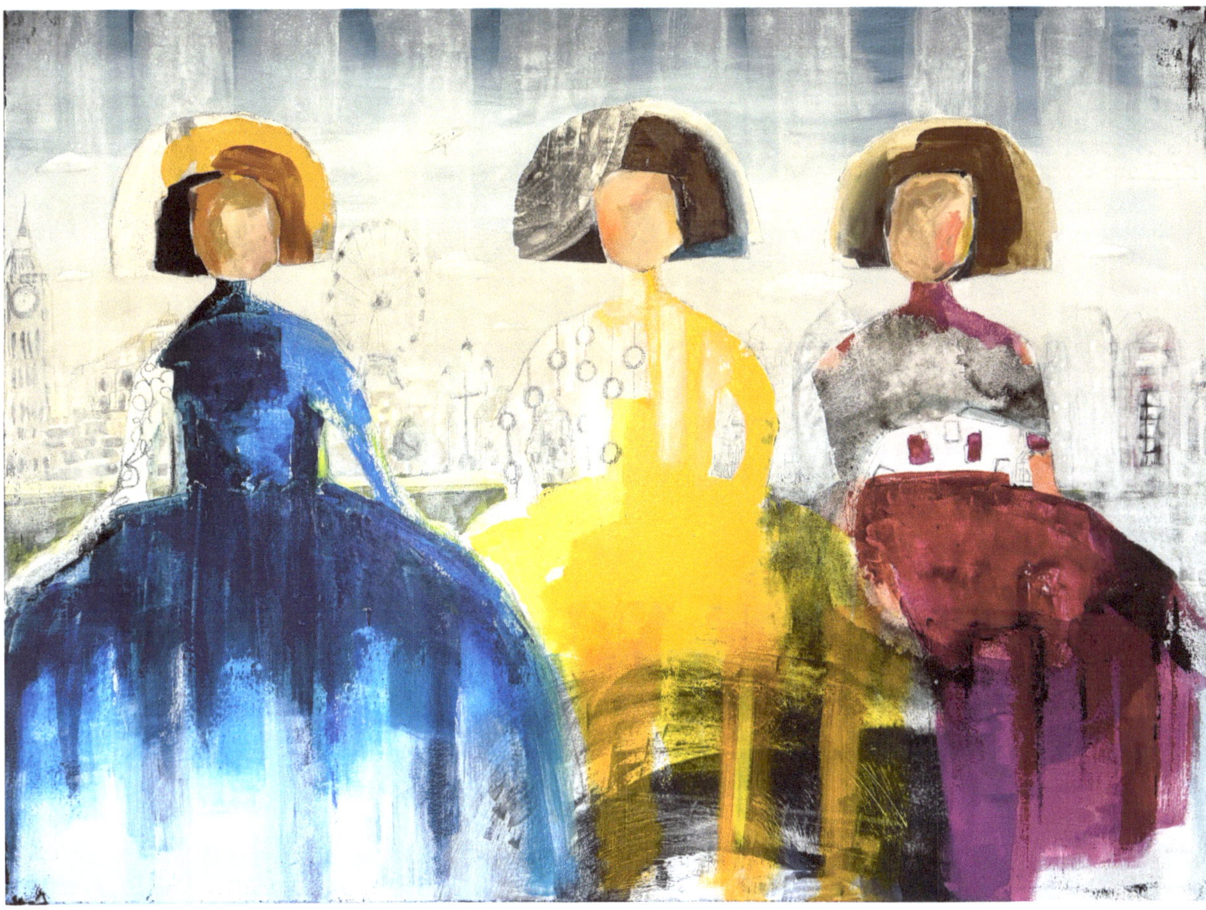

Meninas London Dreaming, 2026, mix media on canvas, 91.4 x 121.9

OENONE HAMMERSLEY

www.oenonehammersley.com

Oenone Hammersley, an internationally recognized mixed-media artist known for her bold use of color, texture, and light. Her nature-inspired paintings—especially her vivid depictions of water—are powerful visual statements about the beauty of our planet and the urgent need for environmental protection. Born in England in 1957 and now living in Florida, USA, Oenone draws inspiration from her background in theatre design and her extensive travels through Southeast Asia, India, Africa, and Latin America. These journeys fuel her creative vision, which she expresses through large-scale oil paintings, collage, and a unique technique that combines hand-painting with multiple paint pours and glossy resin finishes. Collectors of Oenone's art celebrate her ability to transform deep ecological concerns into captivating visual art. Her artworks raise awareness about deforestation, ocean pollution, and overfishing—issues she actively supports through regular donations to conservation organizations. Oenone Hammersley's art is a celebration of nature's beauty and complexity. Her paintings have been exhibited at prestigious galleries and art fairs, including New York, London, Miami, and Washington DC, and are part of important private and public collections worldwide. Artist Statement: Colour and light are used to emphasize the vanishing world of wilderness that implores us to take notice, appreciate the rare and raw beauty about us, and allow our imagination to roam about the abstract compositions symbolizing the unsettled and unsettling world in which man alters nature.

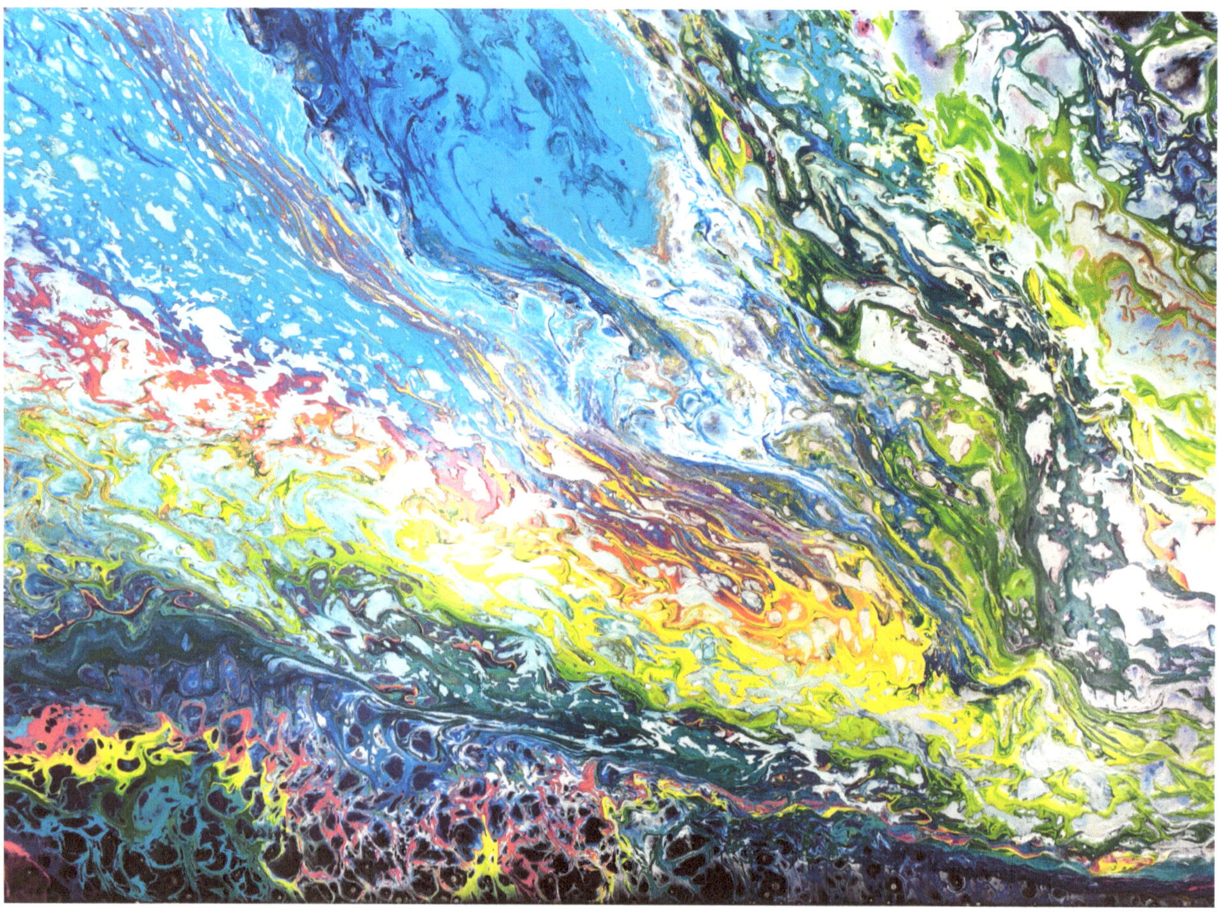

Fire Underwater Tamu Massif 2, 2022, Mixed Media on Canvas, 50cm x 76cm.

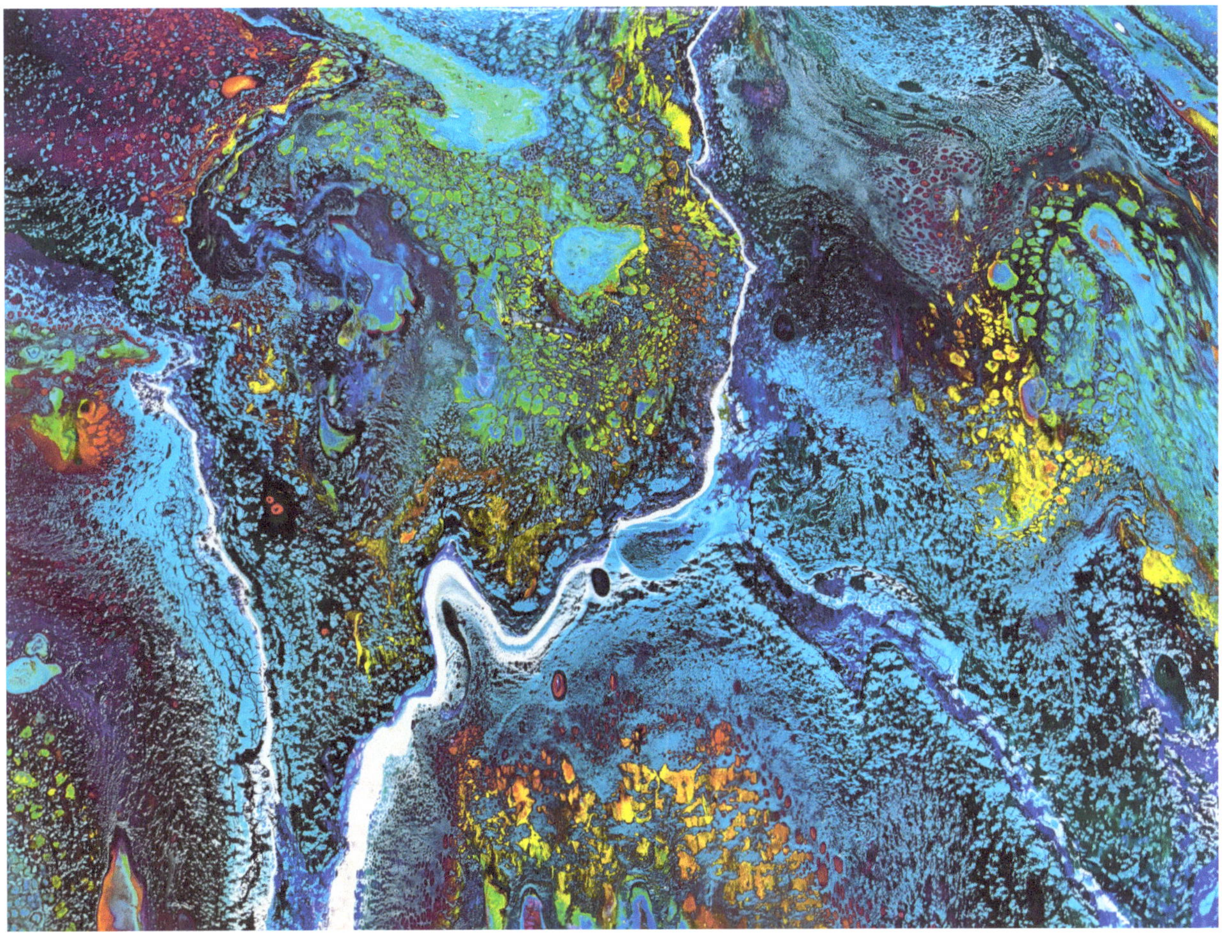

Rainbow River 2, 2025, Acrylic on Canvas, 30cm x 40cm

PAUL HARTEL

HTTPS://WWW.INSTAGRAM.COM/PHARTEL16

Hailing from New York and currently residing in the picturesque West of Ireland, Hartel immerses himself in the world of abstract, neo-expressionist, and art brut styles, using a diverse array of mediums such as oil, acrylic, oil stick, pastels, charcoal, spray paint and pencil. His creative work celebrates a pure, uninhibited essence while also serving as thought-provoking commentary on various social issues. His captivating works are delivered through an energetically raw and improvisational approach. Paul Hartel is a highly acclaimed artist with a strong presence in major cities across the USA and Europe. Hartel's enthralling pieces have been sought after by private collectors and social and professional organizations in Europe, the USA, and Australia. His talent has garnered attention from numerous art publications and magazines, earning him the coveted American Art Award in the Naïve Art Category in Los Angeles, the World Art Award in the Art Brut Category in Los Angeles, Future of Art Global Masterpiece Award in Dubai, the Collector's Choice Award in New York, and the Collector's Vision International Art Award in London. Hartel has recently been included in the 2024 Gold List of Top Contemporary Artists of Today in ArtMarket International art magazine and the Art Investment & Collectors' Guide 2025: Most Investable and Prominent Artists.

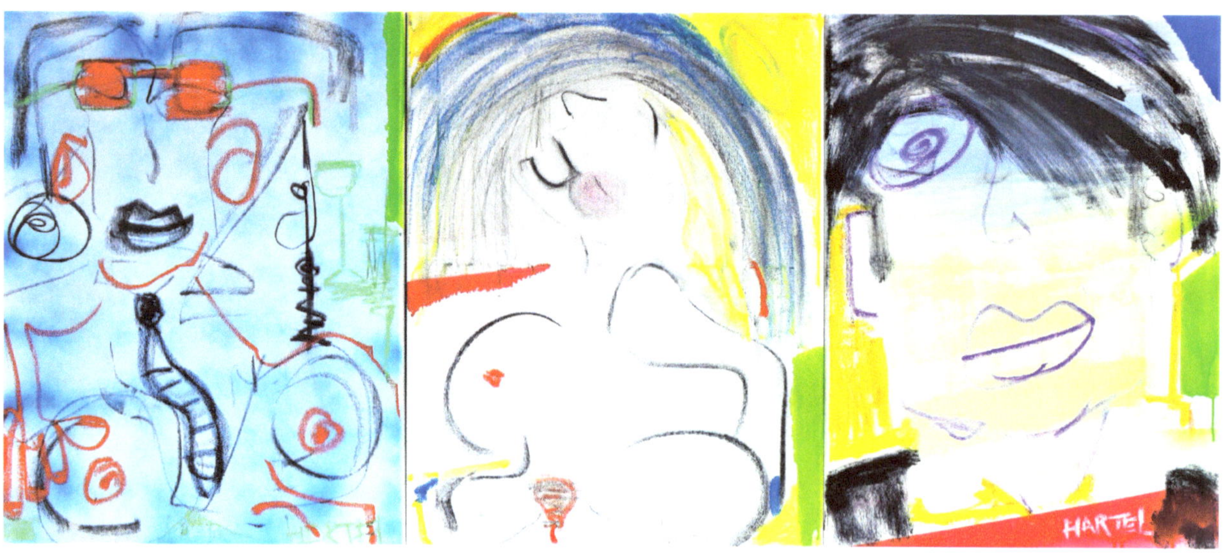

Untitled (from Modern Faces), 2022, mixed media on canvas, 61x152cm

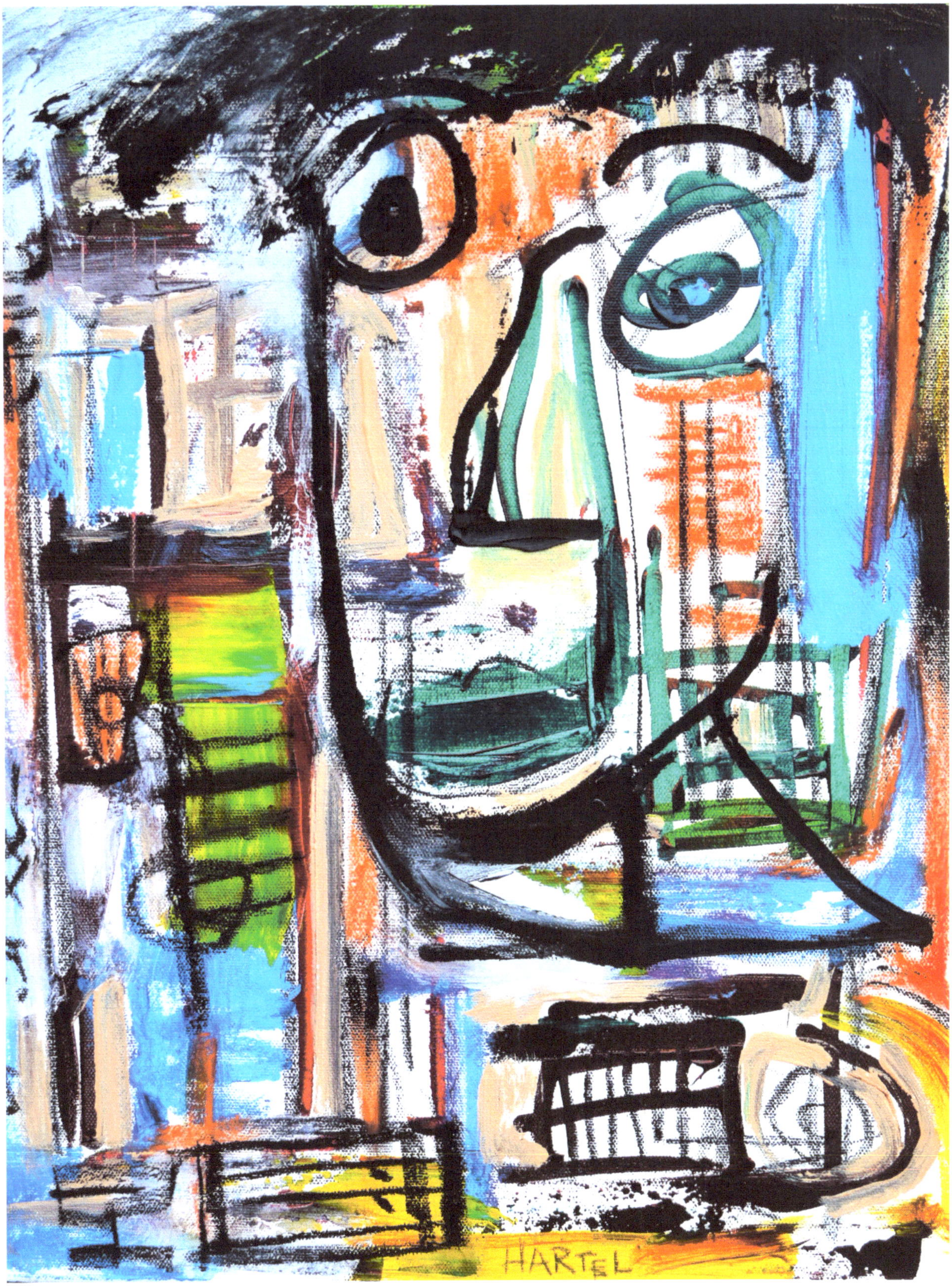

Temporal Executives, 2022, mixed media on canvas, 46x36cm.

PETRA DIPPOLD-GOETZ

https://www.petradippoldgoetz.com

‚Art is a daughter of freedom' Friedrich Schiller

Born near Nuremberg, Germany, Petra Dippold-Goetz grew up in the city of Albrecht Dürer, immersed in a rich artistic tradition. Although painting had always been a deep personal passion, it wasn't until 2014 that she chose to follow it as a calling. One winter evening, she discovered a lifeless white dove in her garden—its blood and feathers scattered in the snow. This haunting moment marked a turning point: from that day forward, art became her way of processing emotion, questioning the world, and engaging with it more deeply. She went on to study Fine Arts at the Academy of Faber-Castell from 2014 to 2018, refining her technical skills while exploring a raw, intuitive visual language. Her work is inspired by visits to museums across Europe and influenced by Informal Art, particularly artists such as Emil Schumacher, Anselm Kiefer, Jackson Pollock, and Franz Kline. Petra's expressive paintings blend gestural abstraction with natural and industrial materials. She works in acrylic and oil, often incorporating sand, wood, plastic, or found objects—especially remnants of human consumption. Her fascination with transformation and meaning-making through discarded matter has led to her participation in several Trash Art Festivals, where she also teaches workshops on turning waste into art. Some of her works are vibrant celebrations of life and beauty. Others carry urgent socio-political messages, confronting ecological destruction, species extinction, and unsustainable consumption. "I see myself as an artist-activist," she says, "wielding my brush not only to adorn the canvas but to awaken the soul." Petra Dippold-Goetz has exhibited in major art cities such as Vienna, Paris, Barcelona, New York, and Tokyo. Her works are part of collections across Europe, the USA, Singapore, and Japan. She has received several honors, including the art prizes Faces of Peace, Voices of Tomorrow, and Global Art Virtuoso. Her artistic mission is both poetic and purposeful: to touch hearts, to question, to awaken reason and compassion. In a global context marked by ecological and social crises, her art becomes a call—to delight in the beauty of our world and to take responsibility for preserving it. Each of her works is a "daughter of freedom": liberated by purpose, yet bound by a deep commitment to insight and care.

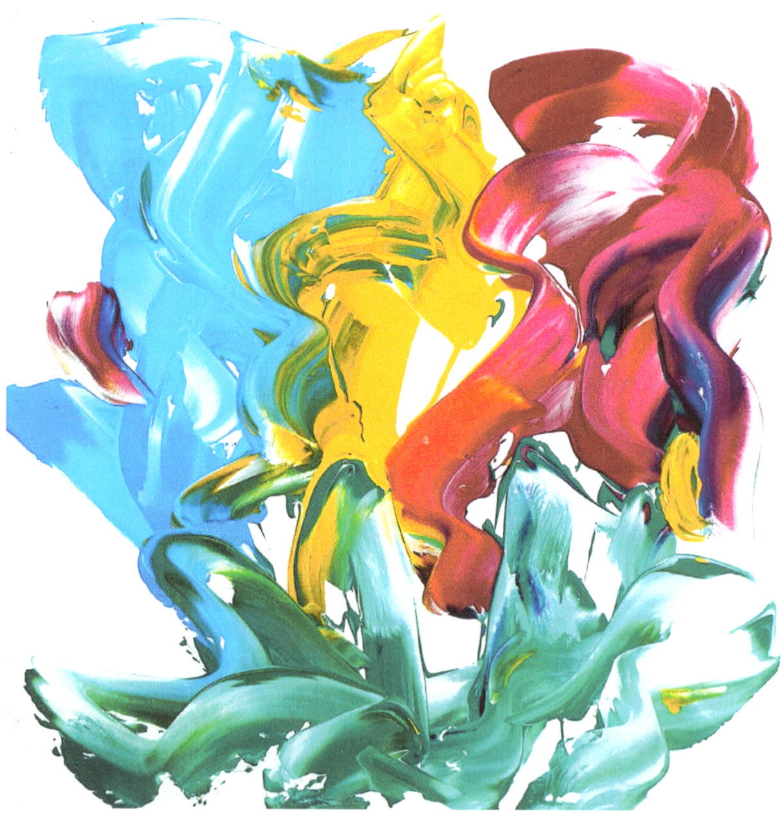

Floral Rhapsody, 2025. Acrylic on canvas, 50 x 50 cm.

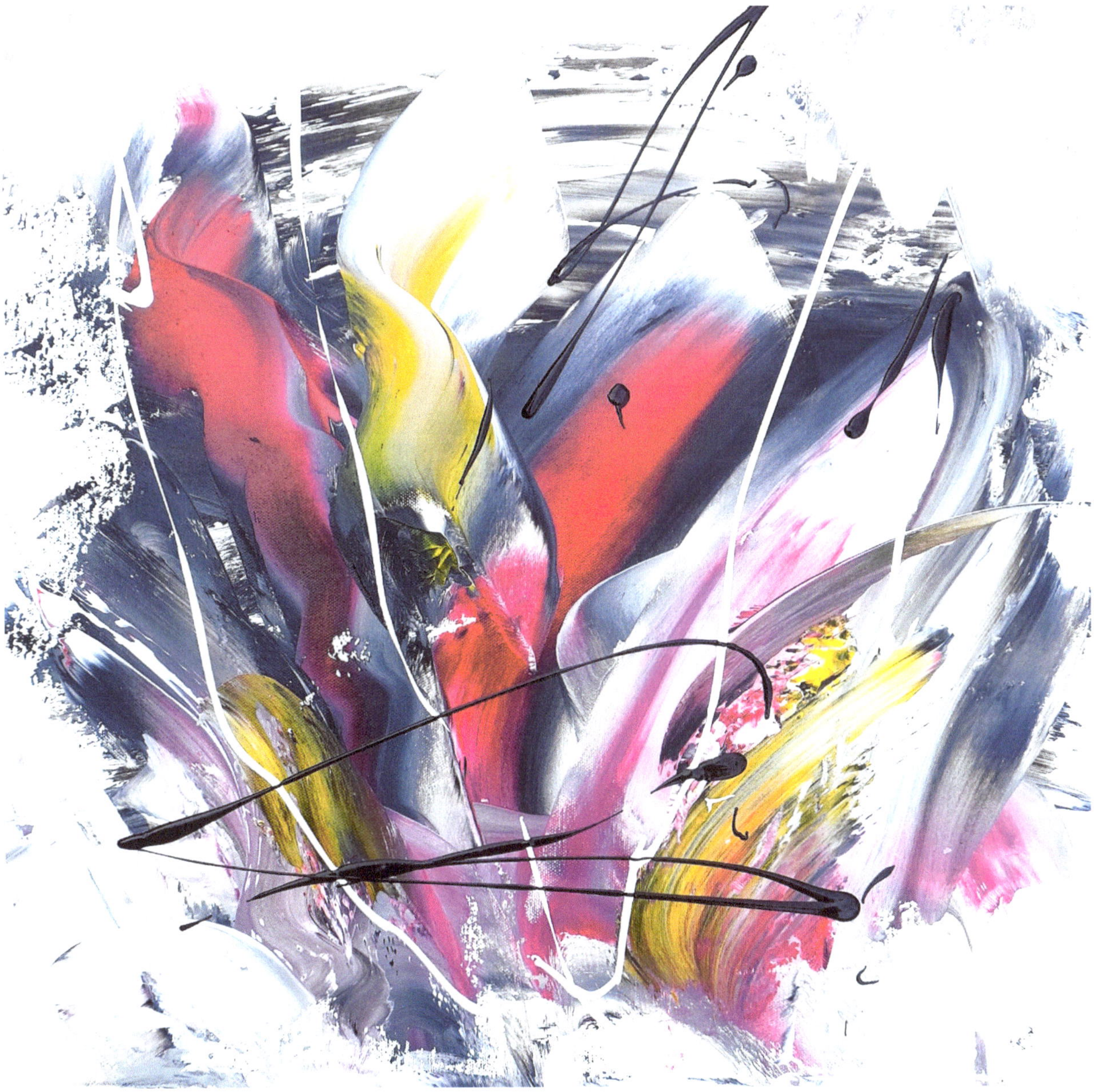

A Whisper of Light and Shadow, 2024. Acrylic on canvas, 50 x 50 cm.

PILAR XERCAVINS CASAS

www.pilarxercavins.com

Pilar Xercavins Casas is an artist from Sant Cugat del Vallès (Barcelona, Spain) born in 1961. Her painting style is abstract and she uses a mixed technique. She went through different learning techniques; pencil, charcoal, oil, coloured chalks and engraving, until she ended up using natural pigments and created her own style. Before creating her own technique she experimented with plants, flowers and leaves from the trees leaving them to act on the canvas under the rain and the sun, this way she discovered an aging texture more similar to nature. Later on a trip to Morocco she discovered the natural pigments that led her to create her own technique. She has exhibited in multiple collective and individual exhibitions in galleries and museums and has received several international awards.

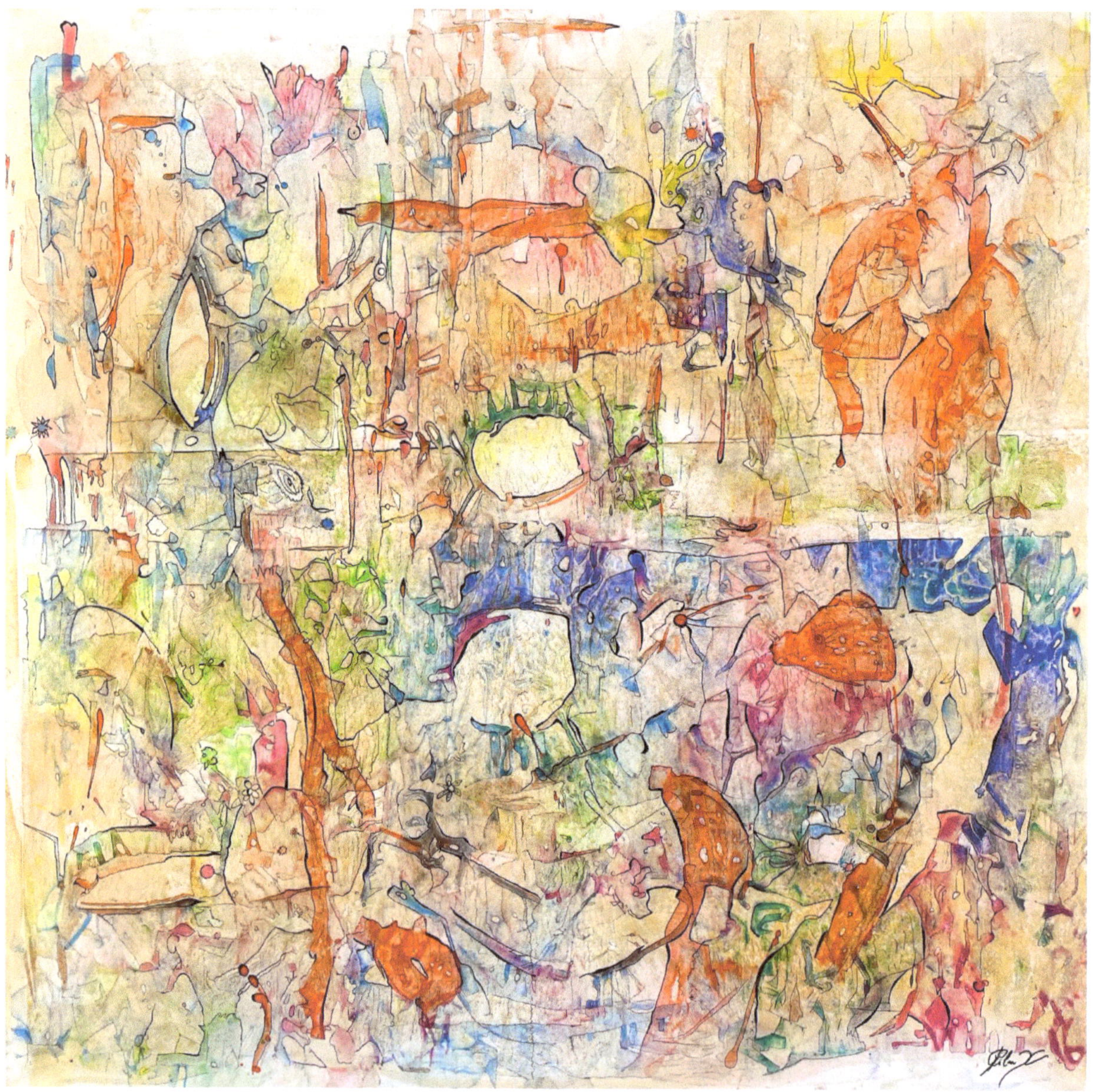

Title: El origen de los grandes genios / Year. 2023 / Technique : mixed / Dimensions: 120 x 120

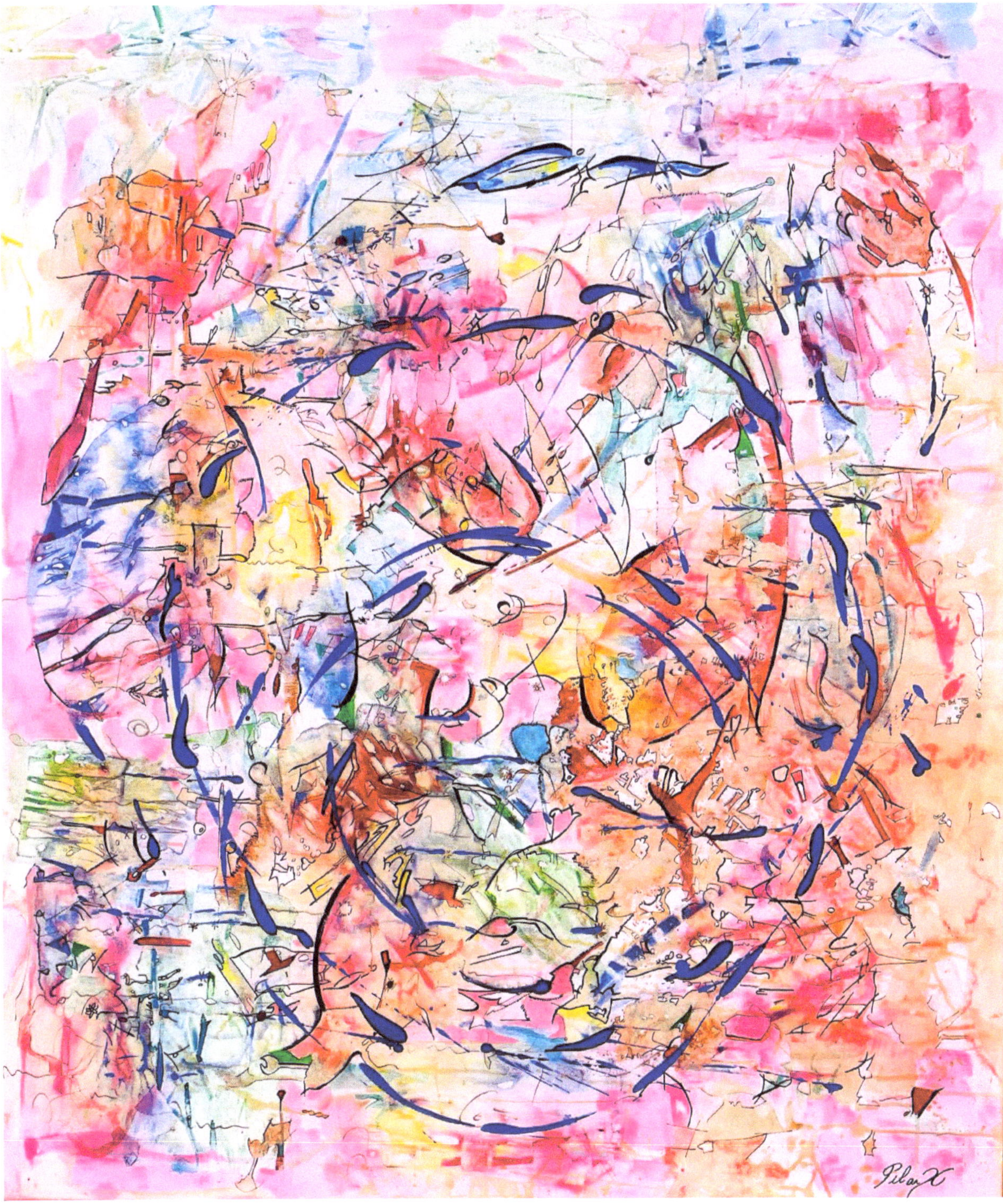

Title: The creator's eye / Year: 2022 / Technique: mixed / Dimensions: 120 x 100

PILBRI BRITTA NEUMÄRKER

https://www.pilbri-artandmore.eu

Britta Neumärker, known in the art world as Pilbri, is a German painter and photographic artist whose creative path has been marked by a profound shift in her worldview. More than two decades ago, a life-changing event altered her perspective—both literally and metaphorically—transforming her perception of light, space, and form.

What could have been a limitation became the catalyst for her artistic voice.Her early works were steeped in the colors and rhythms of Impressionism and Expressionism, influenced by Monet's light sensitivity, Macke's vibrancy, Kandinsky's abstraction, and the poetic boldness of the Blaue Reiter movement.

Over time, she began to interweave painting and photography, creating multifaceted works that exist somewhere between the tangible and the imaginary. Guided by the words from Saint-Exupéry's The Little Prince: "One sees clearly only with the heart; what is essential is invisible to the eye"—Pilbri has dedicated her art to making the invisible visible. She traces the hidden currents beneath the surface: the fragile fragments of human souls, the unspoken dialogue between people, the blurred boundary between reality and the digital world, the silent burden of longing and the glimmer of hope amidst the darkness.

Her working process is one of layering—pigment upon pigment, image upon image, meaning upon meaning. This layering reflects the complexity of consciousness itself, in which memories, desires, fears, and dreams are interwoven. In her paintings, layers of color breathe life into abstraction; in her photographs, textures and transparencies reveal secret dimensions.

Pilbri's work testifies to a deep awareness of the times we live in—an age defined by conflict, disease, and environmental crises—yet she insists on holding on to beauty, compassion, and the quiet defiance of a smile. For her, art and science are not opposites, but allies, both capable of expanding human understanding and shaping a better future.

Each of her series—whether inspired by the raw stones of Stonehenge, the kaleidoscopic geometry of glass, or the refracted visions of "Brain Art"—is an invitation to look closer, feel more deeply, and remember that life itself radiates within the unseen. Her art is not just something to behold, but also something to be experienced—a meeting point between the visible world and the infinite landscapes of the mind.

Pilbri has received numerous awards for her unique art, including the prestigious Future of Art Global Masterpiece Award 2024.Pilbri explores the invisible: emotional fragments, human vulnerability, and the tension between the real and the virtual world. Through her multifaceted techniques—both in painting and conceptual meaning—she reveals hidden beauty. Her work addresses serious themes such as war, disease, and climate change and is rooted in the belief that art and science together can make the world a better place.

The Collectors Art Prize artworks are a blend of painting and digital photography. The digital photographs were created in 2025. They are a combination of a manipulated and a real photograph. Some include parts of the paintings, which are also presented here. The 2025 digital photographs explore the question of how long our brains will be able to distinguish between real and virtual landscapes as the digital world continues to evolve.

Pilbri's creations invite the viewer to look beyond the surface – and never lose the smile.

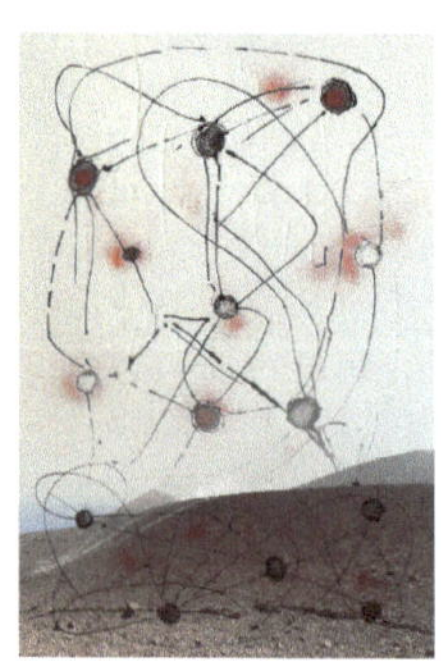

Exploring Network digital photography, containing one real photograph and a processed one of a real painting 100 x 80 cm

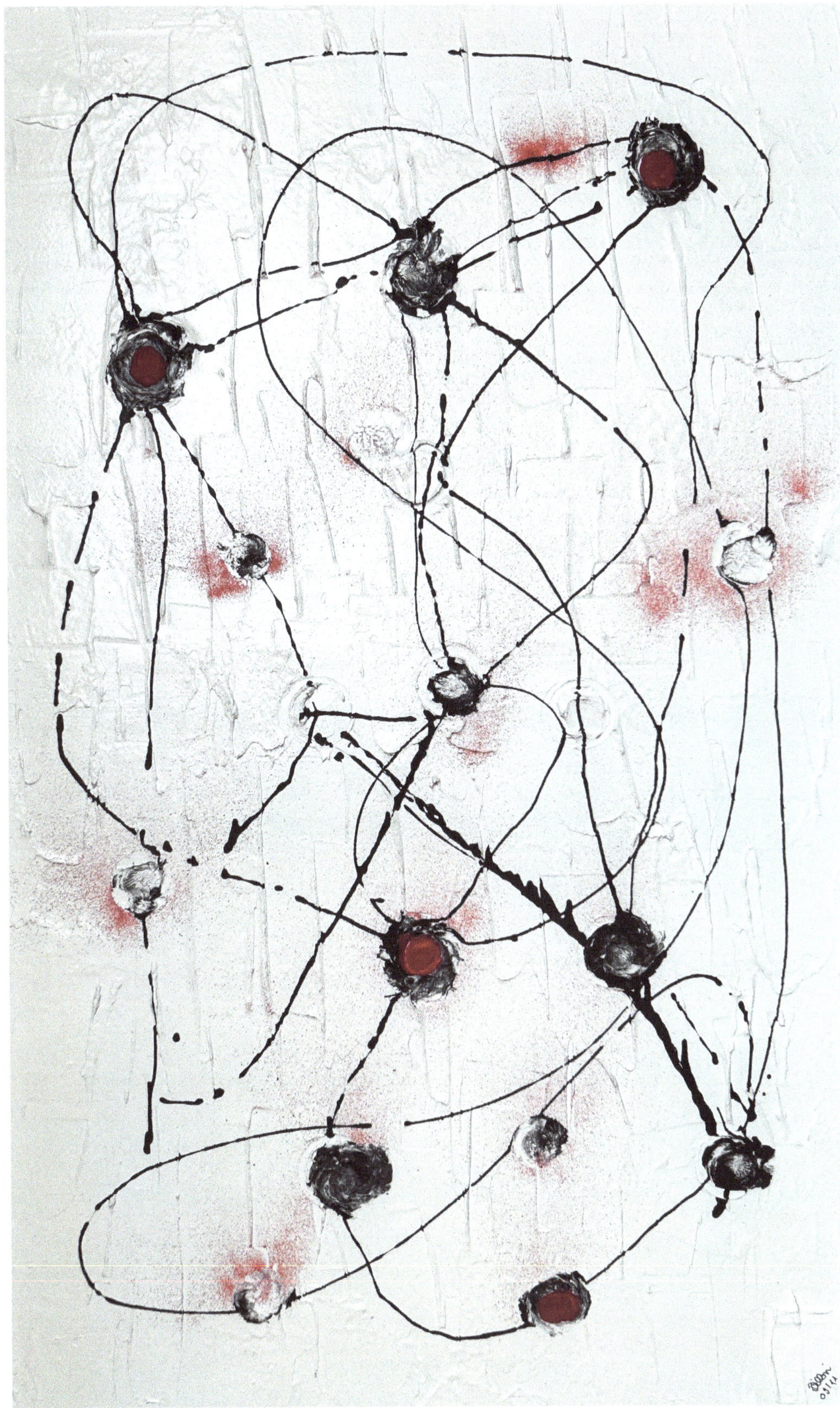

The Net 2 , 2011, Acryl on canvas, 120 x 60 cm

PRUDENCE AU

Instagram: @gallerpru

Prudence Au is a Hong Kong based abstract artist whose work has garnered international acclaim for its emotive depth, lyrical abstraction, and distinctive visual language. Educated in Fine Art in both France and Hong Kong, she brings a nuanced, cross-cultural sensibility to her practice - one that bridges Eastern philosophies of nature and Western traditions of gestural abstraction. Her paintings are not mere representations but meditative explorations of energy, emotion, and elemental form. Working primarily in oil, acrylic, ink, mixed media on canvas. Prudence constructs immersive compositions that pulse with vitality. Her technique is rooted in freehand precision, where each stroke is a deliberate act of expression. Through vibrant color palettes and layered textures, she evokes the raw beauty of the natural world, not as it appears, but as it feels. Since 2022, Prudence's work has been exhibited in leading galleries across Europe, the EMEA region, and Hong Kong. Her rising reputation was solidified between 2023 and 2025, when she received multiple accolades from esteemed international art institutions, recognizing her innovative approach and artistic excellence. These honors reflect not only her technical mastery but also her ability to connect with audiences on a deeply emotional and spiritual level. At the heart of Prudence's practice is a fascination with the invisible forces that shape our world movement, vibration, and transformation. Her compositions often feature nonparallel lines and spatial planes that defy conventional geometry, creating dynamic structures that resist digital reproduction and demand physical presence. In an age of screens and simulations, her work insists on the authenticity of in-person engagement. Each canvas becomes a site of contemplation, inviting viewers to slow down, breathe, and feel. Her visual language is deeply informed by her connection to nature. Rather than depicting landscapes or organic forms, Prudence channels the spirit of matter in its purest state. Her paintings are elemental - earth, water, air, and fire rendered through color, rhythm, and gesture. This approach reflects her belief that nature is not a subject to be observed but a force to be embodied. Through abstraction, she captures its essence: its chaos, its harmony, its quiet power.

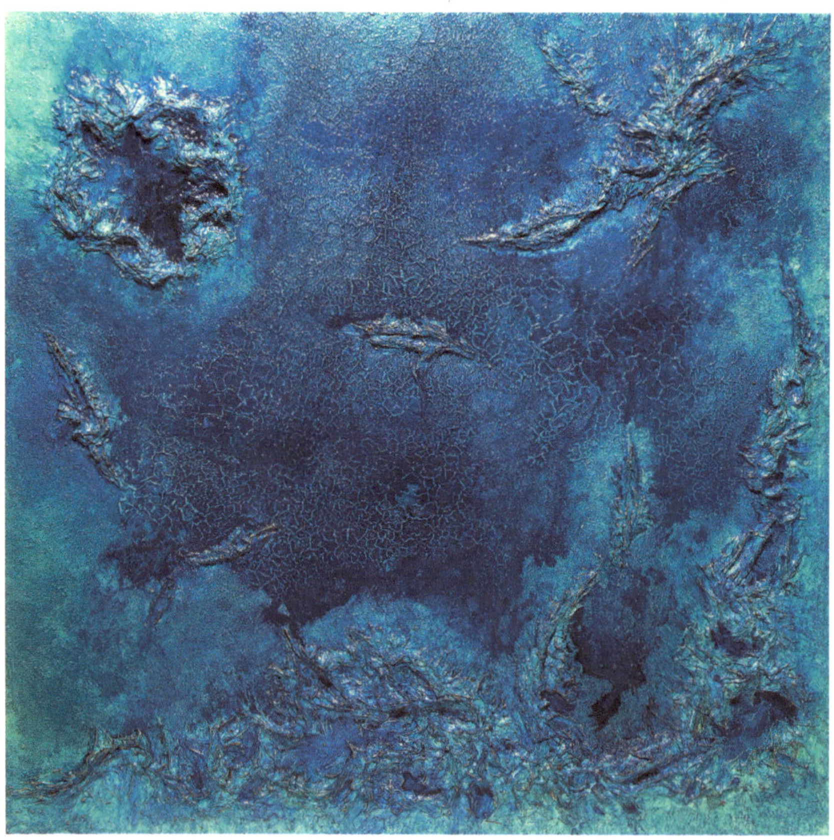

DRAGON DANCING IN THE SEA, 2023. Oil, acrylic, ink, mixed media on canvas, 70 x 70 x 3.5cm

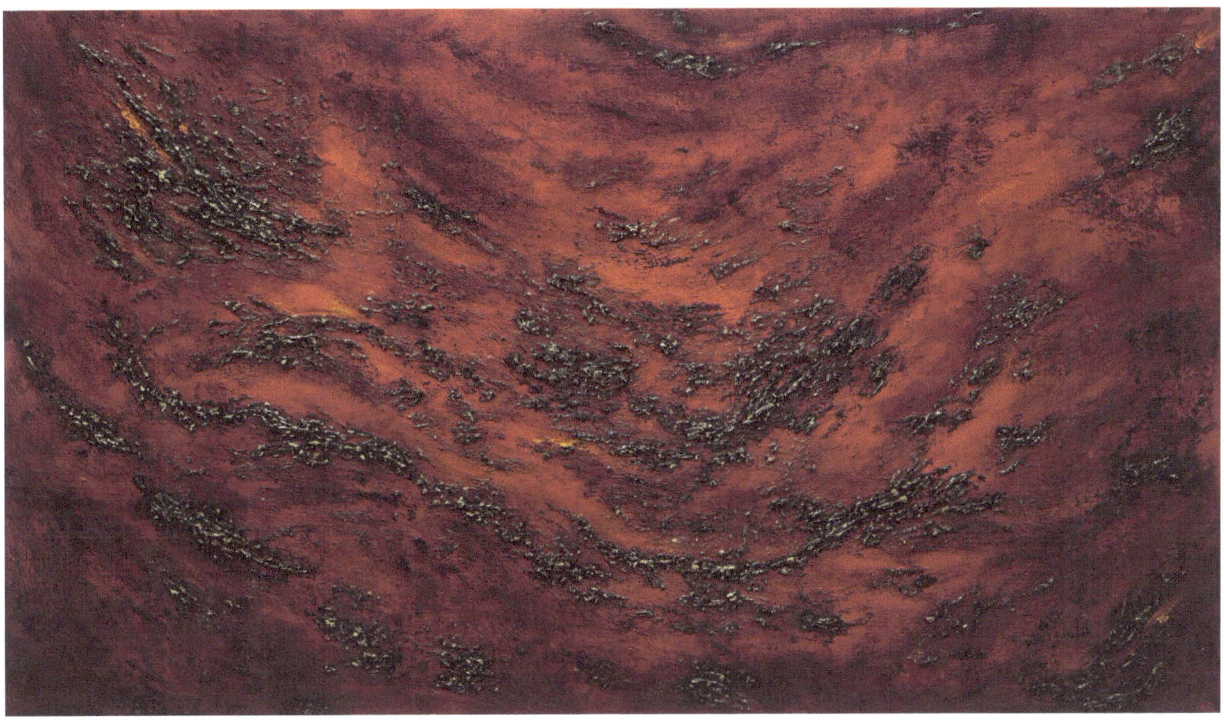

FIRE DRAGON DANCE, 2023. Oil, acrylic, mixed media on canvas, 120 x 70 x 3.5cm

RAMÓN RIVAS

http://www.rivismo.com

Born in Castilla-La Mancha, Spain. His roots are deeply embedded in a land rich in literary and artistic heritage, famous for being the setting of Don Quixote. His family's professional and artistic activities, spanning several generations, have influenced his involvement in the art world since childhood. The multidisciplinary influence of his professional activities in sports, music, engineering, inventions, and art, both in Castilla-La Mancha and Madrid, was decisive in the creation, within the world of art, of a very personal and different style, which has been called Rivismo, based on the application of Experiential Brushstrokes.

Prestigious art professionals have recognized the exceptional originality and aesthetic appeal of his work, sharing some of their reviews: "Ramón Rivas' unique vision and exceptional skills have not only captivated audiences around the world but have also contributed significantly to the enrichment of the art world. His art is not simply a visual feast; it is a revolutionary act, a space where the imagination is set free and the spirits of both the creator and the viewer merge in a dance of vibrant creativity. He proves himself a master of linguistic plurality, developing a language that is his own and unique.
In his visual language, he emphasizes and connects numerous elements such as form, light, color, and energy, extrapolating their emotionality and making it available to the world, imparting sensory and personal development in the observer.
His Rivismo is a declaration of marriage between the artist and the observer, between the material and the spirit, and through it, he has created a new space where creativity and innovation reign supreme. It is not simply a style but a language, distinct and incomparable, marking his works as unique in their innovation and identity.
As a pioneer of contemporary art, his influence is indelible. His contributions transcend aesthetics; they are milestones in the evolution of the art world. In recognizing his profound impact, we celebrate not only the artist, but the pioneer, a visionary who sculpted the future of artistic expression. His work reflects a timeless genius, an unmistakable legacy, and the power to shape art and culture for future generations".

His talent has been recognized through solo and group exhibitions in many countries, with his work featured in several museums. Ramón's artistic contributions have also appeared and continue to appear in numerous books, magazines, and catalogs. In addition, he has been honored with prestigious international awards, further cementing his reputation as a distinguished artist.

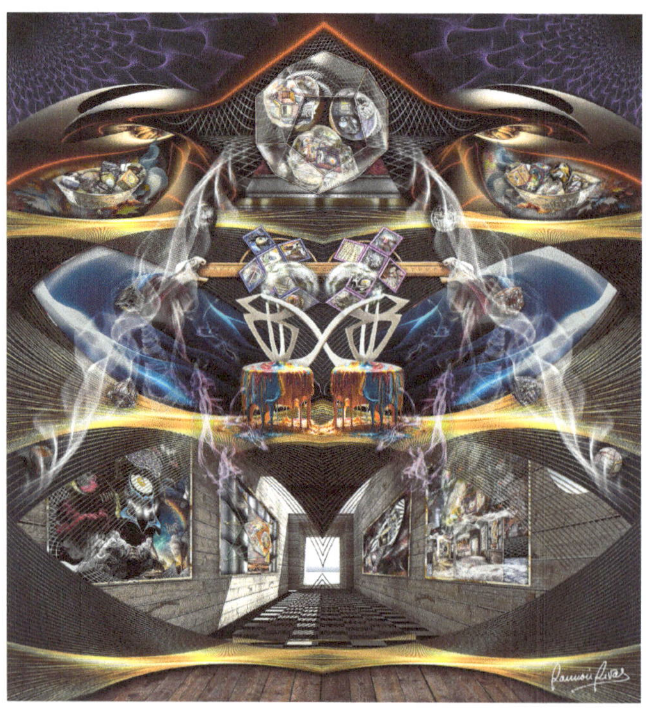

Expo-Park of Experiential Art, 2024. Mixed media-Rivismo, 180x195 cm

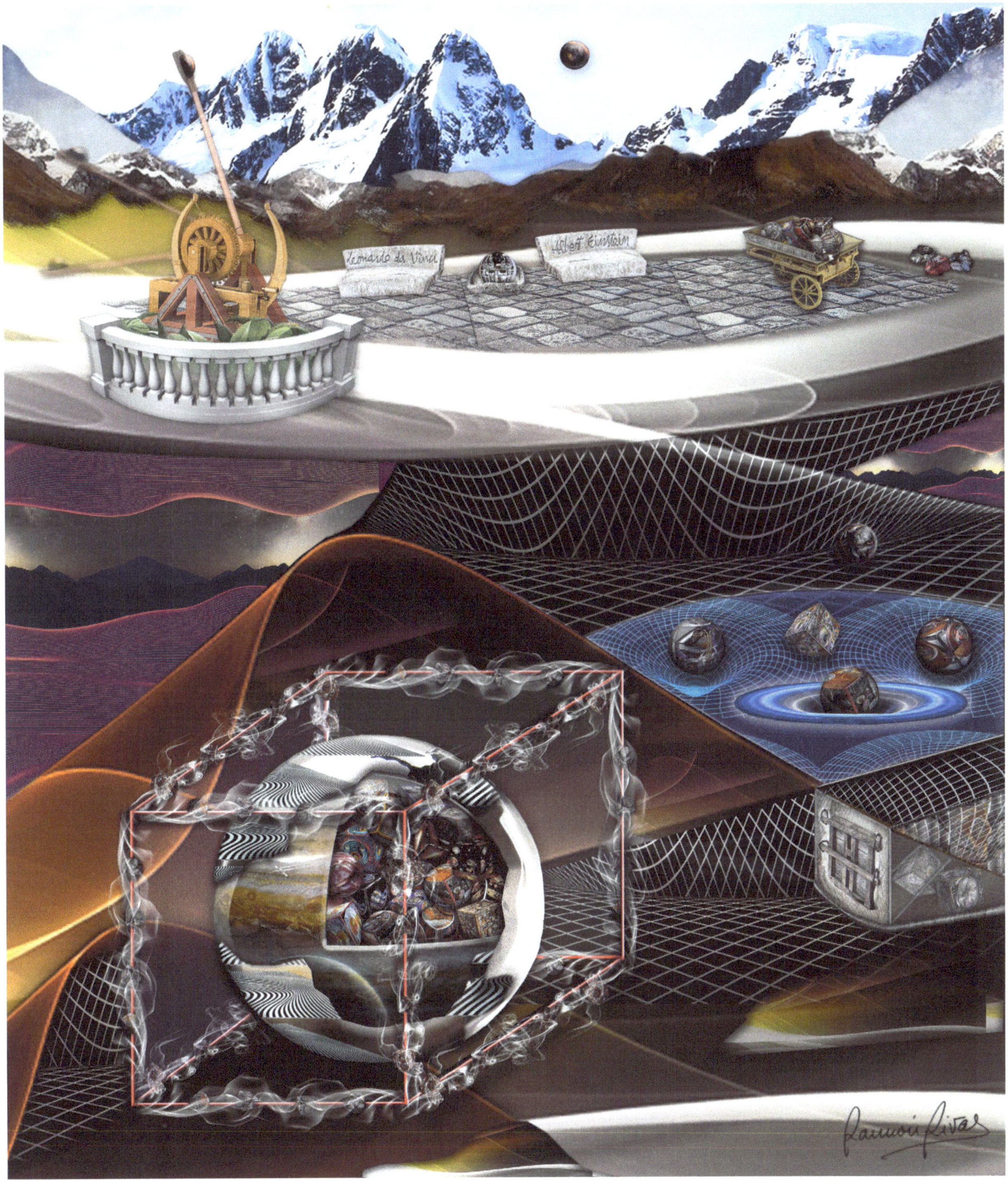

Art between the Catapult and Relativity. Da Vinci & Einstein, 2022. Mixed media-Rivismo, 170x200 cm

RAMSAY ALLAN

https://www.ramsayallan.com/

Ramsay Allan is a versatile oil painter whose artistic journey has evolved over a lifetime of rich personal experience. Initially self-taught, he later deepened his skills through dedicated study and observation of both classical and contemporary masters. His genre focus spans from surrealism to portraiture and beyond—reflecting his versatility and thought provoking engagement with the world. Based in Scotland, Allan continues to explore the boundaries of creativity, drawing inspiration from his heritage, intuition, and a deep-rooted belief in artistic freedom.

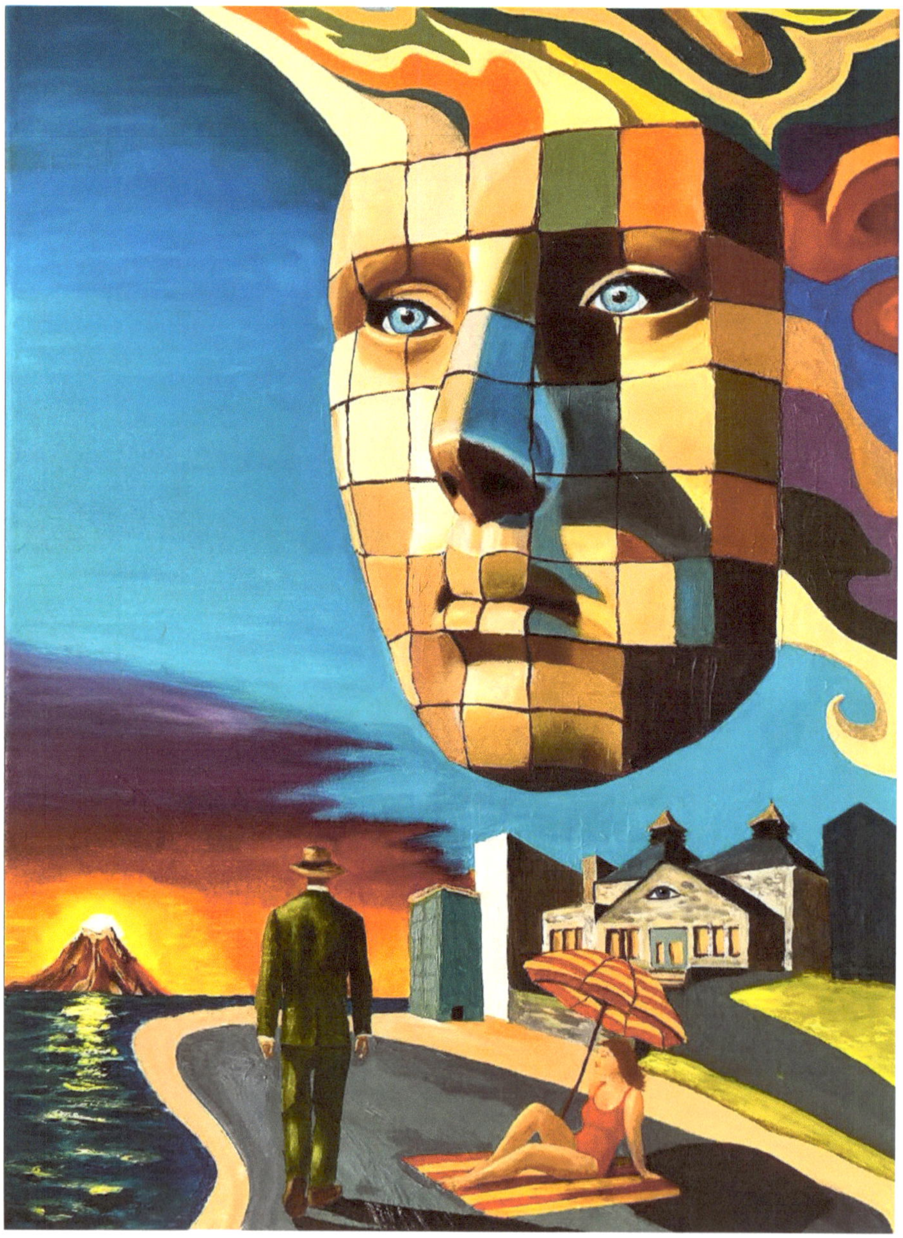

Utopian Dream II, 2025. Oil on canvas, 70 x 50 cm.

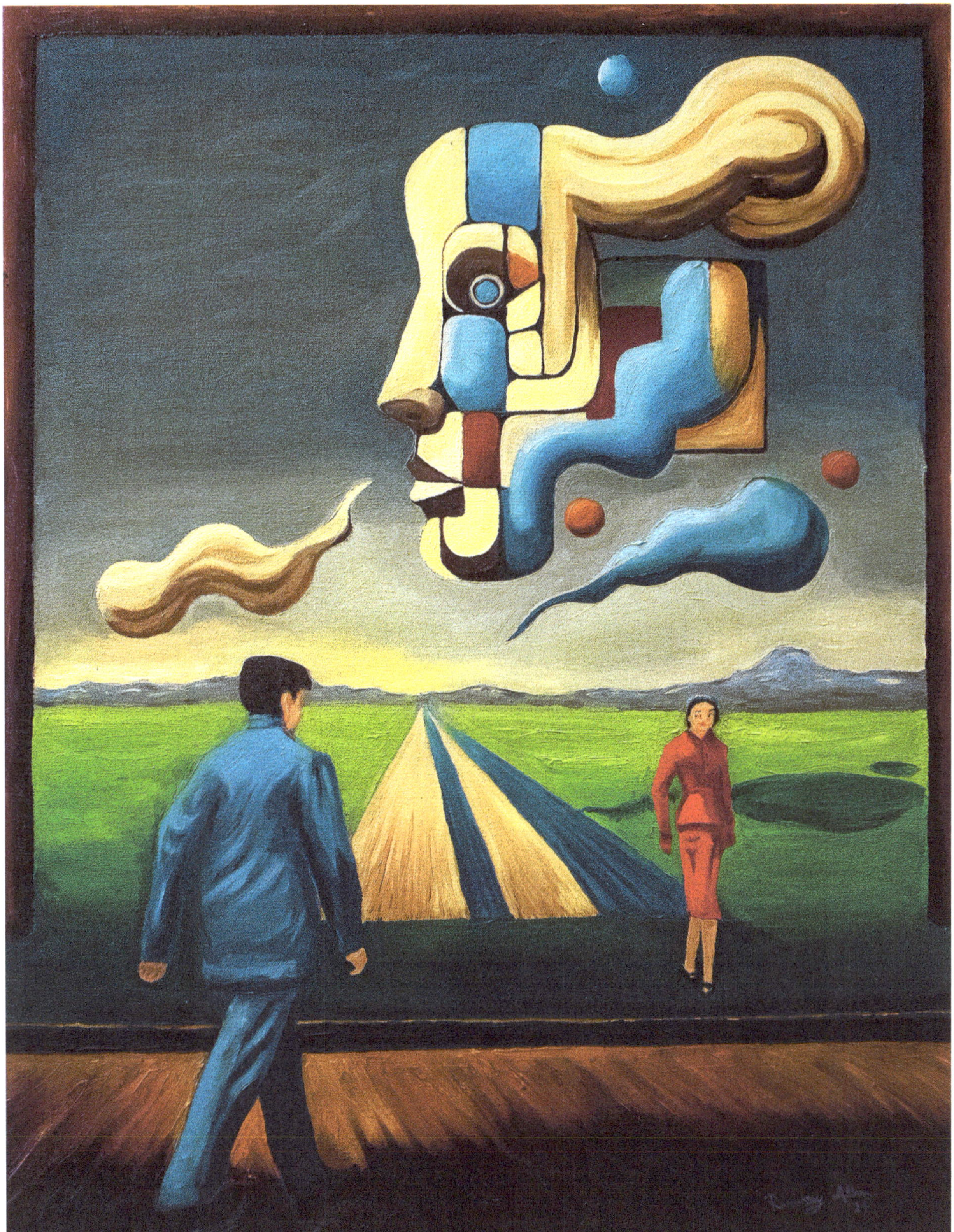

Step into My Utopian Dream, 2024. Oil on canvas, 68 x 52 cm.

RAÚL VEGA

www.raulvega.com

Raúl went to school of Architecture including his 4th year in Florence, Italy. It was during that year that he decided he would become a photographer. More than anything, he has been exposed to art from all periods and has developed a visual sense that he's applied to his work. Raúl couldn't have predicted the work he is currently doing. Raúl's new fine art abstractions re?ect a personal growth resulting from learning the new digital photographic platforms. These innovations allow him the ability to assemble images in new and unexpected ways. Though rooted in a traditional photographic representation of reality, the images, when combined with other elements such as color, texture, scale and varied opacities, allow for a new visual language, Vega's new work ?ips back and forth between and the rigors of representation and the liberating ambiguity of abstraction. Raúl's work deals with the acknowledgement that we live in a rainbow of randomness and chaos.

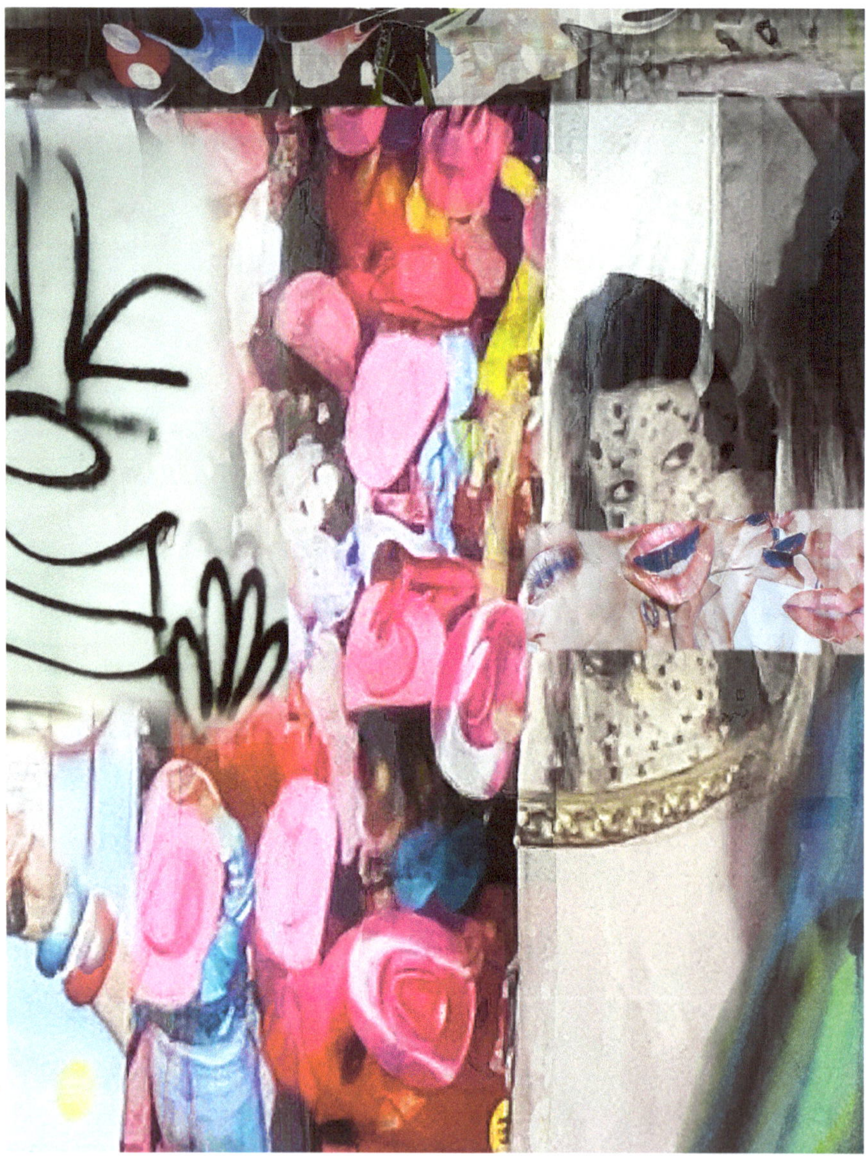

seen, 7.2025, photography, 76.2 x 101.6 cm

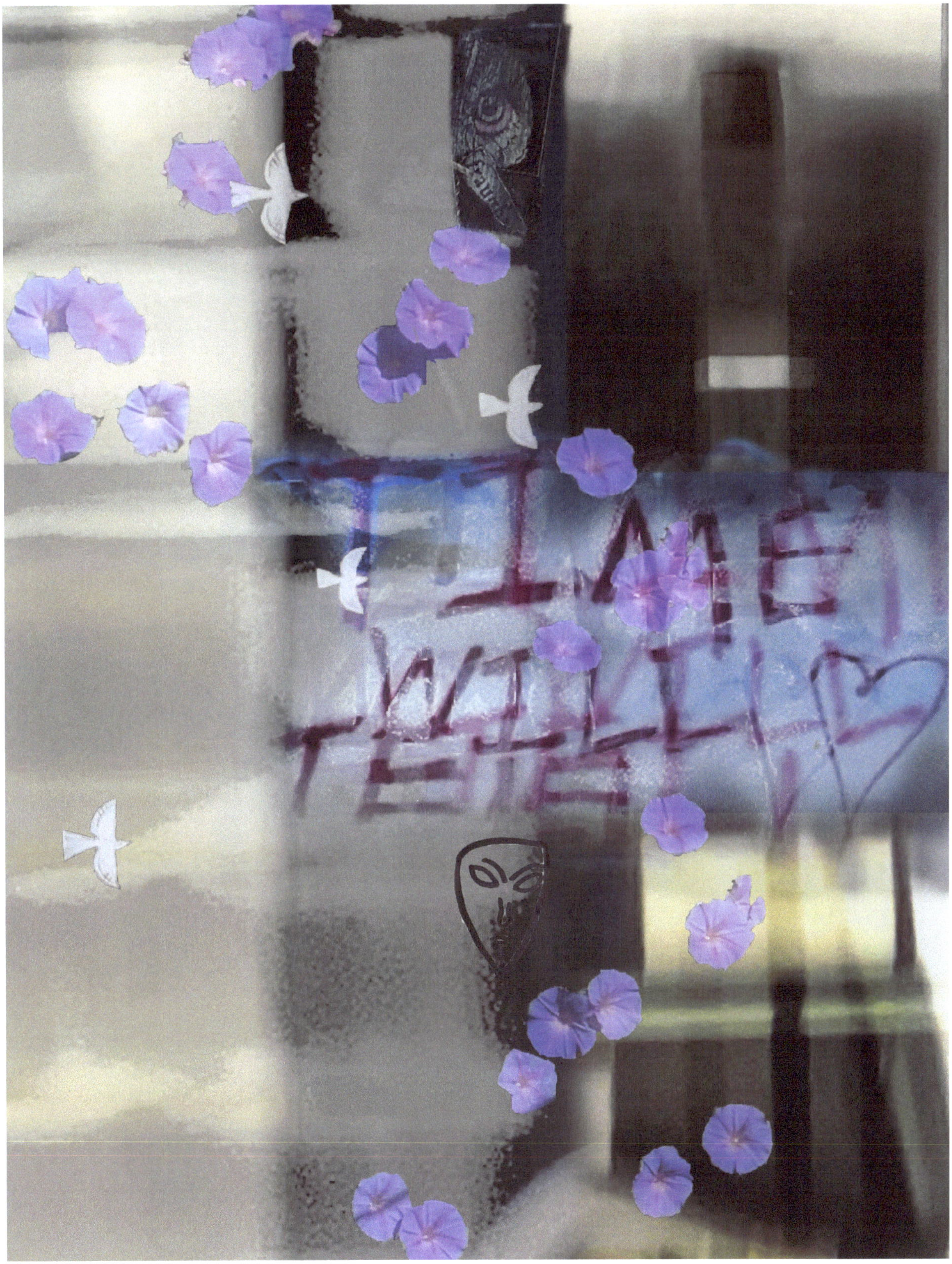

time will tell, photography, 76.2 x 101.6 cm

REBECCAH KLODT

RebeccahKlodt.com

From person to person, each piece means something different. The individualized meaning, and personal interpretation of art is important to me, and I want viewers to be able to interpret my art without context beyond themselves. The majesty of nature is not only all around you but it is within you, express your nature and merge it with the world around you. Rebeccah Klodt is an abstract artist from the Twin Cities area of Minnesota. Her art is on display throughout the United States and Europe. Life's majesty is a key inspiration for Rebeccah. She has worked for over forty years as an interior designer and continues to partner with other designers, artists, and architects.

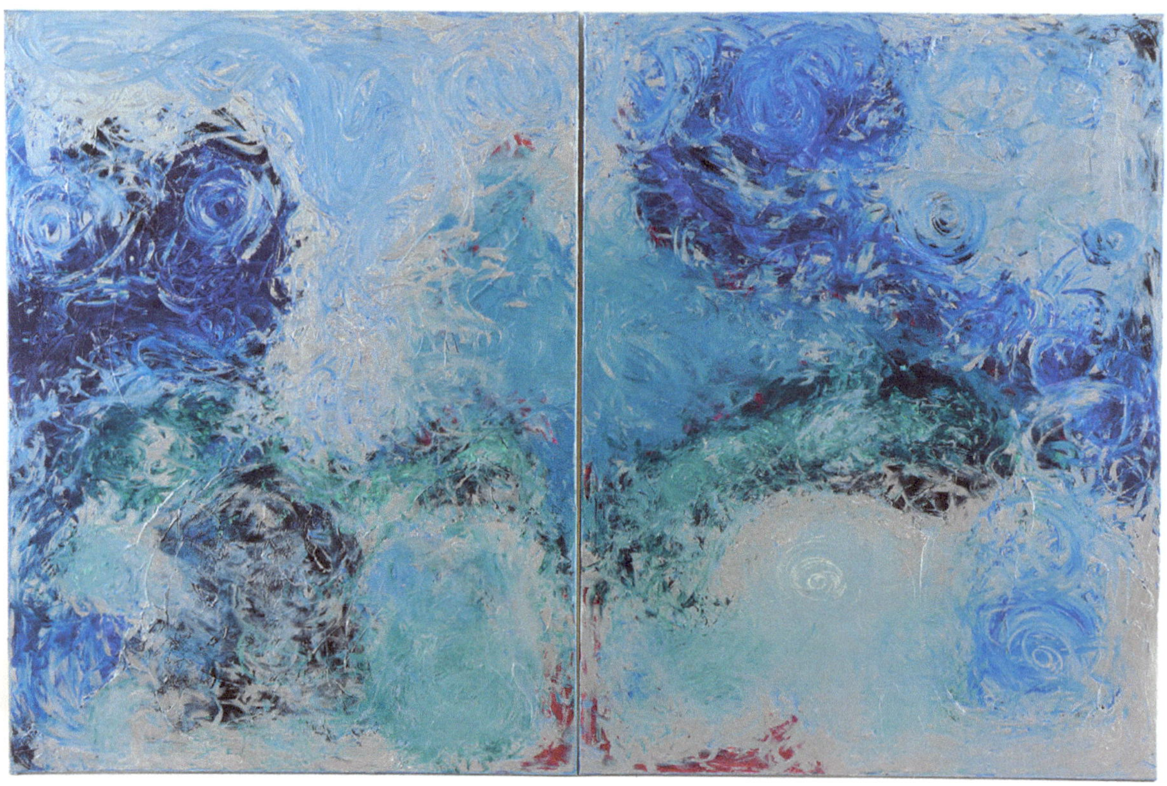

Untitled 72"x48" (2 Panels) Oil on Canvas

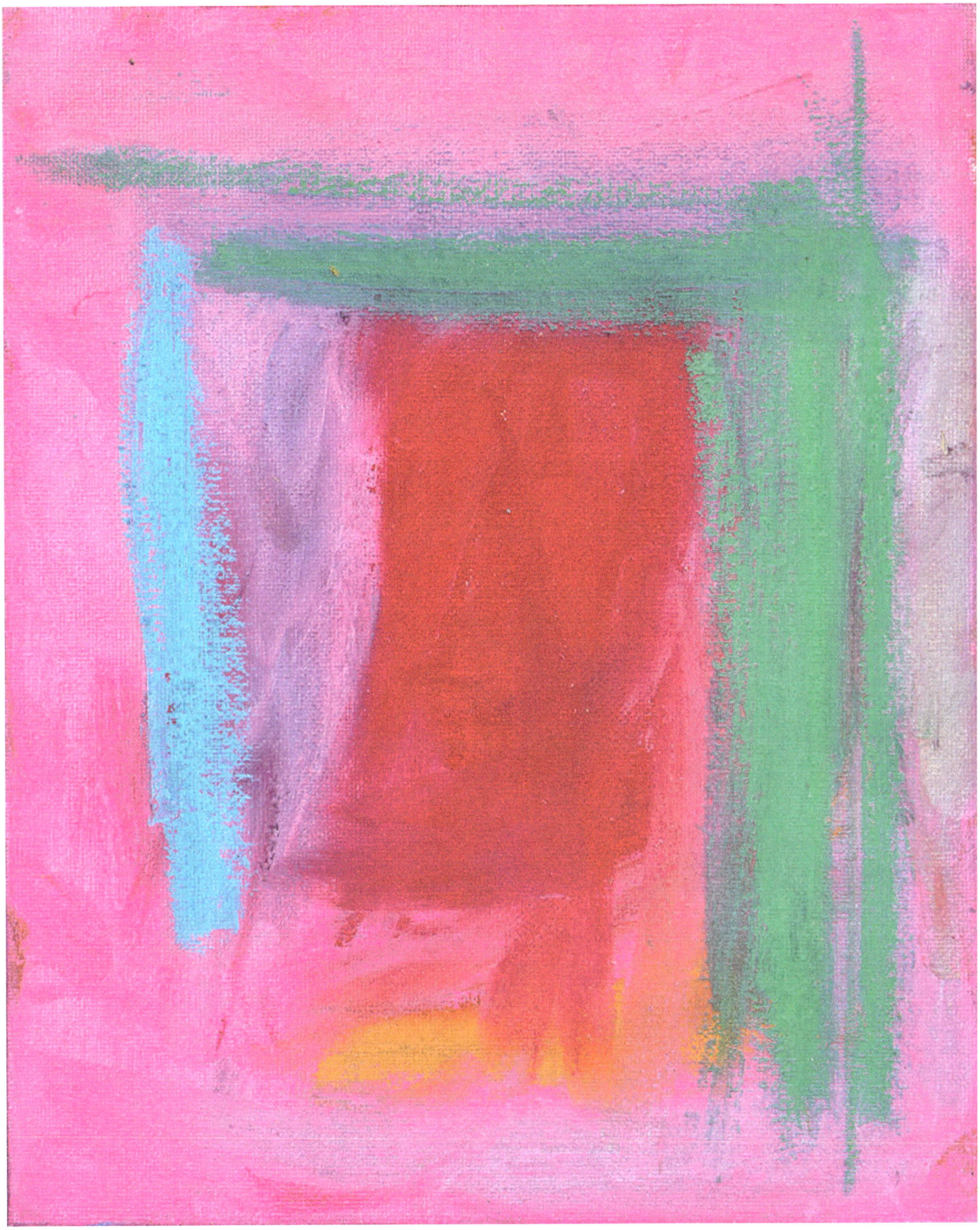

Untitled 2024 9.5"x11.5" Oil on Canvas

RIITTA HELLÉN-VUOTI

www.riittahellenvuoti.fi

Riitta Hellén-Vuoti Biography Riitta Hellén-Vuoti (b. 1959) is a Finnish artist, living and working in Kuopio, Finland. By education she is a licensed medical specialist in psychiatry and psychotherapy. She has been artistic since her youth, and started dedicating more time to painting and poetry around the year 2000. Her artistic focuses remain in painting and poetry. Her artworks have been on display in galleries around Finland since the year 2000 and internationally since 2020. She is now a full – time artist. Statement She is interested in – and inspired by – the human being and the never-ending complexities of life. In art it is possible to deal with all the questions and concepts in a more intuitive way. At first, she mainly worked with oil paint on canvas, but now She also use mixed media. Paintings and poems are inner images. They can sometimes be the same. Layers, textures and metaphors playing together, creating meaning in varying degrees of abstraction.

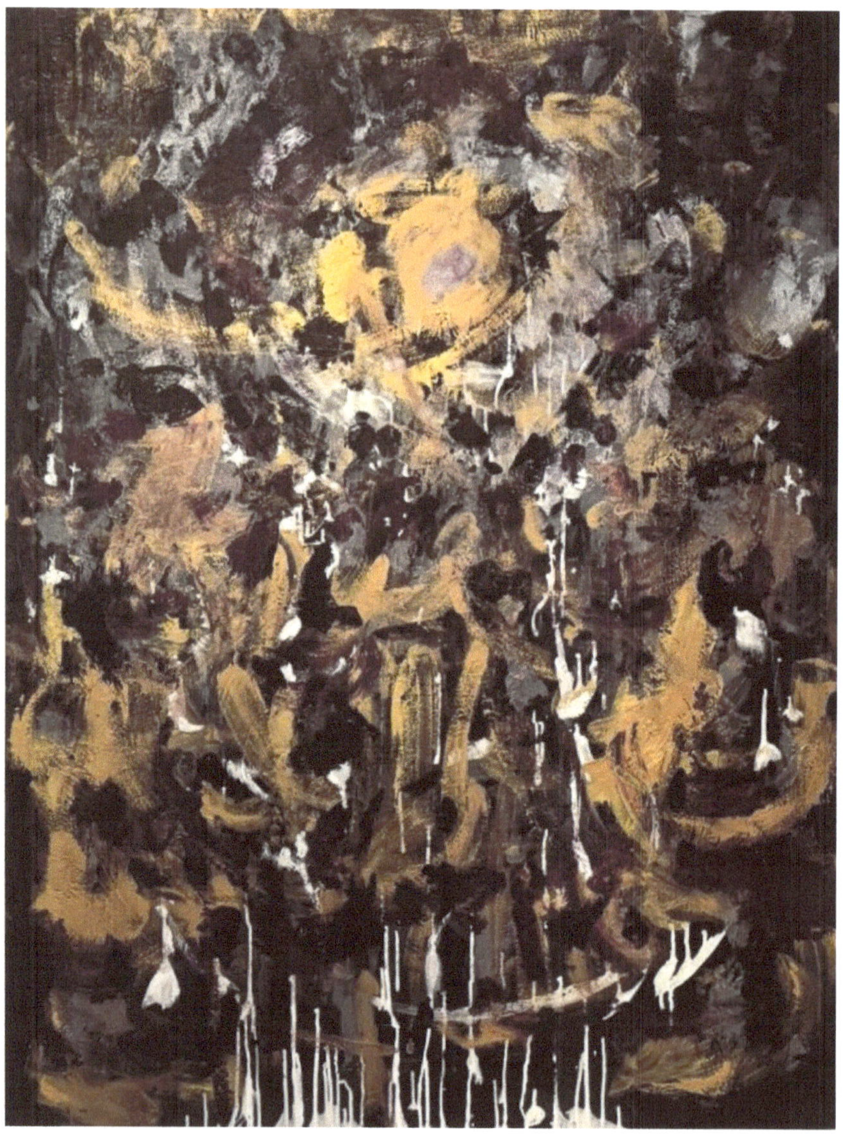

Light in the Darkness, 2025, Acrylic on canvas, 170 x 130cm, from the series Light and Darkness

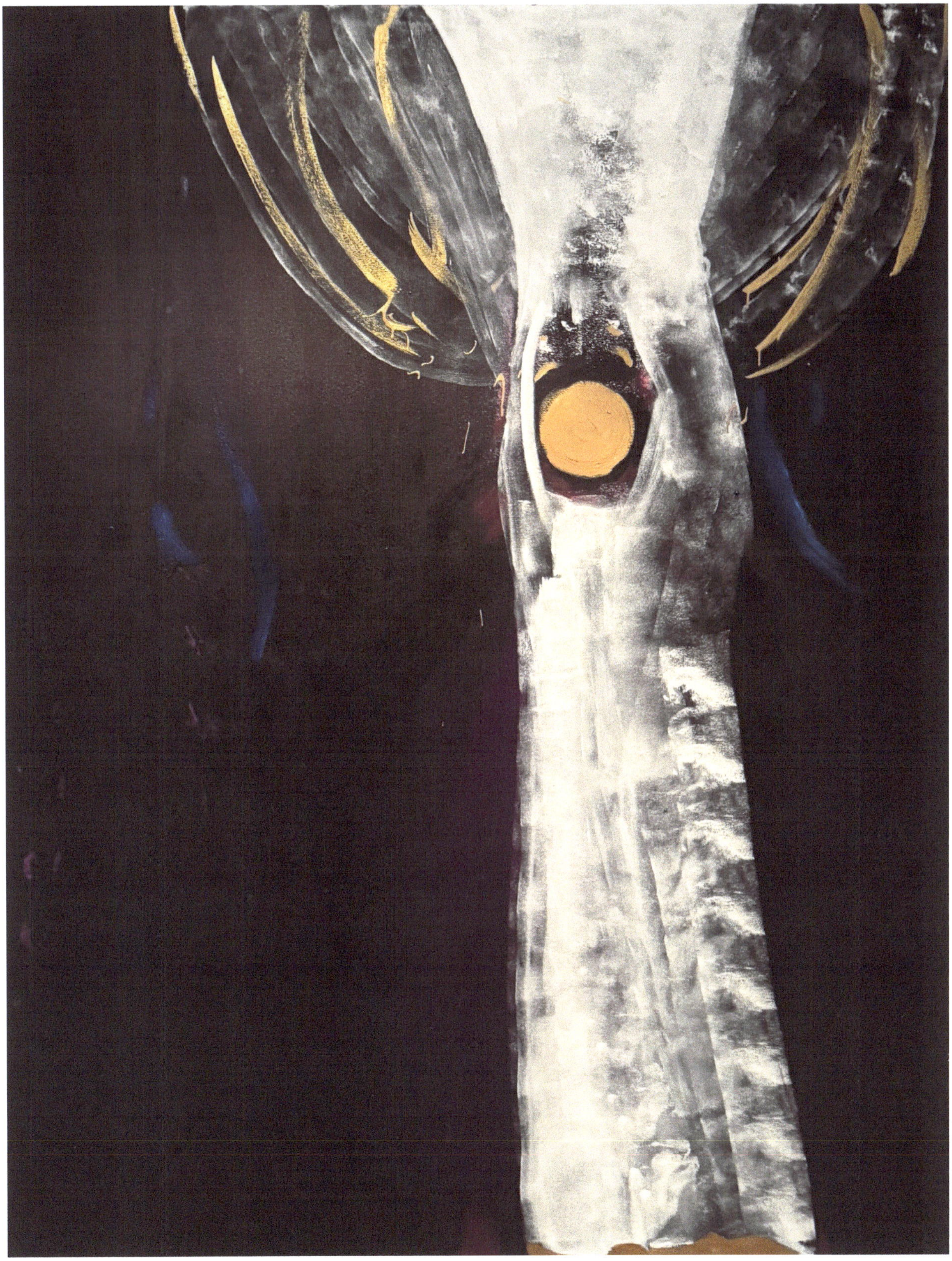

Love is Light, 2025, Acrylic on canvas, 170 x 130cm, from the series Light and Darkness

ROBERT HAWORTH

www.iamthebutterflyman.com

Robert Haworth's new collection MIRACLES HAPPEN Yes, miracles do happen. And, this, my new collection of paintings is proof. You see, my early life was like a helter-skelter, but with even more ups and downs than on Blackpool Pleasure Beach! Actually, my childhood was brutal. And when my beloved mum died when I was just 10, I not only lost her but, through shock, also all memory – all memory – of my passion for art. Then, 12 years later, the first miracle occurred: my mum "visited" me and got me back on track. You see, I'd painted a beautiful picture of a pink butterfly for her, full of sunshine and hope. But after her death, it just disappeared – along with all my childhood paintings. And then, following a mysterious chain of events, the butterfly painting came back to me and, with it, all my memories. In mythology, butterflies are often seen as the souls of the departed bringing gifts and messages to the living. And that's exactly what had happened... my mum, through that butterfly painting, was reaching out to me, nurturing me again... and I began painting, painting, painting. To me, it really was a miracle. And each time I went off the rails a bit, more of those childhood paintings came back to me. Over 20 of them! It was utterly bizarre! It was like she never gave up on me, constantly giving me a loving "kick up the backside"– "Get back to your painting, Bobby!" she was saying. My new collection is the evidence of that miracle. Indeed, it's my art that's taken me from being a damaged "caterpillar", then through times of tumultuous change, to become what I am now, The Butterfly Man. Happy, busy, free, and fulfilled. And you can see this in my paintings. I don't plan them. It's like this: As each day unravels, memories, thoughts and emotions build up inside me ready to express themselves; expressed as layers upon layers of fragmented reality. Every painting tells a story. And that story is always one of Hope; of reaching out to the rainbow that is within us all: the rainbow after the rain. Thank you so much for visiting. I really hope you enjoy the paintings. And if you'd like to see more, visit my website – www.iamthebutterflyman.com – and there's a book telling of my life and art to be published later this year. Robert Haworth, "The Butterfly Man"

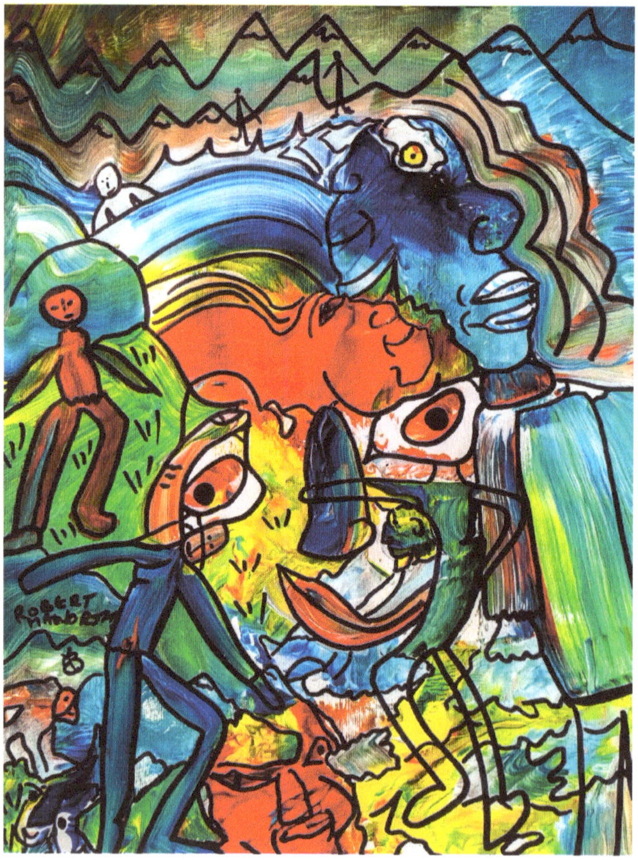

Title happy days medium acrylic year 2025 size a4

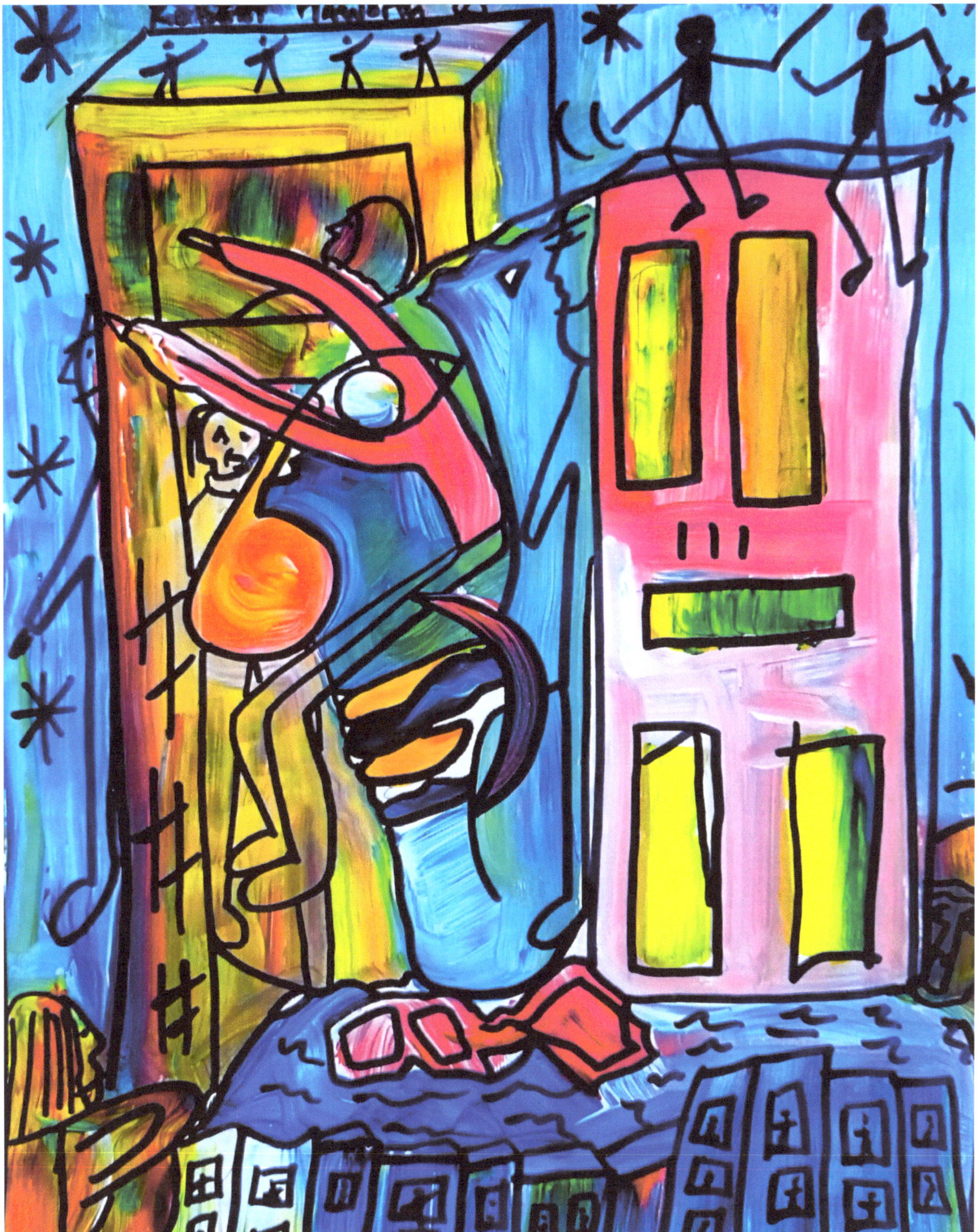

The door two the right 2025 acrylic a3

ROMY PFEIFER

https://www.romy-pfeifer.com

Romy Pfeifer, a German photographer, resides in a rural region south of Stuttgart. Her photographic journey is primarily self-taught, encompassing a diverse array of subjects, including nature, natural landscapes, animals, travel, and portraiture. However, what holds particular significance for her is the realm of experimental and abstract photography, where she employs various techniques and creative approaches. Romy's knowledge and photography expertise continually advance through her independent, self-directed learning. One of her ongoing projects is multi-exposure and ICM photography of nature and natural landscapes. This unique form of photography allows her to emphasize the vibrant colors, captivating light, atmospheric qualities, and the dynamic essence of nature. It represents her distinct perspective on the beauty of the natural world, aiming to encapsulate and unveil the mystical, ever-changing, and fragile aspects of our environment. The line between reality and fantasy becomes blurred in these abstract images, enabling viewers to experience the wonder of nature and comprehend the perpetual state of motion and transformation that surrounds us. Throughout her work, she strives to elicit emotional responses from the audience while upholding the authenticity of her photographic creations. Central to Romy Pfeifer's practice of photographing is her devotion to nature and her dynamic, transformative force. When she is strolling with her dog and her camera through the forests or along a seaside, she has the feeling of being just in the right place. She feels a strong connection to all the beauty that surrounds her: the trees, plants, animals, fields, the sea, and the sky. Making photographs in these landscapes is a kind of meditation for her, and she feels the healing power. Through her art she has found her place in the world. With her way of photographing, she works on our living and connection to nature, on the rhythms of nature, and on the eternal transformations. Her images often force the viewer to look closer. Reality dissolves into abstraction, evoking both the vitality of nature and its ephemerality. In an era of rapid technological change and environmental crisis, she hopes to be able to remind people with her photographs of the enduring beauty of nature and the importance of preserving and protecting it.

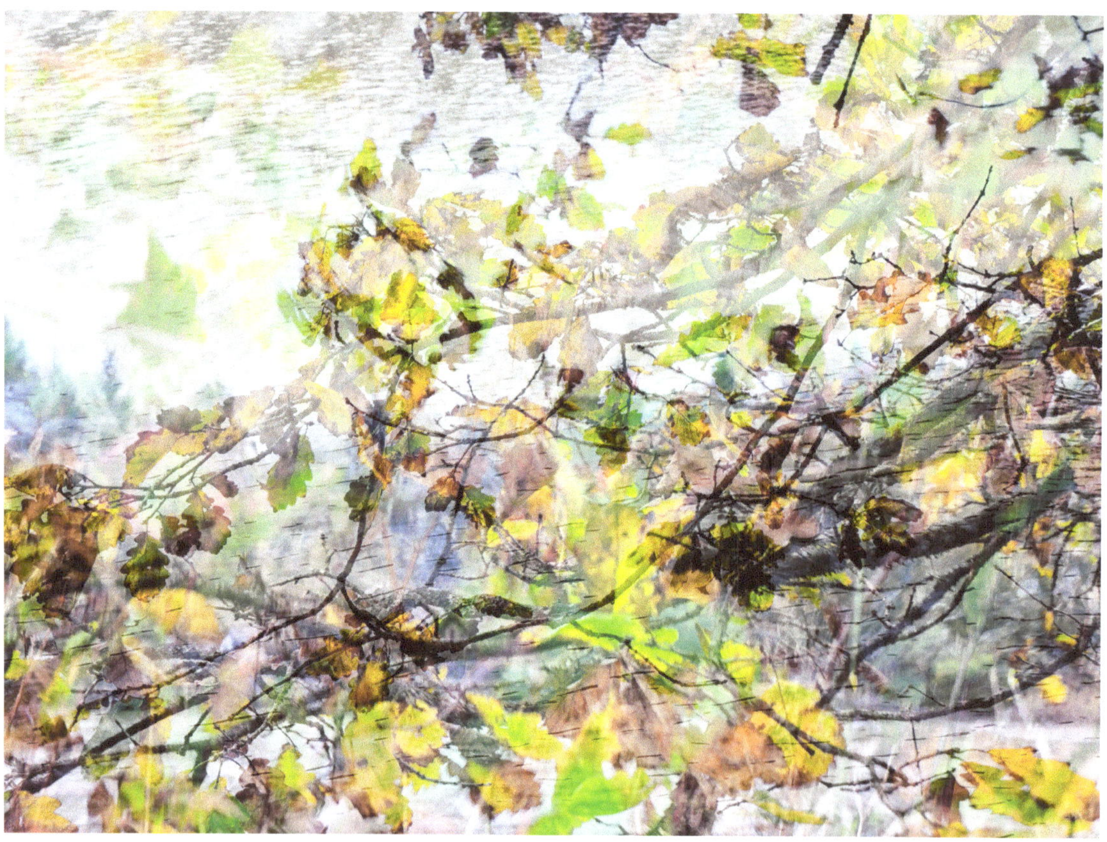

The Beginning of Love, 2024. Photography on Hahnemühle Fine Art Inkjet Paper, 75 x 100 cm

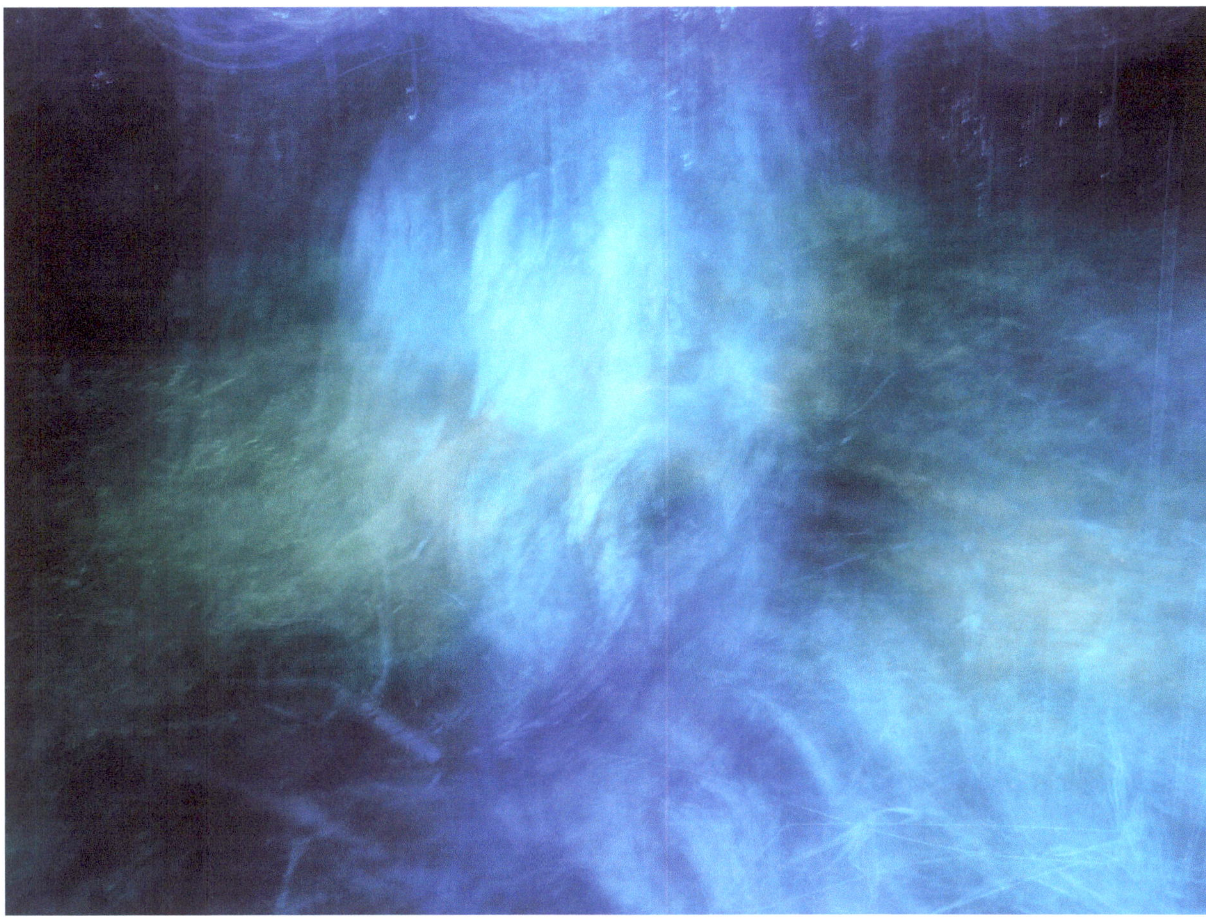

Surprise, 2023. Photography on Hahnemühle Fine Art Inkjet Paper, 75 x 100 cm

ROBERT JOHNSON

roberthjohnson@hotmail.com

After years of teaching student, Robert is on a learning path for himself. This conceptual digital art is driven by his interest in color, shape and light. A final image begins with a single photo, and its path to completion is rarely quick. He revisits it over a period of days or weeks. Robert's work is diverse in its look and presentation, and he wants the colors and subjects to make one pause, to make one think. Experience and experimentation drives the process.

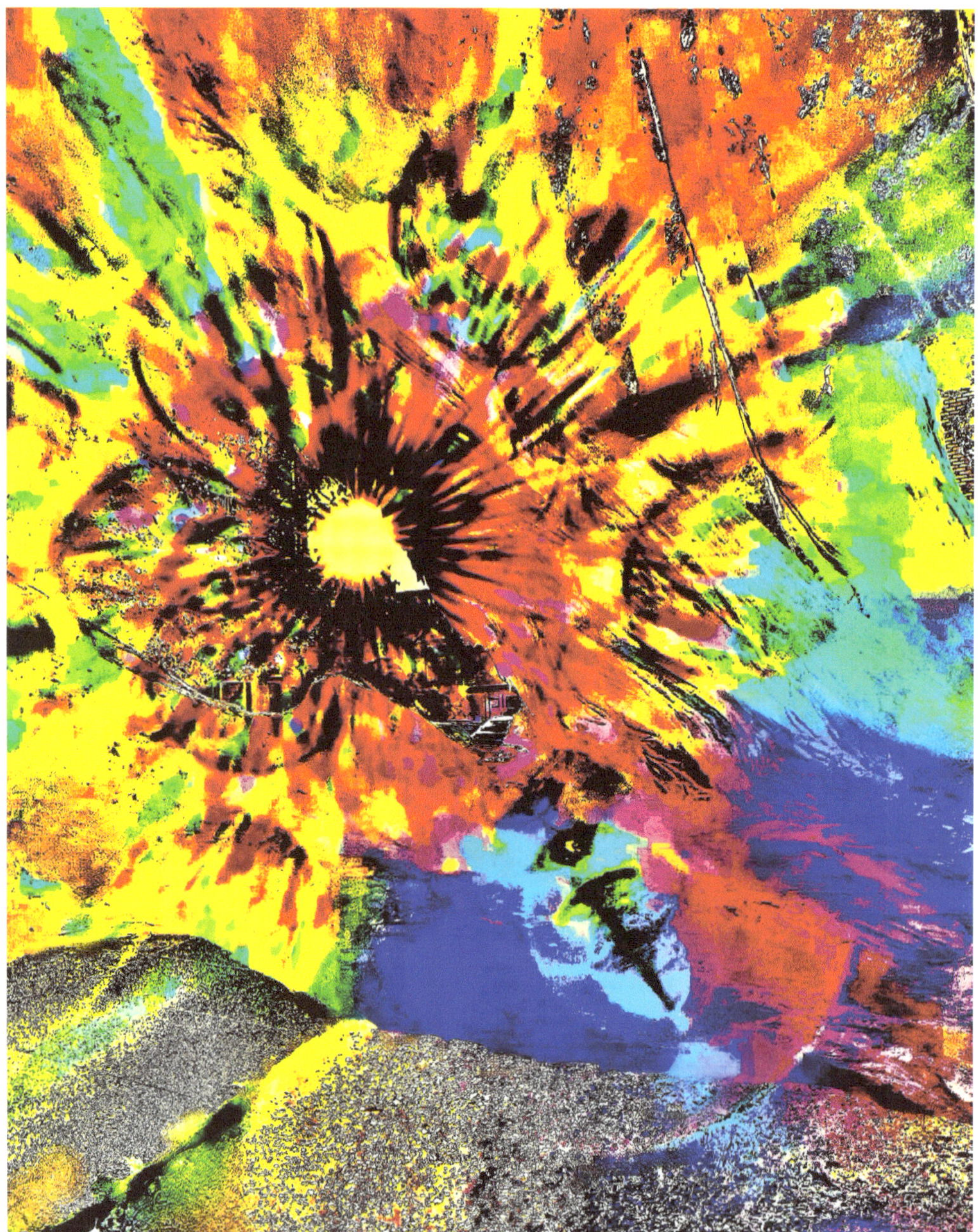

Suspended Again, Robert Johnson, 2024, conceptual digital, 45.72 x 60.96 cm

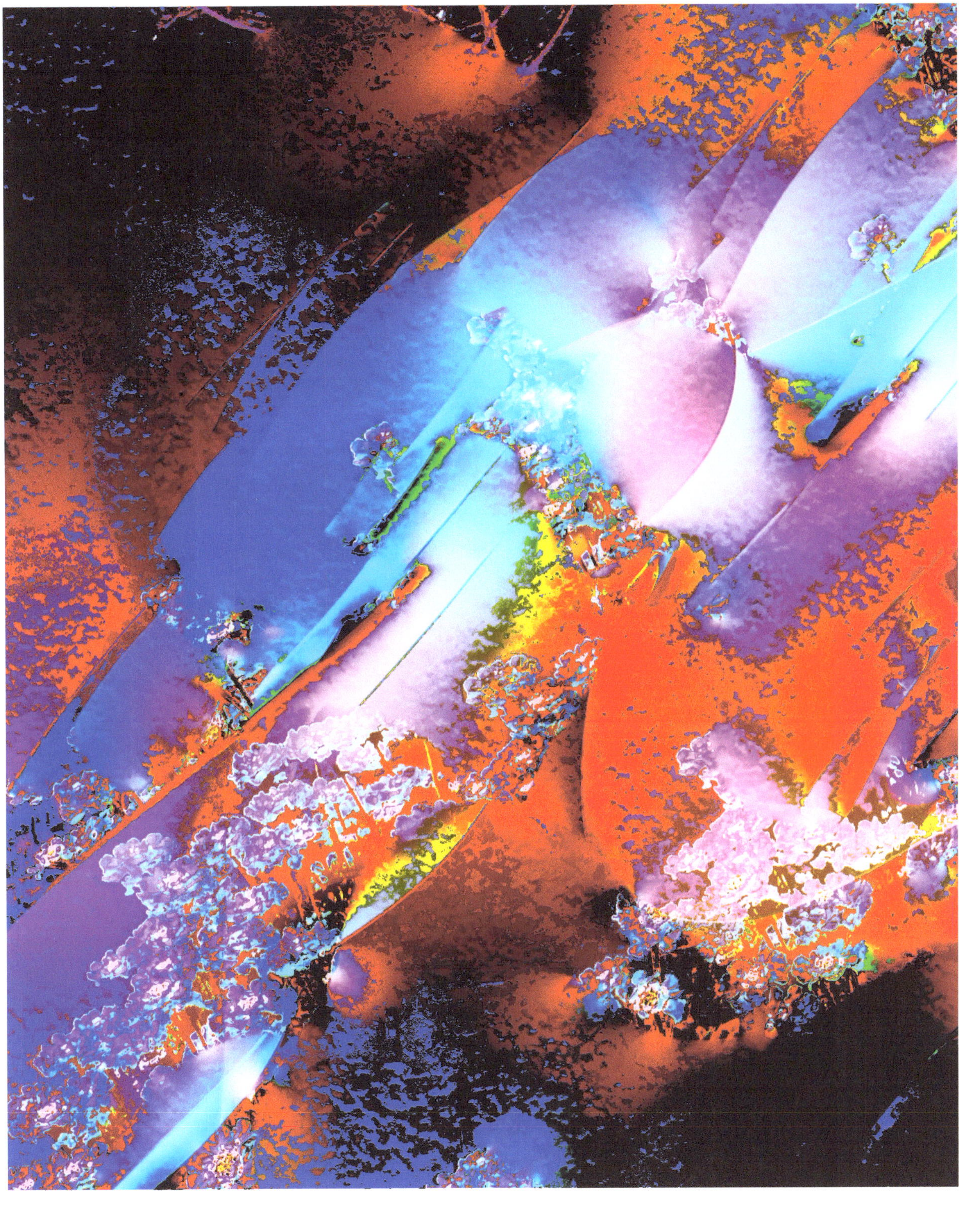

Color World, Robert Johnson, 2024, conceptual digital, 45.72 x 60.96 cm

RUZA SPAK

www.ruzaspak.com

Ruza Spak, born in Poland, studied painting at the Kunstakademie Hamburg and the Akademie der Künste in Berlin. She also received a DAAD scholarship for Rome. She lives and works in Berlin(Germany) and Ibiza(Spain)

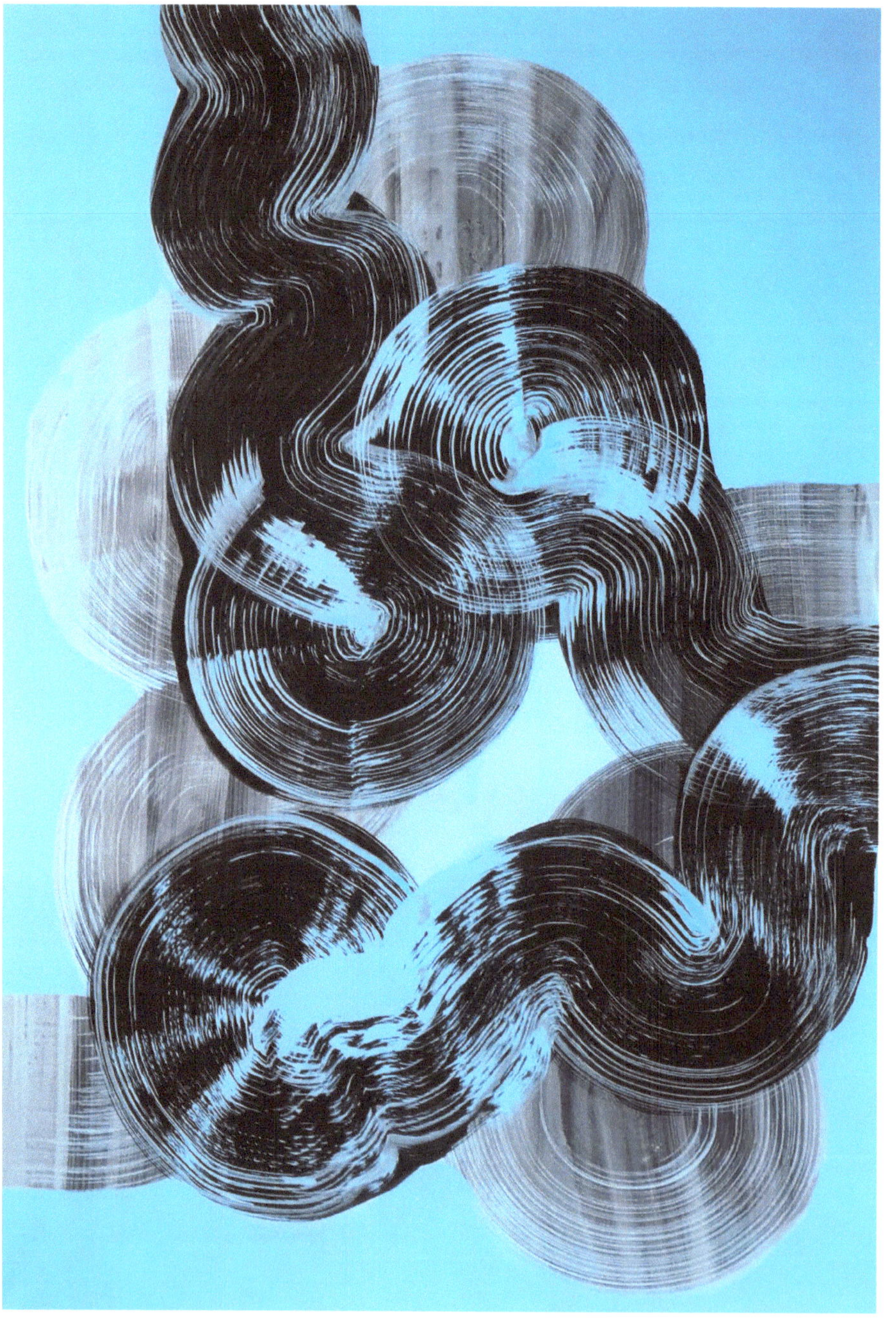

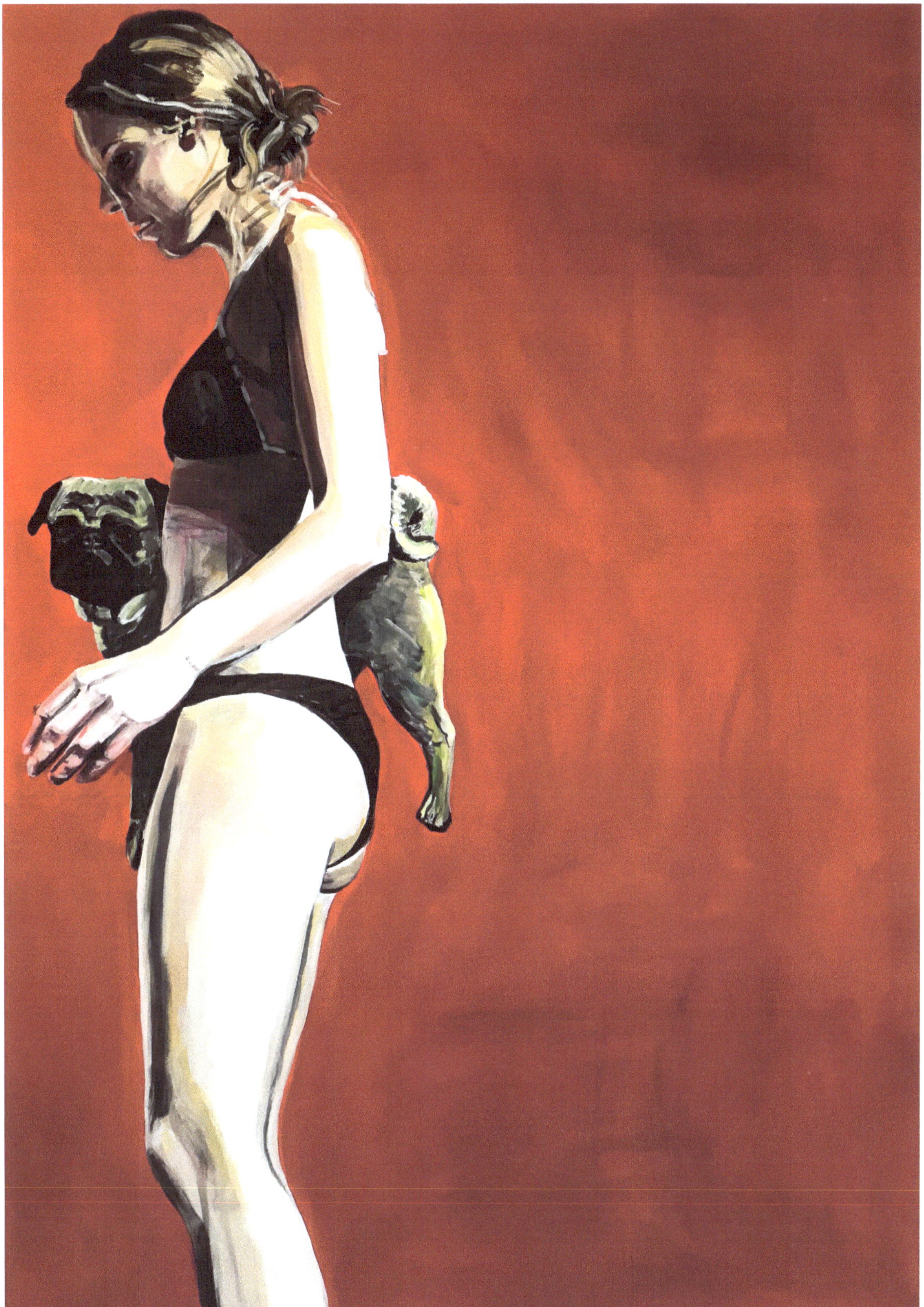

SANDRA BÉDU

sandrabedu@yahoo.fr

Sandra Bédu, born in Tananarive, Madagascar, on January 31, 1967, is a French artist whose work is nourished by contemplation, dreams and a deep connection to nature. A 1989 graduate of the Ecole des Beaux-Arts de Rouen, this painter and linocutter draws on a rich and spiritual imagination, giving rise to works that invite reflection and escape. Dreamy and contemplative, Sandra Bédu sometimes has the impression of "belonging to another planet". This connection with the imaginary and the intangible is evident in every one of her works. Whether through her paintings or linocuts, Sandra enters a creative bubble, a space where she can escape and forget everything else. This introspective approach gives her art a meditative, almost mystical quality. Nevertheless, while many of her works invite us to plunge into an unreal world, others also highlight the fragility of our World and the unconsciousness of some humans in the face of it. Her latest linocuts also draw the viewer's attention to the living conditions of women in certain countries around the world. Expressing this in her works is a way for the artist to feel less powerless, and above all to invite the viewer not to forget.

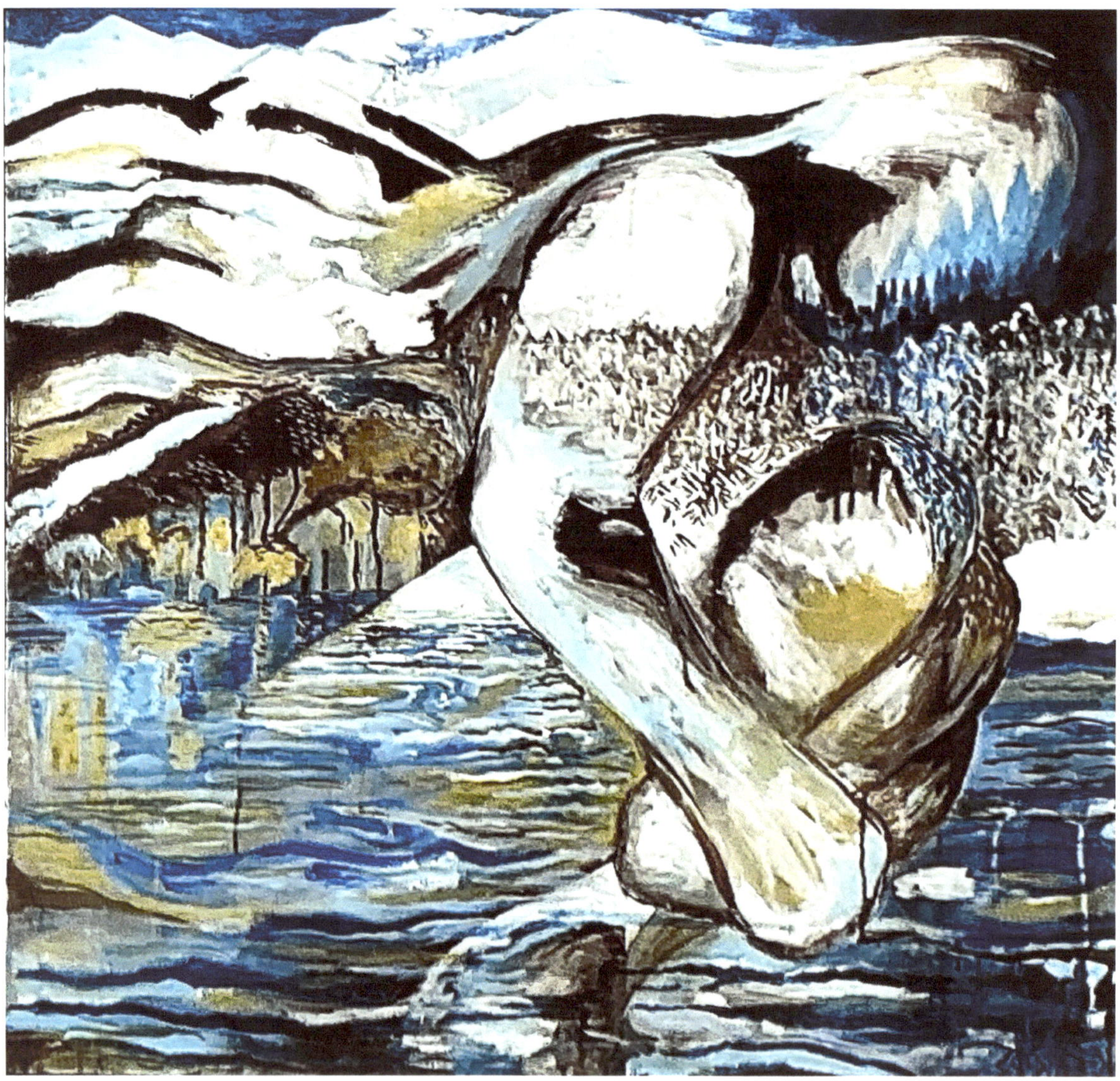

La Nature de l'âme, 2024. Acrylic on canvas, 100x100 cm

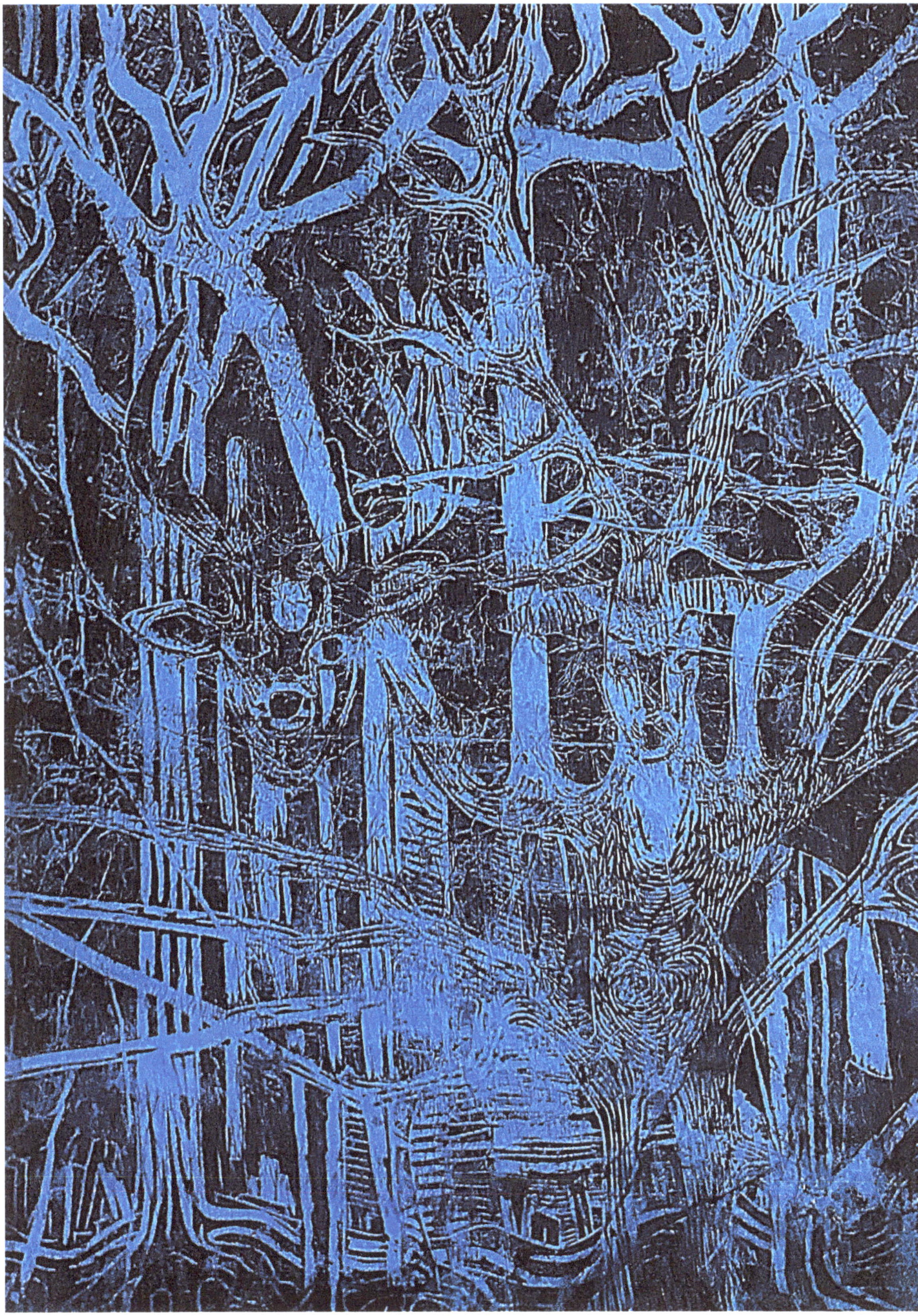

Les âmes de la forêt, 2024. Linocut on silk paper, 30x42 cm

SANDY ISELI

www.sandyiseli.com

Sandy Iseli grew up in Las Vegas, Nevada, USA and graduated from the University of New Mexico. She then came to Switzerland to work as a dental hygienist, married a Swiss and is still there. She completed Interior Design school where her love for beautiful objects and art was awakened. She is a self-taught artist and thanks nature for her inspiration. Her paintings of acrylics or mixed media with oil on canvas invite the viewers to enjoy the peace and serenity that the connection to nature gives.

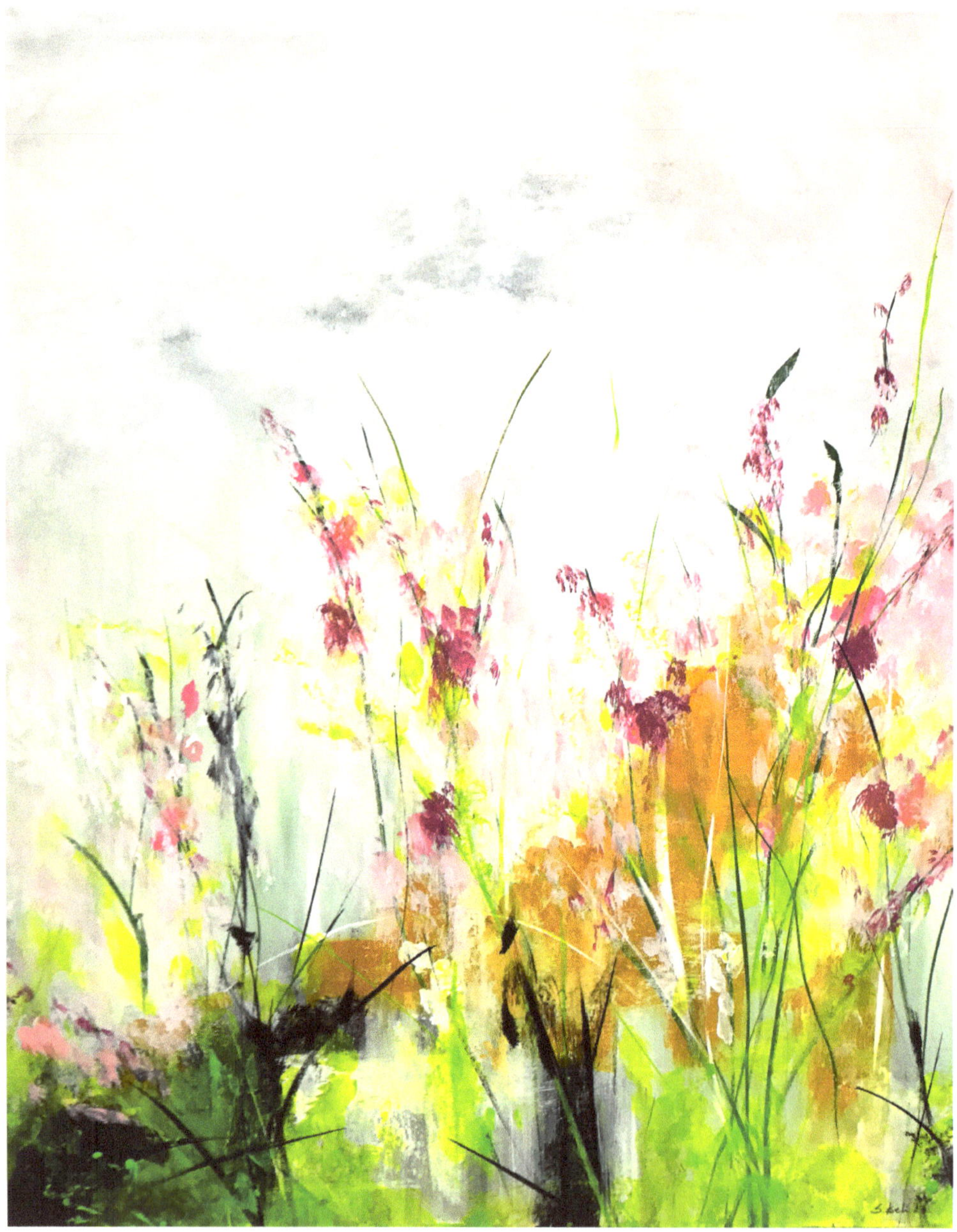

Dainty Ladies 2024, acrylic on canvas, 100 x 80 cm

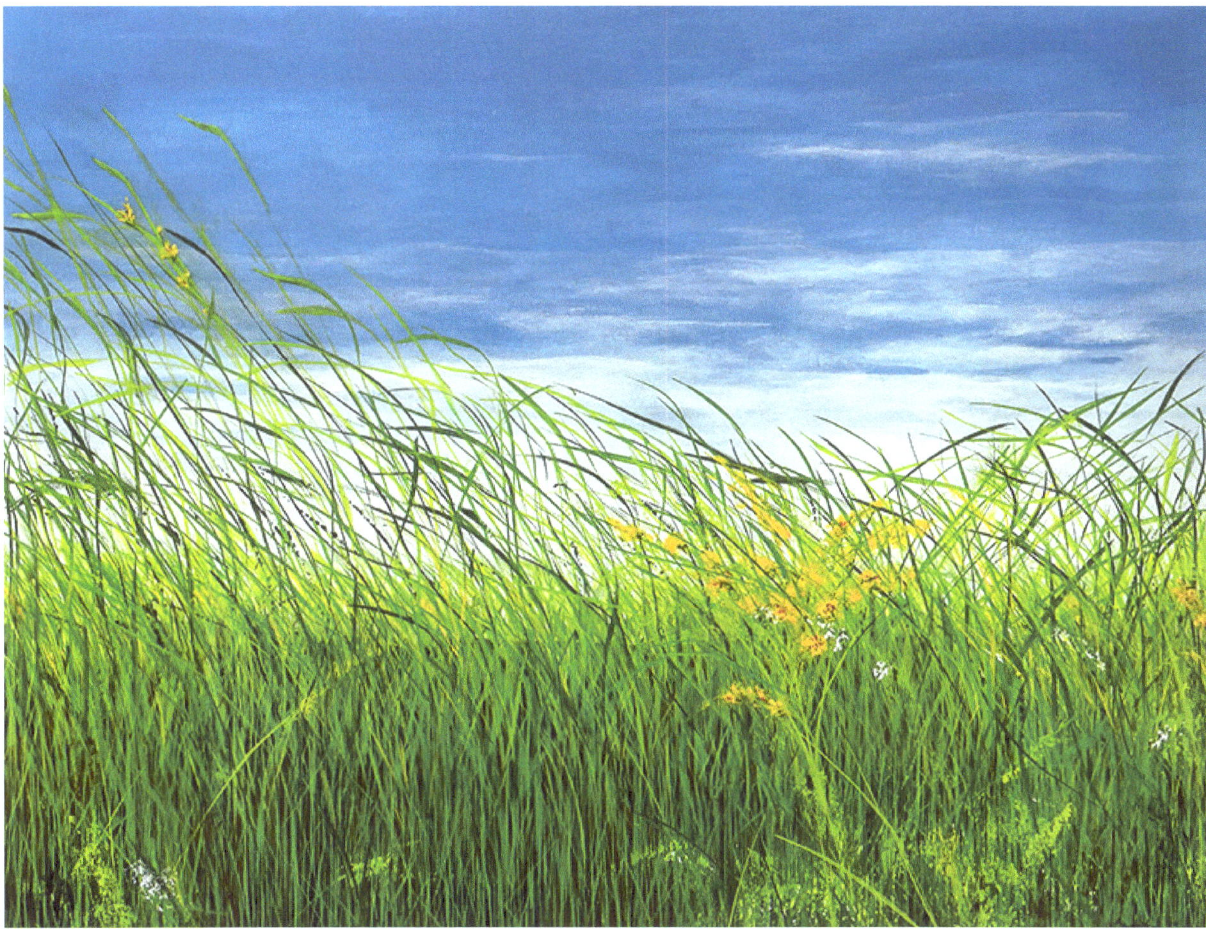

Dancing in the Breeze 2023, acrylic on canvas, 80 x 100 cm

SAVAS DELI

https://www.artmarketexperts.com/most-investable-artists/savas-deli

My art is a mirror of my soul. Through ? spontaneous and intuitive creative processes, I try to process my emotions and experiences and find myself again. It's a way to express my feelings and thoughts and engage with my surroundings. I hope that my art touches the viewer and gives them a glimpse into my world.

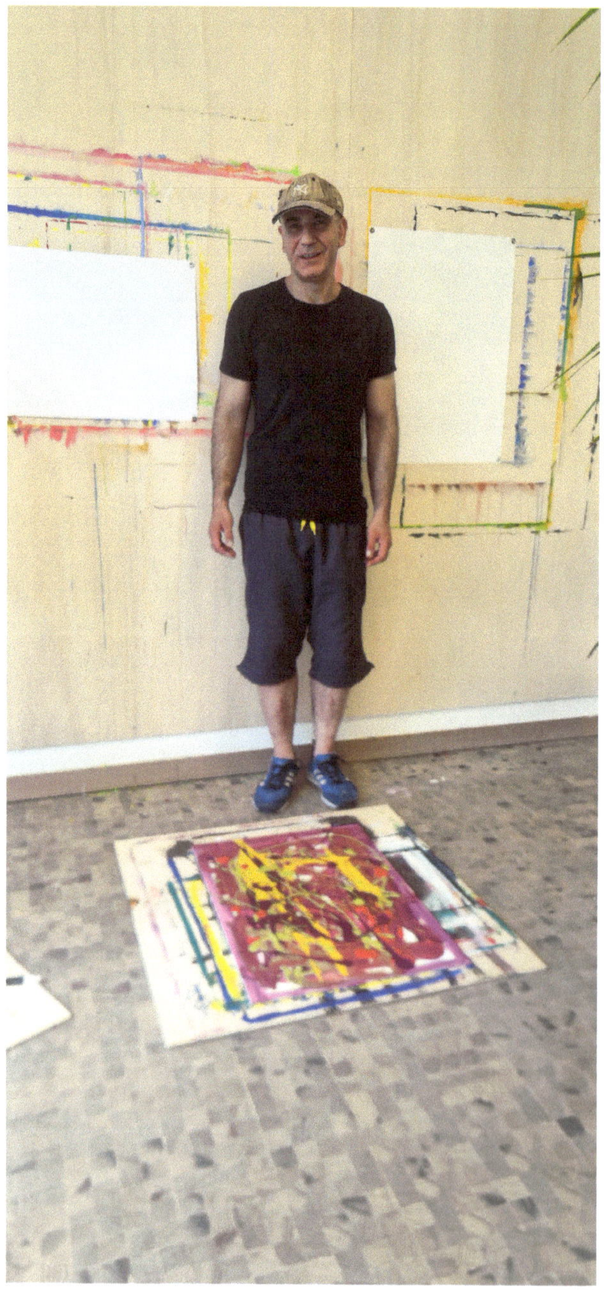

No title

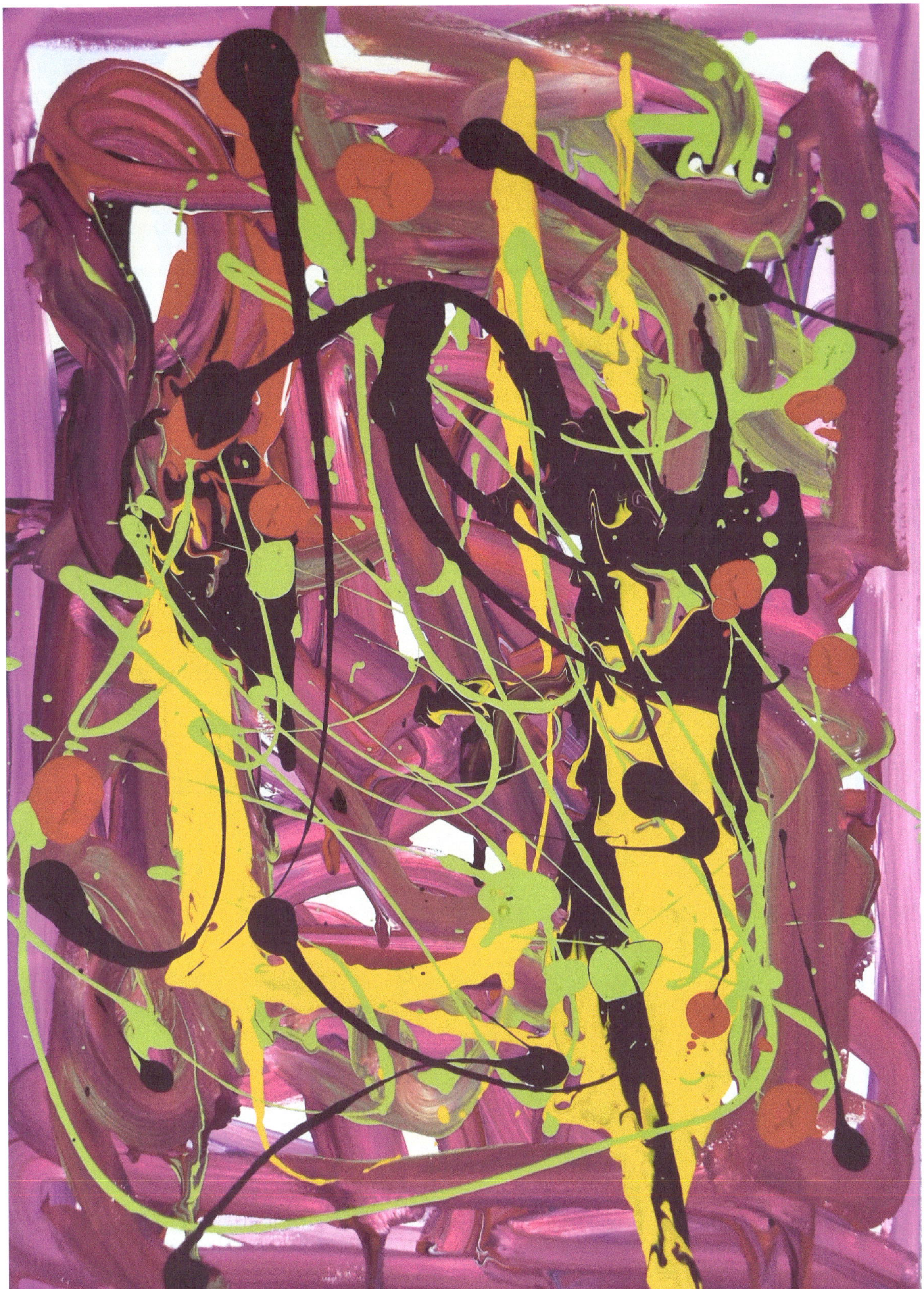

No title

SHANALI PERERA

www.shanaliperera.com

Dr. Shanali Perera is a Manchester-based contemporary artist, author, and former clinician. Born in Sri Lanka, she trained in medicine before vasculitis forced her to leave her clinical career and embrace art as a path to healing. Her work centers on abstract expressionism with figurative undertones, visually interpreting illness, pain, and resilience. With a background spanning global health campaigns and medical humanities, Shanali uses art to spark conversation and drive social change. Her acrylic and digital works have been exhibited at the Women in Art Biennale (London), The Path at Venice Biennale, and in Florence as part of the Artist of Europe Award shortlist. Through her collection "Living Loving Mess," Shanali reclaims identity, transforms pain into beauty, and challenges perceptions of what it means to live with illness. Through her art, Shanali creates a space for dialogue, reflection, and advocacy, positioning her as a trailblazer in combining artistic expression with activism. This dual focus allows her to not only share her personal journey but also inspire others to see art as a transformative tool for empathy and societal impact. Her first book?, "Finding Me Beyond Illness"?explores resilience and transformation through the lens of creativity. As an artist and former clinician, Shanali's practice is rooted in abstract expressionism with figurative undertones, fusing digital and traditional media to reflect the hidden realities of illness, identity, and resilience. Drawing on personal experience living with vasculitis, she explores themes of chronic pain, healing, empowerment, and womanhood—transforming embodied emotion into visual form. Her work invites viewers into the internal landscape of those navigating illness, creating a space where silence gives way to self-expression. Shanali's artistic journey began with digital art, a response to limitations in her hands caused by her illness, vasculitis. Traditional methods became challenging due to pain and numbness, making the digital medium a vital adaptation. Recently, she has ventured into acrylic on canvas as her condition stabilized. The canvases, be it digital, acrylic, or mixed media, are her interpretation as an artist, clinician, and a person living with illness, of these encounters. Driven by raw emotion, Shanali's painting process is intuitive, guided by the flurry of feelings that steer her hand. She is guided by how the canvas takes shape as opposed to her guiding the canvas. "This truly is freeing!" she says. As she still can't use a paintbrush consistently, she throws paint, uses palette knives, rags and her hands to discover how the acrylic pouring technique comes to life. With sticks, she scratches the wet surface, exposing the complexity of layers within. This, to her, is empowering and exhilarating. Her work moves between the intensely personal and the deeply social—each piece a visual act of reclaiming narrative and redefining identity. "My art moves to embrace imperfection, bringing my inner self out. Let it capture your spirit and heart as you see, hear and feel the rhythm of life. See yourself through art. Be inspired. Be moved." ~ Shanali

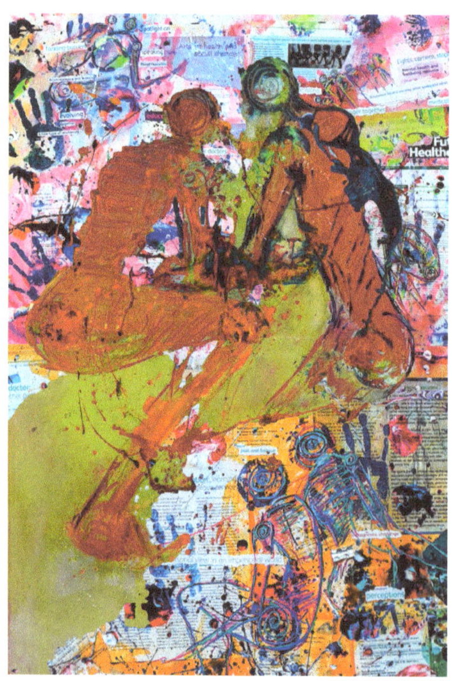

The Mess Reimagined: A Digital-Acrylic Synthesis, 2025. Digital Acrylic Hybrid, 90 x 60 cm.

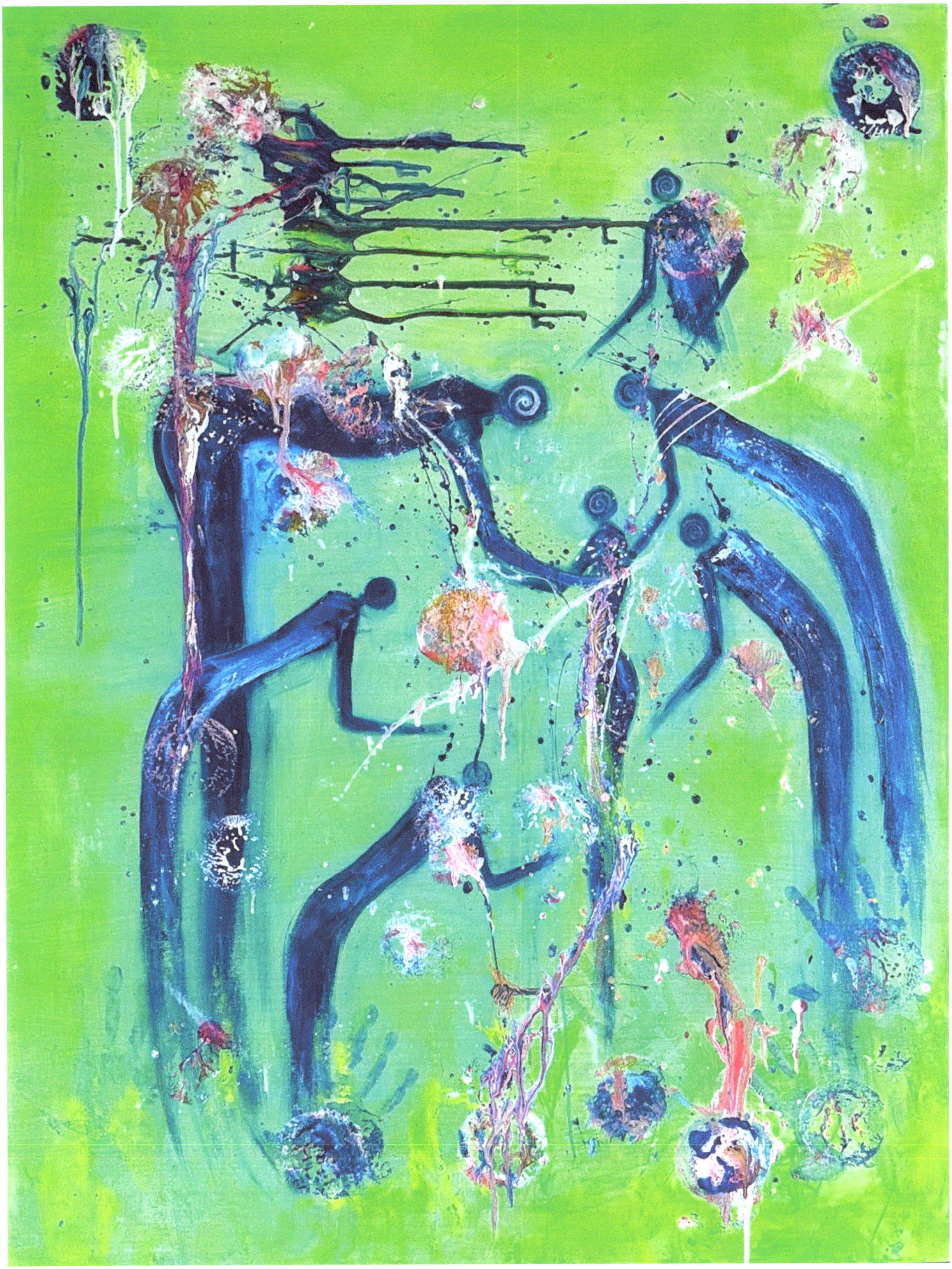

Transforming Mess, 2024. Acrylic on Canvas, 102 x 76 cm.

SHANE ROGERS

https://www.instagram.com/artist.gnesha/

Triumph over oppression, individual freedom, mysticism and magic, introspection, and uniqueness in the universe inspire the surreal, playful, and sometimes foreboding works of the artist GNESHA. Shane Rogers is the artist known as GNESHA. As a mixed media collage artist, scientist and professor of environmental engineering, social activist, and professional musician, his artistic journey is one that intertwines these seemingly disparate roles and grows from their many distinct perspectives, experiences, setbacks and successes. An important element in his art practice that carries over from his role as a scientist is provision of time for experimentation and development of new ideas and techniques, use of new and interesting media, and reflection, practice, revision and refinement of his artwork and ideas. His exploration of media range from the chemistry and staining techniques of his scientific laboratory experience to the basic elements of earth, wind, water, and fire which are sometimes the last resort and sometimes the first. He creates and collaborates with fellow artists sharing techniques, perspectives, and criticism of the works created. Much of his works are an outward expression and release of complex emotions that often cannot be expressed precisely with words. Overcoming powerful challenges in his own life through immersion in art, he gained interest in sharing his creative work publicly. He believes in the power of art to transform thought, inspire action, and manifest a greater consciousness and connection like it did for him while practicing in private. The works of the artist GNESHA have a unique and recognizable creative vision. Recognizable and enduring conceptual elements include expressions complex thoughts and ideas that contemplate themes of introspection, solitude, inner fear, outer courage, triumph, freedom, and the very personal experiences of magic in everyday life. His surreal and playful works portray intersections between fantasy and modern culture, science and mysticism, expression and introspection, and free thought, often with a dark, foreboding element. Much of his work reflects Japanese and American culture and mythology. Formal elements comprising his physical and mixed media digital artworks include hand drawing and painting, staining, interesting, odd, and ancient papers, wood, advertisements and elements from old magazines, vintage photographs, interesting vegetation, feathers, insects, and other found artifacts or original photographs taken by the artist of the same. GNESHA finds inspiration in the curious and the small like odd pictures in vintage magazines and strange artifacts in antique shops, cultural and personal stories of mysticism and mythology, and the intersections between traditional culture and emergent technology. He finds special inspiration in individuals that rise to overcome great challenges and those that are unafraid to express their uniqueness in the universe. His artistic influences sway towards the fantastic illustrations and dreamlike surrealism of classic and contemporary artists such as Heironymus Bosch, Max Ernst, Rene Magritte, and Salvador Dali as well as Japanese Ukiyo-e woodblock prints and paintings by artists such as Utagawa Kuniyoshi, Suzuki Harunobu, Tsukioka Yoshitoshi and Katsushika Hokusai. He is fascinated by the colorful cartoon illustrations of Japanese artist Rokuro Taniuchi (1921-81) and finds delight in honoring his work by reimagining them using found photographs and papers in mixed media and digital collage. ARTIST BIOGRAPHY Shane Rogers is a mixed-media and collage artist, professional singer/songwriter and musician, and classic dancer by education and training. He was born in Des Moines, Iowa in 1972, and currently resides between Germany and New York, USA. Shane holds a PhD in environmental engineering and is a professor of environmental engineering and science in New York. He is internationally recognized for his achievements in environmental and social justice and public health.

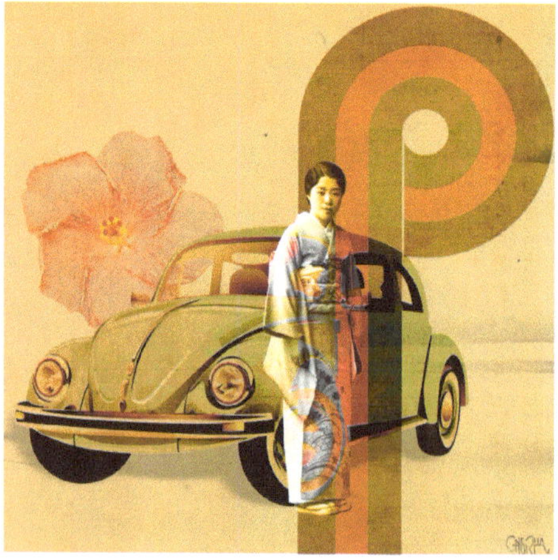

Fantastic Journey (幻想的な旅) *1, 2022. Mixed media and digital collage, 30.5 x 30.5 cm.*

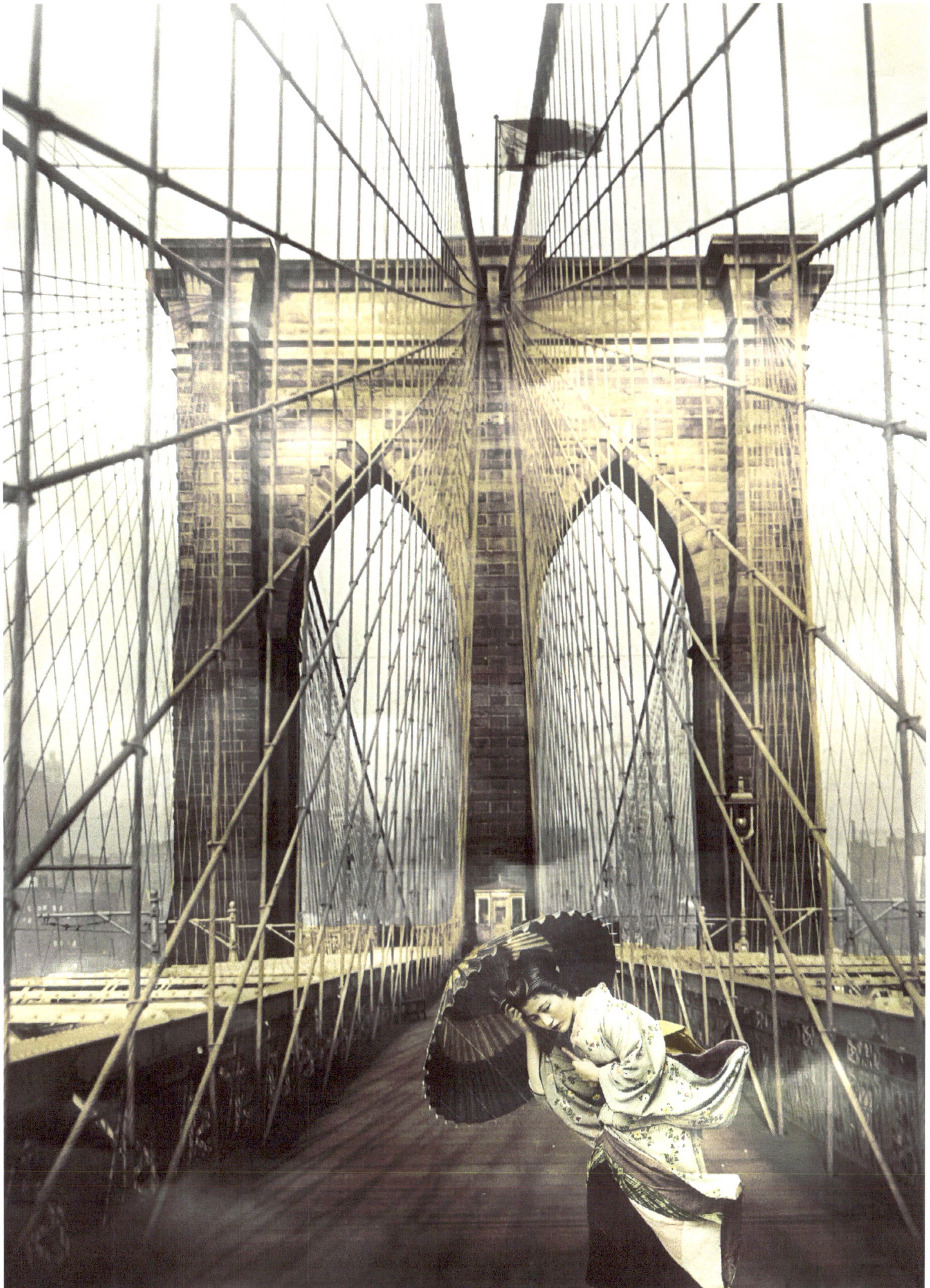

The Crossing **(横断)**, *2025. Mixed media and digital collage, 28 x 40 cm*

SHULAN WANG

instagram: shulan_bnw

Shulan Wang is a fine art photographer hailing from Hangzhou, China. She holds an M.A. in Photography from Spéos International School of Photography, an M.A. from the University of Westminster, and a B.A. from the China Academy of Art. Employing innovative creative approaches, she integrates a variety of techniques—digital darkroom processing, the soft immediacy of Polaroid, paper textures, visual installation, and the emerging language of artificial intelligence photography—each medium a thread in her visual tapestry. Rooted in the timeless motifs of time and nature, she turns her lens into a translator, rendering the quiet tension and profound resonance of life visible through every frame.

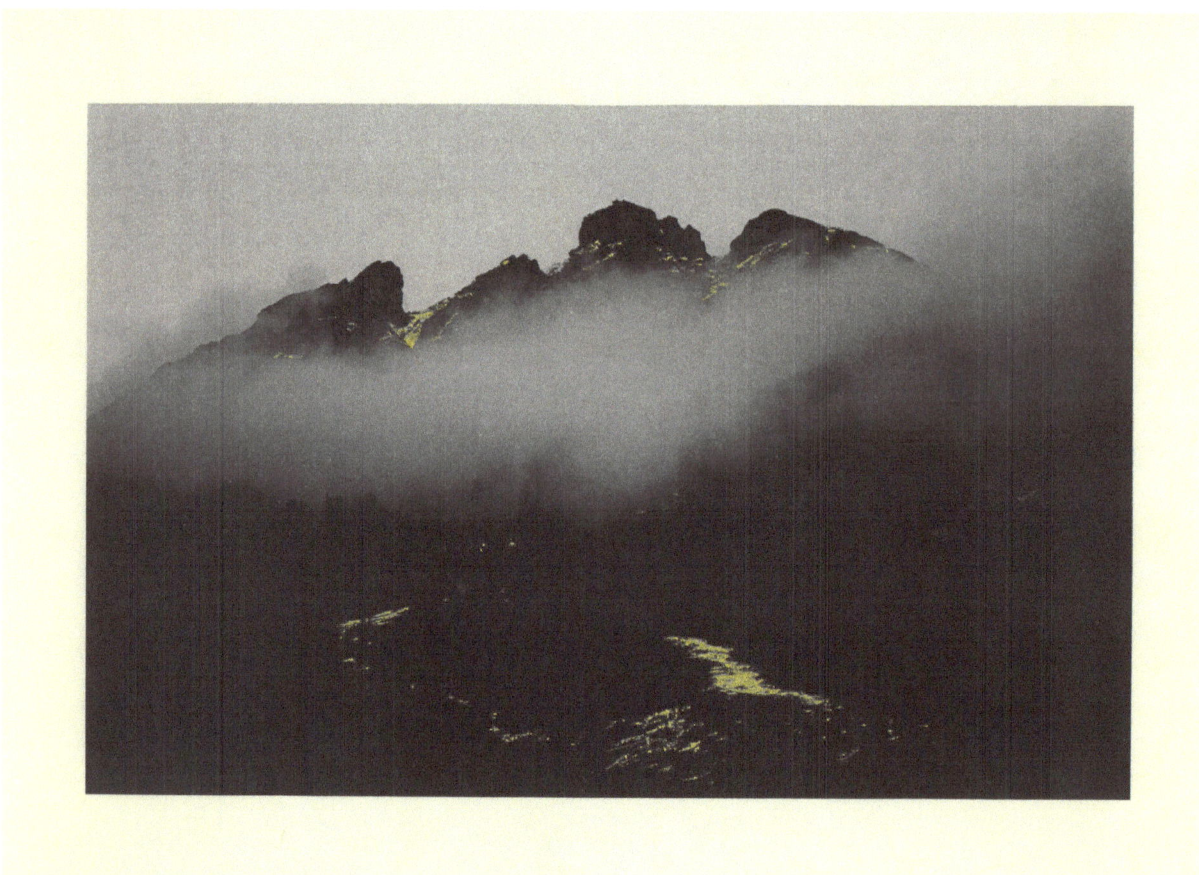

Golden Dreams #2, 2022

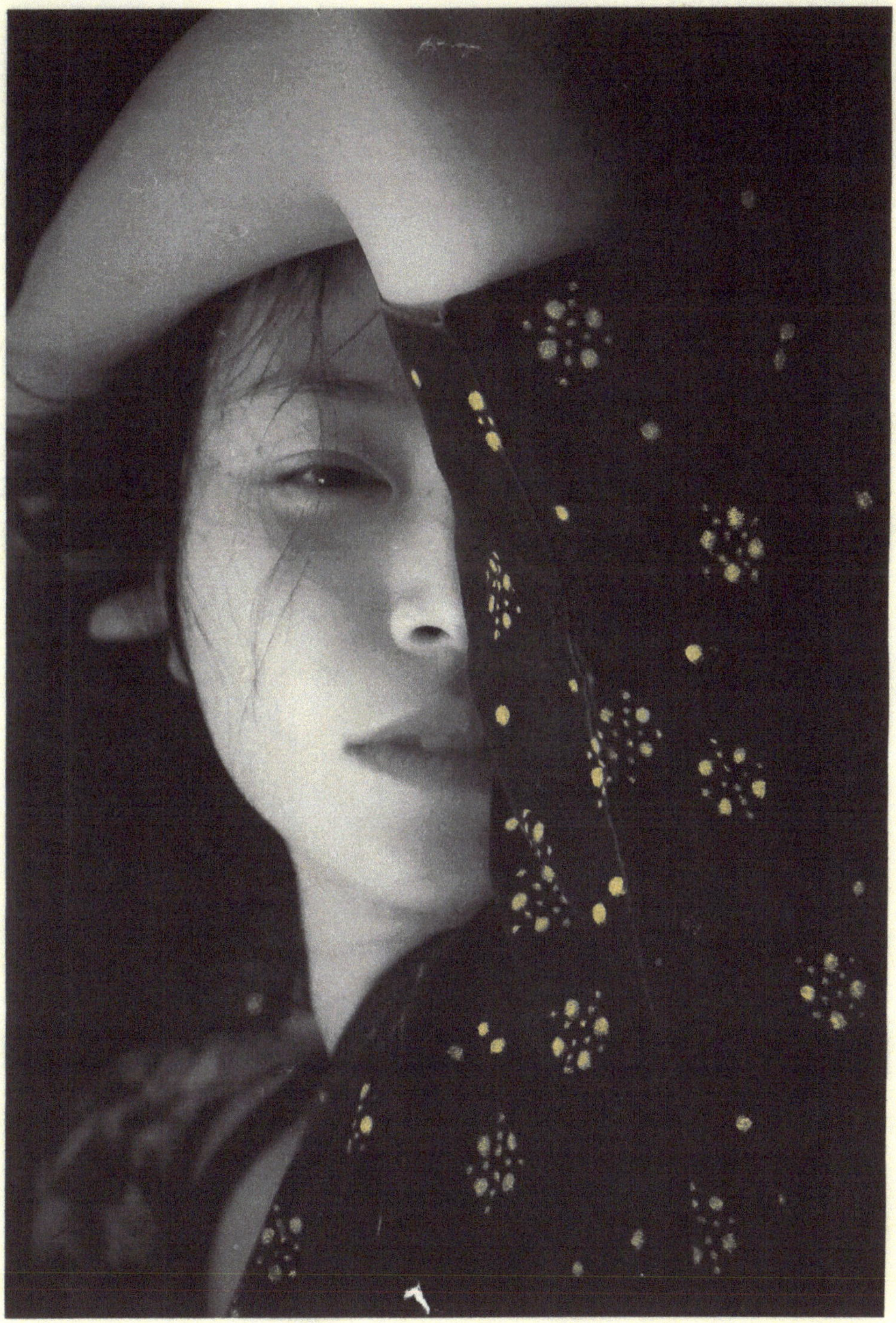

Golden Dreams #21, 2022

SILKE WOLFF

https://www.saatchiart.com/silkewolff

The academical, digital, mediumistic, surreal post pop art fine artist Mrs. Silke Wolff opens a general, secret, supernatural universe with her original graphics. By her broadened consciousness, which she has been developing for 30 years of daily meditative practice, she perceives this sphere of eternal existence. Such unique situations she catches with oil pastel drawings in sketch books. From these ideas for her cycles with series arise, which she creates personally as digital collages, based on drawings and photos, completed with texts. Lacking physical prove you may consider it fantasy. Enjoy :-) Silke Wolff looks forward to reinvest her sales volume from fine arts.

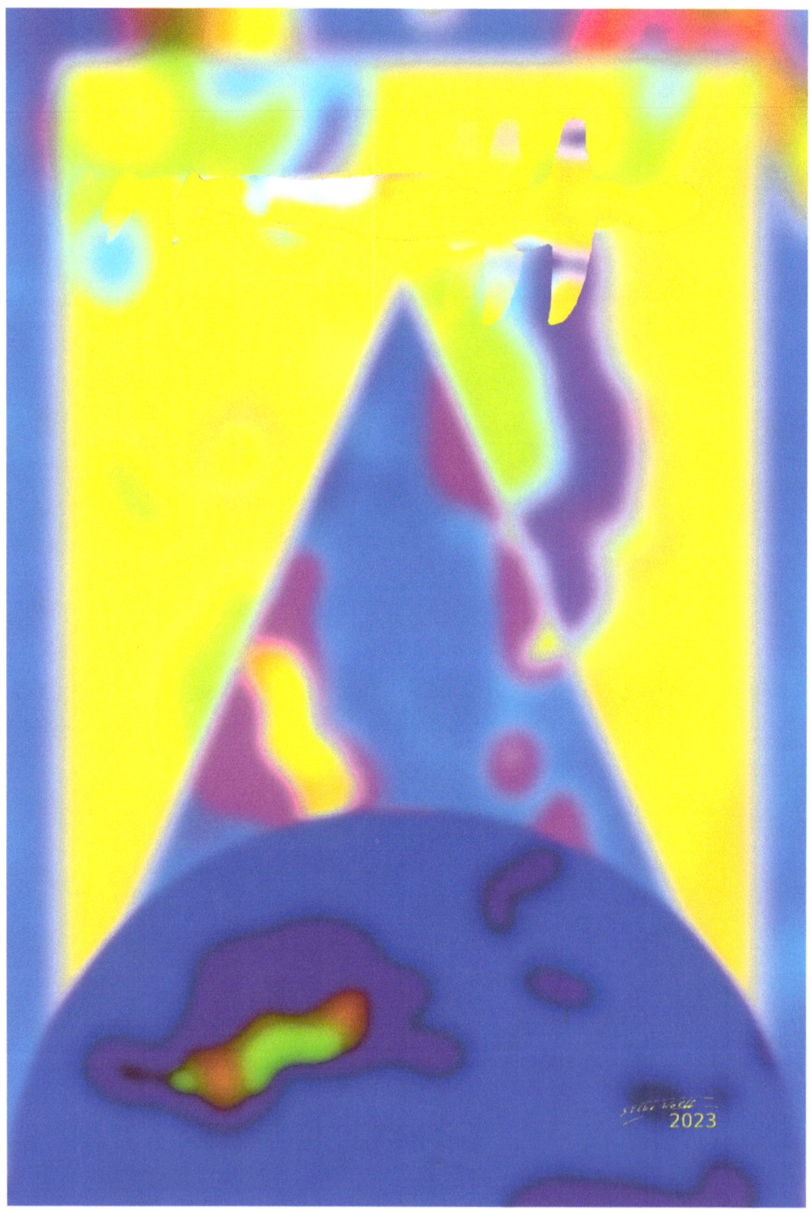

Silke Wolff 2023 Para Flying Opus 3.4.2.1842 original-graphics edition 10, drawings and photos personally processed digital on acrylic glass aluminum, 45x30x3 cm, 500 Euro

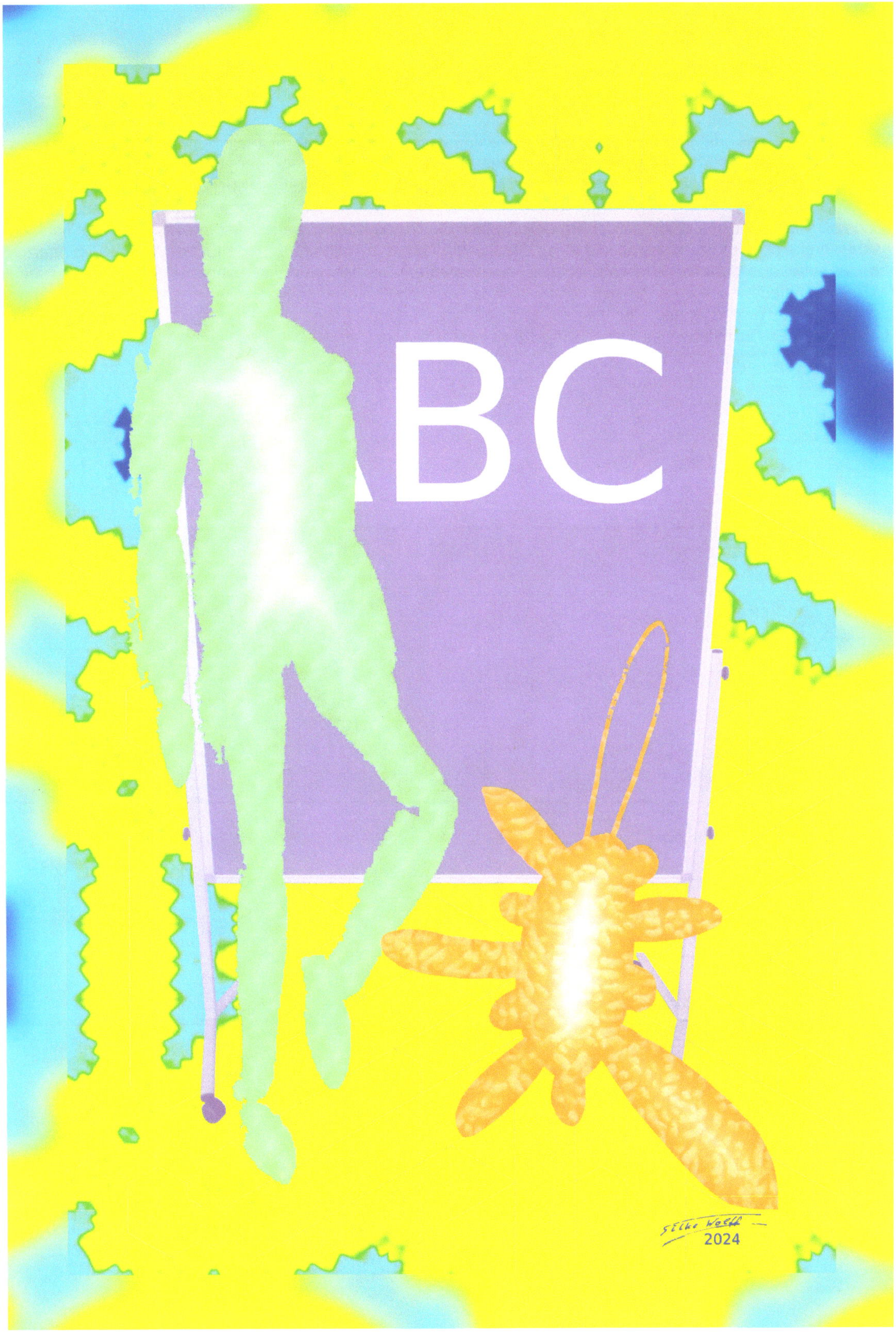

Silke Wolff 2024 PSI ABC Opus 3.5.2.2320 original-graphics edition 10, drawings and photos personally processed digital on acrylic glass aluminum, 45x30x3 cm, 500 Euro

SIMONE VON ANHALT

info@simone-von-anhalt.com

Simone von Anhalt was born in Munich, Germany, but emigrated as a young girl to Brazil. During her several years living there, she was markedly affected by local culture; the people's soul and love for nature remains with her today. Now living once again in Munich with her family, Von Anhalt's work is distinctly inspired by her childhood in Brazil and her cosmopolitan lifestyle. Her works talk silently, touching others with their expressive color and size. Von Anhalt's canvases often focus on gradations of a single color, harmonizing them with languid forms and brushstrokes such that each canvas captures the soulful spirit of Brazil she cherishes so deeply. Von Anhalt is not limited by the formal dimensions of artmaking, and chooses instead to capture the feelings of time and momentariness. Her paintings connect the viewer with their inner being, unfolding reflective and personal emotions within us. Von Anhalt prefers to work in utter solitude, neglecting outside forces to channel her own inner self onto the canvas. She employs acrylic mixed with pigments, gold, sponges, and palette knives to create these lush canvases. Her studio acts as her refuge, and, as a result, her paintings allow the viewer to take refuge in the way they capture peace and encourage subjective emotion.

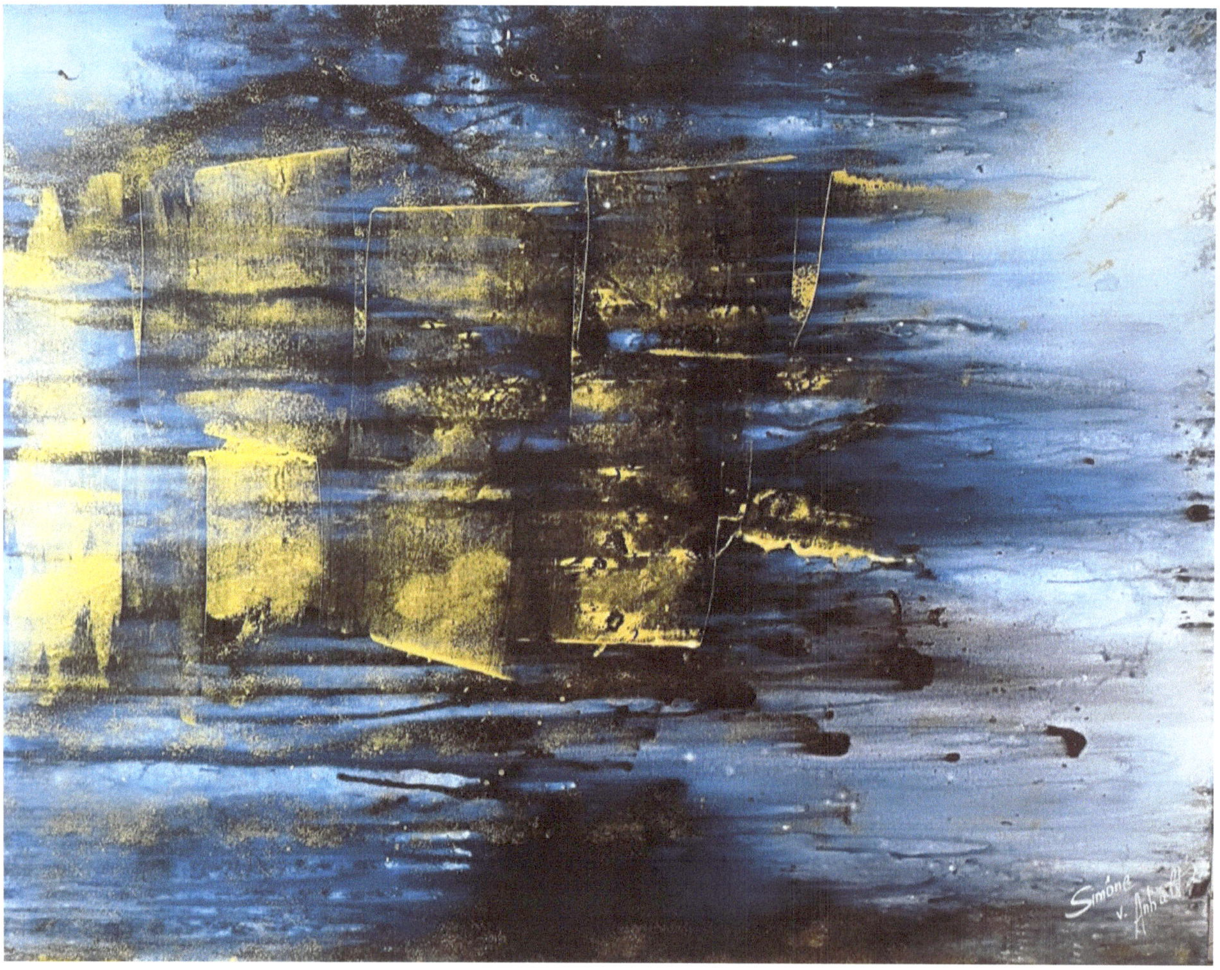

Sky Journey 2022

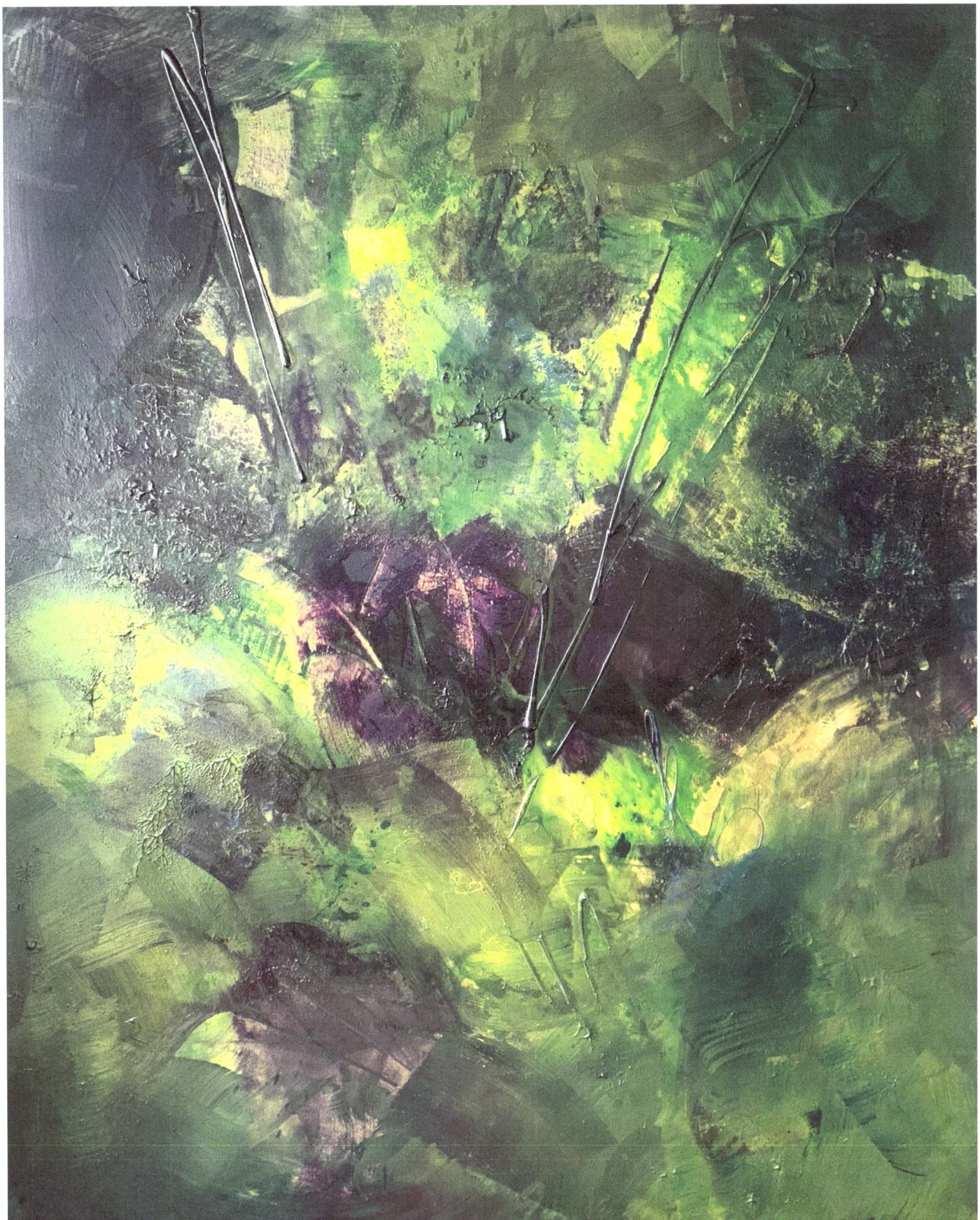

2019 Awakening

SONIA I.ROSEVAL

soniarosevalartist.net

Statement Understanding of the world. Symbolism of Unity and Consciousness: Japanese ink on art paper, created through freehand drawing and inspired by my meditation, is a captivating expression of the my inner world and my connection to the larger universe. The delicate lace-like patterns, formed by circular and geometric shapes with repetitive lines, symbolize the unity of consciousness. Through my intuitive brushstrokes, these forms come together to represent a harmonious whole, reflecting the interconnectedness of all beings. Japanese ink on paper art serves as a reminder of the profound beauty and unity that can be found through artistic expression and the practice of meditation. It invites viewers to contemplate their own place within the interconnected web of existence and to embrace the conscious unity that binds us beings. bio Sonia Roseval, a dynamic artist whose journey spans continents and cultures, was born in Tunis, Tunisia, and moved to Montreal as a child. Influenced by her intellectually inquisitive father and creatively skilled mother, Sonia's early life was filled with wonder and curiosity. At the age of twelve, she began drawing portraits, an early indicator of her artistic path. Self-taught but nurtured by a supportive community, Sonia's techniques evolved organically, heavily guided by intuition and meditation. Her artwork often features intricate sewing patterns inspired by her mother, symbolizing deeper states of consciousness. This personal yet universally resonant approach forms the core of her creative exploration.

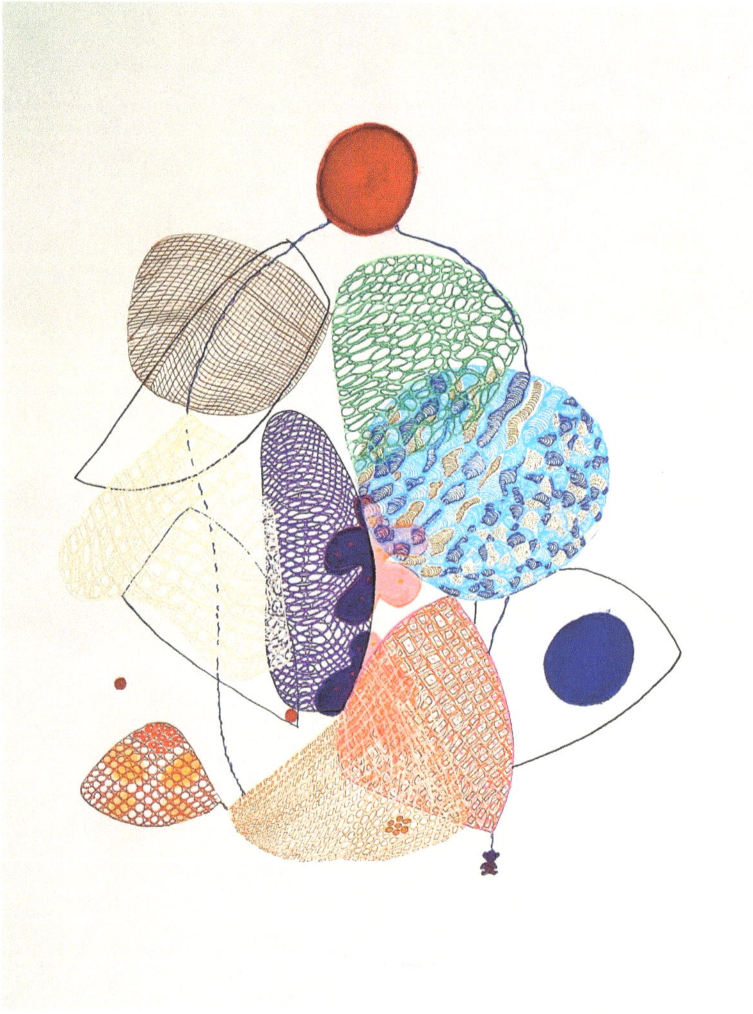

Fusion of Kyoto,2024. Freehand ink drawing on acidfree 300lb watercolor paper.55.88 x71.12 cm

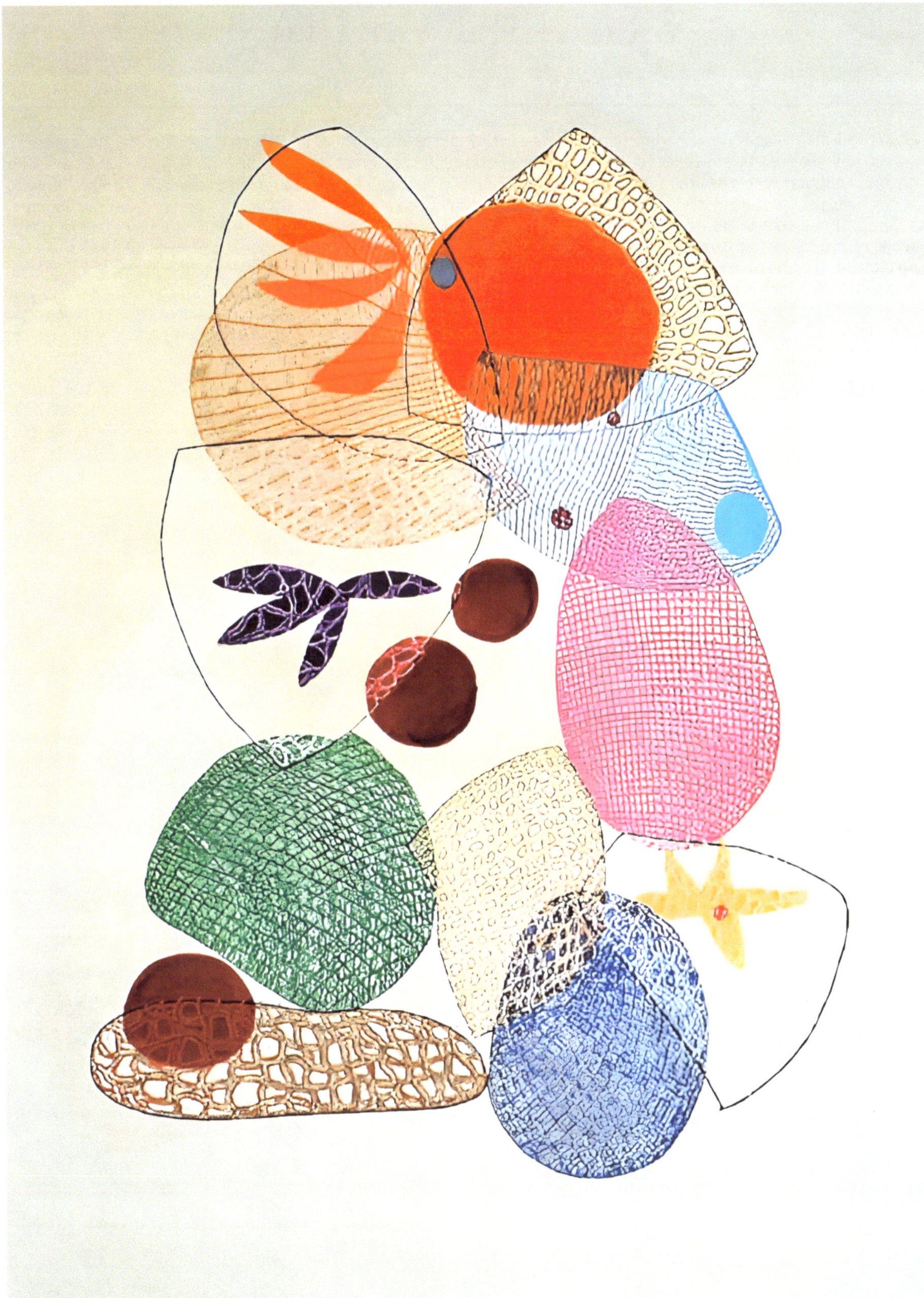

InsanelyBeautifulseries #2,2024. Freehand inkdrawing on Arche acidfree 300lb watercolor paper 71.12 x 55.88 cmd ink drawing on

STANISLAV RIHA

https://www.instagram.com/stanriha/

Stanislav Riha - Standa, Visual artist, photographer and writer. Member of CARFAC, born in 1952 in Prague, former Czechoslovakia. He grew up in Lesser Town (Malá Strana), surrounded by great medieval and modern art and artists, which was great support for his desire to create. In 1980, he lived in Grinzing, Vienna, Austria, for a year, and then he moved to Vancouver, BC, Canada. In the last three decades, Standa has been creating wall-mounted, cast resin, and aluminum sculptures combined with canvas and gold leaf, and I have been exploring the computer as an art tool for creating digital artwork. All his life, he has loved to create art full of emotions and feelings, "soul," with the satisfaction of fun. As well as being interested in the balance and composition of colours and objects, rather than the reality of the items. The direction of the last two decades is aimed at understanding and, through artwork, expressing the human struggle of emotions and adaptations. For the past ten years, he has been polishing his creative work in the Surreal-abstract style. The main motto of his artwork is: Just as in a good story, readers have space to create their own image; in a good impression, viewers can create their own account.

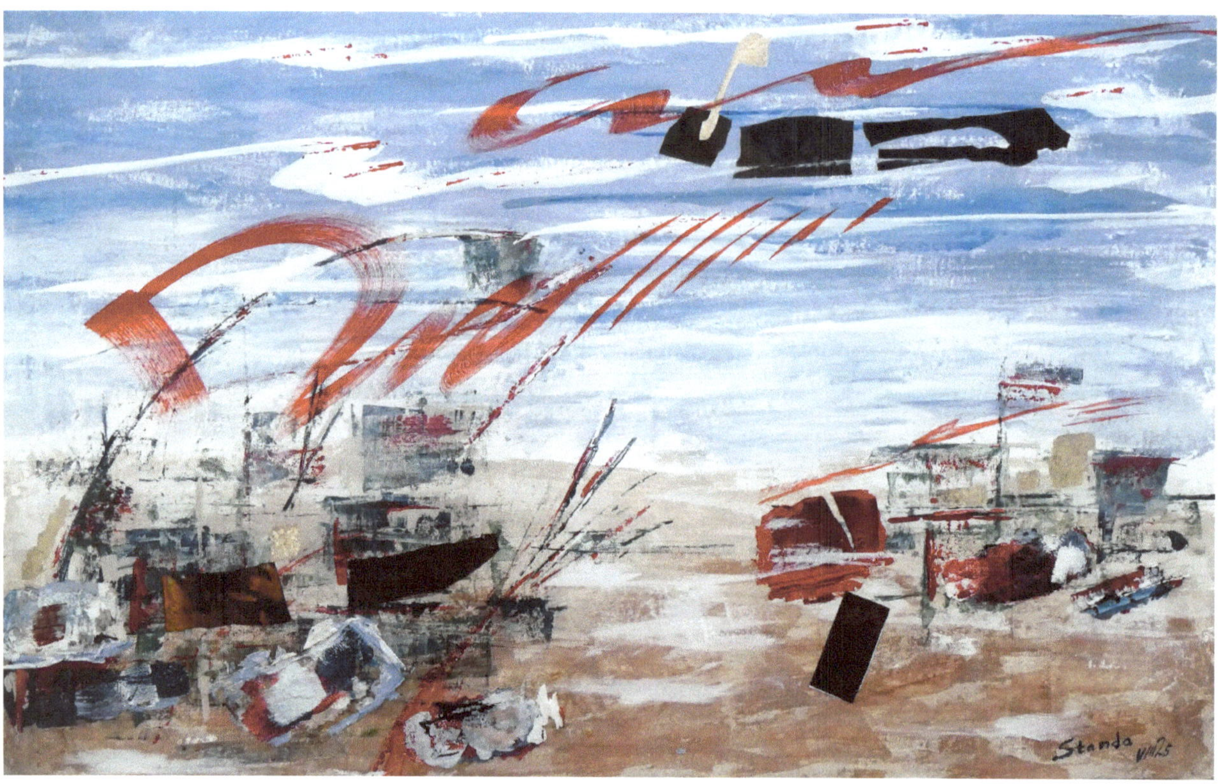

Snorkelling a reef, 2025

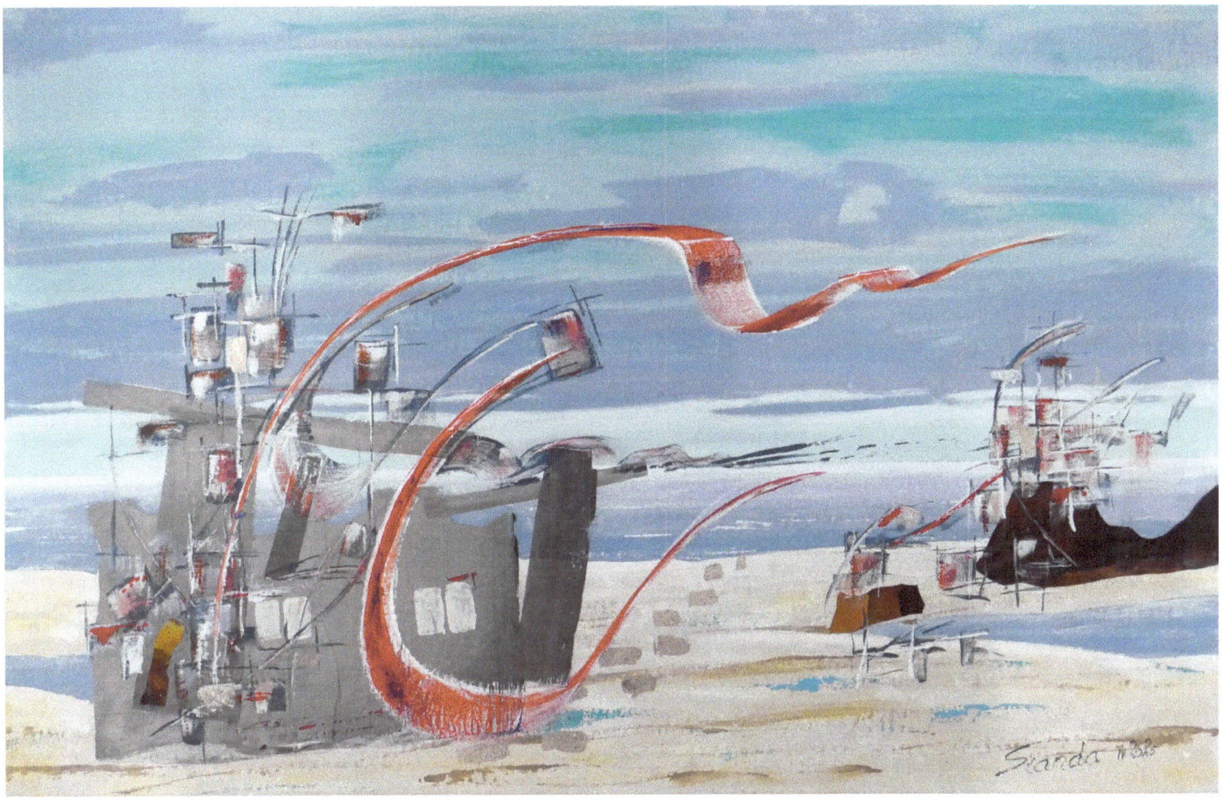

Abandoned beach house, 2025

STEPHANIE BING

Stephanie.Bingo@me.com

Stephanie Bing, born in 1967 in Mannheim, studied fine art, painting, photography, art history, German studies, and literature at Mainz University and Academy of Fine Arts, graduating with distinction. As an associate professor for the Bavarian Ministry of Culture, she taught design, architecture, aesthetic perception, and digital media. Since 1991, her award-winning art has been shown internationally, with physical exhibitions in cities such as Rome, Venice, Milan, Zurich, Basel, Munich, Frankfurt, Vienna, Budapest, Luxemburg, Paris, London, Barcelona, Lisbon, New York, Key West, San Diego, and Los Angeles. Stephanies artistic practice focuses on transforming interiors into vibrant, multi-layered sanctuaries that invite viewers into new perceptual realms. Engaging deeply with art history, composition, color, and symbolism, she incorporates flora, fauna, and historical references into tapestry-like settings that feel both familiar and unexpected. Bing's paintings challenge conventional spatial perception and explore themes of resilience and personal transformation, radiating energy and inviting emotional and intellectual response.

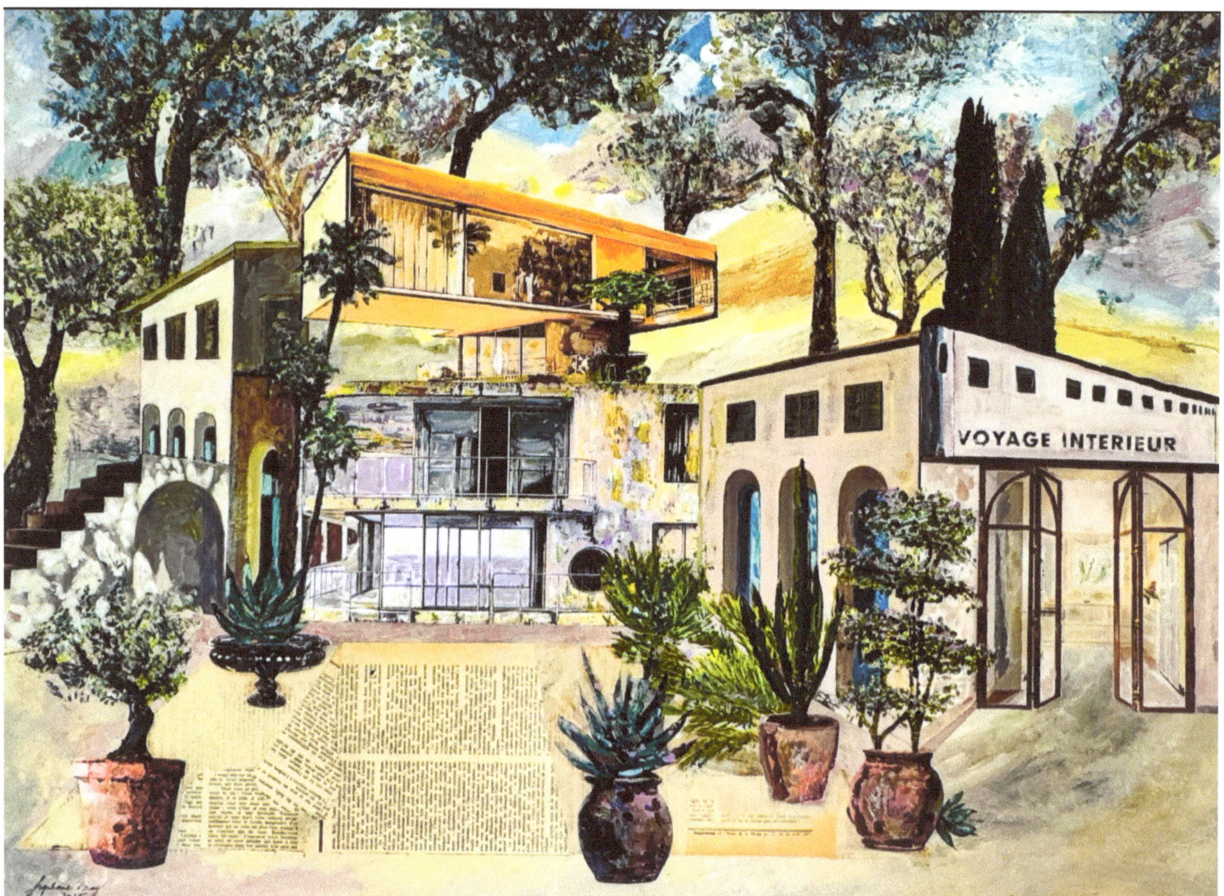

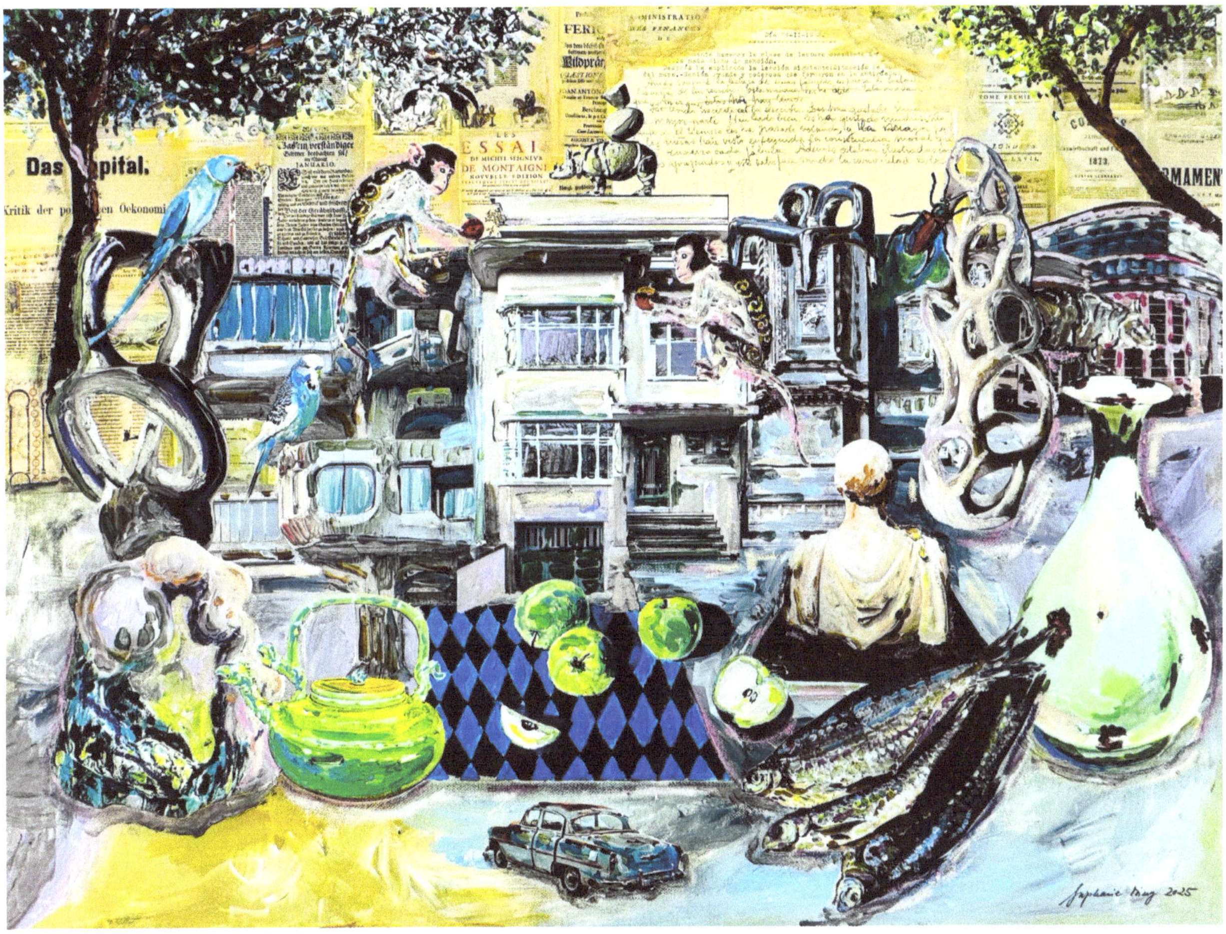

Hortus Conclusus My Mind Mapping 2025

SUKEY CAMACHO

www.sukeycamacho.com

Sukey Camacho It's a self taught Artist and, She is Born in Mexico and Currently living in United States of America. Studied Classical European Art for 4 years at a private school in Sofia Art Academy in Dallas Texas and now she's winning a Multiple International Awards with the most prestigious Elite Certifications Artist merit with the Recognition Globally and Considered ones of the International Investable Artists with the Art Market Experts prestigious Brand for Art Collectors Investment for Her Unique Genuine and Authentic Style Method the Viceversa View and 360°rotation view in the most of her Authentic and Unique Masterpieces of Art. She's characterize her artworks as a expressionist portraits and composition in surreal scenes full of colors with her emotions and well defined lines with geometrical objects and she have her own Genuine and Authentic Style Method "VICEVERSA VIEW"and "360° Rotation View", That it is another kind of perspective in her emotions,Dimensions,Dreams and she mix the reality of her life with her unique vision that is given another parameters of perspectives in every meticulously observation with the emotional experience in every single Masterpiece of Art she creates and involves every human being to connect on her own mystery fascinating revolutionary mind out of this world. She consider herself with very Authentic Evolutionary and Revolutionary Methods and forms with Unique ideas in her own perspective Style in all her creations, because she's follow her own rules and visions,Dreams,Intuitions, Dimensions in everything she saws behind the scenes in her own mind and she's fluid with her freedom technique to bring all that into the reality in every line or stroke she projects with full of Passion, Love or Mystery emotions for transmitting and transferring her Soul, Spirit, thoughts,feelings and all her being from her Highest Consciousness that she's connect with the multiple fresh and unique ideas and subliminal experience messages from the universe or other worlds to keep on process her uniques and authentically Masterpieces of Art to show out for the entire world, because that's why she's born into this new path of her life to be a Genuine and Authentic Artist under the big full of Grace of God in all her Artistic Talent Creations of Art. With Love and Passion! Sukey Camacho The Artist Master Painter.

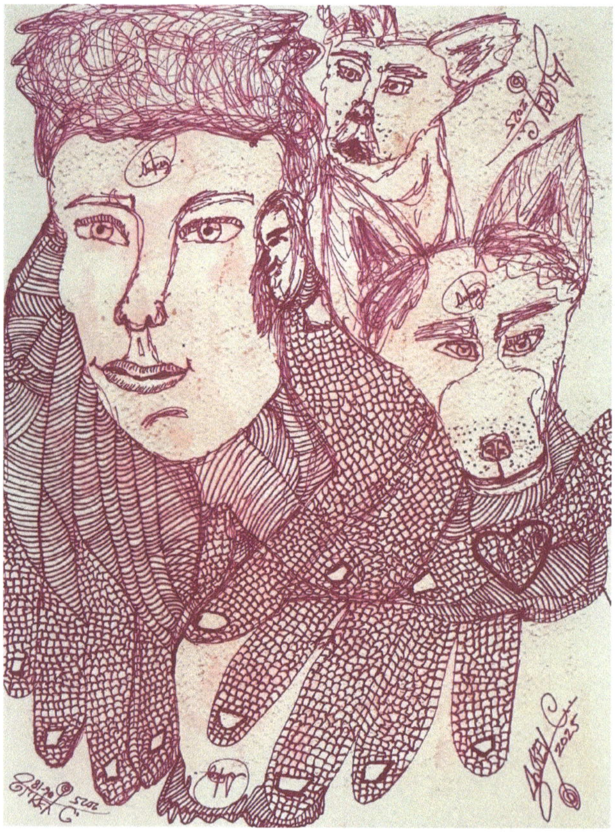

Eleven Fingers 999.9! Year 2025.

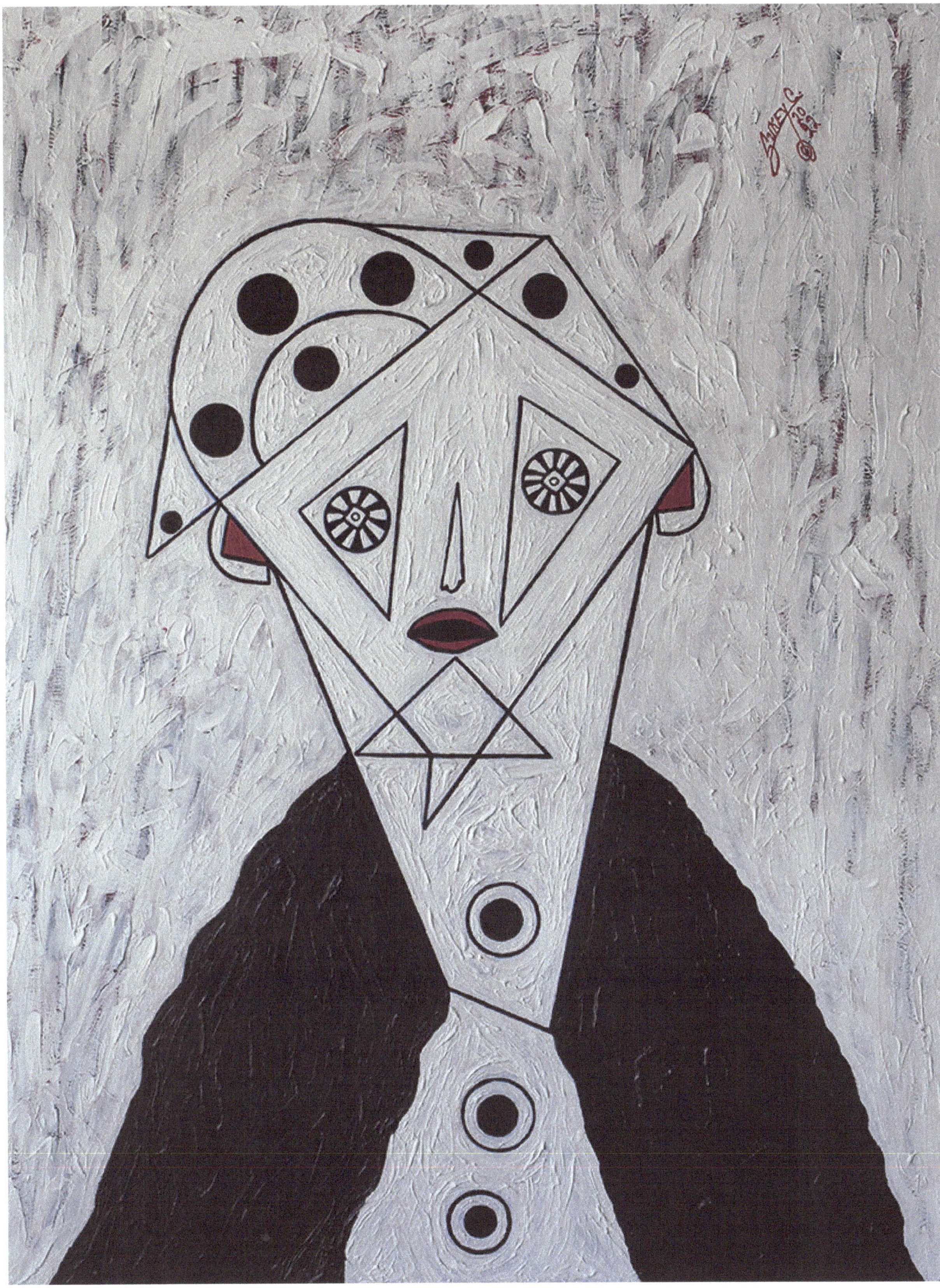

Quhálo 0.0 ! Year 2022.

SUSANA MONCADA

Instagram: ela.luxi

I am a based Visual artist from Panama. She is infatuated with nature, crystal healing, color psychology, chromotherapy, fashion, magic, women empowerment,nature, cosmos,obe experiences, entomology and human evolution. Which she combines with magnificent things she imagines everyday through her art. She writes poetry also and likes to conjure manifestations in her art pieces. Everything she tries to evoke are deep emotions that evolve into creativity implosions and symbiosis. She started to create art since she was 4 years old with fashion figurines that had images inspired in flowers, leafs and nature forms, next she has an incredible granmother that inspire to become the artist she is today due to her flow of creativity expression. She is an accountant and seamstress that adore to draw, then now myself has grown into a multifacetic artist. Not only, drawing and also an expertise in creating collages; she is a performer, she sings, dance and creates without stop !

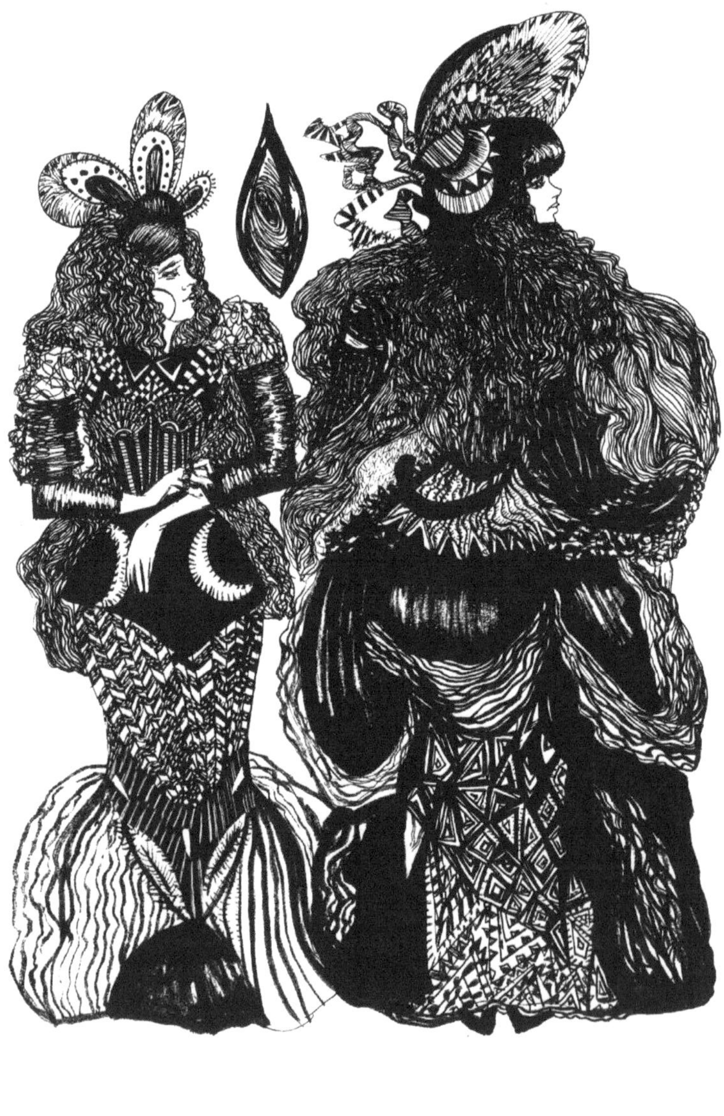

Sisterhood 2015

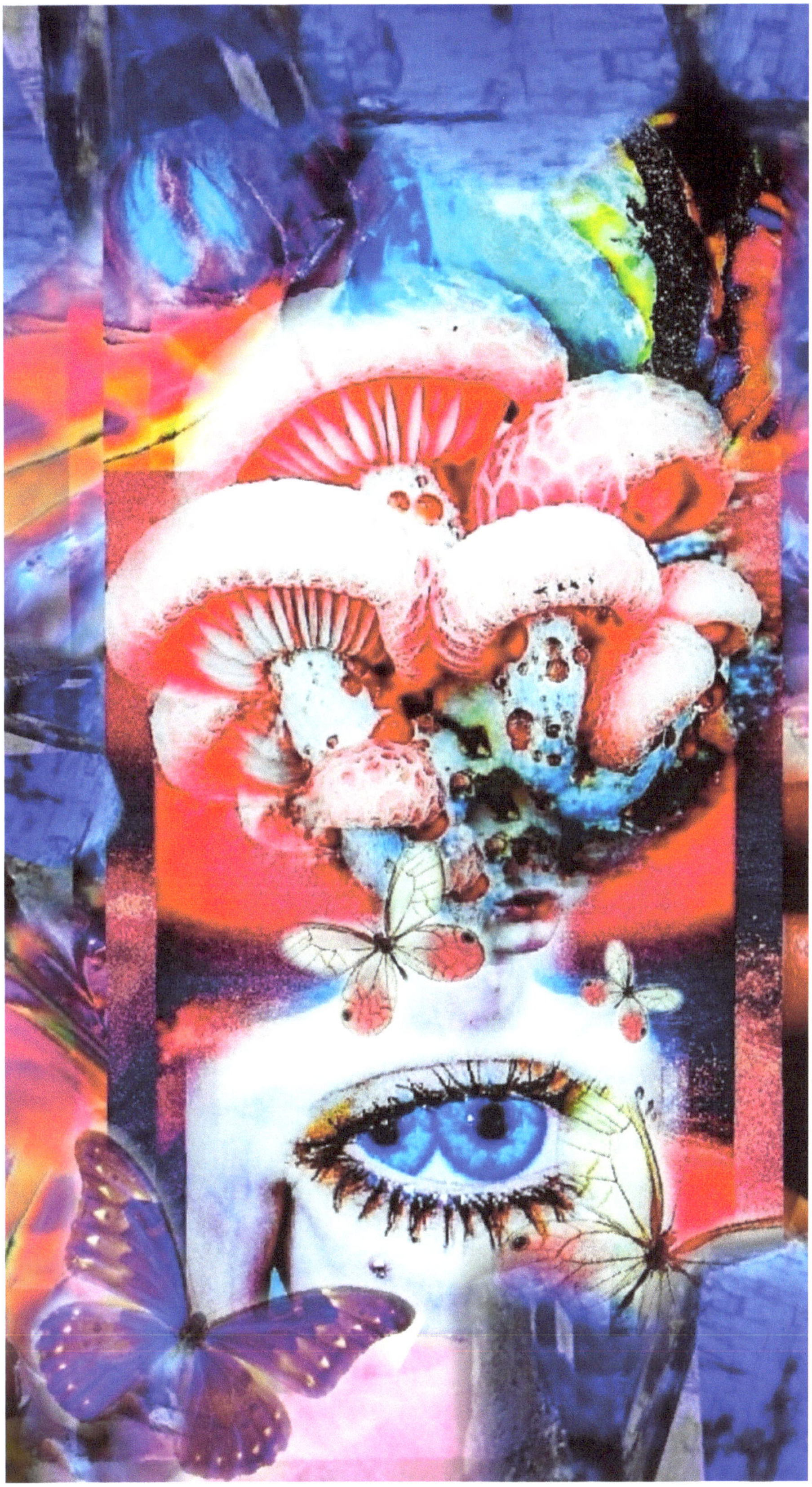

Entomology Fioreskrya

SUZANNE CROSS, PHD

dr.cross.consultant@gmail.com

Suzanne L. Cross's art work represents Native American cultural knowledge which provides an opportunity to moderate discussions of challenging topics i.e., cultural differences, health issues, recovery, loss and renewal of individuals. Often, she is invited to share her artwork with educational presentations to increase an understanding of the purpose of each piece. Secondly, her are is able to share American Indian/Native American cultural differences to develop an awareness of the values and beliefs within the cultures which are reflected in her art. As a young child, she began to learn from elder tribal artists in the areas of basketry, leather work, quillwork, beadwork and traditional clothing design which afforded me valuable life lessons. However, she enjoyed and continues to enjoy the art of beadwork and traditional clothing design. Several of the Elders and Artists shared with her Mother they thought she had an 'old sole' meaning she was more aware of life lessons than most children her age. They not only taught her artistry skills, but the art of living. She learned different methods of beadwork and shawl making; but equally important, she learned the history of her tribal nation, how to protect herself with academic and cultural knowledge, how to share and care for others, and mostly importantly; how to be an American Indian woman. Her artwork (beadwork including jewelry, shawl and ribbon skirts, dressing of dolls) have been shown and purchased in eleven states in the U.S. and two pieces were invited to shows in Canada and Italy. She has also shared and taught her artwork to college and elementary students, Cancer survivors, Native American communities, and exhibited while she presented on topic of U.S. Indian Boarding Schools, Cancer, Heart Disease, Murdered and Missing Native Women, etc.

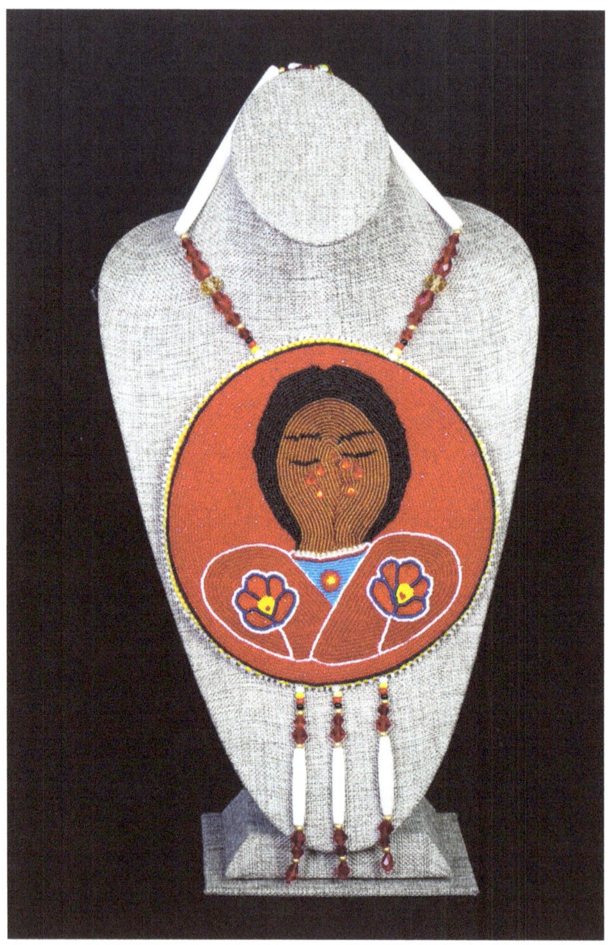

Murdered and Missing Indian Women and Girl, 2022. Beadwork, 16.51cm circumference.

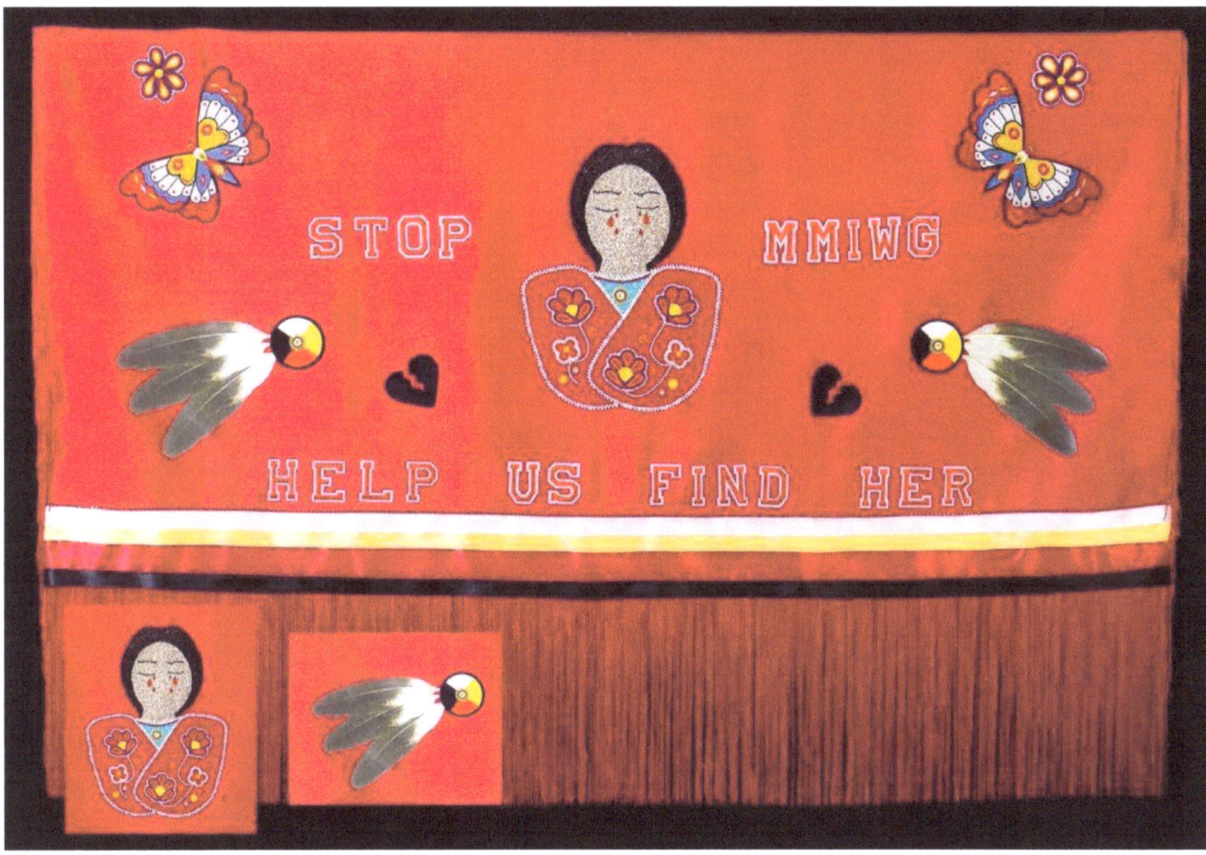

Murdered and Missing Indian Women, 2024. Textile Beadwork.

SYLVIA KÖLBL

http://sylvia-koelbl-ansichtssachen.jimdo.com/

Sylvia Kölbl was born in 9th October 1949 in Vienna, Austria. She studied veterinary medicine in Vienna. She had no education in art, but painting is her passion since childhood. She had five solo exhibitions and participated in more than 90 group exhibitions in different countries since 2013. Her works belong to private and public collections in Austria, Slovakia and Germany. She is an awarded artist. She is a member of vetart-artforum, publicartists and Galeriestudio 38.

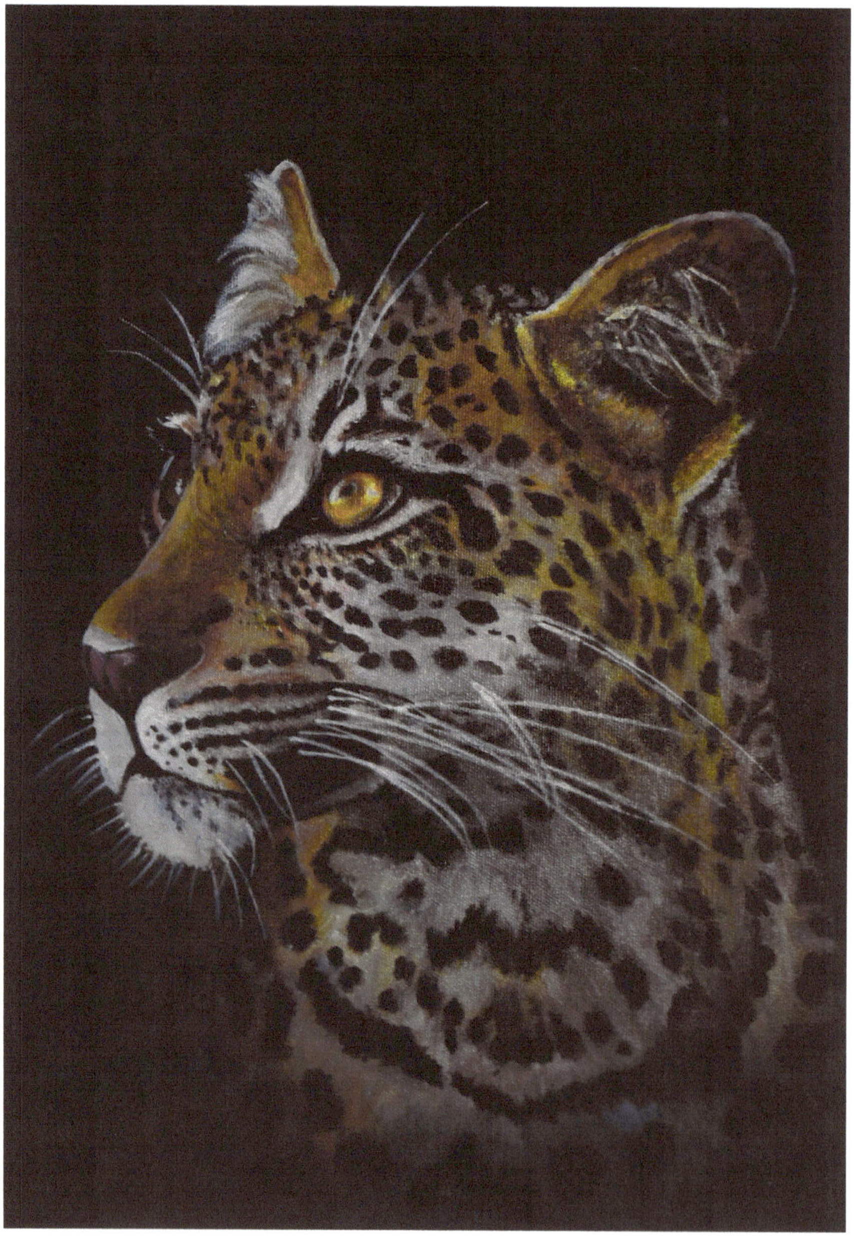

Leopard, 2025. Acrylic on canvas, 50x40 cm

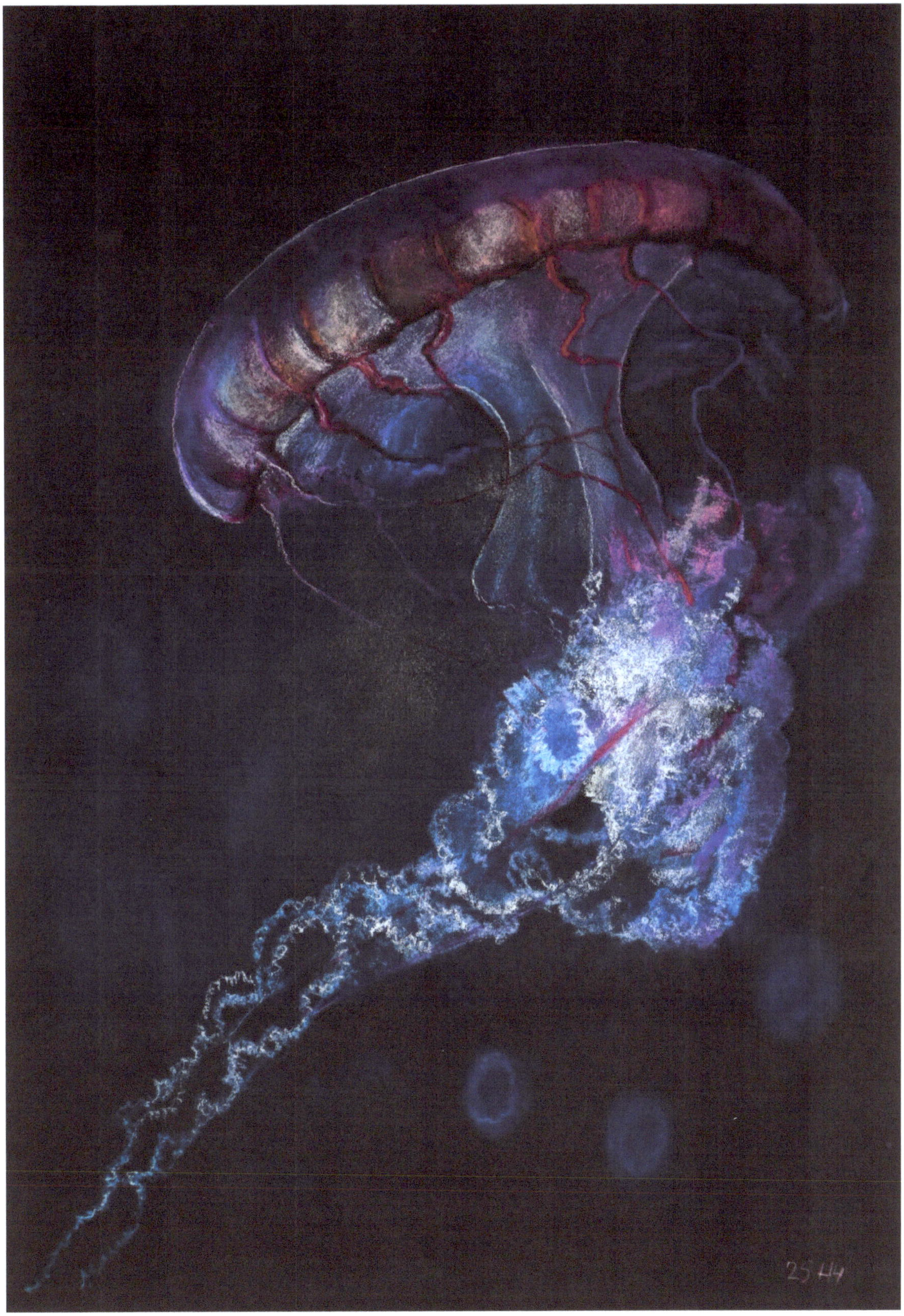

Zarte Schönheit, 2024. Pastel, 60x40 cm

SYMONA COLINA

www.symonacolina.info

A painting is like a window in a blind wall "NOW" ...is that moment in which we fall into the deep end. Holding a line of love and life in the palm of our hand. Where one starts off with a point then follows the line... following the comprehensive wind... As an artist, a visual artist Symona Colina holds the brushes in a steady drumbeat to the canvas. Touching the canvas, as lovers do. Tumbling and falling into the never-ending profound blues ahead... following the burning desire to be united with the rainbow-colored tunes carried by the wind. Songs of Freedom, songs of Ice and Fire... Songs to See... Symona Colina holds the horizon onto the tip of the brush, seeking brightness in the shades of life. As an artist, a visual artist Symona Colina reads between the lines of perspective opening heart and mind to the boundaries of consciousness and perception. Slipping through the doors of perception where time vanishes, finding a deeper awareness of the world and our place within it. To see what cannot be heard... A painting like a window in a blind wall. A painting, a whisper in the wind. A Door of Perception... Looking twice at the empty bottle laid aside, no message can be found. Wise words are spilled all over...

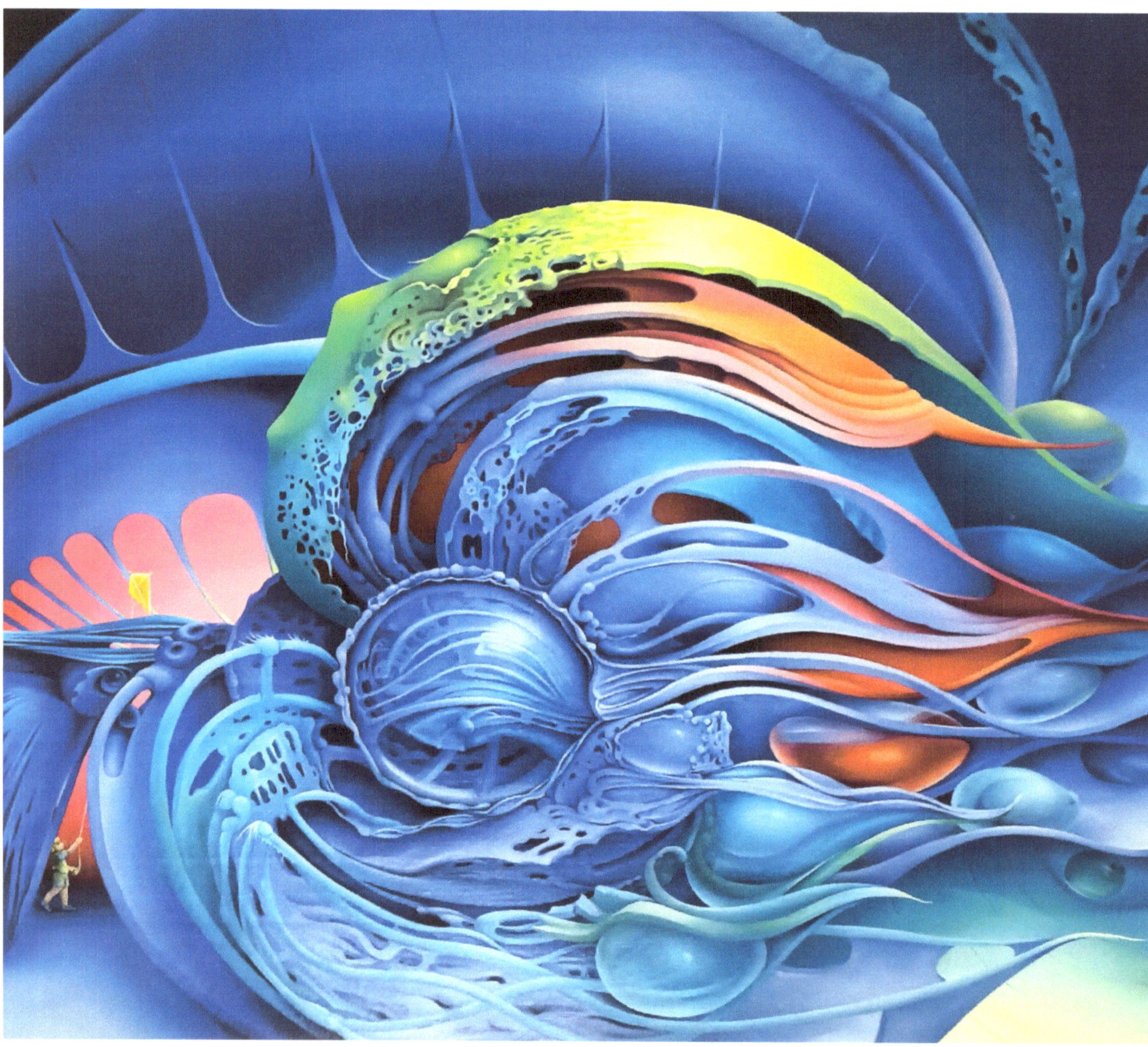

Doors of Perception Oil on Canvas 80x90 cm2025

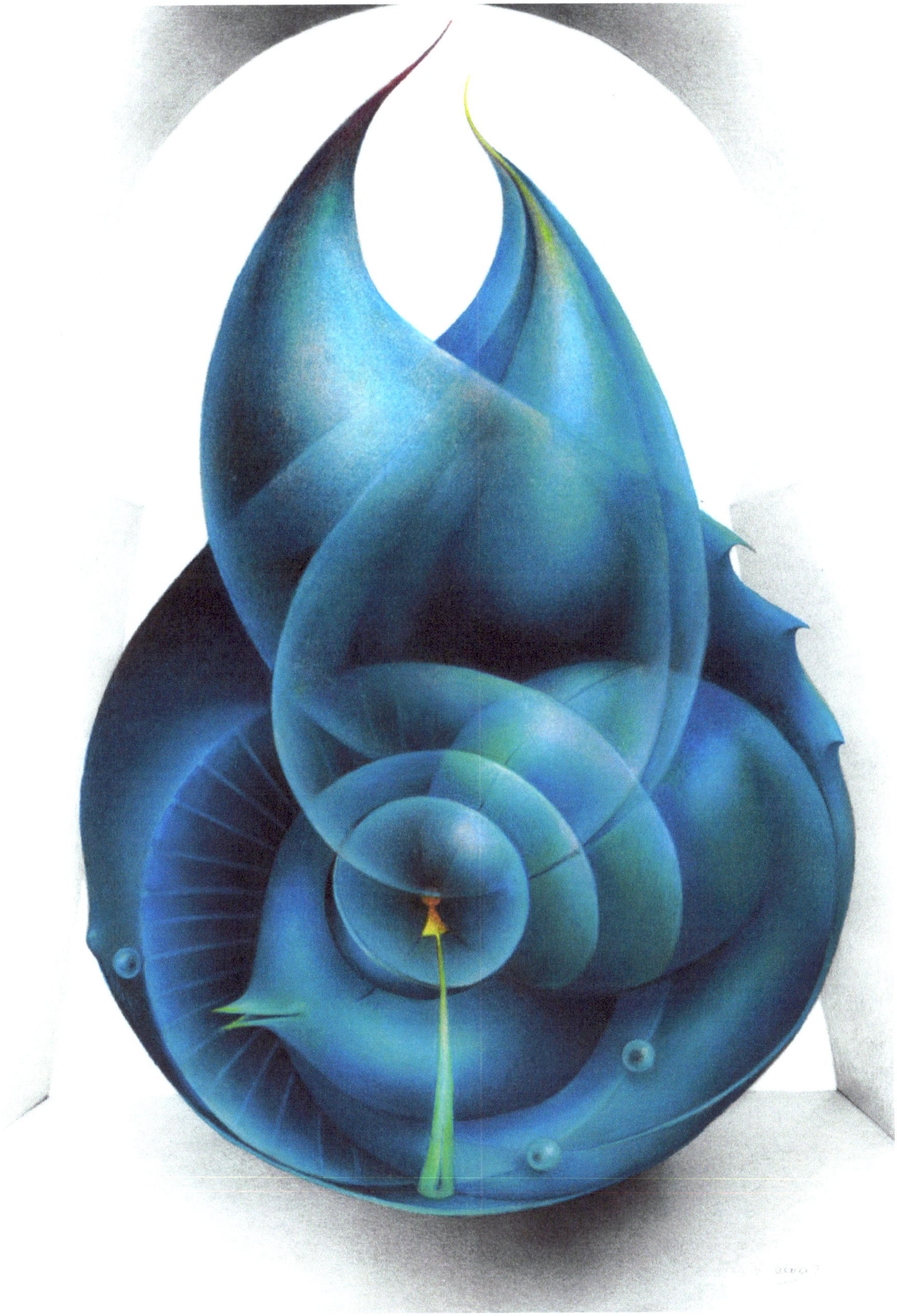

The Shadow Key Colored Pencil on Paper A32025

SYNDY ESTEVES

syndyartist@gmail.com

Cinzia (Syndy) Esteves is an Australian visual artist and has a Bachelor of fine arts with honours from University of NSW, graduating in 2018. Syndy then attended classes at Julian Ashton for human portraiture in 2019/2020. Syndy is an oil painter, draughtsperson, writer and a wild brumby advocate. Her artwork stretches the boundaries between art & politics by giving a voice to the wild brumbies that roam Kosciusko National Park in NSW Australia.

In her love of art, nature, philosophy & political theories, Syndy lends her voice for the Australian brumbies to bring awareness to the human condition that affects flora & fauna by human environmental impact & laws. The Australian political upheaval of the brumbies magnifies the problems of our human condition that governs the environmental management of Australian flora and fauna, especially within the unique Australian landscape, as management is at the forefront for what is considered a 'non-native' species, and the brumbies fall under that label, under Australian laws as wild brumbies evolved from domestic horses landing on Australian shores in 1788. Rehoming of wild brumbies is available but not supported well enough and brumbies that are not rehomed are either ground or aerial culled or sent to knackeries.

The art theories and philosophies attached to the artworks are of Freedom, Speciesism, challenging via juxtaposition the government labelled ideologies. The family and hierarchy of the sentient are thus evoked as well as the rights of animals questioned within our society, all via Portraiture. Each brumby selected for the work, has a family history and backstory behind them, relating the family and sentient behind each portraiture.

It was inevitable that Syndy's art journey of mnemonic experiences and events linked her research of family and the individual of the everyday life starting from a tangent of a childhood love of horses. Her art being based on the ethereal of things, not just experiences, as she is a city-based artist and has no experience with horses as such, hence uses named references of wildlife brumby photographers at times due to this. Syndy's critical thinking has developed the journey and thus relates her writing also to the artworks via discourses or poetry.

The art has expanded to advocacy, and now Syndy advocates with primary rehomers from Clearview Brumby Rescue Queensland and each brumby saved has a story to tell. Syndy's advocacy has taken a tangent, having also spread though social media and to add, runs a brumby transport fund based on donations, there also. But most primarily her advocacy is through her art to envision a different world that works with nature instead of against it.

Syndy expresses her art through traditional forms of oil painting, using restricted palettes and thinner layers of paint to create movement in her paintings. She sometimes also uses a 'alla prima' approach when painting smaller canvases. Her background of architecture relates at times different perspectives and she uses either a realistic approach or an impressionist setting, relating colours to mood and shadows, having also a modern colour palette, as colour & colour theory is one of her forte'. Hence, she mixes most of her colours using a range of primary colours. Traditionalist at heart Syndy also stretches her own canvases using traditional tacks and primes her canvases before she begins her work.

Within drawing she uses graphite, ink, pastel or mixed media, relating her draughting skills from her architectural background, using also technical ink pens. Again, the works are layered and detailed.

Syndy had intended to become a people portrait painter, but her passion for animals and nature has taken front seat, as she found the human faces masked by our human condition, she thus decided to take a not so well travelled road, hoping that it may enlighten a conversation, a thought, a change, in how we view other sentient species.

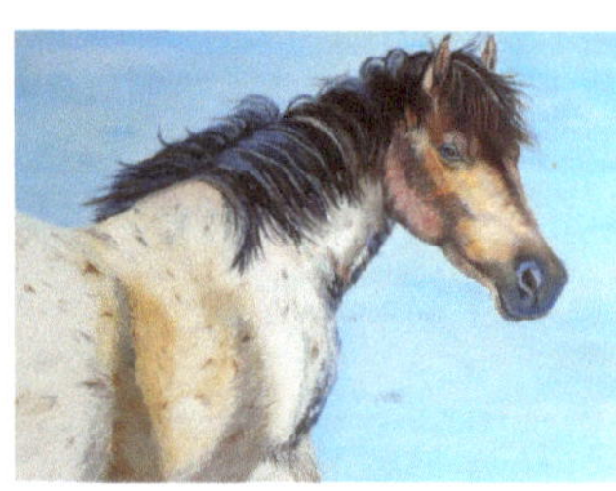

'UNDER BLUE SKIES & ETHEREAL FREEDOM' 2022. WIld Brumby Spirit of the Mountain King Stallion rehomed. Oil on canvas 133 x 96.5 cm

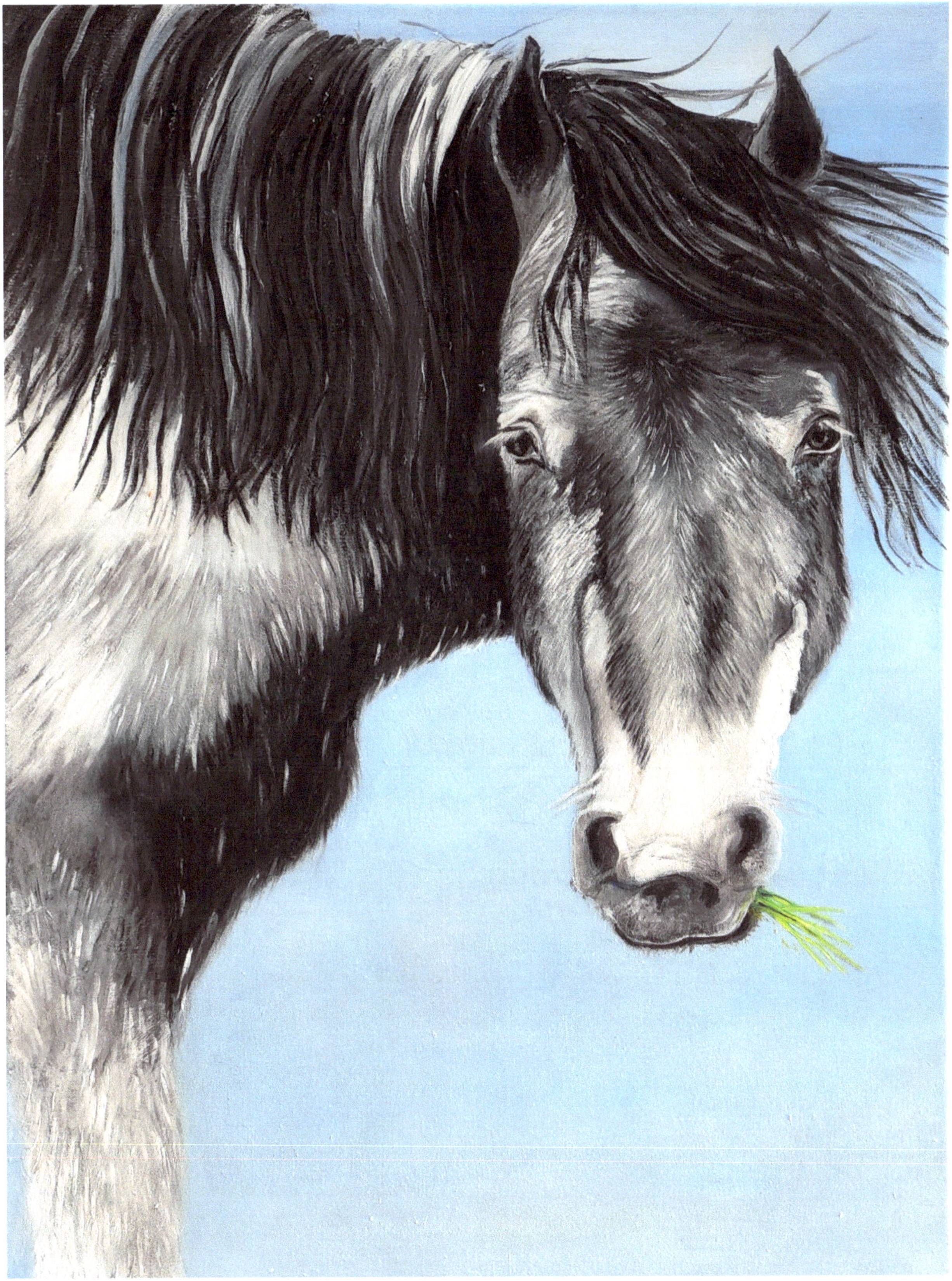

'ARROW BOY & THE DEATH OF KHEIRON' 2022. WIld Brumby Arrow Boy aerial September 2022. Oil on canvas 76 x 56 cm

TAMARA MICHEL

tm339661@gmail.con

Tamara Michel,geboren in Ukraine,studiert in Moskau,seit 30Jahren lebt und arbeitet freiberuflich Künstlerin,sie malt verschiedene Bilder mit Öl,Acryl und Aquarell und tendiert immer zu fröhlichen Farben und Motiven,har eigenen Stiel-zwieschen figurativen und Impressionistischen.Lieblings Motiven sind geheimnissvolle Naturschöncheit.

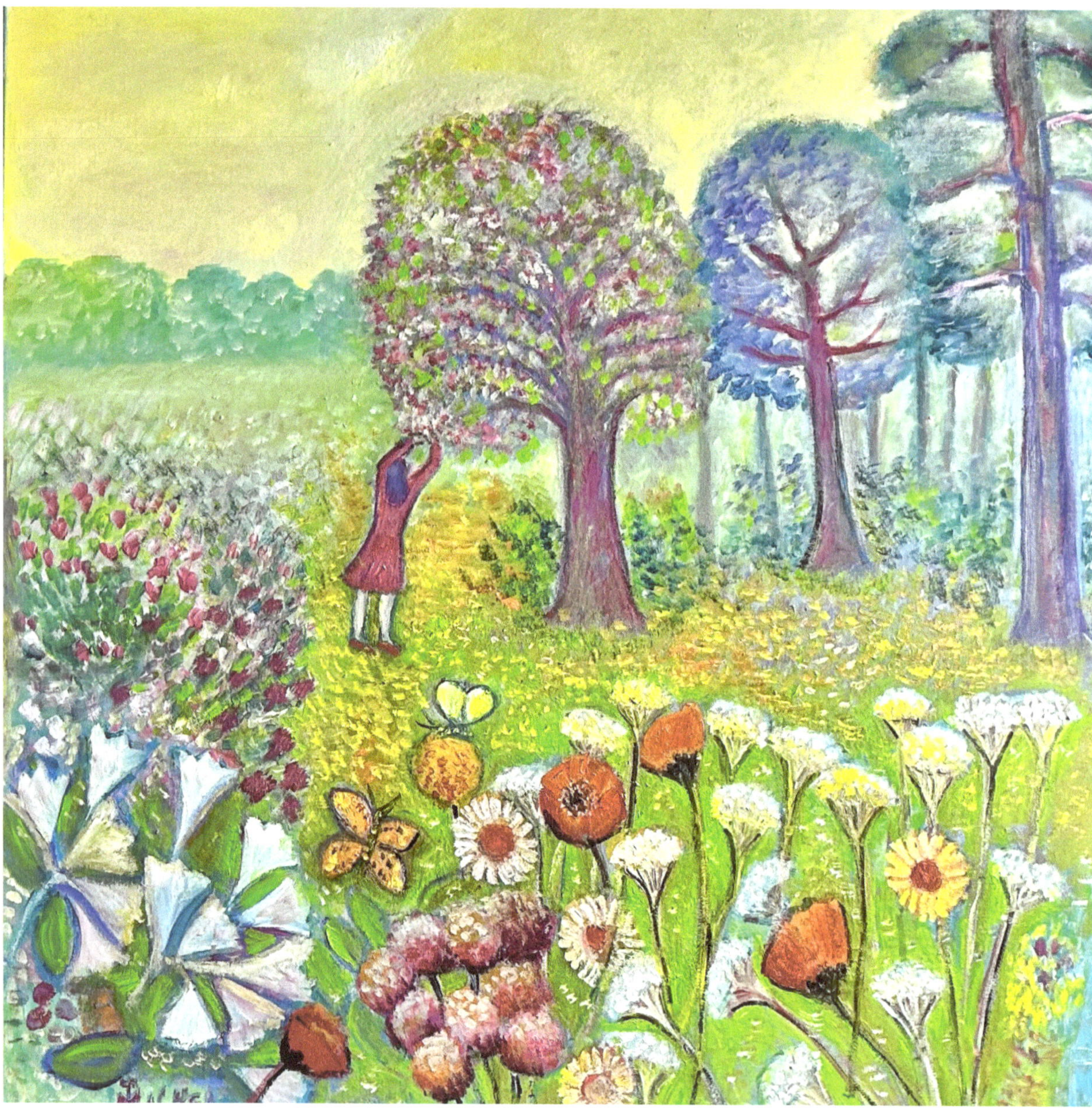

Sommer.2025.Öl auf Leinwand 100/100.

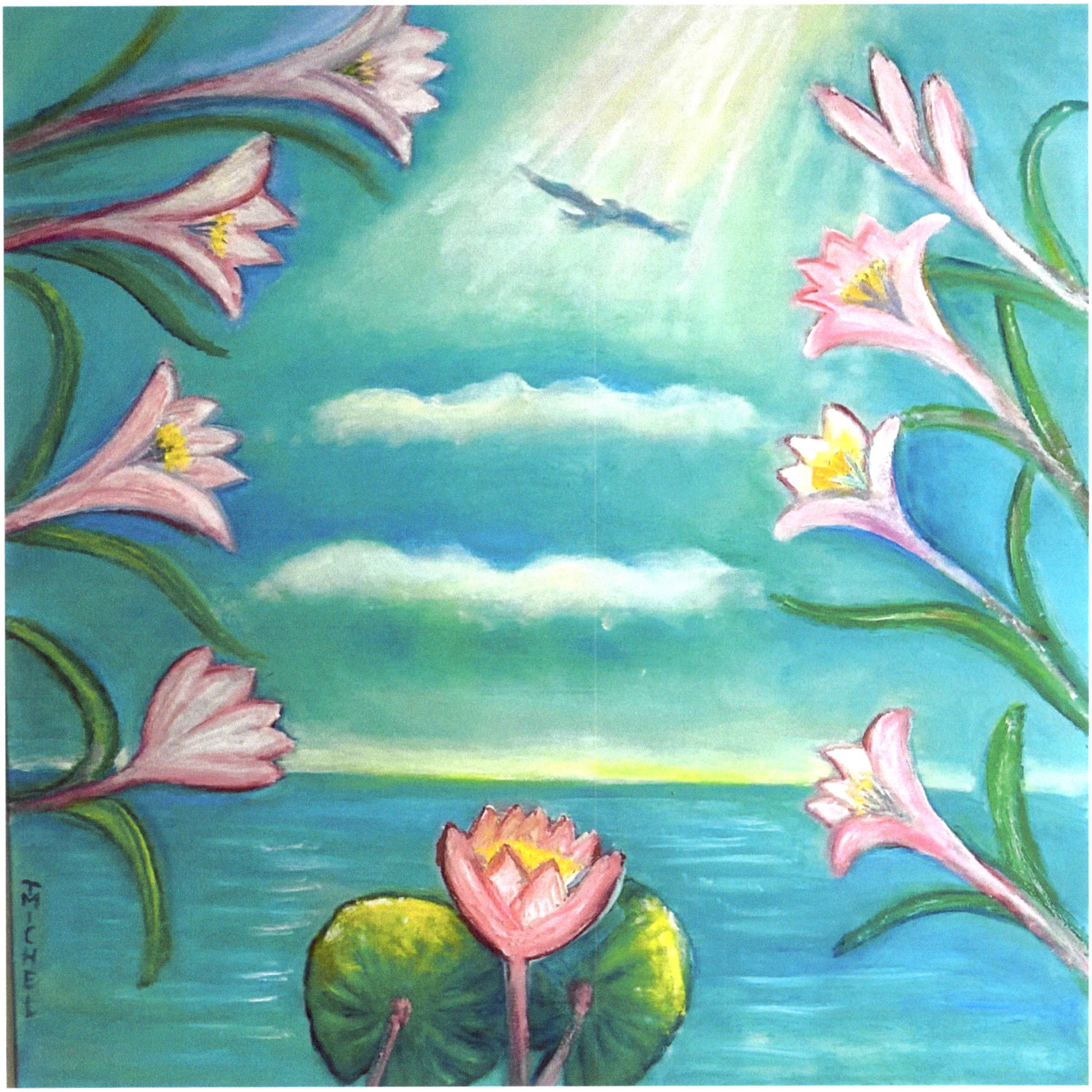

Zurück.2025.Öl auf Leinwand.100/100.

TATYANA PALCHUK

www.tpalchuk.eu

Tatyana Palchuk was born on December 6, 1954, in Riga, Latvia, EU (then part of the Latvian SSR (Soviet Union). Her father was a Soviet soldier who died shortly after World War II, and she was raised by her mother under modest circumstances. Despite financial hardship, her mother encouraged cultural pursuits—Tatyana studied piano and fostered an early love of artistic expression where music notably influenced her later visual art. Education 1967–1973: Attended J?nis Rozent?ls Art High School in Riga, completing a college-level preparatory program for artists. 1975–1981: Studied painting at the Latvian Academy of Arts, earning her first Master of Fine Arts degree (first in class). 1984–1987: Completed postgraduate (aspirantura-masterclass) studies at the USSR Academy of Arts, under academician Eduards Kalni?š. 2003: Awarded a second Master of Arts in Fine Art and Painting (Visual Arts) degree. Her teachers included prominent Latvian masters such as Imants Vecozols, P?teris Postažs, Boriss B?rzi?š, and Edgars Iltners, as well as Eduards Kalni?š, whose mentorship deeply influenced her academic realism and technical mastery Artistic Style & Themes. Palchuk's work is rooted in figurative realism with strong academic foundations. She draws highly on the aesthetic traditions of the Italian Renaissance, Northern Renaissance, and 15th?century French illuminated manuscripts, often invoking a poetic fusion of classical form and spiritual symbolism. Her paintings—often in oil on linen—feature still lifes, musical motifs, birds, and evocative natural elements such as light, skies, and rain. Her compositions are meticulously detailed: one can discover miniature ants crawling over shells, flying grapes, or chiaroscuro interplay between organic and man?made objects—creating surreal yet harmonious tableaux. She describes her process as carefully pre?planned and spiritual, aiming for symbolism rather than mere decoration, with color and composition in service of emotional nuance and timeless resonance. Palchuk has held over 13 solo exhibitions and participated in numerous group shows across multiple countries, including Italy, Spain, Belgium, Germany, the United States, Taiwan, the Czech Republic, among others.She participate in the 58th Venice Biennale (2019) under Musa International and was awarded the Woman Art Award in Venice. Recognized repeatedly in the annual international publication Inspiration Art Book (UK/USA) and received international honors including the Diego Velázquez International Art Award, "Knight of Art", and others from Italian and Spanish foundations during 2016–2018.

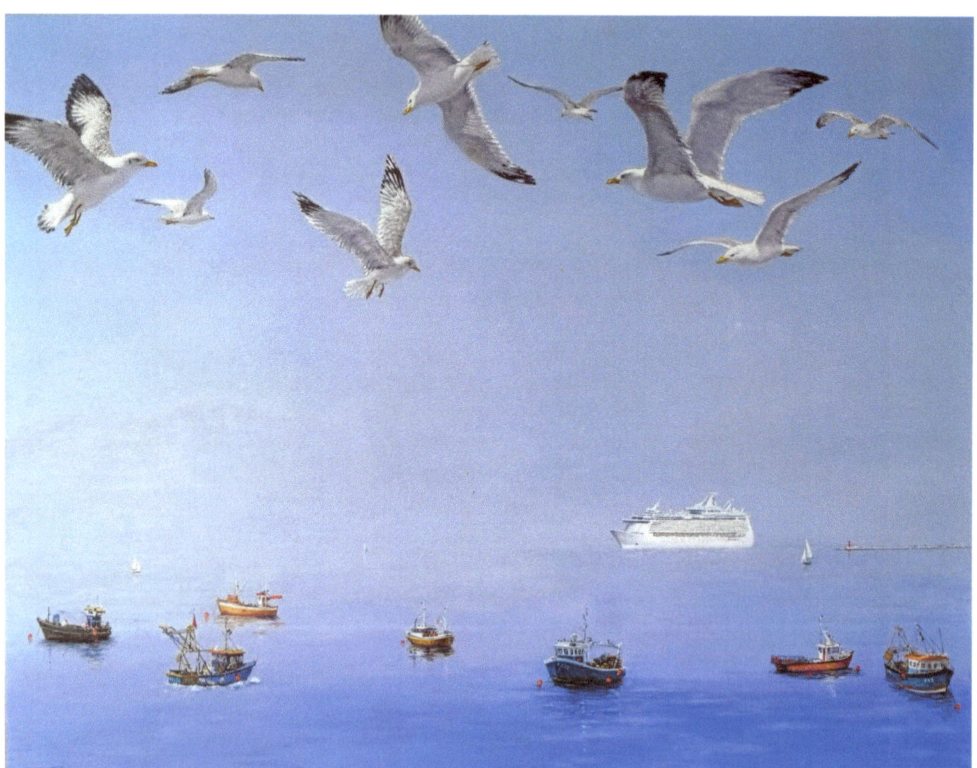

Morning at the the Harbor , 2025. 120x90cm

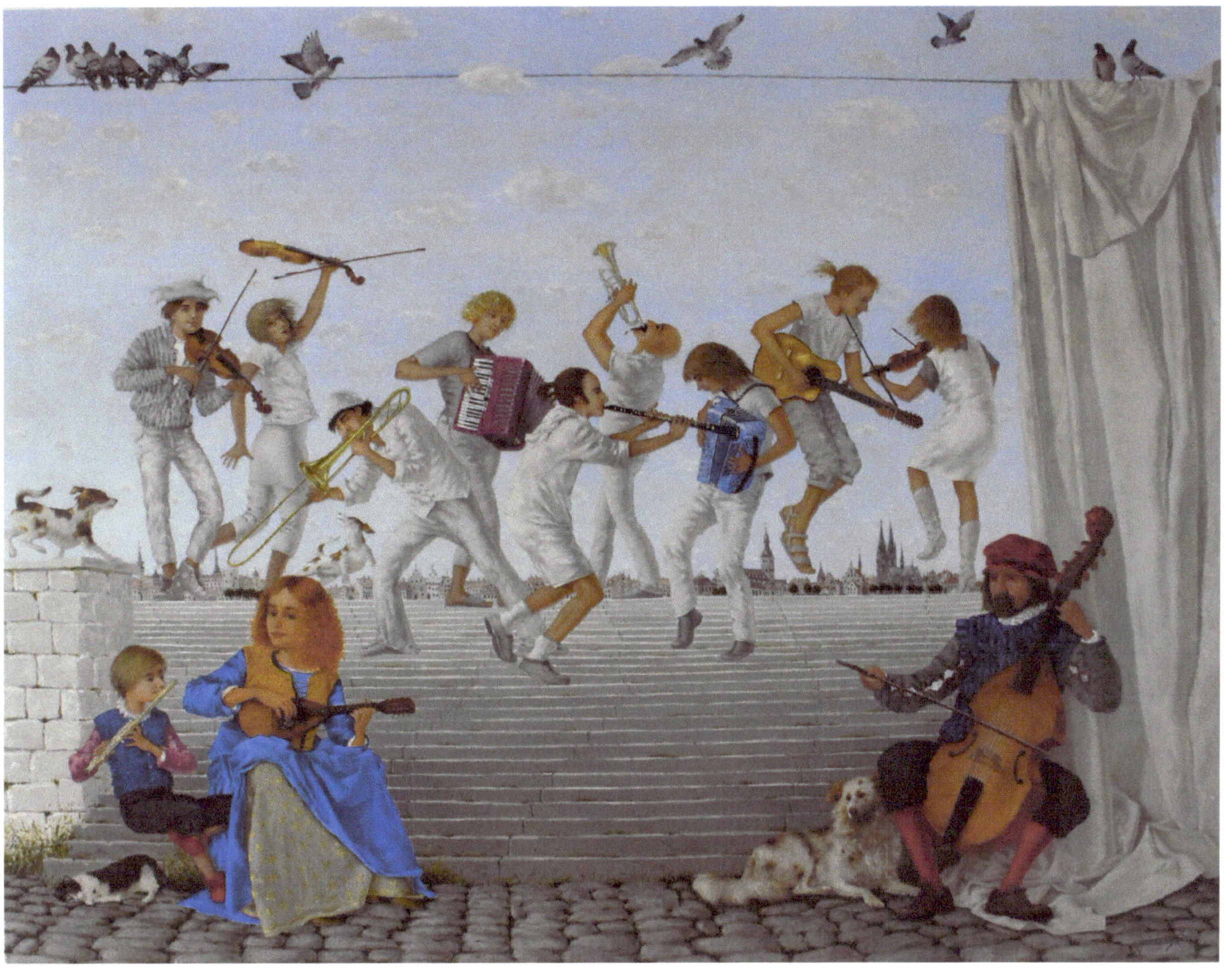

Anthem of Joy *(Allusions to Bethowens music) 95 x 120 cm,2019.oil on linen*

TOM ASHBOURNE SSC SCA OSA

TomAshbourne.com

After intentionally transitioning from corporate executive to sculptor, I'm filled with joy when my artworks resonate with esteemed jurors, discerning patrons, fellow art lovers, and my peers. My love for art and experiences as a collector evolved my artistic eye, deepened my sense of balance and appreciation for texture, shapes, and colour. I naturally think in 3D, a rare but essential gift. I channel strengths that defined my corporate success into my creative process: analytic skills, lateral thinking, attentive listening, and openness to possibilities about how things can coexist or connect in unexpected ways. Great art stirs emotion, it draws you in and makes a personal connection. My goal with every piece is to communicate positive energy and encourage this intimate connection. My love for art and experiences as a collector have evolved my artistic eye, deepened my sense of balance, and appreciation for texture, shapes, and colour. I naturally think in 3D, a rare but essential gift. I channel strengths that once defined my success as a corporate executive into my creative process: analytic skills, lateral thinking, attentive listening, and openness to the possibilities about how things can coexist and connect in unexpected ways. Great art stirs emotion—it draws them in and encourages a personal connection. Through my sculptures and sculptural photography I strive to engage the viewer's emotional energy, creating an intimate connection.

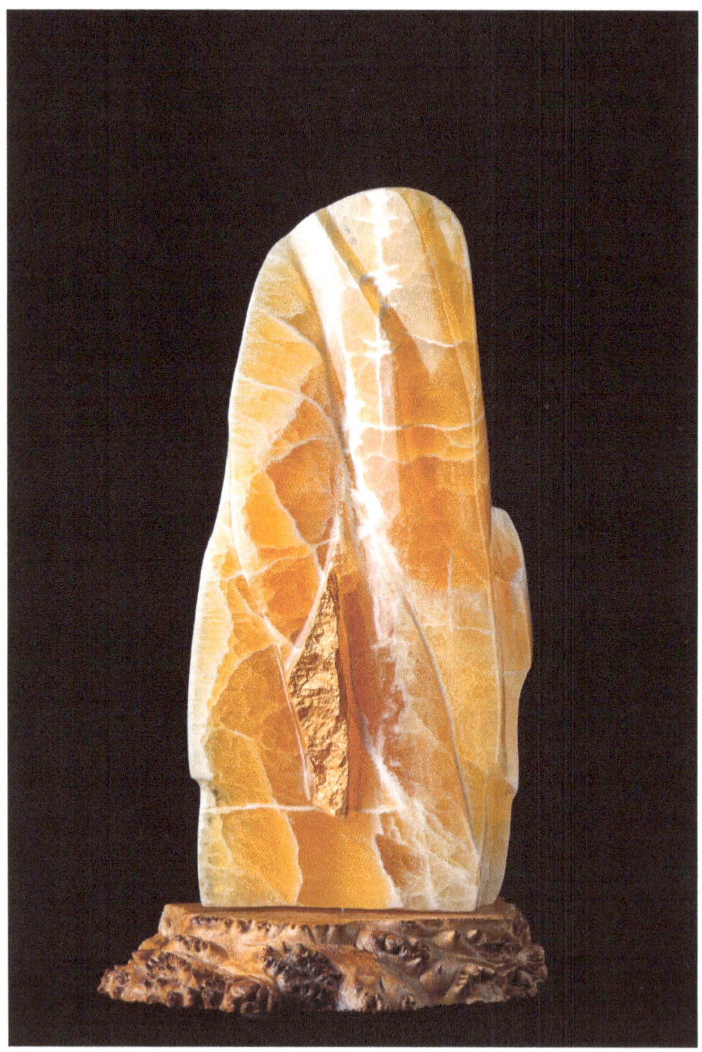

Candle in the Window (2024)

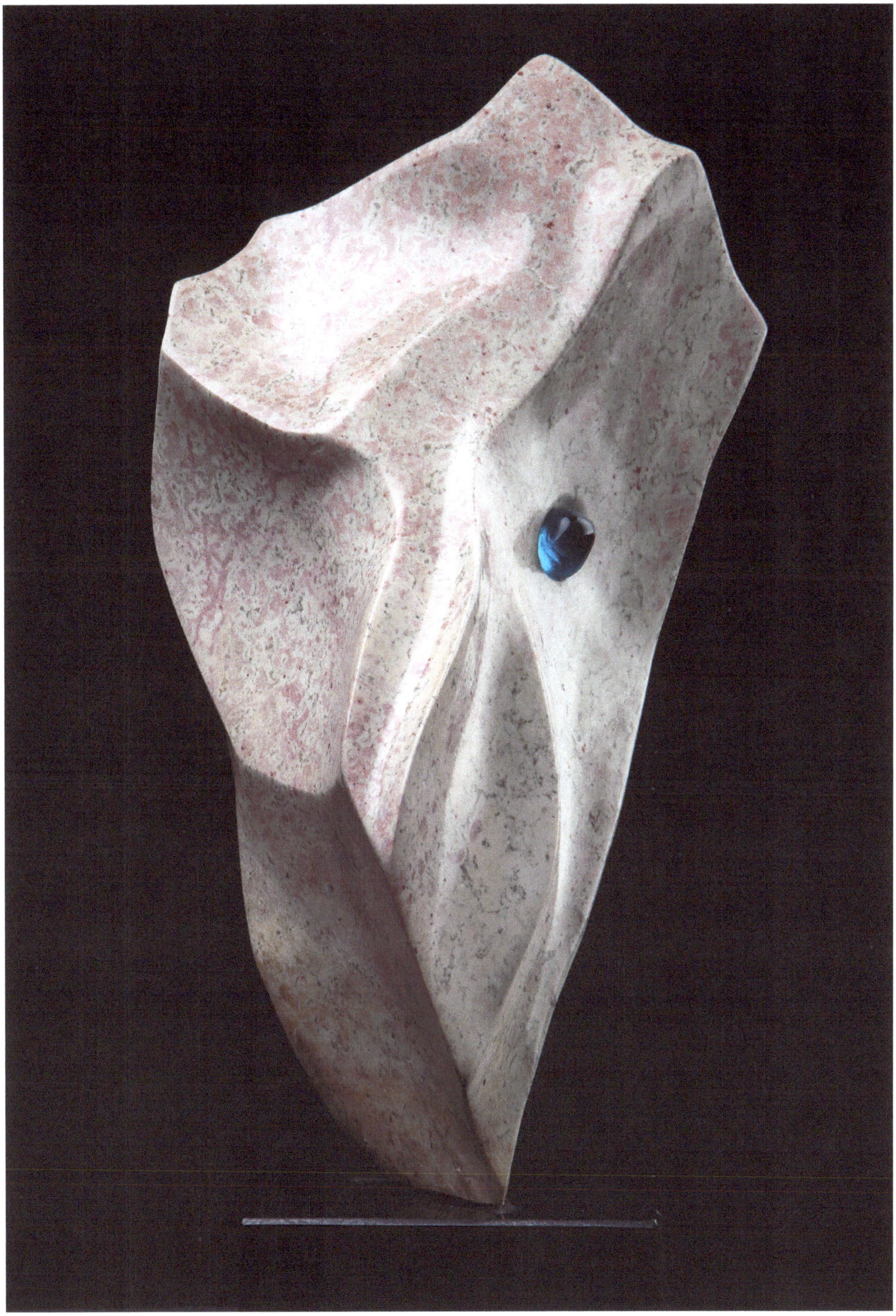

Blue Eyed Girl Too (2023)

TOTI CUESTA

https://www.toticuesta.com

Toti Cuesta is an award-winning Spanish artist whose journey from law and languages to art is one of self-discovery and liberation. Though intellectual pursuits defined her early career, she ultimately found her true calling in watercolor portraiture. Embracing art as more than a passion, Cuesta embarked on a path of introspection that allowed her to break free from the expectations others had set for her. Her training as an Art Therapist underscores her belief in art's transformative power, a central theme in her work. Toti's pieces have garnered numerous international awards and have been exhibited globally, from New York to Venice, celebrating her distinct style that merges hyperrealism with symbolic surrealism. Her work is centered around the female figure, which she uses as a metaphor for life, creativity, and resilience. Her portraits combine elements of nature and human emotion, portraying women as embodiments of Mother Earth, harmonizing the natural and urban landscapes within each piece. Cuesta captures a deep emotional resonance that speaks to humanity's role in nurturing a just and compassionate world through her integration of vibrant colors, symbolic elements, and a balance of warm and cool tones. This thematic focus highlights her dedication to exploring identity, environmental consciousness, and the strength of the human spirit. What sets Toti Cuesta apart is her ability to blend hyperrealism with a surrealist aesthetic, crafting portraits that invite viewers to journey inward. Her work is not just about depicting beauty; it catalyzes self-reflection and collective empathy. Each portrait serves as a portal into the psyche, challenging traditional representations of femininity and inviting viewers to consider their place within the larger life ecosystem. Cuesta achieves a harmonious blend of emotional depth and visual splendor through her art, positioning her as a contemporary artist with a distinctive, thought-provoking vision.

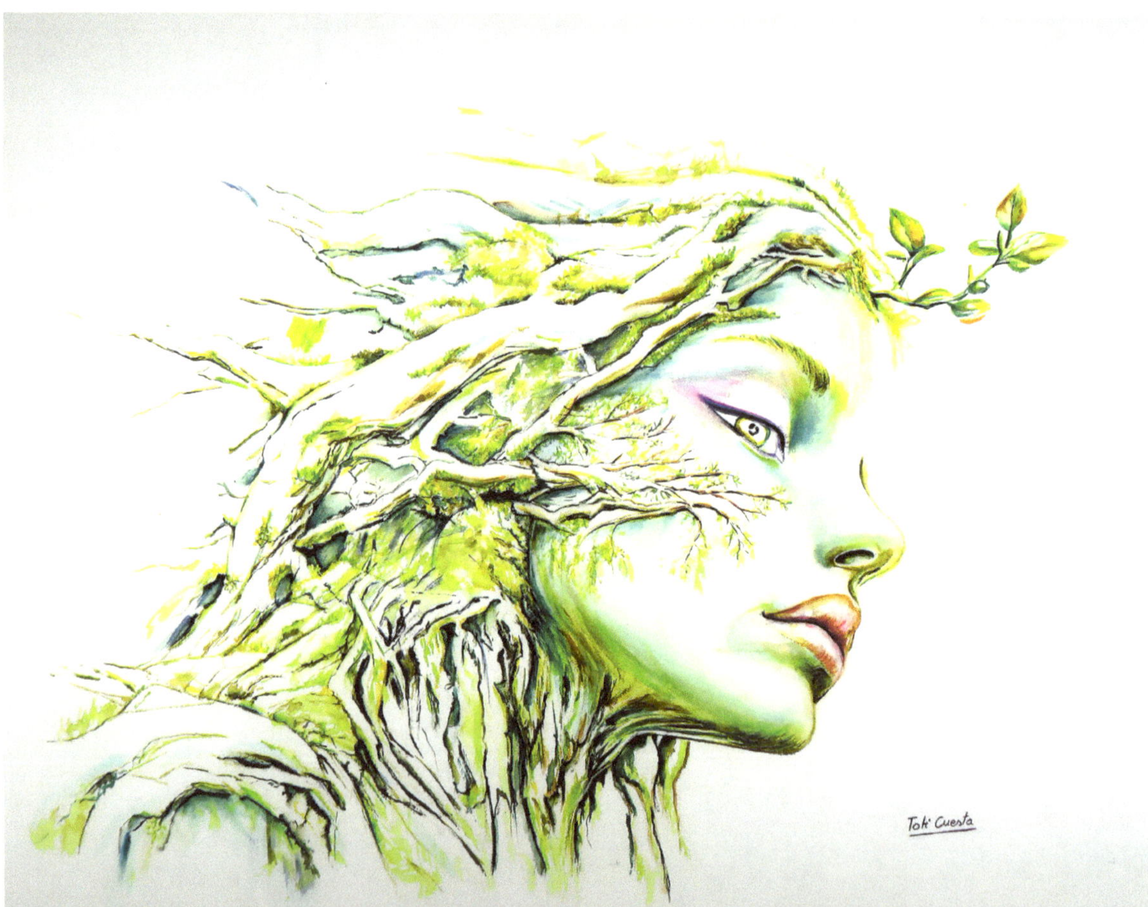

"The new Earth emerging", 2024, 56 x 76 cm

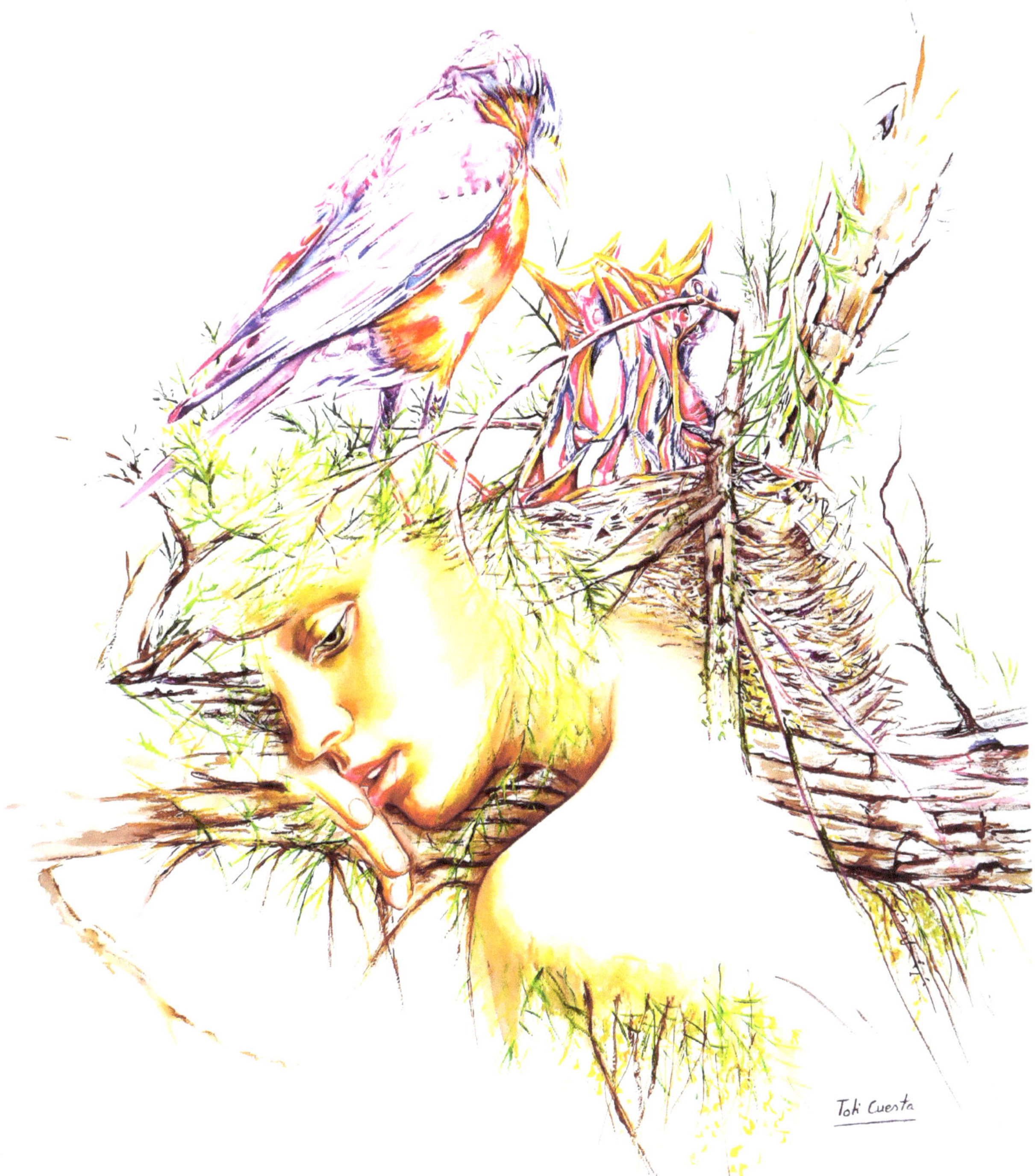

"Upholding Life", 2024, 76 x 56 cm

TRUDE KJØLEN

Www.trudekjolenart.com

Her name is Trude. She was born in Norway but lived in several countries. She has painted since she was 3 years old and went to art schools. She put her brushes on the shelf in 1994. She drew in secret. In 2022 she showed her paintings for the first time. In three years she has won several international awards and exhibited in museums and has had exhibitions in many countries. She especially thanks her son, who made her paint again and show her paintings in 2022. She says painting has been one of her greatest supports and loves in life.

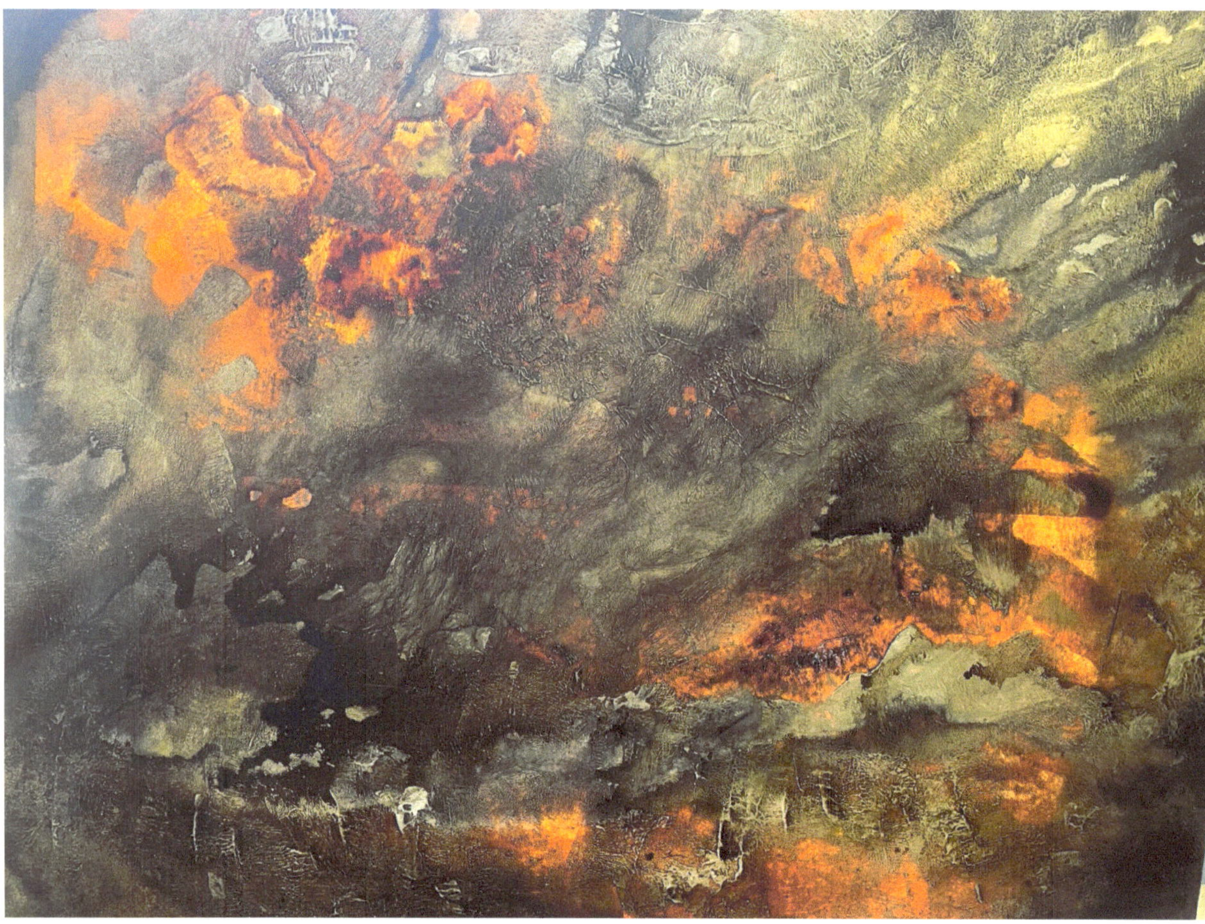

Volcano 2025

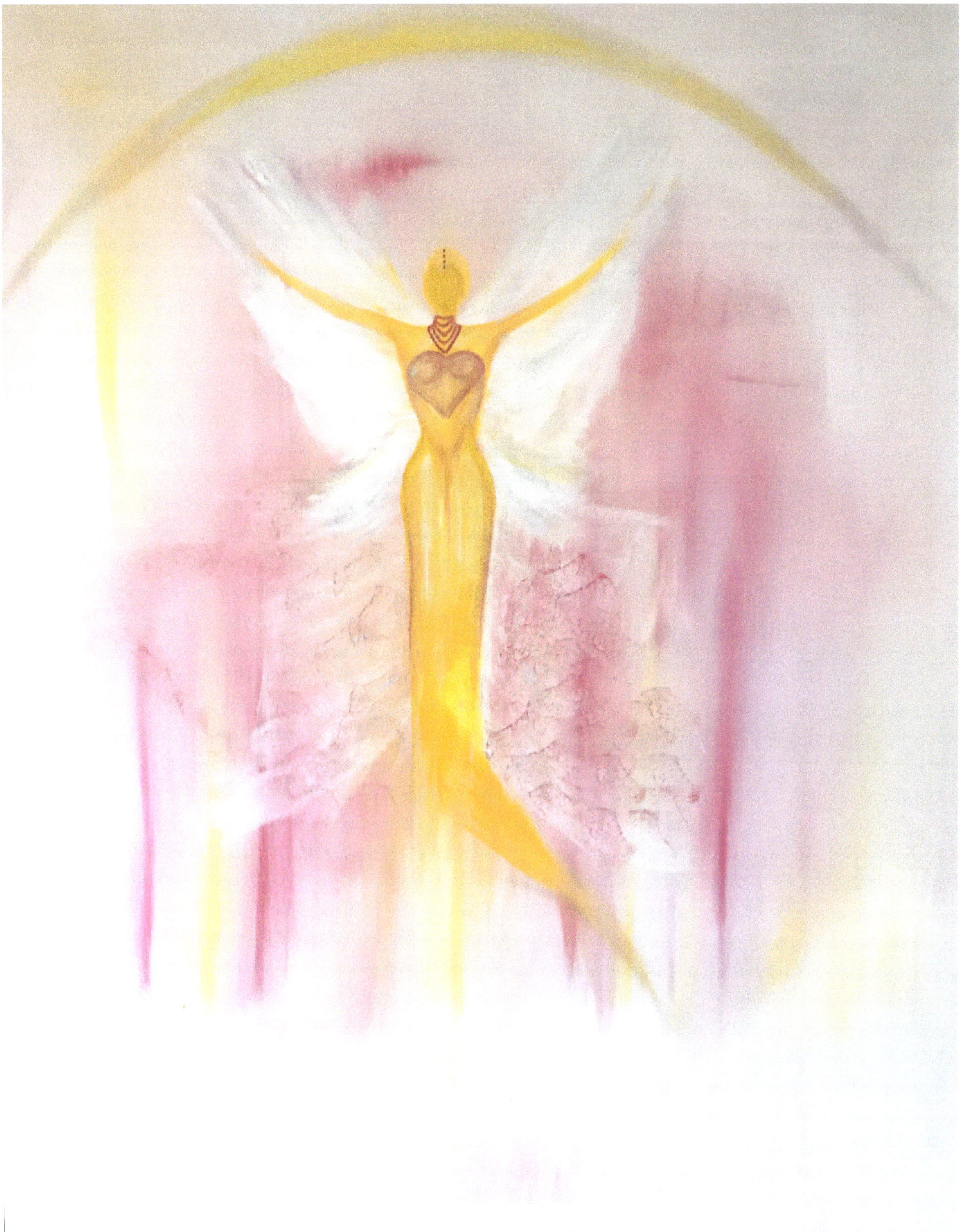

The Goddess of Love 2022

ULLA PLOUGMAND

www.ulla-art.com

ULLA is a Danish-born artist / painter, living and working in London, England. She grew up in the sprawling Danish countryside. Her father was a dedicated country GP, her mother a psychologist, and her upbringing was liberal, but caring. She later studied in Copenhagen. Her colourful and soulful canvases over the years can be found in a number of collections worldwide, public as well as private. Her style is perhaps overall best described as contemporary Impressionism - but broader. She has had a number of exhibitions - often solo - in several countries, mainly in England (London) and the USA. Several works have won prizes. ULLA has travelled the world widely and 'interpreted' her experiences afterwards on canvas. Wherever she went she sketched and took photos - often to never look at them again, it all went into her 'life's computer', as she calls it. Her work now spans three decades, and over the last few years has been increasingly philosophically inspired, often showing fond nostalgia. She may use trees and flowers as metaphors for people. She is showing her passion for a variety of subjects throughout: from her dreamscapes, the female form, the cosmos, and lately to her hope for a better and more peaceful world. She uses an abundance of colours - a result of having lived a colourful life - her 'Danish blues' are a recurring favourite. She relies almost entirely on her mind's eye when she works. As ULLA says, "I paint my life in colour".

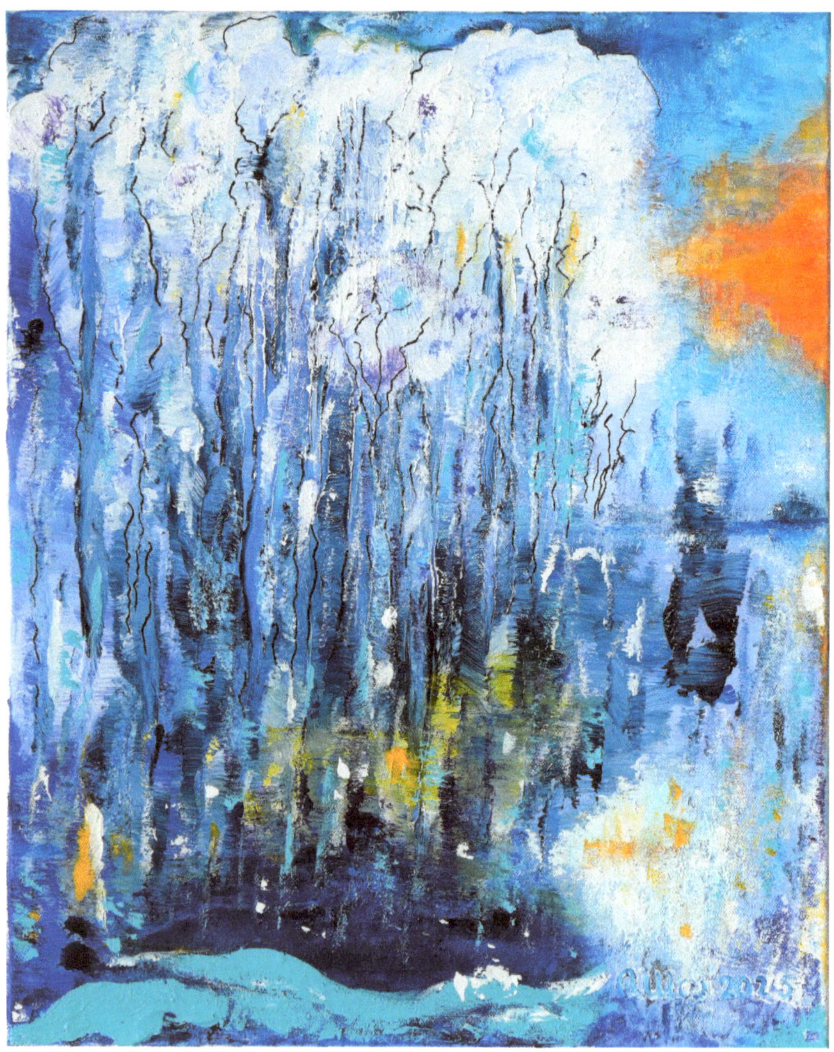

Nordic Nostalgia. 2025. Acrylic on canvas. 41 x 51 cm

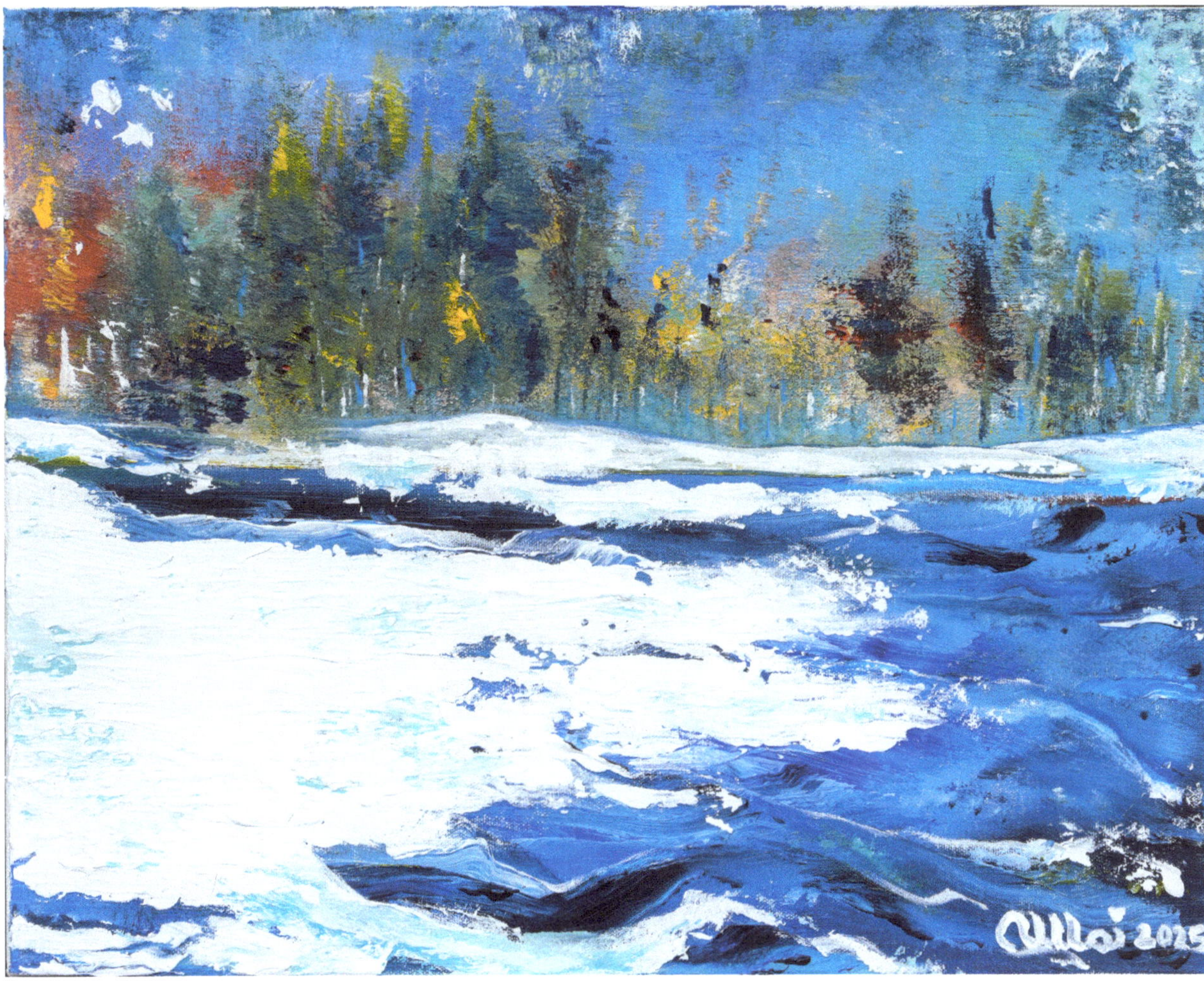

Memories of Scandinavia. 2025. Acrylic on canvas. 51 x 41 cm

URSA SCHOEPPER

https://www.virtuelledenkraeume.de

Ursa Schoepper first completed her studies in Natural Science with state examination. In addition she completed a study in cultural management, state examinaten, with a concentration in fine arts, new media. In her Agentur fu?r Virtuelle Denkraeume she was working as a cultural manager. In 2001 she was awarded the Media Promotion Prize of the German state of North Rhine-Westphalia for „Das Museum der abwesenden Bilder". Since 2003 Ursa Schöpper has been working primarily as a photographic artist. Her artwork has been exhibited internationally and she is the recipient of notable awards. Nothing is as it seems at first; everything is in process and thus in change. Experimental Photography in the Digital Age. Experimental Fine Art Photography a Metaphor of Change. A digital photography is a light image and a data image. As a result, it is material of different systems. It is a preliminary image, a foil of pictorial perception. A mirror is held up to our perception. This always means our perception is in process. In order to gain new perspectives, it sometimes helps to destroy familiar ways of seeing in the figurative sense, to think visually in processes, not in states. Destroying a photographic image by transformation, through a new algorithmic ordering structure, it is a new chance at a new seeing and visual order. An experimental photographic art documents possibilities in the process as an opportunity for innovation. What do we see outside of ourselves, what do we remember? An experimental digital photographic art is not dedicated to realistic reality. The result is a virtual reality, so in possibility existing. It is a transformation of real objects into abstract objects, into an abstract autonomous photographic artwork, in the best sense a visual disturbance, a shift, an unmasking and release of past visions and ways of seeing and viewing. The artistic work can also be called conceptual work with photographic material. It is the observation It is the observation of the environment by Ursa Schoepper and a chance to break up the routines of perception.

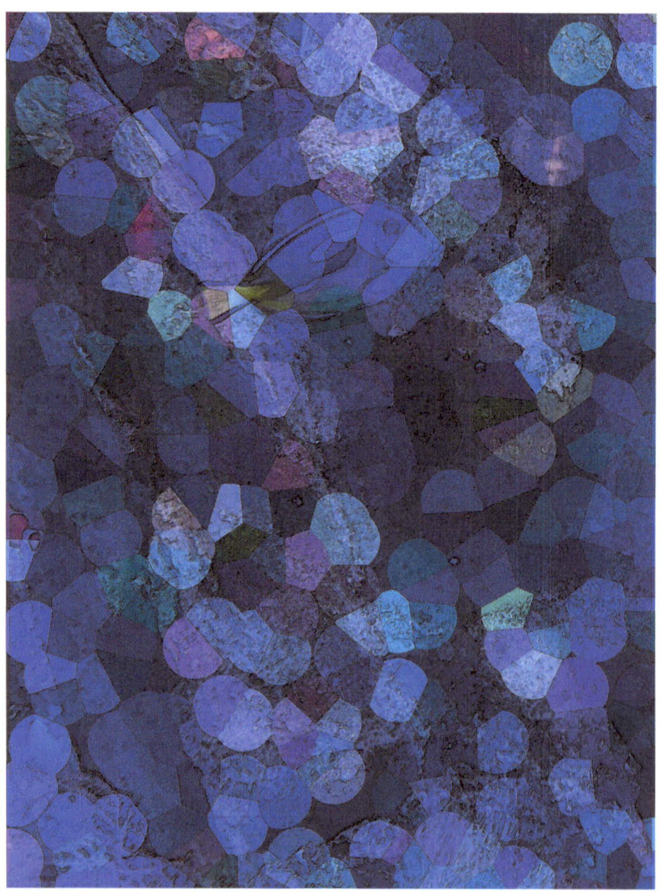

Ursa Schoepper, Pacific blue, 2025, experimental fine art photography Fuji Crystal matt auf Alu Dibond ultra HD framed with shadow gap, Art Box 75 x 55 cm, unique in this size and design signed on the back

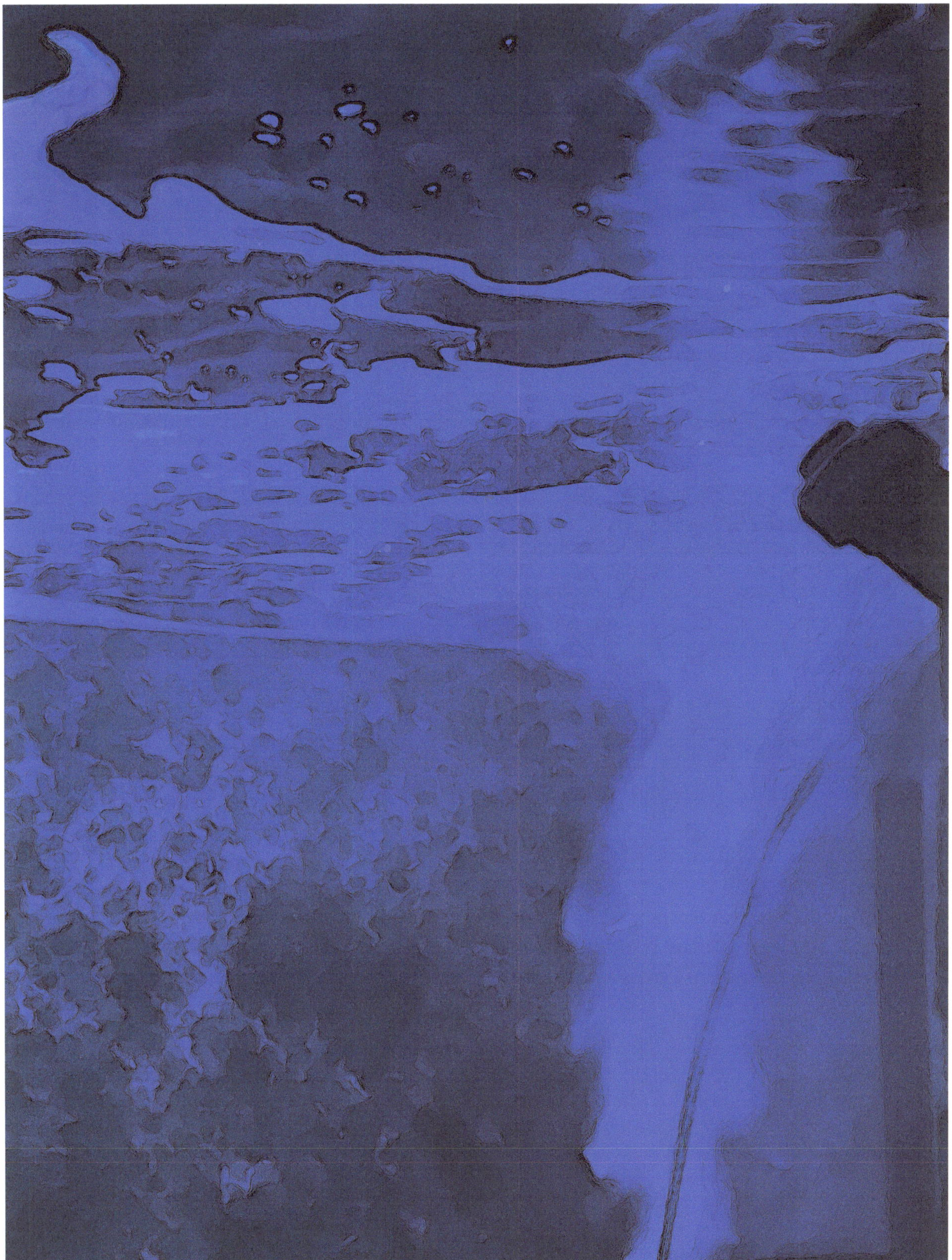

Ursa Schoepper, Current of Sea, 2025, experimental fine art photography Fuji Crystal matt auf Alu Dibond ultra HD framed with shadow gap, Art Box 75 x 55 cm, unique in this size and design signed on the back

VARDA BREGER

varda@vbreger.com

Varda Breger 2025 LEGEND "Civilization ignores the elegies of Mother EARTH" Varda Breger explores in her paintings and poems (in Hebrew and English) ecology and social life on our vulnerable planet. uses mixed media, including transparent and opaque elements, primarily on paper. Streams of spontaneous running paint cages a blurred deer, rudely trodden upon by her shoe or a car tire. An elephant with a broken task emerges from chaos. An abused nude body of a woman, her head hidden with a fig leaf, and a knife and fork beside her to remind us of murder in the family. The threat of nuclear weapons is always on her mind (MSc. Chemistry, Tel Aviv University & BSc., Technion, Israel). The atrocities and the cruel war in my own country, in Ukraine, and other places drive her to act for Peace with her tools. Inspired by the return of migrating birds at the revived Hula Lake, she wrote:

FOLLY WARS
Migratory birds,
from north to south and back,
season after season, millions of miles.
Fraternity of feathers caressing the planet.
No fuel, no flag, no borders, no Gods.
No Folly Wars.

Varda Breger statement: "I believe that all the planet's inhabitants are part of a chain, linked together, and We Humans must keep the future of our unique home-EARTH a planet of life." Varda Breger was born in Israel (1937), and lives and works in Tel Aviv. Married to Dov, three children,8 grandchildren,3 great-grandchildren After a career as a chemistry teacher, always painting, she turned completely to art and poetry. She has been a member of the European Artists and the Tel Aviv Artists and Sculptors Associations since 1986. She was elected to AFC- Artists for Conservation, ANF-Artists for Nature, the General Union of Writers and the Hebrew Writers Association in Israel, and the organization of Women Wage Peace.

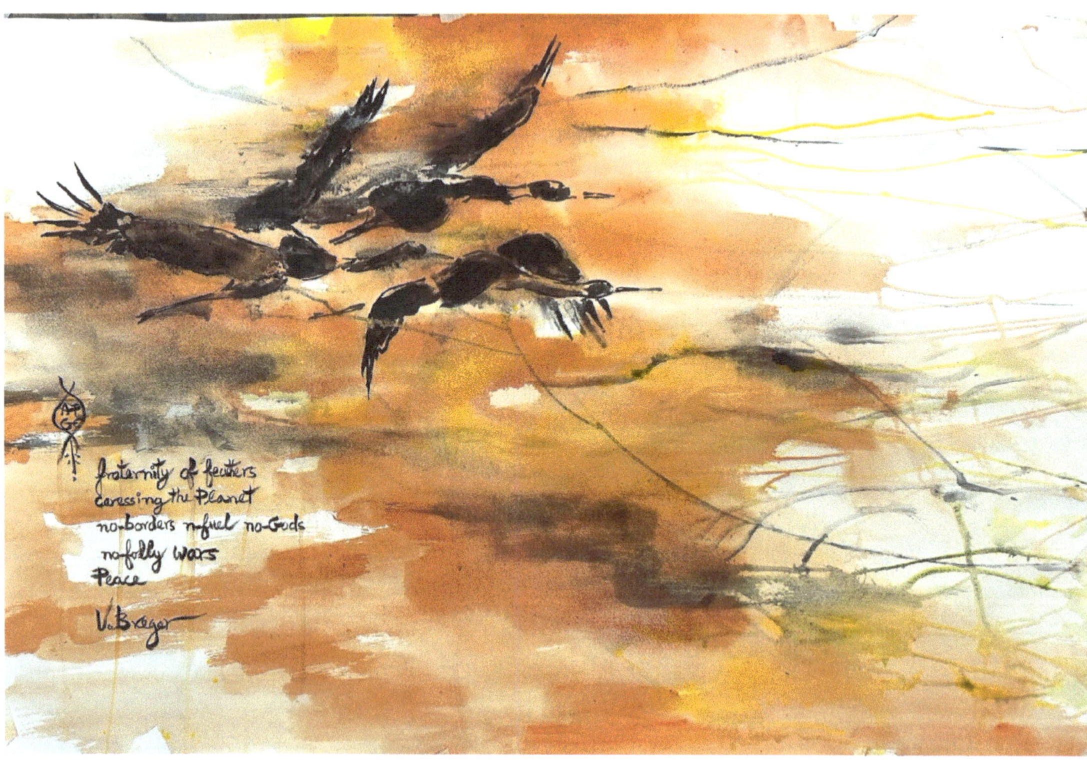

Migratory Birds, 2025.Acrylic on paper.70x100

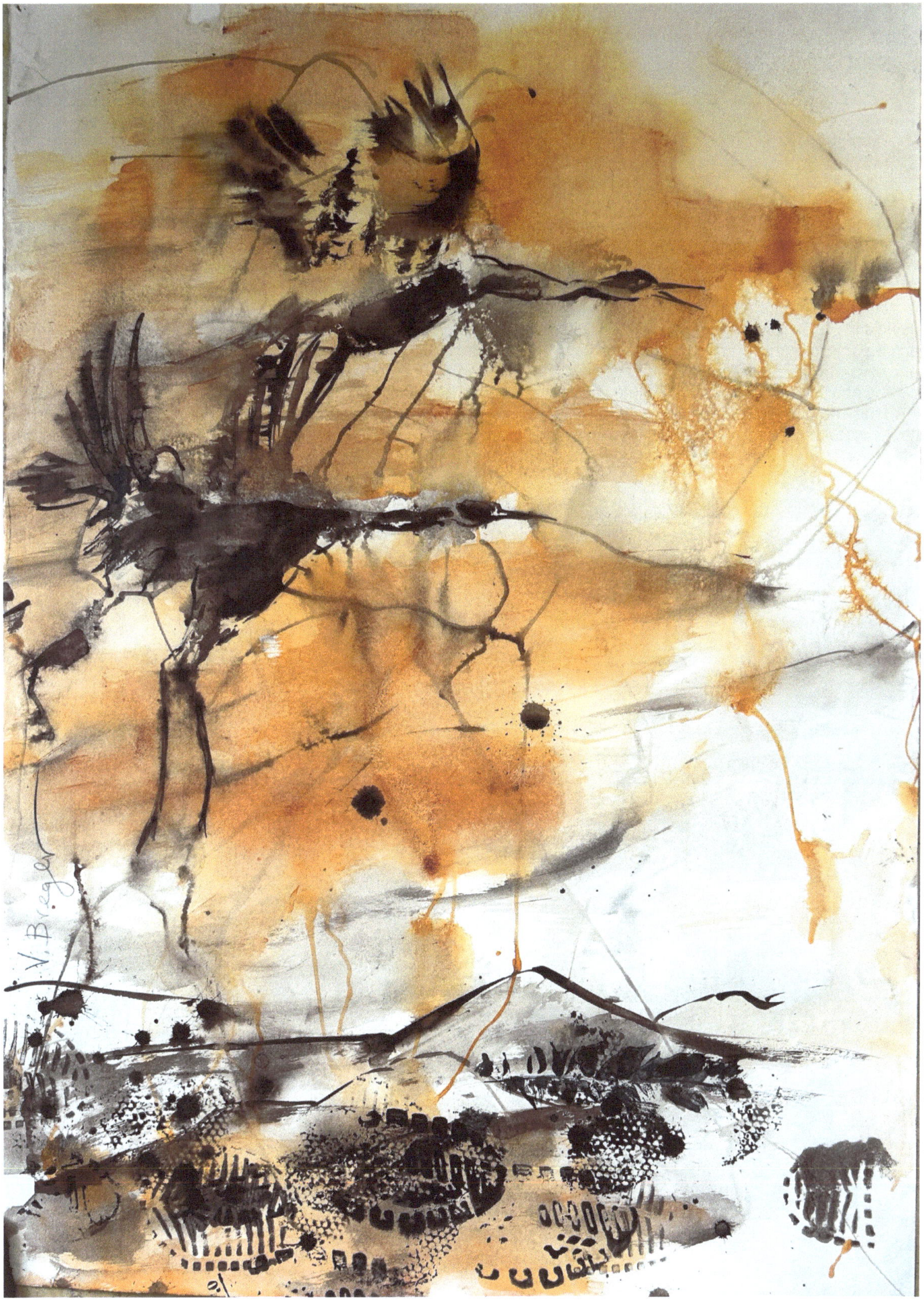

Sunset,2015.Mixed media on paper.100x70

VASCO DIOGO

www.vascodiogo.com

Vasco Diogo was born in Lisbon in 1970. He has a degree in Sociology by Universidade Nova de Lisboa, a Master Degree in Social Sciences by Universidade de Lisboa and a PhD in Communication Sciences by Universidade Nova de Lisboa, with the thesis: "Video: specificity, hybridity and experimentation" (scholarship by FCT, 2008). From 2008 to 2020 he was a professor at University of Beira Interior teaching mainly cinema directing, new cinemas and experimental cinema. After being co-founder of Projecto Teatral (a theatre/performance collective), works, since 1998 in performance, video art and experimental cinema exploring themes such as self-presentation, truth and manipulation. In experimental cinema he has won several international awards, specially with the films/videos: "anexperimentalviralvlog - the movie remix # !", "may I dance?", "may I ? remix#" and "Bakalu Studio Composition". From 2020 till now Vasco Diogo has directed several experimental animation films, namely the Paint On Paint series and the Anima series. He has also directed several mobile phone films such as Mixed Movie and Old New Age. More recently Vasco Diogo has also produced and directed some AI driven experimental films. Vasco Diogo is currently working on a spoken word and electronic project, a short archive and found-footage documentary and several video-performances where he is also the performer. Vasco Diogo other areas of interest and work include drawing and painting and also mixed-media projects. Vasco Diogo is know for crossing boundaries and limits in a quest for experimental freedom where the specificity of each medium is still the main driving force for his work. Co-creation with technology and the process as themes are permanent concerns in his art as well as self-knowledge and spiritual awareness in a post-human age.

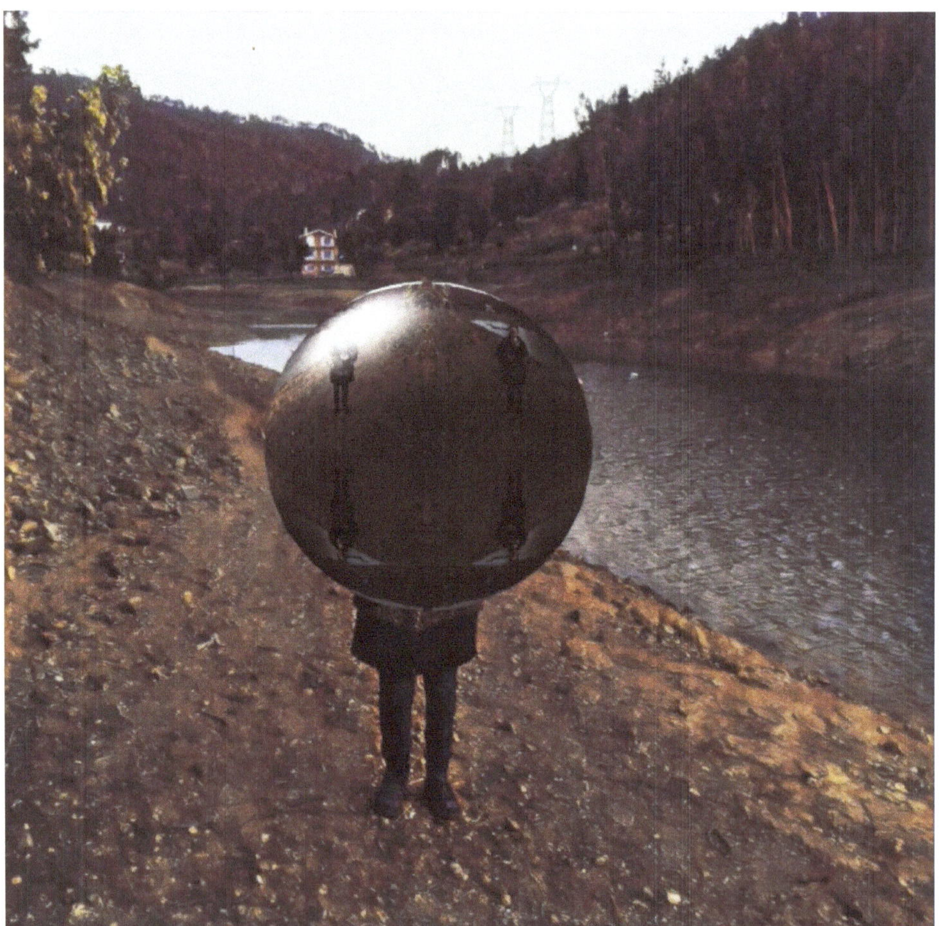

Super Cut Free Way, 2018, video art, mobile experimental cinema

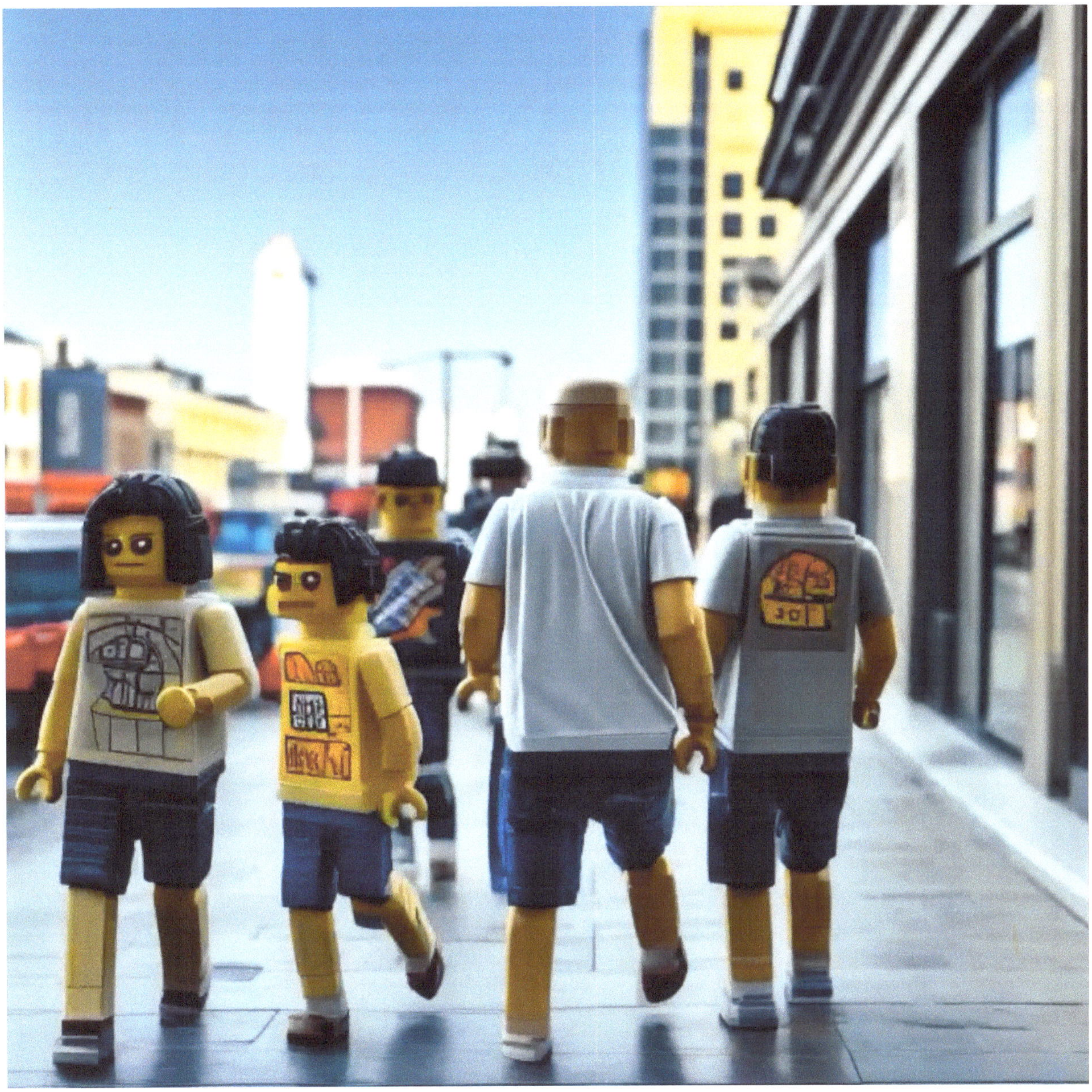

Missing Meaning, 2024, video art, experimental cinema, AI driven

WENDY COHEN

Instagram: wendycohen123

Wendy Cohen is a Sydney-based artist who holds a BFA and MFA degrees. She actively exhibits her works at NYC Art Expo, Art San Diego, Art Spectrum Miami and The Other Art Fair in Sydney. Wendy pushes boundaries with her innovative and inventive style, as she is drawn to the expressive qualities of abstraction, reshaping the indeterminate presence into futuristic shapes, defined by colours, lines and textured forms. She draws inspiration from natural and urban environments to communicate her oeuvre with a painterly abstracted language pulsating with colours and a sense of energy and fluidity. Her aim is to convey her visual poetry and harmonious rhythm to the paintbrush, developing playful imagery with an emotive and inventive sensibility. Freedom of expression reflects her intuition and imagination, unencumbered by conventional rules. As a result, her paintings dance with luminous colours, movement and emotion to transform the canvas into visual symphonies of mark-making, textured gestural brushstrokes and the alchemy of the colour palette. Observation, intuition, and imagination are key to her process as she responds to the interconnectedness of the world

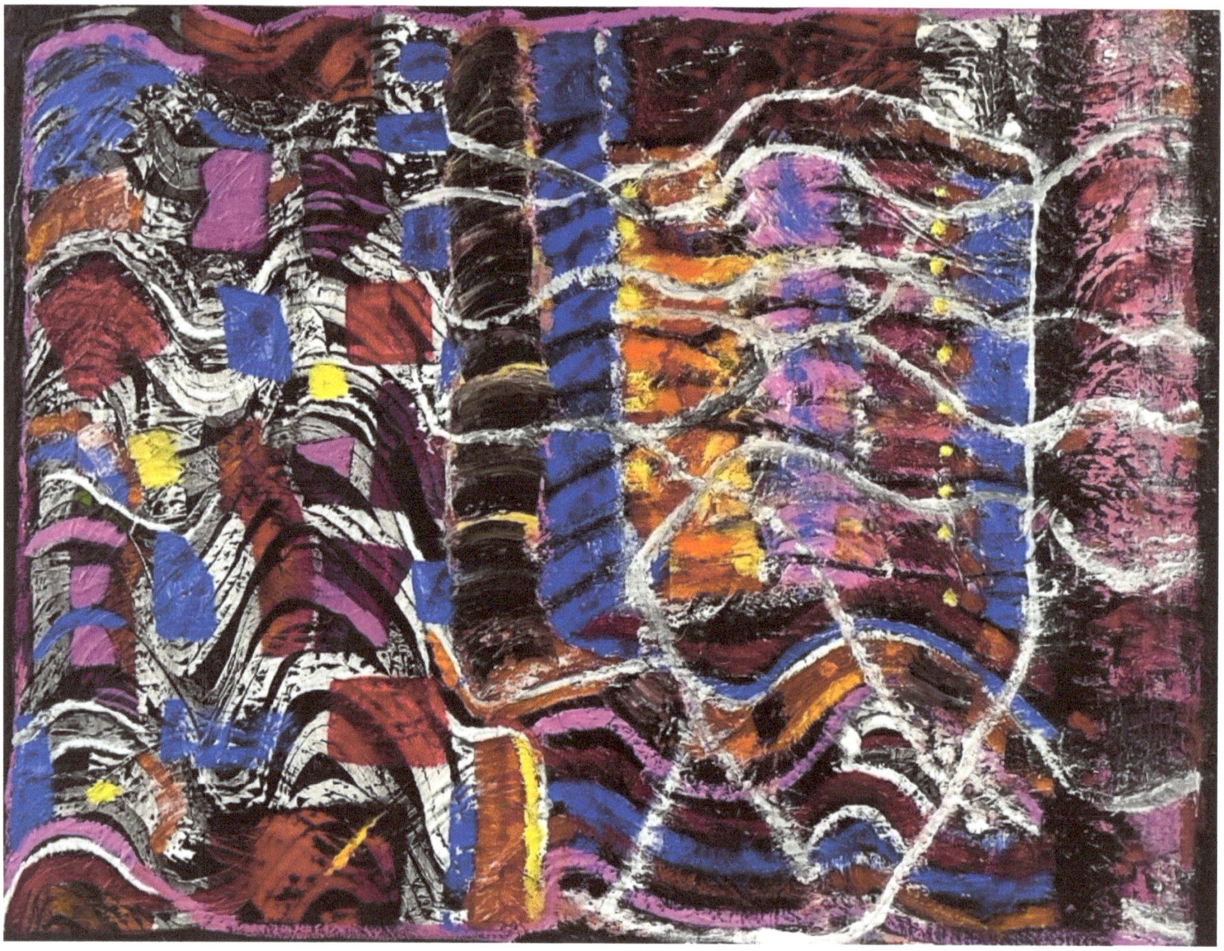

Waves of Colour Waves, 2025

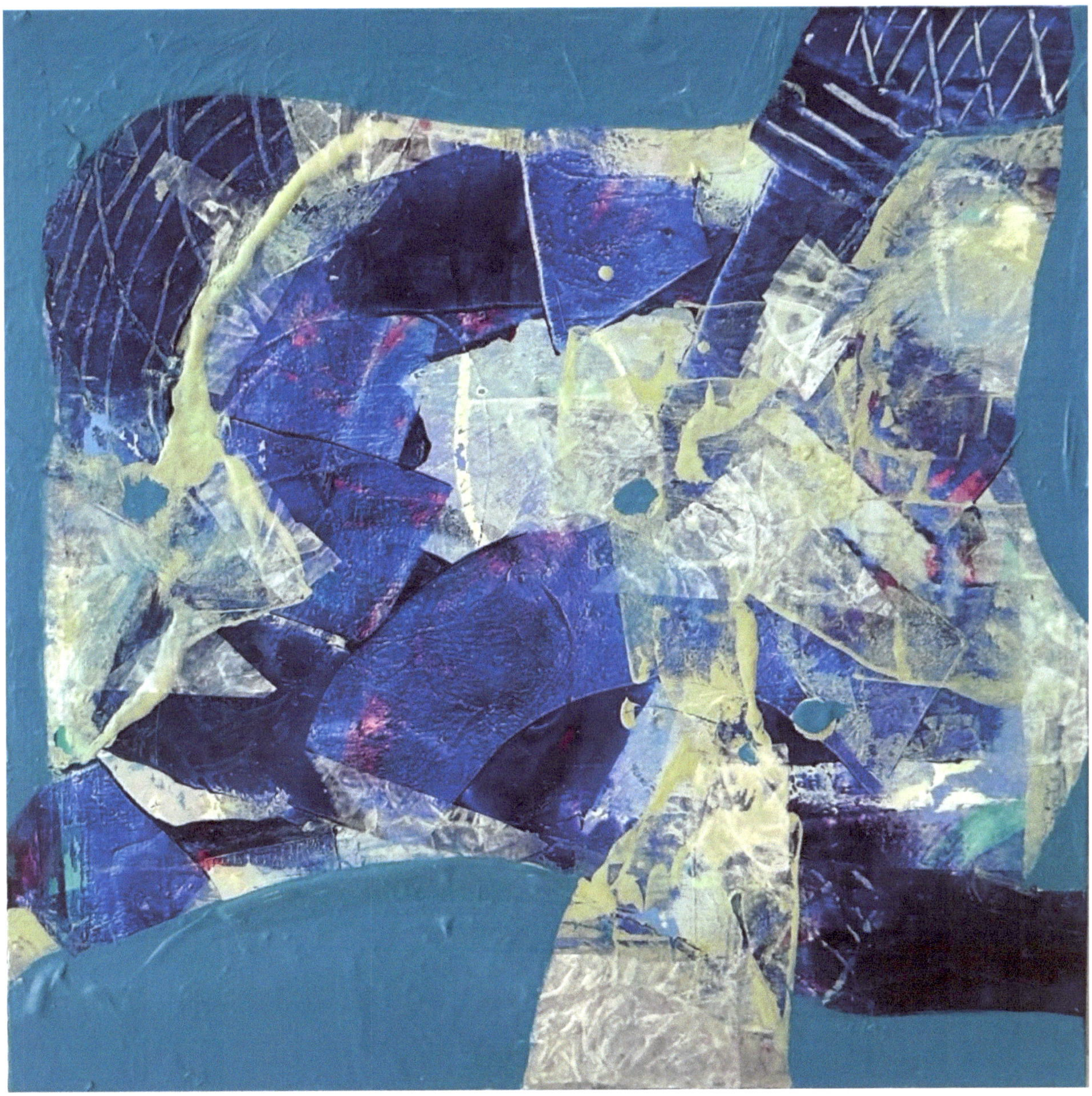

Sonic Blue Hue Waves, 2023

WINSTON TRAGICO

WWW.WINSTON-TRAGICO-ATELIER.DE

Winston Tragico, born in 1959 in Cebu City, Philipines,currently resides in Bad Sachsa, Germany. He studied art at the former East Visayan School of Arts and Trades in Dumaguete City, Philippines, now known as Negros Oriental State University. Tragico has held solo exhibitions in the USA and Germany, and has participated in group exhibitions in France, Great Britain, Germany, and Austria. Notable among these are significant shows at the Carrousel du Louvre in Paris, and with the GAA Global Art Agency at the Oxford International Art Fair Oxford Town Hall, Great Britain. His works are featured in numerous private and public collections worldwide. Tragico has been honored with the International Raffaello Prize in Bologna, Italy. The Premier Artist Prize 2025 in Barcelona,Spain.

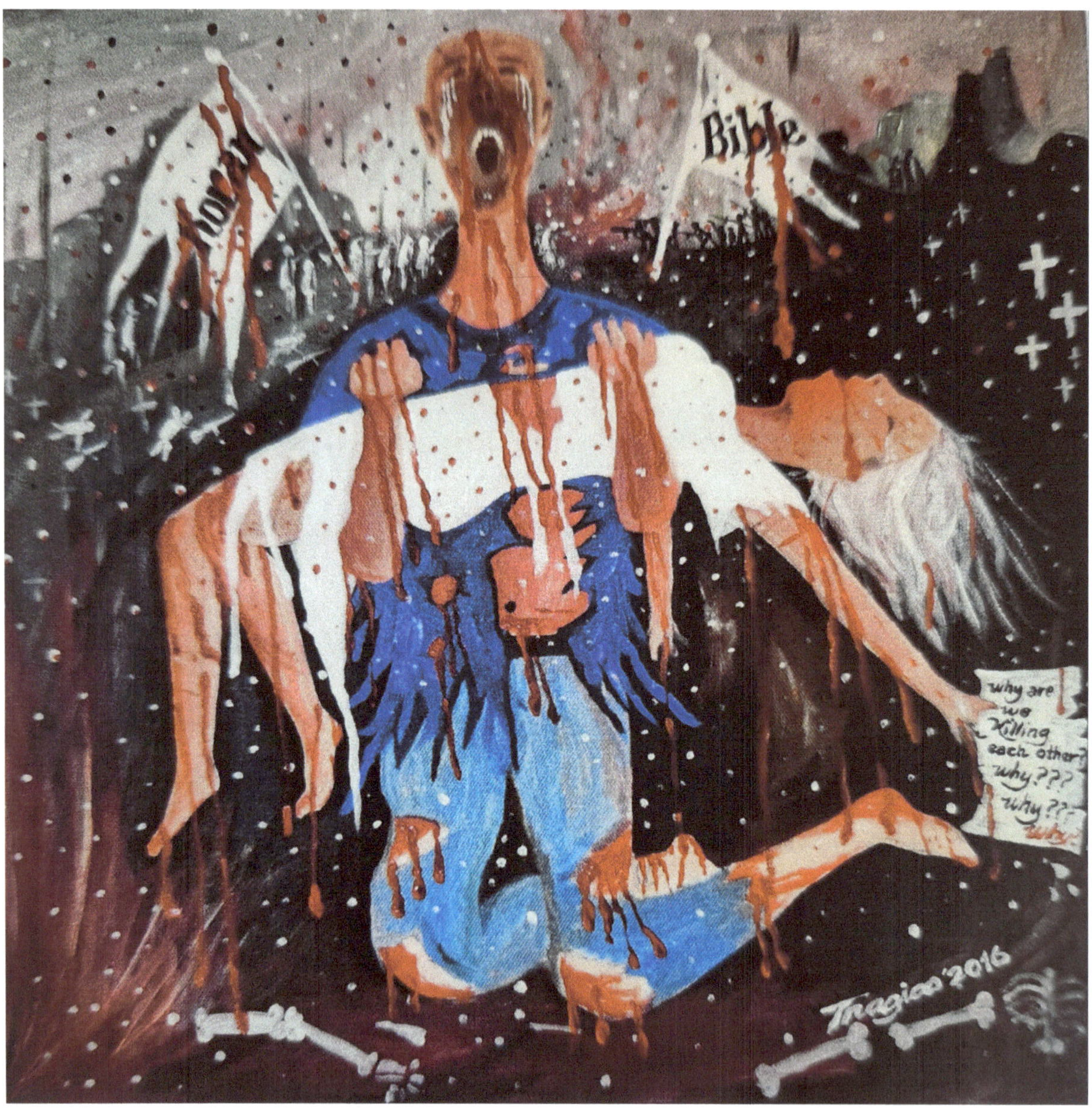

Why? 2016, Acrylic on Canvas, 80 x 80 cm.

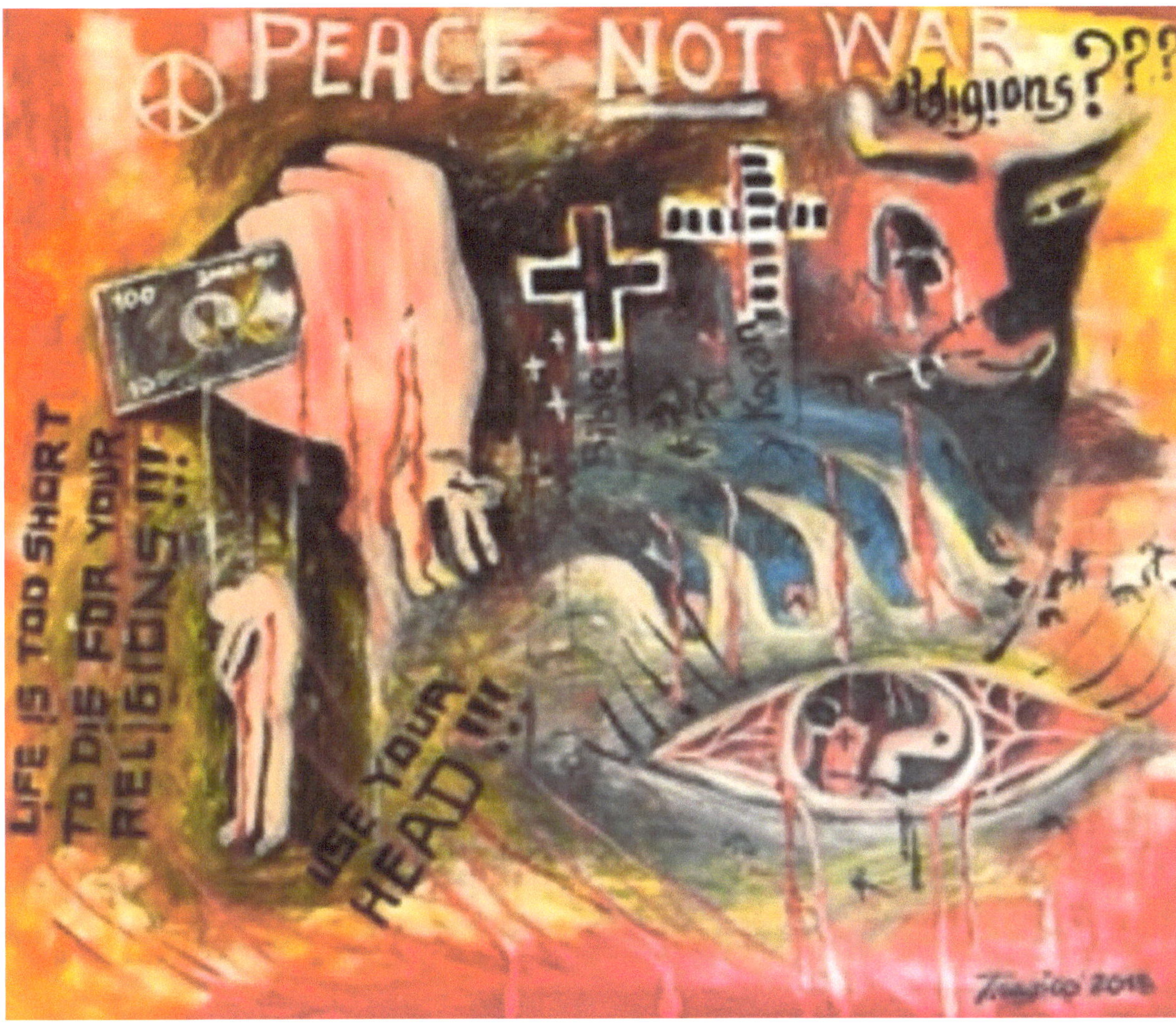

Peace not War , 2016, Acrylic on Canvas, 100 x 120 cm

YVONNE WELMAN

www.yvonne-welman.com

Statement "My work is a personal reaction to social issues." My sense and purpose in life are my paintings. I use them to make people more open minded about social and philosophical issues, to see if they agree or not. Beauty and traditional painting can attract and give more willingness to at least try to understand. Color, composition, materials, icons are used to reach my goal. She wants people to understand that we need a world with high moral standards and to show compassion! Learn from history. She is often indignant about what is happening in society. Yvonne Welman Biography After her education at the academy of arts Tilburg (NL). She worked as a teacher in arts and art history. To improve her qualities as a painter she took lessons in 16e and 17e centuries oil painting techniques. The artist works with open acrylics in a layering technique. She often integrates textile fabrics and other materials from her personal history. Her work has to be realistic, because she creates multifaceted and engaging paintings, that tell visual stories about her experiences and ideas. The stories cover gender equality, social issues, art history and personal issues. She does explore the Zeitgeist from a female view. Serendipity, time and technique each play their part during the process of creating the paintings. It takes a lot of time to create her work, which makes it possible to add a new idea during the process. This stands in strong contrast with all the superficial images that we are surrounded with most of the day. She creates a more complex strip story from all the images we see every day. Inspiration from artists like Breughel, Jeroen Bosch, Georgia O' Keefe, Camille Claudel, Neo Rauch, Lita Cabellut She received awards in France, Swiss, Germany, England, U.S.A. and the Netherland She is a member of the artists societies BOK . Waddinxveense KunstKring , Krimpener Kunstwaard all in the Netherlands, Manhattans art International on line Gallery. U.S.A.,Artboxy-projects Switzerland.

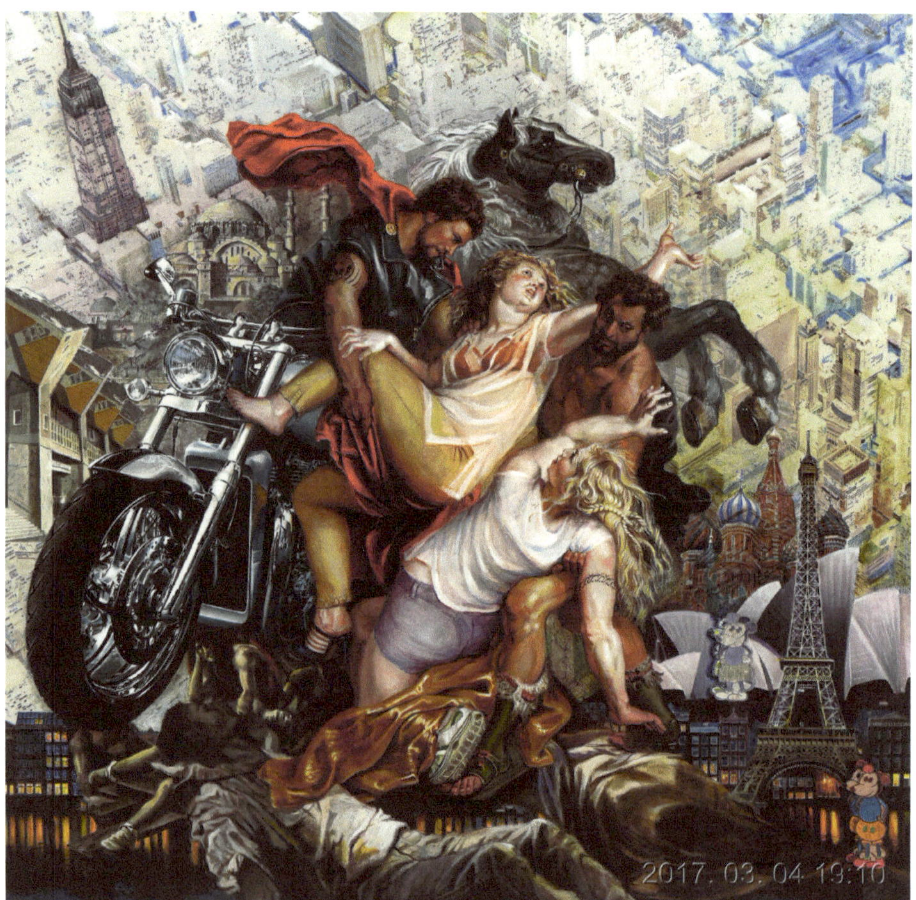

Since Leucippos people are damaged by lust of power 2016 mixed media on canvas 145 x 145 cm

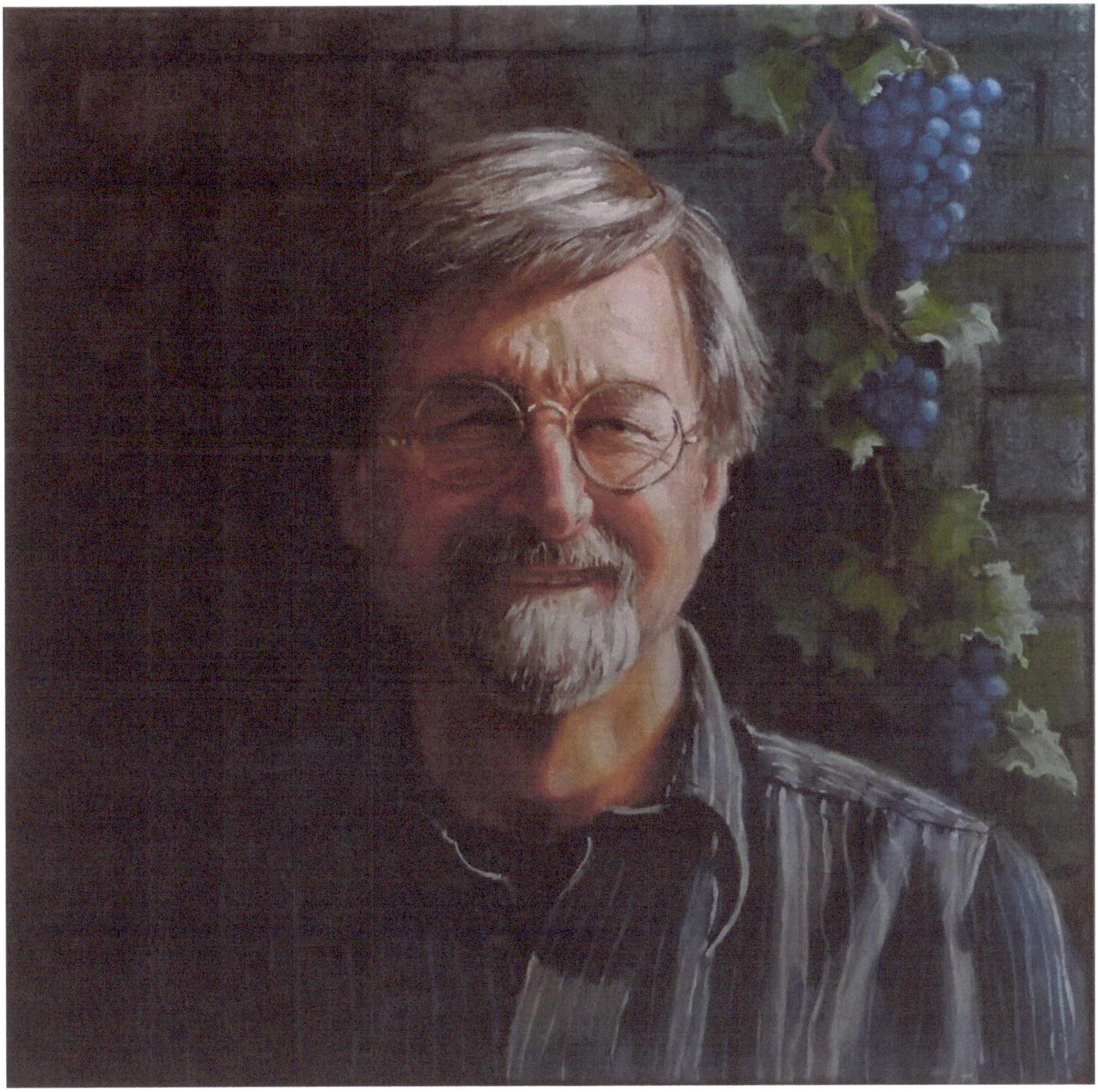

Hans 2024 open acrylic on canvas 60 x 70

婉凝 廖

societyofcanadianartists.com

Liao Wanneng's artistic resume and statement personal information Liao Wanning, female, born in China, is currently living in Toronto, Canada. She is a professional painter. She is a member of the Canadian Artists Association (SCA), the American Portrait Society and the American Oil Painters Association(OPA).American Artists Professional League Membership educational background In 1998, he graduated from the Oil Painting Department of Xi 'an Academy of Fine Arts, studying under famous teachers such as Guo Beiping. In 2000, he received a master's degree in oil painting from Xi' an Academy of Fine Arts, specializing in Impressionist art. Professional experience 1.Art creation and education 2001-2010: Art Director of Love, a large comprehensive magazine in China, planning art columns and special reports. 2007-2010: Signed Hong Kong, China Baoqu Tang Contemporary Art Museum, participated in the planning and exhibition planning work. In 2014, he founded "Wan Ning Art" art school, teaching adult and children's art education. In 2023, I settled in Toronto, Canada and devoted myself to painting. 2.Art creation and exhibition In 2019, he independently completed the oil portrait of 72 academicians of the Chinese Academy of Sciences, which was collected by Yan 'an Museum. 2017: Solo exhibition "Condensation: Portraits and Poems" at Flushing Library, New York. In 2015, I held a personal oil portrait exhibition "A Hundred Faces of All Creatures" in Xi 'an Old Steel Plant Creative Industrial Park. In 2023, his work "Daydream" was selected for the International Art Sand Exhibition in Paris, France. In 2024, the oil painting "Cloud Shoulder" won the Silver Award of INNOART PRIZE International Art Competition; "Women's Life" was selected for the 7th Annual International Exhibition of Women Artists in the United States. Exhibition and award experience In 2023, "Daydream" won the Silver Award of INNOART PRIZE International Art Competition. "Men's Mental Exhaustion" was selected for the International Art Sand Exhibition in Paris, France. In 2024, "Cloud Shoulder" won the Silver Award of INNOART PRIZE International Art Competition; "Women's Life" won the Honorary Award of the 7th Annual International Exhibition of Female Artists in Fusion Art in the United States. "Chinese Coffee Table" won the 2025 Special Art Award from the French Circle of Arts Foundation. Return to Canaan 2, The Eye of the Future, Dad's Baby, Four-Panel Antique and Chinese Shadow Play were selected for the final of the Tajik International Competition in Spain. "Chinese Coffee Table 2" won the grand prize in the challenge of "International Artist" magazine in the United States. 2025 "City Corners" won an honorary award at the LightsPace Urban Landscape Art Exhibition; "The Eye of the Future" was on the cover of Italy's New Tuscany magazine. The Three-part painting "China's Countryside" was selected for the 2025 New England Art Club exhibition. Homecoming Daughter, Collage Drawing, Selected for 2025 London Biennial Artistic statement by Liao Wanneng As a contemporary artist rooted in a female perspective, I consistently use keen social insight and humanistic concern to construct profound reflections on the fate of humanity through visual storytelling. My work not only focuses on the nuanced expression of individual experiences but also aims to reveal the oppression and deconstruction of human nature by power structures within the interplay of history and reality. My works center on female imagery, using a combination of symbolic techniques and realistic brushstrokes to explore the coexistence of memory fragmentation, identity wandering, and vulnerability. In my recent works, I have focused on the global issue of the Russia-Ukraine conflict. Through over 100 pieces, I use the Ukrainian flag as a visual symbol, combining symbolic and imagery to highlight how war erodes the boundaries of humanity and perpetuates the cycle of historical violence. Additionally, by reflecting contemporary conflicts, I emphasize art as a bridge that transcends ideological divides, connecting individuals and collective memories torn apart by war. My artistic practice extends beyond aesthetic expression to include a social critique. I strive to find a balance between vulnerability and resilience in my work. Through the lens of a woman's perspective, I reflect on the complex tapestry of war, history, and human nature, aiming to reconstruct the coherence of meaning in a fragmented reality. My goal is not only to document but also to reshape —— to sow hope in ruins and find empathy in conflict.

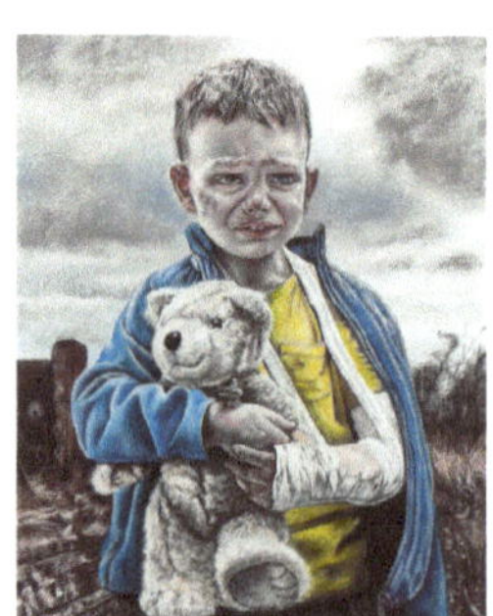

Innocent tears in the silence are louder than gunshots,Paper, chalk, colored pencils, 50×65cm.2025

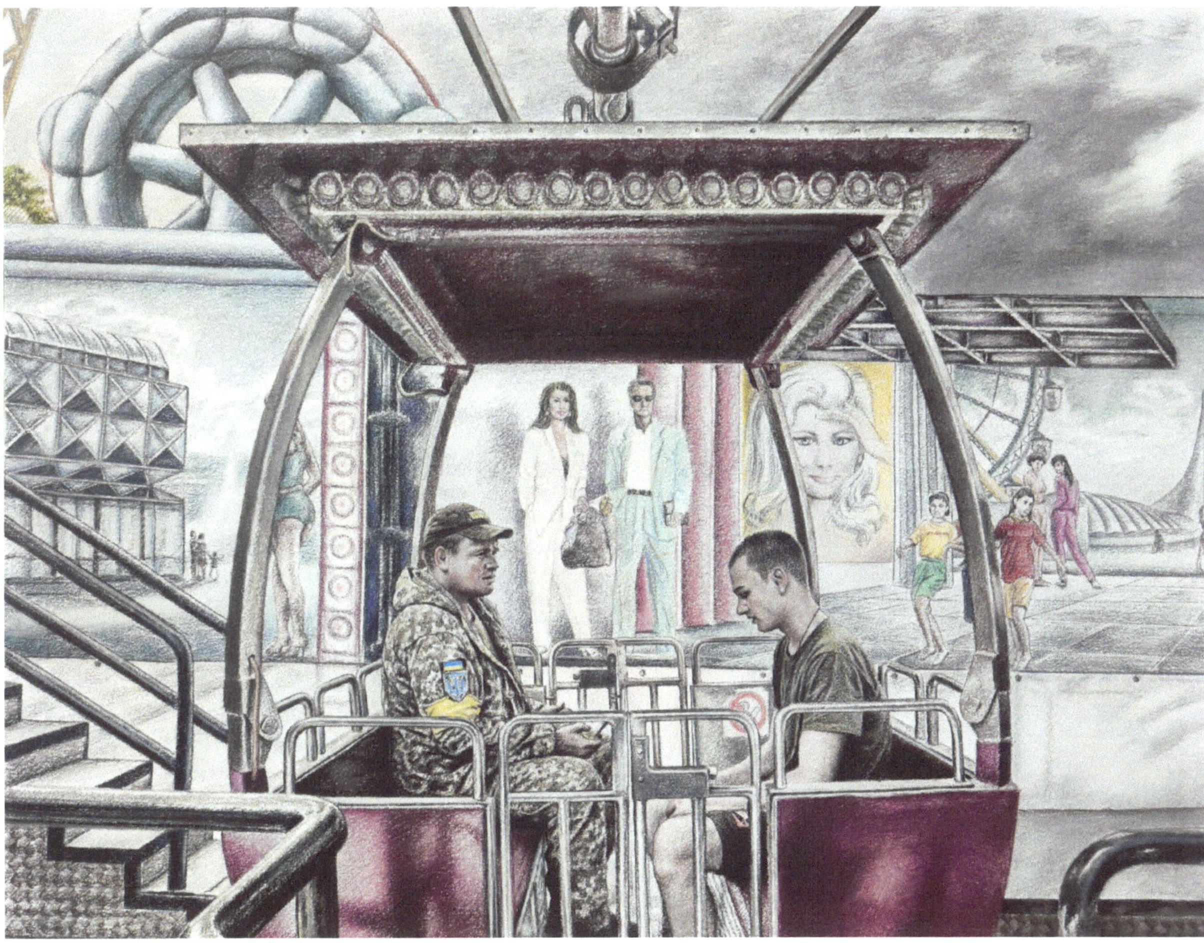

The weekend of two Ukrainian soldiers in the amusement park of Odessa after liberation?Paper, chalk, colored pencils, 50×65cm .2025

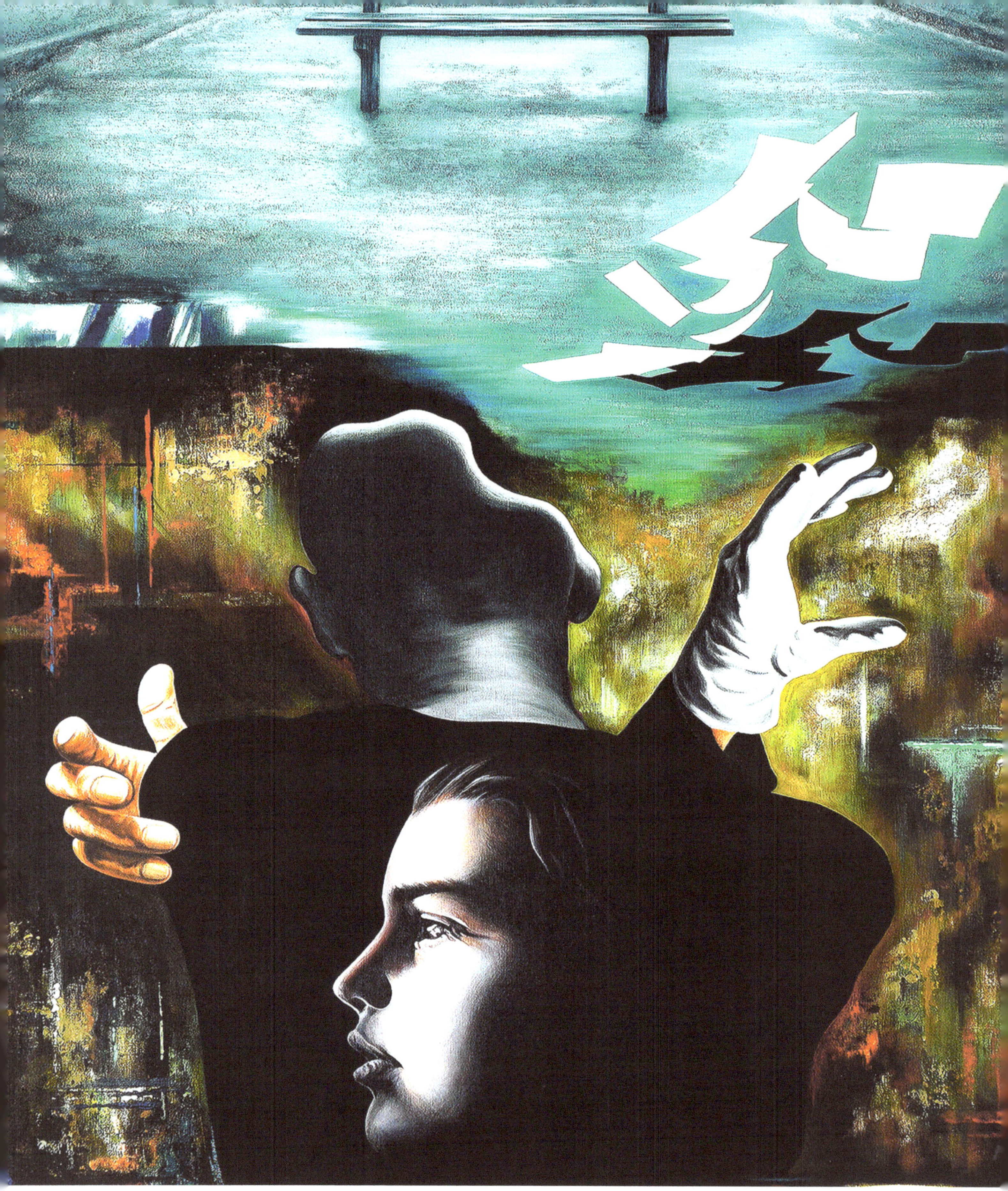

JEONG-AH ZHANG

Gain, Lose, Abandon, Accept. 2011. Acrylic on Canvas. 117 X 81 cm

www.ingramcontent.com/pod-product-compliance
Lightning Source LLC
LaVergne TN
LVHW071952080226
831166LV00014B/122
9789699893308